THE WORKS OF

ORESTES A. BROWNSON

COLLECTED AND ARRANGED

BY

HENRY F. BROWNSON.

VOLUME XVII.

CONTAINING THE THIRD PART OF THE POLITICAL WRITINGS.

DETROIT:
THORNDIKE NOURSE, PUBLISHER.
1885.

CONTENTS.

THE HIGHER LAW.*

[From Brownson's Quarterly Review for January, 1851.]

PROFESSOR STUART appears to have written this pamphlet from patriotic motives, with an earnest desire to allay the uncalled for popular agitation on the subject of negro slavery, and to contribute his share towards the maintenance of domestic peace, and the preservation of the Union. His chief purpose appears to have been to remove the scruples of some of his friends, by showing that a man may with a good conscience support the federal constitution although it recognizes slavery, and requires the slave escaping into a non-slaveholding state to be given up on the demand of his owner ; and though he is no great proficient in moral theology, and his style is prolix, prosy, and at times even garrulous, he has shown this to the satisfaction of all but mere factionists and cavillers.

We do not think that the learned professor has made out his case as conclusively as he might have done. He is a man of respectable ability and attainments, but not remarkable for the strength or acuteness of his logical powers. He makes now and then a slip, of which an uncandid critic might take advantage. He is strongly opposed to slavery, but wishes at the same time to prove that the Christian may with a good conscience be a slaveholder. In order to prove this, he asserts and proves that slavery is not *malum in se*, and therefore, if a sin at all, it is so only accidentally. But in order to justify his sincere aversion to slavery, he maintains that it is always and everywhere an evil, and excuses the old patriarchs for holding slaves only on the ground of invincible ignorance ! In the darkness of those early ages men knew and could know no better ! This we need not say is in contradiction to his assertion that slavery is not *malum in se*. But passing over slips of this sort,—somewhat common in all Professor Stuart's writings that have fallen under our notice,—and looking only to the main design and argument of the pamphlet, we can very cheerfully commend it to our Protestant readers.

---

* *Conscience and the Constitution, with remarks on the recent Speech of the Hon. Daniel Webster in the Senate of the United States on the Subject of Slavery.* By MOSES STUART. Boston: 1850.

For ourselves we agree with Professor Stuart that slavery is not *malum in se.* We hold that in some cases at least slavery is justifiable, and to the slave even a blessing. To the slave it is always good or evil according as he wills it to be one or the other, or according to the spirit with which he bears it. If he regards it as a penance, and submits to it in a true penitential spirit, it is a blessing to him, a great mercy,—as are on the same condition to every one of us all the sufferings and afflictions of this life. We should covet in this world, not happiness, but suffering, and the more grievous our afflictions, the more should we rejoice and give thanks. Christianity does not teach carnal Judaism, but condemns it, and commands its opposite as the condition of all real good, whether for this world or for that which is to come. To the master, slavery is not an evil, when he does not abuse it; when he has not himself participated in reducing those born free to servitude; when he treats his slaves with kindness and humanity, and faithfully watches over their moral and religious well-being. The relation of master and man, as to the authority of the former and the subjection of the latter, differs in nothing from the relation of father and son while the son is under age, and there is nothing which necessarily makes the relation less advantageous to either party in the one case than in the other.

That slavery as it exists in the southern states is an evil, we do not doubt; but it is so accidentally, not necessarily. The evil is not in the relation of slavery itself, but in the fact that the great body of the masters do not bring up their slaves in the church of God, and train or suffer them to be trained to observe the precepts of the divine law. The mass of the slaves in this country grow up in heresy or heathenism, to the everlasting destruction of their souls. Here is the evil we see and deplore,—an evil, however, which none but Catholics do or can feel with much vividness. It is an evil which does not and cannot weigh much with Protestants, for the slaves in general are as little heathen and fully as orthodox as their masters. If the masters were good Catholics, as they ought to be, and are under the condemnation of God for not being, and brought up, as they are bound to do, their slaves in the belief and practice of the Catholic religion, there would be no evil in negro slavery to disturb us. The only evils we see in it are moral and spiritual, inseparable from heresy and heathenism. The physical and sentimental evils, or pretended evils, about which abolitionists and philanthropists keep up such a clamor, do not move us in the least. We place not the slightest value on what the men of this world call liberty, and we are taught by religion that poverty and suffering are far more enviable than riches and sensual enjoyment.

But conceding the evil of slavery as it exists in this country, it is far from certain that it is an evil that would be mitigated by emancipation, or that emancipation would not be even a greater evil. The negroes are here, and here they must remain. This is a "fixed fact." Taking the American people as they are, and as they are likely to be for some time to come, with their pride, prejudices, devotion to material interests, and hatred or disregard of Christian truth and morals, it is clear to us that the condition of the negro as a slave is even less evil than would be his condition as a freedman. The freed negroes amongst us are as a body, to say the least, no less immoral and heathen than the slaves themselves. They are the pests of our northern cities, especially since they have come under the protection of our philanthropists. With a few honorable exceptions, they are low and degraded, steeped in vice and overflowing with crime. Even in our own city, almost at the moment we write, they are parading our streets in armed bands, for the avowed purpose of resisting the execution of the laws. Let loose some two or three millions like them, and there would be no living in the American community. Give them freedom and the right to vote in our elections, and the whole country would be at the mercy of the lowest and most worthless of our demagogues. With only Protestantism, indifferentism, infidelity, or savage fanaticism to restrain them, all their base and disorderly passions would be unchained, and our community would be a hell upon earth. No; before we talk of emancipation, before we can venture upon it with the least conceivable advantage to the slaves, we must train them, and train the white American people also, to habits of self-denial and moral virtue under the regimen of the Catholic Church, which alone has power to subdue the barbarous elements of our nature, and to enable men of widely different races, complexions, and characteristics to live together in the bonds of peace and brotherhood. We cannot, therefore, agree with Professor Stuart in his demand for emancipation, and we are decidedly opposed, for the present at least, not only to the fanatical proceedings set on foot by our miserable abolitionists and philanthropists to effect emancipation, but to emancipation itself. In the present state of things, emancipation would be a greater evil than slavery, and of two evils we are bound to choose the least. We have heard enough of liberty and the rights of man; it is high time to hear something of the duties of men and the rights of authority.

We write very deliberately, and are prepared for all the obloquy which may be showered upon us for what we write. The cry of liberty has gone forth; we, as well as others, have heard it; it has gone forth and been echoed and reëchoed from every quarter, till the world has become maddened with it. The voice of law, of order, of wisdom, of justice, of truth, of experience, of common sense, is drowned in the tumultuous shouts of Liberty, Equality, Fraternity!—shouts fit, in the sense they are uttered, only for assembled demons declaring war upon the eternal God. But this should be our shame, not our boast. It ought not to be, and, if the world is to continue, must soon cease to be. Society cannot subsist where the rights of authority are forgotten, and loyalty and obedience are foresworn. There is no use in multiplying words on the subject. Man is a social being, and cannot live without society; society is impracticable and inconceivable without government; and government is impossible where its right to command is denied, or the obligation to obey it is not recognized. It is of the essence of government to restrain, and a government that imposes no restraint, that leaves every one free to do whatever seemeth right in his own eyes, is no government at all. The first want of every people is strong and efficient government,— a regularly constituted authority, that has the right and the power to enforce submission to its will. No matter what the form of your government, no matter in whose hands the power is lodged,—in the hands of the king, of the lords, or the commons,—it must, in so far as government at all, be sovereign, clothed, under God, with supreme authority, and be respected as such, or society is only Bedlam without its keeper.

This is the great truth the American people, in their insane clamor about the rights of man and the largest liberty, that is to say, full license to every man, lose sight of, or in reality deny; and it is on this truth, not on liberty, for which all are crying out, that it is necessary now to insist, both in season and out of season. There may be times and countries when and where the true servants of God must seek to restrict the action of government, and lessen the prerogatives of power ; but assuredly here and now our duty is not to clamor for liberty or emancipation, but to reassert the rights of authority and the majesty of law. You will be decried if you do so. No doubt of it. But what then ? When was it popular to insist on the special truth demanded by one's own age ? When was it that one could really serve his age or country without falling under its condemnation ? When was it that the multitude were known to applaud him who rebuked them for their errors, exposed to them the dangers into which they were running by following their dominant tendencies, and presented them the truth needed for their salvation ? What great or good man ever proposed to himself to serve his fellow-men by following their instincts, flattering their prejudices, and inflaming their passions ? Who knows not that error and sin come by nature, and that virtue is achieved only by effort, by violence, by heroic struggle against even ourselves ? Is not the hero always a soldier ? Let then, the multitude clamor, let the age denounce, let the wicked rage, let earth and hell do their worst, what care you, heroic soldier of the King of kings ? Go forth and meet the enemy. Charge, and charge home, where your immortal Leader gives the word, and leave the responsibility to him. If you fall, so much the greater glory for you, so much the more certain your victory, and your triumph.

But we are straying from the point we had in mind when we set out. Our purpose was, to offer some remarks on what is termed " the higher law " to which the opponents of the recent fugitive-slave law appeal to justify their refusal to execute it. Mr. Seward, one of the senators from New York, in the debate in the senate during the last session of congress on the fugitive-slave bill, refused to vote for the measure, although necessary to carry out an express constitutional provision, on the ground that to give up a fugitive slave is contrary to the law of God ; and the abolitionists and free-soilers refuse to execute the law, and even in some instances resist its execution, on the same ground. When the senator appealed from the constitution to the law of God, as a higher law, he was told by the advocates of the bill, that, having just taken his oath to support the constitution, he had debarred himself from the right, while retaining his seat in the senate, to appeal from it to any law requiring him to act in contravention of its provisions. The abolitionists and free-soilers immediately concluded from this that the advocates of the bill denied the reality of any law higher than the constitution, and their papers and periodicals teem with articles and essays to prove the supremacy of the law of God. The question is one of no little gravity, and, to our Protestant friends, of no little perplexity. We may, therefore, be allowed to devote a few pages to its consideration.

We agree entirely with Mr. Seward and his abolition and free-soil friends, as to the fact that there is a higher law than the constitution. The law of God is supreme, and overrides all human enactments, and every human enactment incompatible with it is null and void from the beginning and cannot be obeyed with a good conscience, for "we must obey God rather than men." This is the great truth statesmen and lawyers are extremely prone to overlook, which the temporal authority not seldom practically denies, and on which the church never fails to insist. This truth is so frequently denied, so frequently outraged, that we are glad to find it asserted by Mr. Seward and his friends, although they assert it in a case and for a purpose in which we do not and cannot sympathize with them.

But the concession of the fact of a higher law than the constitution does not of itself justify the appeal to it against the constitution, either by Mr. Seward or the opponents of the fugitive-slave law. Mr. Seward had no right, while holding his seat in the senate under the constitution, to appeal to this higher law against the constitution, because that was to deny the very authority by which he held his seat. The constitution, if repugnant to the law of God, is null and void, is without authority, and as Mr. Seward held his seat by virtue of its authority, he could have no authority for holding his seat, after having declared it to be null and void, because the constitution is a mere compact, and the federal government has no existence independent of it, or powers not created by it. This is an inconvenience he does not appear to have considered. The principle that would have justified his refusal to obey the constitution would have deprived him of his seat as a senator. Moreover, the question of the compatibility or incompatibility of the constitution with the law of God was a question for him to have raised and settled before taking his senatorial oath. Could he conscientiously swear to support the constitution? If he could, he could not afterwards refuse to carry out any of its imperative provisions, on the ground of its being contrary to the higher law ; for he would in swearing to support the constitution declare in the most solemn manner in his power, that in his belief at least it imposed upon him no duty contrary to his duty to God, since to swear to support a constitution repugnant to the divine law is to take an unlawful oath, and to swear with the deliberate intention of not keeping one's oath is to take a false oath. After having taken his oath to support the constitution, the senator had, so far as he was concerned, settled the question, and it was no longer for him an open question. In calling God to witness his determination to support the constitution, he had called God to witness his conviction of the compatibility of the constitution with the law of God, and therefore left himself no plea for appealing from it to a higher law. If he discovered the incompatibility of the imperative provisions of the constitution only after having taken his oath, he was bound from that moment to resign his seat. In any view of the case, therefore, we choose to take, Mr. Seward was not and could not be justified in appealing to a law above the constitution against the constitution while he retained his seat under it and remained bound by his oath to support it. It is then perfectly easy to condemn the appeal of the senator, without, as abolitionists and free-soilers pretend, falling into the monstrous error of denying the supremacy of the divine law, and maintaining that there is no law above the constitution.

What we have said is conclusive against the honorable senator from New York, but it does not precisely apply to the case of those who resist or refuse to obey the fugitive-slave law now that it has been passed. These persons take the ground that the law of God is higher than any human law, and therefore we can in no case be bound to obey a human law that is in contravention of it. Such a law is a violence rather than a law, and we are commanded by God himself to resist it, at least passively. All this is undeniable in the case of every human enactment that really does command us to act contrary to the law of God. To this we hold, as firmly as man can hold to any thing, and to this every Christian is bound to hold even unto death. This is the grand principle held by the old martyrs, and therefore they chose martyrdom rather than obedience to the state commanding them to act contrary to the divine law. But who is to decide whether a special civil enactment be or be not repugnant to the law of God? Here is a grave and a perplexing question for those who have no divinely authorized interpreter of the divine law. The abolitionists and freesoilers, adopting the Protestant principle of private judgment, claim the right to decide each for himself. But this places the individual above the state, private judgment above the law, and is wholly incompatible with the simplest conception of civil government. No civil government can exist, none is conceivable even, where every individual is free to disobey its orders whenever they do not happen to square with his private convictions of what is the law of God. The principle of private judgment, adopted by Protestants in religious matters, it is well known, has destroyed for them the church as an authoritative body, and put an end to every thing like ecclesiastical authority; transferred to civil matters, it would equally put an end to the state, and abolish all civil authority, and establish the reign of anarchy or license. Clearly, if government is to be retained, and to govern, the right to decide when a civil enactment does or does not conflict with the law of God cannot be lodged in the individual subject. Where then shall it be lodged? In the state? Then are you bound to absolute obedience to any and every law the state may enact; you make the state supreme, absolute, and deny your own principle of a higher law than the civil law. You have then no appeal from the state, and no relief for conscience, which is absolute civil despotism. Here is a sad dilemma for our uncatholic countrymen, which admirably demonstrates the unsuitableness of Protestant principles for practical life. If they assert the principle of private judgment in order to save individual liberty, they lose government and fall into anarchy. If they assert the authority of the state in order to save government, they lose liberty and fall under absolute civil despotism, and it is an historical fact that the Protestant world perpetually alternates between civil despotism and unbridled license, and after three hundred years of experimenting finds itself as far as ever from solving the problem, how to reconcile liberty and authority. Strange that men do not see that the solution must be sought in God, not in man! Alas! reformers make a sad blunder when they reject the church instituted by God himself for the express purpose of interpreting his law,—the only protector of the people, on the one hand, against despotism, and of government, on the other, against license!

But the people cannot avail themselves of their own blunder to withdraw themselves from their obligation to obey the laws. Government itself is a divine ordinance, is ordained of God. "Let every soul be subject to the higher powers; for there is no power but from God; and the powers that be are ordained of God. Therefore he that resisteth the power resisteth the ordinance of God. And they that resist purchase to themselves damnation." We do not say that all the acts of government are ordained of God; for if we did, we could not assert the reality of a law higher than that of the state, and should be forced to regard every civil enactment as a precept of the divine law. In ordinary government, God does not ordain obedience to all and every of its acts, but to those only of its acts which come within the limits of his own law. He does not make civil government the supreme and infallible organ of his will on earth, and therefore it may err, and contravene his will; and when and where it does, its acts are null and void. But government itself, as civil authority, is a divine ordinance, and, within the law of God, clothed with the right to command and to enforce obedience. No appeal, therefore, from any act of government, which in principle denies the divine right of government, or which is incompatible with the assertion and maintenance of civil authority, can be entertained. Since government as civil authority is an ordinance of God, and as such the divine law, any course of action, or the assertion of any principle of action, incompatible with its existence as government, is necessarily forbidden by the law of God. The law of God is always the equal of the law of God, and can never be in conflict with itself. Consequently no appeal against government as civil authority to the law of God is admissible, because the law of God is as supreme in any one of its enactments as in another.

Now it is clear that Mr. Seward and his friends, the abolitionists and free-soilers, have nothing to which they can appeal from the action of government but their private interpretation of the law of God, that is to say, their own private judgment or opinion as individuals; for it is notorious that they are good Protestants, holding the pretended right of private judgment, and rejecting all authoritative interpretation of the divine law. To appeal from the government to private judgment is to place private judgment above public authority, the individual above the state, which, as we have seen, is incompatible with the very existence of government, and therefore, since government is a divine ordinance, absolutely forbidden by the law of God,—that very higher law invoked to justify resistance to civil enactments. Here is an important consideration, which condemns, on the authority of God himself, the pretended right of private judgment, the grossest absurdity that ever entered the heads of men outside of Bedlam, and proves that, in attempting to set aside on its authority a civil enactment, we come into conflict not with the human law only, but also with the law of God itself. No man can ever be justifiable in resisting the civil law under the pretence that it is repugnant to the divine law, when he has only his private judgment, or, what is the same thing, his private interpretation of the Sacred Scriptures, to tell him what the divine law is on the point in question, because the principle on which he would act in doing so would be repugnant to the very existence of government, and therefore in contravention of the ordinance, therefore of the law, of God.

Man's prime necessity is society, and the prime necessity of society is government. The question, whether government shall or shall not be sustained, is at bottom only the question, whether the human race shall continue to subsist or not. Man is essentially a social being, and cannot live without society, and society is inconceivable without government. Extinguish government, and you extinguish society; extinguish society, and you extinguish man. Inasmuch as God has created and ordained the existence of the human race, he has founded and ordained government, and made it absolutely obligatory on us to sustain it, to refrain in principle and action from whatever would tend to destroy it, or to render its existence insecure. They who set aside or resist the fugitive-slave law on the ground of its supposed repugnance to the law of God are, then, no more justifiable than we have seen was the honorable senator from New York. In no case can any man ever be justified in setting aside or resisting a civil enactment, save on an authority higher than his own and that of the government. This higher authority is not recognized by the abolitionists and free-soilers; they neither have nor claim to have any such authority to allege; consequently, they are bound to absolute submission to the civil authority, not only in the case of the fugitive-slave law, but in every case, however repugnant such submission may be to their private convictions and feelings, or what they call their conscience, for conscience itself is respectable only when it is authorized by the law of God, or is in conformity with it.

That this is civil despotism, that is, the assertion of the absolute supremacy of the state, we do not deny ; but that is not our fault. If men, by rejecting the divinely authorized interpreter of the law of God, voluntarily place themselves in such a condition that they have no alternative but either civil despotism or resistance to the ordinance of God, the fault is their own. They must expect to reap what they sow. They were warned betimes, but they would heed no warning; they would have their own way ; and if they now find that their own way leads to death, they have only themselves to blame. It is is not we who advocate despotism, but they who render it inevitable for themselves, if they wish to escape the still greater evil of absolute license. As Catholics we wash our hands of the consequences which they cannot escape, and which any man with half an eye might have seen would necessarily follow the assertion of the absurd and ridiculous, not to say blasphemous, principle of private judgment. We have never been guilty of the extreme folly of proclaiming that principle, and of superinducing the necessity of asserting civil despotism as the only possible relief from anarchy. We are able to assert liberty without undermining authority, and authority without injury to liberty; for we have been contented to let God himself be our teacher and our legislator, instead of weak, erring, vain, and capricious men, facetiously ycleped *reformers.* As Catholics, we were not among those who undertook to improve on infinite wisdom, and to reform the institutions of the Almighty. We are taught by a divinely authorized teacher, that government is the ordinance of God, and that we are to respect and obey it as such in all things not repugnant to the law of God ; and we have an authority higher than its, higher than our own, to tell us, without error, or the possibility of error,—because by divine assistance and protection rendered infallible,—when the acts of government conflict with the law of God, and it becomes our duty to resist the former in obedience to the latter. Civil authority is respected and obeyed when respected and obeyed in all things it has from God the right to do or command ; and liberty is preserved inviolate when nothing can be exacted from us in contravention of the divine law, and we are free to disobey the prince when he commands us to violate the law of God. We then do and can

experience none of the perplexity which is experienced by
our uncatholic countrymen. We have an infallible church
to tell us when there is a conflict between the human law
and the divine, to save us from the necessity, in order to
get rid of despotism, of asserting individualism, which is
the denial of all government, and, in order to get rid of
individualism, of asserting civil despotism, that is, the supremacy of the state, the grave of all freedom. We have
never to appeal to the principle of despotism nor to the
principle of anarchy. We have always a public authority,
which, as it is inerrable, can never be oppressive, to guide
and direct us, and if we resist the civil law, it is only in
obedience to a higher law, clearly and distinctly declared by
a public authority higher than the individual, and higher
than the state. Our readers, therefore, will not accuse
us of advocating civil despotism, which we abhor, because
we show that they who reject God's church, and assert private judgment, have no alternative but despotism or license.
They are, as Protestants, under the necessity of being slaves
and despots, not we who are Catholics. We enjoy, and we
alone enjoy, the glorious prerogative of being at once freemen and loyal subjects.

There is no principle on which the abolitionists and free-
soilers can justify their resistance to the fugitive-slave law.
They cannot appeal to the law of God, for, having no authority competent to declare it, the law of God is for them as if
it were not. It is for them a mere unmeaning word, or
meaning only their private or individual judgment, which
is no law at all, and if it were would at best be only a human, and the lowest conceivable human law. The highest
human law is unquestionably the law of the state, as the
state is the highest human authority conceivable. No appeal can then lie from the state to another human authority,
least of all to the individual ; for appeals do not go down-
wards, do not lie from the higher to the lower, as ultra democracy would seem to imply. The highest conceivable
human authority has passed the law in question, and in so
doing has declared it compatible with the law of God ; and
as its opponents have only a human authority at best to reverse the judgment of the state, nothing remains for them
but to yield it full and loyal obedience.

We have dwelt at length on this point, because it is one
of great importance in itself, and because we are anxious to
clear away the mist with which it has been surrounded, and

to prevent any denial on the one hand, or misapplication on the other, of the great principle of the supremacy of the divine law. The misapplication of a great principle is always itself a great and dangerous error, and often, perhaps always, leads to the denial of the principle. Mr. Seward and his friends asserted a great and glorious principle, but misapplied it. Their opponents, the friends of the constitution and the Union, seeing clearly the error of the application, have, in some instances at least, denied the principle itself, and their papers North and South are filled with sneers at *the higher law* doctrine. The one error induces the other, and we hardly know which, under existing circumstances, is the most to be deprecated. Each error favors a dangerous popular tendency of the times. We have spoken of the tendency, under the name of liberty, to anarchy and license ; but there is another tendency, under the pretext of authority, to civil despotism, or what has been very properly denominated *statolatry*, or the worship of the state, that is, elevating the state above the church, and putting it in the place of God. Both tendencies have the same origin, that is, in the Protestant rejection of the spiritual authority of the church on the one hand, and the assertion of private judgment on the other ; and in fact, both are but the opposite phases or poles of one and the same principle. The two tendencies proceed *pari passu*, and while the one undermines all authority, the other grasps at all powers and usurps all rights, and modern society in consequence is cursed at once with the opposite evils of anarchy and of civil despotism. The cry for liberty abolishes all loyalty, and destroys the principle and the spirit of obedience, while the usurpations of the state leave to conscience no freedom, to religion no independence. The state tramples on the spiritual prerogatives of the church, assumes to itself the functions of schoolmaster and director of consciences, and the multitude clap their hands, and call it liberty and progress ! We see this in the popular demand for state education, and in the joy that the men of the world manifest at the nefarious conduct of the Sardinian government in breaking the faith of treaties and violating the rights of the church. When it concerns the church, the supremacy of the state is proclamed, and when it concerns government or law, then it is individualism that is shouted. Such is our age, our boasted nineteenth century.

Now there is a right and a wrong way of defending the

truth, and it is always easier to defend the truth on sound than on unsound principles. If men were less blind and head-strong, they would see that the higher law can be asserted without any attack upon legitimate civil authority, and legit-imate civil authority and the majesty of the law can be vin-dicated without asserting the absolute supremacy of the civil power, and falling into statolatry,—as absurd a species of idolatry as the worship of stocks and stones. The assertion of the higher law, as abolitionists and free-soilers make it, without any competent authority to define and declare that law, leads to anarchy and unbridled license, and therefore we are obliged, as we value society, law, order, morality, to oppose them. On the other hand, the denial of the higher law as the condition of opposing them asserts the supremacy in all things of the state, and subjects us in all things un-reservedly to the civil power, which is statolatry, and abso-lute civil despotism. No wise and honest statesman can do either. But—here is the difficulty—the Protestant states-man is obliged to do one or the other, or both, at one mo-ment one, at the next moment the other. This is what we have wished to make plain to the dullest capacity. Protes-tantism is clearly not adapted to practical life, and its prin-ciples are as inapplicable in politics as in religion. There is no practical assertion of true liberty or legitimate author-ity on Protestant principles, and neither is or can be asserted but as men resort, avowedly or otherwise, to Catholic prin-ciples. Hence the reason why we have been unable to dis-cuss the question presented, and give a rational solution of the difficulty, without recurring to our church. In recur-ring to her, we have, no doubt, offended the friends of the constitution and the Union, the party with whom are our sympathies, as much as we have their enemies; but this is no fault of ours, for we cannot go contrary to what God has ordained. He has not seen proper so to constitute society and endow government that they can get on without his church. She is an integral, an essential element in the con-stitution of society, and it is madness and folly to think of managing it and securing its well-being without her. She is the solution of all difficulties, and without her none are solvable.

For us Catholics, the fugitive-slave law presents no sort of difficulty. We are taught, as we have said, to respect and obey the government as the ordinance of God, in all things not declared by our church to be repugnant to the divine law. The law is evidently constitutional, and is necessary to carry out an express and imperative provision of the constitution, which ordains (Art. IV. Sect. 2), that " No person held to service or labor in one state, under the laws thereof, escaping into another, shall, in consequence of any law or regulation therein, be discharged from such service or labor, but shall be delivered up on claim of the party to whom such service or labor may be due." This is imperative, and with regard to its meaning there is no disagreement. By this the slaveholders have the right to claim their fugitive slaves in the non-slaveholding states, and the non-slaveholding states are bound to deliver them up, when claimed. For the purpose of carrying out this constitutional provision, congress passed a law, in 1793, which has proved ineffectual, and it has passed the recent law, more stringent in its provisions, and likely to prove efficient, for the same purpose. We can see nothing in the law contrary to the constitution, and, as high legal authority has pronounced it constitutional, we must presume it to be so. Nobody really regards it as unconstitutional, and the only special objection to it is,—what is no objection at all,—that it is likely to answer its purpose. Now as the law is necessary to secure the fulfilment of the obligations imposed by the constitution, and as our church has never decided that to restore a fugitive slave to its owner is *per se* contrary to the law of God, we are bound to obey the law, and could not, without resisting the ordinance of God and purchasing to ourselves damnation, refuse to obey it. This settles the question for us.

As to Protestants who allege that the law is contrary to the law of God, and therefore that they cannot with a good conscience obey it, we have very little in addition to say. There are no principles in common between them and us, on which the question can be decided. We have shown them that they are bound to obey the civil law till they can bring a higher authority than the state, and a higher than their own private judgment, to set it aside as repugnant to the law of God. This higher authority they have not, and therefore for them there is no higher law. Will they allege the Sacred Scriptures? That will avail them nothing till they show that they have legal possession of the Scriptures, and that they are constituted by Almighty God a court with authority to interpret them and declare their sense. As this is what they can never do, we cannot argue the Scriptural question with them. We will only add, that there is no passage in either the Old Testament or the New that declares it repugnant to the law of God, or law of eternal justice, to deliver up the fugitive slave to his master; and St. Paul sent back, after converting him, the fugitive slave Onesimus to his master Philemon. This is enough; for St. Paul appears to have done more than the recent law of congress demands; he seems to have sent back the fugitive without being requested to do so by his owner; but the law of congress only requires the fugitive to be delivered up when claimed by his master. It will not do for those who appeal to the Sacred Scriptures to maintain either that St. Paul was ignorant of the law of God, or that he acted contrary to it. This fact alone concludes the Scriptural question against them.

But we have detained our readers long enough. We have said more than was necessary to satisfy the intelligent and the candid, and reasoning is thrown away upon factionists and fanatics, abolitionists and philanthropists. There is no question that the country is seriously in danger. What, with the sectionists at the North and the sectionists at the South, with the great dearth of true patriots, and still greater dearth of statesmen, in all sections of the Union, it will go hard but the Union itself receive some severe shocks. Yet we trust in God it will be preserved, although the American people are far from meriting so great a boon. After the humiliation of ourselves, and prayer to God, we see nothing to be done to save the country, but for all the friends of the Union, whether heretofore called Whigs or Democrats, to rally around the Union, and form a grand national party, in opposition to the sectionists, factionists, and fanatics, of all complexions, sorts, and sizes. It is no time now to indulge old party animosities, or to contend for old party organizations. The country is above party, and all who love their country, and wish to save the noble institutions left us by our fathers, should fall into the ranks of one and the same party, and work side by side, and shoulder to shoulder, for the maintenance of the Union and the supremacy of law. We see strong indications that such a party is rapidly forming throughout the country, and we say, let it be formed,—the sooner the better. Let the party take high conservative ground, against all sorts of radicalism and ultraism, and inscribe on its banner, THE PRESERVATION OF THE UNION, AND THE SUPREMACY OF LAW, and it will command the support, we doubt not, of a large majority of the American people, and deserve and receive, we devoutly hope, the protection of Almighty God, who, we must believe, has after all great designs in this country. Above all, let our Catholic fellow-citizens in this crisis be faithful to their duty, even though they find Mr. Fillmore's administration and our Protestant countrymen madly and foolishly hostile to them ; for on the Catholic population, under God, depend the future destinies of these United States. The principles of our holy religion, the prayers of our church, and the fidelity to their trusts of the Catholic portion of the people, are the only sure reliance left us.

THE FUGITIVE-SLAVE LAW.*

[From Brownson's Quarterly Review for July, 1851.]

THIS singular sermon was called forth under the excitement occasioned by the arrest in this city, last April, of a fugitive slave, named Sims, and the determination to give him up to his owner in Savannah, Georgia. Two attempts had been previously made here to execute the recently amended fugitive-slave law, but without success. In the first case, that of Crafts and his wife, the officers did not succeed in making an arrest, and the fugitives, it is supposed, were shipped off by their free-soil or abolition friends to England ; in the second case, that of Shadrach, an arrest was, indeed, made, but the fugitive was rescued from the custody of the United States marshal by a mob, and probably made his escape to Canada. In the case of Sims, better precautions had been taken against a rescue by a mob, whether black or white, and on the day this sermon was preached, it was highly probable that the law would be executed, and the fugitive given up to his master.

This probability threw all our free-soilers into a perfect frenzy. They called public meetings, harangued the mob, made the most inflammatory appeals to passions already

---

*The Chief Sins of the People: a Sermon delivered at the Melodeon, Boston, on Fast Day, April 10, 1851. By REV. THEODORE PARKER. Boston: 1851.

greatly excited, and would, most likely, have attempted another rescue by force, if the vigilance of the police, and the military under arms and advantageously posted, had not made it pretty evident that it could not be done without serious inconvenience. Every method, short of physical violence, to intimidate the authorities, and to induce them to desist from the performance of their duties, was resorted to, and all that rare professional ability, craft, cunning, and unscrupulousness could do to evade the law was done ; but all in vain. On the day of our annual state fast, though the case was not yet decided, the friends of the Union, the supremacy of law, and social order, began to breathe more freely, and felt it to be reasonably certain that at length something would be done towards wiping out the disgrace which our city had incurred from the fanatics she had madly cherished in her bosom. The fanatics were disappointed, and deeply mortified, and Mr. Parker availed himself of the occasion of the fast to pour out their wrath and bitterness, as well as his own, in the sermon before us, which is equally remarkable for bad taste, bad temper, bad logic, bad religion, and bad morals. It professes to treat of the chief sins of the people, but finds the chief of these to be suffering the law to be executed.

We are not called upon to discuss the merits or demerits of slavery as an abstract question. If slavery did not exist in this country, we should oppose by all lawful means in our power its introduction ; but it is here, one of the elements of American society, and directly or indirectly connected with the habits and the interests of the whole American people, and the only question for the moralist or the statesman is, How shall it be dealt with ? Even supposing it to be evil, and only evil, the question as to the treatment of it where it exists is very different from the question of introducing it where it does not exist. To suffer a wrong to remain is not always to commit a wrong ; for often in the complicated affairs of this world it is impossible to remove a long or widely existing evil, without causing a still greater evil. Be it that slavery is as great an evil as free-soilers pretend, it by no means follows that they are bound, or even free, to bring the political or social power of the country to bear on its abolition. Undoubtedly, we are never to do wrong that good may come, and if slavery is evil, and only evil, no advantages likely to result from it can ever justify us in introducing it ; but of two evils we must choose the least, and when slavery cannot in all human probability be abolished without producing a greater evil, we are not even free to abolish it, and must tolerate it till it can be abolished without such result.

In this world, we must, to a greater or less extent, tolerate even moral wrong. It is a great moral evil that in the spiritual field the cockle should spring up to choke the wheat, and yet our Lord commands us to let both grow together, lest in attempting to root up the cockle we root up also the wheat with it. Infidelity, heresy, irreligion, are sins, and very grievous sins, and yet it is not lawful to extirpate them by fire and sword. The magistrate may, undoubtedly, repress their violence, and protect Christain faith and social order from their disorderly conduct; but their extirpation must be the work of the missionary, not of the magistrate, —for faith and obedience must be voluntary, a free-will offering to God. There were zealous disciples of our Lord, who would have called down fire from heaven to consume his adversaries; but he rebuked them. "Ye know not of what spirit ye are. The Son of Man came not to destroy souls, but to save." To a greater or less extent, we must tolerate sin, not in ourselves assuredly, but in others, and bear with transgressors, even as God bears with them. We must respect their free will, leave them the responsibility of their own misdeeds, because this is what God himself does, and because to attempt to root out all sins by violence, whether physical or social, for there is a social as well as a physical violence, would in the end only render matters infinitely worse, by destroying virtue itself. We cannot make this world a paradise, and all its inhabitants saints, as foolish Puritans dream. As long as man retains free will, there will be abuses, there will be wrongs and outrages, and the sooner we come to this conclusion, and conform ourselves to it, the better will it will be for all concerned, and the more real progress will there be made in virtue.

We have no quarrel with free-soilers for being hostile to slavery. We have as little sympathy with any species of slavery as they have, and perhaps as deep and as true a devotion to freedom. They are far from monopolizing all the love of freedom and all the hatred of slavery in the community. "Brave men lived before Agamemnon," and love of freedom and hatred of slavery were born before Gerritt Smith, Robert Rantoul, William Lloyd Garrison, Wendell Phillips, Theodore Parker, or Abby Folsom, and would suf-

fer little diminution were these choice spirits to die, and
leave no heirs. It is very possible to oppose them and their
proceedings without thereby opposing freedom, sympathizing with tyrants, or adding to the burdens of the oppressed.
We oppose them, not for opposing slavery, but for the
principles and methods by which they oppose it. These
principles and methods are repugnant to freedom, and as
friends of freedom we oppose them, and must oppose them.

Nothing in the world is easier than to get off stale commonplaces against slavery and in favor of liberty; but the
man who deals largely in these commonplaces is always a
tyrant in his heart, and one whom it will never do to trust
with power. The essence of all slavery is in the predominance of passion over reason, and passion predominates in the
community over reason in the exact ratio in which law is
weak or wanting; for law is the reason of the community.
As the individual can be free in himself only by the predominance of reason in his interior life, so can a community
be free in its members only by the supremacy of law in its
bosom. The maddest madness conceivable is that which
proposes to abolish slavery and secure freedom by abolishing law,—or government, without which the supremacy of
law cannot be maintained. It is this madness that has
seized the free-soilers or abolitionists. Their principles
strike at the foundation of all government, and therefore
are repugnant to the indispensable conditions of freedom.
Without government, strong and efficient government, it is
impossible to maintain the supremacy of law, and without
the maintenance of that supremacy, there is no guaranty of
freedom either for black man or white man. The supremacy
of law is as necessary to secure the freedom of the slave
when emancipated, as to preserve the freedom of the master
now. Without it there is only anarchy, in which might
usurps the place of right, and the weak are the prey of the
strong. You do not advance freedom when you emancipate the slave from his master by overthrowing government;
you only render thereby freedom impossible, and introduce
the most detestable species of tyranny conceivable, of which
your emancipated slave will be the first victim, because the
least able to defend his liberty.

The cause of freedom is never aided by injustice; and
yet the free-soilers, who, in principle, are not at all distinguishable from the abolitionists, are urging the commission of open, palpable injustice. Slavery exists in this

country by law, and by law which is enacted or sanctioned by the American people in their highest legislative capacity. Suppose that law is unjust, still its injustice is on the part of the law-making power. Before that power the master who owns slaves is not unjust; as before it, he has justly invested his capital in slaves, and therefore it cannot justly require him to free his slaves without full compensation. The people, who have authorized him to hold slaves, cannot cast the burden of their wrongs on him. If they have sinned, they must bear their sin in the same capacity in which they have committed it. If they wish to repent and repair it, they must indemnify the master for the property they have authorized him to hold, and now require him to surrender. To propose, after having authorized it, the abolition of slavery, without proposing a just compensation to the master, is to propose a scheme of public robbery, is virtually to deny private property, and to claim for the state the right to plunder its subjects. And yet our free-soilers will not listen a moment to the proposal to indemnify the owners of slaves. They are urging the people to compel the masters to emancipate their slaves without compensation. Between the proprietor and the state, the property in slaves, whatever view we take of slavery itself, is as sacred and as inviolable as any other species of property, and to attack it is, in principle, to attack every species of private property, and to make the state the only proprietor,—the extreme of despotism, hardly reached by the pretensions of the Grand Turk. And yet the men who propose this do not blush to talk of justice, and to insist on being honored as friends of freedom !

We bring no unfounded charges against the free-soilers. Whoever has any acquaintance with their real principles and proceedings knows that what we allege is true. Mr. Parker is one of their most gifted leaders, and a faithful exponent of their doctrines, and he fully bears us out in what we say. He plainly counsels resistance to the laws, downright treason, and civil war,—only not just yet. The hour is not yet come, and armed resistance might be premature, because just now it might be unsuccessful ! The traitorous intention, the traitorous resolution, is manifest, is avowed, is even gloried in, and nothing is wanting to the overt attempt to carry it into execution but a fair prospect of success. And what is of more serious consequence, the party of which this fierce declaimer is an accredited organ is now in power in this state, and has the governor and the majority of the representatives in both houses of congress. It rules or misrules the great state of Ohio; it is numerous in Pennsylvania, almost the majority in New York, triumphant in Vermont, and, we can but just *not* say, also in New Hampshire. Its principles are entertained by men who do not profess allegiance to the party. Nearly every member of congress from this state, with the exception of Mr. Appleton of this city, is in reality as much of a free-soiler as Horace Mann or Robert Rantoul. Mr. Winthrop, the Whig candidate for the senate, was not a whit sounder than Mr. Sumner, his successful free-soil competitor, and would have made a far more dangerous senator. The party has absorbed in its bosom all the separate fanaticisms of the free states; and all who, like ourselves, have watched its growth from 1831, are well aware that it has been steadily advancing, that it has never lost an inch of ground once gained, and that it has never for a moment met with a serious check. It is as certain as any thing human can be, that, if it is not speedily resisted, and resisted as it never yet has been, it will in a short time possess the power in nearly all the free states, and consequently in the Union itself. To what then are we coming?

This statement will, no doubt, gratify and encourage the party; but the party has already become too strong to be pushed aside as contemptible, and we must not deceive ourselves as to the magnitude of the danger that threatens us. Both parties, Whigs and Democrats,—Whigs more especially till lately,—have criminally tampered with it, and aided it to acquire its present formidable power,—a power which, perhaps, is no longer controllable. The measures hitherto taken against it have thus far only exasperated and strengthened it. The "compromise measures" of the late congress, which it was hoped would allay the excitement, and extinguish the party by depriving it of all pretence for further agitation, have had only a contrary effect. We do not agree with the so-called disunionists of the South, for we are unionists, but it must be confessed that they have been the only considerable party in the country that has had any tolerable appreciation of the free-soil movement. They were correct in their predictions that the compromise measures would be ineffectual, and they have not overstated the danger. We say not danger to the institution of slavery, for the question of slavery loses itself in a much higher question, even higher and more important than the simple maintenance of the Union,—in the question of the maintenance of society itself. The free-soilers are to American society what red-republicans and socialists are to European society, and their triumph is the triumph of anarchy and despotism.

Good, quiet, easy men, looking over their ledgers, or sipping their wine, may flatter themselves that there is no serious danger, and tell us that we are unnecessarily alarmed ; but in all human probability, if the fugitive slave Sims had not been given up on the claim of his owner, the American Union had now already ceased to exist. It is all very well to talk of "southern bluster," and the " Hotspurs " of the South, but there is something more than bluster just now. The southern people are as virtuous and as patriotic as we, and their statesmen are as enlightened and sagacious as ours. They see what, with individual exceptions, we do not permit ourselves to see, that the free states are fast losing all their respect for law, and becoming unfaithful to their solemn engagements, and blind to all the claims of religion and morality. They see that the abolition of slavery at the bidding of our fanatics would be the dissolution of American society itself. They see the disorganizers steadily advancing, and that we are taking no efficient means to repress them, and they very naturally consult secession from the Union as the only means of self-preservation that remain to them. They may be wrong, but we of the North have no right to blame them for doing what we are forcing them to do, if they wish to retain any semblance of freedom.

We regard the Union as we do marriage, that is, as legally indissoluble. We deny in the one, as in the other, the lawfulness of divorce, and therefore are not accustomed to dwell on the advantages of the Union, or to speculate on the consequences of its dissolution. We will not so insult the friends of the Union as to enter into any argument to prove its absolute necessity to the well-being of the people of this country ; but we may be permitted to say, that if the slaveholding states secede in a body, and form a southern confederacy, they will not be the greatest losers. In all the free states, the moment the conservative influence of the Union is withdrawn, free-soilism triumphs, and under the reign of its principles civilized society cannot subsist. The wild radicalism that underlies it, and which is suspected as yet, no doubt, only by a minority of those rallied under the

free-soil flag, will not be slow to develop itself, and to carry
on with it even the mass of those who are unprepared at this
moment to follow it to all lengths it may go.   That radicalism, being in principle sheer anarchy or despotism, cannot
serve as the basis of a civilized state.   The free states, paradoxical as it may seem to them, are, by the prevalence of
this radicalism, deprived of the social and political virtues
necessary to found or preserve civilized society.   In an industrial and commercial point of view, the southern confederacy would have the advantage over the northern.   It
would include the great exporting states, and could therefore always trade more to its advantage in European markets than in ours.   We are now the factors and manufacturers for the South, but we should not be when we come
to sustain to it the relation of a foreign government.   We
should lose two-thirds of our foreign exports, a very large
proportion of our internal trade, and the best markets for
the larger portion of our manufactures.   What, in case of
division, would naturally form the southern republic or
kingdom, would have more fully the elements of national
greatness in itself than the northern, at least, till some great
change should come over the present state of commerce and
industry.   These considerations can have no weight with
the fanatics, but they should have weight with our cool-
headed business men, and with all that portion of our population that have not yet entirely lost their senses.

   It is well known that the union of the American states could
never have been formed if the free states had not consented
to the insertion in the constitution of the provision in regard
to the surrender of fugitive slaves, and no man who is really
aware of the feelings of the South can doubt that its preservation in any thing like its original character is impossible
unless the free-soil fanaticism is effectually suppressed, and
the fugitive-slave law faithfully executed.   This law, which
Mr. Parker and the more open and honest of the free-soilers counsel us to resist, and the more shrewd and cowardly
portion tell us must be repealed, is now a test law.   Let us,
however, be just to the South.   They, no doubt, are attached
to the institution of domestic slavery, at least determined to
follow their own judgment in regard to it, but they do not
insist on this law merely on account of the protection it affords to negro slavery, and we much mistake their character if we suppose they would secede from the Union, or
hazard a civil war, for the sake of a few dozens of runaway

slaves. They never seem over-anxious to recover the slaves that escape into the northern states, and it costs in general more to reclaim one, even when no resistance is offered, than his services are worth. That it is not the value of the runaway slaves they mainly consider, is evident enough from the fact, that the feeling on the subject is deepest in those very states from which the fewest slaves escape, or are likely to escape. They insist on the law because it is constitutional, because in executing it we give them assurance that we are willing and able to abide by our constitutional engagements, and are not disposed to abuse the power of the federal government, now passing, once for all, into our hands. They want some pledge of the ability and determination of the free states to restrain the wild radicalism so rife amongst them, and which laughs at constitutions and laws, and in its onward career is madly sweeping away in them all the defences of personal freedom and social order instituted or preserved by the wisdom of our fathers. They take their stand on this law as a frontier post, which, if carried, admits the enemy into the interior, and leaves them no alternative but to surrender at discretion,—not merely negro slavery, which, comparatively speaking, were a small affair, but liberty itself, to the unrestrained despotism of an irresponsible and fanatical majority.

Let no man deceive himself with the vain hope that this radicalism now represented by the free-soil party would stop with the mere abolition of negro slavery. It is the persuasion of so many of our citizens that it would, which renders it so dangerous. The abolition of slavery by violence, against the will of the masters, and without compensating them for the property we compel them to surrender, would be a great evil, but it is one of the lightest evils to be expected from the progress of free-soil fanaticism. We assure the public,—and it is the point we wish particularly to impress upon our readers,—that the abolition of negro slavery is only an incident in free-soilism. Neither the free-soilers nor we can foresee where they would stop. Combining as they do in one all the several classes of fanatics in the country, and being the party opposed to law, to constitutions and governments, certain it is they would not stop so long as there remained a single safeguard for individual freedom, or a single institution capable of imposing the least restraint upon lawless and despotic will. No doubt there are honest, but deceived, individuals in the

party, who will not go all lengths with it; but they will be
impotent to restrain it, and the party itself, augmenting its
forces as it marches, will on whithersoever its licentious and
despotic principles lead, unless speedily and effectually resisted by the sounder part of the community, or by the
merciful interposition of divine Providence.

The essential principle of the free-soil party, that which
gives it so terrible a vitality, is not, we repeat, exclusively
or mainly, opposition to slavery. Half unknown to itself,
it is a party organized against law in all its forms, against
all the principles and maxims of the past, and all the moral,
religious, social, and political institutions of the present. It
is a party formed against the common reason, common
sense, and common interests of mankind. With the cant of
religion and morality on their lips, its leaders are, almost to
a man, infidels and blasphemers, as well as traitors and disorganizers. They are men for whom it is not enough to
sin from appetite or passion, but who must sin from principle,— for whom it is not enough to see the good, approve
it, and yet pursue the wrong, but who must pervert conscience itself, erect evil into good, and make sin pass for
virtue. They aim at reversing all the judgments of mankind, and brand the Christian virtues as vices, and exalt the
vices opposed to them to the rank and dignity of Christian
virtues. Whatever has hitherto been counted sacred they
pronounce profane, and whatever has been hitherto counted
profane, they command us to respect as sacred. They say
with Milton's Satan,—

> "All good to me is lost;
> Evil, be thou my good."

They carry their zeal for reversing so far as to seek to reverse the natural relation of the sexes, to dishonor woman
by making her the head, and sending her to the legislature,
the cabinet, or into the field to command our armies, and
compelling man to remain at home, and nurse the children,
wash the dishes, make the beds, and sweep the house. Already are their women usurping the male attire, and beginning to appear in our streets and assemblies dressed out in
full *Bloomer* costume, and little remains for the men but to
don the petticoat and draw the veil over their faces.

Let no man accuse us of exaggeration. We do not exaggerate in the least, and are only giving our readers a sober
statement of the spirit and tendency of the great movement party of our times,—red-republicans and socialists in

France, Italy, and Germany, *progresistas* in Spain, radicals in England, free-soilers and abolitionists just now, in the United States,—destructives everywhere, borne forward by the under-currents of nearly all modern societies, glorified by all the popular literature of the age, defended by the newspaper press generally, and with us in the free states already able to blast the reputation of almost every public man who ventures to assail them. We speak of a party which we have long known, and which, we grieve to say, we ourselves, when we had more influence with our countrymen than we can ever hope to have again, supported, under more than one of its aspects, with a zeal and an energy worthy of a better cause. Alas! men are often powerful to do evil, but impotent to repair it. Now that our eyes are open, and we are able to see the mischief we did, we have no power to undo it, and if we are permitted to speak out freely and boldly, as we do, against the party, it is because that party can afford to let us say what we please. No voice raised against it seems to be any longer heeded, and if a man of standing and weight in the community assails it under one of its aspects, he must save himself and friends by giving it a new impetus under another, as we see in the case of Mr. Webster, who apparently writes his letter to the Chevalier Hülsemann, to atone for his speech in the senate chamber on the 7th of March, 1850. He appears to have felt that the only way in which he could obtain a popularity for the administration, to balance the popularity lost by its adhesion to the compromise measures, was to express sympathy with radicalism and revolutionism abroad. In this he may have judged patriotically, if not wisely and justly; for to sympathize with foreign radicalism is less dangerous to us for the moment, than to sympathize with domestic radicalism. Now it is the progress and triumph of this wild radical party that the South really dread. They see it under the free-soil and abolition aspect, but also—though less clearly, perhaps—under other aspects, and they see that they have every thing to fear and nothing to hope from it. Hence the firmness with which they insist—and we, too, ought to insist, for we are as deeply interested as they—on the faithful execution of the fugitive-slave law; for if the party cannot be successfully resisted on this law, it is idle to think of resisting it at all. We and all the members of the Union are then without protection, and at the mercy of the worst and most frightful despotism, under the name of liberty, that it is possible to conceive.

But the fugitive-slave law, Mr. Parker and his associates tell us, is unjust, and they add, that. if the Union cannot be preserved without sustaining an unjust law, let it go to pieces.

"Quicquid id est, timeo Danaos et dona ferentes"

However that may be, we distrust Satan, even when he preaches morality ; for he never preaches morality unless to persuade us to outrage it. We cannot prize very highly the moral lectures of those who are daily and hourly violating all social morality, and counselling us to do the same,— who are undeniably traitors, really guilty of treason, by their combined and persevering resistance to the execution of a law of congress. No lawyer of character can doubt for a moment that persons associating together for the express purpose of permanently defeating the execution of any law of the state or of congress, and in their conventions passing resolves to resist it, incur the guilt of treason ; and treason, whatever some people think, is a violation of the moral law, a sin against God, as well as a crime against the state. It is a sad day for both public and private morals, when treason is regarded as a virtue, and the traitor punished for his treason is looked upon as a martyr. Men have, no doubt, been unjustly accused of treason, and punished as traitors when they should not have been ; but this does not in the least lessen the crime of treason, and should not in the least screen from punishment those who are really guilty of it. It seems to be forgotten by the great mass of our people, that treason is a crime under our form of government, as well as under other forms, and that to sympathize with traitors, whether at home or abroad, is not even here a virtue. Perhaps the government would do well, if, instead of sending out ships of war to bring foreign traitors into the country, it would make examples of some few of our domestic traitors, and thus remind the people that here no more than elsewhere is it lawful to conspire to resist the laws. Perhaps some examples will have soon to be made, if the government intends to maintain itself. But be this as it may, it is certain that the free-soil resistance to the execution of the fugitive-slave law is treason as defined by our laws, because it springs not from a momentary impulse or sudden exasperation, but from a settled purpose of defeating the law, not in one instance only, but in every instance in which there shall be an attempt to execute it.

We must be pardoned, then, if we are not disposed to listen to lectures on morals from the free-soil leaders, especially when the morals they would teach us are only such as they need to save their own necks from the halter.

The fugitive-slave law is not unjust. It is a constitutional law, so declared by Judges Woodbury and Nelson of the United States circuit court, and by the supreme judicial court of this commonwealth. Chief Justice Shaw, than whom it would be difficult to find a higher legal authority, in giving the unanimous opinion of the court, said that the law was not only constitutional, but necessary, and congress was bound to pass it. In principle it does not differ from the original law of 1793, and differs from it at all only in devolving on officers of the federal government certain duties which that law devolved on officers of the state governments. The amendment became necessary in consequence of several of the states having prohibited their officers, under heavy penalties, from performing those duties. The amendment which transferred these duties to officers of the federal government cannot in the least affect the constitutionality of the law, and therefore, since no one can pretend that the original law of 1793 was unconstitutional, the amended law of 1850 must be conceded to be constitutional. The law was enacted by the proper authorities, according to the forms prescribed by the constitution, for the purpose of carrying into effect an imperative provision of the constitution, and, after the decisions of the several tribunals, its constitutionality must be held to be settled, and no longer an open question. Unjust, then, it cannot be, unless the constitution is unjust. The constitution is not unjust, unless it contravenes the law of God. That the constitution does contravene the law of God, no religious man can pretend, for men of all religions have approved it, and men of no religion have nothing to say on the subject, since for them there is no law of God, and therefore no conscience.

The constitution ordains that persons held to service in one state escaping into another shall be given up on being claimed by those to whom such service is due. An independent state in the absence of treaty obligations, or with us in the absence of constitutional obligations, is not bound to give up fugitive slaves, or even fugitives from justice ; but it is free to do so, for reasons satisfactory to itself. To reduce a freeman to slavery is a sin, so declared by the highest religious authority, and accordingly our government prohibits the slave-trade under its flag, and declares it piracy. But to give up a slave to his owner is by no competent authority declared to be a sin. To give up a fugitive slave is not to reduce a freeman to slavery ; it is simply not interfering to liberate a slave. The slave in escaping does not become a freeman, nor in the least alter the relations between him and his master. So far as he is concerned, the master has the same right to reclaim him when he has escaped into another state that he would have if he had only escaped to a neighboring plantation in the same state. The right that debars the master from asserting his claim is not the slave's right, but that of the state into which the slave has escaped, which prohibits the assertion of the claim, because it cannot allow the laws of another state, however just, to operate by their own force within its jurisdiction. The question is not here between master and slave, but between two independent states. The state may, if it chooses, waive its rights, and permit the master to reclaim his slave, without adding to or taking from the previous right of either slave or master, as between themselves. Its waiving of its territorial jurisdiction is only not interposing it, and is therefore simply non-intervention, or not asserting, when it might, its right to intervene. It simply remains neutral, and leaves the relation between the master and slave as it finds it. This is all that the fugitive-slave law requires of any of the states, for the process it prescribes, and the powers it requires to be exercised, have for their sole object, on the one hand, to prevent a freeman from being taken under pretext of recovering a fugitive slave, and on the other, to maintain the neutrality of the state by preventing any portion of its citizens or subjects from interfering to prevent the recovery of his slave by the master.

Thus viewed, the question, even supposing slavery to be wrong, is simply, Has a state the right to remain neutral between two foreign parties, and suffer or permit the party assumed to be in the wrong to bear down the party assumed to be in the right? If the state has this right, it of course has the right to take all the necessary measures to compel its citizens or subjects to remain neutral. Has the state this right? It certainly has the right, for it is idle to pretend that we are bound, either as states or as individuals, to interpose to redress all wrongs, real or supposed, committed or tolerated by others. The question is not as to the *right*, but as to the *obligation* to intervene. There may be cases when we are free to intervene, and others when we are bound to intervene; but the former are not numerous, and the latter are very rare. The experience of our Puritan ancestors proves this very clearly as to individuals, and that nothing is worse than to make every individual in a community the guardian of the morals of every other individual. It leads every one to mind every one's business but his own, establishes a system of universal espionage, and sacrifices all individual freedom and independence. It destroys all sense of individual responsibility, precludes all firmness and manliness of character, and superinduces the general habit of consulting, not what is true, what is right, what is duty, but what is popular, or rather, what will escape the censure of one's neighbors. Whoever knows what our society was under the strict Puritan regimen knows well how fatal to virtue is the system. The New-Englander of to-day bears but too many traces of the system, which makes him but too often a hypocrite at home or in public, and somewhat of a rowdy in private or abroad. The whole system, out of which free-soilism undeniably springs, is false, of immoral tendency, and founded on a misapprehension of the nature of man and the government of God. We must leave scope for individual freedom ; we must trust somthing to individual responsibility, and place our main reliance on the principles we early instil into individuals, the religious influences with which we surround them, and the workings of their own consciences. It will not do to keep them always in leading-strings, or under lock and ward. If we do, we shall never have any strong or masculine virtue ; never have any men on whom in the hour of temptation and trial we can rely. No doubt, outbreaks of passion, of wild and exuberant spirits, there will be ; no doubt, disorders will occur, scenes of personal violence will be exhibited, scandals will be given ; but these things, however much to be deplored, no human foresight or power can prevent, and we must make up our minds to bear with them. To attempt, as Calvin did in Geneva, and as our fathers did in New England, to guard against them by an all-pervading espionage and minute legislation, descending even to prescribe the fashion of cutting the hair, only substitutes a darker and more fatal class of vices and crimes, such as can be practised in solitude or carried on in secret. We must bear with them,—knowing that, if there is less virtue than we wish, what virtue there is will be genuine, and able to abide the test.

The same principle applies to nations, for nations are only individuals to each other. As long as they remain unaggressive, disposed to live in peace with their neighbors, and to fulfil the obligations of good neighborhood, they must be left to stand on their own individual responsibility, and each to be supreme, under God, in managing its own internal affairs. To make them guardians of the morals and policy each of the others, would result only in evil. It would excite perpetual jealousies and heart-burnings, give the strong and grasping a pretext for interfering with and subjugating the weak, rendering peace impossible, war, rapine, and oppression permanent and universal. We deny, then, the moral obligation of independent states—unless it be in certain rare cases, when the very existence of society itself is threatened, and a given state is really waging war against social order and the common interests of mankind, and therefore really attacking the common right of nations—to interfere to redress even the moral wrongs which may be perpetrated in the interior of each other. Granting, then, —what we certainly do not grant,—that slavery is a moral wrong in itself, one state is not bound to interfere for its abolition in another. Then it is free to preserve in regard to it a strict neutrality, and to enforce that neutrality on its citizens or subjects. Then, as what is called giving up a fugitive slave is really nothing but remaining neutral between the master and slave, for by it the state only refuses to interpose its territorial jurisdiction as a bar to the recovery of his slave by the master, the state is not bound to prohibit the recovery of fugitive slaves; and in permitting and compelling its citizens to permit them to be recovered, it does not, and requires no one to do a moral wrong. It is false, then, to pretend that the fugitive slave law or the constitution in requiring it is unjust,—contravenes the law of God. The states, then, in forming this Union, had the right to stipulate that fugitive slaves should be given up, and their stipulation binds all their citizens or subjects.

The free-soilers and abolitionists profess to appeal from the state to what they call the higher law; but no such appeal as they, in fact, contend for, is ever admissible. There is certainly a higher lawgiver than the state. God is the supreme Lawgiver for states and individuals, and no civil enactment contrary to his law is obligatory,—not precisely because his law is a higher law, but because such an enact-

ment is no law at all, and is null and void from the beginning. God as universal sovereign ordains civil government,
clothes it with authority, within the limits of his law, natural and revealed, to govern, and we must never forget that
it is by his authority that it governs. Consequently its enactments, within these limits, are, in effect, the laws of God,
and being his laws, there can be no higher laws on the matters they include to override or annul them. They are by
the will of God supreme in their province, and bind us as
laws of God; and they can no more be disobeyed without
sin against God, than they can without crime against the
state.

But the free-soiler alleges that the fugitive-slave law
transcends these limits, and ordains what the law of God
prohibits; and concludes, therefore, that it is no law, and
he is not only free to disobey, but even bound to resist it.
This is not true, as we have shown in proving that an independent state has the right to remain neutral in the question
between the master and slave of another state, and therefore
the American states, in forming a federal union for their
common weal, had the power to bind themselves to give up
fugitive slaves. If they could not, as we know they could
not, secure the advantages of the Union without so binding
themselves, they had the right to do it, and a sufficient
reason for doing it, and this obligation is binding in conscience upon all their citizens respectively. But let this
pass. The burden of proof is on the free-soiler. Civil government exists and governs by divine appointment, and
therefore the presumption is always that its acts are in accordance with the divine will, till the contrary is shown.
Consequently, they who allege that they are not, must prove
their allegation. It is not enough to say, that all civil enactments in contravention of the law of God are null; therefore the fugitive-slave law is null. The fact of its contravening the divine law must be proved as the condition of
concluding its nullity. This the free-soiler does not even
attempt to prove, or, if he attempts to prove it, it is simply
by alleging in proof his own private opinion, private judgment, or, as he says, conscience; that is, by adducing in
proof the very matter to be proved. The conscience he alleges is his private conscience, and private conscience is
simply one's private judgment of what is or is not the law
of God, and may be true or false. To allege this is only to
allege private judgment, and to allege private judgment is

to allege the very matter in question; for the very matter in question is the truth or validity of this private judgment of the free-soiler, that the fugitive-slave law contravenes the law of God.

Here is precisely where the free-soiler breaks down. His declamation is superior to his logic. He professes to appeal from the civil enactment to the law of God, but in reality appeals only to his own private judgment, and this appeal is not admissible; because it is not an appeal to a higher court, or to a court competent to interpret and declare the will of the higher Lawgiver. The state is the lawgiver for individuals, not individuals for the state. The judgment of the state in all cases overrides the private judgment of individuals, and the individual is bound to submission, whatever his private convictions, unless he can back his private convictions by an authority paramount to that of the state, and which states as well as individuals are bound to obey. Such an authority the free-soiler has not, as we may presume from the fact that he does not attempt to allege it. His pretence is, that his private convictions themselves are the higher law, and override all civil enactments opposed to them, which is manifestly false, as well as repugnant to civil government itself.

Mr. Parker tries to prove that a man's private convictions are themselves the higher law, from the example of the early Christian martyrs, who absolutely refused to sacrifice to idols at the command of the emperor. But this example is not to his purpose; for they offered only a passive resistance, and did not refuse to obey the emperor on the authority of private judgment or private conscience, but on an authority which the emperor himself was bound to obey, that is, the authority, not of private, but of universal reason, which forbids idolatry, and an express revelation of the will of God to the church infallibly interpreted to them. When the free-soiler will bring these authorities, or either of them, —that is, the authorities themselves, not merely his notions of them,—to back his private convictions or conscience, that the fugitive-slave law contravenes the law of God, then we will concede his right, and even his duty, to disobey it; for it is necessary to obey God rather than men. But this he cannot do, for if he could, he would have done it long ago. Conscience is the law for the individual in the absence of all other law, but is sacred and inviolable before civil enactments only when supported by the law of God; for it is not itself the law of God, but simply one's judgment of what that law does or does not command. The appeal to it, then, can never avail the free-soiler; for of itself it can never override a civil enactment.

The appeal to the supreme Lawgiver is compatible with civil government, but the appeal to private judgment, or conviction, as to a higher law than that of the state, is not; for it virtually denies government itself, by making the individual paramount to it. The free-soiler, then, by the very fact that he appeals to private convictions or private conscience as the higher law, proves, what we have alleged, that his principles strike at the foundation of government. He asserts the supremacy of private opinion, and exalts private judgment to the dignity and authority of the law of God. If this pretence that private judgment is the law of God were an isolated fact, if it were a temporary resort of a party hard pressed, we should smile at its absurdity, and pass it over as harmless. But it is a settled doctrine, received as an axiom, as a sacred dogma, as their fundamental principle, by the universal radical or movement party of our times, and holds with them the rank and authority which the dogma of the infallibility of the church holds with the Catholic. They seek to make it the basis of all ethical and legislative codes. Strange as it may seem, whatever minor differences there may be among the members of the party, they all agree in setting up man—humanity, as they say—in the place of God, and man's will—that is, their own—in the place of the divine will. As if preluding Antichrist, they have the incredible audacity to allege that they do this in the name of our blessed Lord himself. The sacred mystery of the Incarnation, they tell us, symbolizes the divinity of man, and signifies to all who understand it that God is *for us* only in man. Man is the only God for men, and man's will is for men God's will, therefore the supreme law, *lex suprema*, to which all creeds, codes, hierarchies, and states must conform, or lose their right to be. This is the doctrine of red-republicans and socialists on the continent of Europe, to a great extent of the radicals and chartists in England, and of the free-soilers or abolitionists of this country. There can be no question of the fact. It is read in all the literature of the party; it is plainly taught in the sermon before us; it is clearly implied in this very appeal to private conviction as to the law of God, which is made by even the more moderate of the free-soilers. Nor is the doctrine entertained simply as a closet theory. It is no longer a mere speculation; it is no longer confined to books, pamphlets, or newspapers; it has come forth into practical life, organized parties, formed conspiracies, produced revolutions, expelled sovereigns, convulsed all Europe, kindled the flames of civil war, and, if defeated on some points, is as yet nowhere subdued. It is here, laughing at constitutions, collecting mobs, arming a party to resist the constituted authorities, undermining the state, corrupting public and private morals, and preparing the way for the horrors of anarchy. It has become an organized party, and as such we have now to meet it, not in the schools only, but in the field, and with something more than syllogisms or moral protestations.

We shall not undertake to refute this doctrine, for they who entertain it are past being reasoned with. Reason and argument were thrown away upon them. But we do entreat such of our countrymen as have not yet entirely lost their senses to open their eyes to the dangers that threaten us. This terribly destructive doctrine takes possession of people in the name of liberty, and it captivates because it is supposed to exalt the individual, and to guaranty his freedom. But it does no such thing. It destroys all individual freedom. It magnifies the individual in the face of government, indeed, but it is only, after having used him to break down government, to crush him beneath the despotism of what it calls society. Why advocate we so strenuously, in season and out of season, the sacredness and inviolability of government, and inscribe LAW AND ORDER on the banner we throw out? Is it because we have no sense of individual freedom, because we would sacrifice the individual to the state, because we would have government everywhere, and suffer no one to sit down or rise up but at the bidding of a master? Let no one be so foolish as to do us that injustice. We are freeborn Americans; we have battled for liberty all our life, and were never more resolute to battle for it than we are now. We love liberty, and would leave always a large margin for individual freedom. We oppose socialism, because it destroys individuality, and is nothing but despotism; we oppose radicalism, because it is despotism; we oppose free-soilism, because it is despotism; and we assert the necessity of government, because without it there can be no margin left for individual liberty. Tell us, ye wise ones, ye enlightened reformers of the nineteenth century, when ye have succeeded in making way with government, what protection ye will have left me for my individual and personal freedom? Whither, then, shall I be able to fly to save myself from being crushed beneath your huge, social despotism, rolling on under the impetus of lawless passion and irresponsible demagogues? What refuge can there be for personal freedom, when what is called society, as distinguished from government, is supreme, without law, without restraint, but the will and passions of the radicals who are at its head? A cruel and despotic public opinion, variable and capricious as morbid feeling, will then become supreme, universal, all-pervading, and overwhelm every individual who has the hardihood to hesitate for a moment to comply with its imperious demands. What now takes place on a small scale in your voluntary associations for reforming society, will then be exhibited on a large scale. The capricious despotism will not stop with putting chains on the limbs, and a padlock on the lips, but it will enter into the soul, penetrate into the very interior of man; all free thought will be stifled in its conception, all manliness, all nobility of character, depart, virtue be unheard of, and men become a race of mean, cringing, cowardly slaves of an intangible despot, and wild and lawless passion revel in one universal and perpetual saturnalia. It is to prevent this fatal result that we demand government, strong and efficient government,—not to crush the individual, but to save him from being crushed under the tyranny of an ungoverned society, by restraining social action and influence within their legitimate bounds. Let the principles of free-soilism, of the fanatics, become predominant, as they are becoming, and government cannot be maintained, or, if maintained, only as an instrument of oppression. We demand, therefore, in the name of liberty, that the movements of the fanatics be repressed, and that the utmost rigor of the laws be enforced against their leaders. Lenity to them is cruelty to the people, and irretrievable ruin to the country.

Some cowardly but crafty free-soil leaders counsel, it is true, not resistance to the fugitive-slave law, but agitation for its repeal. We confess that we respect in comparison with these the bolder traitors, who advise open and unremitting resistance. The highwayman is less despicable than the swindler, and of all traitors those who practise treason under cover of law are the most detestable. The man who, in our times, agitates for the repeal of the fugitive-slave law, is as much of a traitor in his heart as he who bids it open defiance. Why repeal it? It is constitutional. Would you have another more efficient? It is not needed. One less efficient? that is, one that you can evade, one that will not compel you to comply with the solemn obligations of the constitution? So you would evade obedience to the constitution, but without endangering the safety of your necks? No doubt of it. But agitation in the sense of free-soilism is precisely what now creates the danger, and every man who would keep it up in that sense is morally a traitor to his country.

But our limits are exhausted. We have not said half of what we intended to say when we commenced; but we have said perhaps enough. The question is one of vital importance to the republic. We have spoken strongly, but far less strongly than we feel. We see not in free-soilism a single redeeming element. It is wild, lawless, destructive fanaticism. The leaders of the party that sustain it are base and unprincipled men, whose morality is cant, whose piety is maudlin sentiment, and whose patriotism is treason. A more graceless set of deluded fanatics or unmitigated hypocrites could not be found, were we to search the world over. Some worthy persons may have been attracted to the party by their horror of slavery, and by their belief in the loyal intentions of its leaders; but no religious man, no loyal citizen, can, after the developments the party has recently given, any longer adhere to it, or afford it the least conceivable countenance. Whoever continues to support it can be excused from treason only on the ground that he is insane, or else that he stands too low in the scale of intelligence to be responsible for his acts.

Whether there is sufficient political virtue or intelligence remaining in the country to meet successfully the crisis, time must disclose. We hope there is, but we certainly have our fears. Matters have gone so far, that it will be no child's play to arrest them. The South must not now desert the North. They have their faults as well as we ours, and have erred as much in their encouragement of the "expansive democracy," as we by our disregard of constitutional engagements. But their interests must prompt them to discountenance internal radicalism, and to exert at home a conservative influence. Without them there is no hope for us, but with them, with their hearty coöperation with the friends of the Union yet remaining in the free states, we may outride the storm ; we may preserve the Union, check radicalism, and save American society from utter dissolution, and the liberties transmitted us by our fathers from utter annihilation. But we can do so only by waiving all minor issues, disregarding old party organizations, dismissing old party animosities, and bringing the whole conservative party of the republic to act together with one heart and soul, as one man.

SUMNER ON FUGITIVE SLAVES.*

[From Brownson's Quarterly Review for October, 1854.]

WE have no disposition to treat Mr. Sumner, one of our senators in congress, otherwise than with the respect due to his station, to his learning and ability, and his private virtues. But with the party he has joined, and to which he gives an earnest and energetic support, we have not the least conceivable sympathy. We are, as our readers well know, utterly opposed to that party, not from sympathy with slavery, but from love of liberty and from devotion to the constitution. As the friend of social order, as the advocate of wise and practicable government, and as the defender, according to the measure of our poor ability, of genuine American republicanism, we are obliged to oppose with all our might the anarchical and despotic doctrines it holds and seeks to propagate, because those doctrines cannot prevail in this country without involving the subversion of constitutional government, the disruption of society, and the destruction of all possible guaranties of freedom, whether for white men or black men.

It is by no means our present purpose to discuss the question of slavery on its merits. We are personally, in feeling and principle, as much opposed to slavery in any and every form as Mr. Sumner and his party, and take as deep an interest as they in the real welfare of the negro race. We do

---

* *Speeches of the* HON. CHARLES SUMNER *on the Memorial for the Repeal of the Fugitive Slave Bill, and in Reply to Messrs. Jones of Tennessee, Butler of South Carolina, and Mason of Virginia.* In the Senate of the United States, June 26 and 28, 1854.

not admit that free-soilers and abolitionists enjoy a monopoly of the love of liberty, or of interest in the slave population. We are men as well as they ; we are human, with human understandings and human hearts, as well as they ; and nothing human is more foreign to us than to them. We throw back upon them their charges against those who do not see proper to join them, and assure them that we are as far from conceding either their infallibility or their impeccability as they are from conceding ours. We recognize in no self-constituted party, sect, or association, the authority to declare the moral law binding in conscience. According to their own rule of private judgment, we stand on as high ground as they, and deny to them the right to make those arrogant assumptions in which they so liberally deal. If private judgment is good for them, it is good for us, and our private judgment, since opposed to theirs, reduces it, even if theirs reduces ours, to zero.

But we are not among those who say, *Finis justificat media,* or who under pretext of philanthropy hold themselves at liberty to trample down more good in going to their end than they could possibly secure by gaining it. It is never lawful to do evil that good may come. There is a wrong as well as a right way of seeking even lawful ends, and he may well distrust his intentions who seeks to realize them by means obviously unjust, imprudent, or rash. Men are held to be prudent as well as just, and there is seldom gross imprudence where there is not some lack of a clear perception or a sincere love of justice. The end proposed by abolitionists and free-soilers is the emancipation of the negro slaves in the United States. This end, in itself considered, is lawful ; for all men, under the law of nature, are born free, and slavery is the normal condition of no man or race of men. The negro is a man, a man sprung from the same original stock from which the whites have sprung, and the same blood courses in his veins that courses in our own. He had the same first parents on earth, he has the same Heavenly Father, and the same Redeemer ; he is placed under the same moral and religious law, and may aspire to the same heaven. We should belie our convictions as a man, and our faith as a Christian, were we to deny this, and we should disgrace our manhood, and sink into a miserable moral coward, were we to fear to assert it when or where its assertion is required. That negro slave is my brother. For him as well as for me Christ has died on the cross. He has an immortal soul as precious as my own, and he may reign with the saints in heaven, while I may be doomed to suffer eternally with the devil and his angels in hell. Nothing shall make us forswear the unity of the race, or fear to assert the common brotherhood of all men, white, red, or black.

But what conclude from all this? That no man, in any circumstances whatever, can have a good title to the bodily services of another? By no means; for otherwise the father could have no property in the bodily services of his son, the master in those of his apprentice, the creditor in those of his debtor. Nothing can be concluded but that one cannot have the dominion of the soul or the conscience of another, that the property of the master extends only to the bodily services of his servant, and that he must leave him his moral freedom unabridged, and full liberty to obey in all things the natural and divine laws obligatory alike upon all men. The master may have property in the bodily services of the slave by various titles, among which is that of services rendered him, benefits conferred on him, care taken of him in his infancy, maintaining him, nursing him when sick, or making provision for him in old age. It may be in the actual state of things the best practicable condition of the slave that he should remain under the guardianship or as the ward of the master, who, in consideration of the right to his bodily services, shall take upon himself the whole charge of his care and maintenance, on the same principle that minors and persons not regarded as competent to manage for themselves are, even in the free states, placed by the law under guardians. In a state which authorizes slavery, or recognizes property in slaves, the master has a title, whatever it be as against the slave, that is good against the state. If the public has by its laws permitted slavery, recognized the master's title as good, it cannot in justice abolish it, without full indemnification. If the state has legalized a wrong, it may undoubtedly undo it, and is even bound to do so, but not at the expense of the individual citizen. The abolitionist, therefore, who calls upon the public authorities to emancipate the slaves without just compensation to the masters, calls upon it to commit gross injustice. This should for ever shut the mouth of every abolitionist, for every one, without exception, we believe, holds that compensation would itself be a wrong, as it would recognize the title of the master.

But waiving this for the moment, we may oppose the free-soil and abolition movements on the ground that their complete success would, in the present state of things, prove a serious injury to the negro race on this continent. We have no great admiration for the so-called " patriarchal institution " of slavery, and we think that many ameliorations of it are not only possible, but imperatively demanded. But we must treat it as a practical question. The negroes are here, and here they will remain, unless exterminated; for the project of sending them all back to Africa is perfectly visionary. Now, no man of ordinary sense and judgment, with some little knowledge of the subject, can for a moment doubt that the best practical condition of the negro race here is, for the present at least, that of slavery, or that they should remain, as Mr. Calhoun liked best to express it, *wards*, under the guardianship of the masters. Our foreign friends may throw up their hands in holy horror at this statement, and declaim lustily against our American prejudices; but it is possible that we are as sincere friends of liberty as they are, and that we understand the question even better than they do. The most degraded race, morally and physically, among us, are the free negroes in the free states. The slaves, if emancipated, thrown upon their own resources, and compelled to provide for themselves, would very generally sink to the level of these free negroes. They would have all the responsibilities of freemen, and all the disadvantages of slaves, without any of the compensating advantages of either. The simple difference of color alone would suffice to keep them a distinct and degraded class, and therefore a dangerous class in the republic. You may tell us that this ought not to be so; but it is so, and you cannot make it otherwise. In Europe, where a black man is a sort of curiosity, the prejudice against color may not be very strongly manifested; but here it is, humanly speaking, invincible, and in none more so than in European settlers and northern abolitionists. Certainly, then, if emancipation, as there is every reason to believe, would prove a serious injury, a real calamity to the slaves, we show no lack of humanity in refusing to labor for it.

The evils of slavery, as it exists amongst us, are moral, not physical. Physically considered, the negro slaves are in a better condition than any other class of simple laborers in the country. As a general thing, they are treated with humanity, are sufficiently fed and clothed, and not overworked.

They are free from all care and anxiety as to their means of living, which is, for poor people, even in this land of plenty, no small thing ; they are light-hearted and merry, and the only class of laborers we have ever seen in the country that have the heart to sing at their work, or that are not too much exhausted by the labors of the day to join in the evening dance and frolic. Their physical sufferings are nothing in comparison with those of free laborers at the North or on our numerous public works. But the moral evils connected with slavery are great. The principal of these are the lack of proper Christian instruction, the want of respect paid to the sacrament of marriage, and the separation of husband and wife, and parents and children. But these evils are not inherent in the system. They are abuses which might be corrected without weakening the system, or in the least impairing the value of the services of the slave to his master, and they probably would have been corrected to a considerable extent before this, if the movements of the abolitionists had not compelled the slaveholding states to direct all their energy to the preservation of the system itself. These movements, being directed not to the amelioration of the institution, but to its destruction, have operated, and still operate, to make the lot of the slave much worse than it would otherwise be.

Thus far we have considered the abolition and free-soil movements solely as they affect the slave population ; but we have no right to leave the white population of the country entirely out of the account. The freedom and well-being of the whites are as dear to humanity as the freedom and well-being of the blacks. Let slavery be as great an evil as it may, we have no right to abolish it by means that would inflict a still greater evil on the country at large. Of two evils we are bound to choose the least. It will not do to seek freedom for either white man or black, by means which destroy the very conditions of freedom. Freedom in our country, whether for black or white, depends on the maintenance of our constitutional order. The abolition and free-soil movements tend directly to destroy that order, for they are based on the denial of all political authority, all civil rights, and all political justice. If successful, they would render power arbitrary or null, destroy all the guaranties of freedom, and leave the whole population of the country a prey, now to despotism, and now to anarchy.

So much on the general question. We can now easily

dispose of the special question, that of the rendition of absconding slaves, or the fugitive-slave law, which some of our citizens, not well knowing what they are about, are endeavoring to get repealed. It is always well to understand the state of the question before proceeding to discuss it. If Mr. Sumner had taken this precaution, he would have saved himself and us a good deal of trouble. The constitution of the United States ordains, that "no person held to service or labor in one state under the laws thereof, escaping into another, shall, in consequence of any law or regulation therein, be discharged from such service or labor, but *shall be delivered up*, on claim of the party to whom such service or labor may be due." The rule here is, that the civil constitution binds in all things not repugnant to natural justice or the law of God, declared by the competent tribunal. The rendition of the fugitive slave, then, is obligatory on us in conscience, unless to do so is repugnant to natural justice or to the law of God; neither of which can be pretended, for St. Paul sent back to St. Philemon his fugitive slave Onesimus.

If the master has a title to the bodily services of his slave which is good in morals, as he certainly may have, he has the right in justice to recover his slave, the same as he would have in the case of any other species of property. In such case, the slave would himself be bound in conscience to return to his master, unless his master had forfeited his title by abusing it, by inhumanity, or the denial to his slave of his moral freedom. The master may forfeit his title, and in such case the slave is free from all obligations to him, on the same principle that the tyranny of the prince forfeits his title, and absolves his subjects from their allegiance. But in case there has been no abuse of the title, and there is no proximate danger to the soul of the slave, he would be bound to return, on the same principle that he who should entice away a slave from his master, or prevent the master from recovering him, would be held in justice to restitution.

But if the master has no title in justice, or that is good as against the slave, he nevertheless has a good title as against the state, and this title every American must concede. As it concerns the slaveholding states themselves there can be no doubt, for these states have certainly by their laws recognized and guarantied property in slaves. The citizen who has inherited his capital in slaves holds his property in them, as against the state, by as good a title as he holds or can hold any other species of property. The state is bound in justice to protect him in that property, although his title to it as against the slave is vicious. The state may, if the title is not good as against the slave, abolish it, and ought to abolish it, but it cannot do so without indemnifying the master; for if it had recognized and guarantied an unjust title, that is its fault, and the maxim of law and morals, that no one can take advantage of his own wrong, is as applicable to the state as to the individual. The state, then, is bound to deliver up the slave, or to pay his ransom. The obligation of the state binds all its citizens, and they must either permit the master to recover his slave, or, like the state, pay his ransom. Such is the obligation in morals of the slaveholding states and their citizens to the master.

Now, by ratifying or acceding to the constitution, which contains the provision we have cited, each state has recognized the master's title, and guarantied it so far as delivering up the slave on claim of the master is to guaranty it. To this extent, then, the title of the master, even though vicious as against the slave, is good against every state in the Union and the citizens thereof. The state has no option in the case. It must deliver up the slave when claimed by his owner, or pay his ransom. The citizen must do the same. If his conscience will not permit him, he must negotiate his freedom, which in all ordinary cases may be done at a reasonable price. But if it cannot, if the owner refuses to put his slave at ransom, or if the citizen is unable to pay it, he must permit the master to take him back, and submit to it as he is obliged to submit to a thousand other evils which he would, but cannot redress.

But let us understand precisely what *delivering up* a fugitive slave means. Even if the master's title were good as against the slave, I am not bound to send him back, for I am not the keeper of his property. All I am bound to do is not to deprive him of his property, or to hinder him from recovering his man. My duty is simply that of non-intervention. It is the same under the constitution. We are sustained by the supreme court of the United States,* when we say that the constitution does not impose on the state into which the slave escapes any obligation to send him back to the master, and therefore, of course, no obligation

---

* *Prigg vs. Commonwealth of Pennsylvania,* 16 Peters, 539.

on its citizens to do it, or to aid or assist in doing it. The right secured to the master is the right to come and take his absconding slave where he can find him, and the duty imposed on the state and the citizens or subjects thereof is to suffer him to do it in all freedom, and to interpose no obstacle, to offer no resistance of any kind to his doing it. The obligation is not to assist, but not to resist.

We may now understand the fugitive-slave law. This law does not confer on the master the right to come and take his slave, for that right he has under the constitution, nor does it impose on the state or its citizens any obligation to *send* back or restore the fugitive slave. It creates no positive rights, and the obligations it imposes are, in relation to the recovery of the slave, strictly negative. Its objects are two : — 1. To prevent the master, under the plea of recovering his slave, from taking back with him to servitude a man to whose services he has no claim under the laws of his state ; and, 2. To prevent the state or its citizens, or any portion of them, from hindering him or interposing any obstacle to prevent him from coming and freely taking back with him the one to whose services he has such claim. The law aims to enable the master to exercise his constitutional right against all opposition, and only that right. It imposes no active duty on the part of the state or of its citizens, except in case of resistance, and then to suppress the resistance, not to send back the slave to servitude. The law is for strictly constitutional purposes, and, as experience proves that it is not more stringent than is absolutely necessary to effect its purpose, it is ridiculous, or worse, to pretend that it is unconstitutional. No law is or can be unconstitutional that is *necessary* to secure the exercise of an acknowledged constitutional right. The clamor set up against it, that it does not give the alleged slave the benefit of a jury, is, in our judgment, worthy of no attention, because the question at issue before the magistrate is not that of freedom and slavery, as Mr. Sumner would persuade us, but simply whether the master has a *claim* under the laws of his state to the services of this man, say, Anthony Burns. There are but two questions for the magistrate to determine ; — 1. Has he who claims the man, as an absconding slave, a *claim* under the laws of his state ; and, 2. Is this Anthony Burns the man to whom he has such claim? The record of the court of the slaveholding state answers the first question, and evidence of identity settles the second. There is no sitting in judgment on the claim, any further than to see that it is made under the laws of the state from which the alleged master and alleged fugitive come. Judgment on the claim itself can be rendered only in the courts of that state, where the alleged slave has the benefit of a jury secured to him. But as there is no trial on the claim before the magistrate, but a simple inquiry as to the fact that the claim is made under the laws of that state, Virginia for instance, the proceedings are ministerial, not judicial, and the introduction of a jury would be an unheard-of anomaly. Why not insist on a jury in the case of the rendition of absconding apprentices, or of fugitives from justice? The demand for a jury is not, when made by a lawyer, honest, because he knows that the proper matter for a jury does not come before the magistrate, and can be an issue only before the courts of the state from which the slave has escaped, where only "the great question of human freedom," as Mr. Sumner calls it, can be tried. The only thing a jury could do, and the only thing, we suspect, that a jury is desired for, is to interpose an additional obstacle to the exercise of his constitutional right by the master.

We can now appreciate Mr. Sumner's defence of himself. He was asked, by Mr. Butler of South Carolina, if, in case congress should repeal the fugitive-slave law, " Massachusetts would execute the constitutional requirements, and send back to the South absconding slaves?" Mr. Sumner answered, " Do you ask if I would send back a slave?" Mr. Butler replied, "Why, yes." Mr. Sumner answered, " Is thy servant a dog that he should do this thing?" Taken literally, Mr. Sumner's answer, though not marked by proper senatorial courtesy, is defensible, and we could say as much ourselves; for neither in morals nor under the constitution are we bound to *send* back absconding slaves. This has been settled, we suppose, by the supreme court of the United States, in its decision affirming the constitutionality of the fugitive-slave law of 1793. We understand the *delivering up* to be a passive, not an active, delivering up, and consider that the constitution recognizes and guaranties the right of the master to recover or take back his slave, but does not impose upon the state or the citizens thereof the active duty of sending him back. Judge Butler must permit us to say that his question was framed without sufficient regard to the precise obligation in the case. He should have said, "I would like to ask the senator if congress should repeal the fugitive-slave law, would Massachusetts *comply* with the requirements of the constitution and leave the master free to take back to the South his absconding slave ? "

Mr. Sumner.   Do you ask, if I will suffer, as far as depends on me, the master to take back his slave ?

Mr. Butler.   Why, yes.

Mr. Sumner.   Is thy servant a dog, that he should do this thing ?

Now, if the question had been put in this form and Mr. Sumner had answered as we have here supposed, his answer would unquestionably have been indefensible, and in direct conflict with his oath to support the constitution.   But as the question was put, he escapes the charge of declaring his willingness to perjure himself, at least in so many words. But his answer is evasive, almost a verbal quibble, and his defence of it is by no means successful, or creditable to a senator in congress.

Mr. Sumner defends himself on the ground that, in swearing to support the constitution, he swears simply to support it as he understands it, not as others understand it, and cites General Jackson as his authority.   But this ground of defence, if taken without any qualification, is untenable.   That every public officer, in the discharge of his official duties, is, to a certain extent, free to interpret for himself the constitution imposing them, we do not deny ; but this is only in those cases where his duty is not defined by law, and the meaning of the constitution has not been judicially settled. But even here he is bound to understand the constitution in its plain, obvious, or natural sense, and is never at liberty to understand it in some out-of-the-way sense, in a non-natural or an arbitrary sense of his own.   But will Mr. Sumner maintain that, as a citizen, as a lawyer, or as a senator, in swearing to support the constitution, he does not swear to support it as authoritatively defined by the proper tribunal ? We grant that he does not swear to support the constitution as interpreted by the private judgment of individuals, for his private judgment is to be regarded as the equal of theirs ; we grant that where the meaning is doubtful, and is an open question, he is free to follow his own judgment, that is, his own honest judgment, which must be judgment, not caprice ; but will he venture to say that he does not, according to the honest intent of his oath, swear to support the constitution or to understand the constitution as interpreted by the supreme court of the United States, declaring its meaning on the points formally brought before it for adjudication ? Will he say, that the sense of the constitution thus declared does not bind him as a citizen, as a lawyer, and as a senator ? If so, will he tell us where in our political system is lodged the supreme judicial authority ? What is the province of the supreme court, or the value of its decisions ? In every government there is lodged somewhere a supreme judicial authority, whose decisions in the civil order are final. In our political system this authority is separated from the legislative power, and also from the executive, and is vested in a distinct department, called the judiciary. In every question of a judicial nature, the judiciary is supreme, the highest civil authority in the land, and the meaning of the constitution as involved in a legislative or executive act is by its own nature a judicial question, and comes within the legitimate province of the judiciary, unless expressly excepted by the constitution, as perhaps it is in cases of impeachment, when the judicial functions are by express constitutional provision transferred to the senate. The constitution says : " The judicial power shall extend to all cases, in law or equity, arising under this constitution, the laws of the United States," &c. Now in every one of these cases there may arise the question of the constitutionality of the law under which the case is brought, and the judiciary has, as a matter of course, supreme jurisdiction of that question, as long as the constitution remains what it is, and its decision is final, and ends all litigation. So at least we understand the matter. Does the senator mean to deny this, and to maintain that the question, though a *res adjudicata*, is still an open question, and that with regard to it the *civil* conscience remains free ? If so, we should like to know by what right the judgment of the court can in any case be pleaded, or how any case can ever be settled, or a sentence of the court be regarded as the sentence of the law.

The act of congress, if unconstitutional, is null and void, is no law at all. It is impossible, therefore, to decide whether it is law or not without deciding the question touching its constitutionality. If then the supreme court has not jurisdiction of this question, it can decide no case, and can perform no judicial act, that is to say, is no court at all, and if its decision is not conclusive on the constitutionality of the law, it cannot be on the matter in issue under it. The consequence would be, that there is, under our system, no su-

preme judicial power, no provision for terminating litigation, or coming to a final decision in any case whatever.
There can be no final award, and no judgment that can be
enforced ; which would be simply tantamount to no government at all.   If there is no authority to determine the law,
there can be no judgment, and we are as if we had no law
at all. If there be such authority, it must be binding, not
only upon every private citizen, but also upon every public
officer, and the true sense of the oath to support the constitution is *to support it as authoritatively defined or declared
by the supreme judiciary*, or as subject to the interpretation
of the supreme court of the United States.

To take Mr. Sumner's ground, if that be really his ground,
that each public officer is his own judge of the meaning of
the constitution, is to clothe each public officer with supreme
judicial authority in his own case, which were a supreme
absurdity.   To compel a man to swear to support the constitution as he sees proper, in the exercise of this supreme
judicial authority, to interpret it for himself, is nonsense, for
such an oath binds him to nothing, and leaves him as free
as before taking it.   If the man interprets the oath for himself, and there is no authority but his own private judgment
to declare its sense, how would you ever be able to convict
a man of perjury ? or how would you ever be able to bring
his oath home to his conscience ?   Moreover, if the constitution may be interpreted by each individual for himself, it
can be practically only the private judgment of each individual.   It has no practical significance beyond that judgment.
By what right then do you call it a constitution, or a fundamental *law* of the state ?

Mr. Sumner in his defence appeals to the law of humanity
as superior to the constitution.   Be it so.   But that is to
appeal from the civil constitution to the principles of natural
justice.   We allow the appeal, and we maintain that no oath
does or can bind any one to do any thing against natural
justice, for such oath is unlawful, and the oath to support
the constitution is taken with the limitation, *in so far as not
repugnant to natural justice, or the law of God, authoritatively declared by the proper tribunal*, for the individual
has under the superior no more than under the inferior law
supreme judicial functions in his own case.   But in the case
of the fugitive-slave law, this appeal will not avail him.
Grant for the sake of the argument, that the master has in
natural justice no title to the services of his slave, as against

the slave himself, yet he has a good title as against the state, or the Union, under the constitution which recognizes and guaranties it. The constitution recognizes the title, and as against it the title is sacred in natural justice. The state may declare that to be property which is not and cannot be so in natural justice, but the state cannot take advantage, as we have said, of its own wrong, and therefore as against it the claim of the proprietor is as much a claim in natural justice as though the property itself had been property under the same natural justice. Grant that justice to the slave requires his liberation, justice to the proprietor requires that he shall not be liberated without indemnification. It is idle, then, to appeal to the law of natural justice against the master, for justice in his case is justice as much as in the case of the slave, and the superior law itself commands you either to deliver up to him his slave who has taken refuge with you, or, if your conscience or your humanity will not allow you to do that, to pay his ransom. The appeal to the law of conscience is good, but it cannot be made as an excuse for doing injustice, or withholding justice.

Does Mr. Sumner concede that the master has a title to the services of the slave which he as a citizen of Massachusetts or as a senator in congress is bound to recognize and respect? If not, he denies the authority of the constitution, and has no right to hold his seat in the senate. If he does, he must concede that the master has the right in morals to claim his slave where he can find him, and that he cannot be deprived of him without injustice, save on the condition of full indemnification; for private property is sacred in natural justice. No reasonable man can deny that the title of the master under the constitution is valid, and that congress is bound to protect him in the enjoyment of it. Congress had then the right, and it was its duty, to pass the fugitive-slave law, and resistance to that law is a crime, and, if an organized, deliberate, determined, and persevering resistance, it is treason, whatever be the value of the master's title as against the slave.

This conclusion rests, it will be seen, on the principle that every title to property, whether originally vicious or not, recognized and guarantied by the state, is good as between the holder and the state, and cannot be lawfully suppressed by the state without indemnification. The several states in acceding to the constitution of the United States have recognized and guarantied the title of the master to the services of his slave. If the slave absconds, it is not the duty of any one of the free states, or of any citizen thereof, to hunt him out and restore him to his owner, for the guaranty extends only to delivering him up, that is, permitting him to be taken and carried back on the claim of the master. If the state refuses to do this, it is the right and the duty of congress to compel it to do it or to pay the slave's ransom, because the constitution is the supreme law of the land. If a portion of the citizens oppose the master in the exercise of his right to recover his property, they disturb the peace, they do an illegal act, and either the state or the Union has the right to use force to suppress the opposition, and preserve the peace, and both are bound to do it. In the fugitive-slave law the Union takes this duty on itself, and leaves the state to aid or not, as it sees proper. Now under this law every citizen is liable to be called on to assist, not in restoring the slave, but in suppressing the opposition to the exercise by the master of his constitutional right to take his slave. The law does not require me to send back or to aid in sending back the slave, but it does call upon me not to hinder, and may call upon me to aid in preventing lawless abolitionists from hindering, his being taken back. If Mr. Sumner had paid attention to this, he would have spared the heroics with which his speeches so abound.

With regard to the memorial for the repeal of the fugitive-slave law, we have not much to say. It was got up in a moment of excitement, and we have no doubt that most of those who signed it are before this heartily ashamed of having done so. The repeal of the fugitive-slave law could have only one meaning, that of practically expunging from the constitution the clause which requires fugitive slaves to be delivered up, and to petition for it is simply to petition to be released from a duty imposed by the constitution ; for nobody is such a fool as to suppose that, without that or some other law equally offensive to the anti-slavery feeling of the free states, a single absconding slave would ever be recovered. The simple question raised by the memorial, then, is, Will we stand by the constitution as it is, or will we not? For ourselves, we raise no such question. We shall stand by the constitution, and as far as depends on us keep our plighted faith, and when our conscience becomes so tender on the subject that we feel it necessary to interpose and prevent the master from recovering his property, we will do so only by purchasing the slave's freedom, or paying his ransom. This we find is the course that the church has always pursued. It is the morality which we have learned from her, the morality of common sense.

We have nothing to say here of the question debated in the senate as to the comparative strength or merits in past or present times of the different sections of the Union. We have no occasion to defend the North, and we shall not volunteer a defence of the South, unless we see that she needs it. We cannot conclude these remarks without expressing our gratification at finding the national administration finally taking a decided stand in defence of the fugitive-slave law. On this question, notwithstanding certain questionable manœuvres in the beginning, we are happy to see that it stands firm, and is likely to secure the confidence of a large portion of the Union. Many of its appointments have been bad, many of the doctrines it has put forth are highly objectionable, but it will come out much better than we at one time feared, and we shall be much disappointed if it does not prove to be the strongest and upon the whole the most popular administration the country has had since General Jackson's time. All our readers know that we are of no party, not neutral indeed, but independent. What we ask is an honest and intelligent administration of the government according to the constitution. Beyond that, we care not whether it is administered by Whig or Democrat. But one thing is certain, a Democratic administration will generally be stronger than a Whig administration, and possess to a far greater extent the confidence of the American people, therefore is more able to repress evil and do good. We think we hazard little in saying, that the measures of the present administration which its opponents think they can use with killing effect against it will turn out to have contributed greatly to its strength. The Nebraska bill will prove popular, and if it frees Central America from British *protection*, we can assure its party a long lease of power.

SLAVERY AND THE INCOMING ADMINISTRATION.

[From Brownson's Quarterly Review for January, 1857.]

THE Democratic party have succeeded in electing their candidates for the presidency and vice-presidency of the Union. They have won the victory at the polls, but the far more difficult task awaits them of turning that victory to the common good of the country. Mr. Buchanan is a man of experience and ability, but he assumes the reins of government in circumstances of no ordinary difficulty, and which are well fitted to try the best of men, and to call forth the firmness, energy, and decision of the greatest. If he proves equal to his position, carries the government safely through the present crisis, and leaves at the end of four years the party of the Union united and strong enough to administer the government on constitutional principles in spite of all sectional opposition, he will render his administration memorable in our annals, and deserve to be ranked as the second father of his country.

The most of us who at the North voted for Mr. Buchanan did so on Union principles, for the purpose of defeating what we regarded as a northern sectional party on the one hand, and an intolerant, un-American party on the other. We ourselves supported him not from any attachment to the Democratic party as such, but as the candidate opposed to know-nothingism and abolitionism, the two most threatening dangers that existed prior to the election. But there are other extremes also to be guarded against. Know-nothingism we regard as dead and buried. The danger now arises almost solely from the question of negro slavery,—a question which has no place rightfully in our federal politics, but which has found a place there through the fault of the South as well as of the North, and cannot without a fearful struggle now be excluded. The incoming administration cannot prudently stave off this question, but must meet it boldly, firmly, and dispose of it, or it will dispose of the Democratic party. The Cincinnati platform endorses the policy embodied in the Kansas-Nebraska bill, but unless the administration gives to that policy a very liberal interpretation, it will prove the rock on which the party will split, and perhaps the Union itself.

The Kansas-Nebraska policy, not, however, adopted for the first time in the Kansas-Nebraska bill, was designed to combine the slave states as a solid phalanx in support of the Democratic party, so as by the aid of two or three Democratic states in the non-slaveholding section of the Union, to secure the election of its candidates for the presidency against all the rest, and even against the majority of the popular vote. There may be political conjunctures, when such a policy is excusable, but regarded as the permanent policy of a party that professes to consult the welfare of the whole Union, we want language to express the abhorrence in which it should be held.

We shall be believed when we say that we do not oppose this policy on slavery or anti-slavery grounds. We condemn that policy solely for its bearing on the distribution of power, and on the administration of the government. The slave states constitute not the strongest section of the Union, but the slave interest is stronger than any other one interest in the country, and is more than a match for all the others taken singly. It can combine a larger political minority in its favor than any other, though after all only a minority. To combine all the slaveholding states around that interest, and secure them the administration of the government by the aid of one, two, or three Democratic free states against the votes of all the rest, is really to place the government in the hands of the sectional, slaveholding minority, because that minority is the immense majority of the party that elects the president. To suppose such a policy to be permanent is to suppose that the slave interest is to govern the country, and that the majority of the Union is to submit to the slaveholding minority. If fully carried out and consolidated, the policy would virtually disfranchise, as to the general government, the majority of the American people, and render the non-slaveholding states the subjects, ultimately the slaves, of the minority, held together by a particular interest, and that too an interest which has no right to enter into the politics of the Union. No statesman, worthy of the name, can for one moment believe the free states would long submit to be thus deprived of their legitimate influence in the affairs of the country, and quietly acquiesce in the domination of some three hundred thousand slaveholders, in a single geographical section. Having, as they well

know, the absolute majority, having also, as they fully believe, the power, they would rebel against their southern
masters, and form a northern sectional party, do their best
to defeat and subject the slave interest, and in their turn
attempt to bring the slaveholding states under the domination of the northern manufacturers, bankers, brokers, and
stock-jobbers.

There are anti-slavery men at the North,—and we have
found anti-slavery men also at the South,—but it would be
a great mistake to suppose that it is a real anti-slavery feeling that has in the late elections given the so-called Republicans their immense majorities in the free states. It is no
such thing. The large majority of the electors in the non-
slaveholding states are neither " nigger-drivers " nor "nig-
ger-worshippers," to use the homely but expressive terms
of the *New York Herald*, and while strongly opposed to
the extension of the area of slavery, they have no disposition
to interfere with it where it now legally exists. It is in the
power of the South to make every man, woman, and child,
north of Mason and Dixon's line, an abolitionist, but as yet
the majority are not so, and are willing to leave slavery to
the disposition of the several states in which it exists. The
real struggle between the North and South is a struggle
for power. The South seeks to extend and consolidate the
slave interest, because that interest gives her a power in the
Union to which she is not entitled by her numbers, and the
North opposes slavery, not because of its alleged sinfulness,
but because it would prevent it from becoming predominant, and excluding the free states from their legitimate influence in the Union. Here is the significance of the struggle
that is now raging, and which the incoming administration
will be obliged to face as best it may.

The Kansas-Nebraska policy may be thought to have
elected Mr. Buchanan, and his natural temptation may be
to administer the government in accordance with the southern interest which has contributed the most to his election.
The southern minority is the immense majority of the party
that has elected him. In all except two or three free states
the Democratic party is for the present in a hopeless minority; a very large majority of the popular vote of the Union
was cast against it, and without the union of the South,
where is Mr. Buchanan to look for support for his administration? And how is he to retain the South united, without supporting the policy of the slave interest ? But, if he

does support that policy, if he makes it a point to favor that
interest, and carry out the views of those who aim through
it to control the administration, as Nicholas Biddle hoped
to control the credit system of the world by buying up the
cotton crop of the South, he will not only administer the
government as a southern sectional president, but inevitably
prepare the way for the accession of a northern sectional
president in 1860. The experiment of the last election is
one that cannot be repeated with success. There is a spirit
aroused at the North, whether good or bad, that cannot prudently be tampered with, and Mr. Buchanan's safety lies
alone in administering the government on strictly Union
principles,—justice to all sections of the Union, but partiality to none. He must interpret the Kansas-Nebraska policy
to mean really and truly the non-intervention of congress in
the question of slavery, the complete exclusion of that question from federal politics.

The Kansas-Nebraska bill professed, but falsely professed, to be framed on the principle of non-intervention.
Slavery, we hold, is a local institution, and not placed
within the province of the federal government. That government is bound to respect it where it legally exists, as
it is bound to respect all the laws and institutions of the
several states, not in derogation of the constitution and
laws of the United States, and to provide for reclaiming
by their owners persons held to service in one state and
escaping into another; but further than that it has no constitutional power over it. It can neither abolish it where
it exists, nor authorize it where it does not exist, unless it
be in the District of Columbia. The Kansas-Nebraska bill
is opposed to this principle, and is an attempt on the part
of congress to enable slavery to gain a legal introduction
into new territory, under the pretence of leaving it to the
territorial people to decide for themselves whether they
will have slaves or not. But the people of a territory not
yet erected into a state, have no political or civil powers,
except those conferred by congress, and congress can confer
no power which it does not itself possess, or authorize them
to do any thing which it has not the constitutional right to
do itself. Congress having itself no right to say whether
slavery shall or shall not be allowed, it cannot, of course,
authorize the people to do so.

The attempt to get over the lack of power on the part of
congress, by the recognition of so-called "squatter sover-

eignty," is unworthy of high-minded and honorable statesmen.   Squatter sovereignty is an absurdity, and repugnant
to the first principles of all legal order.   Under our system
of government the people as states possess original and underived sovereignty, and sovereignty, under God, in its
plenitude, save so far as by their own free and irrevocable
act they have delegated its exercise to the Union.   But the
inhabitants of a territory have no original and underived
sovereignty at all; they have no existence as a sovereign
people, and no inherent political or civil rights and powers.
Whatever legislative authority the territorial legislature
may have, it holds it as a grant from congress.   To recognize
in the people of the territory original and underived legislative power is a contradiction in terms; for it is to recognize them as a state, while they are only a territory.   When
they receive permission from congress to organize themselves as a state, and to form a state constitution preparatory
to admission into the Union, they may authorize slavery or
not as it seems to them good, for then they act as a state,
from their own inherent sovereignty, but not till then; for
till then, they can act only under the authority of congress.
The clause in the bill remitting the decision of the question
of slavery to the territorial people is, therefore, in our judgment, totally unconstitutional, and all acts done under it are
null and void from the beginning.
    Congress can neither legislate slavery into a territory nor
out of it, because slavery is not within the scope of its constitutional powers, and is a matter over which the states
have supreme and exclusive jurisdiction.   This, as we understand it, is southern doctrine, and we believe it sound.
Let the South and the North each have its advantages and
submit to its disadvantages.   The slaveholding states ought
to be satisfied with it, and the free states, if they love the
constitution, have no reason to object to it, for it excludes
slavery from all territory under the Union, till it becomes a
state.   The supreme court of the United States has decided
that slavery is a local institution, and exists only by virtue
of local law.   The right of the master, then, to his slave is
not a right that adheres to him, and which he can carry
with him into other territory, or a foreign locality.   Hence
all our courts hold that a slave brought by his owner into a
free state ceases to be a slave, and he would be free the
moment his master carried him across the frontier even into
another slave state, if the positive law of this latter state

did not renew and confirm the master's right. The principle on which our courts proceed is, that every man is born
free, and can be deprived of his natural freedom only by a
positive local law. Every man is in presumption of law a
freeman, and no one can be treated otherwise than as a freeman, except where a local law making him a slave can be
pleaded. The slave carried by his master, or were it not
for the constitutional provision with regard to fugitive
slaves, escaping from that locality into another where no
such local positive law can be pleaded, resumes his natural
freedom, and reënters the class of freemen. Nature knows
no slaves. By the law of nature all men are born free and
equal, and man has no *jus dominii* in man. The common
law, in so far as it does not consist of local customs and
usages, is coincident with the law of nature or natural right,
and customs and usages have the force of law, only in their
particular locality. There is no American law common to
the whole Union that authorizes slavery in the absence of
the statute law prohibiting it, because such law could proceed only from some act of the states forming the Union,
and no such act can be pretended. The argument based on
the obligation of congress to protect the right of property,
which we used in 1847, in our article on *Slavery and the
Mexican War*,* is rendered invalid by the decision of the
supreme court, of which we were then ignorant, that slavery
exists only by virtue of local law. Therefore the right of
property held by the master in his slave is a local right, and
has no existence out of that locality. If we understand
the decision, the federal courts can recognize the right of
the master only in cases that come under the *lex loci.*
Hence the courts of law in Kansas, were a suit brought involving the point, would be obliged, we doubt not, to declare the alleged slave a free man, whatever may have been
the action of the people or the territorial legislature. We
deny that slavery does or can legally exist in Kansas, so
long as Kansas remains a territory under the United States.

The great objection to the Kansas-Nebraska bill is to the
clause authorizing the people of the territory to decide
whether they will allow slavery or not. We deny the
power of congress to authorize them to do so. In so far as
the bill touches slavery, it provides for its possible introduction into territory where it cannot go legally or constitu-

---

*Brownson's Works, Vol. XVI., p. 25.

tionally. It was an attempt to impose upon the Democracy, by confounding the people as a territory with the people as a state, although by no means the first attempt of the kind. It hoped, because the people as a state are sovereign, to have it pass without opposition that they are sovereign as a territory, or have as a territory inherent and underived legislative authority,—an absurdity equalled only by the so-called Missouri compromise, which we are glad to see struck from our statute books. We reject with indignation this abominable doctrine of "squatter sovereignty," and oppose the Kansas-Nebraska policy still more for its recognition of this doctrine than for any advantage it is likely to secure to the slave interest. Yet, as a recognition of it in favor of that interest, it is also objectionable.

Our readers know that we are no abolitionists, and no one can suspect us of any sympathy with them. We say distinctly that we are strongly opposed to all efforts made in the non-slaveholding states to abolish slavery where it now legally exists. We have no right or wish to interfere with it in a single slave state. It is, in those states, an affair of their own, and to their disposition of it we feel ourselves bound to leave it. We always have defended, and always shall scrupulously defend, to the best of our feeble abilities, all the constitutional rights of slaveholders as well as of non-slaveholders; we will not interfere with the free development and expansion of slavery within its legal limits; but we are not and never have been the champion of slavery; we have never been and never expect to be captivated by its beauties; and, in common with the great body of the people of the free states, we are personally opposed to its extension beyond the limits of the states in which it now legally exists, and we cannot condemn those who believe themselves bound to use all their constitutional rights to resist its further extension. We will scrupulously respect all the rights of the slave states, but we expect them to respect equally all the rights of the free states, and we are unable to see why it is not as honorable and as chivalric to labor to extend the area of freedom as it is to labor to extend the area of slavery. If we are opposed to the subjection of the South by the North, we are equally opposed to the subjection of the North by the South. We deem it the part of all wise American statesmanship to resist by all constitutional and honorable means, the building up in any section of the Union of a great consolidated sectional interest, able to control and subject all others.   The slave interest is as legitimate as the banking or the mercantile interest, but it is everywhere one and identical, and is already the most powerful interest in the country, and if it comes into federal politics, it is able through the division of other interests, to control the policy of the general government.   As far as this interest is legitimate, and is wielded in a constitutional way, we have nothing to allege against it; but as a citizen, looking to the welfare of the whole Union, we may well be opposed to its growth and expansion beyond its legal limits ; we may well be disposed to use all our constitutional rights to restrict it and to keep it out of the arena of politics, and on the same principle, and for nearly the same reasons that General Jackson opposed the old United States bank.

We enter here into no inquiry as to the party that first brought slavery into federal politics. Very likely the North in this respect is the principal offender.   But whoever was the first aggressor, the question has now to be met on its merits, as at present before the public, and treated in reference to its bearing on the future peace and integrity of the Union.   There is a party at the North, resolved at all hazards to effect the complete abolition of slavery,— a party that may become strong, but which as yet is comparatively weak.   There is also a party at the South, or a so-called southern party, that avails itself of the aggressions of the North as a plea for extending and consolidating the slave interest.   Its members are called disunionists, and perhaps do now and then threaten secession ; but their real policy, as we regard it, is not disunion, but, through the slave interest, supremacy.   It enters into their calculations by filibustering or other means to annex Cuba, all southern Mexico, and Central America, as slave states, and they are taking their measures to force the North to aid them, apparently to take the lead, in doing it.   Cuba is to be annexed to prevent it from becoming a free colony, and also to add another slave state to the Union.   If the Spanish laws and edicts on slavery were executed in Cuba there would remain very few slaves in that island.   I am told that by far the larger part of the black population of the island are legally entitled to their freedom, and that the reason why the Cuban creoles wish to be annexed to the Union, is the fear that the mother country, the moment she gets matters settled at home, may take it into her head to

see that her laws and edicts in favor of freedom are enforced, and thus deprive them of their slaves.   This is the
Spanish tyranny of which we hear so much.   It is pretty
certain that slavery will not much longer exist in Cuba, if it
remains a colony of Spain.   Hence the desire of the Cuban
slaveholders to be annexed to the Union ; and to avoid
another example of emancipation in their immediate neighborhood is one strong reason why the people of the southwestern states entertain the same desire.   Reopen the slave
trade, annex Cuba, Mexico, and Central America, these last
after having been first organized into a southern republic
by Walker or some other equally worthy adventurer, apparently hostile to the United States, so as not to excite the
opposition of France and England, and the slave interest
will have so extended and consolidated itself that it can not
only defy, as it is trusted, the attacks of northern abolitionism, but also dictate as a master the policy of the federal
administration.   This, we take it, is what the so-called
southern party, really not more southern than northern in
its composition, is pursuing.   It is, also, a policy not absolutely impracticable, if its abettors can, by alarming the
friends of the Union as to the danger of northern sectionalism, prevent the sound portion of the people from interposing in time to thwart it.   Northern speculation has a hand
in it, and its most efficient supporters we presume are to be
found in this city.   The Cincinnati platform, with its en-
dorsement of the Kansas-Nebraska bill, the strong emphasis
placed on the so-called "Monroe doctrine," and the recent
movement towards the revival of slavery by Walker in
Nicaragua, are all significant, and indicate pretty plainly
what is intended and what is expected.

We do not pretend that this policy finds its support only
at the South, or that there are not northern demagogues
and speculators in abundance leagued with the southern:
nor do we pretend that the South is unanimously in favor of
it.   The mass of the people both South and North are really
and firmly attached to the Union, and ask nothing more
than to have the government administered in accordance
with Union principles, leaving all sectional interests to be
disposed of by the several state governments.   But the advocates of the policy we have under consideration are
laboring through the slave interest to combine the whole
southern people in its favor, by making them generally believe that their only security for their slave property is in

its realization. The leaders of the party are, perhaps, northern, rather than southern men, and the whole scheme looks to us like the product of a northern, rather than a southern brain. It smells of Wall street. These leaders care no more for one section of the Union than another, and their aim is simply to use the South through the slave interest to further the purposes of their own selfish ambition and personal aggrandizement. They wish to build up a single permanent interest strong enough to dictate the policy of the government, and the slave interest is the one which seems to them to have the requisite capabilities. By combining slavery with democracy, and democracy with the extension of territory and therefore with the interest of the speculators, they hope to succeed in their plans.

The danger in this case, as in most others, comes from creating false issues. The party we oppose labor at the South to confound the security of slave property, where it is legally recognized, and which is all that the great body of the southern people ask, with slavery extension, or the enlargement of the area of slavery; while at the North they labor to confound opposition to the extension of slavery into new territory, with abolitionism, or a determination to interfere with slavery in the slave states themselves. They will not suffer either at the South or at the North the proper issue to be made before the public. Hence the danger. The first thing for Mr. Buchanan to do, is so to shape his administration as to bring the question in its proper form before the American people. He must show the South that the security of slave property and the extension of slave territory have no necessary connection, perhaps are incompatible one with the other, and the North that opposition to the extension of slavery into territory where it cannot go constitutionally does not involve abolitionism, and may be consistent with the most scrupulous respect for the rights of slave property in its own locality. All the great body of the southern people want is security for their property in slaves; all the great body of the northern people think of asking is security that slavery shall not leap its present bounds, and become the dominant interest of the country. Mr. Buchanan, then, must make his appeal distinctly to the great body of the people both North and South, and show by his appointments and the measures he adopts or recommends that, as far as depends on his government, the slaveholding states shall be protected in all their constitutional rights, and no countenance will be given either to the party of abolition or the party of extension. This is what is imposed upon him as a constitutional president, and if distinctly adopted and carried out with resolution and impartiality, the administration will be brought back to Union principles, and the demagogues whether northern or southern will be defeated.   This is the work Mr. Buchanan has been elected to perform, and which he must perform if he means even to retain power in the hands of the Democratic party.

In urging this Union policy upon the incoming administration against the abolition party on the one hand and the slavery extension party on the other, we are warring against the just rights of no section, we are simply warring against sectionalism, whether northern or southern.   The federal government was instituted for the common weal of all the states, and its utility depends on its confining itself to the interests common to all sections of the Union.   We do not, in asking the administration to discountenance the slavery extension party, ask it to interfere positively to prevent the extension of slavery to new territory, but not to interfere to favor it.   Slavery cannot extend legally beyond the present slave states into territory not yet erected into states, without the positive action of the federal government; and the only concession to the North we ask is, that that action shall be withheld, for it is both dangerous and unconstitutional.   All the concession we ask for the South is, that the question of slavery be excluded from federal politics, and left to be disposed of by the states, by each state, when a state, for itself, and as regards the territories by the federal courts.   More than this neither the North nor the South has any real interest in demanding, and to demand more may be to get less.

The admirers of slavery, whether northern or southern, must know that they stand very much alone, and that it is too late to attempt to make converts to the slave system. Say what we will, slavery is regarded by the civilized world as an odious institution, as well as by the great mass of the people of the free states, and even the people of the slave states themselves are very far from being unanimous in their admiration of it.   We have found as much genuine, honest abolition sentiment in the slave states as we have ever found in the free states, and the southern politicians, who talk so violently against the northern Yankees, know very well that it requires the most strenuous efforts on their part to retain their hold on their constituents. Most of their declamation is intended for effect at home, rather than abroad. For ourselves personally, we would not emancipate the slave population at the South, if we had the power, not, indeed, because we like slavery, but because with all the study we have been able to give to the subject, we can discover no condition possible at present for the mass of that population superior to that in which they now are. Humanity towards that population, if nothing else, would prevent us from being an abolitionist. But the South cannot be ignorant that she has the civilized world against her, and if she seeks in earnest to foist her domestic institutions on territory under the constitution now free, she will meet in the free states a resistance, which even her chivalry will not be able to withstand. The free states are determined that there shall be no further extension of slave territory to the North or to the South, and the immense pluralities in the late election for Colonel Fremont prove that their resolution in this respect is not to be despised ; and yet Colonel Fremont himself did not command the full vote of the party opposed to slavery extension. If his election had turned on that question alone, he would have swept by overwhelming majorities every non-slaveholding state in the Union, and perhaps have carried two or three even of the slave states. This should admonish the incoming administration that no strengthening and consolidating of the slave interest beyond its strict constitutional rights, can be prudently attempted. The free states will not consent to be governed by that interest. Southern politicians and southern journals may threaten secession, may talk disunion, may advocate a southern slaveholding confederacy, but it will not move the mass of the people in the free states. If the controversy proceeds to blows, they will give as well as receive, and perhaps not be the first to yield. If worst comes to worst, the old battle of the Puritans and the Cavaliers will be fought over again, and the party opposed to slavery extension will then, in spite of all that can be said, be an abolition party, and the cry will be " freedom to the slave," instead of the old cry of "a godly reformation of the church and state." The South cannot afford to provoke such a conflict, for in it the moral sense of the civilized world would be with the North, which would be cheered on as the champion of freedom.

But we have not the slightest fear of a civil war. There is too much good sense and good feeling in all sections, and too ardent a love for the Union to permit it; and on neither side will it get beyond the bullying point. Yet the South can no more safely press slavery extension than the North can abolition principles and movements. Either is pregnant with danger, and should be abandoned. Let the abolition movement be restrained, and the slavery extension movement can be easily defeated; let the slavery extension policy be withdrawn, and we can easily confine abolitionism to a few harmless men and women who find their dissipation in philanthropy instead of theatres, routs, and balls. Both movements must be suppressed, and the policy of the incoming administration must be to suppress them by favoring neither, and by resisting each when it seeks either to control or to embarrass it. In doing so, we do not say Mr. Buchanan will escape opposition or obloquy; he will no doubt be accused of want of fidelity to the Cincinnati platform, of betraying the South, or of courting the North; but he will, if he does it openly, decidedly, bravely, be sustained, for the people know that the only platform he is at liberty to consult is the constitution, and the only party to which he is responsible is the party of the Union. He has not been elected to carry out the will of any sectional party, northern or southern, eastern or western; but to administer the government for four years on constitutional principles, and with sole reference to those rights and interests which are common to all the states. Let him feel that, and take his stand above party, command party, not serve it, and the country will sustain him, and honor him as one of her greatest and most deserving presidents.

We know the slavery question is one of great delicacy, but it must be resolutely faced, and both sections must give up something. The South must yield its assumed right to transport slave property into territories not yet erected into states, and the North must yield its pretension to the right of congress to refuse to admit a state into the Union, whose constitution does not exclude slavery. The southern claim is unfounded because the right of property in slaves is local, not general; and the northern pretension is unconstitutional, because congress has no right to examine the constitution of a sovereign state any further than to ascertain that it is not anti-republican or incompatible with the constitution of the United States. Under our system it is neither anti-republican nor unconstitutional for a state to authorize slavery. The people of the state, not of the territory, have the undoubted constitutional right, within its own jurisdiction, to establish or to prohibit slavery as they please; and to the people of the state,—not of the territory, as says the Kansas-Nebraska bill,—the disposition of the question must be left. This may not prevent the extension of slavery into new states after their formation as states; but it will prevent its extension by the aid of the federal government, which is all that the anti-slavery extension party can constitutionally insist upon, or attempt by political action. With this both sections must be contented. Any claim on either side beyond will only provoke exaggeration on the other, and render internal peace impracticable.

There must, again, be no talk of reviving the African slave trade. The slave trade is placed by the constitution under the authority of congress, and the Union has the constitutional right to act on it. No doubt our northern and eastern cities swarm with mammon-worshippers anxious to have the trade reopened, and ready to enter into it with all their Yankee energy and perseverance; but that traffic is infamous, and by nearly all civilized nations is declared to be piracy. Were we to reopen it we should become for ever infamous. It is almost enough to make an honest man turn abolitionist to find slavery so blunting the moral sense as to permit men otherwise honorable and high-minded to broach, even in conversation, a thing so infamous. We confess what we have read in respectable southern journals, and heard talked by men of high character in regard to reopening the African slave trade has shocked us, and greatly modified our feelings on the subject of slavery. That traffic was condemned by the church as long ago as 1482, and the condemnation has been renewed by successive popes down to our own times. The Catholic who engages in it, who reduces the African negro to slavery, or who buys and holds as a slave any one so reduced from a state of freedom, is *ipso facto* excommunicated. No class of citizens have more uniformly or more faithfully supported the constitutional rights of the slaveholding states than Catholics, both North and South. With us it has been a point of conscience, of religion to be loyal to the Union, loyal to the constitution, and it has been a sense of duty to the Union, to the constitution, that has made us here at the North vote in almost one solid phalanx for Mr. Buchanan, against what we regarded as northern sectionalism. None of us like slavery, none of us wish to perpetuate it; we all of us love freedom, and hold all men to be equal under the law of nature; but we all respect vested rights, and our respect for the constitutional rights of the slaveholding states, has led us to vote, often much against our personal interests, with the South. But we can never support any party in so infamous a project as that of reopening the African slave trade, a trade which our religion condemns, and which has brought a curse upon every Catholic state that has permitted it. We regard it with horror, and must oppose it to the last gasp, let the cost be to us what it may. If you insist on it, you will compel us to vote as Catholics, as well as citizens, against you, for you then insist on a matter that our religion as Catholics condemns. You touch our consciences, and compel us for religion's sake to cast our votes against you, and there is not a non-slaveholding state in the Union, without us, on whose vote you can count. You would make a northern sectional party a duty as well as a necessity, and commit the honor of the country to the keeping of the North. This were moonlight madness, and we do not believe that the high-minded and chivalric, the moral and Christian South will itself consent to it.

The project of reopening the slave trade, advocated, we regret to see, by the governor of South Carolina in his recent message to the legislature of that state, if seriously entertained, will give to the question of slavery a new face, as well as new and startling dimensions, and convert every northern Union man into a decided anti-slavery man. Northern Union men do not love slavery, and they submit to it where it legally exists, only as they submit to a lesser in order to avoid a greater evil. Impose upon them the additional burden of bearing the infamy of the slave trade, and you will find them entirely unmanageable. They will, in their indignation, throw off that burden and the other too. Constitutional scruples will no longer restrain them, and they will pour down upon the South as an army of veritable northern Berserkirs, whose fury no earthly power can restrain or withstand. Is it prudent on the part of the friends of slavery to push us so far, to exact so much of us? Is it wise to take away from us all middle ground, and force us either to become propagandists of slavery or to join with the abolitionists? Can they not see that, if compelled to take sides, we shall deem it more Christian, more honorable, more chivalric even, to make common cause with the abolition movement than with a movement for reviving and legalizing the African slave trade? Cannot these so-called "fire-eaters" understand that we at the North, especially we who have always stood by the Union and resisted all encroachments on the constitutional rights of the slave interest, have the principles of religion and of honor in as high a degree at least as they have? Can they not understand that we have defended the South from loyalty to the constitution, and not from any good will we have to slavery? Do they expect to convert us to their slavery worship, and to make us admirers of the concealed beauties of negro slavery? If they have so expected, it is time for them to be undeceived.

We know the enemies of the Union at the South and at the North labor with all their might to force the party whose candidate Mr. Buchanan was into one extreme or the other, and to compel it to be either an abolitionist or a pro-slavery party. They are determined that there shall be no Union men. The wider they can make the breach the better are they pleased. The abolitionists hope by so doing to compel all the free states to take up their cause, and the pro-slavery men hope by the same means to combine all the slave states, and through them either rule or split the Union, and form a grand southern republic in which slavery may be developed and expanded without the restraints necessarily imposed by their connections with the free states. But if the South follows the lead of these "fire-eaters," who look for a grand field for slavery expansion in yet unannexed Mexico, Central America, and the West Indies, the abolitionists will prove the successful party, for they will have the federal government and the moral sympathy of the world on their side. Cotton, rice, and tobacco are very important, we own, in regulating our exchanges, but not so important as they were before the California gold discoveries, and California will not go with the slavery republic. The immense Republican vote in the free states proves, among other things, that exchanges do not depend as exclusively on southern products as they did a few years ago. The great West is opened, and its products are every day becoming a more and more important element in trade, domestic and foreign. The great agricultural free states, in the valley of the Mississippi, all Republican states, with two exceptions, not to be counted on, will never suffer the mouth of the Mississippi and the southern outlets of their trade to be held by a foreign state, though of kindred blood, especially if that foreign state depends on slave labor.   The southern confederacy would find itself opposed not only by the Northeast, but by the still more formidable Northwest, and brave as are the southern chivalry, and as handy as they are in using gutta-percha canes, they would be powerless before the two united, acting by authority of the federal government, with the war-cry of freedom.

No; the interest of the South as well as of the North is in loyalty to the Union, and she should be as careful to avoid the issue the "fire-eaters" and abolitionists are forcing upon her as we of the North, and perhaps even more so.   She must, then, for her own sake discountenance all movements towards reviving and legalizing the slave trade, and be contented with our fidelity to our constitutional engagements.   If she finds the slave interest too weak for her ambition, it is a misfortune from which she has no right to expect the free states to relieve her.   She takes her chance with the rest, and must bear her share of her own burdens. We do not reproach her with her slavery, but we owe her no aid beyond letting it alone where it is.   With that she must make up her mind to be satisfied, and so much the free states are, in that case, bound to give her.

We have been discussing slavery merely as a political question, in relation to federal politics; we have not felt called upon to consider it in its moral aspects.   As a Catholic the moral question has long since been settled for us. We have no vague, floating, or uncertain doctrines on the subject. We do not agree with the abolitionists that slavery is *malum in se*, and that one cannot with a good conscience be a slaveholder.   We do not any more believe that slavery is an unmixed evil, or that in private morals, or the Christian virtues, the southern people are one whit inferior to their northern brethren.   As a general rule, we believe the slaves are treated with kindness and humanity, sufficiently fed and clothed, and not over-worked.   We believe they are morally and physically better off, with individual exceptions, than they would be if emancipated; and therefore we would not, as we have said, disturb the relation which exists between them and their masters, if we had the power and the constitutional right.   Nevertheless, the more we have seen of slavery under its most favorable aspects, the more satisfied are we that it is an evil to be borne, rather than a good to be sought, to be confined rather than extended.

We are not writing in a spirit hostile to southern interests. We have dwelt indeed more on the danger of movements to strengthen and consolidate the slave power than
on that of the northern abolition movements, because we
have for years dwelt on the latter, and because we think it
always the part of wisdom to guard first against the danger
that is nearest and most pressing. The nearest and most
pressing danger is that of converting the party which in the
late election supported Colonel Fremont into a strictly
anti-slavery party, and this can be guarded against by no
efforts so to extend and strengthen the slave power as to secure to it the administration.   All efforts of that sort will
tend only to precipitate the danger, for it is precisely
against such extending and strengthening of the slave
power that that party is organized.   The moment the
United States bank entered the arena of politics and attempted to obtain a power too strong for the government
to resist, although apparently in self-defence, its doom was
sealed, because the people, moved by an instinct of freedom, would not suffer the existence of a moneyed power
outside of the government strong enough to control it.   It
will be the same with slavery.   Its safety depends on its
weakness, not in having or in appearing to have the power
to shape the policy of the government.   It has reached the
extent of its power, and to seek to make it more powerful,
is precisely to excite a more determined hostility to it, and
a hostility that under no circumstances it will become
strong enough to subdue. If slavery, where it exists, cannot
find security without governing the Union, it will not be
permitted to exist in the Union at all.

It must never be forgotten that slavery is repugnant to
the moral sense of the civilized world.   It belongs to a past
age, to the heathen rather than the Christian republic,
and no free state will consent to place the interest of slave
labor on a par with the interest of free labor.   The thing
is not to be thought of.   To administer the government in
the interest of the free laboring classes is wise and just, in
harmony with the best and strongest spirit of modern times ;
to administer it solely in the interest of capital, especially
when that capital consists of slaves, human beings, men like
ourselves, descended from the same stock, and redeemed
by the same God become man, is repugnant to that spirit,
and to the uniform tendencies of our holy religion.   Such
is the fact, war against it as you will.   It is, then, in vain

that you brand as aggressive any constitutional action of the
government intended to affect favorably the interests of
free labor, or claim in the name of equal rights a like action
in favor of slave labor. The equality in the case is not and
will not be conceded, for freedom is the natural right of
every man, and slavery its abridgment by positive law. In
the case of free labor the law must be interpreted liberally
in its favor; in the case of slave labor it must be construed
strictly, and favor as little as possible the owner of that
labor. The policy of the law is to favor freedom and to
restrict slavery. This being the case, free labor may develop and expand itself anywhere and to any extent not
prohibited; slave labor only where and to the extent authorized by positive law. There is no aggression on the rights of
slave labor in seeking to keep slavery out of all territory now
free, while there is a direct aggression on free labor in seeking to subject that territory to the slave interest, for in all
cases slavery is the abridgment of the natural rights of man.
Hence the efforts of the South to expand her system of
slave labor against free labor, where free labor has not been
by law deprived of its natural freedom, will be counted a
positive aggression and resisted as such. Therefore we
maintain that the security of slave property consists in its
not attempting to extend or strengthen itself beyond its
present limits, and in submitting without resistance to the
free and full development of free labor within its constitutional bounds. To do otherwise were to provoke a contest
in which slave labor would be deprived of all its rights,
even where it now has rights. Any man who knows the
country and is capable of putting two ideas together cannot
fail to see and admit this.

We, therefore, regret the policy shadowed forth in the
Cincinnati platform, which, under pretence of non-intervention by congress in the question of slavery, contemplates
in reality the strengthening of slavery by the addition of
new slave territory not as yet within the limits of the Union.
The Ostend conference, the emphasis laid on the so-called
"Monroe doctrine," the obvious wish on the part of our
late minister to England to break up the Clayton-Bulwer
treaty, and the filibustering clauses of the Cincinnati platform taken in connection with Walker's movements in Central America, the effort made by General Quitman and
others in congress for the repeal of the neutrality laws, and
the advocacy at the South of the revival of the African

slave trade, all indicate a policy, the character of which it is impossible to mistake. The policy is not to press the extension of slavery in any of the present territory of the Union now free, but to indemnify the slave interest by annexing, at the earliest practicable moment, Cuba, Central America, and Mexico as slave states. This will give the South the predominance in the Union, or at least afford her security against any growth or expansion of the free states. The national greediness for territorial aggrandizement, the filibustering spirit now so rife, the speculators now so numerous in all sections of the Union, the strength of the existing slave interest, the love of democracy of the American people, and their confidence in their manifest destiny, it has been supposed would, all combined, secure the adoption of this policy against all possible opposition.

It would now seem that the plan is, in the first place, by the aid of the filibusters, transit companies, or other corporations and speculators, to organize Mexico and Central America into a great Anglo-Saxon republic, as a duplicate of our own. In the beginning, in order not to excite the hostility of Great Britain and France, it will be organized ostensibly for the purpose of interposing a barrier to the further progress of the Union to the South. It contemplates, we presume, adding to this southern republic California and all the territory of the Union west of the Rocky Mountains, and as many of the southern states as choose to secede, and aid in forming a slaveholding republic. But ultimately it is to be joined to the present Union, so as to extend the Union over the whole North American continent, together with the West India Islands. A grand scheme, we admit, and one which we do not doubt is seriously entertained by men who are not yet in a madhouse.

Even were this policy practicable, it should be opposed by every patriot, every friend of morality, by every man who has the least regard for national honor. The true policy of this country is undoubtedly to prevent Cuba from passing into the hands of a first-class European power, but not to take possession of it ourselves, even if we could do so with the consent of Spain herself. It would add nothing to our strength, and in fact as an outlying post, incapable, in case of war with a great European power, of defending itself, would much extend and weaken our system of military defences. In regard to Central America, through which lies one of the great highways of the future com-

merce of the world, all we want is that it should not be
held by a power able to close that highway to us. Of
course, we cannot consent to let Great Britain, France, or
Russia have possession of that highway, and for the same
reason we can never suffer to grow up a rival power, Anglo-
Saxon or not, able to dispute with us the transit across the
isthmus. These are fixed points in our national policy,
which we shall maintain, if need be, with the whole moral
and material force of the Union. But beyond we need
nothing. A free transit across the isthmus for our commerce we demand, and we shall do our best to exclude the
settlement of any power there strong enough to deny it to
us. Our interest requires nothing more, and this interest
would exclude the grand Walker empire just now talked
about, as much as it would England or France. The policy
of our government has never gone, and we much doubt if it
will go any further. General Pierce came into power with
certain filibuster proclivities, and his foreign appointments
were all such as to create the impression that he intended
to pursue a policy of territorial aggrandizement. But
events proved too strong for him, or experience soon taught
him a sounder policy. He has succeeded in giving his administration, with a few exceptions, the right position in regard to foreign powers; the end of his government has
well-nigh retrieved the errors of its beginning, and we regret that he is not to be at the head of the administration
for the next four years, unless Mr. Marcy be retained as
secretary of state. But whatever may have been Mr. Buchanan's views at the Ostend conference, or as minister to
England, we cannot believe he will aim at more in regard
to Cuba or Central America, than simply to carry out as
occasion may require, and as he has power, the so-called
"Monroe doctrine," and this much even we should insist
upon.

The free transit across the isthmus for our commerce is
necessary to enable us to keep up the balance of the New
World with the Old. Great Britain is not at present ambitious of extending her power in the New World. She has
turned her attention to the East, and hopes to monopolize
the trade of entire Asia. She is aiming at the commerce
of the Black Sea, and to gain a position in Sicily and also
on the Persian Gulf, so as to check Russian advances towards India, and to neutralize France in Africa, Syria, and
Egypt, and by means of the Euphrates railroad, and a rail-

road, or a canal, if she can control it, across the Isthmus of Suez, to place Asia in competition with America. This is the only way in which she can maintain herself for any great length of time against our commercial rivalry. We can meet her policy only by a ship canal across the Isthmus of Central America, and a railroad through our own territory to the Pacific Ocean enabling us to compete advantageously with her in eastern Asia. Great Britain having turned her attention eastward, and being likely for some time to come to have her hands full with France and Russia, whom in the late war she adroitly played off one against the other, our filibusters seem to fancy that there is a chance of founding, by aid of the slave interest, a southern republic unconnected with the free states of this Union, and of securing the commercial advantages to which Central America is the key. Hence the opposition of the South to the Pacific railroad, unless it is made so far South as to come within what is intended to be the southern republic. But this southern republic is a dream that will never be realized. The whole power of the federal government in the hands of the free states, will be exerted, if necessary, to prevent it. Those southern states, not yet within the limits of the Union will, if they change their present condition, be annexed to our confederacy. No matter what the journals may say. No administration will favor or suffer such a republic independent of the Union.

To the annexation of these states there are several weighty objections. One is that we have no right to them, and cannot do it without tarnishing our national honor. Another reason is, the South will oppose their annexation unless they are annexed as slave states, and to their annexation as slave states the North will never consent, and the North is wrought up to that degree of heat, and is so confident of its strength, that it will have its way. It counts its late defeat a victory, and it will yield hereafter to slavery nothing not contained in the bond. In all the Spanish American republics slavery has been abolished, and we shall never consent to take the retrograde step of reëstablishing it. The progress of the whole civilized world since the introduction of Christianity has been towards the abolition of slavery. To reëstablish it where it has been abolished is to take a step backwards towards barbarism and paganism. It would be a fine compliment to American democracy to say that wherever it extends it carries slavery with it. It will do very well for our southern "fire eaters" to tell us slavery is the basis of freedom, and the cement of the Union, but no man of ordinary intelligence and right feeling can be expected to believe it. The states in question may ultimately be annexed to the Union, but not till they can be annexed as free states. Some of the slave states may threaten secession, and may even take measures to secede; but they will soon be glad enough to return, for if they secede they will leave the Union behind them, and by no means carry it with them. We have confidence that this grand filibuster and annexation scheme will find no favor with the incoming administration.

The true policy for us towards our Spanish American neighbors is to respect their rights as independent states, to suppress all invasions of them by our citizens, to protect them, aid them to recover from their internal distractions, and stimulate them by our trade and good offices to maintain well ordered governments, and to develop their internal resources. In this way we shall best promote both their interest and our own. At any rate, the incoming administration must put down filibustering. Filibusters are simply freebooters, pirates, thieves, robbers, murderers, and it is any thing but creditable to us, that they are able to awaken the sympathies of a people like the American. They are corrupt and corrupting, and already have they had a most deleterious effect on both the public and private conscience of large masses of our citizens. No doubt they have gained sympathy chiefly because they have given themselves out as the soldiers,—irregular soldiers it may be,—but the soldiers of liberty. Walker's conduct in Nicaragua in revoking the decree abolishing slavery, and practising the most cruel despotism, strips them of that mask, and they will henceforth, we hope, be held in the horror and detestation they deserve.

Some things more we had intended to say, but we have said enough. We have written for the purpose of throwing out a few suggestions which we hope the incoming administration will regard as those of a friend and not an enemy, but as those of one who loves truth and justice even more than the material interests of his country, and his country more than party, and who asks nothing of any administration for himself. Wiser suggestions may be made; none more honest or disinterested will be offered. We follow no party lead; we go with party as far as it goes with us,

and no further. We reluctantly voted against Col. Fremont, for we feared the influence of the abolition leaders
who surrounded him, but we are as loath to support a southern as a northern sectional party, and though we voted for
Mr. Buchanan, we will support him only so far as he proves
himself a Union president.

THE SLAVERY QUESTION ONCE MORE.

[From Brownson's Quarterly Review for April, 1857.]

WE have been told that our remarks on Slavery and the
Incoming Administration gave great offence to some of our
readers, and we have found ourselves denounced in a Virginia journal of note and influence as on the verge of black-
republicanism.   We are not surprised at this, for partisans
can rarely understand the position of one who holds himself independent of party, and who assumes the right to
judge all parties.
Our views on slavery itself were given in April, 1838,*
and were such as to secure us the friendship of the late
John C. Calhoun, and of several of the more eminent statesmen of the slave-holding states.   We are not aware of having changed our views on that subject since.   We have
never professed to admire slavery, or to wish its continuance; we have uniformly expressed ourselves as in opposition to it, wherever it is an open question, whether it shall
exist or not.   Thus we say to the South, January, 1841,
" Slavery we cannot advocate, for we can see no affinity between slavery and democracy.   We shall undoubtedly speak
out unquestioned, and unobstructed, in favor of universal
freedom to universal man."   " You must not think that we
advocate slavery on principle, that we love the institution.
There is not a Democrat north of Mason and Dixon's line
that does not loathe it, and believe it a crime against humanity.   We refrain from meddling with it, simply because
it is a matter which concerns states of which we are not
citizens, because we can reach it by no constitutional action,
and because we believe liberty is more interested at present
in preserving the constitution, in maintaining state rights,

* *Slavery—Abolitionism*, Brownson's Works, Vol. XV., pp. 45 *et seq.*

than in attempting the doubtful good of emancipating the slave without making any provision for him after his fetters have been knocked off." * Substantially the same views we have always expressed whenever we have alluded to the subject. We have maintained and still maintain that a man may hold slaves with a good conscience, in opposition to abolitionists who maintain that slavery is always and everywhere and under all circumstances a sin, but we have never approved it.

We have, ever since 1838, uniformly opposed,—no man more strenuously, whether efficiently or not,—the whole abolition movement, on legal, moral, economical, and political grounds. Touching the question of slavery the several states are, in relation to one another, independent sovereignties, and must be regarded as so many independent foreign nations. New York has the same right to take cognizance of slavery in South Carolina that she has to take cognizance of any domestic institution of France or Great Britain, and no more ; that is to say, no right at all. As a citizen of New York I am not responsible for the existence of slavery in any other state in the Union, and I cannot, further than the expression of my individual opinion, interfere with the relation existing between the master and his slave, without violating international law, striking at the mutual equality and independence of the states, and sapping the constitution of the Union. The whole abolition movement of the non-slaveholding states as it has been carried on for now nearly thirty years we regard and for nearly the whole of that time have regarded as immoral, illegal, and its abettors as punishable by our laws.

We deny, and always have denied, the right of congress to legislate on the subject. The fugitive-slave law is simply a law for executing a clause in the constitution, which is in the nature of an extradition clause, in a treaty between independent sovereigns. We always regarded the so-called " Missouri compromise " as unconstitutional. Slavery with us is purely a STATE institution, deriving from state sovereignty alone, and there is under our system no power to authorize or to abolish it, but the state itself, that is, the people in their state as distinguished from their federal capacity. The state may or may not, as it chooses, authorize slavery, forbid it, or abolish it, without leave asked or ob-

---

* *Ibid*, pp. 131–2.

tained from the Union, or from her sister states. Congres
has, then, no power to say to the states on one side of a given
parallel of latitude you may, and on the other, you shall not,
hold slaves.   The constitution gives it no such power either
in respect of old states or new states.   New York has been
a slaveholding state since my recollection, and may become
so again if she chooses.   Congress has nothing to say on the
subject, one way or the other.   In the admission of new
states, it has no right to say the state must come in with or
without slaves.   The state does not become a state by the
act of admission, for it is admitted, and can be admitted, into the Union only as a state, and therefore must exist as a
state before admission.   When leave is given to a territory
to form a state constitution for itself, and it has in accordance
with the leave obtained formed its constitution, and organized its state government, it is a state, a free sovereign state,
and till its admission, as independent of the Union, as
though it were a foreign nation.   If congress refuses to admit it, it does not fall back under the territorial government,
and become subject again to the Union, but remains a state
outside of the Union, free and independent, with all the
rights and capacities of a sovereign community.   Congress
then cannot dictate to the people of the territory the provisions of the constitution they adopt, and must treat them in
relation to their constitution, precisely as it must treat the
states already in the Union.   It has then nothing to say in
the formation of their constitution on the subject of slavery.
When they have organized their state government, they
have the right to apply for admission into the Union, and it
is obligatory on congress to admit them, if they have adopted a state government republican in its form.   This settles
the question as to the Missouri compromise, and proves it to
be unconstitutional.

The only case in which it can be pretended that congress
may interfere with the slave question is in the organization
of territorial governments ; but it cannot even in this case
interfere with it, because under our system slavery is purely
a state question, and has no existence where there is no state.
The federal government is a government of express powers,
and among its express powers there is none which gives it
authority to introduce or abolish, to authorize or prohibit
slavery.   Its powers in regard to territories not yet erected
into states are restricted to the necessities of the case, and
must be exercised in accordance with the general principles

of law. It may enforce the natural law, and is bound to protect all the rights which exist under the common law; but it can go no further, except by special constitutional provision. It has no authority to create new rights or to derogate from existing rights. But as slavery exists neither by the common law nor by the natural law, congress cannot introduce it in a territory; and as slavery exists only by virtue of municipal law, it cannot enter legally into any territory while a territory. So in no case has congress or the Union any power over the question of slavery, and hence both the Missouri compromise and the Wilmot proviso are unconstitutional, and ought never to have been adopted.

The South agree that congress has no power to legislate slavery into a territory, and the ground we took in our article is, that without the legislative action of congress slavery cannot legally go into any territory, while a territory. This ground we did not indeed take in 1847, in an article on *Slavery and the Mexican War.* We changed our ground in 1854, on being assured that the supreme court had decided that slavery is a local institution, existing only by virtue of positive law,—a fact of which I was not aware in 1847. I am told the decision of the court does not go to the extent alleged. This may be so, but whether so or not is nothing to my present purpose. If the court has not so decided, the opinion is incontrovertible, and although the alleged decision was the occasion of my adopting it, it is not the authority on which I defend it. Slavery is, whether the supreme court has so decided or not, a local institution, rightfully existing only by virtue of municipal law. Under the law of nature, there are no slaves, for all men are created equal, and one man has no *jus dominii* over another. Hence all Americans maintain that power, in whose hands soever lodged, is a trust, and a trust to be exercised for the good of the governed, for whose benefit the trust is created. Neither the civil law nor the common law authorizes slavery, and every lawyer knows that all the presumptions of law are in favor of freedom. There remains then no possible legal sanction of slavery but that of municipal law, which has no force out of the municipality. It exists with us, if it legally exists at all, by virtue of the local law of the state, and that law has and can have no extra-territorial jurisdiction. How then is it possible for slavery to have a legal *status* in territory included within no state, and subject, aside from the laws of congress, to no law but the law of nature?

We have been told that slavery exists in the Union by usage, and that the usage which obtained in all the colonies from the beginning authorizes it to go wherever it is not forbidden. But we deny that slavery exists in the Union by usage, for it does not exist in the Union at all. It exists in the states by usage, if you will, but not in the Union. Slavery is a state, not a federal institution. It was, we believe, introduced into the colonies without any positive law, and it continues to exist, as a matter of fact, in all the states that have not by positive law abolished or prohibited it. But the usage was that of distinct, and in relation to one another, independent colonies. The usage of one colony had, *per se,* no force in another, and though in fact it obtained in them all, it was never the common usage of the whole, but the particular usage of each. The usage in question may or may not legalize slavery in the states which have not abolished it, but as law it is confined to each state separately without extra-territorial force or vigor. It cannot legalize it in a territory not yet erected into a state, because territories have and can have no local usage. Usage itself, moreover, is not law, and is recognized by the courts as law, only because its long existence warrants the presumption that it has received the express or tacit sanction of the law-making power; and therefore no usage can have the force of law where there is no legislative authority competent to pass a law to the same effect. Give, therefore, to the usage or custom alleged all the force you can, since it is the usage or custom only of distinct colonies or distinct states, it can never authorize slavery, which does not exist by virtue of natural right or the *jus gentium,* out of the territorial jurisdiction of the particular state or colony. It is simply in its nature a municipal usage, and of no force save within the municipality.

We are told, again, that slaves are property, and the Union is bound to recognize and protect slave property as much as any other species of property. Very true, where slave property exists, but not where it does not exist. In the states where slaves are property, the federal courts are bound to treat them as property, and cannot discriminate between them and other species of property; but not therefore does it follow that it must treat them as property in the territories, where no local law makes them property.

The territory of the Union, not yet erected into states, belongs, we are further told, to all the states in common, and as all the states are equal, the citizens of slaveholding states must have the same right to migrate to them and settle on them with their property, that the citizens of the other states have to migrate to them and settle on them with their property. Most certainly, with that which is property out of their own state or in the territory. No discrimination can be made between the citizens of one state and those of another. The citizen of South Carolina must be as free to settle in Nebraska, for instance, as the citizen of New York, and to carry with him every species of property that his New York brother can carry. The citizen of New York cannot carry with him his real estate, or as the French law terms it, his immovable property, though he may retain the title ; neither can the South Carolinian carry his real estate with him, and we believe negroes are counted by the laws of his state, real, not personal property. He may sell them, and carry with him the proceeds, which is all the New Yorker can do with his real or immovable property. The prohibition to the South Carolinian to hold his people in Nebraska as property only places him and the New Yorker on a footing of equality. But, if the South Carolinian asks to carry his people with him and to hold them as property in Nebraska, he asks more than he concedes to his New York brother, for as his people are property only by virtue of the laws of South Carolina, he asks simply that the municipal laws of his state shall *pro tanto* at least, have extra-territorial force, and operate as law in Nebraska. What he really asks is, that the legislation of South Carolina shall extend by its own force over territory not within her jurisdiction, for by no other law than that of South Carolina are his people property. Why shall he have the right to extend over Nebraska the South Carolinian legislation which creates his slave property, any more than the New Yorker to extend over it the New York legislation which abolishes and prohibits such property ?

It is alleged again, that if debarred from migrating with their slaves to the new territory, the citizens of the slaveholding states are deprived of their equal right in the common property of all the states. But not any more than the citizens of the non-slaveholding states would be deprived of theirs, were the privilege conceded, for the existence of slavery is as repugnant to the latter as its non-existence is to the former. The existence of slavery has shut out emigration from the North to the rich lands of the South and

Southwest, as effectually as the prohibition of slavery has shut out emigration from the South to the rich and fertile lands of the Northwest.

The mistake of so many of our own statesmen on this subject grows out of the assumption that the title to slave property rests on the same foundation as does any other species of property. We deny, and all along have denied, this assumption. The slaveholder's title to property in his people rests solely on municipal law, not on natural right. We dispute not its validity within the jurisdiction of the state enacting that law; but we deny it in toto out of that jurisdiction. The right of property is, indeed, anterior to civil society, and is a natural and divine right, but the right to property in human beings is only a municipal right. God gave the earth to the children of men; he made man the lord of the lower creation, and gave him dominion over the beasts of the field, the fowls of the air, and the fishes of the sea, for they were created for man. In them man has a natural right of property, which civil society may indeed define and regulate, but which it does not create, and which it is bound to recognize and protect. But God, as Pope Gregory the Great* has declared, never gave to man dominion over man, nor to one man the right to lord it over another. He has never created some men to be kings and others to be subjects, some to be masters and others to be slaves; but he has created all men equal, and therefore Pope Alexander III. asserts, that by nature all men are free. This is the teaching of Catholic doctors, and of all Christian expounders of the law of nature. It flows naturally and necessarily from the Christian doctrine of the unity of the race. Man has naturally, by the law of nature, no right of property in man, and one man has the right to the services of another only in consideration of benefits conferred, or a debt voluntarily contracted. Here then is a broad distinction between slave property and other species of property. Man has a natural right to property in his lands, his house, his sheep and cattle, and the products of his own skill and industry, and in the absence of municipal prohibition, and in so far as movable, he may carry them with him wherever he goes. But the case with slave property is different. Slaves being property only by virtue of municipal law, they cease to be property when transported out of the jurisdiction of the state which creates him a property in them.

---

*Moral. lib. xxi. cap. xi.

Certainly, if the South Carolinian claims the right to transport his people to Nebraska, and to hold them there as property, he must claim to do it by virtue of some law. We ask him, by virtue of what law? The law of nature? No, for under that law all men are equal, and one man has no property in another. By virtue of the civil law, the "written reason" of continental Europe and parts of America? No, for that law proceeds on the principle that every man is born free, and holds every man to be a free man till the contrary is proved. By virtue of the common law, the *lex non scripta* of England and of most of the states of the Union? No, because in this respect the common law and the civil law are coincident. By virtue of the laws of South Carolina? No, for the laws of South Carolina have no force beyond the territorial limits of South Carolina herself. By virtue of the territorial laws of Nebraska? No, for Nebraska, while a territory, has no original legislative power, and none at all, except what is conferred by congress, and therefore, of course, none which exceeds the legislative power of congress itself. But congress, the South Carolinian himself maintains, has no power to legislate on the subject. Will he tell us then, how in the absence of congressional legislation directly, or indirectly through the territorial legislation, authorizing slavery in Nebraska, he can claim to hold his people in that territory as property? Of course he cannot do it, and therefore we maintain that the non-intervention of congress in the slavery question necessarily excludes slavery from the territories so long as they remain under territorial governments, not indeed by depriving the citizens of the slaveholding states of rights which they possess, but by not creating for them rights where they never possessed them.

We take, it will be seen, in the whole course of our argument the southern doctrine of state rights, and of the powers of congress. We defend the southern doctrine of non-intervention, in opposition to the abolitionists and so-called Republicans. We are faithful to the principles we learned from Mr. Calhoun and the state-rights party, which has always been our party, so far as party we have had; but we arrive, we grant, at a different conclusion from that insisted on by our masters. They held and hold that slavery may go wherever it is not forbidden by municipal law; we, that it can go only where authorized by municipal law, or municipal usage having the force of law. We are right, and they wrong, if, as we maintain, under the law of nature all men are free, and man has by natural law no *jus dominii* over man, as all Catholic morality teaches, as was declared by the American congress of 1776, and as is implied in our whole system of jurisprudence, and assumed as unquestioned by nearly the whole modern world. The negro is a man, and has all the natural rights and freedom of any other man. I cannot, as a Catholic, deny this, and am obliged to assert it as a man. The negro is free unless deprived of his freedom by municipal law, or by his own misuse of his freedom. That a man can forfeit his freedom by his offences nobody doubts; that the state may place some men in the ward of others, and give them a valid title to their bodily services, we do not question; but where neither of these conditions is present, we do and can recognize no slave property. How far the laws of Spain and France authorized slavery in the territory acquired from those two powers before it was erected into states, we shall not undertake to decide, but we do say, and this is our doctrine, that under our system, slavery can have no legal existence in any free territory, while that territory remains under a territorial government. Texas was annexed as a state, and slavery was legal in it by virtue of its own laws prior to its admission, and therefore, though a slave state, was legally admitted. There is very little territory now belonging to the Union likely to be affected one way or the other by our doctrine, and its only practical importance is, as it regards territory which may hereafter be acquired on our southern border.

It will be seen that we have thus far been discussing the constitutional and legal rights of slavery. Slavery is under our system purely a state institution, and strictly a state institution we wish to keep it. As a state institution, whatever may be our private opinion of it, we are bound to recognize, respect, and, when the occasion calls, defend it, as we are any other legitimate state institution. We oppose the so-called Republicans, not because they are opposed to the extension of the area of slavery, but because they claim for congress the power to prevent it by legislation. The power to legislate against implies the power to legislate for its extension, and the Republicans in reality claim for congress full jurisdiction of the slavery question in the territories. This we deny. We say congress has no jurisdiction in the case. Slavery is not a federal question. If, as the South contend, and as several of our statesmen have ad-

mitted, slavery is free to go where no municipal law prohibits it, we cannot deny that it is free to go into any territory of the Union not yet erected into a state. Congress
has no authority to forbid it, and we ought to submit to its
extension, as a less evil than the exercise of an unconstitutional power by the federal legislature. Whether slavery
can or cannot legally exist in the territories, is a question for
the federal courts, and if these courts decide against the
ground we have taken, we shall submit. Meanwhile we
must be permitted for the reasons we have alleged to believe
that they will not and cannot so decide.

We have scouted so-called "squatter sovereignty," but
we have not the least scruple in maintaining that the people
of the territory in forming, by permission of congress, a
state constitution, have the right, and that they only have
the right, to say whether they will or will not authorize
slavery. The people of a territory in meeting in convention and forming a state constitution, have all the powers
of a free, independent sovereign people, and are competent
to decide whether involuntary servitude shall or shall not
be permitted, and we know under our American system no
other power competent to decide that question. To them
we wish to leave it, and to them the people of the Union
should leave it. The northern Democrats, at the head of
whom stands our new secretary of state, are wrong in their
assertion of "squatter sovereignty," which is the extreme
of radicalism, and, in principle, incompatible with the assertion of any legitimate government; the South are wrong,
in our judgment, in asserting that slavery is free where no
municipal law prohibits it. But we regard the abolitionists
and free-soilers as still more dangerously wrong than either;
for the doctrine of federal sovereignty and consolidation
underlies all their proceedings. Their tendency is to centralize all power in the federal government, and make the
states derive from the Union instead of the Union from the
states. We know the tendency of the modern world is to
centralize power, and to render the sovereign, whether
monarchical, aristocratical, or democratical, absolute; but we
are old fogyish enough to oppose all absolute governments,
and to contend for the old doctrine of a limitation of the
sovereign power, whatever its form. Democracy, as popularly understood and defined, is as fatal to freedom as autocracy, and perhaps practically even more so. There is no
limitation of power where the limitation and the power have

one and the same basis. If the states derive from the Union, they are no limit to the power of the Union, for they depend on it, and have no independent basis of their own. Were the Union dissolved, we should not, under the state-rights doctrine, be thrown into a state of complete anarchy, because each state would still exist, at least theoretically, as a complete political community, with all the rights and capacities of a free, independent and sovereign state. But on the abolitionist and free-soil doctrine, the dissolution of the Union would carry with it the dissolution of all government, and we should be thrown into anarchy even in the bosom of the states as well as of the federation. It is the consolidation tendencies of the so-called Republican party, rather than their anti-slavery doctrine, that renders it impossible for us to go with them. The evil that would result from their triumph would be greater than any evil likely to result from any probable extension of slavery, unless that extension be effected by the action of the federal government.

Our remarks in our last article were addressed mainly to the party, whether at the South or at the North, seeking either to extend slavery within the Union, or to build up a great southern slaveholding republic, and had, as was evident on their face, for their purpose to warn the incoming administration against throwing itself into the hands of that party, for should it do so it would be impossible for it to gain the support of the Union. Such is the temper of the people of the non-slaveholding states, that their suffrages cannot be obtained for a pro-slavery administration, or an administration controlled by the slave interest. We ventured to do this, because we had been so long identified with the opposition to abolitionism and free-soilism, that we did not suppose any one would be likely to misconstrue our motives or views. We say of the whole anti-slavery movement to-day, what we said nineteen years ago, when we first discussed the question in its political bearings. We suffer a little humiliation, we admit, when we find that twenty years of steady devotion to the rights of the states, and of opposition on state-rights principles to the consolidation tendencies of the anti-slavery party, can have no weight in saving us from the suspicion of being a black-republican. Certainly we are no "nigger driver," but we are just as little of a "nigger worshipper." We are no advocates of slavery, but we are at the same time no abolitionists: we do not assent to the southern doctrine insisted upon in late years, that slavery is an excellent institution, but we acknowledge the right of every state in the Union to maintain or establish it, if such be its choice, and we will defend that right to the death against any interference with it by the Union. But we will go just as far against any extension or positive support of slavery by the action of the federal government. While we sustain in favor of slavery all the rights it has by virtue of positive law, we shall maintain with equal earnestness all the presumptions of the natural law in favor of freedom. This is our position, and if it displeases our friends at the North or our friends at the South, we cannot help it, and shall regard the fault as theirs, not as ours.

We take the liberty of referring our readers to an article we wrote in 1838, on Slavery and Abolitionism,* when the consolidation or centralizing tendency of the anti-slavery movement had hardly been alluded to. That article shows the ground on which we then placed our opposition to the movement, and from that ground we have not deviated to our knowledge since.

There may be some incidental opinions which we should not now accept without some important modifications, for we are not now a Protestant, as we were when we wrote it, and we recognize now, as we did not then, a power distinct from both the state and the individual competent to decide for the state and the individual, the morality of acts and institutions. But the substance, and all that has any bearing on the question before us, we accept. The reader will also see that the ground on which we oppose the abolition societies and the anti-slavery agitation, is a ground which compels us to oppose equally all our recent filibustering tendencies and movements. We recognize the right of religious propagandism by divinely commissioned missionaries, but we deny all propagandism on mere human authority against the wishes of the political sovereign. All human powers, however constituted, are in relation to one another independent and equal, and the law which binds the sovereign against intervention binds the citizen or subject,—a fact which our Anglo-Saxon race, through all stages of its historical existence, seems never to have duly considered. It may be called the filibustering race. The South as well as the North have favored the filibustering expeditions against Cuba, Mexico, and Central America, and in so doing have

---

* Brownson's Works, vol. xv., pp. 51–63.

given countenance to the very principle on which the abolition societies defend their intermeddling with slavery in
the southern states. It was filibustering coupled with pro-
slavery tendencies, that we more especially condemned in
our article on the incoming administration. If you accept
the filibustering clauses of the Cincinnati platform, we cannot defend your opposition to the anti-slavery party, for
you accept the very principle which justifies that party.
The anti-slavery movement and the filibuster movement
originate in the same tendency, and proceed from the same
principle. If we are to defend slavery against the abolitionists on the principles of international law and state sovereignty, you must not embarrass us by defending the filibustering movement, which denies international law, and
the independence of states. There is nothing less justifiable
in the formation at the North of a party to abolish slavery
at the South, than in the expeditions which have sailed
from our ports against Cuba and Central America. If you
encourage the latter, how can we in your favor oppose the
former? If the South encourages the filibusters with a
view to the acquisition of new slave states, what can we say
against movements at the North for the abolition of slavery?
If the South expects the North to respect international law
in her favor, she must respect international law herself.

Thus far we had written before the decision of the supreme court in the Dred Scott case was rendered. We
have read an abstract of that decision as given us in the
columns of the *New York Herald*, with great satisfaction
in some respects and great surprise in others. It sustains
us on all points except one, and the dissenting opinion of
Judge McLean sustains us even on that; but the opinion of
the majority, as given by Chief Justice Taney, on several
incidental points, we cannot regard as worthy of the high
source whence it emanates, and we are sure it will be very
far from acceptable to a very large class of American citizens who are free from the slightest taint of abolitionism.

As to the precise question before the court the decision
is final, and we have no disposition to criticise it, even if it
were becoming in us to do so. We suppose the court is the
judge of its own powers, and was competent to dismiss the
case as not coming within its jurisdiction. We cannot understand on what ground it could claim jurisdiction in the
case, since, if we understand it, it was purely a question for
the state courts of Missouri, and surely these courts were

competent to decide whether Dred Scott was or was not a slave under the laws of Missouri. Scott was a slave before he left the state, and we can understand no reason why his temporary residence at the United States military posts in Illinois or other free states, should have operated his freedom, so that on his return to Missouri he could not be legally held as a slave under her laws. His being employed at the United States military posts makes in our judgment some difference in the case, for while residing at them he was still constructively in Missouri. Had he chosen when in Illinois to leave his master, a question, however, might arise, whether he could have been recovered as a fugitive slave. But he having remained with his master and returned with him to Missouri, we think the court was quite right in still regarding him as a slave.

We are disposed to agree with the court, that a slave brought by his master into a free state with a view merely of a temporal sojourn there does not recover his freedom, so that if he returns to the state in which he was a slave he becomes there a free man. He is free only in the sense that so long as he resides in a free state he cannot be recovered under the fugitive-slave law. We do not think that New York can endow a person held as a slave in South Carolina with any rights of citizenship which will make him a free citizen everywhere in the Union. If this is the opinion of the court we do not see that it can be objected to. But the doctrine that persons of the negro race are not included in our political community and cannot be citizens of the United States, we are not yet prepared to accept. Negroes are men, and may be freemen, and the essential character of a citizen is that he is a freeman. Every freeman born within the jurisdiction of the United States, of parents not citizens or subjects of a foreign state, is a citizen in every state of the Union, whatever was the condition of his ancestors or the race from which he sprang. This is necessarily so because our institutions recognize among freemen no distinction of rank or race. There were free negroes in several, perhaps in all the states at the time of forming the Union, and they were an integral portion of that people of the states who formed the Union and for whom it was formed.

The negro being a man, a human soul, endowed by the law of nature with all the rights of a white man, he must in all things be held the equal of white men, except where the municipal law makes a distinction to his prejudice. Is there any clause in the constitution which excludes negroes from our political community, or that restricts that community to the white race? The court will not pretend it. Is there any clause which recognizes negroes, as such, as slaves, and declares them incapable of being freemen? Certainly not. How then can the court pretend that negroes born in the country and born free or freed by their masters or by the operations of law are not citizens? They may be, we need not tell the court, citizens, entitled to the protection of the Union, and capable of holding and transmitting real estate, and of suing and being sued in the courts, state and federal, without being electors.

New Hampshire, Massachusetts, and New York confer on negroes the right of suffrage, and make no political or legal distinction between them and white citizens. Suppose one of these negroes, whose ancestors were indeed imported from Africa as slaves, but have never themselves been slaves in other states, should emigrate to Kansas and seek to beome a landholder there, could he not do it? Will the court say that he would be incapable of owning and transmitting landed estate, or maintaining actions in the federal courts of the territory? What rights has a white man in that territory that he would not have? How then say that negroes are not citizens of the United States? Mr. Chief Justice Taney rests the opinion of the court on the estimation in which the negro race was held at the time the Union was formed. They were regarded as no fit associates socially or politically for white men, as having no rights which white men were bound to respect, while nobody denied that they might be bought and sold as an ordinary article of merchandise. Suppose such was the fact, what has that to do with the question? Is it any where incorporated into the constitution of the Union, or recognized by the laws of the United States? Of course not. Then it cannot be cited against the rights of free negroes under the federal government.

But we dispute the fact. There can be no reasonable doubt that Mr. Jefferson and many others when they declared all men created equal intended the principle they asserted after Pope Alexander III., should apply in its fullest extent. Mr. Chief Justice Taney is a Catholic, and knows that from 1482 the popes have condemned, on pain of excommunication, the reduction of African negroes to slavery, and he knows that Mr. Jefferson, in his draft of the declaration of independence, enumerated among the things which justified the colonies in severing the tie which bound them to Great Britain and in casting off their allegiance to the British crown, the fact that the crown had refused its assent to the laws prohibiting the importation of negroes from Africa to be held as slaves. There was too at the adoption of the federal constitution already rising throughout the civilized world a strong opinion against the justice of negro slavery. The right to buy and sell negroes, already slaves, as an ordinary article of merchandise, was very generally held, I grant, but the right to buy and sell free negroes, or to reduce free negroes to slavery, was denied by the Catholic Church, and was, I would fain believe, held by very few. There were then free negroes as well as now; if everybody regarded it lawful to reduce negroes as such to slavery, or looked upon them as having no rights which white men were bound to respect, what was the difference between a free negro and a negro slave? How can a man who has no rights which all others are bound to respect be said to be free?

Mr. Chief Justice Taney seems to us to proceed on the assumption that negroes are politically and legally a degraded race in the Union; but such is not the fact. They may be so in some of the states, but they are not so in the Union, nor indeed in all the states. We regret that in giving the opinion of the court the learned judge did not recollect what he is taught by his religion, namely, the unity of the race, that all men by the natural law are equal, and that negroes are men, and therefore as to their rights must be regarded as standing on the same footing with white men, where there is no positive or municipal law that degrades them. Here is what we dare maintain is the error of the court. We admit that negroes, but not negroes any more than white men, may be reduced by positive law to slavery, but planting ourselves on the constitution, and natural right as expounded by the church and the common law, we maintain, and will maintain in face of all civil courts, that where no such law reduces the negro to slavery, he is a free man, and in the absence of all municipal regulations to the contrary has equal rights with the white man. Neither race nor complexion disables a man under our federal system. That negroes may be citizens and possess equal rights with white men is proved by the fact that we have made them so in the territories acquired from France, Spain and Mexico, by the very treaties by which we acquired those territories. The opinion of the court belongs to an epoch prior to the introduction of Christianity, and is more in accordance with the teaching of Aristotle than with that of the Gospel. We have no more disposition to interfere with slavery where it legally exists than have our southern friends, but we do protest against an opinion which places negroes as such not only out of the pale of our republic, but out of the pale of humanity. If opinion once went that length, it was the business of the court to brand it with its disapprobation, and not to recognize it as law. The court should lean to the side of the weak, and set its face against oppression. The negro race is, no doubt, inferior to the white race, but is that a reason why they should be enslaved, or why the court should join the stronger against the weaker?

The opinion of the court which allows the slaveholder to sojourn temporarily with his slaves in a free state, or to hold them *in transitu* through a free state, we think is just; but the opinion incidentally expressed, that a slaveholder may settle with his people and hold them as slaves in any territory of the United States, we cannot accept, for reasons assigned in the earlier part of this article. We have anticipated, and we think we have refuted, the reasoning of the court on this point. If we have not done it, Judge McLean has, and effectually.

These are some of the exceptions we have felt bound to take to the opinion of the court, as it has been reported to us. Of course, we are aware there is no appeal from the supreme court, and its opinion must stand as law till it is set aside. Though we take exceptions to it, and believe it in several respects erroneous, we trust we shall not forget our duty as a loyal citizen. For ourselves personally, we believe liberty is more interested in the preservation of the Union than even in preventing the extension of slave territory, since, if the slave trade be not revived, the extension of slave territory involves no real extension of slavery. But we regret the decision, for we foresee that it will be impossible to prevent the anti-slavery agitation from being pushed on with new vigor, and with more danger than ever. The decision will be regarded as an extreme southern opinion, and the dissent from the majority by the ablest judges from the free states will deprive it of all moral force out of the slave states. We almost fear for the safety of the Union. Yet we believe Almighty God has great designs with regard to the American people, and we will trust in his good providence to carry us safely through the present crisis, the most dangerous that has as yet occurred in our history.

POLITICS AT HOME.

[From Brownson's Quarterly Review for July, 1860.]

THOUGH open to essays on political science and the relations of politics to religion and morality, the pages of the *Review* are for the most part closed to the discussion of the respective merits of political parties, or of political questions which involve no great and important social principle ;— not indeed because we hold the triumph or defeat of this or that party to be a matter of indifference, or because we hold it lawful to be unmindful of one's rights or duties as a citizen of a great and growing republic ; but because we have not found a public sufficiently enlightened and tolerant to permit us to engage in party politics without detriment to the more important religious and philosophical purposes to which they are primarily devoted. The constitution and laws guaranty us the most perfect freedom of thought and speech, but public opinion, which in a democracy is supreme and reigns as a despot, exercises here a more effectual restraint on both thought and speech than is or can be exercised by the most arbitrary and despotic government in the Old World. The journal that undertakes to enlighten and correct the opinion of its own public has no lease of life, and it will be as speedily and as effectually suppressed with us, as by the police in France would be a journal that should dare question the wisdom or justice of the imperial *régime*, or the imperial policy. No periodical with us can live except on condition of pleasing the special public it addresses, and that public, be it what it will, is impatient of contradiction, and requires the journal it supports not simply to tell it what is true, right, and just, but to defend its opinions, prejudices, sympathies, and antipathies. It supports a journal only on condition that it is devoted to its cause, or its convictions and sentiments. A slight exception, no doubt, must be made in the case of the Catholic public, which has some conscience, but even the Catholic public would soon drop a journal that constantly contradicted its political convictions and sentiments, however conclusive the reasons it might give, or however unexceptionable in a religious point of view it might be, while its devotion to the Catholic cause would effectually prevent its circulation among non-Catholics, however acceptable it might be under the point of view of politics.

Moreover, we are opposed to the alliance of the Catholic cause with political parties. The church is self-sufficing, and we wish her cause to be compromised by no real or apparent league with monarchies or republics, aristocracies or democracies,—the Republicans or the Democrats, the Americans or the Nationals. No one of these parties is Catholic, and no good can come to religion by making the prosperity of the Catholic cause dependent on the success or defeat of any one of them. Catholics have the same political rights and duties with other citizens, but the interest of their church does not require them to throw all their influence on the side of any one of these parties, not even in case it promises to elect now and then a nominal Catholic a member of congress or of a state legislature, or give to a few brawling politicians, whose fathers were Catholics, a place in the customs, or a clerkship in the public offices. With the strong anti-Catholic sentiment of the country, no Catholic known to be firmly devoted to his religion, and publicly associated with the defence of Catholic interests, can be elected or appointed to any office of importance. To succeed politically, except in one or two localities, one must be an indifferent Catholic, and an indifferent Catholic in office is of less service to Catholic interests than the most bigoted non-Catholic. Nor is it a sufficient reason for opposing a party that it refuses to elect or appoint Catholics to office. To be elected or appointed to office is no man's natural right, and should never be regarded as the chief end of politics. No man has the right, prior to his election or appointment, to depend on office for a livelihood. Offices are created or supposed to be created for the public good, not for the private benefit of individuals, and the man who cannot get his living without an office, has rarely the right to get it at all.

We have always considered it, under a Catholic point of

view, a gross blunder on the part of those twenty-one Catholic members of the British parliament, who by their votes
threw out the Derby ministry, and put in the Palmerston-
Russell ministry. The Derby ministry did not appoint
Catholics to office, but they conceded more to Catholic interests than has ever been conceded by all the Whig minis-
tries that have ever governed the United Kingdom. What
they lost by displacing Lord Derby and installing Lord Pal-
merston and Lord John Russell,—two of the worst enemies
Catholicity has in Great Britain, and the very worst men
for Catholic interests to be at the head of the government
in the present state of affairs on the continent,—was poorly
compensated by having four or five Catholics appointed to
subordinate places in the ministry. If the Derby ministry
had remained in power we should not have seen central
Italy annexed to Sardina, or Æmilia wrested by an unprincipled revolution from the Holy Father. So far as Catholic
interests are concerned we should have little to regret in our
country were the so-called American party to rise to place
and power. Its open and avowed hostility is less to be deprecated than the coquetry of the Democratic party, every
whit as hostile, and coquets with us not indeed because we
are Catholics, but because the great body of us are naturalized citizens and cast what is insultingly called "the foreign
vote." They appeal to us as foreign voters, as Irishmen or
as Germans, not as Catholics.

There should be no distinction made between naturalized
and natural-born citizens. Their rights are equal, and there
should be no more objection to the elevation of the one than
of the other to any office to which either is constitutionally
eligible. The objection is not that a citizen of Irish or
German birth or descent votes or is voted for, but that he
votes or is voted for as an Irishman or as a German, that
the appeal is made to him on the ground of his former, not
of his present nationality. The evil is in the naturalized
citizens being made or treated as a class by themselves—in
their acting or being induced or forced to act as a distinct
class of citizens. No American can object to the election
of a citizen of Irish or German birth; but every American
ought to feel indignant at being called upon to select or to
vote for a candidate because he is a German or an Irishman.
As a German or an Irishman he is a foreigner, and is in-
eligible. Nothing is more injurious to American politics
than the practice into which we have fallen of treating

naturalized voters as a separate class, and of soliciting their suffrages under foreign appellations. It introduces into our politics a foreign element, and one which cannot fail to be an element of corruption. Nothing can be worse than for political parties in selecting candidates, or in proposing measures of policy, to feel obliged as the condition of success to consult the "foreign vote," the tastes, inclinations, passions, or prejudices of naturalized citizens. Now each party bids for the "foreign vote,"—is anxious to secure the vote of our "adopted citizens," just as if they remained foreigners after adoption! The evil is a great one, and has done much to bring our country to the verge of ruin. It has virtually given the balance of power to a class destitute of American traditions, and who, however worthy they may be as individuals, lack necessarily American habits and associations. Nobody questions their readiness in case of war to fight or die for the country, but the country of their heart, as it must be with all true men, is the land of their birth, the land consecrated by the joys and sorrows of their ancestors. We are all creatures of habit, and none of us by crossing the ocean can jump out of one national character into another,—be a German or an Irishman one month and an American the next.

We simply state facts. We say nothing in disparagement of American citizens of foreign birth. No man can leave the old homestead, find himself in a new and strange country, surrounded by new and strange faces, away from all his early associations, and all that goes to the making up of home, without some shock to his moral being. We ourselves, feel this, in removing even from one state to another within the Union. The migratory habits of the American people, whether the effect of choice or of necessity, make a large portion of us strangers even in the land of our birth, and give us more or less the character of adventurers, restrained by few ties or associations of early home; and to these habits is due much of the rash and adventurous character of our politics, and not a little of the growing corruption and immorality of our public men. I am, where I now live, as much a stranger, as much an exile from home, as the Irishman or German in New York, Philadelphia, Baltimore, or Boston. I may demean myself as a loyal citizen of New Jersey,—a state in which it is still possible to enforce the laws, punish criminals, and hang murderers, instead of electing them to offices of honor, trust, or emolument,—but I

am no true Jerseyman, and shall remain to the day of my
death a genuine Green Mountain Boy. A Vermonter is
something more to me than the native of any other state in
the Union, and when I meet him in another state, I am
ready to embrace him as a brother. It is a great trial to be
unable to support for the next presidency, my countryman,
Stephen A. Douglas. Now what should be thought of me,
if I, as a citizen of New Jersey, insisted on acting or on being treated as if my rights came from New Jersey, and my
duties from Vermont, on having my vote regarded as the
"Vermont vote," or what should be thought of the Jersey
demagogues,—for unhappily, even New Jersey has demagogues,—if in selecting candidates or shaping the policy of
parties, they should have special reference to gaining my
"Vermont vote"? Add a few thousands from the Green
Mountains, and you would have just what we complain of
in the practice of treating the votes of naturalized citizens
as the "German vote," or the "Irish vote."

The evil, however, is not exclusively nor chiefly in the
fact that the citizens treated as a distinct and separate class
are naturalized and not native-born citizens. It would be
nearly as great, except as a matter of sentiment or prejudice,
were the class native-born. It does not, moreover, grow
out of the fact that naturalized citizens are specially ignorant, immoral, corrupt, or corruptible, but the simple fact
that they are treated as a distinct and separate class of citizens. Politics soon become corrupt, and parties lose all regard for principle, when success in elections is sought by
appeals to other than legitimate political and patriotic motives. It would not help the matter if the object were to
secure "the Presbyterian vote," "the Methodist vote," "the
Baptist vote," "the Quaker vote," "the Catholic vote," or
"the native vote," supposing the natives in the minority.
It grows out of the introduction into politics, of a non-
political element, and the attempt to secure success by appeals to non-political passions, prejudices, sentiments, or
convictions, and it is equally injurious to the naturalized
citizens and to the country at large. The citizens of foreign
birth are not specially to blame for the evil; they cannot
help the fact of their not being natural-born citizens. The
great mass of them have no wish to be treated as a distinct
class, and would prefer to be regarded simply as American
citizens, and to be addressed as such, without any reference
being made to the fact of their foreign birth or the nation-

ality they have abjured. The fault is that of the demagogues, some of home manufacture, some imported, and all
of whom should be transported,—who find it convenient for
them as a means of enhancing their power or personal importance to have a foreign element, that is, a non-political
element, which they can appeal to and turn to a political
account.

As Catholics, it is our duty to keep Catholic interests as
far as possible, independent of all political parties, and therefore as such, we avoid in conducting a Catholic periodical,
as far as we can, all party politics; but the present is one of
those times of political crisis and confusion, when every
citizen who retains some coolness and impartiality owes it
to his country to do what he can to aid in clearing up and
setting matters to rights. The country is now divided into
three prominent parties, each split up into two or more sections,—the Democratic, the Republican, and the Know-
nothing, or so-called American party. These parties are
now struggling with one another for the mastery, and though
to us simply as Catholics, it is of little direct consequence
which of them proves successful, it may be of great and lasting consequence to us as citizens and patriots.

The American or Know-nothing party is not dead, as some
of our friends imagine, and will not die so long as the other
parties continue to make appeals to naturalized citizens as
such, or so long as the naturalized citizens allow themselves,
without indignantly resenting it, to be addressed as Germans or Irishmen, and their vote to be solicited as "the foreign vote," "the German vote," or "the Irish vote." As
long as naturalized citizens regard themselves or are regarded by others as a distinct political class, out of whom
political capital is to be made, or so long as in politics their
foreign nationality is not lost in the common character of
American citizenship, the Know-nothing party, that is, a native American party, under some name or other, will exist;
for so long it will have a principle of vitality and a reason
for existing; so long it will have and must have, to a greater
or less extent, the sympathies of the great body of our citizens who have been nurtured with American traditions. It
appeals to a sentiment common to all the descendants of the
original colonists, and in that sentiment, though it may seek
to use it for an unholy and even an un-American purpose,
it has an element of life and strength, which it will not do
to despise, and which, considered in itself, all Americans

must respect.   Our foreign-born editors may sneer at it as
the *natyve* party, may vituperate it, may get in a rage against
it, but they will not thus extinguish it; for it is never of
any use to abuse a man for being a native in the land of his
nativity, around which cluster all the fondest associations of
his heart, and to which his loyalty is due.   The party lives
and will live till the aliment that sustains it is removed.   Its
measures, its errors, its violence, must prevent all candid,
thinking, and unfanatical Americans from supporting it, but
it is a party that we must count with, as an important element in American politics, for it has at least one side of an
element of truth and justice, though unhappily perverted
and rendered inoperative for good, by virtue of the errors
and false Americanism which overlay it.   Its condemnation
is that it is not truly American, and proposes a remedy for
an evil which every American deplores, that would prove
far worse than the disease.   What would have been in the
beginning the wisest and best policy for the government to
adopt it is too late now to inquire.   The government in its
outset saw proper to adopt a policy of extreme liberality
towards persons migrating hither and settling among us,
and it is too late to change that policy now, even if we think
it was injudicious.   Circumstances at home and abroad, have
sent us foreign settlers by the millions.   They are here, and
to a great extent naturalized citizens, and whether you like
it or dislike it, here they are, and here they will remain,
and form for good or for evil an integral portion of the
American people.   To pursue towards them a hostile policy,
to organize a party to abridge their rights, to curtail their
privileges, and make them feel that you intend to treat them
in a legal and political point of view as an inferior class, as
"hewers of wood and drawers of water," as a sort of pariahs,
or to place them on a less favorable footing before the state
than natural-born citizens, is simply to force them to band
together, and to act as one body in self-defence.   You create
for them a distinct and separate interest, and compel them
by the instinct of self-preservation to feel and act in the
very way that produces the political evil you seek to redress.
Treat them in the spirit of justice and equality recognized
by your laws and institutions, and they will have no motive
for acting as a separate class, and will be content to act in
their simple capacity of American citizens, feeling that they
have the duties as well as the rights of Americans.   The
whole evil comes from their acting as a distinct and separate

class. We have no right to blame them for so acting, if we treat them as such a class. If the naturalized citizens acted in politics, and a great portion of them do so act, as simple American citizens, without reference to their former nationality, their early naturalization would be no disservice to American politics. They would in such case exercise the elective franchise perhaps as wisely and as honestly as natural-born Americans in the corresponding ranks of social life. The natural-born citizens must not suppose that we monopolize all the wisdom, all the virtue, or all the intelligence of the American people. We may smile indeed,—we need not allow ourselves to be indignant,— at the pretence of some Irish-American journals, that the native Americans are "cowards and the sons of cowards," and that we owe every thing honorable in our history, or worthy of esteem in our institutions, in our literature, art, and science, to the foreigners naturalized or domiciled among us. Such pretence is simply ridiculous, and is less due to the vanity of our foreign settlers than to the suspicion we provoke, that we are indisposed to give them the credit to which they are justly entitled. They claim much in the expectation that we shall concede them something. Yet all exaggeration apart, for honesty, integrity, fidelity to their trusts, it may safely be conceded that the naturalized citizens are on a par with our natural-born citizens, and where they are corrupt, they have in great measure been corrupted by our example, and the position they have occupied, and in some sort been forced to occupy, among us.

There is no doubt that what is called the foreign element in our elections is a disturbing element, an element productive of immense evil, but it is so through our fault infinitely more than through the fault of the naturalized citizens themselves. The way to correct that evil is not in any alteration of the naturalization laws, which would be now very much like locking the stable-door after the colt is stolen,— not in organizing parties against them and their religion, giving them thus an importance, and even a power they would not otherwise have ; but in treating them with equal justice, in forbearing to address them by their former national appellations, and in soliciting their suffrages, precisely as we do the suffrages of others, only in their simple character of American citizens. Give them reason to feel that they are recognized as full American citizens, that it is an honor to be an American citizen, and that they, thought not born here, are regarded as brothers and equals as if they were, and the evil we complain of will disappear, and they will prove to be a most valuable accession to our population. No doubt, coming in large numbers as they do, they are destined to modify to a considerable extent our national character, but the *London Times*, in its vaticinations as to Ireland becoming Saxon, and the United States Celtic, forgets that the Celt here after the second generation, loses much of his original character, which is not always an improvement, and that the German immigration at present is more numerous than the Irish, and brings in the Teutonic element to balance the Celtic, and to keep up the original equilibrium. The Celtic character is more flexible, and less persistent than the Teutonic, and we may trust Dutch phlegm to restrain within due bounds Celtic levity. Should all Ireland empty itself into these states we should still remain, like our English ancestors, a mixed people,—a people of Germanic and Celtic origin, and the main elements of our national character would remain substantially unchanged. But even if not, perhaps there would be no great harm. Much of the best blood we boast has flowed in the veins of Irish ancestors, and we know not that Celtic blood is less red or pure than Teutonic blood. The influences on national character to be dreaded are not Celtic or Teutonic, but those of our democratic politics. These are already working a change, radical changes, which may well excite in the breasts of every man with American traditions and patriotic sentiments the most lively alarm.

Recognizing, as we have frankly done, the evil the American party seek to redress, and doing ample justice to the American sentiment in which they find their only element of strength, we confess, all American as we are, we cannot support the party even under its new names, and with its modified policy and its moderated tone. Whether it has really abandoned its element of secrecy and ceased to be "the dark-lantern party" or not, we do not now inquire. Under its best aspect it is narrow-minded and bigoted, and its platform is too weak and too narrow for a full grown man to stand on. As a separate party it is comparatively powerless, and is mischievous only as it pervades and influences the policy of the other parties of the country. It is undoubtedly hostile to our religion, but more because the mass of adult Catholics with us happen to be of foreign birth than because it is Catholic, and as hostile as it may be, it is really no more hostile than either of the other two parties.

The real struggle in the present campaign is between the Republican party and the Democratic party. If the Baltimore convention had nominated Sam Houston for president, instead of Senator Bell, the nationals, the union or modified American party, would have made a respectable show of strength, for the hero of San Jacinto has in him the elements that appeal to popular enthusiasm, although he is no favorite of ours. But the ticket headed by Bell and Everett, is not fitted to call forth any enthusiasm, and only those are likely to vote it, who feel they must vote, and can in conscience vote for neither the Republican nor the Democratic party. The candidates are respectable, the platform adopted and promulgated commits one to nothing, and as the ticket is sure not to succeed one may perhaps vote for it, without sacrificing to any great extent his loyalty or his conscience. Our readers know that for ourselves, though strongly republican, we are no democrat, do not accept the democratic theory of government, although the only candidates for the presidency we have ever supported in this *Review* have been candidates of the Democratic party. We honestly believe that we have more to fear from democracy than from all other causes combined, and we believe the evils in our country, if the democratic tendency of our people be not checked by the elevation to power of a really conservative party, will go on increasing year by year till the only remedy will be in the establishment of something like the imperial despotism introduced by the Bonapartes into France. Things cannot go on as they are now going, without becoming worse, and if they become much worse our society will have no resource but in a military despotism. But the democratic theory has become so strong in the convictions and sentiments of the people, that we fear it is too late to think of restraining it or of preventing them from pushing it to its natural and necessary conclusion.

In these remarks, let it be understood, we have no special reference to the party called Democratic, for we are not aware that the party so called is less conservative or more radical than the so-called Republican party. Indeed, of the two we think the Republican party is the more ultra in its democracy, and this is one reason why we cannot more fully sympathize with it. The Democratic party is, no doubt,

corrupt, but the Republicans when in power or place have
not proved themselves purer, and in their recent nomination
of a presidential candidate they have proved that they are
infected with that curse of democracy, which places availability before fitness.   We do not doubt that Mr. Abraham
Lincoln is a very worthy man, an honest man, and a man
of good natural parts, but we must say of his nomination,
as Daniel Webster said of another, "it is a nomination not
fit to be made."   An honest party, wedded to principle,
and having in itself an element of life and permanent success, will put forth its representative man and stand or fall
with him.   We have no partiality for Wm. H. Seward, but
a party that will reject such a man and take up such a man
as Mr. Lincoln, we think, is governed by a short-sighted
policy, is a party of to-day, expecting to dissolve and vanish
in thin air to-morrow.   The nomination has weakened our
confidence in the Republican party, and dampened whatever hopes we might have placed in it.   But we pass to the
principles and policy of the two great parties now pitted
one against the other.

The two parties are both to a great extent sectional parties, and in them we have the North against the South, and
the South against the North.   The dispute between the two
parties, as between the two sections, turns on negro-slavery,
and we cannot discuss the merits of either party without
discussing the political bearings of the slave question.
Both our northern and our southern friends must allow us
to speak freely on this point, and receive in good humor
any remarks we may make that run athwart their respective
interests or prejudices.

We hold that we of the North have no right to be *political* abolitionists, for in our states slavery does not exist, and
the federal government has no power over it in any of the
states.   We have no right to get up a political party in a
non-slaveholding state for the abolition of slavery, for there
is in such state no subject on which such a party can act,
and to act on it politically in another state is not permitted,
for it is in violation of the principle that all the states in
the Union stand on an equal footing.   We have no right to
get up a federal party, or a party to force the federal government to abolish it in the slave states, for the states in
forming the Union reserved the question of slavery to
themselves in their separate and independent capacity.   All
political abolitionism is contrary, therefore, either to the

federal constitution or to the mutual equality and independence of the states. The abolition of slavery is a legitimate
question for political parties within slaveholding states, but
never within non-slaveholding states. Whatever, then,
may or may not be our views of slavery, we who belong to
non-slaveholding states have no right to make it a political
question, or the basis of a political party, either state or
federal. We may say slavery is an evil, a sin, but that is a
moral question, and under our system of government not to
be reached by political action. So we may say Presbyteri-
anism or Methodism is an evil, a sin, and one that will ultimately bring down the judgments of God upon the people
that sustain it, but we have not therefore the right to form
a political party for its suppression.

Furthermore, though strongly opposed to the extension
of slavery beyond the limits of the present slaveholding
states, we hold that we have no right to form and support
a political party for the prevention through the action of
congress of its extension to new territory. The territories
of the Union are the common property of all the states,
and congress has no right to pass any act or ordinance
that prevents the citizens of one state as well as those of
another from entering and settling them with their property.
Congress has no right to discriminate between different
species of property, but is bound to regard as property,
whatever is property by the laws of the states or any one of
the states. Here we agree entirely with the southern statesmen, and hence we deny to congress the constitutional right,
either to authorize or to prohibit slavery in the territories
no less than in the states themselves. The only doubt we
could entertain on this point arises from the fact, that till
quite recently, congress has uniformly in organizing a new
territorial government, claimed and exercised the power to
permit or to exclude slavery. Should not this fact be taken
as evidence that congress has the power, at least by prescription? But the doubt must vanish the moment that we reflect that the federal government is one of express powers
under a written constitution, and that no prescription can
authorize the exercise of power not expressly conceded it by
the states creating it. Here we differ not only from the
Republican party, but also from what is understood at the
North to be the doctrine of the northern Democrats headed
by Mr. Douglas. The Republicans generally hold that
congress in organizing the territories may either permit or

forbid slavery till the territory becomes a state. Mr. Douglas is understood to deny this power to congress, and to assert it for the people of the territory, under the head of what is called "squatter sovereignty." We know nothing more discreditable to a man who has had the honor to be a judge even in an inferior court. It is decidedly opposed to that clear, logical understanding, boasted not in vain, by the people of the Green Mountain State, and especially by old Windsor County, from which both he and we hail. The people of a territory have no powers except such as are conferred by congress in the organic act, and congress can confer no power which it does not itself possess : *Nemo dat quod non habet.* Squatter sovereignty is a fiction, and a fiction of that ultra-Democratic school which justifies John Brown's raid into Virginia. Congress cannot authorize another to do what it has no right to do itself, and Mr. Douglas's doctrine, if conceded, supposes congress has the power to permit or prohibit slavery in the territories,— in principle the doctrine of the Republican party, or else that the people are sovereign without reference to legal organization, what we call John Brownism. If we believed congress had the power, we should of course demand its exercise to prevent the further extension of slavery, for we claim to be heart and soul an anti-slavery man. But not believing it has the power, we deny the right of any class of American citizens, to form a political party, for the express purpose of exercising it through congress.

So far we go with the Democratic party South, and dissent from both the Republicans and the Douglas Democrats. The Republicans on this point, we believe are wrong, but they are intelligible, logical, and are sustained by the almost uniform practice of congress, ever since we had a congress. If they err it is in respectable company, their error, as far as an error can be, is a respectable error. The Douglas Democrats are neither one thing nor another, "neither fish, flesh, nor fowl, nor yet good red-herring." It involves the error of filibusterism, and if analyzed and reduced to some degree of consistency, it will be found to be John Brownism. But while we so far agree with the South and honor the southern delegates in the Charleston convention, for their refusal to nominate Mr. Douglas for the presidency, we are, as all our readers well know, opposed to slavery itself, in any form, and especially opposed to the further extension of its area. We have heard all that has

been said in its favor, but nothing can reconcile us to slavery
in any form or for any race, red, white, black, or yellow.
We deny that we have any right to interfere politically with
it where it has a legal existence, though we maintain our
right to entertain and express our convictions in regard to it
as a moral question when and where we please, and this
right no power on earth shall ever force us to surrender.
But this has nothing to do with the question before the
American public. We hold that slavery does not exist by
what theologians call the law of nature, and that under that
law all men, as to their rights, are equal. One man has no
dominion in another, and no right to exact his bodily services, except in consideration of benefits conferred, or
wrongs received and to be redressed. Any right or dominion beyond is acquired, and rests on positive, or what is
technically called, municipal law, in distinction from the
jus gentium of the Roman jurists. The presumption is
always in favor of freedom, and where there is no positive
or municipal law authorizing it, slavery has no legal existence, and no man can be held as the bondman of another.
Congress having no power to pass laws establishing slavery
in either state or territory, and the territorial legislature
having no legislative powers not derived from congress,
there is, under our system, no power that can enact a law
authorizing slavery in a territory, before it becomes a sovereign state. As state laws have no extra-territorial vigor,
the slave, carried by the voluntary action of his master into
a territory where no municipal law authorizes slavery, must
in that territory be held to be a free man, because there is
there no law that makes him a slave, and the master carrying him where there is no such law must be held to have
emancipated him. In a case properly brought before the
federal courts, the court would declare and ought to declare
him a free man. This is the ground, and we believe it a
strictly legal ground, that we take. At any rate, it is a
question not for congress, but for the courts, and when
brought fairly before the supreme federal judiciary and distinctly and formally decided, we shall hold ourselves bound
to abide by the decision of the court whether it be for us or
against us. The decision in the Dred Scott case does not
settle the question, for the precise point we raise was not
the question before the court. The precise question before
the court in that case was, whether a slave or person held to
service in Missouri, of which state his master was a citizen,

carried by his master out of that state into a state where
slavery was prohibited, or into a territory where no law
authorized, but the ordinance of 1787 excluded it, and
brought back or voluntarily returning to Missouri, reverted
to his original condition of a slave or not,—clearly a case for
the state courts of Missouri, not a case for the federal
judiciary, and therefore the court very properly dismissed
it for want of jurisdiction.   As to the arguments or opinions
advanced by the court in arriving at the decision, that it had
no jurisdiction, they may have been good or bad, but they
have no legal force, and in no respect bind the courts below.
They are the arguments and opinions of distinguished jurists,
but not legal decisions.   The court simply decided that it
had no jurisdiction in the case.   The reason assigned by Mr.
Chief Justice Taney for dismissing the case for want of
jurisdiction in the court, namely, that negroes are not citizens of the United States, is not, in our poor judgment, a
good reason, for we have always understood that in our
courts, as in the English courts, a foreigner even is free to
bring an action either against a citizen or another foreigner.
Besides, no such reason was needed in the case, for the case
was clearly within the jurisdiction of the courts of Missouri,
and was improperly carried before the federal court.   But,
however this may be, the question, whether a person held to
service, or as a slave in a state, by the laws thereof, voluntarily taken by his master to a territory of the United
States, not yet organized into a state, is, while remaining
there, and within that territory, a slave or not, has not yet
been before the courts, and till it has been and formally decided we cannot regard it as *res judicata*, or as no longer an
open question.

We do not agree with the eminent chief justice, however
presumptuous it may be for us to differ from him, in the
opinion that free negroes are not citizens of the United
States.   All native-born citizens of any of the states of the
Union are citizens of the United States, and all free persons
born in any one of the states of parents owing no allegiance to a foreign power are citizens thereof, unless excluded
from citizenship by express law,—*citizens*, we say, not necessarily voters, for women and children are not voters, yet
are citizens.   In all those states where the law does not
prohibit negroes from being citizens, they are citizens on
the same conditions that white men are citizens, and entitled to the rights and subject to the duties of citizens.   If

so, they are citizens of the United States, and entitled by the constitution to be treated as citizens in the several states. The complaint we made of Mr. Chief Justice Taney was that he neglected or denied the rule of law, that the presumption is always in favor of liberty, as it is in favor of innocence, and that odious laws are to be strictly construed. All laws in favor of slavery, or that deprive any class of citizenship are in their nature odious, and the courts are bound to restrict their meaning or application as much as possible without violence. As a Catholic, Judge Taney is bound to regard negroes as men, men sprung from the same stock and having the same natural rights with himself, and therefore he should regard all laws creating distinctions to their prejudice as odious, and to be strictly construed, as he would in the case of white men. He seemed to us to reverse this, and to labor to give to the laws prejudicial to the negro race the broadest signification they could possibly bear, and thus to neglect the duty of the court to protect to the full extent of its legal power the weak and the oppressed. He reasoned as if the opinions and laws degrading negroes were favorable, benign, or as if to be slaves or outlaws were their normal condition, and therefore were to receive the broadest and most extensive application possible.

We are aware that southern statesmen and their northern sympathizers have latterly pretended to set forth slavery as the normal condition of the African, and to defend it as a noble, a Christian, a divine institution, which can hardly be opposed without sacrilege, or at least, fighting against the manifest will of Providence. We shall not undertake to refute them, because we think the common sense of mankind has settled the question, and because were we to attempt it, our *Review* would soon be excluded from every southern state, as an incendiary publication, likely to stir up insurrection among the slaves. We might not like this, we might think it unfair, and impolitic for the South to have all the argument on their own side, but each state is the judge for itself what publications it will or will not allow to circulate among its citizens. Congress can make no law abridging the freedom of speech or of the press, but the states, each for itself, can make as stringent laws on the subject as they please. Each state has the sovereign control over its own internal police, and, although it may exercise its powers, in our judgment, unwisely, or even unjustly, we cannot, so long as it keeps within its own bounds, quarrel with it, unless we are prepared to trample constitutions and laws under our feet and defend filibusterism on principle. Opinions are free, and if the South chooses to hold slavery as good, and to regard laws favorable to liberty as odious, she has a perfect political right to do so, only we insist that she shall not cram that doctrine down our throats by the action either of congress or the federal judiciary. As much as we detest slavery in any and every form, whether for white men or red men, for black men or yellow men, we will defend for the slave states every clear constitutional right that they have, though it make one half of the American states slaveholding states for ever; for we will never willingly seek what we hold to be even a good end by unlawful means, or in contravention of vested rights; but on the other hand we will not yield one iota of our constitutional rights against slavery. We believe in the moral obligation to keep our plighted faith, and that it is for the interest of the human race, for the interest of liberty, alike for black man and white man, that this Union should be perpetuated, and that it cannot be perpetuated unless the constitution be rigidly observed and all departures from it be promptly repelled, whether on the side of one section or on the side of another. We will not knowingly trespass one hair's breadth on the rights of the slaveholding states, nor will we submit willingly to their trespassing one hair's breadth on the rights of the free states. The rights of liberty do not change, nor the duties of the courts change, because southern or northern statesmen change their opinions on negro-slavery, or on any other subject.

Southern Democrats, and a considerable portion of their brethren at the North, as we have seen in congress, and in the Charleston convention, are now demanding, and demanding under threats of secession from the Union, that congress enact, not as is sometimes pretended, a slave code, but laws for the protection of slave property in the territories. Such demand is unconstitutional, and on the part of the South suicidal. If congress has no power over the question of slavery, and cannot discriminate between one species of property and another, by what right can it pass laws to protect slave property, any more than it can pass laws to abolish it? Slaves carried by their owners from a slave state into a territory not yet erected into a state either remain property, that is, slaves, or they do not. If they do, as the South contends, then no special laws for the protection of slave property are needed, for the common law as to the protection of property administered by the courts is amply sufficient; if, as we contend, they do not, but are emancipated by the voluntary act of the master in carrying them beyond the jurisdiction of the state law by virtue of which he held them as his property, then for congress to pass the laws demanded would be simply establishing slavery in the territory, which we say it has no power to do. If congress has power to establish slavery in a territory, it has power to prohibit it, which is precisely what the Republicans and free-soilers assert, and what the slaveholding interest denies. In demanding such laws the southern gentlemen place themselves in a fatal dilemma, from which they can never logically extricate themselves. Do they not, moreover, in demanding laws for the protection of slave property in the territories, virtually abandon their doctrine, that slavery exists legally in the Union wherever not prohibited by state law, and concede our doctrine that it exists nowhere, unless authorized by state law or long usage?

Are we told that the South need the legislation they ask, only to protect slave property against hostile territorial legislation? Be it so. Do they admit the people of a territory have the attributes of sovereignty, and, therefore, legislative power? If they do, then congress has no right to pass the laws in question, and could not do it without violence to the popular sovereignty of the territory. But, if they deny what is called " squatter sovereignty," and maintain, as is undoubtedly the fact, that the territory has, and can have, while a territory, no legislative authority, and that the acts of a territorial legislature are laws only by virtue of the express or tacit approval of congress; they need no law in the case, for the courts would treat the act of the territorial legislature as unconstitutional, as null, or *non avenu*. There is no doubt that the Kansas-Nebraska act contains, as we contended at the time it passed, elements practically hostile to slavery. It is susceptible of two different interpretations. Its plainest and most natural interpretation is, that it remits the question of slavery to the territorial legislature; that is, authorizes the people of the territory to decide whether they will permit or exclude slavery. According to this interpretation, the act assumes for congress the power to authorize, and therefore, if it chooses, to prohibit slavery in the territories—the Republican or free-soil doctrine. If it be interpreted to mean that in remitting the question to the people of the territory, congress does not authorize the people, but simply recognizes their inherent power to decide for themselves whether they will have slaves or not, the Kansas-Nebraska act simply recognizes the so-called "squatter sovereignty," or the sovereignty of the people irrespective of constitutions, civil or political organizations, and therefore that any number of people, wherever found, have the right to combine together, and do all that may be done by a sovereign state,—the doctrine on which John Brown and his black and white followers acted in their raid into Virginia. The Kansas-Nebraska act we have always understood was dictated by southern influence, and we know, as well as we can know any thing of the sort, that it was designed to combine the South as one man, so that any aspiring demagogue, who, by favoring the slave interest, could get the southern nomination for the presidency, would need to carry only one or two non-slaveholding states in order to be elected. It was an artfully contrived plan for throwing, for all future time, the power of the federal government into the hands of the slave interest, and no man deserves more the execration of the whole American people than its projector, or the senator who engineered it through congress. And yet in that act, in our judgment, the South was overreached, or overreached itself, and if carried out and abided by, it would be more effectual, in practice, against the further extension of slavery than any measure the Republicans, if they come into power, are likely to adopt. We object to it, because we regard it wrong in principle, and because, if it secured the end we approve, it could do so only by unconstitutional means. It has already made the South dissatisfied with northern neutrality, and compelled them, in their own defence, to abandon the doctrine—the strong constitutional doctrine—that congress has no power over the subject, which was Mr. Calhoun's doctrine in the days of our personal intercourse with him, and to demand, not merely that congress shall let slavery alone, but that it shall protect it, which, in principle, yields the whole question to the Republicans.

We are obliged to object to the Democratic party,—for the Democratic party is and will be controlled by the South, where lies its chief strength,—that on the question of slavery it is no longer simply opposed to political abolitionism, and to any unconstitutional use of the federal government against the domestic institutions of the states, but has become a pro-slavery party, and to support it, we must support slavery, whether we wish to do so or not. Formerly, a northern man, though disapproving slavery, could support the Democratic party, because he was required simply to adhere to the constitution, and in his political action, to let slavery alone, and leave it to the slaveholding states to deal with the question in their own way, and in their own time. This is no longer possible, and we cannot see, if we accept the policy adopted by the present administration, or the ground taken by the leading statesmen of the South, how a man can give his vote to the Democratic party unless he means to be practically a pro-slavery man, and to sustain negro-slavery as one of the normal and permanent institutions of the country; or, in other words, unless he is prepared to nationalize slavery, and make it a federal, instead of a merely state or local institution. We deem it more important to preserve the constitution than it is to get rid of slavery; nevertheless, we are not willing to assist in perpetuating slavery.

We have other objections to the Democratic party; the one is its secret, we should rather say, its open sympathy with the revival of the African slave-trade, and the other is its avowed filibuster propensities. When three years and a half ago we assured our countrymen that the reopening of the slave-trade was contemplated, and warned the Democratic party against favoring it, we were hooted at as idle alarmists, and assured that our fears were ridiculous. Notwithstanding the slave-trade has been reopened, that is, if it ever was closed, and negroes are now imported from Africa in American ships, under the protection of the American flag, and sold in our southern slave markets. Either the denials we met were a blind, or we happened to be better informed than they who contradicted us. One federal judge has decided, and we are inclined to think correctly decided, that there is no federal law against importing *slaves* from Africa; that is, negroes who are slaves in Africa at the time of being procured. We have found no Democratic journal or statesmen either objecting to that decision, or demanding the amendment of the federal legislation on the subject. Indeed, if slavery be as the Democratic party both North and South now appear to hold, not abnormal, not an evil, but for the negroes a normal, a noble, a Christian, a divine condition, we see not why the importation of negroes from Africa, whether slaves or free men in Africa, should not rather be encouraged than prohibited. It is idle to make laws against a practice justified by the premises consecrated by the law-makers. The main reason for condemning the slave trade is in the supposition that slavery is an evil, and that it is the duty of governments, while they respect vested rights, to circumscribe it as much as possible, and by a wise policy to render practicable its ultimate abolition. On this point there can be no room for doubt. If, then, you take the present Democratic view of the Christian excellence of slavery, you remove the main reason for prohibiting the slave trade, and its revival is but a logical consequence of the premises you adopt. Let the views recently put forth by Mr. O'Connor, a leading Democrat, and a distinguished lawyer of New York, once become the convictions of the great body of the American people, and it will be impossible to convince them that there is any more reason why it should be piracy, to bring negroes from Africa to our southern ports, than there is that it should be piracy to carry them from Virginia to Texas. The South wants more laborers, and why shall Africa, the vast magazine whence they may be drawn, be closed to them? Just in proportion as you diminish the abhorrence of slavery, do you diminish the abhorrence in the minds of the people of the slave trade. The argument for opening or keeping open the slave trade, is unanswerable, except on the supposition that slavery itself is a wrong, and to be discouraged in every legal and constitutional way. But we cannot defend the slave trade, or support any party that favors it. Our church condemns the importation of negroes from Africa, to be held as slaves on our plantations, as an infamous traffic, and interdicts all her children who directly or indirectly engage in it. Here we can make no compromise; practise no connivance; for the question is a question of conscience. No Catholic can either import negroes from Africa, or buy to be held as slaves those imported by others, under pain of the severest spiritual censures; and we see not how any Catholic, with a good conscience, can support a party that is known to favor or to connive at this infamous traffic. As the constitution gives to congress full power to prohibit the slave trade, we have a right to insist that it shall pass and enforce the most stringent laws needed against it. Here we stand on strong ground, for here we stand on conscience, and ask only what it is confessed on all hands congress has the constitutional power to do; and unless the Democratic party purge itself of the vehement suspicion of favoring the slave trade, and show itself in earnest to do all in its power to suppress it, no Catholic who loves his church more than his party, can, save through ignorance, it seems to us, still continue to support it.

The Democratic party, North and South, to a great extent, sympathize with the filibuster movements so disgraceful to the country, so damaging to our national character and reputation. We do not regard all, who sustain the Democratic party, as favoring filibusterism, any more than we regard all of them as favoring the African slave trade. There is yet a strong element in the party opposed to both; but both are legitimate logical consequences of the principles avowed and sustained by the leaders of the party. The South, less than the North, can afford to countenance filibusterism. Their immense property in slaves is an aquired, not a natural, right, and is protected by the respect entertained by the American people generally, for international or inter-state law and vested rights. Filibusterism is the denial, in principle as in practice, of the sacredness of vested rights, of state constitutions, and international laws. Let the anti-slavery population of the North, or non-slaveholding states, once be fully satisfied that filibusterism is just and honorable, and we know nothing that would prevent them from pouring into the slave states by thousands and hundreds of thousands to liberate the slaves and plunder the inhabitants. We read the defiant answer of the southern man in the indignant flash of his eye and the motion of his hand towards his revolver or his bowie-knife; but, without questioning his courage, and without doubting that men will fight more bravely to make or keep than to emancipate slaves, yet it must be remembered that there is booty in the case, and that men will fight harder and more daringly for plunder than for any thing else. We question not the bravery or military capacity of the South. We cannot sit down and coolly calculate the chances of a death-struggle between the two sections, or speculate as to which would come off conqueror; but this we will say, that erect filibusterism into a principle, destroy in the northern mind, as democracy is fast doing, our traditionary respect for constitutions and laws, for vested rights, and international laws, which require the citizens of one state to forbear all hostile invasions of another, save as led on by legitimate authority in lawful war, and the South will find men in numbers large enough, and brave enough, to give them no little trouble and vexation; indeed, more daring fellows to follow some John Brown into Virginia or Kentucky to liberate the slaves, than your General Walkers can find to invade Mexico or Central America to reëstablish slavery, especially when, in addition to liberating the slaves, they have the attractions of a rich country, populous and wealthy towns to ravage and plunder. And why not? If William Walker may lawfully invade Nicaragua like some adventurous Norman knight of the middle ages, to take possession of the land for himself and followers, and to reduce the inhabitants to slavery, and reopen the African slave trade, which he tells in his late *History of the War in Nicaragua*, was what he understood by introducing the American element into that republic, why may not another John Brown invade any of our southern states with a view of liberating the slaves? What is the difference in principle between John Brown's raid into Virginia, and Sam Houston's filibustering operations in Texas, Lopez's invasion of Cuba, or Walker's murderous expeditions to Nicaragua? We can see none, or, if any, it is not in favor of the latter.

The pretence on which our democrats justify these piratical expeditions, that they are intended to emancipate a people ground down by tyranny, and to extend the area of freedom, is equally available in the case of the John Browns. No people are more completely deprived of their liberty than are negro slaves, and if we may bid defiance to constitutions, and trample on the rights of independent states in the name of liberty, we see not why we may not do it to liberate the domestic slave as well as to liberate the political slave. Our sins, like chickens, come home to roost, and we can never violate justice, and teach that it is honorable and praiseworthy to violate it, without having, sooner or later, in one form or another, our own rights set at naught. Nations have no life in the world to come, and national sins must, sooner or later, meet their punishment in this world. The South, so long as it suffers its craving for more territory suitable for slave culture, to induce it to countenance or to connive at filibuster expeditions against Cuba, Mexico, or Central America, can never successfully appeal to law, to the constitution, or to the sacredness of vested rights, to protect her in the peaceable possession of her negroes. Nor can northern men feel that they hold their property by any other tenure than the strong hand, so long as they suffer their greediness for land speculations to make them forget to respect the rights, the territory, and the possessions of others. In itself considered, John Brown's raid was no great affair, but viewed in connection with the doctrines as to popular sovereignty, entertained in all sections of the country, and which form the democratic theory, unhappily, embraced by all our political parties, and which justify it, it is a symptom of what we are to expect, and deserves all the importance that has been attached to it.

We write with deep feeling, but without any sectional or party animosity. Filibusterism, as it is understood and practised among us, is the legitimate child of the democratic theories of popular sovereignty, which have gained such ascendency in the country during the last twenty or thirty years, that came into place with General Jackson, and that were so strenuously warred against by that greatest and most accomplished of our statesmen, John C. Calhoun, to the day of his death. It is the direct offspring of the Jacobinism of the old French revolution which pervades, more or less, all classes of European society, embodied by the Carbonari and other secret societies, led on in one form by Louis Napoleon and Victor Emanuel, and in another by Joseph Mazzini and Louis Kossuth, and preventing the establishment of peace and legal order in every European continental state. It is justified by that very democratic theory which, in our own country, has already destroyed in most of the states the independence of the judiciary, corrupted the sources of justice, swept away the safeguards of individual liberty retained by our fathers, identified the people with God, made public opinion, or rather the opinion of each man's special public, the rule of right, and success the standard of merit; which has thrown the power into the hands of the most numerous, and therefore the least intelligent class, who can understand in politics only a trade to be carried on for each one's private benefit, banished alike public spirit and public virtue, and filled the public offices with men, at best, of only average capacity, who are venal, insensible to the honor and glory of the country, and whose principal study is to derive all the pecuniary profit possible from their office and position during the brief period of their official life. Each party claims to be democratic, and each in its greediness for power and place outbids the other. Not all of any party, we would fain believe, have as yet adopted this wild and destructive democratic theory, or are prepared to follow it to its last logical results. But if entertained in its principles, there is an invincible logic in the popular mind that will, before we are aware of it, under pain of the sin of inconsequence, which the human race never pardons, force us to adopt even its remotest consequences, however repugnant they may be to common sense, or revolting to common honesty. The Democratic party is not alone in fault, but of all our parties it is the more deeply committed. Its name alone is fatal to it, for there is a logic in names which, in the long run, will prove invincible, and compel the party that bears the name to accept the thing. The Republican party may be nearly as far gone as the Democratic, but its name does not commit it, and it would be possible for it to become a truly conservative party without any change of name. Its name is a good one.

Now the South freed by slavery from that modern curse, universal suffrage, by the independent position of her leading men as planters and large property holders, forming a sort of aristocracy in a too democratic country, ought to furnish a conservative element in our American politics, and prove a restraint on the democratic tendencies of the free states. We have looked to it for this, and felt at times in our hatred of democracy—which we have no wish to disguise —half reconciled to the existence of slavery, if it should be indirectly the means of saving us from the wild radicalism which we have so much reason to fear. But, unhappily, the South has not been true to her mission. She chose to ally herself with the democratic party of the North, and by that alliance has forced all parties hoping for success to become democratic, and we therefore hold her to a great extent indirectly responsible for the democracy that now threatens the whole country with ruin. We regret it, for the evil has gone so far as to seem to us well-nigh irreparable.

We have stated our principal points of agreement and disagreement with the Democratic party North and South, and we leave them to the judgment of our readers. We say nothing of the present administration, except that it has realized our worst fears. We say nothing of the candidates of the Democratic party for president and vice-president, for at the time we are writing, the party has not made its nominations. We will only say that with our view of the case we could neither as a northern nor as a southern man support Mr. Douglas, for we regard his policy as alike false to both sections, although we have nothing to say against him as a man and a citizen, and we honor him for the pluck he has shown in maintaining the fight between him and Mr. Buchanan. If the administration has damaged him, he has prostrated the administration. Our views of the Republican party may be gathered from what we have already said. As far as it has Whig antecedents we are not hostile to it; as far as it is the free-soil party under a new name, we have no sympathy with it. In its opposition to the further extension of slavery we believe it right and just, and go with it heart and soul, but in the respect that it proposes to prevent its further extension by Wilmot provisos, or congressional action, we dissent from its policy, for we regard such legislation and such provisos as unconstitutional. Inasmuch as it is a sectional party, though in reality no more so than the Democratic party, we are not pleased with it. Its position on the question of slavery is too far one way, while the position of the South is too far the other way. On the question of slavery, like the Democratic party, it is partly right and partly wrong, and is preferable to the Democratic party only in the respect that it is not proslavery, and if we must violate the constitution, or usurp for congress powers not conceded it, it is better to do so in favor of, than against, human liberty. Aside from the slavery question the Republican platform strikes us as in the main not objectionable, and free from the filibuster element that we detect in the platform of the Democratic party, and by no means necessarily commits the party to the ultra-democracy we so earnestly oppose. Yet the elevation of the party to power with Horace Greeley as one of its most influential leaders, without a southern state or the hope of attaining the vote of a single slaveholding state, unless the little state of Delaware, is a serious matter, and one must think twice before he makes up his mind to support it. It is not the secession of the southern states or the dissolution of the Union we fear, but the want of a proper conservative element. We do not like to have power as now wholly in the hands of the South; we should dislike equally to see it exclusively in the hands of the North. We should regret the defeat of the Republican party, for that would involve the triumph of the slave interest, and subject to it the policy of the government; and we should regret its success, for that would open the door for the reappearance of political abolitionism.   The candidates of the party are not such as we prefer, but perhaps they are better than the Democratic party will support.   Turn the question which way we will, which side in or out, up or down, it has an ugly look, and whichever of the two parties accedes to power, we must expect trouble, confusion, and not much good to compensate for it.

However, the end of the republic is not yet, nor will the coming election, however it terminates, decide its fate.   We may trust something to the " chapter of accidents," that is, to Providence, and in the meantime instead of staking all on the success or defeat of this or that party, we shall do well to labor to clear up the questions now agitated, and present the true issue before the people for a future election. Let the South abandon all filibustering tendencies, all disposition to reopen the slave trade, cease to ask the North to favor slavery, and leave the question of slavery in the territories to be decided by the courts, and all disputes on the slavery question, so far as we are concerned, would cease, that is, as a question to be carried into politics ; or, let the Republican party agree to the same, or cease to claim for congress the power to legislate on slavery anywhere, and the North and the South may once more act together.   Slavery would gain nothing but what it is entitled to, and the welfare of the whole people, the cause of republican government would gain much.   Neither the North nor the South is a complete or whole people without the other.   It is, no doubt, too late for the voice of reason to be heard in the present canvass ; but let those who really love their country hold themselves ready, when the contest is over, to place American politics on a new and better footing, and so to organize parties that an honest man may find a party he can support without violence to his conscience.

THE GREAT REBELLION.

[From Brownson's Quarterly Review for July, 1861.]

THE closing days of Mr. Buchanan's administration, which had managed to bring the country to the brink of ruin, were gloomy and sullen, and we were disposed to take a somewhat desponding view of the crisis in our national affairs. The Republicans, who had triumphed in the election of Mr. Lincoln, were apparently divided among themselves as to the course the new government should take; there seemed nowhere, either North or South, any decided attachment to the Union: and rebellion was as openly avowed, and almost as fiercely defended in Philadelphia, New York, and Boston, as in Baltimore, Charleston, and New Orleans; there was a general distrust of the officers of the army and navy; traitors were everywhere; wisdom, energy, patriotism, nowhere. The gulf states pretended to have seceded, and had formed a provisional government under the name of the "Confederate States of America." North Carolina, Virginia, and Maryland, if not Kentucky and Tennessee, it was known were ready to withdraw from the Union the moment that it was clearly ascertained that they could no longer effectually serve the cause of rebellion by remaining in it. Arkansas was pledged to the confederacy, and there was a strong secession party in Missouri. A confederate army was organized, and the rebels had plenty of arms, taken from the forts and arsenals of the United States. The treasury was empty; the credit of the government was low; and the feeble federal army and navy were so dispersed as to require months to concentrate them, or to render them of any efficiency in supporting the Union. A long peace and a general belief that wars on this continent were no longer to be apprehended, had left our militia without effective organization, and, for the most part, nothing more than the mere raw material of soldiers. The great bulk of the people seemed to be wholly engrossed in trade and speculation, selfish, and incapable of any disinterested, heroic, or patriotic effort. What wonder, then, that we were despondent, without hope for the future?

But since then the whole aspect of affairs has changed, and we are obliged to confess that we had underrated the patriotism and attachment to the Union of the people of the non-slaveholding states. The administration has been able to replenish, not on very unreasonable terms, the exhausted treasury, and the call of the president for seventy-five thousand volunteers to save the national capital and stay the tide of rebellion, was within three weeks responded to from the several free states, it is said, with an offer of the services of more than half a million of men. States and municipalities, within the same period, voted, as a free gift to the government for arming, equipping, and training volunteers or supporting their families, over twenty-three millions of dollars. Party lines were obliterated, divisions were healed, and there was an outburst of patriotism such as the world has rarely, if ever, witnessed, from twenty millions of freemen. The star-spangled banner was thrown to the breeze from every public edifice, from every church steeple, and almost from every house; and from the mighty heart of all the free states rung out the battle-cry, "The Union must and shall be preserved." Since the fall of Sumter on the 14th of April, up to the 1st of June, an efficient land force of not less, it is said, than a hundred and fifty thousand men has been organized, armed, and equipped, and is either on the frontiers or drilling in the different camps in the several states. Another levy of a hundred thousand men, if made, would be cheerfully responded to, as indeed would be a levy of twice that number. The only embarrassment of the government thus far has grown out of its inability to accept the numbers of volunteers offering. Ships-of-war have been recalled, a powerful fleet fitted out, and nearly all the ports of the states in which rebellion is rampant, are effectually blockaded. Nearly all the strategic points are guarded, the advance of the rebels effectually checked, the posts in the rebellious states that continued in the possession of the government effectually reinforced, and a forward movement commenced. All this has been done in six weeks. The simple enumeration of these facts proves that we, as well as others, had wronged our countrymen, and that our fears for the safety of the Union were uncalled for.

We do not believe that the history of the world presents an instance of so much having been done and in so short a time by any people. The uprising of the free states in defence of their government and flag is unprecedented, and proves that however the American people may have degenerated during fifty years of peace and unbounded prosperity, they are still a people who have a future and are far from having fallen into the past; that they are full of life and energy, of ardor and hope, and have a long and, if they choose, a glorious career before them. As to the military spirit of our people, we have never doubted it. We have said on more occasions than one, that give the American people a cause, an occasion, a battle field, and they would prove themselves the first military nation in the world. They have in their composition the activity of the Frenchman, the reckless daring of the Irishman, the steadiness of the German, and the pluck of the Englishman; they have combined in them in admirable proportions the peculiar military virtues of the several nations of Europe. But we had feared that, made up to a great extent as they are from all the various populations of Europe, and possessing a sort of cosmopolitan character, they would be found in the hour of trial deficient in patriotism, especially in loyalty to the government of the Union. We think the events of the last six weeks ought to dissipate all fears of this sort, at least so far as the real American people, the people of the non-slaveholding states are concerned. We feel for ourselves that we still have a country, and whatever may be the future, we are proud of our countrymen, and still glory in being an American.

It is too late to discuss the merits of the controversy between the United States and the rebels now in arms against the government. Our views with regard to that controversy are well known to our readers. No man in the Union, according to his ability, and sphere of influence, has done more to prevent the spread of abolitionism, or to defend against fanatics of either section of the Union the constitutional rights of the South or slaveholding states. From 1828 down to the present moment, the editor of this *Review* has never faltered or wavered in his defence of state rights, or in his opposition to centralism or consolidation. He was, as is well known, the personal and political friend of John C. Calhoun, and for a time defended even his doctrine of nullification. His sympathies have always been with the South, and his warmest personal and political friends have been in that section of the country. But he owes it to himself to say that he has always been attached to the Union of these states, and felt that his loyalty as a citizen was due to

the federal government.   He has always looked upon the
several states as integral parts of one common country, and
whether in Wisconsin or Michigan, in Ohio or Indiana,
Illinois or Missouri, Kentucky or Tennessee, Louisiana or
Alabama, South Carolina or Virginia, Maryland or Pennsylvania, New York or Connecticut, Rhode Island or Massachusetts, Maine or Vermont, he was still in his own
country, on his own native soil, among his own countrymen
and fellow-citizens.   Patriotism, with him, has always meant
love to the whole country under the jurisdiction of the federal government.   He has never understood it to be restricted to his native state, or to the state of which, for the
time being, he might be a citizen.   In his patriotism he has
known no North, no South, no East, no West.   For him
every man was his countryman who was born under the flag
of the Union.   He has always regarded the federal government, though a government of express and delegated powers, as possessing, within the sphere of its constitutional
powers, the character of a real government, vested with
true sovereignty.   Though formed by sovereign states, by
mutual compact, he has never held it, when formed, to be a
simple league or confederation of states, but a proper national government, and entitled to the allegiance of every
American citizen.   He has never admitted the actual right
of any state to secede from the Union, and the doctrine of
nullification which he at one time held he had disavowed in
these pages so long ago as in 1847.

We owe it furthermore to ourselves to say that though
opposed to the abolition party movement, we have never
approved of slavery.   Regarding slavery as a local institution existing only by municipal law or usage, we have always treated it as a subject over which the Union had, in
the ordinary exercise of its powers, no authority, and as
lying in our political system wholly within the jurisdiction
of the state in which it is established.   In our political action we have insisted on leaving it to the slaveholding
states themselves, to be disposed of as they should judge
proper.   But as a man, as a philosopher, as a Christian, and
as a statesman, we have always been opposed to it.   We
have regarded it as a flagrant violation of those fundamental rights of man on which our republic professes to be
founded, no less than of that brotherhood of the human
race asserted by the Gospel.   We have believed it wrong in
principle, mischievous in practice, a grave evil to the slave,

and a graver evil to the master. We have always believed it a grievous moral, social, and political evil, and hence we have always been opposed to the extension of its area. Our policy has always been to circumscribe it within the narrowest limits that we could constitutionally. We have believed it more important to maintain the Union of these states under the existing constitution, and more in the interest of liberty, than to seek the extinction of slavery by unconstitutional action, or by the political interference of the citizens of one state with the institutions, domestic or social, of another. As far as slavery could extend itself legally under the existing constitution, we have always deemed it our duty to refrain from interfering with it. But we have never contemplated with any degree of satisfaction to ourselves the probability, or even the possibility, of the permanent existence of negro slavery in any part of the American republic. We have always held it to be the duty of the slaveholding states to take at the earliest moment the most efficient measures in their power for educating and preparing their slaves for freedom and the final extinction of slavery. Such have been our views ever since we have been old enough to reflect and form opinions on the subject, and such have been and are the views of the great majority of the people of the non-slaveholding states. The great majority of us have always detested slavery, and deeply regretted its existence within the limits of the United States, but we have always been willing to discharge to the letter all our constitutional duties towards the slaveholding communities of the South, and notwithstanding all the provocation and insults heaped upon us by our southern brethren, we are still prepared to discharge faithfully all the duties in regard to slavery that any fair and honest interpretation of the constitution imposes upon us.

If the slaveholding states had been satisfied with this, and asked nothing more of us in the free states than the simple discharge of our constitutional duties, or if they had been content with the simple legal rights of slavery, there would have been no collision between the two sections of the country. The cause of the southern rebellion is not in the aggressions of the North, nor in the movements of northern abolitionists. We must seek it in the fact that the slaveholding states wished through the slave interest, or the interest of capital invested in slaves, to control the policy of the country and administer the government in their own favor, and in the further fact that they felt they could have no adequate security for the capital so invested while the wealthier and more populous section of the Union entertained opinions and convictions hostile to slavery. No modification of the constitution, however favorable to slavery, would have satisfied them so long as they felt themselves the weaker party. Nothing would satisfy them but the conversion of the North to their views of slavery. They knew perfectly well that slavery could not long exist in a country unless it were its controlling interest. It can flourish only so long as it governs, and must die out when the supremacy passes from its hands. Hence these states made at first a desperate struggle through the northern Democracy, which almost from the origin of the government had been allied with them, to retain their supremacy. They made afterwards a still more desperate struggle to change the opinions of the North with regard to slavery itself. But, failing in both attempts, and seeing that power must pass from their hands, and henceforth be wielded by a party that would not consent to be governed by the interests of the capital invested in slaves, they felt that their only security lay in breaking up the Union, and forming a separate confederacy of their own, based on slavery as its corner-stone. They would, whatever they pretended, accept no compromise, and the free states had no option but to submit to their dictation, abdicate their own rights in the Union, and recognize slavery as a Christian institution, as existing by divine right, and as forming the basis of our republic, or to assert their own manhood, their equal rights as members of the Union, form a really constitutional party, carry the elections, and administer the government for the common interests of the whole country, and not for the special interest of a particular section, and that the slaveholding section. This they did in the last presidential election. No intelligent man at the South believed that the success of the Republican party threatened directly the institution of slavery; but the whole South saw in it the fact that the political control of the Union had passed from southern hands, and that henceforth the slaveholding states would be obliged to be contented to stand on a footing of equality with the non-slaveholding states. There was no fear that the slave interest would be deprived of any of its legal rights, but there was a certainty that henceforth it would not be supreme in the councils of the

Union ; that, however scrupulously it might be respected within the slaveholding states themselves, the extension of slavery into new territory where it had no legal existence, would be effectually checked ; that no more territory could be acquired and annexed to the Union in the interest of slavery ; that the flag of the Union would be no longer permitted to cover the piratical slave-trade, and that all hopes of reopening the African slave-trade must be abandoned. Here, in our judgment, is, in brief, the real cause of the present collision between the United States and the southern rebels. The cause, we repeat, is not in northern aggression, but in northern emancipation from southern domination. We told the South in 1857* what would be the consequence if she persisted in seeking to make the Union the mere instrument of advancing the interest of capital vested in slaves, of her attempting to convert the Democratic party into a party for slavery propagandism, and of her attempt to establish the doctrine that the constitution carries with it slavery wherever it goes.

Well, it has come to this. The South has appealed from ballots to bullets, and forced upon the North an issue which the people of the free states could not refuse to accept without abdicating their manhood, and standing branded in history as the most miserable cravens and dastards that the world has ever known. The war has come, and come none too soon. The issue had to be tried, whether the New World was to be a land of freedom, sacred to free institutions and self-government, or whether it was to be a land of slavery, where man was to be treated no longer as man, but as a mere chattel, with no soul, no reason, no conscience, no immortality. It has come, we say, none too soon, for already were we beginning to lose our freedom of speech even in the free states, and there was growing up everywhere a fear to speak out the great truths of religion and morality, of philosophy and political science, lest, forsooth, we might irritate our southern brethren and endanger the trade between the North and South. When we wrote our articles on slavery in January and April, 1857, a committee from highly respectable and most influential gentlemen in this city was sent to remonstrate with us, and to urge us either to retract what we had said or carefully refrain for the future from alluding to the subject of slavery in our

---

*Slavery and the Incoming Administration; ante, pp. 64–65

pages. It was hazardous to our reputation with our own northern fellow-citizens to publish on the question of slavery what has always been the doctrine of the church, that all men by nature are free, that man has received from his Maker no dominion over man, and that slavery can lawfully exist only as a penalty or a discipline. Slavery was penetrating everywhere, and we were fast becoming slaves, even while boasting our freedom. Thank God, we are now emancipated, our lips are unsealed, and we are no longer debarred from speaking the language of reason and common sense for fear of irritating some southern slaveholder or trafficker in human flesh. The shots that struck Sumter knocked off our chains, and enabled us of the North to spring to our feet as freemen, and to feel for the first time in our history as a nation, that we are really free and no longer under southern tutelage. It was this sense of freedom, this sense of their emancipation, the assurance that henceforth they had no terms to keep with slave-drivers or slaveholders, that called forth that universal burst of enthusiasm, that unanimous response to the call of the government for volunteers, that has surprised ourselves, and called forth the admiration of the civilized world. Whatever be the result of the present struggle, one thing is certain, southern domination is gone and gone for ever, and with it northern servility and northern cowardice. If in this struggle we secure not the freedom of the negro population of the South, we shall at least secure our own.

  The war now raging is no doubt to be deeply deplored, or rather the causes which have led to it ; but in this war the United States are in the right and the southern rebels wholly in the wrong. The rebels, by aid of their Democratic friends in the non-slaveholding states, have had the administration of the government, have shaped its general policy at home and abroad, and wielded its patronage, with hardly an interval of time, since the inauguration of Mr. Jefferson in 1801. They have had almost every thing their own way. The South have had no wrongs from the government, and no grievances from the North to complain of. The federal government has, from the first, faithfully performed all its duties with regard to the question of slavery. It has fully protected the rights of the slave-owner, and has enacted and executed the most stringent and offensive laws in his favor. The southern section of the Union has had far more than its share of officers in the army and navy, as well as of the diplomatic representatives of the country. Of the two foreign wars in which we have been engaged since the adoption of the federal constitution, the first was forced upon us by the South for the purpose of ruining the commerce and influence of the northern and eastern states; and the second, that against Mexico, was undertaken wholly in the slaveholding interest of the South. Though more than three-fourths of the revenues of the federal government have been collected in the ports of the free states, nearly two-thirds have been expended in and for the slaveholding states, and these states have held their slave property in security and been protected in their peculiar institutions, solely because they were regarded by foreign nations and by the citizens of the free states as integral parts of the great American republic. No portion of the United States have received so great and so many benefits from the federal Union. Of what, then, do they complain? What grievance have they had, not of their own creating? Some of our journals, indeed, in all sections of the country say "the South has had wrongs," but we confess we do not know what those wrongs have been. For over thirty years we of the North have been obliged to vote under threats of a dissolution of the Union by southern politicians, if we did not vote to please them. Since the Missouri compromise in 1820, there has been on our part but one continued series of concessions to the slaveholding South. If the free states showed any disposition to adopt a governmental policy not likely to strengthen and consolidate the slave power and to render it permanent, they were branded as "sectional," denounced as "aggressive," as trampling on the "compromises of the constitution," and met with loud and angry threats of secession. If any party, then, could complain of wrongs, it is not the South, but the North.

We have carefully read the public declarations of the rebel governments, and, we confess, we have been able to find, even in their one-sided representations, no serious grievances enumerated. They speak of protective tariffs: but they forget that the tariff policy was originated by southern statesmen, or rendered necessary by southern policy. The capitalists of the North were forced to engage in manufactures by the war of 1812,—a southern measure intended to destroy the commerce of New England. The first tariff for protecting these manufactures, introduced at the close of the war, was introduced, or at least supported by John C. Calhoun, subsequently the great freetrader and nullification leader of South Carolina; the most strenuous, energetic, and successful advocate of the policy was Henry Clay, a slaveholder and the representative of a slaveholding state; and a majority of the votes of the New England states was never given for any tariff bill in congress prior to that of 1842. Whether, then, the protective policy be favorable to the North and oppressive to the South or not, the South is at least as deeply implicated in its adoption as any other section of the Union.

These governments also complain of the personal-liberty bills passed by some of the free states: but they should remember that these bills were passed chiefly in retaliation for laws enacted in the slaveholding states, imprisoning free citizens of the North acting as sailors on ships trading to southern ports during the period of their remaining in port, and authorizing them to be sold into slavery for the expenses of their imprisonment; and also to protect their own citizens from being arrested and carried away into slavery by southern kidnappers. They should also bear in mind that these personal-liberty laws have never prevented the return of fugitive slaves. No state is bound by its own officers or action to return fugitive slaves on claim of their owner; this duty the supreme court, as well as congress, has decided devolves on the federal government, and the federal government has never failed to discharge it.

A careful reading of these official declarations, in connection with well-known facts, proves that the only grievance the South has to complain of in us in the non-slaveholding states is, that we are not charmed with the beauties of the slave system; that we do not regard slavery as a Christian institution existing by divine right; that in fact we dislike slavery, that we detest it and take the liberty to say so. Here is the head and front of our offending. But even in this respect we only retain and express the views and feelings entertained and expressed, till quite recently, by the prominent statesmen and leading men of the slaveholding states themselves. It amounts, then, to this, that the people of the slaveholding states have rebelled against the federal government because the majority of the people of the non-slaveholding states differ from them in opinion on the subject of slavery, and insist upon treating black men, as well as white men, as belonging to the human family, in a word, as men created with rational and immortal souls and redeemed by the passion and death of our Lord; —because, in fact, we include them in the great brotherhood of humanity. This is their grievance for which they have seen proper to rebel against the federal government, and attempt to efface from the map of the world the great republic of the United States.

The federal government is manifestly in the right; for whether the federal government derives its powers by delegation from sovereign states, or directly from the people politically divided into states, it is, within its constitutional sphere, a government with all the rights and immunities of government, and, like every government, must have that first of all rights, the right of self-preservation. The question as to the source of its powers is and can be of no practical importance, when once its powers are ascertained and defined. The people of the United States, in forming the federal Union, did not form a mere league or confederacy of sovereigns; they formed a government, a government with limited powers indeed but still a government, supreme, sovereign within its constitutional limits. They formed a union and not a confederacy. From this union no state, any more than an individual, has the right to secede; for they expressly ordain that the "constitution, and the laws of the United State which shall be made in pursuance thereof; and all treaties made, or which shall be made, under the authority of the United States, shall be the supreme law of the land; and the judges in every state shall be bound thereby, any thing in the constitution or laws of any state to the contrary notwithstanding." There is no getting over this: the federal government, within its constitutional limits, is the supreme government of the land, and paramount to all state constitutions, authorities, or laws. Any act of secession by a state is an act of rebellion, and therefore null and void, not only as against the Union, but in relation to its own citizens; and the attempt of the people, or any portion of the people of any state by force of arms to carry such an act into effect, is manifestly a levying of war against the United States, and therefore an act of treason. Even if it were conceded that the sovereignty theoretically still vests in the states, its exercise within certain limits is delegated to the Union and incapable of being revoked without a manifest breach of faith. Say that the Union is a "constitutional compact," it is one of those compacts in which all the parties are bound to each and each to all. Such a compact can be

dissolved only by the unanimous consent of all the contracting parties, while from its very nature the parties remaining
faithful to it must necessarily have the right to enforce its
observance upon any party seeking to evade its provisions.
So, whether we take the northern or the southern view of
the federal Union, secession is illegal, is in violation of the
constitution, nothing more or less than an act of rebellion,
and as such the federal government has not only the constitutional right, but the constitutional duty, to put it down,
if it has or can command the means to do it.

The federal government, in the present war, is not warring against any state, or seeking to coerce any state as such,
into submission; for no state, as a state, has withdrawn or
could withdraw from the Union, since any action of the people of any state to withdraw itself would exceed the constitutional right of the state, and be a simple usurpation of
power. No states have seceded, for no state, by the constitution of the United States or by its own constitution, could
secede. The so-called Confederate States of America have,
therefore, no legitimate authority either within the states
themselves or as against the Union. This southern confederacy is simply a league of conspirators and rebels. The
federal government in making war against them, therefore,
only makes war in its own defence and in vindication of
the constitutional rights of the several states; and in doing
it, it is only performing its own imperious and constitutional
duties. The war is not a war between the North and South,
between the free and the slaveholding states, for or against
slavery, but is, on the part of the government, simply a war
against traitors and rebels to the states and the Union.

The fact that the rebellion is confined principally to one
section of the Union, or the fact that a considerable portion
of the Union are involved in it, makes no difference as to
its character. The right of the government and the essential character of the war remain the same, whether the rebels are few or many, whether they are northern or southern,
slaveholders or non-slaveholders. If it be the right and
duty of a government to maintain itself and to put down
armed conspirators and traitors against it, there can be no
question that the government has the right and the duty to
put down this southern rebellion, and that all loyal citizens
are bound to aid it in doing so with their property and with
their lives. There never was a more causeless rebellion,
one more unprovoked, more unjustifiable, or more guilty.

There is not one word to be said in defence or in extenuation of the actors in this foul conspiracy. Consequently no war on the part of a government to put down a conspiracy against its own rights and existence, to vindicate itself and maintain the supremacy of the laws, ever was or ever could be more just and deserving of the support of all loyal subjects and good citizens.

The rebel forces are not only forces arrayed against legitimate authority, but they are forces so arrayed under circumstances of peculiar aggravation. The government they seek to cast off or to overthrow is a free government, under a constitution that provides for its own amendment. If the people of the slaveholding states had wished to separate from the Union, and to form themselves into a separate and independent government, or to become a nation by themselves, there was a legal and constitutional way by which they could have been gratified. If they had felt that their interests, their peculiar institutions, their sentiments and convictions made a longer connection with the non-slaveholding states undesirable, they might easily have obtained a convention of all the states, which, no doubt, would have authorized their separation, and enabled them, in a legal and peaceful way, to have established themselves as a separate nation. If they had made their request known in a legal way, and had made it manifest that a separation was their unanimous, or very general desire, we are confident that the majority of the non-slaveholding states would have permitted their separation, and consented to a proper boundary line and to a just and equitable division of the public property and of the public debt.

But they did nothing of this. They first attempted to gain the supremacy of the Union, and, failing in that, they attempt violently its dissolution. They respect no oath of allegiance which they had taken to the Union, and begin by taking possession of the public property, the forts, arsenals, and mints, and trampling the laws of the Union, as well as the rights of property, under foot. Their first acts are acts of plunder and robbery; their second proceeding is, in the most open and avowed manner, a levying of war on the Union and threatening its destruction. No attempt at a peaceful separation was made till after they had committed gross acts of aggression, violence, and plunder, and they had trampled on the federal laws, and broken all their obligations as loyal citizens to the federal government, as well as to their own state governments. These are aggravating circumstances, and mark the character of the chief actors in the conspiracy with a degree of atrocity that does not attach to ordinary rebels. They might have had all they wished, without violence or wrong done. But their acts show clearly that their object was not so much separation from the Union and the formation of a new government for themselves, as the subjection by force, or humiliation of the federal government and its loyal supporters. Evidently their *animus* was bad, not so much to form a southern confederacy as to subject the Union to their domination and to force their policy and respect for their institution of slavery upon the people of the non-slaveholding states. It was not so much a new government they proposed to themselves, as the possession of the administration of the existing government, which they had failed to secure at the ballot-box, or a reconstruction of the Union under their dictation on the basis of negro slavery. They counted, but vainly counted, as the event has proved, on being able by aid of their Democratic friends at the North, to bring into their scheme all the states of the Union, with, perhaps, the exception of the New-England states. Could any government that had the least consciousness of its duty or the least respect for itself stand still, look quietly on, and suffer this nefarious plan to be carried into execution without offering the least opposition? Would it not have been to fail in its most imperious duty, to abdicate itself, or to commit suicide?

The fault of the government is not that it has called loyal people to the support of their own government which they themselves have constituted, but in suffering the conspirators to work so long without any serious attempt to arrest them. During the four years of Mr. Buchanan's administration, they not only worked without opposition from the government, but even made use of its authority, its offices, and its patronage, to further their purposes. We will not say that Mr. Buchanan was himself a rebel, we will not say that he favored the plans of the conspirators, but we will say that, down to nearly the close of his administration, he gave them free scope for their operations, and protected them by his authority. He kept their chief instruments in his cabinet and suffered in their interest their agents to deplete the treasury and bankrupt the government; to deprive the forts in the slaveholding section of the Union of all sufficient garrisons; to leave the arsenals, mints, and public property in the same section, for the most part, under the command of officers of doubtful attachment to the Union, and exposed to easy capture by a handful of rebels ; to transfer arms, ordnance and military stores very unnecessarily from the northern to the southern states, thereby depriving the loyal section of arms and munitions of war, and furnishing them to the disloyal populations ; to scatter the small federal army at the most distant points, whence many months must elapse before they could be collected in defence of the government ; to disperse our few war ships to the most distant quarters of the globe, or to place them within reach of the intended rebels. He used all the patronage of the government and all his personal influence to prevent the selection of a Union candidate to succeed him ; and when pretended secession broke out, though he feebly remonstrated against it, he declared officially that no coercion must be used. No one man in the country is so responsible for the present war as the late president of the United States, for it was his duty and it was in his power to have dismissed at an early day the traitors from his cabinet, to have supplied their places by loyal and honest men, to have foreseen the coming danger, and to have effectually guarded the government against it. He might and he should have suppressed the conspiracy before it came to a head, or been ready to have crushed the rebellion at the very instant of its breaking out. Unhappily he did no such thing, and his name must go down in our annals branded with infamy, or with imbecility.

The fault of the present administration, if any is to be laid to its charge, is not in the resistance it offers to rebellion, but in its having too long followed the do-nothing policy of its predecessor, or in having been too timid, hesitating, or uncertain, during the first weeks of its existence. Yet, if it were so, something can be said in its excuse, perhaps its justification. It came into power under all the embarrassments which the previous administration had created for it, without an army or navy, with an exhausted treasury, with a majority of the people on a popular vote against it, with all the civil offices of the government at home and abroad filled with its enemies, and ignorant of what military or naval officers it might or might not trust. It might have distrusted, as we ourselves did, the loyalty of a large portion of the citizens of the non-slaveholding states, and doubted whether its call for forces to put down the rebellion would have been generally responded to. The event, as we have seen, shows that if it ever entertained this doubt or this distrust there was no solid ground for it, and since it has shown itself determined to resist the rebellion, to use all the forces military and naval of the loyal states to crush the rebels and save the Union, it has risen in the respect and in the affections of the nation, at the South no less than at the North. If there still lingers a doubt or a distrust in its regard, it is not because it makes war on the rebellion, but because it is feared it is not prepared to make it with sufficient boldness, energy, and determination. Yet the doubt or fear which may still linger in some minds, we think, is unjustifiable. The administration understands its duty, and is prepared to perform it. That in the beginning it was timid, hesitating, uncertain as to the policy best to be adopted, is possible; but assured now of the support of the loyal American people, even of the great majority of those in the non-slaveholding states who, in the late presidential election, voted against it, it feels its strength and understands what its dignity and honor as a government demand ; its timidity has passed away ; it no longer hesitates, and is determined to vindicate the constitution, to preserve the Union, and to crush speedily and for ever its foes. In this it is manifestly right, and every American is not only free, but bound in conscience to support it to the full extent of his ability.

Yet, in thus vindicating the government and its determination to put down the armed rebellion against its authority, we by no means express or feel any hostility to the people of the slaveholding states; we regard them, as we do the people of the non-slaveholding states, as our countrymen, and feel that in supporting the government of the Union we are not invading, but defending their rights and interests. We deny that they have received any wrongs worth mentioning from the North. There is not, and there never has been, any intention on the part of the citizens of the free states to violate or misinterpret the constitution against them. There is not, and there never has been, any determination or wish on the part of the Republican party even, to interfere with their peculiar institution, or to deprive them of their property in slaves. This party has not been organized to deprive them of their equal rights under the constitution, but to resist the aggressions of the slaveholders upon the equal rights of the non-slaveholding states.

Where slavery has a legal existence, the Republican party by its own doctrines respects and defends it; but where freedom is the law, there the party defends and respects freedom,—resists and repels the attempt to displace it for slavery. But the people of the South have been misled by their disloyal and ambitious leaders, and also by the anti-Republican journals like the *New York Herald* and *Express*, of the North, who, for partisan purposes, have misrepresented and most foully calumniated the Republican party. They have been misled and drawn into their present rebellious position or hostility to the Union by the exaggerations, perversions, and falsehoods of their northern friends and allies, who have assured them that the Republicans, if attaining to power and place, would abolish slavery or encourage insurrections among the slaves, and induce them to reënact the horrors of St. Domingo. All this is false. Even the wildest and maddest of the abolitionists of the North, with a very few individual exceptions, would shrink with horror from any thing of the sort.

For thirty years or more the South have been taught to regard the North as their enemies, and made to believe that they could not live in peace with us; they have been taught that we of the free states are mere money-makers, destitute of any high moral or religious principle, selfish, calculating, cold-hearted, and worse than all, mere cowards. Their teaching has been bad and has led them into grave mistakes. For those who have misled them we have no excuse, no palliation to offer, not a word in extenuation of their offence to utter. They knew better, and have sinned against light and knowledge. For them we have no mercy; let them meet, as they deserve, a traitor's doom; not because they are southern men, or slaveholders, but because they are conspirators and rebels, bent on destroying the government under which they were born, to which they owe allegiance, and which, with all its faults of administration, is the freest and best government ever instituted by man, and which, from its foundation, has been, with that of Great Britain, the hope of the friends of liberty throughout the world. It is not against a despot or a tyrant, or a foreign domination that they have conspired, but against their own legitimate government, whose only defect, if defect it have, is that it claims too little power for itself, and leaves too much freedom to the citizen. The American citizen who seeks to overthrow the American government is not only a

traitor, but a liberticide, a dis-humanized monster not fit to
live or to inhabit any part of this globe : he has no suitable place this side of hell.

We fear no longer the ultimate fate of the Union ; we
feel full confidence that it will be preserved, and be henceforth stronger and more beloved than ever.   The South will
come to know the North better and to entertain for it a
much higher esteem.   It will learn that all the chivalry of
the Union is not confined to the slaveholding states.   It
will find that, if the people of the North are an industrious
and business people, if they are principled against duels,
loath to believe in the necessity of war, and slow to engage
in a fight, it is from no lack of the sense of honor, from
no deficiency of courage, or want of pluck.   It will learn,
we doubt not, that the people of the free states, though
they can bear much, are not all-enduring ; that with them
even there is a point where forbearance ceases to be a
virtue ; and that they can give as well as receive blows.   It
will learn, perhaps to its cost, that there is as much high
spirit, gentlemanly feeling, chivalric sentiment, and noble
daring, among our farmers, mechanics, merchants, shop-keep-
ers, and cotton-spinners, as among its own slave-owners,
nigger-drivers, and clay-eaters.   It will learn that its estimate of our character has been founded on ignorance and
prejudice ; and, when the federal armies have defended the
government, defeated and annihilated the rebellious forces
arrayed against it, preserved it, and caused once more its
time-honored flag to float in the breeze from the capitol of
every state in the Union, it will feel that we are not only
fit foemen, but a people that they may well be proud to
own, love, and respect, as their friends and countrymen.
Far be it from us to undervalue the fine qualities of the
southern people, their frankness, their spirit, their generous
and elegant hospitality ; but they will be taught before the
end of this war that the freemen of the North have qualities
in no sense inferior, and which when known, will probably
prove equally attractive.

It is customary to speak of war, especially of civil war,
as a great calamity ; but the war itself is not the evil.   The
evil is always in the causes that lead to it, in the humors
that are in the system ; war itself is but the effort of the
constitution to throw off these humors and to regain its
soundness and strength.   Peace is always more corrupting
than war; for in peace are generated the humors that ren-

der war necessary. The civil war in which we are now engaged, though the effect of great and deplorable evils, baseness, and criminality, will not itself prove a calamity. It will be the thunder-storm that purifies the moral and political atmosphere; it will enable us to see and understand the wrong principles, the mischievous principles we have unconsciously fostered, the fatal doctrines we have adopted, the dangerous tendencies to which we have yielded. It will teach us that a majority of votes cannot make a statesman out of a pot-house politican, or give a man any additional quantity of brains. It will teach us that henceforth it will be necessary to seek honesty, loyalty, ability, fitness in our candidates for office, not mere availability. It will also teach us that republics, no more than monarchies, can safely preach the divine right of revolutions; that loyalty is as necessary a virtue under a republican as under a monarchical form of government; that every government must be based on right and not on mere opinion, and be able to use force to protect itself against all classes of enemies, domestic as well as foreign; that mere public sentiment is never sufficient to protect or sustain it; and that there must always be placed a sufficient armed force at its command. It will teach us, that while the people may be the motive power, they can never be safely the governing power of the state.

We, as a people, have had much need of this lesson. In asserting popular sovereignty, in appealing to the people, and exaggerating both their wisdom and their virtue, we have overlooked the necessity and authority of government; we have forgotten that freedom is impossible without order, and order impossible without authority, and authority able to make itself respected and obeyed; we have forgotten that *demagogie* is not statesmanship, that liberty is not license, and that the elevation of our party to power does not necessarily secure good government or promote the welfare of the country; we have forgotten that the first necessity of every people is authority, and the first duty of every citizen is obedience to law. Here has been our first and greatest mistake, into which we have been led by the wild democratic doctrines of European liberals warring against the authority of absolute princes. We have approved the rebellion of the Tuscans against their legitimate government, the secession of the Æmilian provinces from the pontifical state, the rebellion of Sicily and Naples against their king, the hostile attitude of Hungary against her lawful sovereign.

But, if in this we have been right, by what right do we complain of the secession of South Carolina, Georgia, Louisiana, Virginia, or Tennessee? Secession and rebellion were all well enough when they took place only in Europe; but we see at once that they cannot be tolerated for a moment when they are attempted among ourselves. We shall learn, then, from the present contest that we have very unjustly, and imprudently asserted the " sacred right of insurrection," and henceforth be prepared, while we fearlessly maintain the rights of the people, to respect and vindicate the rights and authority of governments.

We, as a people, have fallen into another grievous error. We have depreciated and ridiculed the military. We have fancied that the great business of government could go on, internal and external peace be maintained, the laws executed, the honor and dignity of the nation asserted and vindicated without an armed force; we have been afraid of increasing the army and navy, and have proceeded on the assumption that no emergency could arise when either would be necessary. But with a sufficient army and navy at the command of the federal government, this civil war could never have broken out. Even Mr. Buchanan would have suppressed the rebellion in its very inception, and millions and millions of property, as well as thousands and thousands of lives, would have been saved to the nation. Henceforth, we trust, we shall cease to fear to sustain a large and respectable military and naval force, both as a necessity of authority and as an economical arrangement. We are far less likely to fall under military rule with a large military force at the disposal of the government, than we are by having it unarmed and at the mercy of unprincipled adventurers like Jefferson Davis and his associate conspirators. We shall henceforth be obliged to maintain a large, well-disciplined and well-appointed naval force in order to recover our prestige, and to exert our legitimate influence among the great and leading nations of the world. We showed our weakness under Mr. Buchanan's administration, when we dared not reinforce or provision a federal garrison against the protest of one of the pettiest states of the Union. We gave the European nations just cause to despise us, and to treat our power with contempt. The military spirit awakened and the military resources of the nation called forth by the present administration, have done something, perhaps much, to raise us in the estimation of foreign powers ; but fully to regain and preserve our rightful position, we must, after the present war is over, keep on foot an army of not less than a hundred and fifty thousand men, and have a naval establishment that will enable us to assert equality with the first maritime powers of Europe.

We write with a full conviction that the United States, in this civil war, will succeed in suppressing the formidable rebellion against their authority ; but we do not expect them to succeed without a long, severe, and bloody struggle. We do not think lightly of the resources of the rebels, or of their courage and resolution. We think they will not only be able to bring large forces into action, but that they will fight skilfully and bravely. Their commander-in chief, who, we understand, is Mr. Jefferson Davis himself, is not a man of high military character, or in himself a very formidable general ; but he has under him a large number of able officers, educated at our national military academy, trained and disciplined in the federal army, and ranking among the first and best of the officers of that army. These officers have military science, military skill, and their military reputation to sustain. The men they will lead into action, though not taking discipline kindly, and not the best materials in the world for regular soldiers, are strong, alert, and brave, accustomed from their childhood to the use of arms, generally good marksmen, and must be expected to fight desperately and often successfully. We do not persuade ourselves that they are to be easily beaten, or that the rebels can be subdued in a single campaign by any force the federal government is likely to bring against them. Indeed, it is better for the country that they should not be. The practical lessons of the war will be lost for both North and South, unless it is long and severe, making a large portion of our young men practical soldiers, and imposing upon the whole country great privations and manifold sufferings.

The true way to regard this war is to regard it as a chastisement from the hand of divine Providence, as a just judgment from God upon our nation for its manifold sins ; but a judgment sent in mercy, designed not to destroy us, but to purify and save us, to render us a wiser, a better, a more virtuous, a more elevated, and a more powerful people. It is intended to try us, to inure us to hardship, to make us feel that all mere worldly prosperity is short-lived and transitory, and that no people that departs from God, neglects eternal goods, and fixes its affections only on the low and perishing goods of sense, can ever hope to be a great, a strong, and long-lived people. Let us then welcome the sufferings, the privations, the hardships, the toil, the loss of affluence, the poverty that this war is sure to bring upon no small portion of our population. Let us welcome them as a severe but necessary chastisement, and let us wish the chastisement to be severe enough to correct us and to ensure our amendment and our future progress. Unless such be the case, no cause of the war will be removed; its seeds will remain, and at the first favorable opportunity will germinate anew, grow up, blossom, and bear their deadly fruit.

What will be the final effect of the contest on the slave question, we pretend not to predict. Nobody has engaged in the war with the intention of putting an immediate end to slavery ; all who have responded to the call of the president and buckled on their armor, have done so to vindicate the constitution, to enforce the prevailing laws, and to preserve the Union. But if the rebels prove themselves able to protract the struggle and to gain some victories, if they carry on the war in the manner indicated by the murder of the lamented Ellsworth, and large numbers of our fathers, husbands, brothers, or sons fall, and the passions of the non-slaveholding states become roused and embittered, slavery must go, and the war will be in effect a war of liberation. We, for ourselves, seek not this result, for we see not what disposition could be made of the slaves, if emancipated. But that this result will come, we think by no means unlikely. In the meantime, let us say distinctly that while we should disapprove of all attempts to excite the negroes to insurrection, we earnestly protest, in case insurrections among them should take place without our agency, against employing federal troops in suppressing them. As long as the slaveholders are in rebellion against the Union, we say let them employ their own forces in keeping their slaves in subjection. If this weakens their force against us, so much the better for us and so much the worse for them. We are not enough in love with slavery to volunteer it any protection. The " pound of flesh " stipulated in the bond we will pay to the exact scruple ; but if the slaveholder asks for more, let the penalty fall on his own head. While he remained a loyal citizen and discharged his obligations to the Union, we were bound to give up his fugitive slave; but when he turns rebel, and arms himself to overthrow the Union, we are by his act absolved from that obligation, and he must expect from us no assistance in recovering or in keeping his slave property. If his slaves run away, escape from his control, they are for us free, and we shall bid them take care and not be caught; and if, in order to preserve the Union, it is necessary to allow the slaves to emancipate themselves, we shall not grieve, but shall be much better pleased than we are with the necessity under which our fathers felt themselves, in order to found the Union, to bind themselves to give up to his owner a fugitive slave.

But we have exhausted our space. It is a trying moment for our republic. Popular institutions themselves are on trial. The cause of self-government throughout the world is at stake. But let not absolute monarchs, the *oscurantisti*, or the friends of despotic power rejoice or persuade themselves that the cause of liberty is lost. The republic yet stands, and with the brave old veteran, the well-tried soldier, the hero of so many battles who now commands her armies, and who is more than a match for any military skill or science that can be brought against him, continue to stand it will. It has, we think seen its darkest day. The New World will yet prove true to its mission, and be, as it has been from the first, the asylum of the oppressed, and the home of freedom. We bid our friends abroad, who are struggling for free governments or constitutional guaranties for liberty, be of good heart, keep up their courage, continue their efforts; we shall not fail them, but prove ourselves firmer and more efficient friends of the cause than we have ever heretofore been.

SLAVERY AND THE WAR.*

[From Brownson's Quarterly Review for October, 1861.]

WE have not been able to do more than look at a few of the pages of the admirable work by our highly esteemed friend M. Augustin Cochin, on *The Abolition of Slavery.* We have, however, read enough to enable us to judge of its general character, and to pronounce it a work of rare merit.

The first volume gives the result of the abolition of slavery by France and England in their colonies, and establishes the fact that it has been effected without ruin and without disturbance. A storm, an insect, a year of drought would, in a material point of view, have caused more evil; while, in a moral and religious point of view, the good has been immense, although few precautions had been taken to secure it. The second volume is devoted to the United States, Holland, Brazil, the Spanish and Portuguese colonies, the slave-trade, Africa, and the influence of Christianity on slavery. We have noticed a few trifling inaccuracies in regard to our own country. The author reckons Wisconsin among the slave states; but we are happy to say that Wisconsin is not only a free state, but one of the most decided anti-slavery states in the Union. He says New York was originally settled by Germans—it was originally settled by the Dutch from Holland, who are not usually called Germans by us, though of the Germanic family. Maryland was not colonized by *Irish* Catholics, but by *English* Catholics and Protestants. George Calvert had an Irish title, but was himself an Englishman. These errors, however, are very slight, and detract nothing from the real value of the work. As far as we have been able to read it, we have found the views of the author very just, philanthropic, liberal, and truly Christian. Two abler or more intensely interesting volumes on the subject of the abolition of slavery, it has not been our good fortune to meet; and they are creditable in the highest degree to the ability, industry, and noble sentiments of their distinguished author.

---

* *L' Abolition de l' Esclavage.* Par AUGUSTIN COCHIN, ancien Maire et Conseiller de la Ville de Paris. Paris: 1861.

The question of the abolition of slavery is becoming with us a practical question in a sense it has never before been. The rebellion of the slave states, which has for its object, not so much the dissolution of the Union, or the separation of the South from the North, as the reconstruction of the Union on the basis of slavery, or, as the vice-president of the Confederate States has it, with "slavery as its corner-stone," and therefore the extension of slavery over the whole country, cannot fail to force this question upon the grave attention of every citizen of the loyal states, who loves his country, and believes in the practicability of freedom. The slave states, by their rebellion and war on the Union, are compelling us to regard this question as one which must soon be practically met, and are forcing all loyal citizens to make their election between the preservation of the Union and the preservation of slavery. This, whatever the federal administration, whatever individuals or parties in the free states, with or without southern or pro-slavery proclivities, may wish or desire, is pretty sure to be the inevitable issue of the terrible struggle in which our glorious, and hitherto peaceful republic is now engaged. Perhaps, at the moment we write, the last of August, a majority of the people of the free states may not only shrink from this issue, but even honestly believe it possible to avert it altogether. The bare suggestion of the abolition of slavery may shock, perhaps enrage them; but events march, and men who mean to be successful, or not to be left behind, must march with them. Another disaster, like that of Bull Run, or another unsuccessful action, like that of Wilson's Creek, where the brave and noble-hearted Lyon fell, a martyr to the cause of his country, and a victim to the failure of his government to send him timely aid, will do much to change the feelings and convictions of the loyal citizens of the free states, and, perhaps, force them to give up the last hope or thought of preserving both the Union and the institution of slavery. It requires, however chary our public men may be even of whispering it, no extraordinary sagacity or foresight to perceive that, if the present war is to be continued, and the integrity of the nation restored and maintained, the war can hardly fail to become a war of liberation, or that the northern blood and treasure, which it demands for its successful prosecution, will demand in return, as their indemnification, the emancipation of the slave, and the universal adoption for the South as well as the North of our free-labor system.

We need not say, for the fact is well known to our read-ers, that no man, according to his ability and opportunity, has, since April, 1838, more strenuously opposed the aboli-tion movement in the free states than we have ; not because we loved slavery, or had any sympathy with that hateful institution, but because we loved the constitution of the Union, and because we believed that liberty at home and throughout the world was far more interested in preserving the union of these states under the federal constitution, than in abolishing slavery as it existed in the southern section of our common country. But we believe, and always have be-lieved, that liberty, the cause of free institutions, the hopes of philanthropists and Christians, both at home and abroad, are more interested in preserving the Union and the integ-rity of the nation, than they are or can be in maintaining negro-slavery. If we have opposed abolition heretofore be-cause we would preserve the Union, we must, *a fortiori*, op-pose slavery whenever, in our judgment, its continuance be-comes incompatible with the maintenance of the Union, or of our nation as a free republican state.

Certainly, we said in the article on *The Great Rebellion*, the North has not taken up arms for the destruction of negro-slavery, but for the maintenance of the federal gov-ernment, the enforcement of the laws, and the preservation of the Union. This is true. The liberation of the slave is not the purpose and end of the war in which we are now en-gaged. The war is a war against rebellion, an unprovoked and wicked rebellion, engaged in by the rebels for the pur-pose of making this a great slaveholding republic, in which the labor of the country shall be performed by slaves, either black or white; and if, to defeat the rebellion, the destruc-tion of slavery be rendered necessary and be actually effect-ed, it will change nothing in the character or purpose of the war. It will have been necessitated by the rebellion, and the rebels will have only themselves to thank for the destruc-tion or abolition they force us to adopt in defence of lib-erty, the Union, and the authority of the government.

The real question now before the loyal states is not, whether the rebellion shall be suppressed by force of arms, or a peaceful division of the country into two separate and independent republics submitted to. Any one who has any knowledge of the plans and purposes of the rebels, knows well, that the division of the territory of the Union into two independent republics is far short of what they are aiming at. The leaders of the rebellion, they who planned it, they who have stirred it up, and armed it against the Union, have worked themselves into the conviction, that slavery is not to be looked upon as an evil, under certain circumstances to be tolerated, but as a good to be desired, which religion and humanity require not only to be perpetuated, but extended the furthest possible. Their doctrine is, that liberty is not practicable for a whole people, that it is practicable only for a class or a race ; and that republicanism can subsist and be practically beneficial, only where the laboring class is deprived of all political and civil rights, and reduced to slavery. Their plan, their purpose is, the reconstruction of the federal government in accordance with this theory, not merely to cut themselves loose from all companionship, with the non-slaveholding states of the North and Northwest. They propose to extend slavery over the whole Union, and, in those states where negroes cannot be profitably employed as laborers, to reduce, perhaps gradually, but ultimately and effectually, to the condition of slaves, the present class of free white laborers, who in the free states are, to a great extent, Irish and Germans, by birth or immediate descent.

The reconstruction of the Union on the basis of slavery is the real aim of the chiefs of the southern rebellion, which reconstruction would give them a government similar in its essential features to that of ancient pagan Rome, and a government, if the states held together, prepared for future conquest. The Union reconstructed, it could proceed to the conquest of Mexico and Central America, and reduce their negro and colored populations to slavery, which would be counted their americanization. This done, it could proceed, beginning with Cuba, to the annexation, one after another, of the West India Islands. It then could extend its power over the whole continent of South America, and threaten an advance upon eastern Asia, and the annexation of all the cotton-producing countries and tropical regions of the globe, and through the monopoly of cotton, rice, and tropical productions in general, to obtain the control of the commerce and credit of all nations. Such, to a greater or less extent, is the dream which southern statesmen have indulged, and which they have taken the first step towards realizing. In its full extent no sane man supposes the dream practicable ; but its practicability, up to a certain point, has been demonstrated by the success which has hitherto attended the rebellion, for, up to the present, successful it undeniably has been. The confederates have brought into the field a more effective, if not a larger force than the federal government has thus far brought against them; and, from the Potomac to the Mississippi, they hold the strategic lines, and can be met by the federal forces only at great disadvantage. As yet not one of those lines has been wrested from them.

Now, suppose we adopt the policy urged upon us by the peace-makers, traitors, and cowards of the loyal states, consent to a peaceful division of the United States, and recognize the southern confederacy as a separate and independent nation, what would be the result? Two comparatively equal independent republics, existing side by side? Not at all. Spread out the map of the United States before you, and see which republic would have the advantage in territory, soil, climate, productions, and all the sources of national wealth, strength, and material greatness. You would give to the southern republic full three-fourths of the whole territory of the Union; for the South would consent to no division now, that did not include the states of Delaware, Maryland, Kentucky, Missouri, and all the territory south of the line running due West from the Northwest angle of Missouri to the Pacific. You would give up to the South, to what would then be a foreign power, the whole gulf coast, and the whole Atlantic coast, except the narrow strip from the Penobscot to the Delaware. You would leave the North a majority of the present population of the country, and nominally the superiority in wealth, it is true: but as the present superior numbers and wealth of the North depend chiefly on our superiority in commerce and manufactures, their superiority could not be long maintained. The southern republic, producing raw materials consumed chiefly in Europe, would be a great exporting republic, and would naturally in its policy favor exports to European markets. From those markets where it disposes of its raw materials, it could, by means of a lower tariff on imports than the northern republic could afford to adopt, more easily and cheaply supply its own demand for imports than it could from our northern markets. It would thus drive our manufactures from its markets, and, by importing from abroad for itself, greatly diminish our manufactures, and at the same time both our foreign and domestic trade. In addition, we should not only lose our southern market for our imports and manufactures, but should hardly be able to keep our own. Imports would seek southern ports, and, in spite of any possible cordon of custom-houses and custom-house officers, would find their way into all the border states of the northern republic and up the Mississippi and Ohio into the great states of the West and the Northwest, to the most serious detriment of our own trade and manufactures, and consequently to the retention of our relative superiority in wealth and population. In spite of our industry and our enterprise, we should soon find ourselves a state far inferior in wealth and numbers to our southern neighbor.

Moreover, the great agricultural states of the Mississippi valley, finding the natural outlets for their productions held by a foreign power, and themselves unable to wrest them from it, would be compelled by their own interests to secede from the northern republic, and to join the southern confederacy. The secession of these, which would be followed by that of all the states West of the Rocky Mountains, would necessarily compel the secession of New York, New Jersey, and Pennsylvania, and their annexation to the same confederacy. This would reduce the northern republic to the New-England states; two of which, Connecticut and Rhode Island, would, most likely, follow New York, and there would remain for the northern republic only the states of Massachusetts, Vermont, New Hampshire, and Maine, which could escape absorption in the confederacy only by its refusal to accept them, or by joining with the Canadas and the other British provinces, and coming again under the British crown. Such would be the inevitable result of the proposed peaceful division of the United States, and the formation of two separate and independent republics out of their territory, if the southern confederacy held together; and such is substantially the plan of reconstruction contemplated by the southern statesmen, as is evident from their leaving their confederacy open to the accession of new states; as was avowed in New York, last December, by Mr. Benjamin, now the attorney-general of the Confederate States; and as asserted openly by southern sympathizers everywhere at the North. All this is notorious, and is only what any man accustomed to reason on such subjects, and familiar with the geography, soil, and productions of the Union, sees must and would inevitably result from the policy recommended by our peace-men, cowards, and traitors.

But peace, even on as favorable terms as we have supposed, cannot now be made. Six months ago, perhaps it might have been; but now, flushed with their recent successes, in possession of the principal strategic lines, and able to prosecute the war with more vigor than we have yet shown, the rebels will entertain no question of peace short of our subjugation, or, what is the same thing, disbandment of our armies and quiet submission to the principles and theory on which their confederacy is founded. Look at the question as we will, we have now no alternative but to subdue the rebels or be subjugated by them. We must either depose that confederacy, and enforce the authority of the federal government over all the rebellious states, or it will enforce its authority over the free states, and impose upon them its system of slave labor. If it enforces its authority over us, there may still, perhaps, be liberty for a class or caste, but our laboring classes will no longer be freemen; they will be placed on a level with the negro slave on a southern plantation. For the Christian commonwealth founded by our fathers, toiled for, and bled for, we shall have reëstablished a pagan republic more hostile to the rights of man and the rights of nations, than was ever pagan Greece or pagan Rome. We put it to our Christian countrymen, if such is the commonwealth their fathers fought and suffered through the long seven-years war of the revolution to establish, and if they can be contented to let the hopes of liberty in the New World set in a night of blackness and despair.

We know very well that we have fallen far below the virtues that founded this republic, and gained this New World to civilization; we know that a long career of uninterrupted prosperity and unbounded luxury has done much to corrupt us; we know that the labor in one-half of the republic being performed by slaves, and the greater part in the other half performed by emigrants from foreign countries, has caused a lamentable forgetfulness of those principles of liberty so dear to our fathers, and produced amongst us a laxity of principle, an indifference to law, a disregard for personal rights and personal independence, without which no republic can long subsist and prosper; but we are not yet willing to believe that we have fallen so low, become so corrupt, so indifferent to liberty, or so dead to all moral considerations, as to be prepared to submit, for the sake of gain, or of preserving our manufactures, without a struggle, to the indignities the southern confederacy would heap upon us, or to the adoption of the base and inhuman principle on which that confederacy is avowedly founded. If we retain any thing of our manhood, or any memory of the Christian virtues of our ancestors, we can never submit to be slaves ourselves, or to take part in reducing any portion or class of our fellow-men to slavery. If there is any virtue left in us, we must resolve that we will be free ourselves, and do all in our power to secure freedom to all other men, whether white or black, yellow or copper-colored. If we do not, we are indeed "degenerate sons of noble sires," and deserve, as we shall receive, the scorn and derision of the whole world. Political and party leaders, greedy for the "pickings and stealings" of office, who are innocent of ever having entertained a statesmanlike idea or a moral conception, may cry, like the false prophets whom the Lord, in Holy Scripture, rebukes, "Peace, peace," and seek to embarrass the government and give aid and comfort to its enemies; but we hope there is still virtue enough left in the people of the loyal states to estimate them at their true value, and to treat with indignation and scorn their counsels. Whatever the result of the contest, the vocation of these leaders is gone; and the best use to which you can put a man who now cries out for "peace," for "compromise," for "submission," and charges the government with having provoked an "unholy and unnecessary" war, is to treat him as loyal Union men in the South are treated by the confederates. Such men, whatever their pretensions, are really traitors, and deserve a traitor's doom; or, if not traitors, they are idiots and lunatics, and should be provided for in asylums. It is no time to mince our words, or to study out honeyed phrases; we must call things by their right names, and treat all who are not for us, as against us. We have something more than even the constitution and laws to maintain; the very existence of the nation is at stake; and, as no means are scrupled at to destroy it, we have the right to use all the means which the law of self-preservation renders necessary or expedient.

We wish our readers and the public at large to understand that we are in war, and to let it get through their heads that the war which the rebellion has forced upon us, is no mimic war, is no child's play, and is not to be conducted to a successful issue on the principle of treating the rebels as friends, giving them every advantage, and doing them no harm. They are in downright earnest, and are putting forth all their strength, and doing their best to subjugate us ; and we also must be in downright earnest, put forth all our strength, and do our best to subjugate them. War cannot be conducted on peace principles, or successfully conducted by men who do not enter into it with spirit, resolution, and energy. We have no disposition to censure the civil or military authorities of our country ; they have labored under great embarrassments, and have had no ordinary difficulties to contend with ; but we must be excused, if we say that as yet they have given us little evidence of their being in earnest, or of their believing in the reality and important character of the war. Up to the disaster of Bull Run, military operations seem to have been conducted in subordination to the projects of politicians and the especial benefit of contractors. The war was apparently treated as a secondary affair, a mere bagatelle, or a toy for children to amuse themselves with ; in scarcely an instance was it treated as a grave affair, demanding for its prosecution the whole strength and energy of the country. Some doubted if the South would really fight, and it seemed to many, that all we needed to rout their armies, suppress rebellion, and reëstablish over the seceded states the authority of the federal government, was a large number of regiments having no existence except on paper or in the imagination of those who wished to sport the epaulettes of a colonel. This delusion has passed away. But still, at the time we are writing, it has hardly got through our heads that we are really engaged in war, and a war involving the very life or death of the nation. The mass of those who really believe we are in war, still think the war is one that may be carried on without any serious detriment to our ordinary avocations or pleasures, and one not likely to come home to our own bosoms and business. Very few of us see that every thing we hold dear in this world is at stake, and that we have to struggle not only to defeat a foreign enemy, but to defend our own firesides and altars, our own wives and children, and our own personal liberty. Country gone, all is gone ; and unless we become more in earnest than we have hitherto been, and put forth a civil and military force and energy which we have not yet displayed, nor judged it necessary to display, our country cannot be preserved.

We cheerfully concede that much allowance is to be made for the administration, in the novel and unexpected position in which it has been placed. With no preparation to meet a rebellion on a formidable scale, with doubts as to how far the patriotism of the loyal states could be relied on, with the army and navy filled with traitors, or with officers at best indifferent to the cause of the Union, surrounded by weak, timid, and corrupt politicians, and the important, though subaltern, offices of the various departments of the civil government filled with men desiring success to the rebels, and ready to use all the opportunities afforded by their position to secure that success, the administration may be excused for having hesitated, before feeling the public pulse, to adopt the bold, energetic, and decisive measures the crisis demanded. It was embarrassed by the legacy left it by its predecessor, and also by the fears, timidities, hopes, and advice of the Union men in the border states, who begged it not to be precipitate, lest it should plunge those states also into open secession. This fear of driving the border states into secession has been from the first the bugbear of the administration, and its chief embarrassment. It prevented it from taking, at the outset, those bold and decisive measures which would have forestalled the rebels, and confined the rebellion to South Carolina, Georgia, and the gulf states. Its efforts since to organize and strengthen the Union party in western Virginia and eastern Tennessee, have impeded, rather than aided, its military operations, and lost it a campaign, without gaining it any real additional strength.

There is only one way of dealing with rebels; it is for the government to be prompt, to strike quick, and to strike hard. If it hesitates, if it temporizes, if it seeks to conciliate, or shows that it fears to strike lest the blow recoil upon its own head, it is only by a miracle that it can be saved. Its policy will be set down either to conscious weakness or to conscious wrong, and the rebels not only gain time, but, what is even more important to them, they gain confidence in their own cause, which more than doubles their forces, while the friends of the government are disheartened, rendered timid, if not alienated. A bold, energetic man at the head of the government, one year ago, would have crushed out rebellion before it could really have come to a head even in South Carolina. A man able to create public opinion, not merely to follow it, at the head of the government last March, would have confined the rebellion within the limits it then had, and, long before this, would have reduced Florida and Louisiana to their allegiance, and thus have broken the back-bone of rebellion, and prepared the way for its speedy and utter annihilation. Hesitation and delay in dealing with rebellion, is the worst policy possible.

That its dilatory and timid policy was on the part of the government a mistake, a blunder, no one can reasonably doubt. But it would be a mistake, a blunder no less fatal, for the friends of the Union to blazon it forth so as to weaken the confidence of the people in the administration, and diminish its power for good. The president is worthy of all confidence for his honesty, integrity, and patriotism ; and if he will rid himself of the embarrassment of political jobbers and tricksters, dismiss and visit with adequate punishment all secessionists, traitors, or lukewarm patriots in the employment of the government, and put honest and capable men in their places, men who know their duty, and have the courage to perform it, who love their country and are ready, if need be, to sacrifice themselves for it, he may retrieve the past, recover all the ground that has been lost, conduct the war to a successful issue, and, if not precisely the man best fitted to the crisis, yet stand in American history second only to Washington, if indeed second even to Washington himself. Never had a president of the United States so glorious an opportunity to prove himself a man, a statesman, a true civil hero. He has, we are sure, the disposition, let him prove that he has the courage and ability not merely to follow public opinion, not merely to follow the people, but to go before them, and, by kindling up a resistless enthusiasm in them, lead them on to victory.

The American people, especially of the North, are a susceptible people, and can feel and respond to the force of genius as readily and as heartily as any other people on the face of the globe. No people in the world are susceptible of a deeper or more abiding enthusiasm ; no people better appreciate the value of a good battle-cry; and it has been a mistake on the part of the administration, not to have better appreciated their real character. It has failed to give them that battle-cry. It has been too cold, too prosaic, and has pronounced no spirit-stirring word. Instead of kindling up the enthusiasm of the people, it has looked to the people to quicken its own. Instead of inspiring them, it has waited for them to inspire it. This has been a grave mistake. Men placed at the head of affairs, are placed there to lead, not to follow, to give an impulse to the people, not to receive it from the people. If the administration has life and energy,

if it has ability and genius, let it no longer hesitate to use
them, but put them forth in that free, bold, and energetic
manner which will carry the people with them, and command victory.

We insist the more earnestly on this, because the mass of
our people have so long been accustomed to sympathize
with rebels, to aid and encourage revolutionists abroad, and
to visit with their severest denunciations the acts of the legitimate government to suppress insurrection, to put down
revolutionists, and vindicate its authority, that they cannot
be rallied with much enthusiasm under the simple banner
of Law and Order. Their first emotion is to sympathize
with rebellion, wherever it breaks out, even though against
their own government. They hold as a principle, as that on
which their very national independence is based, the " sacred
right" of revolution ; because they generally take it for
granted that all rebels and revolutionists are the party of
liberty, warring against despotism, and for the rights of man.
Would you rally them and render them invincible against
the foe ?   You must give them another battle-cry than that
of " Law and Order," or you will not stir their heart, that
mighty American heart which conquered this country from
the savage and the forest, proclaimed and won its independence, constituted the Union, and made the American nation one of the great nations of the earth.   It is not for us,
even if we were able, to give that battle-cry ; it must be
given by genius in authority, and fall either from the lips
of the president, or the commander-in-chief of our armies.
Neither may as yet be prepared to utter it ; but, if this nation has a future, if its destiny is, as we have hitherto boasted, to prove what man may be when and where he has the
liberty to be himself, uttered by one or the other it ere long
will be, and in tones that will ring out through the whole
Union, and through the whole civilized world now anxiously
listening to hear it.   The Union is and must be sacred to
liberty.   Here man must be man, nothing more, and nothing
less.   Slaves must not breathe our atmosphere ; and we
must be able to adopt the proud boast of our mother country, "The slave that touches our soil is free."   This is the
destiny of this New World, if destiny it have, —the destiny
our fathers toiled for, fought for, bled for, and to this we
their children must swear to be faithful, or die to the last
man.

We have spoken thus far as the American, the patriot,

and the devoted defender of republican institutions; but we must be permitted also to speak as the Catholic publicist. We have, from the first, maintained, and with the fullest approbation of the Catholic authorities in this country, that Catholic morality enjoins upon all Catholics, whatever their rank or dignity, to be loyal to the legitimate government of their country, and to be ready to defend it, when called upon, at the sacrifice of their property, and even of their lives. That the federal government is the legitimate government of the American nation, no Catholic can reasonably doubt. We may, as Catholics, lawfully resist tyranny or usurpation, but we cannot conspire to overthrow a legitimate government, which has not transcended its constitutional powers, or resist its authority without failing not only in our civil, but in our Catholic duty. The federal government is no usurpation; it is a legitimate government; and it has never lost its legitimacy by any act of tyranny or oppression. No such act has been or can be pretended. Rebellion against it, therefore, is not only a crime, but a sin. The principle here asserted is that which we defended for years against the revolutionists in Europe, and it has been on the ground that such is the teaching of the Catholic religion, that we have repelled with indignation the charge brought against us by Know-nothings, that Catholics are not and cannot be loyal American citizens. We have labored, in opposition to the Know-nothings, to show that Catholics are bound by their very religion to be loyal; and we have ventured to assert that, if the republic were threatened, or an attempt made to dismember the Union, Catholics would be the first to rush to its rescue, and the last to desert it.

The assertion we ventured has not been entirely justified. The conduct of our Catholic population, especially that of their leaders, has not wholly answered our expectations. Of the twelve journals in the English language, published in this country, and professedly devoted to Catholic interests, we can name only *The Catholic*, published at Pittsburg, and the *Tablet*, in this city, as decidedly loyal. The *Telegraph and Advocate*, published at Cincinnati, is occasionally loyal, and so also, perhaps, is the *Buffalo Sentinel*. The *Metropolitan Record* was, when last we read it, striving hard to be on both sides. All the rest are really secession sheets, and exert, whether avowedly or not, all their influence against the federal government, and in favor of that of the southern confederacy; for we count every journal favorable to the secessionists, that opposes the war, and clamors for peace. Of the clergy, the greater part of whom have been born or educated abroad, a large majority have southern sympathies, and a portion of them, a small minority, we hope, are decidedly disloyal. The bishop of Charleston, South Carolina, sang, we have been told, the *Te Deum* over the fall of Sumter. Much allowance, no doubt, must be made for bishops and priests residing in rebel states, and it would be too much to ask them to proclaim on all occasions and under all circumstances Union sentiments ; their silence may often be excusable, and sometimes justifiable. Still they are bound by their religion to instruct their own people in their duty of fidelity to the government of the Union, and they have and can have no authority under that religion, or in consonance with it, to hold disloyal sentiments, denounce the loyal states, and sing *Te Deums* over the defeats of the government to which they owe allegiance. The bishops both of Charleston and of Richmond appear to have done this; and, if they have done so, no reverence or respect for their episcopal character should be allowed to excuse their treason, or make us hesitate to charge them with violating their Catholic duty, and doing all in their power to justify the Know-nothings in their grave charges against the loyalty of Catholics. Catholic morality is as obligatory on priests and bishops as it is on laymen, and from its obligations they can neither absolve themselves, nor be absolved even by the pope. The right of the supreme pontiff to absolve from their oath of allegiance the subjects of a prince who, according to the law of God and the constitution of the realm or empire, has forfeited his right to reign, we have uniformly maintained, and still hold ; but we have never maintained, and cannot maintain, that he has .the right to absolve from their allegiance the subjects of a prince who holds his power legitimately, and has done nothing to forfeit his trusts; and certainly we cannot concede to simple bishops and priests a power which we do not and cannot concede to the supreme pontiff himself. We do not, in such a case, deny the absolving power to their chief in order to claim it for them.

But we are gratified to know that the Catholic people, moved by their loyal and patriotic instincts, are nobly redeeming their church from the false position in which the disloyalty or mistaken policy of the majority of their journals, and a portion of their bishops and clergy, have had a tendency to place her. Though for the most part, wedded to the Democratic party, which has brought the country to its present critical state, and bitterly prejudiced against the party that elected our present chief magistrate, and especially against New-England Yankees, regarded by them as fanatics, bigots, and the enemies of all good, they have nobly volunteered to fill the ranks of our army, and generously shed their blood in defence of the Union. No class of American citizens have, in this respect, surpassed them, and indeed they have set an example worthy of all imitation. Catholics have, considering their numbers, more than their proportion in the regular army and volunteer forces of the Union, and Catholic soldiers, whether we speak of officers or men, are surpassed by no others now in the field. The loyalty of the majority of the Catholics of the North must be held to efface the disloyalty of the few Catholics of the South ; and when this war has been prosecuted to a successful issue, we doubt not that the loyalty of Catholics will cease to be called in question, and both Catholics and non-Catholics will mutually feel that they are citizens of a common country, and form but one political people.

That the attempt of some of the so-called Catholic journals to make Catholics believe that the so-called confederacy is less anti-Catholic in its sympathies than the North, and that the North, when the rebellion is suppressed, will turn its arms against Catholics, may have influenced, and may still influence a few, especially Irish Catholics, whose misfortune it often is to trust their enemies, and suspect their friends, we do not deny, and we regret it. But the notion is absurd, and always has been. The South is more infidel or pagan, and far less Christian than the North, and is and always has been, as we might expect, far more anti-Catholic, and, when not absolutely indifferent to all religion, far more bigoted than the North, if, by the North, we refer to New England. There is no part of the Union where Catholics are better treated, and suffer fewer annoyances, than in the New-England states. Nowhere in New England will a Catholic priest or a Catholic layman, if a gentleman, miss the treatment due to a gentleman, whatever some of our journals may allege to the contrary.

It is, no doubt, true that Mr. Wise and Mr. Hunter, who are secessionists, did good service to the Democratic party, —which, by the way, is not the same thing as doing good service to Catholics,—in arresting the Know-nothing movements in Virginia ; but to defeat the Know-nothings was for them a political necessity. Had the Know-nothings triumphed in Virginia in 1855, the chances of either of these individuals becoming a candidate for the presidency would have been less than nothing. Their success depended on the success of the Democratic party, and that party could succeed in no non-slaveholding state without securing the Catholic and foreign vote. Deprived of that vote, the Democratic party was, and still is, in a hopeless minority in every one of the free states. The opposition to the Know-nothings, therefore, no more proved a disposition on the part of Mr. Wise and Mr. Hunter favorable to Catholics, than it proved their loyalty and devotion to the Union. The secession leaders, no doubt, mean to use Catholics in their struggle for a separate nationality, or the reconstruction of the Union; but there can be just as little doubt that, when they have gained it, they mean to proscribe them, as they have openly avowed, for they wish to perpetuate slavery, and the Catholic religion everybody knows is hostile to slavery, and the church everywhere exerts her influence against it. There is no safety in this country for our religion but in restoring and preserving the Union, and securing the liberty of the church not as a political grant or favor, but as one of the inherent and inalienable rights of man.

Still we regret that a certain number of Catholics, misled by their demagogues, unite with the followers of Breckenridge of Kentucky, Bright of Indiana, Vallandigham of Ohio, and the senators from the border slave states not yet in open rebellion, in opposing the war for the maintenance of the Union, and in calling upon the government to discontinue it, and to make peace at once. In this they are the dupes of pretended patriots, but real traitors, and serve the cause of rebellion more effectually than they could if its open and declared adherents. The pretence or the belief that our difficulties could now be settled by a convention, or compromise, or any concessions short of our absolute submission to the demands of the rebels, is the idlest thing in the world. The time for conventions, for compromises, or for conciliatory measures, has gone by, and no man not really in league with the southern rebels, no patriot, no friend of the Union, with the slightest grain of intelligence, can for a moment seriously believe in their practical utility. There has never been a time since the election of Mr. Lincoln when any conciliatory measures, or any constitutional compromises, short of a complete surrender to the demands of the southern leaders, could have been of the slightest avail.   The last congress was disposed to go further in the way of compromise, and to make greater concessions for the preservation of peace, than wisdom or prudence dictated. But there were no terms of compromise the seceded states would accept, short of their full and unequivocal recognition as a separate and independent nation. They openly refused to return to their allegiance, even on the adoption of the so-called " Crittenden compromise," and declared their separation final and irrevocable, leaving it for us to go to them, but absolutely refusing to come to us.   The border state convention, whatever may have been the honest intention of many of its members, was a mere farce; for we doubt not that it was, from the first, the intention of the leading politicians in all the border slave states to make common cause with their southern brethren.   The present government had exhausted all the hopes of a peaceful solution of our difficulties, before it took the step which was made the pretext for war against it.   From the first, Virginia, Maryland, Tennessee, Kentucky, and Missouri were pledged, as far as their leading statesmen could pledge them, to the southern cause, and, from the first, the question with all the slaveholding states was separation, or the reconstruction of the Union on the basis of slavery; and we entirely mistake the temper of the southern statesmen and of the people of the slaveholding states, if we suppose them prepared to make peace on any other terms now.   There is no peace party, no Union party in any slaveholding state, except, perhaps, in Missouri and Kentucky, North Carolina, and western Virginia, on which the slightest reliance can be placed.   The Union men in all the other slave states, or sections of slave states, not excepting Maryland, are the weak, the passive, the imbecile portion of their population. The talent, the energy, the decision, the governing capacity in all the slaveholding states, whether the minority or the majority, are on the side of the secessionists, and secession has a far stronger party in every one of the free states, than the Union has in any of the slave states, except those already named.

There is no use of attempting to disguise the facts from our own eyes.   The slaveholding states constitute really a united people, a more firmly united people in opposition to the government than we of the free states are in support of it.   Any policy, civil or military, based on a contrary supposition will prove a blunder, and disastrous in the end to the federal cause. The South have a fixed and definite policy, which they are enthusiastic in carrying out, and they will stop at no means, however unscrupulous, judged by them necessary to their purpose. They have chosen war, and they will accept peace, until compelled, only on their own terms. Thus far the war has been mainly a success on their part, and they are far from having exhausted all their strength. Indeed they believe they are able to sustain the war as long as we can, and to sustain it successfully to the end. Nothing is more idle, then, than to suppose that the matter can now be conciliated by politicians, or that the government, without abdicating itself, has it in its power to make peace. The government has no alternative, if it would sustain itself, and preserve the integrity of the nation, or even its own honor, but to prosecute the war, and prosecute it with all the vigor and all the forces and means it can command. For men, then, who profess to be attached to the Union, to talk of "peace," of "conciliation," of "compromises," of "conventions," is the veriest twaddle, or would be, if it were not the grossest outrage upon common sense and common decency. As we have said, all these things have gone by; and to attempt to recall them from the dead past, or to galvanize them into life, is only to betray our own stupidity or our disloyalty. No; we must fight, fight manfully to the end, and teach rebellion a lesson that it will not soon forget.

We love peace as much as any man does or can, and no man, in proportion to his means, suffers more by the present war, than we do. But the Scriptures tell us, "Follow after the things which make for peace," not peace at any price; and, now that we are in war, we insist on prosecuting it till the basis of an honorable and durable peace can be obtained. The recognition of the southern confederacy and disbandment of our armies would not, as we have shown, secure this peace; because the project of the southern leaders is not merely a separation from the Union, but a reconstruction of the Union under their control on the basis of slavery. Are we asked, why not quietly submit to the reconstruction demanded? Would there not still be a Union of the states under a federal government? And suppose that it did recognize slavery, what harm in that? Nearly all the states once held slaves, and the southern states have grown and prospered, become great and powerful with the institution of slavery, and even by it; that institution has not only contributed to the greatness, strength, and prosperity of the South, but has been the basis of the commercial and manufacturing prosperity of the North; why, then, should the North oppose it, or hesitate to adopt it? The Union reconstructed on the basis of slavery would be far greater, more homogeneous, stronger, and more prosperous than it has ever hitherto been; and the reconstruction demanded is not merely in the interest of the South, but in the interest of the whole country; why not then accept it? —So we have found men not in a madhouse reasoning here at the North, and so, perhaps, some misguided citizens really believe.

We reply to this reasoning—1. The reconstruction proposed would be the destruction of the present Union, of the Union effected by our fathers, and indeed of the nation which it formed, hitherto symbolized by the "Stars and Stripes." It would be the destruction of our present nation, and, at best, only the substitution of another nation in its place. Now, it so happens that many of us have an ardent attachment to the Union, in which we were born, and under which we have thus far lived, and do not choose to expatriate ourselves, or to be forced to become the subjects of another government. For ourselves, we were born an American citizen, and, wherever the vicissitudes of life may cast our lot, an American citizen we will live and we will die, and no consideration under heaven shall ever induce us to abjure allegiance to the federal government, or swear allegiance to any other sovereign. Except for gross tyranny or oppression, we deny the right of expatriation, just as we deny the right of secession or revolution. This feeling which we express may be treated lightly by traitors, rebels, and peace-men, and sneered at as mere sentimentality; but we must be permitted to say, that, where it is wanting in any considerable number of the population of a country, there is and can be no real loyalty, no genuine patriotism, and therefore no firm support for a national government, no secure reliance for the nation in its moment of peril. To transfer our allegiance from the present Union to a new Union not growing out of it, but established in spite of it, and on its ruins, would be to convert us into foreigners in our own country; it would wound, in its most sensitive part, the patriotism of the people, and obliterate from their hearts all sentiments of national honor and loyalty, and therefore the very condition of the existence and durability of the nation, and consequently of the reconstructed Union.

2. A nation to be great, to be strong and what the true patriot desires it, must have a solid foundation in truth and virtue, and aim at something higher, nobler, more spiritual, than mere material conquest, or material wealth and prosperity. Whatever southern slaveholders or northern merchants and manufacturers may think, there is a moral Governor of this world, and the nation that constitutionally and habitually violates the great law of right and wrong, and contemplates only material grandeur and material goods, either will not long subsist, or subsist only as the scourge of the nations. We want not that paganized republic of which the southern leaders dream, and with which they seek to allure us to union with them, even were it to become as great, as powerful, and as magnificent as was ancient Rome, once the haughty mistress of the world. Such a republic would contribute nothing to modern civilization, nothing to the intelligence, the virtue, or the happiness of mankind. It would be at war with all Christian principles and tendencies, and could only prepare the world for a return of heathen darkness and barbarism. It would be anachronous. It would be out of place in modern society, and out of time in the progress of civilization. It would be a retrograde movement, and therefore a movement against the laws of Providence, as well as against the true interests of mankind.

3. There are some among us who still retain a conscience, and are foolish enough, if you will, to believe that all men are created equal, and have certain inalienable rights, of which civil society cannot divest them, except in punishment for crime. There are people who believe in the practicability of republican institutions, which, though not securing to all men equality of rank or condition, shall yet secure to all their native and inherent rights as men. Such people are honestly opposed to slavery, and can never, without the last struggle, submit to the formation of an aristocratic state with slavery for its corner-stone. It might have been wise and prudent to acquiesce in the institution of slavery as a local institution in some of the states of the Union, where it existed prior to the Union itself, or had since been suffered to acquire, a legal, or *quasi*-legal existence, so long as it could not be reached without doing violence to the constitution ; but it would be something very different to consent to the reconstruction of the Union on the basis of slavery, and to give it through the constitution a legal *status*. Slavery, say what we will of it, is a great

moral, social, and political wrong, and that, too, whatever be the complexion of the slave. If there be any truth in Christianity, if there be any truth in the teachings of the great fathers and doctors of the church, God never gave to man the dominion of man; and hence St. Augustine, St. Gregory the Great, and others, tell us that the first rulers of mankind were called *pastors* or *shepherds*, not *lords* or *dominators;* and that God gave to mankind dominion over the irrational creation, but not over the rational. The church has tolerated slavery, where she lacked the power to abolish it; but her whole history proves that she sets her face against it, and uses all the means at her disposal, without shocking the public peace, or creating tumults and disorder, to prepare the slave for freedom, and to secure his ultimate emancipation. The negro is a man—is a human being—a member of the human race; and, whether naturally inferior or not, to the boasted Caucasian variety, he has the same natural and inherent right to liberty that has the white man, and the wrong of enslaving him is just as great as it would be if he were white. The laboring man, whether white or black, may be a poor man, but God has given him the right to be a free man, to be his own man, not another's.

As to the argument of our southern slaveholders, and apologists for slavery, that the slave is better cared for, better fed, and better clothed than our poor laborers at the North, they weigh nothing with us; because they relate only to the human animal, and not to the man. If the slave were a mere animal, had no rational soul or moral nature, if he were indeed an ox, a horse, or a dog, we should not complain of his condition, or offer any objection to slavery. We believe that the *animal* in the slave is often better provided for than the animal in the poor white laboring man; but the *man* is and must be neglected. It is the *man* that is wronged and outraged, the *man* that is debased and enslaved; and the slaveholders know very well that, in order to keep their slaves in subjection, they must close to them, as far as possible, all the avenues to intelligence, debar them from all intellectual and moral culture, and keep them as near the level of brutes as they are able; they must stifle in them the *man*, and prevent the development in them of that "image and likeness" of God after which they were created. It is this that renders slavery an outrage upon humanity, and has excited against it the indignation of the whole Christian world.

We cannot, therefore, consent to the reconstruction of the Union on the basis of slavery. We believe in the rights of man ; we believe in liberty ; we would secure to all others that liberty which we demand for ourselves ; and we believe slavery a great wrong, a sin against humanity, which is sure, sooner or later, to bring down the vengeance of God upon every people that adopts and insists on perpetuating it. The nations of antiquity had slaves ; where are those nations now ? Pagan Greece and Rome had their slaves ; and where are Greece and Rome to-day ? The Ottomans have had their slaves, and the Ottoman empire is now in its agony. Spain became a great slave power through her colonies. Most of those colonies has she lost, and she herself has fallen from the first power, below the rank of a second-class power of Europe. The same may be said of Portugal. Only those nations in Europe, which have emancipated their slaves, freed, or are freeing their serfs, show any signs of longevity. Let the fate of all slaveholding nations be a warning to all those weak, cowardly, or traitorous men at the North, who would consent to the reconstruction of the Union on the basis of slavery. Let them reflect that " the wicked shall be turned into hell, and all the nations that forget God ; " and every slaveholding nation, whatever its spasmodic piety, or its hypocritical professions, does forget God, who never refuses to hear and ultimately to avenge the slave.

4. Finally, passing over all thus far adduced, we cannot consent to such a reconstructed Union, because it would contain in it no element of strength and durability, but the seeds of its own dissolution. It would be based not only on slavery as its corner-stone, but on the right of any or every state to secede, whenever it should choose, without the other states having any right to call it to an account for its secession. This recognized right of secession may work no great harm to-day, while the Confederate States are united in a grand struggle for separate existence, or national reconstruction ; but the moment that struggle is over and peace is restored, it would begin to operate, and render the confederate bond a mere rope of sand. State jealousies would spring up, and new secessions would commence ; the Union would hardly be reconstructed before it would be redissolved into its original elements, and there be as many separate and independent governments as there are individual states. We tried confederation before constructing the

Union, and found that it would not work; and the Union itself, if it has any defect, is in the fact that it leaves the federal power too weak for an effective central power, or to constitute the people of the several states really and practically one political people. The new confederacy would be still weaker, exaggerate this defect, inasmuch as it would recognize the right of every individual state to secede whenever it should judge it for its own interest, convenience, or pleasure to do so. Is it to be hoped that the confederacy would be conducted with so much wisdom and propriety as never to give umbrage to any state, or that disappointed and ambitious politicians in any state would never find or make a cause for dissatisfaction, and, like the politicians of South Carolina, whirl their state out of the reconstructed Union? Even now, we are told, South Carolina and Georgia are beginning to manifest symptoms of dissatisfaction with the confederate government, and we can readily believe that, if the pressure of a common danger were removed, each of them would lose no time in raising the "lone star" of independence, and seceding from secession.

However attractive, then, might be the dream of a reconstructed Union on the basis of slavery, we could never hope to realize it; for we could never hope to preserve it for any considerable length of time in its integrity. There would soon be disaffection at the South; there would be disaffection at the North; and there would always be disaffection in the consciences of all good men, of all true Christians in all sections, created and sustained by the moral and social plague of slavery. Here are reasons amply sufficient why we should not discontinue our efforts to preserve the Union as it is, and why we should not make peace with the rebels on their own terms, or accept their proposition of substituting the constitution of the confederated states for the constitution of the United States.

The government, we insist, had no alternative in the outset but to abdicate itself, or to resist the rebellious movements with all the forces at its command. It has no other alternative now, and the men who would urge upon it any other policy can be commended for their loyalty only at the expense of their intelligence. The only fault of the government has been in having too long pursued a conciliatory policy, in having delayed too long the necessary measures to vindicate its own dignity and authority, in

adopting timid and half-way measures, and in having prosecuted the war with too little vigor, and with too great tenderness towards the rebels. But it is no time now to call
up its past delinquencies, and parade them before it.
Nothing remains for it but to let the past go, and henceforth treat secession as rebellion, and the seceders and their
aiders and abettors as traitors. We wish it to prove that
it has the courage and the disposition to treat them as
traitors, wherever it meets them, or is able to seize them.
We desire it to understand that there is war, real war,
downright earnest war, and a war to be conducted not on
the principle of respecting the feelings of the enemy, and
of doing him no harm, but on the principle of striking him
where he is weakest and sorest, and availing ourselves of
every advantage against him allowed by the laws of civilized warfare. The rebels offer no advantage to us ; they
avail themselves of every advantage against us in their
power, respect none of our susceptibilities, and take no
pains not to wound our feelings; we must mete them the
measure they mete. They allow in their states, where they
have the power, the utterance of no Union sentiments, of
no Union speeches, or Union harangues, and they hang,
imprison, or banish every Union man they can lay their
hands on, who keeps not his Union sentiments to himself.
We must mete out a like measure to every rebel or secessionist we find in the loyal states, and silence every voice
raised against the right of the government to vindicate and
preserve the Union by force of arms. It is madness to
send our sons and brothers to fight rebels in Virginia, Tennessee, or Missouri, while we suffer their friends, aiders,
and abettors to spout their treason and disloyal sentiments
here at home. It is not only madness; it is a moral wrong ;
it is, as some would say, worse still,—it is a blunder.

Do not tell us that this would be contrary to the constitution and the free expression of opinion. Traitors and
friends of traitors have no constitutional rights, for they are
in rebellion against the constitution itself, and no man can
stand on his own wrong. Free expression of opinion ! Just
as if the question between lawful authority and rebels were
a question on which there could be two honest opinions !
Is it a question of opinion, when a nation is engaged in a
struggle for its very existence, whether its children shall
support it or not ? Is it a matter of opinion whether the
nation shall be preserved or not ? Is it a matter of opinion,

when I am assaulted by an assassin, whether I have the right to resist him or not; whether I shall quietly submit to be assassinated, or snatch the dagger from his hand, and plunge it into his own heart? Have men lost their senses? Are we to argue the question whether the sun shines in the heavens or not, when we see it with our own eyes? Down with such intolerable cant about "constitutional liberty," and "freedom of speech or opinion!" How, if the constitution is gone, trampled under foot by rebels, do you expect to maintain constitutional liberty, or any other kind of liberty worth having? Understand at once that we are in war, and in a war for the preservation of the constitution, for the preservation of liberty, political, moral, mental, civil, and social, and that it is never permitted to plead the constitution and liberty against the measures necessary for their maintenance. Do understand, if understanding you have, that we are in war for the very existence of the nation, and that, if the nation goes, constitutions and liberty go with it. It is only by preserving the nation in its integrity and its majesty that the constitution can be maintained, and the liberty it secures enjoyed. Neither the nation nor the constitution can afford protection to those who would only use their liberty and the constitution to destroy them.

The measure we suggest may be severe, and such as in ordinary cases of rebellion ought not to be resorted to by a free government. But we are engaged in suppressing no ordinary rebellion; we are engaged in suppressing a rebellion of vast proportions, of vast resources, and of strength hardly inferior to that of the loyal states themselves. We can put it down; and, God helping, we shall put it down; but not without exerting all our strength, and availing ourselves of all the means to suppress it authorized, we will not say by the constitution, but by the recognized laws of war. War has its own laws; and, while it lasts, it overrides all other laws, and, if need be, places the constitution itself, so far as it would be a barrier to its success, in abeyance. *Salus populi lex suprema* is a universally received maxim, and the safety of the nation is the only law which can control military operations, or determine the measures necessary or proper in the prosecution of the war.

It is all very well for your Breckenridges, your Burnetts, your Brights, and your Vallandighams, *et id omne genus,* to prate in congress and elsewhere about the unconstitutionality of the acts of the president; we know not, and care not, whether those acts were constitutional or not, so long as we know that they were necessary to the maintenance of the Union, the majesty of law, and our national existence itself. How long must it take the petty political attorneys to learn that the nation is above the constitution, since it makes the constitution, and its preservation is more than the preservation of the constitution, and therefore that all acts necessary to maintain the integrity of the nation and its authority are always lawful, authorized by the highest of all laws? Only they who uphold the constitution, sustain the Union, and labor to save the constitution, can plead the constitution and laws in their favor. They who rebel, or aid and abet rebels, by their very act of rebellion put themselves out of the protection of the constitution and laws, and cannot demand their protection, and should not be permitted to expect that it will be extended over them. The constitution and the laws are for loyal citizens,—not for rebels and traitors. Let, then, the measures suggested or recommended be severe, let them be such as in peaceful times, when the constitution and laws are unresisted and everywhere cheerfully and respectfully obeyed, would be unconstitutional and indefensible, that, in times like these, when the very existence of the nation is at stake, is no objection to them. The first law of nations, as well as of individuals, is self-preservation. It is unconstitutional and illegal to hang innocent and peaceful men; but it is neither illegal nor unconstitutional to hang murderers. It is unconstitutional and illegal to shoot down innocent and peaceful men arrayed in the field before you, even though they have arms in their hands; but it is not unconstitutional or illegal to shoot them down in self-defence, or in defence of the constitution and laws. Let us, then, hear no more about the constitutionality of this or that measure clearly necessary to the safety of the nation, and the preservation of the Union under the existing constitution.

In a state of war every thing has to give way to military necessity, private property, liberty, and even life itself. The state may take, if its necessities demand it, the private property of its citizens to the last cent, and it can command any citizen it sees proper, to march to meet the enemy, and, if need be, and the fate of war so decide, to lay down his life and, what is dearer than life, his liberty, for his country. On this principle the federal government now calls for troops, and imposes heavy taxes on our property for the support of the war; and loyal citizens cheerfully respond to its call, because they know it has the right to do it, and because they know that, if the country be lost, all is lost, life, liberty, and property themselves.

A heavy tax is imposed by the present war on the citizens of the loyal states, although the war has been brought about without any fault of theirs, or any act of theirs having rendered it necessary. Are they to bear the whole burden it imposes, without any indemnification, or without any attempt, at least, to make the rebellious states, whose treachery has created the necessity for it, bear any portion of it? Shall not they who dance pay the piper? In preserving the Union, do we not do it for the benefit of the disloyal, no less than for the benefit of the loyal states; and must we, because we are loyal, bear the whole burden of preserving it? The Union has as much right to tax disloyal as loyal citizens, and to collect the tax from the disloyal in the most ready and practicable way possible. Hence congress, at its last session, passed an act confiscating the property of disloyal citizens of the states now in rebellion, and authorizing its seizure wherever it can be found. This is only simple justice. They whose misconduct has created the war, should be made, as far as possible, to bear its burden, or to indemnify the loyal states for the expenses it compels them to incur.

But military necessity may require us to go even further than this late act of congress. The laws of war and military prudence authorize us to strike the enemy where he is most vulnerable, and where the blow will inflict on him the greatest damage. No just war is ever prosecuted for the sake of war. War, for the sake of war, is in all cases unjustifiable. War is justifiable, and can be engaged in by a Christian people, only when it looks to peace for its end, or, which is the same thing, the removal of the causes which have rendered it necessary. If it may be justly resorted to, it is always lawful so to conduct it as in the speediest and most effectual manner possible to remove those causes, to redress the wrongs for which it is waged, and to bring about the desired peace. We are never morally obliged to meet the enemy on his own chosen ground, or to fight him with an equality of forces or weapons. We have the right to choose our own time, place, and mode of attack, and to choose such time, place, and mode as will be the most inconvenient or distressing to him, and the most effectually cripple his resources, crush his power, and compel him to surrender. If he has a weak spot, one weaker than another, we have not only the right, but in common prudence and common humanity are bound to seek out that spot, and there strike our heaviest and deadliest blow. Thus, if there is a disaffected party in the enemy's country, we have the right to encourage and strengthen that party. Hence the government has labored to strengthen and encourage the Union men in western Virginia, eastern Tennessee, Maryland, Kentucky, and Missouri, and by so doing has prevented these states and parts of states from joining openly in the rebellion. On the same principle it has a right to go further, and make friends and allies of all classes of the population of the rebellious states that it can influence, and that, too, without reference to the condition in which they have heretofore been placed by the laws or usages of those states themselves.

This brings us to the question of the slave population in the rebellious states. In these states there are over three millions of the population held by the laws or usages of those states as slaves. These people are an integral portion of the people of the United States, owe allegiance to the federal government, and are entitled to the protection of that government. The government has the same right to make friends and allies of them, and to enroll and arm them against the rebellion, that it has to make friends and allies, or to enroll and arm the white population of western Virginia or of eastern Tennessee. It makes nothing against this that these people have heretofore been slaves by the laws or the usages of the states in which they reside; for those laws or usages are deprived of all force against the Union by the very act of rebellion. Rebellion dissolves all laws for the protection of the life or property of the rebels. By the very act of rebellion, the rebel forfeits to the government against which he rebels both his property and his life, and holds henceforth neither, save at its mercy or discretion. If it were not so, the government would have no right to confiscate the property of rebels, or to attempt to suppress a rebellion by force of arms. If the slaves held in the rebellious states are property, they are forfeited to the government, and the government may confiscate them, as cotton, rice, tobacco, or any other species of property found in the hands of the rebels. The same principle that gives to the government the right to confiscate a bale of cotton owned by a rebel, gives it a right to confiscate every negro slave claimed by a rebel master. This is perfectly clear, and is implied in the recent act of congress on the subject. But if these people held as slaves are not property, they are and should be regarded as citizens of the United States, owing allegiance to the federal government, liable to be called into the service of the Union in the way and manner it deems most advisable, and, if loyal, entitled to the same protection from the government as any other class of loyal citizens. Nobody can pretend that the federal government is obliged, by virtue of the laws or usages heretofore existing in the slave states, to treat these people as property. Whatever might have been its obligation before the rebellious acts of those states, that obligation is now no longer in force.

But if it be required to treat them as free and loyal citizens by the military operations for the preservation of the Union, or even to remove the causes of the present rebellion, the government is bound so to treat them. The only doubt that can arise is as to the fact, whether it would or would not prove useful to this end. It may be objected to such a measure that it would deprive us of the aid of western Virginia and eastern Tennessee, and drive into open hostility to the Union Maryland, Kentucky, and Missouri. This objection deserves grave consideration. But it is in substance the objection that has embarrassed the government from the outset, and compelled it to take only half-way measures to suppress the rebellion. For ourselves, we cannot respect the fear to which this obligation appeals. Fear is the worst possible counsellor in the world, and the government that hesitates to adopt the best policy for fear of alienating its friends, is lost. Let the lines be at once sharply drawn between our friends and our enemies. In a crisis like the present, lukewarm friends, or friends who will be our friends only by virtue of certain concessions to their interests or prejudices, are more embarrassing than open enemies, and do more to weaken our forces than if arrayed in open hostility against us. If these states are for the Union they will insist on no conditions incompatible with the preservation of the Union; they will make sacrifices for the Union, as well as the other loyal states, and there is no reason why they should not. There is neither reason nor justice in Massachusetts, New York, New Jersey, Pennsylvania, and the great states Northwest of the Ohio, pouring out their blood and treasure for the gratification of the slaveholding pretensions of Maryland, Kentucky or Missouri. The citizens of these states who own slaves, are as much bound, if the preservation of the Union requires it, to give up their property in slaves, as we at the further North are to pour out our blood and treasure to put down a rebellion which threatens alike them and us. If they love their few slaves more than they do the Union, let them go out of the Union. We are stronger to fight the battles of the Union without them, than we are with them.

But we have referred only to the slaves in the rebellious states, and, if it is, or if it becomes a military necessity to liberate all the slaves of the Union, and to treat the whole present slave population as freemen and citizens, it would be no more than just and proper that, at the conclusion of the war, the citizens of loyal states, or the loyal citizens of loyal sections of the rebellious states, should be indemnified at a reasonable rate for the slaves that may have been liberated. The states and sections of states named have not a large number of slaves, and, if the Union is preserved, it would not be a very heavy burden on it to pay their ransom; and to paying it no patriot, or loyal citizen of the free states would raise the slightest objection. The objection, therefore, urged, though grave, need not be regarded as insuperable; and we think the advantages of the measure in a military point of view, would be far greater than any disadvantage we have to apprehend from it.

Whether the time for this important measure has come or not, it is for the president, as commander-in-chief of our armies, to determine. But, in our judgment, no single measure could be adopted by the government that would more effectually aid its military operations, do more to weaken the rebel forces, and to strengthen our own. Four millions of people in the slave states, feeling that the suppression of the rebellion and the triumph of the Union secures to them and their children for ever the *status* of free citizens, are more than a hundred thousand men taken from the forces of the enemy, and twice that number added to our own; for they would not only compel the rebels to keep a large force, that might otherwise be employed, at home, to protect their own wives and children, but would deprive them of the greater portion of that labor by which they now subsist their armies. Now slavery is to them a source of strength; it would then be to them a source of weakness. Its abolition would, in our judgment, be striking the enemy

at his most vulnerable point, precisely where we can best
sunder the sinews of his strength, and deal him the most
fatal blow.

Moreover, it would not only bring to the assistance of
the federal arms the coöperation of the whole colored race
in the Union, but would secure us, what we now lack, the
sympathy and the moral aid of the whole civilized world,
and remove all danger of our coming into conflict with
either France or England.   The war would be seen then
likely to effect a result with which Englishmen and French-
men could sympathize, and, instead of wishing for the success of the southern confederacy, they would wish with all
their hearts for the success of the federal arms.   It would
do more than this.   It would bring to the aid of our volunteer force from one hundred to two hundred thousand brave
and stalwart volunteers from the free states, aye, and even
many from the slave states themselves, who will not, and
cannot be induced to volunteer their services in a war which,
even if successful, promises to leave the institution of
slavery not only existing, but more firmly established than
ever.   Everybody knows that slavery is at the bottom of
the whole controversy, and that the real object of the southern leaders is not simply to protect slavery against abolition
movements where it exists, but to extend it over the whole
Union, and make the American republic a great slaveholding republic.   And there are men in large numbers amongst
us, men who have had no sympathy with abolitionists, who
see and understand very well that, even were we successful
in putting down the present rebellion, no real union between
the North and the South could be restored, and that no durable peace between them could be reëstablished, if slavery
continued to exist.   These men enter not and will not enter
heartily into the war, unless they see clearly and feel fully
assured that it will result in the final and total extinction of
slavery throughout the Union and all the territory it may
now possess or hereafter acquire.

The present rebellion proves, what thoughtful and far-seeing men in all sections of the Union have long seen and
said, that the preservation of the Union with the slave system of labor extending over one half of it, and the free
labor system over the other half, is, in the ordinary course
of human affairs, an impossibility.   Senator Seward, or
rather Mein Herr Diefenbach in "Conversations of our
Club" before him, was right in saying there is an " irre-

pressible conflict" between the two systems. They cannot long coexist together in peace and harmony; there is an irrepressible tendency in each to exclude the other; and no possible wisdom or prudence, on the part of any administration, can harmonize their coexistence under one and the same government. You must make your election between the systems, and adopt for the whole country either the slave system, or the free-labor system; and the real significance of the contest in which we are now engaged, is as to which of these systems shall be the American system.

However homogeneous in race or character, habits or manners, may be the people of a country in the outset, they separate, and grow gradually into two distinct peoples, with almost entirely different ideas, habits and customs, if one half of them in the one section adopt the slave system, and the other half in the other the free-labor system. We have already in the United States, notwithstanding our common origin, our common language, the similarity of our laws, and our habitual intercourse, grown almost into two distinct nations. The confederates are Americans indeed, for they have been born and bred on American soil; but they no longer retain the original American character; while in the free states, bating the alterations effected by foreign immigration, that character is substantially preserved. We of the North are the same people that made the revolution, won American independence, and established the federal government. This divergence showed itself even at the time of the revolution; and it has been growing greater and greater from the beginning of the present century; and if the two systems of labor are continued on American soil, must continue to grow still greater and greater, till the people of the two sections grow up into two absolutely distinct and mutually hostile nations, no longer capable, but by the subjugation of the one by the other, of existing under one and the same government. The only way this divergence can be checked, the unity and homogeneousness of the whole American people recovered and preserved, is by the assimilation of the labor systems of the North and the South.

We of the North cannot and ought not to accept the labor system of the South. But the slave states, by their unprovoked rebellion, have given us an opportunity of performing an act of long delayed justice to the negro population of the Union, and of assimilating the southern labor system to ours. This assimilation is at the bottom of the southern rebellion, and the South has risen in arms against the Union, chiefly for the purpose of extending her labor system over all the free states. In doing so, she gives us the right, in our own self-defence, to extend our free-labor system over all the slave states,—a right which, but for her rebellion, we should not have had under the constitution.

If this prove a disadvantage to the southern states, owing to the peculiar character of their laboring population, they have no right to complain, for it is a disadvantage they have brought upon themselves. But this will be a disadvantage only as compared with us of the North; for it will be better for the South herself to have her negro population free laborers, than it is to have them slaves. In counting the population of the South, we must count not merely her white, but also her black and colored population. The moral, spiritual, and material well-being of her four millions of black and colored people must be considered, as well as the moral, spiritual, and material well-being of her eight millions of whites. These black and colored people are as much human beings, whose welfare is as important and as necessary to be consulted by the statesman, the political economist, the moralist, and the Christian, as that of any other portion of her population; and what they would gain by their emancipation should be thrown into the balance against what might be lost by their former owners. But even the three hundred and forty-seven thousand slave proprietors would, in reality, lose nothing, or gain in moral more than they would lose in material prosperity. We do not believe southern society would, in case of emancipation, be equal to what it would if the whole population were of the white race. The negro element would remain in that society, and, wherever it remains, it will be an inferior element; but far less so as free, than as enslaved. The white population of the South must always suffer this drawback for having collected, or submitted to the collection of a large African population on their soil, and they have no right to complain if obliged to make expiation, as long as the world stands, for having introduced and sustained the institution of negro slavery. But aside from the disadvantage of having its laboring population of a race with which the white race will not mingle, the South would gain by the assimilation of her labor system to that of the North.

M. Augustin Cochin has proved, in the work before us,

that slavery can be abolished, and the slaves converted into free laborers, without any serious detriment, even to the former slave proprietors. We all know that free labor is more economical than slave labor, and therefore that a free man is worth more, under the point of view of national wealth, than a slave. The conversion of the four millions of slaves now in the southern states into freemen, would very much increase, instead of diminishing, the aggregate wealth of those states; and if a portion of this increased aggregate wealth should pass from the hands of a few slave proprietors, and into the hands of those who have heretofore been allowed to hold no property, the aggregate well-being of the whole community would also be augmented instead of diminished, and therefore the South, regarded as a whole, or looking to her whole population, would be unquestionably a great gainer by the change. She would not in any respect be depopulated or impoverished, but would be in the way of a more rapid increase of her population, and of that wealth which constitutes the real strength and prosperity of a state. What we propose, then, would in no respect be ruinous, or even injurious, to the southern states themselves, but would be a real advantage to them, and secure them after the peace all the real greatness, strength, and prosperity states with a mixed population of white and black are capable of. The proposition, then, involves no wrong, no injustice, no injury to the white population of the southern states; while it would be an act of justice, though tardy justice, to the negro race so long held in bondage, and forced to forego all their own rights and interests for the pride, wealth, and pleasure of their white masters.

It seems to us, then, highly important, in every possible view of the case, that the federal government should avail itself of the opportunity given it by the southern rebellion to perform this act of justice to the negro race; to assimilate the labor system of the South to that of the North; to remove a great moral and political wrong; and to wipe out the foul stain of slavery, which has hitherto sullied the otherwise bright escutcheon of our republic. We are no fanatics on the subject of slavery, as is well known to our readers, and we make no extraordinary pretensions to modern philanthropy; but we cannot help fearing that, if the government lets slip the present opportunity of doing justice to the negro race, and of placing our republic throughout in harmony with modern civilization, God, who is especially the

God of the poor and the oppressed, will never give victory
to our arms, or suffer us to succeed in our efforts to suppress
rebellion, and restore peace and integrity to the Union. We
have too long turned a deaf ear to the cry of the enslaved;
we have too long suffered our hearts to grow callous to the
wrongs of the down-trodden in our own country; we have
too long been willing to grow rich, to erect our palaces, and
gather luxuries around us by the toil, the sweat, and the
blood of our enslaved brethren. May it not be that the cry
of these brethren has already entered the ear of Heaven,
and that he has taken up their cause, and determined that,
if we refuse any longer to break their chains, to set them
free, and to treat them as our brothers and fellow-citizens,
we shall no longer exist as a nation? May it not be that,
in this matter, we have him to reckon with, and that the
first step toward success is, justice to the wronged? We
confess that we fear, and deeply fear, if we let slip the opportunity which the southern rebellion gives us to do justice
to the slave, or to make his cause ours, in vain shall we have
gathered our forces and gone forth to battle. We fear God
may be using the rebels as instruments of our punishment
—instruments themselves to be destroyed, when through
them our own destruction has been effected. We speak
solemnly and in deep earnest; for he fights at terrible odds
who has the infinite and just God against him. It may be
that an all-wise Providence has suffered this rebellion for
the very purpose of giving us an opportunity of emancipating rightfully, without destroying, but as a means of preserving, the Union, the men, women, and children now held
in bondage, and of redeeming our past offences. If so, most
fearful will be his judgments upon us, if we neglect the opportunity, and fail to avail ourselves of the right. Now is
our day of grace. This opportunity neglected, our day of
grace may be over, and our republic follow the fate of all
others, and become a hissing and a by-word in all the earth.
Which may God in his infinite mercy avert.

ARCHBISHOP HUGHES ON SLAVERY.*

[From Brownson's Quarterly Review for January, 1862.]

ANY apology due to our readers for calling their attention to a weekly sheet like that of the *Metropolitan Record*, may be found in the fact that this sheet is the "Official Organ" of our most reverend archbishop, and that the article *à propos* of this *Review*, in its number for the 12th of last October, has been publicly stated, and as far as we know, not contradicted, to have been written, dictated, or at least inspired by the most reverend archbishop himself. To take notice of an article written by the ostensible editor of that journal would indeed be a derogation from the dignity of a quarterly reviewer; but there can be no derogation from that dignity in taking even the most formal notice of an article written, or approved, by so distinguished a prelate as the illustrious archbishop of New York. The respect is then paid not to the weekly newspaper, or to its comparatively unknown editor, but to one of the most widely known and influential prelates of the American church. Any remarks by a writer occupying so elevated and so commanding a position among Catholics as the Most Reverend Archbishop Hughes, even though published in a weekly newspaper, deserve the attention, and even the grave consideration of the Catholic reviewer, whoever he may be.

That the article in question was actually written, dictated, or inspired by the most reverend archbishop, we have no positive proof; but it has been ascribed to him; it bears all the internal marks of genuineness; and, even if not actually written by him, it is too elaborate and too important to have appeared in his "official organ" without his knowledge and expressed approval. It has the stamp of his peculiar genius, the well-known characteristics of his somewhat original mind, and is what we should expect him to write on the subject discussed. There can, then, it seems to us, be no impropriety in assuming it to be substantially his, or in awarding him the credit due to its author.

We know very well that the archbishop's authorship of

Metropolitan Record. October 12th, 1861. New York.

the article in question has been gravely disputed by some
of the public journals, and various reasons have been assigned
why he could not have written it.   But to us none of these
reasons, however weighty, are conclusive. They proceed on
the assumption that the article, or the chief portion of it at
least, is a defence of slavery and an apology for the slave
trade ; and therefore conclude that it could not have been
written by him, for no Catholic archbishop would or could
defend the one, or apologize for the other.   But this conclusion is drawn from an erroneous assumption, for, as we
hope to be able to show, the article neither defends slavery
nor apologizes for the slave trade.   His authorship has also
been denied on the ground that its style is deficient in that
dignity and classic purity always to be presumed in the
writings of an archbishop, and is a closer imitation of the
"slang and billingsgate" of the *New York Herald* than
could be expected in a writer who for years was on no
friendly terms with its editor, and persistently refused to
suffer a copy of it to enter his palace.   But this imitation is
not so close as is pretended, and, even if it were, it would
not necessarily be conclusive against his authorship.   The
man who writes not merely to prove that he is a fine writer,
but to produce an effect beyond his personal glory, adapts
his style to the understanding and taste of those he seeks to
influence ; and it may be said in the archbishop's defence, if
he indeed wrote the article, that he was writing in the columns of a newspaper, and for a public whose taste and
judgment had, to a great extent, been formed by the *New
York Herald*, and kindred journals.

It has, furthermore, been objected that the article could
not have been written by the archbishop, because it is written against this *Review*, the only Catholic review published
in the United States, and which, it is to be presumed, a
Catholic archbishop would be more ready to uphold and defend than to oppose and denounce.   But we know no reason why an archbishop should not write against this *Review*, as against any other periodical, in case he disapproves
it, or thinks it necessary to put the faithful or any portion
of the community on their guard against what he judges to be
erroneous or dangerous in its pages.   The article, however,
is not written against us, or against any principle or doctrine
we have set forth or maintained ; and we are very far from
accepting the sympathy of those of our friends who pronounce it "a brutal attack" upon our *Review*.   The arch-

bishop, we believe, has usually expressed himself, publicly and privately, in terms of warm commendation of this periodical, and we have received, even since the publication of our last number, on very respectable authority, the gratifying assurance that he has "no doubt of our personal orthodoxy," and that he does not deem it expedient for either the Propaganda or himself to write any thing against us. This assurance would, no doubt, be conclusive against the supposition that he is the author of the article in question, if it were really written, or intended to be written, against us. But such is not the fact, as we trust we shall soon make evident.

Undoubtedly, there are points on which there are differences of opinion between the writer of the article and ourselves. We are both independent thinkers; and as neither is personally infallible, it is hardly possible that we should not now and then take different views, and fail occasionally to arrive at the same conclusions. But this is not to be taken as a grave objection either to him or to ourselves. He does not fully approve every judgment of ours, any more than we approve every judgment of his. He insinuates a doubt whether the answer we gave to various objections and criticisms against us "will prove satisfactory to the Catholic portion of our readers;" but this does not necessarily imply that it ought not to be satisfactory to them, and we presume it is satisfactory to his own mind, or else he would not, as he does, assert positively that we do "*really* answer" them in "a way which is satisfactory to" ourselves. He says, indeed, of Gioberti, whom many people admire as an able writer and a profound philosopher: "he has written as much philosophical trash as any of his contemporaries, and an attempt at refutation, here or there, would be only a multiplication of that same trash." But he and we may differ on a literary and philosophical question, or as to what is or is not "philosophical trash," we presume, without mutual hostility, and without impeaching the orthodoxy or the Catholic standing of either. He says, again, in relation to our article on the *Reading and Study of the Scriptures*, that there is "a conglomeration of opinions on that subject, all of which are antagonistic to the *Catholic* sense and meaning of the Holy Scriptures;" yet he cannot expect us to understand him to assert any antagonism between our views and the real Catholic sense and meaning of the Holy Scriptures. He can only mean to assert an antagonism between our literary sense or taste and that of some Catholics; for he is well aware that we entered into no discussion of the sense and meaning of the Holy Scriptures, and confined our remarks simply to the respective literary merits of different English translations of the sacred volume. We preferred, and we must still prefer, the *English* of King James's version to that of the Douay version. If he does not, then his taste in English and ours differ, and there is an old maxim, *De gustibus non est disputandum.* But these differences of taste or judgment are perfectly compatible with mutual confidence and esteem.

But it is said that the main portion of the article is directed against our views in the article on *Slavery and the War*, which, we have been told, it refutes in a masterly and triumphant manner. But this is a mistake. The article is written *à propos* of ours, but not against it. It is written almost exclusively against the abolitionists, with whom it would be ridiculous to seek to confound us, and, if it objects to our article at all, it is only as inopportune, and, as the writer fears, may be "mischievous" because "untimely." He controverts none of its principles, and does little more than question the fact that we assert, that slavery is at the bottom of the rebellion, or the cause of the war in which we are now engaged.

The writer says against us, "that slavery is the cause of the war * * * happens to be simply impossible, except in the sense that a man's carrying money on his person is the cause of his being robbed on the highway!" But we cannot accept this assertion. Cause, strictly taken, is that which produces an event or thing, and without which it could not happen or exist. No man can doubt that in this sense slavery is the cause of the rebellion and therefore of the war, for if there had been no slavery in the country, there would have been no rebellion,—and no rebellion, no war. Even the writer's own theory of the war, which attributes it to northern abolitionism, virtually makes slavery its cause; for, if there had been no slavery in the country, there would have been no abolitionism. We all know that slavery is at the bottom of the whole controversy between the North and the South, and is the real cause of that divergence of feeling and interest, of which the civil war now raging is the bitter fruit, and therefore, if not its immediate, is at least its remote cause. That it is the cause of the war is implied in the public speeches and declarations of southern statesmen.

For, why have the South seceded or attempted to secede from the Union, and taken up arms against the federal government, but because they asked, and because the North refused to grant, or, in the election of Mr. Lincoln, showed that it was disposed to refuse to grant, through the federal government, protection to the institution of slavery in territory where, as we hold, it has no legal existence?

The writer has been led to his conclusion by not observing that the war has been brought on not by the abolitionists wishing to rob the man who carried the money on his person, but by the North showing itself determined to refuse to suffer the power of the federal government to be used to protect those who insist on taking and carrying away other men's money, and using it as their own. No doubt if the North had passively submitted to the extension of slavery, and suffered its friends to have their own way in regard to it, there would have been no rebellion and no civil war. So, if the traveller should offer no resistance to the highwayman, but passively submit to have his pockets and valise rifled, there would be no strife between him and the robber. The writer overlooks the fact that the North is not the robber rifling the pockets of the innocent traveller, but the innocent traveller seeking to recover his own from the robber, and protect himself from future robberies. This slight oversight, which is no more than any of us are liable to, is the reason, we presume, why he has differed from us as to the cause of the war.

The archbishop, or whoever was the writer, says: "Dr. Brownson maintains that the end and purpose of the war is not, or at least should not be, merely to sustain the constitution, government, and laws of the country, but to abolish slavery in the southern states;" that is, beyond maintaining the constitution, government, and laws of the country, the war should be prosecuted for the abolition of southern slavery. This proposition he undoubtedly controverts; but his assertion that it is ours must be regarded as made in his character of a newspaper writer, and be taken in a newspaper or "Pickwickian" sense; for he knew very well that we had maintained nothing of the sort. We say expressly in our article: "The liberation of the slave is *not* the purpose and end of the war in which we are now engaged. The war is a war against rebellion, an unprovoked and wicked rebellion, engaged in by the rebels for the purpose of making this a great slaveholding republic, in which the labor of the country shall be performed by slaves, either black or white; and if, to defeat the rebellion, the destruction of slavery be necessary, and be actually effected, it *will change nothing in the character or purpose of the war.*" Such being our own express language, and which was, undoubtedly, before the eyes of the writer, we must, in simple justice to him, suppose that his real purpose in attaching our name to the offensive proposition was not to assert it as ours, but to assert it as the one he proposed to controvert.

As to the proposition the archbishop or the writer in the *Record* so elaborately controverts, there is no difference of opinion between him and us. He denies that the federal government can rightfully carry on a war for the abolition of slavery, and so do we; and he concedes that it has the right to abolish it under the pressure of military necessity, as a means of preserving the Union, and maintaining the integrity of the nation. This is all that we ourselves have maintained. The federal government has the constitutional right to maintain itself, and the constitutional duty to maintain inviolate, as far as in its power, the Union of these states formed by our fathers. It has, therefore, the right to use all the means at its command necessary to maintain this right and to fulfil this duty. If the abolition of slavery is necessary to this end, it has the right, and is bound, to abolish it. The archbishop's "official organ" concedes all this. It does not oppose the liberation of the slave; it does not oppose his liberation by the federal government as a necessary means to a lawful end, but only as an end in itself. Hence it says: "In the progress of the war it is difficult to foresee what turn events may take in the South under the pressure of military necessity;" and again, after asserting the legal right of the planter to hold slaves, it says: "It is only under pressure of military necessity during a war that even the federal government or the federal troops would have any right to deprive him of his lands or of his servants." This is very true, but it plainly implies that such pressure of military necessity is possible, and that under it the planter may rightfully be deprived of his servants or slaves. This is all we have asserted, and all we pretend to assert; and we therefore maintain that the article in the *Record* was not written against us, or intended to controvert our position as to the right and duty of the federal government to recognize under the war power the freedom of the slave, and to call upon him, if it judges proper, to assist it in maintaining the integrity of the nation.

Undoubtedly, the archbishop and we differ as to the fact whether the pressure of military necessity actually exists or not. He honestly believes that there is as yet no such military necessity as would justify the liberation of the slaves under the war power. He, we presume, believes it still practicable to save both slavery and the Union, and therefore that the recognition of the slaves as freemen is not called for, and would be manifestly unlawful. We think differently. We think that persistence in the effort to save the Union without calling the slaves to our assistance must result in the destruction of the Union and the complete success of the confederates. There is here, no doubt, a wide difference of judgment between us. Events may prove that he is right and we are wrong; they may also prove that he is wrong and we are right. Each of us makes up, and must make up his judgment from the facts and probabilities in the case, and neither he nor we can form or pretend to form an absolutely infallible judgment on the subject. But there is, however, this difference between our respective judgments; if ours be acted on and found erroneous, the most serious consequence would be that four millions of people, who like ourselves are of the human race, and for whom, as well as for us, our Lord was incarnated, suffered and died on the cross, would be converted from slaves to freemen; while, if his should be acted upon and prove to be faulty, the consequence would be that rebellion would be successful, the laws would be trampled under foot, the constitution would be overthrown, the integrity of the nation itself would be destroyed, and that liberty so prized by our fathers, and from which the friends of humanity throughout the world have hoped so much, would in all probability be rendered henceforth for ever impossible on this continent. Evidently, then, it would be better that the administration should err with us than err with him.

We are, we grant, opposed to slavery in any and every form; but, if we believed it practicable to secure the end and purposes of the war,—the maintenance and defence of our constitution and government, which imply the maintenance and defence of the integrity of the nation and the sovereignty of the Union—without abolishing slavery, or calling the slaves to our assistance, our respect for legal forms and vested rights would compel us to deny the right of the federal government or any branch thereof, to declare

them free. We urge their liberation only as a war measure, a measure necessary to save the nation, justified and
called for by military necessity. We believe it necessary
to save the integrity of the nation, to put down effectually
rebellion in the slaveholding section of the Union. On this
ground, we urge it; that is, as a means necessary to secure
a lawful end, but not as an end in itself, or as an end which
congress or the administration might legally attempt to
effect in ordinary times with or without war. As a necessary means to such an end the archbishop concedes that it
would be lawful, and should be adopted; but he is apparently satisfied that it is not necessary as a means, and that
the Union can be restored, and peace reëstablished without
resorting to it. Although we think him wrong, he may be
right. It may be that loyal blood, and loyal treasure, and
northern skill and bravery will prove amply sufficient to
put down the rebellion without recognizing the slaves as
freemen, and availing ourselves of their services and sympathies, and that hereafter, as heretofore, the Union and
slavery may continue to exist together. If so, we shall
glory in the generosity and bravery of the loyal states, and
rejoice that the Union is restored, and make, as we have
heretofore made, no efforts to abolish slavery by the action
of the federal government. We shall regret the continuance of slavery, but shall stir up no war for its abolition.
We shall console ourselves and the poor negroes as well as
we can with the scathing lines of the poet:—

> " Yet, yet, degraded men ! th' expected day,
> That breaks your bitter cup, is far away ;
> Trade, wealth, and fashion ask you still to bleed,
> And holy men give Scripture for the deed."

The archbishop very properly maintains that Catholics
have not enlisted and will not enlist in a war for the abolition of slavery, and we fully agree with him when he asks
in one of his most eloquent strains :

"Was it for this our dauntless soldiers fell in battle ? Was it for this
that many of them, together with their brave officers, are now pining
away in the captivity of a southern dungeon ? Take, for instance,
Colonel Corcoran and his gallant fellow-prisoners of the 69th. Was it
for this that Cameron fell on the battle-field, without any friendly eye
to gaze on his countenance whilst he lay

> " ' Like a warrior taking his rest,
> With his martial cloak around him ? '

Was it for this that the noble-hearted and gallant Ward was, we might say, assassinated on the deck of his vessel ? Was it for this that the unyielding patriot and heroic commander of Fort Sumter, as well as the equally heroic Mulligan at Lexington, no less than the brave General Lyon who fell on the field, were so cruelly neglected and left to their fate until reinforcements came too late ? Was it to carry out the idea of abolitionism that these noble warriors, and thousands of less distinguished names, have already given their lives, as they imagined, for the support of the constitution and the preservation of the Union ? "

But neither was it, we may add, to defend slavery, or to protect the property of rebel masters in their slaves, that those brave men fell, or languish in southern prisons. Catholics, at least foreign-born Catholics, are not pro-slavery men, and if many of them have been found opposed to abolitionists, it has been from a scrupulous regard for the constitution and the Union, not from any love for slavery itself, or wish to see it perpetuated here or elsewhere. The great body of our German population, it is well known, are strongly anti-slavery ; and there are no people on earth whose heart beats more warmly or vividly for liberty, or which has a deeper horror of slavery, than the Catholic Irish. Catholics by their religion are inspired with sentiments of loyalty and with respect for the sacredness of the oath of allegiance, and know that they may never do evil that good may come. They have believed it far better for the interests of liberty and humanity to endure the existence of negro-slavery in our southern states, than to attempt to remove it by unconstitutional means, or by means which would endanger the safety of the Union and the integrity of the nation. But, judging them by ourselves, and we may so judge them, for the same heart that beats in our bosom beats no less warmly in theirs, they will not hesitate a moment when they see that the alternative is presented, that either slavery or the Union must go by the board, to say, and to say with an emphasis not to be mistaken : " Let slavery perish, but the Union—it must and shall be preserved."

This undoubtedly is the sentiment of the archbishop himself. Though not born in the country, he has so long lived in it that he feels that it is his own native land, and takes his stand for the Union against the southern slaveholding. rebellion. No doubt he treats the rebels with tenderness, for he comes of a nation in which rebellion, or what England treats as rebellion, has been chronic for nearly eight

centuries ; still more, because his ministry is one of peace
and love, and he looks to the future peace and harmony between Catholics of the North and Catholics of the South ;
but he still, as a right loyal citizen, insists that the rebellion
must be put down, and that private friendships and private
interests, if need be, must be sacrificed on the altar of the
country. He opposes the abolitionists indeed, but he does
not, as it has been charged against him, defend slavery. He
is a Catholic prelate, and declares true our proposition that
" the Catholic Church is opposed to slavery." He is a man,
and says : " We are not the friends of slavery. If it were
still to be introduced, we would resist the attempt with all
our might." He regards slavery as " a calamity," and speaks
of American slavery as " terrific." He objects to it on the
score of morality, the disrespect by the masters of " the marriage bond creating man and wife among slaves," the breaking up " of families, the selling of the husband in one direction, the wife in another, whilst their children are disposed
of according to the highest price offered from any point of
the compass." It is evident then, that he is not favorable
to slavery, that he regards it as an evil, the introduction of
which should be resisted *à outrance*. Certainly, then, he
would not make, nor urge others to make war in its defence,
or condemn honest folk for simply wishing to abolish it. If
he speaks now and then apparently in its favor or extenuation, he does so not because he approves it, but because he
regards its abolition as impracticable, or the evil as irremediable. " The church," he says, " is opposed to slavery, but
only in the sense that she is opposed to the calamities of
human life, which she has no power to reverse." Believing it an irreversible calamity, an irremediable evil, an evil
which is fixed upon us for ever, he seeks, very wisely and
justly, to reconcile us to its existence. To this end he shows,
on the one hand, its redeeming features, and, on the other,
that, however terrific a calamity it may be, " It is not alien
from the condition of mankind in general," that it is only
one of those calamities which original sin has entailed upon
mankind, and therefore to be borne with patience and resignation. It is always the characteristic of a wise man to
reconcile himself and others, as far as possible, to the existence of inevitable evils, and to endure without a murmur
what cannot be cured, trusting that the wrong will be made
right, and full indemnification be granted in another and a
better world. This is pious, is wise, is just, that is, in the

case of really incurable evils, and implies no approbation of the evils themselves.

The archbishop, we doubt not, would, could he see any legal and practicable way in which slavery could be abolished without entailing a greater evil than itself, not only be willing to see it abolished, but would earnestly engage in the great and noble work of abolishing it. He is animated by the spirit of his religion, and like his church, in earnest to remove every evil that is removable. "The church," we said in our article, and he will not deny it, "has tolerated slavery where she lacked the power to abolish it; but her whole history proves that she sets her face against it, and uses all the means at her disposal, without shocking the public peace, or creating tumults and disorder, to prepare the slave for freedom, and to secure his ultimate emancipation." The church never enjoins resignation to evils which are removable, and she never, whatever too many of her children, whether cleric or laic, may do, tolerates any evil which she has the power to remove without creating a greater evil. Resignation to evils which afflict our brethren, or even ourselves, when not voluntarily assumed as penances, when we have it in our power to remove them, is not and cannot be either a human or a Christian virtue. Catholicity requires us to love all men as our brethren, and to labor earnestly and perseveringly for the good of society, the progress of civilization, and the freedom and manly development of mankind, as well as to cultivate the pious affections and the ascetic virtues. The latter we are to do, but not in doing it to leave undone the former. For he who says he loves God, and hateth his brother, is a liar and the truth is not in him. All this the archbishop knows far better than we do, and we must therefore presume that, were he to see his way clear, he would labor as earnestly and as persistently for the abolition of slavery as would any of those abolitionist themselves, against whom he so vehemently directs his cutting irony and his biting sarcasms. To say less would be to doubt his Catholic spirit, and his devotion to the religion of which he is regarded as so bright an ornament and so illustrious a champion.

The archbishop, in opposing the abolitionists, does not oppose them on the ground that they are opposed to slavery and seek its abolition. He opposes them, as we understand him, on the ground that they fail to recognize the right of property which the law secures to the master in his slaves, that they seek the abolition of slavery by unconstitutional means, and that their success would endanger the peace of the Union, and work no real benefit to the slaves themselves. On this same ground we ourselves have for twenty years objected to them, and opposed their movements. This ground of opposition is legitimate, and implies no approbation of slavery itself. The only fault with it is, that it has now ceased to be true in its more essential parts. It is inopportune, and can no longer serve the sacred cause of Union. The disruption of the Union apprehended has actually taken place, the peace of the Union is broken, and the slaveholders cannot be more embittered against the North than they already are, and they can attempt nothing worse than they are now doing. When the work was to preserve peace and union, it was well to oppose abolitionists, but now when peace and union are broken, and the work is to restore them, such opposition is mistimed and altogether misplaced. It creates divisions among loyal citizens, and weakens our strength to put down the rebellion.

After all, neither the archbishop nor we can object to the principle of abolitionism or the end it seeks; for we both believe slavery an evil, a wrong, opposed by the church, and as men and Catholics must believe that it ought to be abolished in case it can be legally and constitutionally. We can really object to abolitionists only their too little respect for the alleged right of property in man and for legal forms and constitutions. Their error was not in seeking the abolition of slavery, but in seeking it by improper and unjustifiable means. This is all that we can say against them, for neither he nor we do or can wish the perpetuation of negro-slavery. The negro, as we never cease to repeat, is a man, a man of the same race with ourselves. He, like us, belongs to the genus HOMO, and all men are members of the body of humanity in the natural order, as all Christians, in the regeneration, are members of the body of Christ, and members one of another, and no member can suffer without the whole body suffering with it. This great truth he and we must hold. Both he and we, then, must oppose slavery, for it is the greatest possible outrage upon the rights and dignity of man, and even an outrage upon the Creator himself, whose image and likeness it debases and disfigures in his creature. But the abolitionists are not now seeking the abolition of slavery by any illegal, improper, or unjustifiable means. They ask no violation now of the constitu-

tion, and waive the question of property, for the slaveholders by their rebellion have forfeited whatever right the law
secured to them as loyal citizens. They are contented to
accept abolition under the war-power, as a military necessity. There is, then, no longer any solid reason for warring
against them.

Grant, as the archbishop alleges, that the abolitionists or
some of them have said hard things against the constitution
of the United States; they have done so only on the supposition that the constitution was in the way of redressing
what they and we also regard as a great moral, social, and
political wrong. They have, however, confined their opposition to words; they have never risen in rebellion, or labored to induce others to rise in rebellion against the constitution. They have never made, and never proposed to
make war on the Union for the sake of emancipating the
slaves. They have used, and they propose to use against
slavery only the freedom of speech and the press, which
congress is forbidden by the constitution itself to make any
law against. They may have said or may have written and
printed many foolish, many imprudent, or many unpleas-
ant, or even incendiary words against slaveholders and
pro-slavery men; but they are not and never have been
guilty of treason. Treason, according to the constitution of
the United States, consists only "in levying war against
them, or in adhering to their enemies, giving them aid and
comfort." The abolitionists have never done this; they
have never levied war against the United States; they have
never adhered to their enemies, or given them aid or comfort. The raid of John Brown and his band into Virginia
is no exception to this statement. John Brown and his
handful of adherents acted on their own responsibility,
without the approval and without the knowledge of the
great body of abolitionists, as well as contrary to their
avowed principles and mode of abolishing slavery. That
they sympathized with the end, to wit, the freedom of the
slave, is no doubt true; that they believed John Brown's
motives were good, is possible; that they approved the
means he adopted is untrue, and they are no more to be
held responsible for his action, than the archbishop, who
wished to see Ireland free, and generously contributed five
hundred dollars to purchase her a shield, but disapproved
of the Young Ireland party, is to be held responsible for
the Irish rebellion which terminated so sadly at Sliev-na
Mon in 1848.

The archbishop intimates in his letter to Bishop Lynch, and he or his "official organ" insinuates in the article we are examining, that the chief blame of the present war rests upon northern abolitionists, not on the southern rebels themselves. We cannot agree with him in this; nor can we believe it wise or just on the part of the loyal friends of the Union to indulge at the present time in violent and bitter vituperations against any portion of our loyal citizens. That the *New York Herald* should do this, is in character, and can excite no surprise, hardly any indignation, for many persons honestly believe that it is really as much in the interest of secession, and working as earnestly for the success of the southern confederacy now, as it was avowedly before the assemblage of New York citizens one day required it to raise from its office the flag of the Union. That those who for years gained political notoriety and influence by denouncing as black republicans or as abolitionists all who opposed the extension of slavery, and sought in a legal and constitutional way to resist the encroachments of the slave interest, should continue on in their old way, and repeat their old slang phrases, unconscious of any change in public affairs, was to be expected, and can surprise no one. A change in them would be the surprising thing. But, we confess, it grieves us to find our own archbishop, or even his "official organ," joining with them, castigating or ridiculing the loyal North, and holding it up as responsible for all the calamities which have befallen our beloved country. We are grieved, because it, to some extent, places our religion in a false position, and can hardly fail seriously to impair the reputation of one of our most eminent Catholics, and most distinguished and highly esteemed prelates. His reputation is not a thing to be trifled with. It is the property of the church, and is dear to every true-hearted Catholic, who cannot but be deeply grieved to find any thing occurring to impair it, or to lower his position, or lessen his influence in the American community.

We are confident that, in his war upon the anti-slavery party, the archbishop has had no disloyal purpose, has been moved by no improper motive, and has had no wish but to serve the best interests of his country; but we beg his permission to say, and with all deference and respect, that he appears to us to have neglected to consult chronology, and has not noted with his usual care and sagacity the changes in the bearing of great public questions which one or two years have effected. He has suffered himself to be betrayed into the adoption of a policy manifestly behind the times, —a policy which, when there was no rebellion in arms against the government, and no danger of any serious disturbance of the public peace, might have been judicious or, at least, harmless, but which we fear can now be regarded neither as the one nor the other. It seems to us now fitted only to give indirectly, if not directly, aid and comfort to the enemies of the United States; and we have no doubt that, were we to adopt it, we should find ourselves suddenly arrested for treason, and sent to keep company with some of our old friends at Fort Warren. Few things could more effectually aid and comfort the rebels than articles and speeches by men in the loyal states exonerating them, and throwing the blame of having caused the rebellion on the citizens of the loyal North, now in arms and pouring out their blood and treasure in defence of the constitution and the integrity of the nation.

This is a matter which cannot be passed over lightly, and these are times when it will not do to study to keep up old party feuds and party animosities. These are times when all loyal men must sacrifice on the altar of their country their party and even their private loves, and, what to most men is still more difficult, their party and their private hatreds; for the Union can be saved only on condition that the whole North present an unbroken front and, to use a fine Scriptural expression, march " as one man " against the enemy, to put down the wicked and unprovoked rebellion. The South had never dared to bring her conspiracy to a head, to appeal from ballots to bullets, and to attempt by force of arms to reconstruct or destroy the Union, had she not counted on a divided North, and support from a party which was opposed to abolition and even Republicanism, and in elections had always acted under her dictation, and sustained her policy. She expected to find opposed to her only the non-fighting abolitionists and the Republican party, who both together constituted only a bare majority of the population of the non-slaveholding states; and, if her expectations in this respect had been realized, she would in all probability have been able to succeed. Whatever, then, tends to keep the North divided, and to prevent the loyal states from entering into the contest with the hearty sympathy and coöperation of their whole population is really and undeniably aid and comfort given to the enemy, and is therefore under the constitution of the United States virtually, if nor formally, treason.

Party divisions, and especially party rivalries and animosities, are now mistimed and mischievous. They weaken the friends of the Union, and strengthen the hands of the rebels. We know, and can afford to know, till the rebellion is crushed out, no party divisions, and no division but that between loyalists and rebels. Hushed should be all party strife between loyal men, and even the usual *odium theologicum* should be suppressed. All loyal men, Protestants or Catholics, Republicans, Democrats, or abolitionists, whether black or white, red or yellow, who are prepared to stand by our common country, and defend it, if need be, even to the last gasp, are of our party, are our friends, our brothers, and we give them our hand and our heart. If there are differences between us to be settled, we will adjourn them till we have put down the rebellion, saved the Union, and made it sure that we have a country, homes, and firesides that we may enjoy in peace and safety, and, when that is done, perhaps, it will be found that most of those differences will have settled themselves, or, at least so far as personal or political, are not worth reviving. We must be united, and not like the maddened Jews when their chief city was beleaguered by the Roman cohorts, and Roman battering-rams were beating down the walls of their citadel, divided into factions and wasting in spilling each other's blood the strength needed to save our national existence from destruction.

This is no time for an archbishop or any other man to make war on abolitionists and to crack stale jokes about an " abolition brigade," and the valor or want of valor of its suggested " brigadier." Such things are " untimely and mischievous." The very existence of the nation is threatened, and threatened not by abolitionists or their sympathizers, but by the slaveholding aristocracy of the South, and their dupes, tools, or aiders and abettors in the loyal states,—men who have no abolition sympathies, but as strong antipathies to all abolitionists as John Randolph of Roanoke had to a sheep, which made him say, that he would at any time go a mile out of his way to give one a kick. The danger that threatens is not on the side of abolitionists, but on the side of the friends and supporters of slavery, and very ordinary wisdom would counsel us, if we are true men, to face the danger where it is, not where it is not. There is no use in trying to gain credit with the loyal North by saying the Union must be sustained, and with the disloyal South by vituperating abolitionists, and denouncing as abolitionists all who would not indeed overstep the constitution to abolish slavery, but would abolish slavery as a means of saving the constitution. No man can now be suffered to say, "Good Lord, and Good Devil." He must choose either the Lord's side or the devil's side, and take the consequence of success or failure:

"Under which king, Bezonian ? Speak, or die !"

He who is not with us is against us. No man can now be neutral, and he who attempts to serve on both sides, will in the end be scorned and rejected by both. Are you for the Union ? Then you must be against the rebels and all that favors their cause. Are you not against the rebels ? Then you are against the Union, and are no more a dutiful citizen than he would be a dutiful son who would stand by as a neutral, and see his own mother assassinated. Neutrality in a citizen, when his country is threatened by a foreign or domestic foe, is virtually treason, and more despicable than open treason itself, for it lacks the courage and the manhood to declare itself. We do not charge the writer with neutrality ; we only fear that his desire to keep his friendly relations with his "southern brethren" has made him less warm, earnest, and decided in his efforts to save the Union than we, both as a citizen and a Catholic, might wish to find him.

Nobody can suspect us of any undue sympathy with abolitionists, for no man in the country has more steadily or more energetically opposed their movements for the last twenty years than ourselves; and we should continue to oppose them as steadily and as energetically, if we believed there were the least danger to the constitution, or to the peace and safety of the Union, to be apprehended from them. We, no more than the archbishop, are prepared to abrogate the constitution in order to abolish slavery, and he, as well as we, is prepared to abolish slavery as a means necessary to save the constitution and the nation from the destruction threatened by the southern rebellion, whenever he is convinced that it is necessary to that end. Yet it may be that we have all of us done and are still doing more or less injustice to those whom we have stigmatized as abolition fanatics. It is not our province to defend the abolitionists ;

but we cannot help suspecting, as events are turning out, it would have done no harm to have listened to them with less contempt, and given more heed to their suggestions. They saw clearer than any of us the aggressive strength and tendency of the slave power, and they felt more intensely than any of us the gross outrage slavery itself is upon the rights and dignity of our common manhood. To us they seemed fanatics; but it is possible they were fanatics only in the sense that all living men are fanatics to the dead, all earnest men are fanatics to the lukewarm, all disinterested and devoted men are fanatics to the selfish, and all heroic men are fanatics to the cowardly. Perhaps, if we who have so long sneered at them as fanatics, had studied less to be wise and politic, and been more truly living men, more in earnest to assert and vindicate the rights of our race, more disinterested and less selfish in our disposition and aims, and more truly heroic in our devotion to the right and the just instead of the merely prudent and the expedient, their fanaticism would have revolted us less, indeed have seemed to us no fanaticism at all, and we been saved from the terrible alternative of either succumbing to the slaveholding aristocracy, or of maintaining our freedom and manhood at the expense of millions of lives, and untold treasure. There are few men who are wise betimes, and to most men wisdom comes only when it is too late to profit them. But, however this may be, the war for the Union cannot be successfully prosecuted on pro-slavery principles; and to us it is a "fixed fact" that we must give up either slavery or the Union. Slavery is the bond of union between the rebels, and it is the great instrument on which they rely for effecting their purposes; and they can be defeated and the Union cause secured a triumph, as we view the case, only by calling to our aid the anti-slavery sentiment of the country, and suffering the war to be not in its end and purpose, but in its incidental effect, a war of liberation.

Whatever our politicians may say, whatever the administration may fear, whatever our archbishop may think, the great body of the people of the loyal states are strongly opposed to negro-slavery, and there are few loyal men amongst us who are not anti-slavery men. Though they will violate no constitution or law, or public right, in order to abolish slavery, they will engage with none the less alacrity in the war by feeling assured that it will result in giving to the oppressed and down-trodden millions the opportunity to rise from their degradation, and prove their manhood. The conviction that such a result will come, and come in a legal way, as a means of defeating and punishing the public enemies of the country, will give additional energy to our brave volunteers, nerve them with greater firmness to endure the privations of a soldier's life, and fire them with more heroic courage to meet the foe on the battle-field. They will feel that then some good will come, incidentally at least, from their self-sacrifice, that they will have done something more than preserve the life of the nation so needlessly endangered, and that, if they fall, millions of warm hearts, free hearts, made free by them, will bless their memories, and bedew their graves with tears of gratitude.

O, tell us not that these brave husbands, sons, and brothers we have armed and sent forth to the battle will throw down their arms and retire to their homes, because, if they fight, the chains will fall from four millions of slaves! You who say it know nothing of the human heart, least of all the true American heart. You dishonor your own manhood; you dishonor our common manhood; you belie human nature itself. There lives not the man in whose heart there is not a chord that vibrates to the slightest whisper of liberty,—liberty, man's true dignity, man's greatest glory, that for which God himself descended to earth, and assumed flesh to secure to him,—liberty, for which humanity everywhere pants as the thirsty hart for the water-brook, and for which she never ceases to struggle, and leaves her pathway through the ages red with the blood and white with the bones of its martyrs. Tell us not that men will fight only for legal technicalities and parchment formulas. They will no more fight for these than for so much chaff of the summer threshing-floor, unless as a means necessary to secure liberty,—liberty for themselves, liberty for their wives and children, and, if they have any sense of their true humanity, liberty for all men and for all times.

We know very well that there is a strong prejudice in some minds, assiduously cultivated under southern inspiration, against all men and parties avowing anti-slavery sentiments, affecting a certain number even of the officers of the army and navy. This prejudice has gone far to paralyze both arms of the service, and has had some influence in depriving it of several of its ablest and most accomplished officers, who have been induced by it to regard the Republican party as low, ungentlemanly, and plebeian, and to feel that it would be a degradation to serve the Union, which had nursed, fed, and educated them, under a Republican administration. This has, no doubt, operated unfavorably to the Union cause ; but as the prejudice is unjust, and has no foundation in truth, it cannot long survive, and can, after all, affect only those who are influenced more by artificial society than by the natural sentiments of humanity. Even the slaveholders love liberty, and themselves feel that slavery is unjust, and loathe it even while they arm to defend it. We, some five years since, gave utterance to stronger anti-slavery sentiments in a public lecture, in Charleston, to the very *élite* of Charleston society, than we have heretofore expressed in these pages, and were loudly applauded. Always will the earnest and fearless tones of a freeman, asserting the rights and dignity of man, find an echo from every man's heart, for they touch and stir to the quick the very heart of humanity itself.

Yet, the prejudice we speak of exists, though artificial and unnatural, and is extended to all New England, and to Massachusetts especially, as the chief seat of anti-slavery sentiments and of anti-slavery movements. But for the " fierce democracie " of the old Bay State, it is pretended no resistance would have been offered to the encroachments of the slave power, and there would have been no rebellion of the slaveholding aristocracy, and therefore again, no civil war, and no interruption of trade and commerce. To concede this, which politicians and demagogues who take no note of time or of the changes which it brings, urge as a crushing charge, would be unjust to the patriotism and humanity of other sections of our common country, hardly, if at all, behind her in their hatred of slavery, or their devotion to the Union. Yet New England in general, and the old Bay State in particular, have been surpassed nowhere in hatred of slavery, in disinterested devotion to the cause of humanity, and true-hearted loyalty to the government of the United States. There may be faults in the New England character ; but not for what is faulty in her character is she loaded with reproaches by the slaveholding aristocracy of the South and their northern dupes and lackeys, but for what is noble, generous, disinterested, and manly. These reproaches are her wreath of honor, more enviable than the diadem that circles the brow of king or kaiser.

When, a year ago, it was proposed in this city by Senator Benjamin, the *New York Herald*, and others, in the reconstruction of the Union to exclude New England, a noble young Irish gentleman, now an officer in the federal army, and sure to do honor to himself and the country, replied, " Yes, you may exclude New England, but at the expense of excluding your brains." The New England mind, the New England spirit and energy, took the lead in resisting British tyranny and oppression, in creating the American nation; and it is still in New England that survives in greater purity and vigor than elsewhere, the genuine American national life. There still glows the fire that warmed the hearts of the patriots who signed the declaration of American independence, and of the sages who formed the federal constitution; and till it is extinguished there, the American nationality is not lost, and the hopes founded by the friends of humanity on American civilization may still be cherished. New England is not only the head, but the heart of America; and who knows her not, knows as little of the American nation, as he knows of Great Britain who has visited only Scotland or Ireland. Liberty, when retired from all the rest of the Union, will still find a home on her green mountains, amid her granite hills, in her smiling valleys, on her capes, and along her rivers and bays; and still shall her sons be rocked in the old family cradle preserved in her noble metropolis.

We love the whole Union, and will permit ourselves to draw no invidious comparisons between different loyal sections of the Union; but we cherish as the apple of our eye the fair fame of our own New England, to which, wherever we may pitch our tent for the night or encamp for the day, our heart fondly turns as to a mother's face; and especially do we love and honor the Old Bay State—where we first received that second birth which gives promise of heaven; where first we learned to labor for truth, virtue, and immortality; where reposes, in the hope of a glorious uprising, all that was mortal of our loved ones; and where are the scenes of our deepest grief and our sweetest joys. Men who know her not may revile her, but all real American history centres in or clusters around her. Hers was the first blood shed in the struggle to make us a nation; hers, too, has been the first blood shed in the struggle to preserve us a nation. No braver men have fallen on the field, or are now wasting out their life in southern dungeons, than the sons of Massachusetts; and though others may equal, none

will more distinguish themselves in the holy war in defence
of our glorious Union, and the rights and liberties it secures.

We hope our readers will pardon us these remarks, into
which we have been betrayed by our wish to point out the
madness in loyal men of that bitter prejudice some of our
friends think it wise and politic to excite against New England, and against all who find it difficult to reconcile themselves to the perpetual existence of slavery on this continent,
which should be sacred to liberty. There is no section of
the Union, if we speak as Catholics, from which we have
more to hope, than New England; and we place far more
reliance for the promotion of Catholic interests on the
Catholics of Boston, than on the Catholics of Baltimore.
Catholics of Boston may have less wealth, less polish, and
been less associated with the past history of the country,
than those of Baltimore; but they give more signs of life,
and live in a purer and more invigorating atmosphere, and
are likely at a much earlier day to form the union, so much
desired between our religion and the true, legitimate, un-
mistakable American order of civilization. Ecclesiastically
speaking, Baltimore is our metropolis, for its archbishop is
our primate; but in civilization, in public spirit, in American principle, American patriotism, and American thought
and energy, our metropolis is Boston, though it might be
New York.

Never did our Catholic publicists and political and social
leaders commit a greater mistake, than when they seized
the bait thrown out to catch the Spanish people, and reconcile them to the surrender of Cuba to the southern slaveholders,—that slavery and Catholicity are the only two conservative institutions in the country, and that to strengthen
the slaveholding power would be to strengthen the Catholic
Church, place the country on the side of conservatism, and
secure the salvation of souls. It was a sad mistake. In
this country, as everywhere else, the interests of Catholicity
are linked with the cause of freedom, and the proper alliance of Catholics is not with the friends of slavery, but
with those who love, respect, and are ready to die in defence
of the rights of man. In regard to civilization and the
future prosperity of our religion on this continent, an anti-
slavery Protestant is worth more than a pro-slavery Catholic. It is not from the slaveholding South that we can
hope for accessions to our church; and thus far, experience

shows our accessions are to come, if they come at all, from the free states, and first and foremost from New England and her descendants settled in other sections of the Union. Our religion can prosper in this country only as it accepts and consecrates true American civilization, and that civilization is represented by the free North, not by the slave-holding South. Hence we should resist *à outrance* every pro-slavery tendency that we discover in our Catholic community. The Catholic people are loyal in their intentions, and in their heart deeply and earnestly devoted to the Union; but in consequence of the accidental influence which Maryland has from the first exerted and still exerts, there are many amongst us who fail to perceive that the seat of true Americanism is North of Mason and Dixon's line, and by no means South of it. The present rebellion proves that, though there may still be Americanism in the slave-holding states, the predominant tendency in them is to a nationality foreign from that which formed the Union, and is represented by it. Your southern Americanism is a bastard Americanism, and it feels it, or else it would never have arisen and attempted to murder the legitimate heir. We wish our publicists, our politicians, our influential men, and we may say it, our clergy, to understand this fact, and suffer it to dictate their future policy. To attempt to unite the destiny of our religion on this continent with the inferior civilization of the South, would be manifestly against its true interest, and to provide only for its future failure and extinction. The North may be Protestant, but the South is pagan ; and Protestantism, as much as we may dislike it, is always to be preferred to paganism.

It is easy, therefore, to see why we cannot join with the writer of the article in the *Record*, in his jests and sarcasms against the anti-slavery men of the North, and why, even as a Catholic with the best interests of religion at heart, we must treat the anti-slavery sentiment in the present crisis at least, with no little tenderness and respect. We agree perfectly with the writer, that the laws recognize the master's right of property in his slaves, and that we can, as citizens of non-slaveholding states, no more interfere in the slave states themselves with his property in slaves, than with his property in horses and cattle ; but we maintain, what he seems to forget, the master by his rebellion forfeits that right, and may justly have the forfeiture enforced against him. Had he remained a loyal subject—had he not conspired against the legitimate authority of the Union and taken part in the armed rebellion against it—he might retain that property, and the federal government have no right to interfere with it. But, as the writer well knows, we have the right to deprive the rebel not only of his property in slaves, but even in his cotton, rice, and tobacco. It was, therefore, wholly unnecessary for him to construct his long and elaborate article to establish in the southern states the legality of slave property. The slaves, whether slaves of loyal men or of rebels, whether legitimately or illegitimately held, may under the war-power, be recognized as free citizens, and, under the pressure of military necessity, be called upon to assist, in any and every way that the government judges best, in defending the Union; while the slaves of rebel owners may be declared free not only under the pressure of military necessity, but as a punishment which the sovereign authority has a right to inflict upon them for their crimes, and as a warning to all future rebels. It is on this ground, and on this ground only, that we or any considerable proportion of the North, propose or ever have proposed to interfere with the master's right of property in his slaves, and to recognize the slaves as free citizens, owing allegiance to the federal government, and entitled to protection from it; while the writer himself, as we have seen, concedes that on this ground it may be done, and, at least, hints that, in his judgment, it may be necessary to be done.

But a more serious charge than that of favoring slavery has been urged against the writer, namely, that of apologizing for the slave-trade. We quote the passage from his article on which this charge is founded :—

"Africa, it is well known, is a country of savages, not having the slightest gleam of hope as to prospective civilization. We may say that, in all the southwestern section of Africa, there is no such thing known as the idea of a natural freeman. The tribes in the interior are in perpetual war, and the laws of war among them are, that a prisoner may either be executed on the spot or sold as a slave. It is but lately that the savage called king of Dahomey immolated 2,000, some say 5,000, of his prisoners, or subjects, to crimson with their blood the grave of his equally savage father. This was according to what, in the barbarian spirit of that country, was called 'THE GREAT CUSTOM.' Now, if our philanthropists of the abolition school would pay the slightest attention to the instincts and hopes of human nature, whether in Africa or elsewhere, they would easily comprehend that these two or five thousand victims would prefer slavery to decapitation. This they might understand from what goes on here continually, viz., that a poor prisoner who is condemned to death by the laws of his country, chooses invariably, if mercy should interpose, the penitentiary for life in preference to the hemp of the gallows. This is human nature, of which our abolitionists do not appear to have any adequate conception.

"Now, suppose that the savage king of Dahomey sent his subjects or prisoners to some of the factories on the coast, and sold them as slaves, would he be more guilty than if he had cut their heads off ? Suppose the slavers at the dock should buy them off at $1.25 a head from the massacre of their barbarous tyrant, would they be doing wrong ? They would only have to choose between leaving those wretches to be butchered or transporting them to some of the slave colonies of America. We, of course, believe that no genuine Christian—no decent man— would be engaged in this kind of business, still we cannot discover the crime even of the slaver in snatching them from the butcheries prepared for them in their native land. When they arrive in those colonies would it be a crime for humane masters to purchase them at a sum which prospectively might cover the annual, or semi annual, wages given to laborers in other parts of the world ? These purchasers should be bound, and if they are men of conscience they would be bound, to take care of these unfortunate people. Under the circumstances, it is very difficult to discover in the purchasers any moral transgression of the law of God or of the law of man where that traffic is authorized. The terrific part of the question is, that not only the individuals brought to the American continent or islands are themselves to be slaves, but their posterity, in like manner, for all time to come. This is the only terrific feature about American slavery. And yet it is not alien from the condition of mankind in general. Original sin has entailed upon the human race its consequences for time and eternity. And yet the men who are living now had no part in the commission of original sin. The drunkard, the thief, the bad man of any description, entails upon his posterity evils which the forfeiture of his own personal life cannot prevent or repair."

This, at first sight, looks very much like an apology for the slave-trade, for the writer not only says that he cannot discover the crime in the slaver, or that there would be any moral transgression of the law of God in the act, but even explains away the terrific part of the question that "not only the individuals brought to the American continent or islands are themselves to be slaves, but their posterity, in like manner, for all time to come," by likening it to the "consequences which original sin has entailed upon the human race," and therefore as "not alien from the condition of mankind in general." So understood, the writer has unquestionably incurred the interdict pronounced by the church, for she not only excommunicates all who are actually engaged in the traffic, as he alleges, but "absolutely prohibits and interdicts all ecclesiastics and laymen from maintaining that this traffic in blacks is permitted, under any pretext or color whatsoever; or to preach, or teach in public or in private, in any way whatever, any thing" in its favor or extenuation. To excuse the traffic under any circumstances whatever, and to attempt to lessen our horror of it by likening its consequences to those of original sin, and assuming that the men who actually engage in it are free from all actual guilt in carrying it on, is plainly to do what Gregory XVI., in the words we have cited from his bull given at Rome, the 3d of November, 1839, absolutely forbids and interdicts.

But we are far from believing that it was the intention of the writer, whether the archbishop or some one else, to approve or apologize for the infamous traffic in blacks, for he says expressly: "We of course believe that no genuine Christian, no decent man would be engaged in this kind of business." Every reader of the article will have perceived that the writer adopts a popular newspaper style, and in no respect studies to be precise or exact in his language; as is evident from his saying that "the men who are living now had no part in the commission of original sin." This he cannot be unaware, is theologically inexact; for original sin is really sin and punished as such in all men, to whom it is not remitted, with the loss of heaven, and no man can be punished for a sin of which he is not guilty, or be guilty of a sin which he has had no part in committing. The race sinned in Adam, and we all sin in the race, for we all participate in it, since the race is in us, and we in it. But what he means is, no doubt, true, that is, that we, regarded as individuals, acting as individuals in our purely individual capacity, had no part in the commission of original sin, and therefore original sin is distinguished from actual sin both in its character and in its punishment. His intention clearly was not to represent the act of the slaver as one of the consequences of original sin, for which the slaver himself would not be personally responsible, but the evil which descends upon the posterity of the slaves as the consequence of his act, as descending in like manner as the consequences of original sin descend upon the individuals of the race, and therefore that there is nothing alien in this from the condition of mankind in general, since "the drunkard, the thief, the bad man of any description, entails upon his posterity evils which the forfeiture of his own personal life cannot prevent or repair." Understood in this way, we are under no necessity of so interpreting his language as to make it a defence of a traffic which the church has condemned, and which all civilized nations regard as infamous and treat as piracy.

Newspaper writers and even essayists, who are obliged to write with haste and confine themselves to a limited space, must frequently express themselves without sufficiently guarding their language at all points from misconstruction, and should always be interpreted in a liberal spirit, according to what is their evident scope and intention, and not according to the sense which a narrow-minded and ill-natured critic might extract from their loose and unguarded expressions. An archbishop, however strongly opposed he may be to abolition movements, however fervently he may wish to reconcile us to the existence of an institution or the continuance of a traffic which he believes to be inevitable, or at least not to be suppressed without incurring greater evils and more deplorable calamities than the existence of slavery or the continuance of the slave-trade, it is not to be presumed would, in the free North, where he has perfect liberty to speak or not to speak, as he thinks, knowingly incur the censures of his church, place himself under interdict, or expose himself to excommunication and deposition by defending, apologizing, or in any way whatever justifying, or even extenuating the infamous traffic in blacks. All the presumptions are that, both as a Catholic and as a man, he agrees with his church, and regards that traffic with horror, and nothing but his most formal and express declarations should lead us to a contrary conclusion. It would be most horrible to believe that our illustrious archbishop would or could, either by himself or by his "official organ," commit so gross an outrage upon Catholic sentiment and upon the intimate convictions of the whole civilized world. We can accept no such interpretation of his language, and even if we were unable to explain it away, we would still insist that he did not and could not mean it, and should wait with our confidence in him unimpaired till he should see proper to favor us or the public with his own explanations.

The writer seems at a loss to know what would be done with the slaves if they were freed, and to fear that their emancipation would lead to a repetition of the horrors of San Domingo. In answer, we suggest, as some relief to his mind, that the horrors of San Domingo did not result from the emancipation of the slaves, but from the obstinate refusal of the slave proprietors to recognize the partial emancipation decreed by the mother country. It was not the liberation of the slaves, but the refusal of that liberation by their owners, and their severe and barbarous punishments inflicted on those who simply asked that the laws in their favor should be practically observed, that led to those terrible scenes of pillage, murder, and incendiarism which slaveholders take a savage delight in holding up as the horrors of San Domingo, to discourage all efforts by the friends of humanity in behalf of the poor down-trodden slaves of the negro race. Had the masters done their duty, had they not set an example of greater barbarity than any subsequently practised by their slaves, had they treated the slaves as men, not as wild beasts, for whom hanging, chopping to pieces, or burning was too slight a punishment, we should have heard little of the horrors of San Domingo. The real horrors of San Domingo, those which are most revolting to humanity, and indicate the greatest barbarism, were enacted not by the black slaves, but by the white and polished masters, before the slaves made their fierce and their terrible effort to free themselves.

The horrors of San Domingo read, indeed, a terrible lesson, but it is a lesson to be learned and pondered well in a contrary sense from that in which it is usually taken by our southern slaveholders and our northern apologists for slavery. Deny the slave, even the negro, all hope of being one day delivered from his bondage, and of standing up, sable though be his complexion, as a freeman, drive him to utter desperation, and you make him a tiger in ferocity, and he will rend you in pieces. That the horrors of San Domingo have not been reënacted in some of the southern states, is owing to the influence of these same northern abolitionists whom you vituperate, and to the hope they have enabled the slave to cherish in his heart that one day growing humanity, the progress of civilization, and a deeper sense of the obligations imposed by Christianity, would ultimately bring him deliverance. Beware how you extinguish that hope, and make that slave, who, after all, has a man's heart beating in his bosom, perfectly desperate. We, like others, had doubted whether the chains of the slave had not eaten into his very soul, and extinguished all manly feeling and all desire for freedom ; but a slave in a southern state set us right. He complained not of ill-treatment, of insufficient food, or of being overworked; but, to our enumeration of his advantages and the disadvantages of the free colored population at the North, showing him, as we thought, that he was better off than they, he looked us in the face, and said : " Very true, Massa, but you know a man likes to feel that he owns himself." That answer proved that he was a man and a brother, and that he had not lost all sense of the rights and dignity of manhood. It undeceived us, and corrected our error.

We may add, by way of calming the fears which the writer and many others have of the consequences of emancipation or of the repetition of the horrors of San Domingo, that it is proposed to recognize the slaves as free only in so far as they come within, or are found within, our lines, and therefore only within the power of the federal government. There is no intention of exciting them to insurrection against their masters, or of calling upon them to fight for their freedom where the federal power is not present both to protect and to govern them, and to secure them from the vengeance of their late masters, and to prevent them from doing any thing contrary to the laws of civilized warfare. The knowledge of the fact that all who come or are found within our lines are to be treated as freemen and be protected as such, as far as our government has power to do it, will speedily be conveyed to all the slaves throughout the southern states, inspire them with the hope of freedom, make them our friends, cause them to regard our advance as a deliverance, and, at the same time, alarm the confederates, and compel them to keep a large portion of their forces, many of which they would otherwise employ against our troops, at home to guard against the possibility of a servile war. Feeling that once within our lines they are free, they would hasten to come within them, bringing us most valuable information, and lending us important service as scouts and laborers, if not as soldiers. The great body of them would be practically liberated, or make any serious efforts for their own liberation, only as the federal forces advanced. Our own troops, as they advanced, would serve as a police for them, as for all others in the rebel states, and protect them as they protect all loyal citizens. In this way their liberation would seriously weaken the forces of the rebels, and vastly increase our own, and, at the same time, be effected without any of those cruelties and barbarities which usually accompany a servile insurrection or a war of liberation. In this way, too, their liberation could be effected without breaking up southern society, or preventing it from assuming its peaceful and orderly character when the rebellion shall have been suppressed, and the national flag again loved and honored throughout the whole Union.

As to what will be done with the negro population when emancipated and the rebellion is over, we would leave them where they are, subject to the same stringent police regulations as are adopted in the loyal states in the case of white men. The writer fears they will come North and compete with our northern white laborers; but his fears are idle, for they are remarkable for their local attachments, and their labor will be in greater demand at the South than at the North. They are at home at the South, can more easily support themselves there than here, and their former masters will need, as heretofore, their services both as domestics and field hands. We own that if the slave states had not rebelled and made emancipation a military necessity, we should never have proposed the immediate and unprepared emancipation of the slaves. If we could have had our way, we should have begun by converting them into *adscripti glebæ*, capable of being bought and sold only with the land; we should have secured to them all their moral rights as men and as Christians, and then, as we found them advancing, we would recognize in them the civil right to acquire, hold, and transmit property, and finally elevate them to the full civil freedom of the free peasantry of Europe, with full recognition of their moral rights and obligations as men and Christians.

But it is seldom in this world that the good we seek can be obtained without some mixture of evil, and we are at all times obliged to do not the best we would, but the best we can. The regular, gradual, peaceful emancipation of the slaves is not now practicable, and their emancipation, if it comes at all, must come at once, and be full and complete. But with proper care and honest intentions on the part of those who regard themselves as the superior race, and who certainly have had superior advantages, no great harm need be apprehended either to the blacks or to the whites by emancipation. Great social transitions always involve a certain amount of evil, but we see no reason why the negroes should not after a short time settle down into an honest, peaceful, and industrious peasantry, and the white race, now corrupted and well-nigh ruined, at least in morals, be greatly benefited, for, after all, the chief curse of slavery falls on the slave-owners and their children. The only difference that will then remain between North and South will be, that the South will employ colored laborers, and the North white laborers.

In conclusion, we would say that, while we have frankly acknowledged various points of difference between the writer and ourselves, and given our reasons for regarding the line of policy which he and the *New York Herald* so vehemently defend, as dangerous, and pretty sure, if persisted in, to ruin the country, and prove that we of the North are, as the South pretends, cravens and poltroons, if not on the battle-field, at least in our politics, we have honestly endeavored to clear the writer in the best way in our power from the fearful accusations of defending slavery and apologizing for the African slave-trade. We can well understand that a Catholic, even a Catholic archbishop, may deem it inexpedient and even wrong, under certain circumstances, and in certain times and places, to encourage abolition movements, and we ourselves always discouraged and even opposed such movements till the slave power rose in rebellion against the constitution and the integrity of the nation ; but we must believe that that Catholic has little knowledge of his religion and little reverence for his church who can defend slavery on principle, and vent his indignation and wrath against those who honestly seek to remove it. Such a man has yet to learn that Catholicity requires him to labor assiduously for the progress of civilization as a means of fulfilling the proper destiny of man ; that slavery is in its essence and in all its consequences opposed to civilization ; and that its perpetuation is the perpetuation of barbarism,—the social state directly opposed to the civilized. We could not, therefore, suffer the charge against our archbishop of being a pro-slavery man to go unrefuted.

The civilized world has—with the exception of individuals who for the sake of gain would worship his satanic majesty as God—agreed in denouncing the African slave-trade as infamous ; and the church not only excommunicates those engaged in it, but absolutely prohibits and interdicts all Catholics, ecclesiastics or laymen, from venturing to teach or to preach in public or in private any thing in its favor. She condemns as unworthy of the Christian name not merely those who reduce, or maintain that there is no wrong or crime in reducing men naturally free to slavery, as the writer would seem to imagine, but all who engage in or defend, or venture to maintain that the traffic in blacks is permitted under any pretext or color whatsoever, and without any reference to the fact that the blacks brought from Africa and sold into slavery were born naturally free or in servitude. The question whether the negroes are freemen or slaves in Africa, the writer will see, if he examines the bull of the pope, has no bearing on the lawfulness or unlawfulness of the traffic. The notion which some entertain that the church in her prohibition of the traffic, simply prohibits the reduction of men naturally free, is not correct; she prohibits the entire traffic in blacks, or, what is ordinarily understood by the African slave-trade. The writer, however carelessly or loosely he may have expressed himself, could not have intended to justify or in any sense apologize for that infamous traffic, and therefore be condemned by his church as unworthy of the Christian name. Every friend he has must be indignant at finding such a charge brought against him, and we could do no less than attempt to clear him from it.

The writer differs from us in regard to the policy of calling to our aid in suppressing this wicked rebellion the slave population of the South; and so do many others. We think them wrong, very gravely mistaken in their policy, if they are really in earnest to put down the rebellion, and save the integrity of the nation. Not otherwise do we believe it possible to save the national life, and secure a peaceful and glorious career for American civilization. But we can believe that these people are as honest in opposing as we are in advocating the liberation of the slaves, and, as far as they will engage in downright earnest to defend the Union, and crush out the rebellion, we are ready to accept them as loyal citizens, and to work heartily with them. The life of the nation is at stake, and the salvation of that is now our supreme law. We must, in the forcible language of Cromwell, "secure the *being* of the commonwealth, before proceeding to discuss its *well-being.*

THE STRUGGLE OF THE NATION FOR LIFE.

[From Brownson's Quarterly Review for January, 1862.]

MANY worthy people regard war, especially a civil war like that which is now raging in the American Union, as the greatest calamity that can befall a nation, and so great is their horror of war that they seem willing to purchase peace at any price, even by national dishonor and national degradation, yet war is rather the effect of evil than the evil itself. The real evil is in the causes that precede and lead to it. In our case it is the effort of the sound part of the nation to expel a disease long since contracted, and which was gradually but steadily approaching the seat of life, and threatening us with complete dissolution. To the eye of enlightened patriotism our condition as a people is less deplorable to-day than it was four years ago before the war broke out.

War is never lawful for its own sake, and can be rightfully undertaken only for the sake of a true and lasting peace; but, when necessary to that end, it is not only justifiable, but sacred and obligatory. It is a severe remedy for a desperate disease, what physicians call an "heroic" remedy, therefore good, but one which in certain cases must be resorted to, if recovery is not to be despaired of. Without it, we had no chance of prolonging our national life. With the slave interest in full power in nearly one half of the Union, and by its combinations ruling the councils of the nation; with Young America, reckless and destitute of principle, managing our politics at the North under the lead of Fernando Woods and New York Heralds; with the laxity of morals becoming almost universal in politics and business, in public life and private; with the growing tastes and habits of luxury and extravagance prevalent throughout the land, we were well-nigh a lost people; our destruction as a nation was, if no change came, only a question of time, and thoughtful and far-seeing men were beginning to despair of the republic. The impending ruin, in the ordinary providence of God, could be averted only by the war which has broken out, and is now raging. We deplore with all our heart the causes which made the war

211

necessary and inevitable, but we do not and cannot grieve that it has come, or lament the sacrifices it compels us to make.

War is a less calamity to a nation than the effeminate and luxurious tastes and habits generated by a long peace and its attendant exterior prosperity. It can never be so fatal to a nation as the loss of virtue, courage, manliness, and love of glory, which we had suffered during the thirty years preceding the outbreak of the present rebellion, and which renders it yet doubtful whether we have the moral qualities requisite to restore the Union, and preserve our national existence. What is the loss of blood or treasure in comparison with the loss of country or of national life? What are all the losses war can occasion in comparison with the possession of our manhood, and of those self-denying and self-sacrificing virtues which war demands and seldom fails to develop? Indeed, we look upon the war as our only means of salvation, as sent in mercy to a privileged people to enable them to be a living people, a great, heroic, and chivalric nation, fitted to receive and fulfil the holy mission of proving what is the nobility of man when and where he is free to be himself. Better to be moved by the inordinate love of glory than by the inordinate love of gain or sensual pleasure, and far nobler are the qualities of the soldier than those of the demagogue or even the shopkeeper.

Instead of sighing over the calamities of the war, its disarrangement of business, its interruption of ordinary pursuits, or its expenditures in money and in life, we should bring our minds up to the high thought that there are nobler things than these and far more worth living for. No man ever rises to the dignity of true manhood who has not hovering before him an ideal above all things of this sort, and in whom there has not been developed the power of heroic self-abnegation, and of wedding himself to a cause that transcends all the goods of time and sense, and of counting no loss, no toil, no suffering, no sacrifice in its defence or promotion. Such a cause is religion, and first on the list of those honored on earth and in heaven stand her martyrs. Next to religion, and never separable from it, is the cause of our country, and humanity honors, next to her saints, the brave and heroic soldier, next to her martyrs for the cause of God, those who nobly fall in battle for the honor, dignity, and defence of their country. The church agrees with the human race in all ages in her estimate of the soldier, and bestows peculiar privileges on those who fall in fighting for a just and sacred cause. Let not modern scepticism or mistaken philanthropy attempt to reverse the verdict of the church and of humanity. He who marches to the battle-field, and pours out his life in defence of his country is the* brother of him who marches to the stake or the scaffold, and gives his life for his faith. In both it is the heroism that the world loves and worships, the forgetfulness of self, the power of self-sacrifice, the devotion to the great, the noble, the true, the good. The heroism, in the true and nobler sense of that soul-stirring word, which the war for religion or for country generates or develops is worth more to a nation than all it costs, for, without it, no nation is really a living or an advancing nation. When a nation has ceased to produce heroes, as a religion when it has ceased to produce martyrs, it has culminated, is on its decline, falling or fallen into the dead and putrid state of Turkey, India, or China, and has no longer a work for either God or man.

If we are wise, we shall accept the present civil war as a much needed and a salutary discipline, necessary to arrest us in our downward career, and to recall us to the virtues of our heroic fathers. We shall even accept it with thankfulness, as giving us the opportunity of rivalling, and even surpassing them in glory. It gives us the opportunity to prove ourselves men, and to achieve greatness for ourselves. Our fathers won us a country, we can now prove that we are able to defend, preserve, and ennoble a country. We can now prove that the race has not degenerated in this New World, and that man here is still man in all his vigor, in all his proud daring, and in all his noble deeds. We of the free states have been taunted by the slaveholding South with being cowards and poltroons, with being ready to sacrifice honor, dignity, and glory, for the sake of trade and its profits, and poltroons in our politics we have been; we can now prove that if we have been ready to make any sacrifice, even that of honor, to prevent the dissolution of the Union, it has not been through sordidness or cowardice. Our honor, our very manhood as a free and living people are now at stake, and must be redeemed. We must wipe out the disgrace of our past concessions, our past crouching to the "Barons of the South," and prove that those concessions were not wrung from a timidity that springs from a want of manhood or from insensibility to national honor or national glory; that we have not crouched because we wanted spirit to assert, or strength to defend our own rights and dignity, but because we loved the Union, and are now ready to make any sacrifice to preserve the integrity of the nation. This we can and must now prove. We are now called upon to prove that there still lives and burns in our hearts the spirit of our fathers; that we have the old American energy and indomitable perseverance that won this continent from the savage and the forest, that forced the proud mother country to acknowledge our independence, framed the federal constitution, and made us a nation full of promise to the future of the world.

But to do this we must take the matter in earnest, and understand and feel that the war is a reality, and that it must be conducted on war, not on peace principles. The amiable speculations of our late " peace-men," and the charming sentimentalities of well-meaning philanthropists, with which we wiled away the " piping times of peace," for the want of something more amusing, interesting, or spirit-stirring, must be laid aside for the present, for we are now face to face with the stern realities of war. The real, not the mimic stage is now before us, and the actors are actors in real, not mimic life. The tragic deeds are *doing*, not merely represented before our eyes. They are real, not pasteboard soldiers that pass and repass before us, and the charge sounded is a real charge to a real battle, in which the life of a nation, perhaps the whole future of humanity, is at stake. We are not sitting at our ease in the parterre or a private box, and witnessing a theatrical battle. There is no artifice, no phantasmagoria, no painted scenery here; it is all real, sternly, terribly real. The reality itself is before us, and we must meet it with a sternness, a gravity equal to its own. It is real blood, not red paint that flows, and real life-warm blood must still flow, and flow in torrents. We must have not only the courage to be killed, but we must have for brave and generous souls the harder courage to kill,— not simply to bear, but to do harm, to strike the enemy in his tenderest part our quickest and heaviest blows. War demands not the passive virtues alone; it demands the active virtues, and is the work not of women, but of men,—of men wound up to the highest pitch of their manhood, acting in the terrible energy of their full masculine strength, and the whole directed with an invincible will to the beating down of every obstacle to its advance. There must be no dilly-dallying, no Chinese making up of faces, and trusting to painted dragons and devils, or real noise and clamor. There must be a downright, straightforward, and earnest advance, with all the death-dealing instruments of war. The war, while it lasts, is and must be inexorable. There must be no fear to strike, lest we fell a foe, no fear to fire, lest somebody should be shot. This fear or hesitancy may do when we are playing soldiers, but it is out of place now. The very design of war is, while it lasts, to inflict the greatest possible injury in the shortest possible time, and with the least possible loss to ourselves, on the enemy, in order to force him to submit, and cease resistance. When he submits, but not till then, may pity, compassion, tenderness, love be displayed, and exerted in all their divine sweetness and power.

There is no question that the people of the loyal states are not yet fully wrought up to the stern realities of war, nor fully alive to the gravity and magnitude of the struggle we are now engaged in for the existence of the nation. We are not yet fully convinced that we are in face of a real rebellion, or that the confederates are really attempting any thing more than their old practice of gambling on our love for the Union, and seeking by the game of bluff to force us to make them new and greater concessions. We half persuade ourselves that the war is only a bravado on their part, and that the controversy will be settled, as so many controversies between the North and the South have heretofore been, by some political *coup de main*, by some new "compromise bill," or, at least, by some unforeseen and lucky accident. But the day for concession and compromise has gone by. The rebel states are in earnest, and this time the wolf has really come. They demand our retirement from the family mansion, and the surrender of the family estate to their management, and that we trust to their generosity or their filial piety to dole us out the bare pittance necessary to keep soul and body together. There is no half-way measure possible. They will make the Union theirs, or they will dash it to atoms. In this there is no mistake. Their motto is, "Rule or Ruin."

Even the administration, able and patriotic as it is, we fear is deceiving itself with a specious, but illusory theory. Its theory is, that no state has seceded from the Union, and that the rebels are merely a faction in their several states, who, by a wicked and artful conspiracy, have usurped the functions of their respective state governments, and are exercising a gross and intolerable despotism over the people, who are in general loyal and devoted to the Union. The true policy, it holds, is to strengthen the people in the states where the faction has usurped the government, and to enable them through the ballot-box to recover their political ascendency. Hence while defending itself against the rebels, it must protect the people of the seceding states,—the Union people,—and avoid irritating them, or doing any thing that might drive them to make common cause with the rebels, or prevent them, when the rebellion is suppressed, from readily fraternizing with their northern brethren, and from looking upon them in any other light than that of deliverers. Hence it shows itself scrupulously tender of their feelings and prejudices, and forbears to exercise its full rights, either as a sovereign or as a belligerent, towards even the rebels themselves. It concentrates not its energies on suppressing the rebellion, and saving the life of the nation, but suffers its arm to be paralyzed by vain efforts to protect the constitutional rights of rebel states, and to provide for the well-being of the Union after the war is over.

This theory may have had some reason in its favor last February, perhaps even last March ; but it is worse than idle now. Prior to the breaking out of the war, a majority of the people of nearly all the southern states, very likely would have preferred the Union to secession, and, perhaps, had not secession been attempted, a majority of them would even yet vote against secession ; but we only show our ignorance of the seceded states, if we suppose there is a majority of the people in a single southern state, or even a respectable minority—except, perhaps, in two or three of the border slave states—that is prepared to aid in putting down the rebellion by force of arms, or that would now even give their votes in favor of the Union. We really can count on no Union party in those states, or a party worth naming that really wishes success to the federal arms. If the seceded states return to their allegiance, their government and politics will be controlled as now by the leaders and people who have made, and support the rebellion. There may grow up a Union party at the South, after the rebellion has been suppressed, but it will not find its nucleus in any Union party now existing. The old Union party in them is defunct, and *revocare defunctos* is impossible. Having declared their independence and founded a confederacy of their own, which has successfully resisted all the power of the federal government for nearly a year, state pride, interest, and even loyalty, as they understand it, naturally operate on the mass of those who would have preferred the Union should remain, and compel them now to throw in their lot with the secessionists, and the administration must treat the people of those states as substantially a united people.

As a question of *right*, no state has seceded or can secede, for no state has or can have any right to secede ; but, as a question of *fact*, eleven states have seceded, and are practically as much out of the Union as if they had never been in it.   In these eleven states the rebels are the PEOPLE, and it is worse than useless to proceed as if they were only a faction.   The rebels are, whether we like to own it or not, really rebel or revolted states, not simply individuals acting in their individual capacity.   They are practically communities or provinces in revolt, not simply individuals in rebellion.   They are the vassal at war with his suzerain.   In the technicalities of law no state has seceded, and the theory of the government is sustainable ; but as a matter of fact, the whole eleven are out of the Union, and constitute a confederated power, though as yet unacknowledged, and, God helping, never shall be acknowledged.   We must rise above legal technicalities, and look at the facts as they are.   The rebels are not simple individuals, but communities in revolt, and warring against the legitimate sovereign, and it is as such it is necessary to regard them.   The business of the sovereign is to reduce them by force of arms to their allegiance, or, if unable to do that, to recognize them as an independent foreign nation.

The federal government has the right and is bound, if in its power, to reduce them to their allegiance, let it cost what it may, or whatever havoc it may play with our theories ; but it must not flatter itself with the vain illusion that in this contest it has only a faction, or even a party, in the seceding states to deal with.   It is the people of those states who are in rebellion, and who second their leaders with a zeal and energy, a unanimity surpassing any thing we see in the loyal states in support of the Union, and submit to toils, hardships, and sacrifices to which we have not yet proved ourselves equal.   We honor the government for its respect for the technicalities and even empty formalities of law ; but we should honor it still more, if it would rise above them, and look the facts as they are full in the face.   These technicalities and formalities are wisely devised to restrain its action and limit its power in time of peace, or in the normal state of the country ; but they embarrass it, they paralyze its arm, when it has to put down a rebellion of the formidable proportions assumed by that it has now to struggle with, and the sooner it abandons them, and deals with practical realities, the more easy will it be for it to suppress the rebellion, and restore peace and constitutional liberty. The surest way of building up a Union party at the South is to put down the rebels.

So long as the government proceeds on the supposition that the seceding states are still in the Union, it is bound to treat them in their state capacity as loyal states, and to fulfil toward them all the constitutional obligations it is under to the non-seceding states.   It cannot treat them as states in revolt, but must treat them as equal and loyal members of the Union.   It must respect all their constitutional rights, all their state laws and usages, and exercise its sovereign, or even its belligerent rights, only in accordance with, or rather in subordination to them.   Assuming them to be, as states, still in the Union, it can war only against individuals, and legally let fall its blows only on those who can be proved to be personally involved in the crime of rebellion.   All others it must presume to be loyal, a hair of whose head it can touch only at its peril.   This is a serious embarrassment to the government in its work of suppressing the rebellion. It makes it afraid to strike the rebel lest it should hit a Union man, and will bankrupt the federal treasury, when the war is ended, and the Union men, who will be numerous enough then, make their demands on it for indemnification for losses incurred during the war, whether losses occasioned by federal or confederate troops.   The states having been declared not out of the Union, but loyal states in the Union, their citizens can prefer no claim of indemnity against them for damages caused by the rebels, and consequently they will have the right to claim it from the federal treasury, which will be bound to pay it.

It might have been wise in the outset to set up the theory the administration has adopted, for then public opinion was hardly up to the point of prosecuting the war on national principles.   Public opinion had been so long debauched on the subject of coercing a state, that even we ourselves thought it prudent last June, when writing our article on *The Great Rebellion*, to seek a ground on which we could defend the war without asserting the right of the federal government to coerce a state or the people of a state. But public opinion advances with the war, especially as the war assumes more and more formidable proportions; and experience already proves the inconveniences of the government theory. We are compelled by it to conduct the war on state-rights principles, and to respect and protect the constitutions, laws, and usages of the seceded states, and to enforce the federal laws in their favor, even while arming and putting forth all our military strength against them. It obliges us to respect for rebels the constitutional rights of loyal citizens, while they themselves respect no rights of the government, and seek by every means in their power to overthrow it. This is waging war at a terrible disadvantage, and imposing upon the loyal states a burden as unjust as it is intolerable. It is time, we respectfully suggest, for the government to adopt and act on the principle that the constitution exists only for the loyal, and that rebels, whether states or individuals, by their rebellion forfeit all their constitutional rights, and are placed at the mercy of the sovereign against whom they have rebelled.

The people of the loyal states must understand and feel that they are at war with the political PEOPLE of the seceding states,—so far as any such political people can now be said to exist,—acting illegally indeed, but still acting through their old state machinery, and under their old state organization and officers, not with a disorderly mob to be put down as we put down a mob or riot in one of our great cities. Such, indeed, the rebels are in strict law; but practically they are states combined and acting as a single confederated power. It is this practical aspect of the case that should govern us in our war against them. To concede this, concedes or abridges none of our rights against them as rebels; for we have got beyond the twaddle about coercing a state, and it is now understood that we have as much right to put down a rebel state as we have to put down rebel individuals. States as well as individuals may rebel, and the sovereign has the same right against the one that he has against the other.

The war on the part of the Union is defensible only on the ground that the Union is supreme, and represents the sovereign authority of the nation. If we deny that the American people are a nation, and maintain that the constitution framed by our fathers is merely a league of sovereigns, we must give up the contest, and admit the right of secession. The question whether the United States are or are not a nation represented by the federal government, is precisely the issue between the loyal and seceding states, and which the war must settle. We of the loyal states assert that we are a nation, and that the federal government, though limited in its powers by those reserved to the states so long as they remain loyal, is yet a supreme national government, and all laws and treaties made in pursuance of its constitution are "the supreme law of the land," and override all state constitutions, laws, and usages. In this national character of the federal government is founded both its right and its duty to suppress the rebellion, and the right and the duty are in no sense weakened by the fact that the rebellious party is a state or several states combined. Both the right and the duty are full and undeniable, if the federal government be, as we maintain, a true national government.

We should, for ourselves, take little interest in the war, if it were waged on any but national principles, by the national government, for national existence, and the integrity of the national territory. We support it, and make all the sacrifices in our power to sustain it, as a war for national existence, against a rebellion that seeks to dismember the Union, and destroy our national life. This is what gives to the war its terrible significance, and justifies its demand for every sacrifice needed on every man who loves his country, and would maintain national life and national integrity. We do not believe the war can, and we have no wish that it should, be successfully prosecuted on any other principles. If it does not prove us a nation, if it leaves it to be maintained that we are simply a confederacy of sovereign states, however it may terminate, it will have settled nothing, and all the old sores will remain to fester and break out anew. We should gain nothing by putting down the rebellion on state-rights principles, for the old pretension of the right of a state to secede would be strengthened rather than weakened, and we should have our old battles to fight over again.

As we look deeper into the controversy raging, we think less and less of the effort that has been made to prove that the secession ordinances of the seceding states were not the acts of the people of those states, but of a faction illegally usurping their authority. We deny not that the secession ordinances were, in some instances, perhaps in all, passed in violation of the state constitutions, and therefore are not by state law legally binding on the people of the several seceding states; but we prefer to regard that as a state question, to be settled between the citizens of the state and the authority that professes to act as the state. We prefer that the federal government should regard these ordinances, even if informal, as in fact ratified by the general acquiescence of the people, and therefore treat the rebels as rebellious states rather than as rebellious individuals. We prefer this, because it brings the controversy to a distinct issue, and the war must settle once for all the question whether we are a nation or only a confederacy of sovereign states, and establish the nationality of the government without destroying its federal character.

If we are a nation, we have the same right, we repeat, to coerce a revolted state as an individual into submission. If we have not that right, we are not a nation, and the attempt to enforce the federal authority over the people of any particular state, is, even if defensible in law, worse than useless. A Union which is only a confederacy is, in our judgment, not worth seeking to maintain; for its action will always be impeded, and its wise and salutary administration prevented, or at least embarrassed, by threats of dissolution from one section or another. We have seen it for the last thirty years. The northern states have been more attached to the Union than the southern, and more ready to make concessions for its preservation. Southern politicians and statesmen have known this, and for thirty years have gambled on it. Whenever we showed a disposition not to vote to suit them, or to persist in a policy which, though constitutional, did not happen to meet their approbation, they have resisted us with threats to nullify the acts of congress, or to dissolve the Union. They have at last attempted to carry their threats into execution; and now we wish it settled once and for ever, whether the pretended right of nullification or of secession is to be continually held up, *in terrorem*, to compel the sincere and earnest lovers of the Union to forego their rights, and stultify their own judgments. Ever since we were old enough to vote, we have voted under threats of the dissolution of the Union, if we did not vote to please the slaveholding South. We have borne this long enough. We want an end put to those threats, and to know, once for all, which is sovereign, the state or the nation. We wish, therefore, the issue distinctly made up, so that it shall be decided by the result of the war, whether we are or are not a sovereign nation, with the right of protecting itself against dismemberment or death.

Such being our view of the case, we are anxious that this war should be conducted on strictly national principles, against insurgent states, as well as against insurgent individuals. So conducted, the success of the federal arms will settle the question for ever, and put an end once for all to the threats of dissolving the Union. It will also relieve the administration from numerous embarrassments occasioned by the rights of real or pretended Union men, and the necessity of protecting the constitutional rights of states, practically in revolt. It will much simplify the contest; for it at once, as against the Union, abrogates all constitutions, laws, and usages, in the case of such states, and reverts their citizens to their state government for redress in case of rebel injuries. It would also enable the administration with less seeming impropriety to treat the rebels as belligerents, which they in fact are, and to arrange for a mutual exchange of prisoners according to the usages of civilized warfare. Such exchanges would affect none of our rights toward the rebels that we shall ever seriously insist on exercising. All engaged in the war are rebels and traitors, but nobody supposes that, if the government triumph, and the rebels submit, there will be any executions for treason of persons taken in arms. They will be treated as prisoners of war, and released when peace is made. We should have to depopulate the seceding states if we proposed to shoot or hang all secessionists. We expect the men now in war against us, if beaten, will return to their duty as American citizens. Instead, then, of standing upon a technicality unworthy of a great and strong power, and especially instead of going through the empty formalities of swearing and then releasing them, it would be much better to exchange the confederate soldiers that fall into our hands, for our own who have the misfortune to fall into the hands of the rebel authorities. It will prejudice no right that we need insist on, and will present no obstacle to a final settlement.

But while we are willing to accord the rebels in certain respects the rights of belligerents, we insist that the war shall be prosecuted on war principles, and that we avail ourselves of all the advantages allowed by civilized warfare. We insist that, while we observe toward the defenceless, or those who have ceased to resist, the tenderness and compassion of Christians, we shall conduct the war as a war against public enemies, not against friends, and inflict, till they submit, the surest damage in our power on the revolted states and their supporters.

Parcere subjectis, et debellare superbos.

We must understand that to-day our business is *debellare superbos;* to-morrow it may be *parcere subjectis;* but to-morrow will take care of itself. We need not fear that, if we bring home to the revolted states all the horrors of war, we shall make them one whit more hostile to us than they now are, or more difficult to be reconciled to the Union after the war is over.

We wish the people of the loyal states to understand well that the people of the disloyal states will regard any show of forbearance, tenderness, or magnanimity on our part only as weakness, tameness, or fear of losing them for ever as our customers. These things are thrown away upon them, and injure instead of serving the cause of the Union and reconciliation. The South will never believe in our sincerity and magnanimity till we have given them a sound drubbing, and proved ourselves the better men. Then they will respect us, and consent to live in peace and brotherhood with us. They take every advantage of us, and we must take every advantage of them, and force them by the damage we do them into submission. Nothing else remains for us. They will not submit unless forced to submit; but when forced into submission and fully convinced that further resistance is vain, they will, we doubt not, with far less difficulty than many imagine, become reconciled to national union with us. They have great respect for power, and worship force as a god. With them, as with all men in their stage of civilization, perhaps even in ours, the stronger is the better man, and to real superiority they will deem it no dishonor to yield.

If the contest end favorably to us, as it certainly will, unless we throw away our advantages, we shall lag behind no one in our efforts to make the terms of reconciliation easy; but we urge now the prosecution of the war with all of war's severity, and with all the energy of a free government and a brave and heroic people. Especially do we protest against any compromise. If we are beaten, as we may be, for the race is not always to the swift, nor the battle to the strong, we will submit to the victor, and take what comes.

But we insist on preserving our dignity as men, our honor as states, and fall, if fall we must, with our principles. Let no man dare breathe the word " compromise." The day for compromise has gone by. The man, be he president, or secretary, or senator, or general, who shall propose and effect a compromise, will stand branded in history as an infamous traitor to his country and to humanity. The rights of this nation we hold as a sacred trust from our fathers to be transmitted inviolate to posterity. We have no right to barter them away, or by our cowardice and want of manhood to suffer them to be wrested from us. Private wrongs we may compromise or forgive, but not wrongs to our country.

While we write, the president's annual message to both houses of congress reaches us, and we read it with eagerness. We cannot say much in its favor, and it does not comport with our duty to the chief magistrate of the Union in the present critical juncture of our national affairs to say much against it. Mr. Lincoln, in part, for the moment, represents the nation, and we cannot well stand by the nation without standing by him; certainly not, till it is clear that he is, through incompetency or some other reason, on the eve of betraying it. We believe him patriotic, conscientious, and anxious to do the best for the country in his power, and, although we regard his policy as far less bold and determined than that the danger that threatens us demands, we remember that he is placed by his countrymen in a position which for him is and must be one of great embarrassment,—of great difficulty and delicacy, and we are disposed to give to all his words and actions the best possible construction, and to make the most liberal allowance for what may seem to us low, narrow, defective, or tame in his mode of conducting the war for the preservation of our national existence. We are loyal to the nation, and will be loyal to the administration, so long as it shall be loyal to itself.

The message is comparatively short, and, though it can lay claim to no grammatical purity, or literary elegance, it is a plain, sensible, business-like document, not much above, nor much below what we expected. We believe the president is disposed to save the Union, but, in our judgment, he has no adequate conception of the conditions on which, and on which alone, it can be done. He is timid where we should wish him to be fearless, and fearless where we should be willing he should be timid. He is bold enough before loyal men, timid almost to shrinking before disloyal men. He is afraid to touch with his little finger the "divine" institution of slavery; but has no fear of sacrificing any number of freemen and any amount of national treasure, to prevent a hair of its head from being singed. He would seem to regard it as a more imperative duty to keep the border slave states nominally in the Union, than to suppress the armed rebellion against it. We fear that he has not emancipated himself from the old slavery domination, or risen above the old notion that the government must be administered in the exclusive interest and according to the wishes of southern slaveholders. The rights and interests of millions of freemen he apparently counts for nothing in comparison with the duty of protecting the doubtful rights of slavery. This is sad, and, if persisted in, will render all the efforts and sacrifices we have made, or are making to save the Union, worse than pure loss.

We tell the president, and we desire to do so with all possible respect, that even the restoration of the Union on a policy shaped expressly to conciliate "Ole Kentuc'," or the slaveholding interest of any of the border states, would now, if possible, not be worth effecting. Why was he elected to the presidency? Why have we of the loyal states placed him in his present elevated position? No man better than himself knows, that we voted for him, at the risk of civil war and the dissolution of the Union, because we were determined that the slave interest should no longer shape the policy and govern the councils of the nation. It was this determination on the part of the freemen of the East, the North, and the West that took Mr. Lincoln from his lawoffice, and made him president. He was not elected to preserve slavery, nor to abolish slavery; but he was elected to emancipate the administration and the republic itself from the domination of the slave interest; and we protest, therefore, in the name of those who elected him, against the perpetuation of that domination, even though confined to the slave interest of Maryland, Kentucky, and Missouri. Slavery may or may not continue to exist, but we insist that the government shall cease to be administered in its interest, or under its dictation. The government must be administered in the interest of freedom and loyalty. If not, better yield to the secessionists at once, and take Jefferson Davis for our president. We will not pour out our blood and our treasure, we will not send the flower of our youth and the glory of our manhood to rot in camp, die on the battle-field, or languish in southern dungeons, for the sake of bringing the Union again under the domination of southern slaveholders, and of exposing ourselves to be again insulted and bullied, or cheated out of our rights and our manhood by the Davises, the Toombses, the Hammonds, the Masons, and the Slidells. We have resolved that our government shall be emancipated, whatever becomes of slavery and its worshippers. This is what we beg the administration to bear in mind. We should be glad to believe that the president has not forgotten it, and that he is prepared to assert his own independence of the slave power, and that of the government, for we tell him never will there, and never can there, be a reunion of the separated states under the domination of the slave interest.

We have no concessions to make to Kentucky, or to any other border slave state. The slaveholders have rebelled against the Union, and by so doing have absolved the Union from all obligations to protect slavery in either loyal or disloyal states. If Kentucky, the native state of the president, will not remain in the Union, unless permitted to dictate its policy, and make her slave interest its law, then let her be treated as a rebel state, and coerced as we are coercing the other rebel states into loyalty. We will no more consent to allow Kentucky than South Carolina or Georgia to impose her slave policy upon the government. We of the free states intend to assert and maintain our own freedom, our own rights and dignity, and to be something else hereafter in the government of the country than the mere lackeys of southern slaveholders. We are fighting to vindicate our own rights, and our government must recollect that in this contest it is bound to take our rights, the rights of freemen, into the account. We wish the administration to consider that we of the free states have accepted the issue tendered us, and that we will spend our last dollar and our last life before we will suffer this Union to be sacrificed in the vain endeavor to preserve the infamous institution of negro slavery ; and before the slave interest shall ever again shape the policy of the government, or dominate in its councils. If Mr. Lincoln has not learned this yet, he will, perhaps, learn it before the close of the present session of congress. We have been in bondage to the capital invested in slavery long enough ; we have long enough cowered and crouched under the lash of slaveholding dictators, afraid even to say our souls are our own, lest we should endanger the peace and safety of the Union. We will do it no longer. By the memory of our fathers who fought at Bunker Hill, Saratoga, Monmouth, Yorktown, whose blood yet courses in our veins, we have sworn we will not.   Timid, weak, narrow-minded, pettifogging politicians may quake at these words, or shrink from them as meaning something, but their day is gone.   There is a spirit rising in the free states, that does not believe in "the divinity of slavery," or that all other interests must be sacrificed to it; and, what is more to the purpose, that *does* believe in free-dom, that it is right, is law, and before it slavery must and shall give way.   Events march, as we said three months ago, and they are marching with fearful rapidity.   We are all carried along with them.   To many of us what six months ago seemed the extreme of rashness now appears timid, tame, and cowardly.   The government, if it would guide events, must march with them.   The president, we perceive, marches, slowly indeed; but, nevertheless, he marches, and his message proves that he is at least some steps in advance of where he was at the close of the extra session of congress. He will probably march at a more rapid pace by and by, and perhaps catch up with public opinion.

We do not want the war waged or prosecuted for the abolition of slavery; but we do insist that it shall not be waged or prosecuted for the protection of slavery, and its reinstatement in power.   Slavery has rebelled, and let it pay the forfeit.   We have no confidence in the wisdom, we had almost said in the loyalty, of the statesmen who insist that the government has any further obligation toward it now, than to brush it aside, if found in its way.   We do not sup-pose the president is any more favorable to slavery than we are, but we do fear that he does not perceive that he is un-der no obligation to protect it, and that with less assump-tion of extraordinary power than he has assumed in arrest-ing and incarcerating persons suspected of disloyalty with-out form of law, or bringing them to a speedy trial, a power we do not deny him, he might treat the relation of master and slave as *non avenue*, and declare the slaves free men.   Why can he not be as bold against slavery as against freedom?   Let him go as far in the slavery question as he has gone in many others, and he will satisfy the loyal people who are now in arms to save the life of the nation.   Let him make an end of the "Eternal Nigger," and feel, think, and act as the chief magistrate of a free people, and we shall be content, and not only support him as our chief magis-trate, but do so with cheerfulness and alacrity, with confi-dence and hope that our sacrifices will not be in vain.

STATE REBELLION, STATE SUICIDE.

[From Brownson's Quarterly Review for April, 1862.]

OUR highly esteemed friend of the *Pittsburg Catholic*, the ablest and most loyal Catholic journal at this time published in our country, takes care to tell us that, in his judgment, it is unwise to agitate the slavery question, and that in the present crisis of our national affairs only harm can come of discussing it. He will pardon us, we hope, if we tell him, in return, that we think it both wise and useful for every man who loves his country to agitate that question, and thoroughly discuss it. Slavery has produced our present national crisis. The rebellion itself is at bottom only the armed phase of the slavery question, and to suppose it possible to suppress and extinguish it without touching the question, would be like attempting to cure a man of drunkenness without touching the question of temperance. Slavery is now the question, the great question, the whole question before the American public, and it depends on the disposition we make of that question whether we are or are not to continue to be a nation. We cannot blink it, if we would. It enters vitally into the struggle of the nation for life, and we must dispose of it, so that it can never again come up, or all our efforts will be idle, and all our sacrifices of men and money will be worse than lost.

The southern confederacy, against which the United States are now hurling their armed forces, rests on slavery as its corner-stone, and derives from it its very reason of existence. Grant, if you insist upon it, that the sole object of that illegal and dangerous confederacy is not the preservation or extension of slavery, still the objects of that confederacy, the ends for which it has been formed, demand the continuance of slavery. The preservation and extension of slavery may not be the end the rebels have in view, but slavery is the indispensable means to that end. They would not seek to form a separate and independent republic, if it were to be a republic based on the free-labor system, for they are not such fools as not to know that such a republic would have fewer advantages than the present United States— could never be so strong, never command so high a place in the world's estimation or in the world's history. The whole is, and always must be greater than a part, and a man of real ambition would always say, with the old Athenian, "I would rather be second in Athens than first in Euboea." Even supposing, then, that the rebels had not originally, or that they have abandoned the intention of reconstructing the whole Union on the basis of the slave-labor system, they must still preserve that system as the necessary condition of the separate existence, and of the greatness and power they hope to attain to as an independent people. The abolition of slavery would take away all motive, all reason, and all desire for a separation from the Union. Being unable without slavery to attain to the objects they contemplate as a separate and independent political existence, they would naturally desire to remain in the United States, and share the greatness and glory of one united republic.

The productions on which the seceded states rely as the means of securing to them the hegemony of the commercial nations of the world they would aspire to, they believe, demand the system of slave labor. "The only reason for desiring slavery," said to us an eminent physician of Charleston, and himself the owner of a hundred slaves, "is that in the management of large plantations the planter must be able to command labor when he wants it, and to be always able to do this, he must own it. Aside from this consideration, slave labor is less economical than free labor. Its advantage over hired labor, or your northern system of labor, is in the fact that the planter can command it at the very moment he needs it. If he depends on hired labor, he is likely to find his hands striking at the critical moment, and compelling him either to lose the proper time for planting or for gathering his crops and preparing them for market, or to pay them wages that would swallow up all his profits, and end in his ruin. What is said about the inability of the white man to perform the labor now performed by negroes is worthy of no attention. There is no climate, there is no position in which you can place the negro and the white man side by side, in which the white man will not kill the negro. Negroes are preferred, not because they are hardier or more enduring than white laborers, even in our climate ; but because they can be kept in slavery, and men of the white race cannot. I know no other argument for negro slavery." Now, as the rebels rely principally on their plantations, on growing and exporting cotton, rice, and tobacco, for their greatness and prosperity, it is clear that, in their view at least, slavery is essential to the end they have in view. Free the negroes, and they are deprived of the means to the end for which they have rebelled, and have formed their confederacy.

It is, we suppose, the object of the United States in the present civil war to break up the southern confederacy, to put down, and utterly extinguish the present rebellion, and, as far as human foresight and human ability can go, to guard against any like rebellion in future. The aim of every nation should be, first of all, self-preservation, or the maintenance of its own existence and the integrity of its territory. Our nation can do this only by rendering universal either the slave system or the free-labor system, legalizing slavery everywhere in the land or permitting it nowhere. Were we to beat, as we are beating, the armies of the confederacy, and crush its present military power, we should, so long as slavery occupied its former position, at best gain only a truce for some few years, no solid or durable peace. The embers of the rebellion would still slumber, ready to break out, and burn afresh on the first opportunity. The slaveholding interest might consent again to govern and use the Union for its own ends, but it would not be extinguished, and would break out in a still more formidable rebellion, and again convulse the nation, the moment that the interest of free labor should show itself able and determined to assert its own rights and legitimacy.

It is useless to multiply words about it. There can be no permanent Union of freedom with slavery, no national unity and integrity with slavery in one half of the states and freedom in the other half. We have tried the experiment for the best half of a century, and it has failed, utterly failed. Freedom has made all conceivable sacrifices to slavery. Compromise after compromise has been consented to. We have suppressed the utterance of our noblest convictions, done all that we could to stifle the irrepressible instincts of humanity, lest by some word or deed we might endanger the safety of the Union, and the result has been contempt on the part of the South for the Union-saving North, and the present rebellion. A new trial of the experiment can succeed no better, for the people of the loyal states, if they would retain the slightest approach to self-respect, cannot possibly make greater concessions, or do more than they have already done to render practicable and permanent that union.   The experiment has failed, as fail it always will and always must.   It is not constitutional government, it is not republicanism, as some of our European friends pretend, that has failed ; but the attempted union of freedom and slavery, of two essentially hostile and mutually repellent systems in the same state.

We cannot, then, we repeat, blink the question of slavery, if we would.   It meets us on the very threshold of the controversy in which the nation is now engaged, and they who petition congress to put down the rebellion and let the negro question alone, and they who imagine that the present rebellion can be suppressed and extinguished without disposing of the slavery question at once and for ever, only show, if not their lack of loyalty, that they have thus far comprehended simply nothing of the terrible question which now involves the life or death of the nation.   The advertisement of some players, that they would present on the stage on a given evening Shakespeare's *Hamlet*, with the part of the prince of Denmark left out by particular request, has long been referred to as a capital joke ; but the joke is not half so capital as that of those worthy people who in the discussion of our present national affairs leave out, by particular request, the slave question.   Why, the slavery question is the whole question, that without which there never would or could have been any question at all. To refuse to agitate the question of slavery is simply to refuse to agitate any question at all really important in the present crisis.   The whole question of extinguishing the rebellion, of restoring the unity and integrity of the nation, and of sustaining our national life and securing future glory, turns on the slave question.   You may, as we have said, beat the rebel armies ; you may gain victories by sea and by land ; you may even gain an armistice or a truce ; but to suppose that you can reëstablish peace and be really a nation, unless you go further and remove the cause and mainspring of the rebellion, is sheer folly, absolute fatuity.   The old union of freedom with slavery under one and the same constitutional government has failed.   Slavery, not freedom, has broken it, we would fain hope for ever.   You cannot restore it, if you would, and you should not, if you could. No man is worthy of the name of statesman, who does not assume this as a fixed fact, and take it as his starting-point in all discussions having reference to our present difficulties and their final settlement.   The slave interest, treated with the utmost tenderness, and allowed to have its own way in almost every thing from the very origin of the government, has declared its secession from the Union. It has declared its secession and separation final and irrevocable. It is for freedom to take it at its word. For ourselves, we accept the declaration, and insist that it shall be final and irrevocable. We never loved that Union, but as it had been consented to by the framers of our constitution, we have always felt it our duty to avoid doing any thing to endanger it. The dissolution has been by no act of ours, and by no act of the United States. It has been effected by the act of slavery itself, and since slavery has seen proper to secede, and to declare that it will have no further connection with freedom, we are not sorry, and are resolved on our part also, that they shall never again be united, or their union find a place in the republic.

We have no patience with those politicians, demagogues and pettifoggers, who labor to restore the old Union of slavery and freedom, who believe, or profess to believe, in the possibility of its restoration, and who try to persuade us that on that union depend the future greatness and glory of the republic. The slave interest had always the right to secede from the Union, if it chose, and in this sense we recognize the alleged right of secession; for the United States never made slaveholding obligatory on any particular state, or on any of their citizens. The slave interest had always the right, if it chose, to go out of the Union, to cease to be an interest in or of the nation. It had the perfect right of self-destruction. But having gone out of the Union, and ceased to be an interest in the Union, we deny the obligation of the United States to force it back, or even to permit its voluntary return. It has gone out, and we say, let it stay out. But the right of slavery to secede by no means involves the right of the slaveholding states themselves to secede. Slavery might secede, but it could not carry with it any portion of the national territory, the national property, or the national population, and as the slave has no rights and no property of his own, it could carry no rights and no property with it. Its secession, therefore, leaves to the United States all the territory previously occupied by it, and the plenary right of sovereignty over that territory and the population occupying it. The secession could only dissolve the union between slavery and freedom, it could not abrogate the rights of freedom. It, by seceding, necessarily left to freedom the whole national territory, none of which could ever rightly again become slave territory. Rightly and legally considered, the question of slavery in the seceding states is not, whether it shall or shall not be abolished, but whether it shall or shall not be reëstablished. By the act of secession slavery has no longer a legal *status* in what was the territory of the seceding states, and the population held to service are free, because there is now no law in that territory by which they can be so held. What we demand is, not an act of the government abolishing slavery, but a refusal on the part of the United States to allow the success of their arms over the rebels to be used to reestablish it, or to remand to slavery a population made free by the secession of their masters. Here is the position of the slave question to-day,—a position far in advance of its position yesterday.

While the slave interest, or the interest created by slavery, held fast to the unnatural union of slavery and freedom, and was loyal to the federal authorities, we opposed all efforts for emancipation by the national government, and threw on the slave states themselves the whole responsibility of the infamous system they sustained. We, as citizens of the non-slaveholding states, washed our hands of that system, for we had no rights over it, and were responsible neither for its adoption, nor its continuance. The case is now altered. The slave-owners by their rebellion have unquestionably forfeited their right under the federal constitution to be protected in their slave property, or as to that matter, in any other species of property. If slavery be ever again recognized as legal, therefore, the responsibility will attach not to slave states only, but to the whole people of the United States, and we of the free states will become, clearly and decidedly, *participes criminis.* Here is a very grave consideration for those who insist on letting the slave question alone. If we of the free states suffer the negroes in the seceding states to be remanded to slavery, the crime and the sin will not be the crime and sin of particular states, but of the nation itself, and of the free states no less than of the slave states themselves.

Our readers are aware that we have from the outset maintained that the rebel by his rebellion forfeits his right to property, liberty, and even life, and that states by rebellion are dissolved, or cease to have any laws or usages that anybody is bound to respect. We hold with Mr. Sumner in his noble resolutions, creditable alike to him as a statesman and a lawyer, that the state by rebellion commits suicide, and lapses as a civil and political entity. All laws, customs, and usages depending for their vitality, force, or vigor on the state, are rendered null and void by its secession, and are to be treated as *non avenus.* Slavery exists in any country only by municipal law, in no country by the *jus gentium.* In our political system it exists by the local law, or by the law or usage of a particular state, in distinction from a law or usage of the United States. Even Chief Justice Taney, in his opinion in the Dred-Scott case, does not pretend that slavery exists by virtue of the law of the United States, though he maintains that it has the right to exist wherever it is not forbidden by local law, assuming, it would seem, that it exists by virtue of the law of nature. But as his opinion was a mere *obiter dictum,* we venture to maintain, with a previous opinion of the supreme court, with the decisions of the English courts, with the general principles of law, and with common sense, that slavery being a violation of man's natural liberty, can exist only by municipal law, and in our country only by the law or usage of a particular state. Consequently it lapses when the state itself lapses. The state by the act of rebellion lapses, and consequently the rebellion of the state abrogates the only law by which negroes are held to service, either to persons loyal or to persons disloyal to the federal government; for the federal government never guarantied to any man property in slaves after it had ceased to be property by state law. Any state may abolish slavery within its limits. Should a loyal state even see proper to emancipate its slaves without any indemnification to the owners, the owners have no claim of indemnity against the United States. Their remedy should be only against their own state.

That a state in its state capacity can, under our system, rebel, admits of no doubt, if we concede it to be, though in a subordinate sphere, a civil and political entity, or a civil and political person. It is, if a person, capable of state action, and when as a state it resists the legitimate authority of the general government, and arms its citizens against it, it rebels. If we deny the autonomy of the state, deny that it is a civil and political person, that is, in the sense a corporation is called a person, we eliminate the federal element of our political system, and make our republic not a federal, but a consolidated or centralized republic. If we take this ground, slavery nowhere on our territory has any legal existence. For it is evident there is no law of the national government authorizing it. Taking the other ground, a state can rebel, and its rebellion is and must be its dissolution as a state. It ceases from the moment of its rebellion to have any legal existence. Consequently all that depends on its existence for vitality ceases to live, and nothing lives except the natural law, and the constitution and laws of the United States ; but as no one has under either of them any title to slaves, slavery necessarily lapses with the state authorizing it.

That this doctrine reaches far we do not deny, we maintain that under our system a state may rebel, and that the rebellion of a state, *ipso facto*, dissolves it as civil and political society, and consequently vacates all rights and remedies created or afforded by it. There remains after its rebellion no state law in force. Its rebellion vacates all titles held under it, dissolves all contracts, and annihilates all property created by it, and takes away all civil protection for even natural rights, save so far as that protection is given by the federal government. It abrogates all civil laws respecting marriage, all laws authorizing the transferring, devising, transmitting, or inheriting property, for these under our system are all left to the state government. The courts of law are all dissolved, and the remedies afforded by them can no longer be enforced. The rebellion, in a word, kills the whole state, and every thing dependent on it. Whether the state be revived and permitted to return to the Union depends entirely on the good pleasure of the federal authority. It cannot be claimed as a right by the population of the territory of the defunct state. As they could not take the territory out of the Union, and as they, so long as they remain on it, are within the jurisdiction of the United States, the federal government has authority to govern them, either as a territory or as a conquered province.

We trust the time will come when the defunct states will be revived, or, more strictly speaking, new states be formed with the old names and boundaries, and admitted into the Union on terms of perfect equality, although this ought not to be done till the rebels have unconditionally surrendered. When they have unconditionally surrendered, and thrown themselves on the mercy of the federal government, the United States will, no doubt, after having compelled rebel property to pay the expenses of the war, permit the people to reorganize themselves into states, and confirm all who give evidence of loyal intentions, in their former civil and political rights. It will not restore, for it has no constitutional right to restore, the relation of master and slave. It cannot deprive freemen of their liberty, except for crime. The negroes having been freed by the rebellion of the states whose laws authorized them to be held as slaves, are henceforth freemen, and the federal government must protect and govern them as freemen.

Undoubtedly there is something severe in treating the rebellion of a state as state suicide; but we have yet to learn that the way of rebellion ought to be graded, macadamized, and made easy. We see no wisdom or humanity in leaving a state free to rebel, convulse the nation, create a fearful civil war, with all its sacrifices of men and money, and be free to resume its former *status* the moment it ceases fighting, because fighting ceases to be of any avail. No government that has any self-respect, any consciousness of its rights and duties, any regard for justice or the public weal, can ever allow rebellion such impunity. It will make, as it ought to make, the way of the political transgressor hard. We must not forget that the states forming the southern confederacy have no legal existence and no legal authority to make war or peace. Every soldier in the national army killed in battle by their soldiers is murdered, just as much murdered as I should be, were a robber to break into my house, and kill me while defending the inviolability of my dwelling and my property. We say not that every secession soldier who kills a national soldier in battle is a murderer *in foro conscientiæ*, but we do say the killing of such a soldier is a murder. All our brave soldiers, officers or privates, who have fallen in this civil war have been murdered, barbarously, treacherously murdered; and every man who voluntarily and knowing what he is about, has entered into the rebellion, originated, fostered, or in any way aided and abetted it, is answerable, either as principal or accessory, for their murder, and for murdering them while in the discharge of their highest and most solemn duties to their country. This is undeniable; for they act without warrant of law, and deliberate killing without warrant of law is murder, and murder in the first degree. We hope we shall not be regarded as a moral monster, if we have the harshness to say that we are not willing to pass lightly over the treacherous murder of so many fathers, husbands, sons, and brothers, guilty of no offence but that of rushing at the call of their country to the defence of law, the rights of authority, and the integrity of the nation, against traitors and rebels.

We know very well what the constitution says with regard to the punishment of treason, and also what is the law of congress on the subject; but neither the special clause in the constitution limiting the penalty of treason, nor the special statute of congress, governs the present case. A rebellion, when it rises to certain proportions, and assumes the character of a civil war, is never regarded or expected to be treated as a case of ordinary treason, which can be put down by the civil authority. Besides, the constitution and the law relate only to individual traitors, not to treason committed by a state. The rebellion of a state must be treated according to its natural and legal effects. The court in recognizing those effects to be as we have stated, violates no clause of the constitution and no law of congress. The court deprives no man of his property beyond the term of his natural life, for he has been deprived of all property which it refuses to recognize as his, by the rebellion of his state. In recognizing the suicide of the state, and leaving its citizens to the consequences of that suicide, it does not confiscate the traitor's property; it only refuses to restore to him or his children property which had lapsed by the action of his state, before the national authority took possession of it. The law makes the punishment of treason death. The principle of that law is not violated, but conformed to, by treating the rebellion of a state as state suicide. The deceased state leaves no heir, and the nation in assuming and administering its effects, preserves at least the principle of the law. All lapses to the Union, because under our system a state can have no other successor. Individuals can hold henceforth property once held under its authority only by a law of congress confirming their titles, or under patents granted by the United States. By the lapse of the state, the whole property held under its authority becomes vested in the United States, the only successor of the state. This, we apprehend, is the law in the case, and severe as it is, it inflicts no severer penalty than state treason deserves.

No doubt, the property will, in the case of loyal persons, be confirmed to the former owners, as, to some extent, will be their former property to rebels, after they have given evidence that for the future they will demean themselves as peaceable and loyal citizens. The government will be bound by justice, and the people of the loyal states will require it, to reorganize civil society in the seceded states at the earliest practicable moment, and with as little change in former possessions and social relations as a due regard for the whole people of the Union will admit. The constitution has been violated by the rebels, but nothing we demand or recommend is any violation of that sacred instrument by the federal authorities. All its provisions will remain intact, and it will be, as before, the constitution of the country.

The great danger, now to be guarded against, does not come from the avowed rebels. At the moment we are writing, our victorious armies have penetrated into Tennessee, and taken possession of its capital, and already we hear that a new state government is soon to be elected, and Tennessee is to have her full representation in both houses of congress. The press recommends to the government, that as fast as a state is reconquered, it shall recognize it as loyal, allow it to elect its state and federal officers, and resume its place in the Union. Whether the government will adopt such a policy or not, we know not, for we are not its organ, and are not in its secrets. We hope it will not, for such a policy is, in our judgment, under present circumstances, the shallowest, the maddest, and the most suicidal policy that can be proposed. That such a policy should have been entertained in the beginning of the struggle, can be excused. There was then much to be said in its favor. The administration did not know its own strength, and could not tell how far it could count on the patriotism of the people. It knew there was a strong southern and pro-slavery party in the free states, and it had reason to fear that it would prove a disunion party, and make common cause with the rebels. Besides, it was supposed that there was a strong Union party in the seceding states, whom it was necessary to secure, and who must at any cost be prevented from being irritated and estranged from the national cause. The restoration of the *status quo*, or the suppression of the rebellion without affecting the *status* of persons held prior to the rebellion to service, was all that was generally contemplated, or that, except by the very boldest, it was thought prudent to contemplate. Everybody disclaimed all intention of subjugating the rebellious states, and nearly all were prepared to allow them to return to their allegiance, and to resume their former position in the Union, very much on their own terms. But we are not where we were when President Lincoln issued his first proclamation; we are not where we were even three months ago. Events have marched, and men have marched with them. The policy which might have been prudent in the beginning, would now be a shameful surrender. We are now in a position to enforce the law in the case, and to make the rebels pay the just penalty of their treason and rebellion, and to teach state treason a lesson it will never forget.

But precisely now comes our danger, and never at any moment since the secession of South Carolina has the danger to the republic been greater or more imminent. The old pro-slavery party at the North, aided by the border states nominally in the Union, but in the Union only through fear of our battalions, rears its head, and threatens to render all our sacrifices useless, and all our victories abortive. This party is all the more dangerous, because it professedly adopts what was in the outset apparently the policy of the administration itself, and claims to approve and sustain the executive policy—a policy, the useless and dangerous character of which was first thoroughly exposed by Mr. Conway, of Kansas, in his remarkable speech in the house of representatives on the 12th of last December. Let Tennessee and one or two more of the rebellious states, or even Tennessee alone, be represented, and this party has regained its majority in congress, and the whole nation is brought again under the domination of the slave interest, represented now principally by the border states, nominally loyal, but really disloyal. Here is the danger, which will only be increased by any addition to the representation in congress of the so-called Union men in the seceding states.

We would not be unjust to the border states, but we say frankly we have no confidence in their loyalty. It is "neither fish, flesh, nor fowl, nor yet good red herring." It is the loyalty of neutrality, like that of the affectionate wife in the battle between her husband and the bear, "Fight, husband; fight, bear; I am neutral." Missouri was for neutrality, and three times we have had to conquer her secessionists; Kentucky was neutral, that is to say, against the Union; and Maryland would have openly seceded but for the presence of the federal troops and the timely arrest and imprisonment of a part of her legislature. Both Missouri and Kentucky are represented in the rebel congress, and no doubt would have openly seceded with Virginia and Tennessee, if it had not been for the proximity of the great Northwest and a secret conviction that they would serve the cause of rebellion more effectually in the Union than out of it, or by pretended neutrality than by avowedly taking sides with the rebels. To these may be added western Virginia, treated as the old state of Virginia, and allowed her representation in congress. There are, no doubt, in the border states nominally within the Union, as well as in the seceded states themselves, individuals who are unsurpassed by any in any section, for their loyalty to the Union ; individuals whom we love and honor, and in whose patriotism we would confide as unreservedly as in our own. But in general, the Union men in all the border states, as in the seceded states, are tainted with the heresy of state sovereignty, and are willing to remain in the Union only on condition of dictating its policy, and placing it under the domination of the slave interest. Kentucky never voted to sustain the Union or to discharge her duty to the Union, till the president had modified General Fremont's proclamation, freeing the slaves of rebels, and her prominent men had received assurances that the triumph of the national cause should work no detriment to the " divine and sacred institution " of negro slavery. Protect slavery, and she will be loyal; leave slavery to follow the surcease of the states that authorized it, and she will go over to the enemy. Such is her loyalty, a conditional loyalty, which we treat as disloyalty, and despise more than open treason and rebellion.

Western Virginia has demonstrated the impolicy of treating the professed Union men of a seceded state, as a state, and allowing them a congressional representation. This policy is unjustifiable, and in adopting it, the government sanctions a more fatal revolutionary principle than that asserted by the rebellion we are seeking to suppress and extinguish. Mr. Pierrepont may be a very worthy and respectable gentleman, but who thinks of him as the governor of Virginia, and what court of law would recognize as the acts of Virginia the acts of the pretended government at Wheeling ? The recognition of that government of conditional and revolutionary loyalty by the administration, was worse than a fault, it was a blunder ; and it will not do to repeat it. The administration might have taken, and should have taken military possession of the loyal counties of the Old Dominion, and congress might have provided for their government as a territory. But to recognize them as the state of Virginia, and give them the representation of the state

in the senate, and their proportionate representation in the
house of representatives, without any legitimate state action,
was a blunder in policy, a blow at legitimate state rights,
and an act of gross injustice to the loyal states, on whom,
for the present at least, is thrown the chief burden of saving the constitution and the integrity and life of the nation.

The policy adopted in the case of western Virginia, is
based on the false assumption that a state, as a state, cannot
rebel, and therefore that the several seceding states, as states,
are loyal, and that the loyal people of those states retain all
their constitutional rights unimpaired by the act of secession.
This is the grand fallacy which has embarrassed the administration and congress from the outset, and greatly impeded
military operations.   If the state were, as some pretend, a
sovereign state, it could not, we grant, rebel, for in that
case there would be no superior on earth for it to rebel
against.   But if the state is autonomous, a political entity,
capable of acting as a political person, and yet subordinate to
a superior, it can rebel as well as an individual, and does
rebel when it refuses to obey, and takes up arms against
the legitimate authority of that superior.   The rebellion of
a state carries away all the rights, even of loyal persons, depending on their being citizens of a particular state.   Such
persons are citizens of the United States, indeed, but they
are no longer citizens of a particular state, and necessarily
fall into the condition of persons *squatting* on federal
territory, for which no state or territorial government
has as yet been organized and put into operation.   They
have for the present no political rights whatever, and consequently no right of representation in congress.   This is the
case of the loyal population even of all the seceded states.
Virginia had seceded, and by her act, her whole population
were deprived of all the rights of the people of Virginia,
for by that act, the people of Virginia ceased to exist.

That a state by rebellion, in case it can rebel, loses its *status* in the Union, and therefore all its rights as a federal
state, we presume will not be questioned.   That a state
under our political system *can* rebel, we think is undeniable.
The generic character of our system is that of a federal republic.   We are a nation, one nation, and therefore have
one national sovereignty, but the government is not a centralized or consolidated government.   The government is
formed by the union, not league, of several individual or
particular states, or civil and political communities, and in

relation to one another separate and independent states.
These states have each in its own sphere certain rights,
which are not derived from the national government, or held
as grants or concessions from it. In other words, all rights
and power in the republic, though held in subordination to
the legitimate authority of the national government, do not
emanate from. it, and are not held subject to its pleasure.
The national government recognizes and protects the rights
of the states, but does not create, and cannot abrogate them.
The matter is best explained by regarding the several states
as holding before the federal government a relation analogous to that held by individuals before civil society. Civil
society derives its powers, *mediante* the people as individuals, from God, and hence its legitimacy. But the individual
after the creation of civil society, as before its creation, has
certain rights, called the rights of man, which he holds by
a law antecedent to civil society, which it does not create,
cannot revoke, and is bound to recognize and protect as
sacred and inviolable, among which, according to the declaration of American independence, are "life, liberty, and the
pursuit of happiness." These rights I hold by the patent of
my Creator, by the charter of my manhood. They are inalienable, and so long as I do not forfeit them, the civil society of which I am a member, is bound to protect me in
their peaceable enjoyment. I may hold them up before the
state, and say, "These are mine, touch them not." But I
may forfeit them by my misdeeds. I forfeit my right to life
by murdering my fellow-man, and society may hang me. I
forfeit my right to liberty by abusing it, and rendering it
incompatible with the equal liberty of others. I forfeit my
right to pursue my happiness, when I insist on pursuing it
in a way destructive of the happiness of others, or in a manner dangerous to the existence or peace of society.

The same may be said of the several states before the federal government. The federal government derives its powers from God, through the people as states, and therefore
holds them legitimately. Each state has certain rights,
which it holds by a law anterior to the Union, and independent of it. But the state may forfeit its rights, and even
its existence as a state, because though a state, and in its
subordinate sphere a complete state, it is not a sovereign,
but a subordinate state. It is subordinate, because the
United States are made by the constitution the supreme government. Article VI. of the constitution says: "This con-

stitution, and the laws of the United States which shall be made in pursuance thereof; and all treaties made, or which shall be made, under the authority of the United States, shall be the supreme law of the land; and the judges in every state shall be bound thereby, any thing in the consti-tution and laws of any state to the contrary notwithstand-ing." No language can more clearly assert the constitution-al supremacy of the United States, and therefore the subor-dinate character of each particular state. By making the United States the supreme government, and their constitu-tion and constitutional acts the supreme law of the land, the American people are made one civil and political people or community—not an aggregation of peoples—a sovereign nation whose sovereignty excludes all others, for sovereign-ty is and must be one and indivisible. But the powers of government are, under our system, not concentrated in the same hands, but are divided and distributed among an in-definite number of autonomous though subordinate civil and political communities. These communities, so long as they keep within their sphere, are independent of the federal government, and may resist its invasion of their reserved or antecedent rights, as an individual, so long as he abuses none of his rights, may resist any encroachment on them by civil society. So far we assert state rights as an essential element in our political system, and as an element we can never con-sent to see eliminated. It is the grandest and noblest feat-ure in our institutions. This has always been our doctrine on the subject, and if in some of our writings we have at times seemed to go further, we have seemed to go further than we really intended. We had accepted in early life Mr. Calhoun's theory of state rights, but we never understood this theory to mean the right of a state to secede, or that state sovereignty denied the constitutional supremacy of the federal government. Mr. Calhoun was a nullifier, but when we knew him he was not a secessionist. "You cannot," said he to us in 1841, when authorizing us to speak officially for him,—" you cannot coerce a state, because you can never get power enough to do it. So many other states will make common cause with the state it is proposed to coerce, that the government will be compelled to desist from its attempt, and withdraw the acts that have given offence, and which the state has nullified." Mr. Calhoun did not deny, as he explained himself to us, the *right*, but simply the *ability* of the federal government to coerce a state. The moment it should attempt to coerce the nullifying state, other states would intervene, arrest its action, and compel it to accept a compromise, as in 1832. State sovereignty, in any other sense than that the state derives none of its rights from the Union, and that all the states are independent states in their internal relations to one another, was always, in our judgment, a political heresy; and it is unquestionably this political heresy, that has justified, in the minds of the southern people, the fearful schism they have attempted, and which the federal authorities are now laboring to suppress.

Conceding that a state has autonomy, but denying its sovereignty, we can consistently maintain that a state, as well as an individual, may rebel. Any person, natural or artificial, that owes allegiance to a superior, is capable of rebellion because capable of resisting and warring against the legitimate authority of that superior. The states have a superior, since the constitutional acts of the United States are the supreme law of the land, and override their acts. That government, whose acts are the supreme law of the land, is unquestionably the supreme government of the land; and if the federal government is supreme the states can be only subordinate. If subordinate to the federal government, they owe it allegiance, and are bound to obey it in the constitutional exercise of its authority. They being autonomous, capable of self-action, are capable of resisting that authority, refusing it obedience, and taking up arms against it, and therefore are capable of rebellion. To say a state can do none of these things because they are illegal, is to overlook the reason of their illegality on the one hand, or to maintain, on the other, that an act done illegally is not done at all. Any act done by the political people called a state, acting through their state organization, and by its authority, is an act of the state in the full and proper sense of the term. The secession ordinances were passed not by the people as population, by the people outside of their state organization, and irrespective of state authority, but by the people as the state, acting through the state organization, and according to the forms of state law. They were passed by the highest authority in the state, and have been recognized, acted on, and enforced by all the authorities of the state, legislative, judicial, executive, and military. In the eyes of the state these ordinances, and the acts following them, are not illegal, but legal and valid. The individuals in arms against the federal government are not rebels to their respective states. So far as state acts can go, they are, in relation to their own states, loyal and patriotic citizens, and simply fighting at the command of authority for their country, not against it.

The illegality is not illegality in relation to state authority, but to federal authority. The acts justify the citizen in the state court, and would, in that court, be a valid plea; but they do not justify the citizen, nor can he plead them, in the federal courts. They are illegal and void, not because they are not acts of the state, but because they are acts in violation of the constitution of the United States, and acts in contravention of the supreme authority of the land, which is superior to state authority, and overrides it. They are illegal, and bind nobody, because they are in contravention of a superior authority, not in but out of the state, and to which the state is bound to conform. The citizen is not bound by them, because the allegiance of the citizen is due to the superior authority and he is bound to obedience to his state only as far as compatible with that allegiance. The allegiance that can be claimed by a state is a subordinate and conditional allegiance, and is restricted by the higher allegiance due to the national sovereign. The vassal swears to his immediate lord to be his true liegeman, saving against the lord paramount. The state acts illegally in seceding, but the law it violates is not state law, but United States law; and as that law overrides all state law, her illegal acts can bind no citizen of the United States to obedience, not because they are in the state court *non avenus*, but because they are null and void in the federal courts. Their illegality, therefore, is no proof that they are not acts of the state, or her legal acts, so far as herself is concerned, but a proof that she has usurped the sovereign power, and therefore destroyed herself as a federal state.

Secession, there can be no question, is rebellion, for it is an act of hostility to the superior, the total denial of the superior's authority. The state, then, in seceding, loses all its rights and its very existence as a civil or political community. The population and territory remain within the jurisdiction of the United States, but the entity called the *state* is out of the Union, as completely so, as though it had never been in it, and therefore is no longer a state at all, for a state without population or territory is a sheer nullity. It does not, as it imagines, become by secession a separate and independent state, because its act being illegal, null, and void, as against the superior, cannot carry either the population or territory essential to its existence with it. It does not fall back on the people in their original and primary capacity, because the people in that capacity are simply population, and the people, as population, so long as they remain on territory within the jurisdiction of the United States, are not an independent people, but simply a part of the population of the United States, bound to obey the constitutional acts of the federal government as "the supreme law of the land." Its act of secession is simply an act of self-destruction, and the surcease of its authority. Its secession ordinance has killed it. The population and territory belong to the Union, but are not in the Union as a state, consequently have no right of representation in the federal congress, and, till reorganized into a state or territory, no political or even civil existence whatever.

That congress may reorganize the people of the geographical districts vacated by the decease of the seceding states into territorial governments, and then authorize the territorial people to assemble in conventions, adopt state constitutions, and apply for admission as states into the Union, we readily concede; but we deny the right of congress or of the executive to recognize them as states till they have been so organized and formally admitted. There is now no state of Tennessee. The state of Tennessee has abdicated, and the word is now only a geographical expression. The gentlemen from the geographical district called Tennessee, now sitting in congress, are most estimable gentlemen, but they represent no political entity, and have, so far as we can see, not a shadow of right to the seats they occupy. The same must be said of the gentlemen in congress from western Virginia. Western Virginia is not and never was a federal state. It is included in Virginia, and Virginia as a state is no more. The loyal people remaining in the seceding states lost their federal rights by the suicide of those states. They are not anywhere states or successors of the defunct states, and have no power of themselves to organize themselves into states, with the right of representation in congress.

The policy we oppose, and which we devoutly pray may never be adopted, is to treat the loyal men found in a seceded state as the state itself, and to recognize the defunct constitution as still in force. But this is only an indirect way of imposing a constitution on a state, the capital error of Mr. Buchanan's administration with regard to Kansas. These people are not the state, and the old constitution is not in force. Neither congress nor the executive can revive that constitution, nor organize these people into a state. Congress can organize them into a territory, and pass in their favor an " enabling act," as it is called. But the act of organizing them into a state, and adopting a state constitution, must be the act of the people themselves, though of a legally recognized and defined territorial people. These Union men, or the population on the territory of any of the lapsed states, are not such people. For the federal government to treat them as such, and allow them to act under the old constitution, and elect state and federal officers, as in western Virginia, would strike a deadly blow to constitutional government, and violate in a most flagrant manner our federal system and the rights of the loyal states.

The states that have remained loyal, and that now constitute the political community called the United States, have the constitutional right to settle the affairs of the nation, without the interference of gentlemen who have no constitutional right to seats on the floor of either house of congress. We know to a moral certainty that, if government treats as a state the population of each district it recovers from the so-called confederacy, and concedes them the full state representation in congress, the *status quo* will be restored, slavery be reëstablished, the slave interest again be dominant, and our political condition after the war be more disgraceful and humiliating than it was ever before. In every one of the seceded states there are, no doubt, Union men, and, as our armies advance, they will become much more numerous. Some will be heartily Union men, a much larger number will be Union men because secession is the losing, and the Union the winning side. Nowhere are these men the state ; nowhere can they claim to be the state, or by any state law hold a regular election for either state or federal officers. There is no possible way for them to perform any legal or constitutional state act. All their acts must lack authority, and in their principle and essence be illegal and revolutionary. To allow them to send representatives to congress, is therefore an outrage upon the loyal states, which deprives them of their constitutional rights, for these representatives, though representing population, would be the representatives of no state. It would destroy constitutionalism by placing the unorganized and unconsti-

tuted population of a geographical division of territory on
the same footing with a legally organized and constituted
state. It is states according to population, not population
simply, that is represented in the lower house of congress,
and states alone that are represented in the upper house or
senate.   Let those who are ready to adopt this policy, and
who profess to be the special friends of the constitution,
ponder this well.

These people in Tennessee, North Carolina, and Arkansas, that it is proposed, under these names, to treat as states,
even if loyal, are not and never were states. They are in all
the states named, we presume, only a minority, though that
is not fatal, for it is only the loyal majority of a legally
constituted people that is of moment.   Now, to allow this
population to be represented in congress, is an outrage on
the federal principle of our government.   We then make
population alone, not states, the people represented, and
thus in principle convert our republic from a federal to a
centralized republic, and sanction the wildest and most irregular democracy ever broached by the most rabid Jacobin
or radical. We should not in this way preserve our federal system, our federal constitution, but should revolution-
ize and destroy it.   We should put an end to the republic
of Washington and Adams, Jefferson and Madison, and attempt the dangerous experiment of a pure, centralized democracy.   We are not prepared for such a revolution.   We
love our country with all her faults, for she is *our* country ;
but we love her institutions because we have studied them,
and believe them the wisest and best the world has yet seen.
It is our political civil constitution, not our learning, our
science, our polish, or our personal morals, that places us in
the front rank of the grand army of civilization. To destroy
the federal element in these institutions would ruin them,
and ruin the country no less than secession itself, for all
centralism is absolutism, whether democratic or monarchical centralism.   We should err on the one hand, were we to
adopt it, as much as the confederates do on the other.

Receive back, without territorial discipline, the seceded
states the moment they cease fighting because fighting has
become a losing game, and you simply pay a premium for
rebellion, and make treason more profitable than loyalty.
The border-state representation, aided by Democratic pro-
slavery representatives, and a few renegade administration
members, even now all but control congress, and make it

well-nigh impossible to pass any comprehensive measure for punishing rebels, or for indemnifying loyal men by confiscating rebel property. The slave interest is nearly as dominant in congress now as it was before the secession of Toombs and Davis, Slidell and Mason, Wigfall and Hunter. It must be protected at all hazards. No damage must be done it, whatever becomes of loyalty. It thwarts the patriotic action of congress, and has from the outset paralyzed the arm of the executive, only just now beginning to be emancipated. For a long time every military precaution was neglected lest the border states should be irritated and secede ; and the finest months in the season for military operations were suffered to wear away without any thing being done, and the wisest strategic movements were sternly forbidden to be made, and the most important strategic points were left to the enemy, lest the Union men in Kentucky should vote to join the confederates. Let now Tennessee, North Carolina, Arkansas, and one after another of all the seceded states return to the Union, and send their delegations to congress, and it is easy to foresee the injustice that will be done to loyalty.

If one thing more than another should be insisted on, it is that the expenses of putting down the rebellion should be paid out of the property of rebels, of rebel states and rebel individuals. This is alike the dictate of justice and sound policy. But even as congress is now constituted this could hardly be effected. Let all the seceded states come back, and the United States would soon find that, in addition to the federal debt, in addition to the damages done to the property of so-called loyal men, by either army, federal or confederate, the federal treasury would be drawn upon to pay the scrip of the confederacy, and discharge all the obligations contracted by the rebels in their war against the Union. Some northern " dough-face " say the Honorable Mr. Diven of New York, for instance,—could be found to introduce a bill to that effect, it would be supported by all the Union men of the border states, from interest and the desire to stand well with their neighbors, late rebels to the government, by the whole southern delegation, as a matter of course, and by a fair share of northern men who would be anxious to prove that the era of good feeling had returned, and that they entertained no grudge against their southern brethren, and the bill would be passed, if necessary, even over the presidential veto. As sure as the armies of the Union continue to be victorious, and the seceded states are suffered to return to the Union the moment they lay down their arms, this is what will be done. It will be the rebels, not the loyalists, to whom will enure the victory. Slavery will again be in power, and the cotton lords will dominate as of old in the halls of congress, the executive chair, and the departments, threatening anew, if we of the free states show any disposition to assert our own rights, to secede, to convulse the nation again with civil war, to murder again our fathers, husbands, sons, and brothers, till they break our spirit, and we become as tame and docile as their own negroes.   Is this the premium to be paid for treason? And this the penalty to be inflicted on loyalty?

We trust in God that the federal government will never adopt, or, rather, that it will not persist in so insane and suicidal a policy. We trust that it will abandon the πρῶτον ψεῦδος with which it started, and will understand that a state may secede, that state secession is state suicide, and that the slaveholding states, by seceding, have lapsed as states, and that even loyal men inhabiting the geographical territories once under their jurisdiction have lost by the lapse of their respective states, all right of federal representation; while it itself is absolved from all obligation to protect or to recognize any of their municipal rights derived from state legislation or state authority alone. By the secession of the rebellious states, and by the rebellion of the greater part of the slaveholders throughout the non-seceding slaveholding states, slavery is legally well-nigh extinguished. We earnestly beseech the government, whatever it may do in regard to slavery in Maryland, Kentucky, Missouri, and Delaware, it will never recognize its existence anywhere else, and resist à outrance the return of the slave interest to power. As sure as it exists in the nation, that interest will rule it, for it must rule or die. We plead not now for the black alone, but for the white also; not for the abolition of slavery, but especially against reducing again to slavery the recently emancipated free men of the North. Nowhere on territory within the usurped rule of the so-called confederacy, has black slavery to-day any legal existence. We say to the negroes of all the seceding states, you are free, no law or usage now in force binds you to service. The rebellion of your masters restores you to the ownership of yourselves. Your wives and children are your own. Let the federal government refuse to suffer you to be remanded to slavery, and you will be free, and the poor white men of the North will also be free.

The two most important measures ever introduced into the American congress are, first, the resolutions of Mr. Sumner, in the senate, declaring that a state by rebellion commits suicide, and, second, General Ashley's bill providing for the government of the rebellious states as territories. We fear the democratic and border state influence, aided by a certain number of " dough-faced " republicans, may be too strong for their friends, and defeat the whole utility of the war, by forcing the acceptance of some base, timid, and disgraceful compromise, but they are wise and noble measures, almost the only measures introduced into the present congress that belong to high and comprehensive statesmanship. Let those measures be adopted, and our government will rise from its degradation, will reassume its majestic port and step, and command anew the admiration of the world. Their adoption would save constitutional government, and give new guaranties of man's capacity for freedom. But whether these measures be adopted or not Mr. Sumner's resolutions will serve as a platform on which will take their stand all in the country worthy of consideration for their political sagacity, their wise statesmanship, their disinterestedness, and their nobility of sentiment.

Never have we trembled more for the fate of the republic than we do at this moment when the shouts of victory are ringing in our ears. Yet we do not despair. If the present congress fails in its duty, we shall regret it. If it receives back the revolted states, and restores them to their former *status*, permitting them to remand the persons now legally free to their former servitude, we shall blush for our country, and hold that she knows not how to avail herself of this, her hour of visitation, but we shall not cease to labor for liberty, or to hope for its final triumph. We shall, if slavery be reëstablished in the territory of rebeldom, hold the federal government and the whole nation responsible for it, and therefore treat slavery as a matter that comes legitimately within the sphere of the political action of the citizens of the non-slaveholding states. It will then be our business as much as it would be if we lived in South Carolina or Tennessee. We shall then have the right to agitate the slave question politically, for the adoption of the policy we oppose makes slavery, if it exists anywhere on the territory of the seceded states, henceforth a national and not a

mere state question.   The government and people may be
sure, if the policy we have opposed prevails, they will find
it necessary, though in a different way, to reckon with the
friends of freedom as well as with the friends of slavery.

If the view of state suicide we have taken be accepted,
and the territorial government bill before congress adopted,
the slave interest will be crushed in all except the border
states, now nominally in the Union.   The slavery question,
when confined to these border states, will not amount to
much.   The slaves of rebels may be liberated under a confiscation act, and the few owned by loyal masters may be
liberated under the war power, and their owners indemnified, or they may be purchased and set free, or, in fine, left
as they are.   In these states slavery will not long remain,
after it is abolished further South, and the market for their
surplus stock of slaves is cut off.   Confined to these states,
and forbidden to expand, it will soon die out.   We are far
from being sanguine that there is either statesmanship
enough, or love of liberty enough, left in the country, to
adopt, though evidently legal, constitutional, and just, the
policy we recommend.   There is one cause that operates
powerfully in keeping the negro in bondage, the horror of
africanizing free American society.   This horror is the
greatest obstacle the friends of freedom have to overcome.
The majority of the people in the free states are anti-abolitionists, not because they approve of slavery, but because
they do not like the negro for an associate, a neighbor, or a fellow-citizen.   They believe he is a man, wish him to enjoy the
rights of man, but not in their community.   Not a few of
these believe with the late Mr. Calhoun, that if the two
races are to live on the same territory, it is best both for the
white race and the negro race that the negro should be retained in the condition of a slave.   Here is the great obstacle in the way of adopting Mr. Sumner's and General Ashley's policy.   If the slaves were of the white race, that
policy would be speedily adopted, and our republic made in
reality, as well as in name, a free republic.

We have no space left for the discussion of this question.
We suppose we share in the common prejudice against the
negro race, and have no wish to see our free American society africanized.   But prejudice, however strong, must not
be permitted to override justice.   We are not now pleading
for the abolition of slavery, but against its reëstablishment.
In all the seceding states the slaves are freed, and what we

ask is, that their freedom should be recognized. We want them treated as freemen : of their social and political *status* we say nothing. If recognized as freemen, we think, as white men press in to take their place as laborers, they would gradually, yet effectually, disappear from our republic by emigration to Hayti, or other black communities, where they can be free, and form integral portions of communities of their own race. We would urge no forced colonization; we would compel no emigration, but we believe the force of circumstances would lead them to emigrate, and we should have no objection to the government taking measures to facilitate and aid their emigration, providing their emigration is voluntary on their part, like the emigration hither of Irish and Germans. However this may be, we insist that no prejudice of race or color should induce us to remand to slavery those who, by the crimes of their masters, or the surcease of the state authorities making them slaves, are now legally freemen. We must insist on this as an act of justice to them, as a duty we owe to God, and cannot neglect with impunity, and as the only way of saving the country from the domination of the slave interest, and enabling it to live, flourish, and fulfil its civilizing mission.

EMANCIPATION AND COLONIZATION.*

[From Brownson's Quarterly Review for April, 1862.]

Count Gasparin's book on the "Uprising of a Great People," is a remarkable book for its keen foresight, its broad statesmanlike views, its inspiring eloquence, and its noble sentiments. Our only wish while reading it is, that our countrymen were less unworthy of the high praise the enlightened French nobleman awards them. The election of Mr. Lincoln in 1860 to the presidency was indeed a great event, less indeed on account of the man elected than on account of the cause he represented ; and we are not surprised that foreigners, who are strongly opposed to slavery,

---

* *The Uprising of a Great People.* By Count Agénor de Gasparin. New York: 1862.

should have regarded it with interest, and greeted it with pleasure and hope.   Under the circumstances, it was an act of courage, and not undeserving of admiration.

Yet there was less real courage in the actors generally than appeared to on-lookers from abroad, for comparatively few of those who voted for Mr. Lincoln, believed any real danger was to be apprehended.   The southern politicians threatened loudly, everybody knew ; but not many, if any, in the Republican party believed their threats were in earnest, or were any thing more than a part of the machinery usually put in operation before elections.   The northern politicians opposed to the Republican party assured us that this time the South were in downright earnest ; and that if the Republicans should dare elect their candidate, there would surely be separation or civil war, or perhaps both ; but we believed it only an ordinary trick of politicians to serve their own personal or party purposes, and we could hardly do otherwise, since we found them offering no word of rebuke to their southern allies, and not one manly word in defence of the constitutional freedom of election.   Their warnings we believed selfish, uncalled for, and we felt that, when addressed to Republicans, they were addressed to the wrong party.   The tears they shed over the dangers to the Union, seemed to us only tears shed over their own probable displacement from power ; and history will for ever throw on the Union-loving and Union-saving Democrats and their allies, who would save the Union by surrendering it, bound hand and foot, to slavery, the guilt of the rebellion, which their depravity and want of manhood, of true and enlightened patriotism, encouraged and well-nigh rendered successful.   Yet certain it is that they whose votes elected Mr. Lincoln, did not generally believe that either separation or civil war would follow his election.   They believed the Democratic party, South as well as North, would acquiesce in the election, when it was over and the new administration fairly inaugurated.   This was in accordance with all past experience, and they had no special reason to believe the present election would prove an exception to the general rule.

How many of them would have voted for Mr. Lincoln if they had believed any serious attempt would be made to put the threats loudly vociferated by politicians into execution, or if they had clearly foreseen the course since taken, it is not possible to determine.   It can never be known, and perhaps it is better that it should not be known. The architect sometimes builds better than he knows. But this is certain, that many prominent Republicans, when they saw the wolf had really come, that southern threats were not mere bullying, but did mean something, showed the white feather, and were prepared to avert the coming storm by new and larger concessions to slavery, and to purchase peace at the expense of throwing away the fruits of the victory they had just won after a hard-fought battle. The Republican party were saved from a disgraceful compromise, not, perhaps, so much by their own virtue, as by the madness of the southern politicians, who, disgusted with their Democratic allies of the free states, and resolved on separation and reconstruction, or, if you will, on separation alone, would listen to no compromise, and declared that they would not come back into the Union, even if left at liberty to prescribe their own terms. Their madness, rather than our virtue, saved us at the critical moment, and left us no alternative but to consent peaceably to separation, or to fight for the Union, and to crush out secession by force of arms. The merit of the Republicans is that they had the virtue, the manliness, the patriotism, to choose the latter alternative.

We ourselves voted for Mr. Lincoln, because we felt that it had become necessary for the country to commence the work of breaking and annihilating the political power of slavery, which had almost from the origin of the government dominated in the administration. The domination of the slave interest was corrupting our politics both North and South, was blackening our reputation in the eyes of the civilized world, and undermining the public and private morals of the people. We did not believe secession or civil war, though threatened, would follow, and, even if we had so believed, should still have voted for Mr. Lincoln all the same. We should only have felt it so much the more necessary to do so. We stated in some remarks to our fellow-citizens, urging them to support the Republican party, that we wished the power of the slave interest broken, and that, if civil war should follow, we would welcome and meet it as the sons of the heroes of the revolution should meet it. We wished the question, which was sure sooner or later to come up, to be met and disposed of in our day, so that we might, when called to our own final account, know whether we left our children a heritage of freedom or not. There are, we said, greater evils for a nation than civil war. The loss of liberty is greater, the loss of public and private virtue is greater, and greater by far is the loss of that patriotism which counts it sweet to die for one's country, or that heroism that dares do or suffer any thing or every thing in defence of the just and noble cause. We did not believe the South would secede, openly rebel, but, if they did, if they chose to fight, we were for meeting them, and giving them fight for fight to their hearts' content. Whether the majority of Republicans at that time could have said as much, may be doubted, but their purposes and ours were the same, and they have for the most part shown no deficiency of pluck when they found themselves forced to meet the stern realities of war.

We confess, however, that in voting with the Republican party, we were not moved by any special regard for the negroes held in bondage. We were, as a matter of course, opposed to slavery, and wished there were no slaves, and no negroes in the country. The system was bad, detestable, abominable, but we of the non-slaveholding states were not responsible for it. It was a local matter, and its disposition a matter for the states that authorized it, with which we had no civil or political right to interfere. Our motive was not to abolish slavery where it had a legal or *quasi*-legal existence, but to restrain, and finally abolish the political power of the slave interest, by sternly forbidding its expansion into new territory, and the admission of any additional slave states into the Union. We opposed the extension of slavery, not on abolition principles, not for the sake of slavery itself, but for the sake of emancipating and purifying American politics, because we found the interest created by slavery stronger in federal politics than any other one interest in the country, and able by its combinations and alliances to carry our presidential elections, and to shape the policy of the federal government, in a sense necessarily antagonistical to the general interests of the immense majority of the people of the United States. We found it dominant, and laboring, not without success, to render its domination complete and perpetual. It had the feeble administration of Mr. Buchanan on its side; it had got an opinion of the supreme court in its favor; it had fifteen states out of thirty-three, the majority of voters in three or four, and large majorities in all the other states, pledged to its support, and we felt bound to do all we could constitutionally to overthrow it. It was not liberty for the black race so much as for the white race, that we wished to secure. It was not the abolition of negro slavery, but the redemption and preservation of the glorious republic inherited from our fathers, that moved us. We did not propose to interfere with slavery where it had a recognized legal existence, and were prepared to adhere strictly to the so-called " compromises of the constitution," and to pay the slaveholders their pound of flesh cut from the region nearest the heart. It was only the *political* power of slavery we sought to eliminate. So was it with us personally, and so, we presume, was it with the great majority of those who voted in 1860 for the Republican candidates. The Republican party were denounced at the North as well as at the South by the Bell and Everett men, and by both wings of the Democratic party, as an abolition party; but an abolition party they were not, and had no thought of becoming.

But there is a logic in events, and men who adopt the principles of a movement are carried further than they foresee or are prepared for in the outset. All great movements have their law, and must and will on to their legitimate conclusion. The developments and events since the presidential election, have carried us far beyond the point we had then reached, and have made evident, what should have been evident to us from the first, that it is impossible to annihilate the political power of the slave interest without annihiliating that interest itself, and that it is impossible to annihilate that interest without the complete emancipation of the slaves, and their recognition as free population. We have seen three or four slave states, nominally in the Union, and having, comparatively speaking, only a small number of slaves, for over a year embarrassing the action of the government, preventing much necessary legislation, paralyzing the administration, impeding its military operations, and rendering useless the most costly sacrifices. For six weeks after the inauguration of the present administration, the military defences of the country were neglected, forts and arsenals, the armory at Harper's Ferry, the navy-yard and naval armaments at Gosport, were left unprotected, lest the border states should be irritated and secede, and there was even thought of abandoning on one and the same day Sumter, Pickens, and all the forts still held by the Union in the seceded states. Even after the war had commenced, and we had a powerful army in the field, it was pretended that its principal object was to defend the national capital, while all thought of subjugating the rebellious states was officially disclaimed. Even congress, at its extra session, passed almost unanimously, at least without serious debate, a resolution declaring that the war having been forced upon the United States by the rebels in the seceded states, would be prosecuted solely to the end of putting down the rebellion, without any intention of interfering with the property or institutions of those states. All this was done through the influence of the slave interest in the non-seceding slave states. That interest is hardly less controlling in congress to-day than it was under the administration of the feeble Buchanan. Maryland, Delaware, Western Virginia, Kentucky, and Missouri have inherited the mantle of the more southern states, and succeeded to their power. Even now not a step can be taken without reckoning with the slave interest.

This fact alone suffices to show that there is no way of emancipating the government from the slave power, but by treating slavery as abolished, but by destroying the property in slaves, and never suffering a slave interest again to grow up anywhere within the limits of the United States. This we can now do without any violation of constitutional law, or breach of constitutional duty, for the secession of the slaveholders has given the federal government jurisdiction over the whole subject. Slavery, if suffered to exist in any part of the Union at all, will compel all other interests to succumb to it, because it is antagonistical in its very essence to all other interests. If it exists in the Union at all, the interest it creates must be placed on a footing of equality with every other interest, and be counted as legitimate and as sacred as the interest of freedom. If allowed equality, it will from its nature claim superiority, and dominate, because equality can be predicated only of things homogeneous, and there is no homogeneousness between liberty and slavery. The equality of the slave interest can in the nature of the case mean only the right of slavery to restrain and repress freedom, for the advance of freedom is the destruction of slavery. We can, then, secure an open field for freedom, and prevent the slave interest from domineering, only by abolishing it, and recognizing the slaves as free. The republic to subsist and flourish must either be all free or all slave.

In the slaveholding states themselves the slave-owners

are only a small minority, and yet this minority is the ruling class, and to the interests of slavery the interests of the non-slaveholding whites are sacrificed. The seven and a half millions of non-slaveholding whites are of the same race as ourselves, are, by nature, as hardy, as brave, as energetic, and as ingenious as we are, and yet, even their material prosperity, notwithstanding their more genial climate, and their richer and more productive soil, cannot compare with ours. The blight of slavery is on them, because all their interests must be sacrificed to the interests of the slaveholders. They have comparatively few schools, few private or public libraries, and in many parts of the South are below the level of the most degraded peasantry of Europe. We sympathize with these people, who are fitted by nature, and by their favored climate and soil, to stand in the foremost ranks of the free American people. Not a few of those brave Union troops who fought at Belmont, and conquered at Logan's Cross Roads, at Henry, and at Donelson, were either from their class or their descendants, and are only a sample of what the whole would be, if the curse of slavery were removed, and they lived in a land of freedom. Why shall these seven millions of free whites, of the same stock with ourselves, and by nature every way our equals, be sacrificed to the slaveholding oligarchy which rules them with a rod of iron, and prevents the development and growth of their innate genius and greatness? They, not the slaveholders, are the real people of the South, and, if united heart and hand with us of the North, would contribute their full share toward making the American people the greatest and noblest people on earth.

Now, to emancipate these non-slaveholding whites of the slaveholding states, who, as a population, dislike slavery far more than do the population of the non-slaveholding states, to emancipate national politics, and free labor both North and South, and to make the North and the South really one people, one in their system of labor, one in their institutions, culture, and affections, it is necessary to put an end to slavery, and to induce—not force—and aid, as fast and as far as practicable, the freed men of the African race to emigrate to some tropical region congenial to their constitution and temperament, where they may form a great cotton, rice, coffee, and tobacco growing and exporting people by themselves, leaving the whole territory of the United States to the white race. This is what is necessary, and the assurance of the government that it will adopt and carry out the policy of emancipation and settlement of the blacks in a congenial climate, beyond the limits of the United States, would make these seven millions, or seven millions and a half, of non-slaveholding whites its fast friends, and friends who would fight for it with a heartiness and zeal they have never manifested in fighting the battles of the slaveholders, for it is not slavery they would retain, but the africaniza- tion of free American society they would avert. They hold no slaves; they resist all amalgamation with the negro race, leaving that to slave-owners and overseers; they believe the negro a man with the natural rights of man; they think him different from themselves; do not regard him as a white man; they wish him well; but they do not want negroes for neighbors, associates, fellow-citizens, or voters. They see and know well, if freed and remaining as laborers, they will do so only as a degraded class, and so long as a consid- erable portion of the labor of the country is performed by a socially degraded class, they understand perfectly well that labor will never rise from its degradation, and it be held honorable to labor. It is therefore they join the slave- holders against abolition; but if it could be made clear to them that free American society would not be africanized, and that in a reasonable time the African element of the American population would be eliminated, there would be no more resolute, determined, and invincible abolitionists in the country. To accomplish, then, the destruction of the political power of slavery, and to make the American people really one people, complete emancipation and colo- nization are necessary.

This is the conclusion to which events, our own reflec- tions, and the suggestions of others have brought us. But the greatest obstacle to the realization of the good aimed at, is in the free, not in the slave states. The abolitionists are opposed to the colonization feature of emancipation, as are also the political economists, and most of our old Democratic and pro-slavery politicians. The abolitionists demand the abolition of slavery on the ground that slavery is unjust, a sin, and no people has the right to tolerate it. The slaves must be freed as an act of simple justice to them, and, when freed, they are freemen, and we have no more right to colo- nize them than we have to colonize any other class of free- men. They have the same right to live in the country that we who propose to colonize them have. Besides, if it is necessary to colonize, why not colonize their late masters, whom we can much better spare? The economists add that we need the labor of the blacks, and that to deport four millions of the laboring population, to say nothing of the expense of doing it, would derange the labor market, diminish production, and impoverish the country, almost to a ruinous extent. To the economists it may be conceded that the loss of labor would be great, and be a serious blow to production, if we suppose them all deported at once, and their places unsupplied from other sources. But the process of removal must, on any supposition, spread over a considerable space of time; and as their removal leaves a vacuum, white labor will rush in to fill it, and keep up the equilibrium between demand and supply. There would undoubtedly be for a time some derangement, some difficulty, and some loss; but here, as everywhere else, supply would soon follow the demand, and the labor market of the world is generally overstocked with white laborers.

To the abolitionists it may be replied that the question is not a question of colonizing the freed men of the African race for the interest or pleasure of their late masters. We make little of these late masters, and are quite willing, if thought best, that they should be deported to Africa, to become, if they wish, slave-drivers for their friend and ally, the king of Dahomey. We demand nothing as a concession to their interests and feelings; we consult only the interests of the whole country, and the rights, feelings, and interests of the non-slaveholding whites in the slave states, the seven millions or seven millions and a half, the real southern people, who own no slaves, and are as much opposed to slavery as we are. We think it would be better, as well as easier, to colonize four millions of the African race, than to colonize those seven and a half millions of the white race.

The other objection of the abolitionists cannot be so lightly dismissed. It professes to be founded in justice, and asserts that to deport the slaves after their freedom would be a violation of their liberty, and therefore an act of injustice. This is a grave objection, and should be gravely considered. If the abolitionists are chargeable with having given too little weight to political interests, or political expediency, we who have opposed them are, perhaps, even more chargeable with having made too little account in our political calculations of justice, which overrides, and should override, all other considerations. It will not do for us, when settling

up the past, and taking a fresh start for the future, to neglect the strict and stern demands of justice. We cannot
hope to repair one sin by another, or an act of injustice by
an act of injustice. This is certain. Let justice stand though
the heavens fall; for justice is the basis of all institutions
worth preserving, and the condition of all real prosperity,
social or individual. To forget justice is to forget God;
and all the nations that forget God shall perish, as all history proves.

We grant that slavery is not only a political wrong, not
only an evil to the free whites, but an injustice to the slave
himself, and must be abolished for his sake alone. We are
willing on this point to sing our palinode, and frankly confess that we have never given to this feature in the slave
question its due consideration. Many others are very likely
in the same predicament with ourselves. Slavery is a wrong
done to the slave, the greatest possible wrong that can be done
him. It is an outrage upon his manhood, an outrage which
disfigures and debases in him that very image of God after
which he was created. It is a supreme sophism, utterly repugnant to the dialectic harmony of God's creation. The
negro is a man, and slavery is as great an outrage of the
rights and dignity of manhood in the black man as in the
white man. We have never denied or overlooked this, but
we have not given it in our calculations all the weight it
deserved. On this point the abolitionists have exaggerated
nothing; and they have said no more than the simple truth
when they have said strict justice demands the immediate
and unconditional emancipation of the slave. But, practically considered, the real and complete act of emancipation
is a complex act, and cannot be performed instantaneously
and at once. The act is not, and cannot be, one simple isolated act. It has its relations, and its relations on all sides,
the consideration of which does and must enter into and
form a part of the act itself. In doing even an act of justice to the slave, we must take care so to do it, that if it results in evil to him it shall be through his fault, not ours.
Certainly justice must never give place to expediency, but
we must take care that justice be done in the best practicable
manner, and be as complete as possible. The question of
emancipation, from the abolitionist point of view, is one of
reparation of wrong done to the slave by slavery. This
wrong is not confined to the simple deprivation of liberty,
and is not repaired by simply declaring him free. Slavery

has done him a greater wrong than such a declaration repairs. It has injured him in the habits it has generated, in the obstacles it has interposed to his intellectual and moral development, and in disqualifying him for fair competition, in the race for equality, in a community where the white element predominates. This injury cannot be repaired at once, and by a single stroke of the pen. The obligation of setting about repairing it immediately or at once, is imperative, and all avoidable delay is criminal, is an augmentation of the wrong done to the slave ; but it is not imperative that the reparation should be instantly completed. For completing it time may be demanded, and many things besides declaring the slave free may be necessary to be done, which cannot be done all at once. There are vested rights to be considered and adjusted, the rights of others—we mean not the slaveholders—are to be consulted, and care has to be taken that no injustice be done to other and innocent parties. It is always easier to do a wrong than it is to undo it. We are not at liberty to undo the wrong to the slave by doing a wrong to the free. It is just to abolish slavery against the will of their pretended owners, for their ownership being founded in injustice is invalid save as against the community that authorized it ; but to force upon the free non-slaveholding southern society four millions of negroes, to take their place in that society against its will, on a footing of equality, or, in other words, to africanize free non-slaveholding society against its consent, is not an act of justice, but may be an act of injustice. To do it strikes at the freedom of that society, and without repairing the injustice done to the slave ; for the slaves, liberated by a stroke of the pen, and let loose in such a society, with which they could not amalgamate, would not and could not be really free. They cannot be free and equal members of a society that instinctively repels them, and can remember them only as having been slaves. They can, in the southern states, with here and there an individual exception, be only slaves or pariahs, and to leave them pariahs is not to repair the injustice of slavery. Even not counting for the moment the invasion of the rights of the non-slaveholding people of the South, by the infusion of four millions of blacks into their free society, against their will, the government has the right to treat the negroes heretofore held as slaves, and would be bound to treat them, as wards, so far and so long as necessary for their transition from slavery to freedom, in the best practicable way for their own interest.

We hold the slaves in all the seceded states have been freed from their former owners, whose rebellion has annulled the only law by which they were held to service. The federal government in succeeding to the defunct states cannot remand the slaves to their former condition, cannot hold them to service to the United States, nor sell them as vacated or confiscated property. It cannot treat them as property at all, but must treat them as persons, though persons under its authority, and for whose future *status* and welfare it is bound in justice to provide. They properly become wards of the United States, who have over them the authority, and owe them the duty, of guardians. They are to be regarded in law and even in justice as under age, as not having as yet attained to their majority, and, if the United States as their guardian honestly believe that their colonization in a congenial climate and productive soil, where they may form a civil community and an independent sovereign state of their own race, is practicable, they have the right, and it is their duty, so to colonize them.

We know the answer of the abolitionists. They say, you must immediately and at once recognize the slaves as freemen; and, when you have so recognized them, they stand on the same footing of equality with any other class of freemen. Being freed, to colonize or deport them without their choice and consent, would be to violate the very freedom you have recognized as theirs. When you recognize them as freemen, you recognize in them the inalienable right to "life, liberty, and the pursuit of happiness." You deny that right, when you deny them the right to live, to be free, and to pursue their happiness, where it best pleases them. When you claim the right to deport them, except for crime, you make a distinction between them and white men, as unjust in principle as slavery itself. The abolitionists demand not only the freedom of the slave as a man, the complete and unreserved recognition of his manhood, but the full and unreserved recognition of the equality of the negro race with the white race. They demand freedom for the slave in the name of the universal brotherhood of the human race, as a man and a brother, and therefore demand that this brotherhood be recognized, and the negro be placed on a footing of perfect equality with the white race, in one and the same civil and political community; and therefore they hold that the forced colonization of the African race, in a community by themselves, is an act of injustice to the members of that race, which no plea of expediency or utility can ever justify.

Let no man treat this answer of the abolitionists with contempt. There is in it an homage paid to justice, which commands our reverence. We recognize the brotherhood of the human race, in the sense that all men of whatever temperament or complexion have had the same origin, have sprung from the same original pair, Adam and Eve. So far, as a Christian, a philosopher, a man, we have no doubt or misgiving. But there is the fact of human degeneracy, called by theologians original sin, which must be taken into the account. The fact of this degeneracy is evident to every one who will compare the ideal or typical man presented by his own reason and conscience, with the actual state of men as he finds them. This degeneracy, as sin, or considered in regard to its *culpa*, or guilt, is the same in all men, for it was committed alike by all in Adam. But, taken as simple degeneracy, as a simple fact in man's natural history, it has various degrees, and from these various degrees spring what we call *races*, which are not properly distinct races, but simple varieties in one and the same race. The degeneracy is greater in some, and less in others. Some have departed further than others from the primitive type. Why, or wherefore, we have no space now to inquire. We restrict ourselves to the simple statement of the fact. The least degenerated variety is that commonly called the Caucasian; the most degenerated is the African. The African is the lowest variety, and stands furthest removed from the true ideal or typical man. The Caucasian variety has suffered from original sin, has degenerated from the proper human type, but it has degenerated the least of any of the known varieties of the human family. Whether we consider the Caucasian man, physically, intellectually, or morally, he is the nearest approach to the integral man now to be found.

Between one variety and another there is an interval. This interval is greatest between the negro and the Caucasian, and between these it is too great to be leaped by a single bound. The two varieties do not easily amalgamate. Their amalgamation is in some sense unnatural and violent, and the amalgam is a deterioration. We know amalgamation is not contemplated by the abolitionists generally; but how is it to be prevented? Do you propose to forbid it by law? By what right, if you deny all distinction in the case, and assert the black and white races are equal? Do you say that intermarriage between blacks and whites will not be sought ; that white persons will prefer to marry white persons, and black persons will prefer to marry black persons? You may be right.   We believe such will be the case.   We believe that there is an instinctive aversion on both sides, but especially on the part of the white race, to such intermarriage.   It is doubtful if a white man or a white woman ever cohabits with a black of the other sex, unless moved to it by lust or some morbid affection ; and we believe the black man prefers a black woman for his wife, or a black woman a black man for her husband.   Intermarriage between the two races, we apprehend, strikes both as improper and undesirable, and is pretty sure not to take place to any considerable extent.

But in saying this, we say all ; we settle the question that blacks and whites do not and cannot without more or less violence form one and the same community, and live together in one and the same society on the footing of equality.   There can be no society between persons who have a mutually instinctive aversion to intermarriage ; for marriage is the basis of the family, and the family is the basis of general society ; when therefore the different races or varieties are separated by too broad an interval for the family union, it is clear that they cannot form one and the same society. They cannot live in one and the same civil and political society as equal, but one will be held superior and the other inferior.   There is no real society or community where there is no intermarriage, and if they inhabit the same territory, the blacks and the whites, not intermarrying, cannot form one people.   They will be two distinct peoples in one state, in which the stronger will predominate and oppress the weaker.   This is evident and conclusive against the notion of forming the liberated slaves of the negro family into one people and society with the freemen of the white family.

The amalgamation of the two varieties, separated as they are by so great an interval, would be undesirable, even if it were less impracticable than it evidently is.   Intermarriage between them would deteriorate the superior variety, without a compensating elevation of the inferior.   The mulatto, if in some respects superior to the full-blooded negro, is, as a rule, in all respects inferior to the full-blooded white man.   In all countries where the mingling of the two races has gone on to any considerable extent, we find a great deterioration in the white race, as may be seen in Spanish and Portuguese America. A marked deterioration would result in our southern society, were intermarriages between them to become frequent. But, excluding amalgamation, as to most Americans at least, and especially to the non-slaveholding whites of the South, a thing too shocking to be quietly named, we can see only degradation and oppression for the black race so long as it inhabits the same territory with the white. They can never take their places as equal members in free-white American society; never form with free-white Americans one people, and as they are now in most, and soon would be in all of the states, the minority, poor and uneducated, they would be not only a distinct, but an inferior people, and consequently an impassable barrier to the realization of that idea of right and equality, in contradistinction from mediæval privilege and inequality, on which our American order of civilization is founded.

We do not in this deny the negro to be a man. We recognize distinctly his manhood; we assert for him all the rights of man; and maintain for him all the civil and political rights we claim for ourselves, only not in one and the same civil and political society with white men, because so great is the interval between him and us, that he cannot enjoy the same civil and political rights except in a society of his own, where color will be no badge of an inferior caste. It is not that we ask less for the negro than the abolitionists do, but that we ask more for him, and at the same time pay more attention to the tastes, habits, inclinations and interests of free white American society. We recognize with the abolitionists the original brotherhood of the human race, but we do not recognize the present equality of the black and white varieties, or admit that the two can form in the present state of their respective development society together. For the benefit of each, we wish them to live in free and independent separate communities.

We cannot admit that the government in denying to the liberated slave the right to pursue his happiness where he pleases, necessarily infringes his liberty. No one has the right in all cases to pursue his happiness where he pleases. No one can do it by living against my will on my farm, in my house, in my family, or by eating at my table. Every man's right is necessarily limited by every other man's right. The negro's right to live in free white society is limited by the right of free white society to exclude persons, not born in it, whom its members do not wish to associate with. Nor can we admit that the functions of government are merely negative, and that it can never take in any thing the initiative, and act as a positive providence. We are no admirers of the *paternal* governments of Europe, administered on the principle, "All for the people, nothing by the people;" we defend the largest individual liberty compatible with social order, and social well-being; but individualism may be carried to a fatal extreme, so as to exclude all government, or so as to convert what is called government into a machine to be worked by individuals for their own private benefit, as was rapidly becoming the case with us before the breaking out of the present civil war. The government has positive as well as negative functions, and may even restrain a man's freedom for his own benefit. It may found at the public expense, institutions of learning, universities, colleges, seminaries; it may encourage science and art, this or that special industry for the national independence or prosperity; it may found hospitals and asylums, and establish bureaus of beneficence. It may act, and should act as a general social providence. As the social providence it is the natural guardian of the weak and the friendless. It may, then, without assuming any illegitimate power or violating any individual freedom take the guardianship of the emancipated negro slaves, and exercise over them the control necessary to place them in a condition where their freedom can be practically secured, and their rights and interest protected. On this score we have no scruples, and believe the government might forcibly remove them from its territory to another where they could be better off in a community by themselves, if it saw proper to do so.

But we wish it distinctly understood that we propose no resort to force, and therefore nothing that can be called *deportation*. We rely on voluntary emigration to effect the end we have in view, and to voluntary emigration no abolitionist can object. We want no forced emigration. We demand, first of all, the clear, distinct, and unconditional recognition of the negroes as persons entitled to freedom. We demand this immediately. Slavery everywhere in the United States must be outlawed. We demand this as a political necessity, and as an act of justice to the negro race. Slavery must cease. On this point we are and, God helping us, will be abolitionists, so long as there is a single slave to be liberated.

Heretofore we have demanded the recognition of the slaves as free persons, on the ground of military necessity. Some pretend, since our late victories, that the plea of military necessity can no longer be urged. We do not concede it. The war is not yet ended. We have gained some important advantages over the rebels; but if they have any of the characteristic pluck of the stock from which they have sprung, they will not acknowledge themselves beaten, and are not yet beaten, and will give us some hard fighting yet. We cannot say what a few weeks may bring forth, but at the time we are writing, the early part of March, the shouts of victory appear to us to be premature, and it is not impossible that we shall still find it, in order to secure a complete and final triumph, necessary to deprive the rebels of their slaves. and use the services of these slaves in such way as they can best contribute to the defence of the national integrity and life. But be this as it may, if events have weakened the plea of *military* necessity, they have strengthened the plea of *political* necessity. The total cessation of slavery in the United States is a political necessity. It is absolutely necessary to create union and harmony, to mould the people of the North and the people of the South into one homogeneous people, to consolidate and strengthen the nation, to develop its resources, to provide for the general defence, and to enable the American people to work out the great social and political problem committed to them by Providence for solution. It is, happily, a political necessity to which we can yield without violating any private right, or disturbing any vested interests. Slavery in the adhering border states can present no difficulty, when it is once abolished in the seceding states, and in the seceding states it has now no longer any constitutional rights or legal existence in the way of federal action. It existed there only by local law, and the local law, as we have shown in the foregoing article, has lost its force there; for state rebellion is state suicide. We can therefore yield to political necessity, without compromising private rights or private interests. The whole question of slavery in the seceded states is now within the jurisdiction of the United States. The plea of justice to the slave, like the Irishman's plea, justice to Ireland, always stands good, and never to be disregarded by statesmen, any more than by moralists. On each and all these grounds we demand the total extinction of slavery, and the recognition of all persons heretofore held to service in the seceded states by the laws thereof, as free persons, and as no longer held to service anywhere.

This is the first question, and with this question it would have been well to stop till after the war, and not have inopportunely complicated it with the question, What shall be done with the emancipated slaves? But this latter question has been raised, and we cannot now refuse to consider it, for on its solution depends in no small degree the practical answer that will be given to the question of emancipation. We are disposed to agree with Mr. Lincoln, Mr. Blair, and many distinguished members of both houses of congress, that the best mode of dealing with the emancipated slaves is to colonize them outside of the United States, at the earliest reasonable moment. We do not for ourselves, however, make emancipation turn on colonization. We insist on emancipation for its own sake, colonization, or no colonization. We hold that the government, as the necessary and natural guardian of the emancipated slaves, has the right to insist on their emigration, and that emigration, and colonization after emancipation, is best for both blacks and whites; but we are persuaded if government will secure a territory suitable to their tastes, habits, and temperament, and facilitate their migration to it, the emancipated negroes will, in a reasonable time, nearly all migrate to it of their own accord. We know the strong local attachment of the negro, and his little enterprising or adventurous disposition, but it must be borne in mind that the negroes have leaders of their own race, or with some mixture of white blood perhaps, who are men of ability, intelligence, and enterprise. These men can be nobody in a community where the white race predominates, and therefore can easily be induced to emigrate and to lead their people with them. Many of these, wearing their life out in slavery, are not wholly unfitted by their genius and ability to lead forth the millions of their race to a new territory, and to found there and govern a state. Seeing that they and their people, if remaining in the United States, must remain there, in spite of all philanthropy can do, as slaves or as outcasts, pariahs, as we have said, they will feel for themselves, and without much difficulty make their people feel, that the best thing for them is to migrate to a country where they can live in a community of their own race, or where at least their own will be the dominant race. Such migration or exode will be the beginning of the uprising of their race. It will quicken a new spirit in them, and be the commencement of their return toward the type from which they have departed so far, and their recompense for the long ages of slavery and oppression they have endured from the white race.

Still we do not conceal from ourselves, the opposition of the other class mentioned at the North, not merely to colonization, but to emancipation, under any form or any condition, is the most formidable obstacle to justice to the slave to be encountered. We have been surprised to find how completely wedded to negro slavery have become our old Democratic politicians, and how widely pro-slavery sentiments are cherished in the free states. We had so long been living out of the political world, engrossed with our theological and philosophical studies, that we had taken little note of the changes in public opinion favorable to slavery, which had been effected during the last ten or fifteen years, and we find, very much to our regret, the North, as a whole, less abolition than the South. Our commercial cities had become almost completely southernized in their views of slavery, and opposition to the existence of slavery, or even to its extension into new territory, has had very little influence with the merchants of Boston, New York, and Philadelphia, and the interests of trade, far more than patriotism or loyalty, have moved them to support the administration in suppressing the rebellion. The Morrill tariff moved them more than the fall of Sumter. The commercial class in no country and in no age is remarkable for patriotism, and finds usually its country where its profits are largest, or best secured. It with us seeks to preserve the integrity of the Union, for if that should be lost, they would lose a large portion of their trade. But for the same reason they are opposed to the abolition of slavery. The abolition of slavery, and the great changes it would effect in southern society, would at least, for a time, seriously lessen the amount of business, and diminish its profits. They want the Union restored as speedily as possible, but at the same time they want slavery retained, so that buying and selling may go on as before, and hence as soon as they thought it likely that slavery might be interfered with, and their old customers at the South crippled in their resources, they became less willing to furnish the government with the means of carrying on the war.

But the politicians, to some extent, of all parties, but more especially of the old Democratic party, are the most inveterate enemies of the policy of emancipation, and from them we hear it proclaimed, over and over again, that the armies of the Union will throw down their arms, if the war were made, in any sense, a war of liberation. They keep up a continued howl against abolitionists and radicals, and would seem to regard slavery as more than the Union, as the corner-stone of the republic, as the the essential condition of its prosperity, and the very palladium of its safety. Remove slavery and we should be obliged to sing, in our grief, *Ilium fuit.* These politicians had for some time a great advantage over us, in making it appear that they had the administration on their side, and that we, in opposing them, were deserting the very president we had helped to elect. Since the sixth of March last, this pretense has been taken from them, and the president, by his message to congress on that day, shows that the administration is at least on the side of emancipation, and is prepared to initiate it, if, indeed, it be not prepared to go further.

But the reason of the advocacy of slavery by those old politicians is no secret. If slavery goes, they lose their stock in trade, and their vocation is gone. The Democratic party was always a southern party. It had its chief strength in the South, and its ablest and most important allies. Let slavery go, and that party is defunct. It can no longer rule the nation, and will be henceforth remembered only as the party that, under pretence of fidelity to the constitution, has done its best to sacrifice the life of the nation. If slavery be abolished, it can never have the South with it again. If the Union ceases to be the union of freedom and slavery, it can have no charms for it; for no class of people, than those who composed it, will be more utterly distrusted and despised by the South. They will, therefore, do all in their power to save the " patriarchal institution," and to rear once more their Democracy on the slavery of the negro race, as its basis. But we trust they will fail, and the logic of the movement, represented by the Republican party, will carry the nation on, we had almost said, in spite of itself, to the final emancipation of itself from the political power of slavery, by the complete destruction of slavery as property. We think we have shown how this end can be obtained under the constitution, without violating any constitutional provision or existing law. If we have so done, the way is clear for the final obliteration from our soil of the curse of slavery.

WHAT THE REBELLION TEACHES.*

[From Brownson's Quarterly Review for July, 1862.]

Dr. Keogh, the able and loyal editor of the Pittsburg *Catholic*, has in his popular lecture before the Catholic Institute of Cincinnati, given a very condensed, clear, explicit and just statement of the Catholic principles of government as taught by the greatest and most approved fathers and doctors of the church. To those familiar with the writings of St. Augustine, St. Thomas, Bellarmine, and Suarez his statement contains indeed little that is new, but it presents their doctrine in a popular form, and applies it to the great struggles now raging between legitimate authority and revolutionism both at home and abroad. His lecture, which we should be glad to see widely circulated, is timely, and brings out and enforces certain great principles of which the people, whether orthodox or heterodox, cannot be too frequently reminded, and with which they cannot be too thoroughly imbued,—principles which, if they had been more generally held and more generally understood, would have saved Europe from revolutionary terrorism, and our own country from the fearful evils of the civil war, with which she is now so sorely afflicted.

Men who pique themselves on being "practical men," men of "plain common sense," are apt to treat with contempt those of us who deal with principles, and labor to establish sound and just doctrines; but all experience proves that the people collectively as well as individually are logical, and sure, sooner or later, to draw from their premises their logical conclusion. If they start with a false theory of authority, they are certain to fetch up in despotism, and, if with a false theory of liberty, they are just as certain to fetch up in revolutionism, anarchy, or license. A false theory respecting the divine origin of power has led nation after nation to submit to the misrule and oppression of despots, and a false theory as to popular sovereignty subjects all European society to the terror of revolutionism,

---

* *Catholic Principles of Civil Government. A Lecture,* by Rev. James Keogh, D. D. Cincinnati: 1862.

and in this country leads to rebellion, secession, and civil war. The doctrine of popular sovereignty held and proclaimed by our American demagogues, and heretofore generally insisted on by the American press, both North and South, fully justifies secession, and condemns the federal government for its attempt to coerce the rebellious states into submission. If the people are sovereign, and government is nothing but an agency, created by them for carrying out their will, as modern demagogy teaches, by what right do you deny the people of the slaveholding states the right to secede from the Union, and to form a southern confederacy, if such be their pleasure? Either the theory which you have insisted on in the case of all foreign revolutions is untenable, and should be promptly disavowed, or you are wrong in attempting to enforce the laws of the Union over states that do not choose to obey them. If the Æmilian provinces had the right to secede from the papal authority, and annex themselves to Piedmont, why has not South Carolina the right to secede from the Union, and enter into the southern confederacy? Yet there are men, that hailed the secession of the Æmilian provinces as a glorious assertion of freedom, who are now fighting against South Carolina, and willing to see her annihilated. There are men amongst us, men who applaud to the echo Garibaldi, that prince of freebooters, laud him as a patriot and a hero, who yet demand the capture and execution of Jefferson Davis as a traitor. It is said that even our government actually invited Garibaldi to accept a commission in our army, and there was at one time a report that he was to be its commander-in-chief,—he, a man not worthy to be named in the same breath with even Jefferson Davis, John B. Floyd, or Gideon Pillow!

It is of the last importance that we start with sound and just principles. It is absurd to claim the right to resist government, if it governs by divine right, or to undertake to suppress a rebellion, if the people are above law, and absolutely and persistently sovereign, as our demagogues assert. In either case the inconsistency is too great to be permanently successful. We ourselves support the government, because we believe in government, and do not believe in the demagogical doctrine of popular sovereignty. We love both liberty and authority, and believe in the possibility of neither without the other. We opposed the European revolutions of 1848 and 1849; we opposed the revolution that reëstablished the Napoleonic dynasty in 1852, the revolutionary campaign of the French in Italy in 1859, and have opposed all the Italian revolutions for which it prepared the way, and which it stirred up. We condemned the secession of the Æmilian provinces from the papal authority, and the annexation of the duchies to the Sard kingdom. We justified the attempt of the sovereign of Rome to reduce his rebellious provinces to submission, as we have justified the emperor of Austria in his efforts to save his empire from dismemberment. We are perfectly consistent, therefore, in denying the right of southern secession, and in sustaining the federal government in the use of force for coercing the rebellious states into submission, and in putting forth its full strength to preserve the Union, and save the life and integrity of the nation. We should have been equally false to our country and to our principles had we not done so.

We may be told here in answer to our boast of consistency, that we, also, defended the cause of Italian unity, and recommended the union of all Italy under the sceptre of the house of Savoy. Be it so. We desired and desire Italian unity; we wish Italy to be a united and powerful state. We look upon a united Italy, embracing under a wise, just, and honorable constitutional government the whole peninsula, as a desideratum in European politics. But we were never willing, and are not now willing, to see it effected by revolutionary or despotic violence. We never were willing to encourage secession or invasion as the means of effecting it, though, if effected by such means, we maintained, and still dare maintain, that, when effected, it would be wiser to accept it, as *un fait accompli*, acquiesce in it, and make the best terms possible with it, than to make unavailing attempts to restore the old order of things. This is all that can be said against us, and this much we can maintain in perfect consistency with our principles, even if it be an error of judgment.

Moreover, the reasons which make us wish the unity of Italy, lead us to oppose the disintegration of the American Union. This is the epoch of great states, great powers, as they are called, and small states or powers stand a poor chance of existence, and a still poorer chance of independence. The great powers manage the politics of the world as suits themselves, or, as they can best agree among themselves. Since the popes have ceased to be at the head of the political system of Europe, the division of Italy into a number of petty states has deprived her of political influence, and reduced her to a "geographical expression." We would see, if the thing be practicable (of which we have our doubts, as things go), a united, independent, constitutional Italy, as one of the great powers of Europe. Such an Italy is necessary to keep up the equilibrium between Catholic and non-Catholic Europe, and to secure the balance of power in the Old World. We would preserve the American Union in order to preserve the American state as one of the great states or powers of the world, and to insure to the New World her proper rank and political influence. We oppose the disintegration of the Union, because its disintegration would reduce America to a mere geographical expression and compel the people of this continent to follow the politics and submit to the will or caprice of the great powers of the Old World. We want the United States to remain a great power, so that it may compel respect to its rights and interests, and give weight to its views and wishes in the politics of the European states. We do not want to see our great republic reduced to the rank of a second or third rate power. Our political principles and our patriotism alike make us wish that it should, at least, preserve its rank and its power. So, under any and every point of view, we are consistent with ourselves in opposing secession, and seeking to preserve the life and integrity of the republic.

Secession itself is another illustration of the importance of theory. Secession is only a logical deduction from the theory of state sovereignty, which has been favored to some extent almost from the formation of the federal government, and in the North as well as in the South, and alternately by all parties. Patrick Henry, of Virginia, and Samuel Adams, of Massachusetts, opposed the federal constitution on the ground that it created a national government, and they wanted only a confederacy or congress of sovereign states. Mr. Jefferson inclined to the view that the states retained their sovereignty even after the adoption of the constitution. Such was the dominant view of the Anti-federal party of 1798, which, under the name of Republican, came into power with Mr. Jefferson in 1801, and it has always been the doctrine, or at least the doctrinal tendency, of the so-called Democratic party. President Jackson opposed it when asserted and acted on by South Carolina, and favored it in the adjoining state of Georgia, whose nullification of a judgment of the supreme court was no less reprehensible than South Carolina's nullification of an act of congress.   The New-England states, excepting Vermont, all but ruined by the war forced on the country by the southern and middle states, resorted to it in 1812, and threatened to secede from the Union.   The doctrine has been lurking in the American mind from the first, and the section that felt itself aggrieved has always more or less boldly assumed it.   South Carolina did little more in 1831, than Massachusetts talked of doing in 1814.   If we suppose that the states entered the Union as sovereigns, and that each remains after the union a sovereign state, it will be hard to say that any state has not the inherent right to secede, when she judges it for her interest to do so ; and equally hard to say, that, if she so judges and secedes, the remaining states have the right to use force to compel her to return to the Union.   Moreover, if she remains a sovereign state, she can, by revoking her act of accession to the Union, absolve all her citizens from their allegiance to the United States, and require them to take the oath of allegiance to herself.   You have no right to call the seceders or the confederates rebels, or to treat them as rebels or traitors, if you concede their doctrine of state sovereignty.   In fact, there are few, if any, among them who regard themselves as traitors or rebels.   In their view of the case, they are as loyal and as patriotic as we are in ours.

Let no man mistake us.   We are not justifying the southern rebellion.   The whole country knows on which side we are, and that according to our ability and in our own narrow sphere no man has done or sacrificed more than we for the sake of the Union.   We hold secession to be rebellion, and the seceders in arms against the Union to be rebels; but we can do so only on condition that we reject the theory of state sovereignty on which they act, and which has received too much countenance in all parts of the Union.   The fact that a theory which justifies them, or would justify them if true, has been widely entertained, and entertained by men of eminence, whose loyalty and patriotism are not to be questioned, may have, and, perhaps, should have, some weight with us in moderating our personal feelings toward them, and even in mitigating the punishment we may deem it necessary to inflict on them when the rebellion has been suppressed.   But not for this do we state it.   We state it for the purpose of indicating the danger of false theories, and to rebuke those self-complacent men who are so ready to denounce as vain "theorizers" and "abstractionists" those who call attention to first principles, and seek to establish a sound political philosophy. We have, not all of us, but large numbers of us, cherished two false principles, one in relation to government in general, and the other in relation to the federal government in particular,—principles which we find in this hour of trial we cannot act on, without giving up all government, and suffering the Union to fall to pieces as a rope of sand. The blood and treasure which are so freely poured out by the loyal states in defence of the authority of the government and the integrity of the nation, are the earnest and practical protest of a great and free people against the demagogical interpretation of the doctrine of popular sovereignty, and the disintegrating doctrine of state sovereignty, and it is to be hoped that the war when it closes will have corrected both, the one as fatal to government itself, and the other as fatal to national unity and integrity.

We love our form of government; we want no alterations in the federal constitution, and very few in any of the several state constitutions. We are republican, heart and soul, and far more so than we were before the rebellion broke out. We have had our confidence in popular government incalculably increased by the experience of the last twelve months. The strength and energy put forth by the United States, the mighty army we have been able, within a year, to collect, arm and equip, discipline and place in the field; the large and efficient navy we have been able to create and place on our coasts and mighty rivers, the respectable efficiency of both branches of the service, and the orderly behavior, patience, endurance, and bravery of both our land and naval forces, have, we confess, astonished us, made us proud of our country and proud of our countrymen. A people so long engaged in peaceful pursuits, so long in the enjoyment of peace as to have almost lost the tradition as well as the experience of war, without military organization, without armies, ships, arms, or stores, sending more than a half a million of soldiers to the field, and creating, arming, and equipping an efficient navy of two or three hundred ships-of-war, in so brief a time, may well be called a great people. Blunders there may have been, arising from inexperience; traitors there may have been in and out of office to embarrass our measures, and impede our operations; and much narrow-mindness and inefficiency there may also have been; but after all we have shown an aptitude, an energy, and strength, unsurpassed by any other people in the history of the world. No, this civil war, whether it terminate in a few months, or whether it linger for a dozen years, has for ever settled the question in favor of free government, and rendered the old arguments against it obsolete. It has proved that, if the republic had been united in a war against foreign enemies, it would have been invincible against all Europe, for we count as ours, as American, the skill, the energy, and the strength shown by the rebels themselves.

Universal suffrage, which, we own, we had come to distrust, has vindicated itself, and the people have proved that they are capable of self-government, and can dispense with both kings and nobles. Even our liberal naturalization laws, and our open hospitality to foreigners, which we with many others feared might prove dangerous to our American order of civilization, have been justified, and Know-nothingism has lost its last advocate. In the war natural-born and naturalized citizens have fought with equal bravery and devotion side by side. German, Irish, French, Italian born citizens have proved themselves loyal Americans, have been not the last to rush in where blows fall thickest and fall heaviest, and have contributed their full share to the victories we have won, and to the glory of our arms. All are Americans by loyalty, by common suffering, by common hardships, by common dangers, and by common deeds. They who have mingled their blood on the same battle-field, in defence of the same noble cause, must henceforth be, and be treated, as brothers. The war has made or is making us one people, and has removed or is removing more than one of the old causes of division. No American can forget that chiefly to the sturdy Germans of the West we owe it that the great state of Missouri did not follow her sister slave states into secession, or that in the very darkest hour, when even stout hearts failed, the brave and impulsive Irish were foremost to volunteer in the armies of the republic. No American can ever forget that full one-third of the forces that have won our victories, and saved the life and integrity of the nation were not born on American soil. Disloyal as have been many of those who belong to our own church, and as absurd as are the prejudices of many of our brethren against New England, no loyal Protestant can ever forget that in the nation's struggle for life Catholics have sent to the field both in officers and men far more than their proportion.

The proportion of Catholics in the army is probably more than double the proportion which Catholics bear to the whole population of the country. After this no sane American can ever countenance an anti-foreign, or an anti-Catholic party in politics. Foreign-born citizens have sealed their naturalization with their blood, and Catholics have vindicated their right to civil and political equality in every battle that has been fought, in every defeat that has been suffered, and in every victory that has been won. No blood has flowed more freely or in richer torrents than theirs, and the non-Catholic who forgets it is not worthy the name of American, and should undergo the old Anglo-Saxon punishment of being branded *nidering,*—infamous.

We own, and are glad to own, that the war has corrected many of our own prejudices, and relieved many of our fears; it has given us full confidence in the strength and durability of our institutions. It has, also, corrected many errors the popular mind had imbibed, and exploded more than one popular fallacy. It has proved the necessity of upholding the legitimate authority of government, and therefore refuted the notion that government is a mere agency, with no power, in case of need, to coerce obedience. It has proved that in the freest states loyalty and obedience to law are as necessary, and as indispensable as in monarchical states. It has refuted the popular theories of revolutionists so rife in our times, and proved the necessity of conservative principles, and respect for established authority. Happily the war came in season to arrest our wild radicalism, before the heart of our people had become wholly corrupt, and before they had become as base as the theories of their demagogues. The rebellion has shown, also, that the Union can be saved only by rejecting the interpretation of the constitution that makes the United States a mere congress of sovereigns, and by adopting and adhering to the doctrine that assumes them to be a nation, a real state, one and indivisible. The people in the loyal states have acted right in the present struggle, but they have done so only in opposition to opinions and theories which had gained great credit in all sections of the country. The doctrines that there is a sacred right of revolution, and that a state cannot be coerced, gave the rebellion every advantage under the imbecile Buchanan, enabled it to mature itself without resistance, and to make openly all the preparations supposed to be necessary to secure its success, and paralyzed for months the activity and strength of the present administration. Even stanch Republicans shook before these doctrines, and many of our ablest statesmen and truest patriots feared to grapple with the danger, and talked of " compromise," some even thought we must let the seceding states go. It was doubtful how far the administration could count on the support of the free states themselves in an attempt to put down the rebellion by force of arms. If patriotism had not triumphed over theory, and if the people had not felt it more urgent to maintain the integrity of the nation than to carry out the speculations of their demagogues, the administration would have been unable to collect force enough to defend for a single day the national capital. The danger was far greater than has been told, and, perhaps, than ever will be told. The rebellion is crushed, or is sure to be crushed, if no foreign power intervenes, because the northern Democratic leaders rose above their doctrines, and refused to fulfil the expectations of their southern brethren, who counted on them as friends and allies. The rebellion has proved that the doctrines we refer to are, as far as they go, incompatible with the stability of government, and especially with the maintenance of the life and integrity of the nation, and therefore that they are false and dangerous, and to be abandoned in speculation as we have been forced to abandon them in practice. The war, we hope, will have the effect to conform our theories to the practice which all loyal men now see to be just and necessary, and which the people have so generously and heroically adopted.

The principles of government which are as necessary under a republican as under any other form of government, require us to distinguish between the *power*, and the *person* or *persons* invested with it. The power comes from God, for, as says the apostle, *non est potestas, nisi a Deo ;* but being from God, it is necessarily a trust, not an absolute, inherent right. Here is the real distinction between legitimate authority and cæsarism, liberty and despotism. The prejudice against the divine origin of power grows out of the failure to make this distinction, and of assuming that the assertion of the power, or authority, as from God, means that God has given to certain individuals or certain families, the indefeasible right to govern, an inalienable and inadmissible right, which cannot, whatever the character of the ruler or the intolerable tyranny of his government, be resisted without impiety, and rebellion against God, the doc-

trine known in history as the "divine right of kings and
passive obedience." This doctrine makes the prince the
living law, according to the maxim of the old Roman jurist,
Quod placuit principi, id legis habet vigorem. This is
what we call cæsarism, and oppose as despotism, which is
destructive alike of the best interests of society and the true
dignity of man. It lies at the basis of the old Roman imperialism, under which the emperor was the living law and
worshipped as a divinity. Even the Christian and orthodox
Emperor Theodosius was addressed by his subjects as "your
eternity." This doctrine was revived in the sixteenth and
seventeenth centuries, and in England lost the Stuarts their
throne, and in France provoked the old French revolution,
while it reduced Spain from the foremost power of Europe
to a third-rate state, and Italy to "a geographical expression." No sane man, who knows aught of liberty, can for
one moment countenance the divine origin of government
in the sense of this doctrine.

To get rid of "the divine right of kings and passive
obedience," the friends of freedom went to the opposite extreme, asserted the *popular* origin of power, and made the
people in their own native right and might the living law.
These made the people Cæsar, the popular will the law, and
asserted as a maxim, *Vox populi vox Dei,* or *Quod placuit
populo, id legis habet vigorem,* and therefore in principle as
absolute a despotism as that asserted by the cæsarists they
warred against. This is the condemnation of modern philosophical democracy, as defended by Mazzini and his
friends, who do not hesitate to clothe the people with all the
attributes claimed by the old imperialists for the emperor,
and to say not only " people-prince," " people-king," but
"people-priest," and " people-god." It is in the name of
this " people-divinity " that democratic revolutions in Europe, of late years, have been commenced, and of which
Garibaldi is the soldier, and Mazzini is the prophet. Mazzini
is the Mahomet and Garibaldi the Kaled of this new
worship, a political imposture, for withstanding which any
amount of abuse has been heaped on Pio Nono, Francis
Joseph, and the young king of Naples. It is this political
theory, called by us European democracy, and which like all
the vices of the Old World, has of late years found its way
to our country, that we for nearly twenty years have been
battling with our best ability, and holding up to our readers as wholly incompatible with American republicanism.

American democracy, which, to avoid confusion, we call republicanism, has and can have no affinity with this European democracy, and can no more be reconciled with it than Christianity can be reconciled with demon-worship.

The true theory of the origin of government is dialectic, and harmonizes these two extremes. The power, the right, or the authority is from God, who says " By me kings reign, and lawgivers decree just things," but who shall be the depositary of the power, or exercise the trust, is a matter determinable by the people themselves. The power comes from God, but comes to the prince or government through the people. Since the power comes from God, it comes from a source above the people, and they neither individually nor collectively have any right to resist it, and are bound in conscience to respect and obey it. The law of God settles the authority or right of government, and the people settle the question who shall be governors, or who shall exercise the power. When the people have settled the form of the government, and have legally chosen their rulers, these rulers, within the limits and conditions fixed by the constitution, have the divine right to govern, do govern by authority of God, and the people individually and collectively are bound to obey them, not as the ministers of their will, but as ministers of the divine will, and therefore obedience is due them in conscience, and disobedience is not only a crime against society, but a sin against God. This principle gives authority and stability to government, for it gives it the right to wield the sword, to punish evil doers and to enforce obedience to its acts, while it denies all right of resistance, and binds all subjects in conscience to obedience. It also secures freedom by making the power a trust, and placing in the hands of the people the right to determine who shall and who shall not be vested with it.

The theory of "the divine right of kings and passive obedience," the cæsarist theory, as expounded by James I. of England, Louis XIV. of France, Philip II. of Spain, and the great Bossuet, does not deny that the monarch is responsible to God for the use he may make of his power, or that God will punish him, here or hereafter, in his own person or in his descendants, for any injustice, tyranny, or oppression of which he may be guilty, but it denies that he is responsible to the nation or justiciable by the people. It, consequently, denies to the nation or the people all right of resistance, not simply to legitimate authority, but to tyranny and oppression, and leaves them without any right to demand, and, if necessary, to effect by force a redress of grievances. It, therefore, covers the oppressor with the ægis of religion, and renders oppression sacred and inviolable. The other theory, the European democratic theory, makes the persons invested with authority responsible indeed, but to the people alone, and asserts for the people the right to resist their rulers at any time, in any way, and for any reason they please. It divests government of all moral sanction, deprives obedience of all religious obligation, and makes civil obedience a mere question of expediency, and results necessarily in *mobocracy*, to use a barbarous term, anarchy, or the despotism of the majority. The dialectic theory we adopt makes rulers responsible to God, as all men are, and also to the nation, or to the people. To the people, because they receive their investiture from them, and to God, because the power with which they are clothed is from him, and remains his. What is essential to the existence and maintenance of government, the essential and necessary rights of authority under any and every form of government, are from God, held and exercised by divine right, independently of all popular conventions or popular will. These are the divine or natural rights of government in that it is government. The people may say who shall or shall not be intrusted with the exercise of these rights, but the rights themselves are determined by the very nature of civil society, and depend on the eternal reason or will of the Creator. No popular conventions, however called or constituted, can create them, or rightly abridge them. They rest on the same basis with the rights of man,—rights held from the Almighty in the very constitution of our manhood. All Americans hold the natural rights of man sacred and inviolable; the essential rights, we would say, the natural rights, of civil society should be held equally sacred and inviolable, for they are equally from God. Let our countrymen so hold, and they will hold what we assert in asserting that the power is from God.

What we wish here to assert is that the power is not conventional, nor of popular, nor indeed of human institution, and therefore that it can never be justly resisted by the people either collectively or individually, and that it has the right to command, and the right to use all the force necessary to maintain itself, to suppress all opposition and to make its commands obeyed, however large or small the party opposing it. Even in constituting the government the people have no right to deny it any of its essential or natural rights, or to restrict power beyond the limits of the divine charter. Any clause in the constitution doing this must be treated as null and void, as repugnant to natural right, to the necessary and essential authority of civil society. In other words, there is a higher law than the will of the people,—the original divine law of civil society. The government while obeying this law, without which it would not and could not be government, and keeping within the limits of its conventional restrictions, is legitimate, sacred, and inviolable, and cannot, as we have said, be resisted without crime against the state, and sin against God, since natural law is divine law. This, as we have said, secures the stability and authority of government, by limiting the power of the people over it, and denying the right of popular resistance to it so long as it simply discharges its legitimate functions and does not transgress its legitimate bounds. Yet it by no means demands passive obedience to the tyrant, or forbids popular resistance to wrong and oppression, or what was formerly understood by the right of revolution, for the oppressor or the tyrant forfeits to the people the power that comes from God.

In the modern sense, as now understood by European revolutionists, the right of revolution cannot be asserted, for it denies the right of government. Formerly the right of revolution meant simply the right to resist and overthrow tyranny. This right no lover of freedom can question. A government that abuses and persists in abusing its trusts, that plays the tyrant, that perverts power from the common good, or the good of the community, that makes it a burden and a curse instead of a common benefit, and obstinately persists in so doing, forfeits its rights, loses its authority, becomes a usurper, and therefore may be justly resisted, and made to give place to another, because in resisting it there is no resistance to the power that comes from God. The tyranny of the prince absolves the subject from his allegiance. All that comes from God is dialectic, and his grants cannot contradict one another. His patent of the rights of man to the individual is in harmony with his patent of authority to civil society, and he can give no power of government to society incompatible with the rights he gives to the individual. When the individual uses the rights of man in a sense incompatible with the rights of

authority, he errs, and society may set him right; so when
the government uses its power in a sense incompatible with
the rights of man, it transcends its authority, and may be
corrected by the people. The right of revolution in this
sense we assert. But the right of revolution seems to us,
as popularly understood at present, to mean the right to
overthrow any existing government even by violence and
bloodshed whenever the people, or a portion of them numerous or strong enough to do it, choose to attempt it, simply
for the sake of introducing another and as they believe a
better political organization, although no act of tyranny or
oppression can be alleged against it. In this sense we deny
the right of revolution, as incompatible with the very idea
of government.

One government may be more wisely constituted than
another, and it often happens that the growth and prosperity of a nation demand grave changes in the constitutional
law; but if the government is honestly administered according to the existing constitution, and its administrators
take care to usurp no power, we deny the right of the people
to seek even a desirable change by revolutionary violence.
In such a case the remedy is reform, not revolution,—reform
brought about by peaceful, not violent measures, by the co-
operation of authority, secured by the force of public opinion. The right of resistance must not be confounded with
the present sense of the word *revolution*. The right of resistance to tyranny is a sacred and divine right, as sacred
and divine as the right of legitimate government itself; the
right of revolution as the word is now used has no existence, and revolution is not and cannot be justifiable.

The power in the case of the federal government, as in
that of all other governments, comes from God through the
people, but through the people acting as political communities, not simply as population. These political communities
or states are the successors or continuators of the English
colonies created by the British crown, or under the sovereignty of Great Britain, and therefore, though political
communities or bodies politic and corporate, and since the
revolution no longer colonies, they are not complete or
sovereign states. The sovereignty previously in the British
crown or in the mother country was not assumed or exercised
by the colonies severally, and on becoming independent of
Great Britain they did not each for itself succeed to her
sovereignty, or to any more power than they had possessed

as colonies. That is, the mother country was succeeded not by the states severally, but by the *United States*. The United States as one political people took the place in the new order introduced by the revolution previously held by the mother country, and therefore became in their unity the inheritor of her sovereignty. The revolution simply transferred the sovereignty from Great Britain to the *United States.* Hence, under the old confederation and even after the adoption of the federal constitution, some of the states continued to act under the colonial charters granted by the British crown. The states, have, as had the colonies, certain civil and political rights, but never at any moment have they held or claimed the full rights of sovereignty. As colonies the sovereignty was in Great Britain or the British crown ; under the confederation the sovereignty was claimed, possessed, and exercised not by the states separately, but by the United States, as it is under the federal constitution.

We will not say that, if the several Anglo-American colonies had each in its individual capacity asserted and maintained its independence, it would not have become on its successful assertion of its independence a free sovereign state possessed of the full rights of sovereignty, and the Union formed between them been a congress or league of sovereigns, a union of the nature of the Zollverein formed by the northern states of Germany. But such was not the fact. The independence was declared by the united colonies, which by this fact became united states. The articles of confederation were drawn up by the united states, and the new political power recognized and treated with by foreign nations, and finally acknowledged by Great Britain, was not thirteen independent powers or sovereignties, but one power, one national sovereignty, called the *United States* of America. The people of the United States have, therefore, always been and are one political people, and have never existed as separate, independent, and sovereign states. Under the colonial *régime* the political unity was in the British crown ; under the confederation it was in the United States, and it is in the United States under the federal constitution, and where is lodged the unity, there is lodged the sovereignty of a nation.

Nor will we say that there were in transferring the sovereignty from the British crown to the United States no irregularities, no isolated acts incompatible with the doctrine we

advocate.   Revolutionary times are seldom remarkable for
their order and regularity.   But what is disorderly, irregular, or anomalous in those times establishes no precedent,
and forms no rule of interpretation. With the exception of
Vermont and Texas, not included in the original " Thirteen," no state in this Union has ever existed as an independent sovereign state.   None of them has ever been recognized as a sovereign power by any foreign state, ever
exercised the functions of a sovereign power, ever entered
into relations with foreign powers, negotiated foreign treaties, or had the right to make war or peace.   The supreme
attributes of sovereignty they have never as a fact possessed,
exercised, or, until recently, claimed. Foreign nations have
known and now know only the United States.   All our foreign treaties are negotiated by and with the United States ;
the only flag floating from ships of war or commerce, known
on the ocean, or in foreign ports is the United States flag ;
the United States make war and peace, enter into and discharge national obligations, acquire and hold national territory by purchase or conquest, and stand recognized and
respected by all the nations of the earth as an independent
sovereign nation.   None of the several states, excepting
Vermont and Texas, have ever been so recognized, performed any of these functions, or sustained any of these
relations ; and the exception in the case of Vermont and
Texas amounts to nothing, for in the Union they stand on
the same footing with the original states.   The states have
never exercised the rights of sovereignty, and have remained
political and independent communities only in the sense in
which they were such communities when colonies under the
crown of Great Britain. They hold their civil and political
rights now, as when they were colonies, in subordination to
the national sovereign.

We know there were differences of opinion at the epoch
of the formation of the federal constitution, that some patriots wished to reserve a larger and others a smaller sphere
of action to the states, and some wished, it is probable, to
make the Union simply a congress of sovereigns. There are,
no doubt, in the constitution traces of these differences of
opinions and wishes ; but it is clear that the convention of
1787 intended to frame, and regarded themselves as framing
a constitution of a national government, a constitution for
one political people, and the few phrases or even provisions
that smack of the state sovereignty theory were inserted or

suffered to remain so as to escape the danger of having the constitution rejected by any one of the states. The convention were content to secure the substance of nationality, without pushing the state sovereignty men to the wall. They effected their object, though not without some ambiguity of language, and leaving a chance for cavillers and pettifoggers.

The fact that the constitution was formed by a convention of the people as states, and that the constitution was ratified by the states, or conventions of the people of the several states, has led even some who assert the national character of the government to suppose the constitution emanated from the states severally, and not from the people of the United States, and that the American people became one political people only by virtue of the constitution. This, we believe, was Mr. Webster's doctrine. But this is contradicted by the very preamble of the constitution itself, which says, "We the people of the United States,"—not we the people of the several states,—" do ordain and establish this constitution for the United States of America." The people of the United States are not created by the constitution, for they precede it, and ordain and establish it. Our own former error on the subject grew out of supposing the states succeeded severally not only to the rights of the colonies under the British crown, but to the sovereignty possessed by that crown itself. This was a mistake. The sovereignty of the crown did not fall to the states severally, but to the *United* States, and therefore after independence, as before, the states severally were subordinate, not sovereign political communities, and the people of the United States were one political people with a single national sovereign. This, if we are not mistaken, is substantially the doctrine held by John Quincy Adams, no mean authority in questions of this sort.

Art. X. of the amendments has been adduced in defence of a doctrine opposite to the one we are defending. "The powers not delegated to the United States by the constitution, nor prohibited by it to the states, are reserved to the states respectively, or to the people." Hence it has been argued that the powers of the United States are powers delegated to it by the states, and that all the powers of government not so delegated are reserved to the states severally, or to the people, not of the United States, but of the several states. But this inference is not necessary, and the amendment, though undoubtedly intended as a constitutional guaranty of the reserved rights of the several states, says nothing in favor of state sovereignty. It asserts indeed that the federal government is a government of delegated and limited powers, but it does not assert that the United States are created by state delegation, or that the political people called the United States have only delegated and limited powers. In the amendment the term *United States* must be taken in the sense of the government created or perfected by the constitution. The federal government has only delegated powers, but the powers are delegated by the people of the *united*, not the *several* states. It is a government of limited powers, because the people so willed, not because the powers of the people of the United States are limited by the rights of the people of the several states. The reservation, again, is to the states respectively, or to the people. But what people ? The article does not say, to the people of the states respectively, or the people of the states severally, and therefore we must understand them to be the people of the United States, the very people assembled in convention to constitute the national government.

There is nothing in our view of the unity and sovereignty of the people of the United States to interfere with the federal element of our government. The states severally were never complete, that is, sovereign states, for, as we have seen, the British sovereignty over the colonies did not fall to the states severally, but to the states united, or, the United States. But the colonies, though created at different dates and differently constituted, had by royal grant, charter, or custom, certain political and civil rights, which they retained after independence. These rights rendered uniform in all the states, enlarged in some respects and abridged in others by the federal constitution, are in their substance and in their tenure anterior to that constitution, and are what we called the reserved rights of the states, that is to say, rights which the United States willed should be reserved and guarantied to the states severally. These rights, even as colonial rights, were rights the sovereign was bound to treat as sacred and inviolable, and it was for his alleged violation of them his sovereignty was abjured, and independence declared. Even under the British crown the colonies within the sphere of their rights were legally free and independent political communities. They remain so under the sovereignty of the United States, and the federal government is bound to treat those rights as sacred and inviolable. They are recognized and guarantied by the constitution.

But we may remark that, after all, these rights were not original in the colonies as civil society, and could not be defended by them as their natural rights of government. They were rights held by them as British colonies and as British subjects, and were therefore of the nature of franchises, of chartered, or of vested rights. They were sacred and inviolable only so long as they who held them observed the conditions expressed or implied in the grant. They could be forfeited as all such rights may be forfeited, and the king might issue his writ *quo warranto* against any one of the colonies, and, on evidence of forfeiture, revoke the charter, as in several cases was actually done. The United States holds substantially the relation to the several states held by the British crown to the Anglo-American colonies. The rights of the several states are the rights of those colonies, and are held by them as American states and American citizens, not as original, independent, and sovereign states. As long as the express or implied conditions of their charter or tenure are complied with, they are sacred and inviolable, and within their sphere the states are independent of the national government, and of one another. But if they break these conditions, if they cease to be *American* states, and their people to be citizens of the United States, they forfeit their liberties, and the United States as sovereign has the right to revoke their charters, or annul their state constitutions, and enter upon their possession as upon any other forfeited estate. The state by its own act has lapsed, and the sovereign only resumes what is his own. Hence Mr. Sumner was right in declaring state secession state suicide, as we proved by a slightly different line of argument in our last *Review*.

The right of a state to resist the federal government, in case it becomes tyrannical and oppressive, is precisely the right, neither greater nor less, of individuals to do the same, and what that is, has been already stated. So long as the federal government keeps within its constitutional powers, it governs by divine right, and no state or individual has any moral or political right to resist it. If the free and fair exercise of its legitimate powers bears unequally upon different sections, changes or reforms may be sought, but only in a constitutional way, and by peaceful means. No violence, no insurrection, no rebellion, no armed resistance is lawful. The condemnation of the southern seceders is that they have resisted the federal government in the exercise of its legitimate powers, without having a single act of tyranny or in contravention of the constitution to allege against it. And they could not have such act without condemning themselves, for they have controlled the federal administration, and shaped its policy for more than three-fourths of the time since the organization of the government. For the twenty-four years next preceding the present administration they had every thing pretty much their own way, and if any portion of the people had any right to complain, it was not the people of the slave states. No doubt the abolitionists said and printed many things annoying to them, and some of the free states passed laws not acceptable to them; but the people of the free states had to complain of laws far more objectionable passed by them, and of numerous and gross outrages upon their citizens at the South, such as imprisonment, expulsion, lynching, tar-and-feathering, and hanging, for which no redress could be obtained. Yet the federal government, while it suffered unrebuked southern outrages upon northern citizens, was never restrained by the personal-liberty laws, and executed its own laws faithfully as far as the North was concerned. The South really had no grievance to complain of from the government, and the seceding states have never had a shadow of excuse for their rebellion. If the southern "chivalry" disliked being yoked with northern "mudsills," they were free to seek a separation by peaceful and constitutional means, but not by rebellion and civil war.

Such are the corrections we think are demanded, not of our institutions, but of popular opinion. Let public opinion conform, on the one hand, to our institutions, and, on the other, to the loyal and conservative practice of the people who have volunteered to defend the government, assert the majesty of law, and to save the life and integrity of the nation. We ask no more. These corrections, we trust, the southern rebellion and the civil war which has clothed with mourning almost every family in the Union will induce us to make. The minds and hearts of the people are now open to serious thought and to wise counsels. They are prepared to review the past, and to take a wise and fresh start for the future.

CONFISCATION AND EMANCIPATION.*

[From Brownson's Quarterly Review for July, 1862.]

VERY few of us who call ourselves loyal men and patriots had at the outbreak of the great southern rebellion a perfectly clear and distinct perception of the constitutional principles on which it was to be suppressed. All were anxious for its speedy suppression, and that, too, in strict accordance with the constitution, for, after saving the life and integrity of the republic, our dearest wish was to save constitutional government; but our minds were not clear as to the principles on which it was to be done. To many it was evident that the peace powers of the constitution were not adequate to the exigencies of the case, and to others it was not clear that the war power could be constitutionally invoked and exercised against our own citizens, even though in arms against the government.

The administration adopted in the outset the theory that the rebellion is not civil war, and the rebels are not enemies, but citizens criminally combined to obstruct the administration of justice, and to resist the execution of the laws. This is evident from the president's inaugural address, and his proclamation calling out the militia. Congress itself at the extra session, unless its partial confiscation act be an exception, appears to have adopted the president's theory of the rebellion, and we can call to mind no act of that session incompatible with it. But on this theory the government is restricted to the peace provisions of the constitution. The military forces are not an army operating against enemies, but a *posse comitatus* acting under the orders of the civil magistrate in aid of the civil authority, just as when called out to aid in suppressing a riot. On this theory, any and every assumption of war powers, or appeal to the rights of war would be manifestly unconstitutional, and unjustifiable on any recognized principles of law. Yet the government,

---

* *Indemnity for the Past and Security for the Future.* Speech of Hon. CHARLES SUMNER, of Massachusetts, on his Bill for the Confiscation of Property and the Liberation of Slaves belonging to Rebels. In the Senate of the United States, May 19, 1862.

while apparently adopting this theory, which we call the peace theory, and assuming the country to be at peace, has blockaded the southern ports, has made prizes, sent and received flags of truce, treated captured rebels as prisoners of war, released them on parole, or exchanged them, and done various other things which imply a state of war, and which would be highly improper, in some respects criminal, if the rebels are not enemies as well as criminal citizens.

The adoption of the peace theory by the government as the constitutional theory, and many of its acts being defensible only on the war theory, has continued and increased the confusion in loyal minds, and at the same time given the opposition in and out of congress some show of reason in organizing themselves as a constitutional party, and in professing to oppose the government on strictly constitutional grounds. If the government adopts and insists on the peace theory, many of its acts are undeniably open to the strictures of such men as Powell of Kentucky, Saulsbury of Delaware, Vallandigham of Ohio, and Diven of New York. On this theory the various bills introduced into congress, one of which has passed the house while we are writing, for confiscating the property of rebels and emancipating their slaves, are, if regarded as penal statutes against the rebels, of doubtful constitutionality. It may be plausibly argued, to say the least, that such measures are not within the purview of the peace powers of the constitution, and, if defensible at all, are defensible only under the war power,—only on the supposition that the property and slaves in question, are the property and slaves of enemies.

The constitution says expressly that, " The congress shall have power to declare the punishment of treason, but no attainder shall work corruption of blood, or forfeiture, except during the life of the person attainted." This, taken in an untechnical sense and as usually understood, positively forbids congress to pass any confiscation laws, as a penalty for treason, except during the life of the traitor. Confiscation of rebel property as a punishment for treason for a longer period than the life of the traitor, would, consequently, according to this interpretation, be manifestly unconstitutional, and the courts would be obliged to treat the act of congress authorizing it as null and void. So of emancipation. As a peace power neither congress nor the president has any power over the emancipation question.

Slavery does not exist under or by virtue of the constitution of the United States. So far as it has any legal existence at all in the Union, it exists by the *jus proprium* of the several states, and all the federal government has authority to do with it is, to see that the constitutional provision for the return of persons held to service escaping from one state to another is carried out. If the rebel slaveholders are to be regarded not as enemies, but as simply criminal citizens, an act emancipating their slaves would be undeniably in violation of the constitution, a usurpation of power that no lover of the constitution can for one moment permit. So far we are disposed to agree with those members of congress, who oppose, on constitutional grounds, both confiscation and emancipation.

Yet, we heartily approve a stringent confiscation act, and demand full and immediate emancipation at least of all the slaves claimed by rebels. Both are necessary as a means of weakening the rebels, obtaining indemnity for the past, and security for the future. We demand indemnity for the expenses incurred in suppressing the rebellion. The government has no right to exempt rebel property, and compel the loyal men of the country not only to pour out their blood in its defence, but to bear the burden of the expense necessarily incurred, when there is within its reach rebel property that can be seized as an indemnity. It would be paying a premium for treason, and imposing an almost insupportable tax on loyalty. The rebels have confiscated some two hundred millions of debts due to the loyal men in the loyal states, besides a large amount of property owned by northern men in the seceding states. They have stolen or destroyed many millions of property owned by the United States, and compelled an expenditure by the Union of at least twelve hundred millions, to say nothing of indemnities to private citizens, especially loyal citizens of the rebellious states, which will be found in the end to be nearly as much more. We protest against the whole burden of this immense expenditure falling on the federal treasury. The whole debt contracted, we hold, is a lien on rebel property, and the property of the rebels, as far as it will go, must be made to pay the cost of putting down their rebellion. We hold indeed, that all the property of the rebellious states, and all held under them, has lapsed to the United States by the rebellion of those states, for we hold, as our readers know, that state rebellion is state suicide, the death of the state, and, so far as it depended on the state, the dissolution of all civil society in its territory. But we demand, if congress will not accept this doctrine, that it authorize the seizure of rebel property as a just indemnity, as far as it will go, of the expenses of government and the losses by the rebellion of loyal private citizens.

But we cannot make this demand under the peace powers of the constitution, or on the government theory of the rebellion. We can make it only under the war power, as one of the rights of war, and therefore only on the ground that the country is not at peace, that the rebellion is civil war, and that the rebels are not only criminal citizens and punishable as such, but enemies against whom the government has all the rights of war. We have against the rebels all the civil rights determined by the constitution, and, besides these, all the rights of war against foreign enemies; for all authorities agree that a rebellion assuming certain dimensions is civil war, and the laws of war apply to civil or domestic war in like manner as to a foreign war, or, in other words, that the government has against domestic enemies all the rights that it has against a foreign state with which it is at war. That is to say, it has all the rights of a belligerent in addition to its rights as a sovereign. This clears up the confusion we have referred to, as may be seen in Mr. Sumner's masterly speech in the senate on confiscation, the title of which we have quoted at the head of this article. Mr. Sumner has drawn sharply the distinction between the peace powers of the constitution and the war power, and shown what we can and what we cannot do under each of them. We have done nothing but state in our own way his positions, and we refer to his speech for the authorities he cites in their support, and for the arguments by which he sustains them. In that speech he proves himself to be as scrupulously attached to the constitution as he is ardent and unreserved in his devotion to liberty. He is not merely the warm-hearted philanthropist, the indefatigable advocate of negro emancipation, but also an able and profound constitutional lawyer.

The right of both confiscation and emancipation under the war power is undeniable. The laws of war allow the seizure and appropriation of enemy's property wherever it can be reached without invading the jurisdiction of a neutral power. They also authorize the demand of indemnity for expenses incurred in prosecuting the war, and security for the future. This demand may be complied with by the payment of a sum of money agreed on between the parties, by a concession of territory, or by the concession of certain commercial facilities, as may be stipulated in the treaty of peace. It is on the right to demand indemnity for the past and security for the future, that rests the validity of the title by conquest.

It is true, as Mr. Sumner remarks, that, in modern times the private property of citizens on land is respected, and the rights of war, except on sea, authorize only the seizure and appropriation of the public property of the enemy. This is because the government is held responsible, and because the citizens in their private character are not held to be enemies, or, if so, not by their own choice. This is a modification of the laws of war, which we owe to Christianity. Under the old *jus gentium* as recognized by Roman jurisprudence, all the property, both public and private, of the hostile nation fell to the conqueror. Hence Rome or the Roman emperor was regarded as the sole proprietor of all the land of the conquered provinces, which, if it continued to be held by its former owners, was held by lease or payment of a stipulated rent or tribute. But this restriction of the war power does not apply in the case of rebels or domestic enemies, for they have no legal government, and are held to act individually, from choice, and therefore must be held individually responsible.

This is Mr. Sumner's doctrine, and in most cases of rebellion is unquestionable. But in our case the question might arise whether the rebels are not states rather than individuals. The states have acted in their state capacity, and demanded the support of their citizens by virtue of their allegiance to the state. In such a case the demand for indemnity and security would be against the state, and not directly against the individual citizen. This view was taken and urged at some length in our pages in the article on *The Struggle of the Nation for Life.* But it was taken not so much to meet the present question, as to escape the difficulties we felt in adopting the peace theory of the administration, on which we did not believe it possible to suppress the rebellion. Our thought was, in case of success, to compel the states, as states, to meet the demand for indemnity and security. This, we think, could be defended if it should be denied that state rebellion is state suicide, and it would answer most of the purposes of a confiscation act. But we have since looked more closely into the question of state sovereignty than we had previously done, and have come to the conclusion that the states are not and never were sovereign states either in law or in fact, that the American people are and always have been one political people, and that the undivided allegiance of the citizen is due to the United States, and to the United States alone. The state by rebellion forfeits all its rights, its very existence ceases to be a legal entity, and therefore the citizen is not bound by any of the acts or enactments of the pretended state after its rebellion. Hence he must be held individually responsible for his rebellion, and be accounted personally an enemy. In this case Mr. Sumner's doctrine applies, for the private property of rebels is enemy's property, and may be confiscated as such.

The right to confiscate enemy's property under the war power is indubitable; but the war power itself—is that a constitutional power? As against foreign enemies it is certainly constitutional, and equally so, if the doctrine we have asserted be sound, against domestic enemies. The war power is not, as some seem to suppose, a power above or outside of the constitution. Every sovereign state has, by virtue of the sole fact that it is a sovereignty, the inherent and indefeasible right of self-defence, or of self-preservation, to demand redress for injuries inflicted, and to guard against injuries threatened. In this is founded the right of war, whence flows the war power. The war power is inherent in the United States, as a free, independent, and sovereign state, and is by the political people of the United States expressly vested by the constitution in congress, as any one may see by reading Article I., Section 8. The constitution recognizes the war power, and confers it on congress. It is, then, a constitutional power, as constitutional as any of the peace powers. The war power is recognized and conferred by the constitution, but the constitution does not specify or determine the rights or laws of war. These are determined by the *jus gentium*, or international law, as recognized and enforced by universal jurisprudence, or the jurisprudence of all civilized or Christian states. The rights or laws of war, as recognized by international law, which is a part of the civil law of every nation, are constitutional, and congress can, while the war is pending, as constitutionally exercise them as it can any other rights. The confiscation of rebel property, even if unauthorized, or forbidden under the peace powers of the constitution, is then constitutional under the war power.

So much for the right while the war is pending to confiscate. The expediency of ' exercising the right or not exercising it, or of exercising it only with discrimination, or to a partial extent, is a question for the government to determine. No government is obliged to exercise all its rights, or to push its rights to their extreme. The rebels, while the civil war lasts, are enemies, as much, and as strictly so, as if they were foreigners ; but we expect the government to suppress the rebellion, and the people of the seceding states to return, after a while, to their allegiance, and to demean themselves as our countrymen and fellow-citizens. It is the duty of the government to use against them all the force and all the means authorized by the laws and usages of civilized warfare necessary to induce them to submit, and cease their opposition ; but it is for the interest of the whole country that this should be done with as little injury to them as possible. It could be of no advantage to the loyal states, even if they were so disposed, which they are not, to reduce the great mass of the population of the seceding states to absolute pauperism, to deprive them of all capital, and entirely ruin their industry. It is the duty of the United States to save them, as far as it can, from completely ruining themselves. We do not think interest, humanity, or sound policy, can counsel extreme and indiscriminate confiscation. We, if the matter were left to us, would leave the mass of the people,—who have but small means, and who have been drawn into the rebellion by their leaders rather than by their own malice,—when returning to their loyalty, the undisturbed possession of their little properties. We would exempt them from the operation of the confiscation law.

But we would not spare the leaders and wealthy secessionists, the members of the confederate government, or of the seceding state governments, those who have accepted office under them, and the commissioned officers of the confederate army and navy. On all these we would let the confiscation law fall with its full force. It is due to patriotism and loyalty that it should do so. These should not escape with impunity. There will, of course, be no hanging, no capital punishment for treason. The time has gone by for that. If we intended to inflict on traitors the traitor's doom, we should have begun our hanging under Mr. Buchanan's administration, and Mr. Lincoln's government should have arrested and executed as traitors, the commissioners sent by the so-called confederates to Washington to negotiate the terms of a dissolution of the Union, instead of treating them, unofficially of course, as high-minded, honorable, and accomplished gentlemen. As much as we disapprove the mistimed leniency in the beginning, whether it sprang from policy or cowardice, we should still more disapprove any prosecutions, after the war is over, under the civil law for treason. The legal right to do it we of course maintain, but after the past we believe such prosecutions would be highly dishonorable, and that they would prove to be at best a useless and an impolitic vengeance. Yet some punishment the leaders and influential classes who favored the rebellion should receive. But if the punishment extends to stripping them of all their property, and reducing them to the necessity of earning their bread by the sweat of their faces, it will probably be punishment enough.

The principle on which we defend the constitutionality of confiscation of enemy's property enables us to defend the emancipation of the enemy's slaves as a strictly constitutional measure. We hold, as we endeavored to prove in our last *Review*, that the slaves in all the rebellious states are already legally free. The suicide of those states of itself emancipated the slaves, and the federal government has no authority to remand them to slavery. Strictly speaking, slavery does not exist in the United States, and never has existed in them since the adoption of the federal constitution. The United States knows only persons, whatever their race or complexion, and *persons*, though they may be bondmen, are not slaves. The people of the United States, when they formed and adopted the federal constitution, abolished slavery, by recognizing and describing those who had been slaves as "*persons* held to service," and thus raising them, though they might be bondmen, from chattels to men. It would be a nice question, whether the constitution did not also abolish hereditary bondage. Hereditary bondage is founded on the legal fiction that the mother is a chattel, a thing, and that the offspring belongs to the master as the natural increase of property, which cannot be alleged if the mother is recognized as a person. If hereditary bondage has any legal existence in any of the states it must be by what lawyers call *jus proprium*, some special or express local statute, or custom having the force of law, not by the *jus gentium*. We apprehend, if we should inquire, that a great deal in regard to slavery alleged to be legal would be found to be in reality illegal, without even the shadow of a law, national or municipal, in its support. But be this as it may, it is undeniable that congress under the war power, as a war measure, has the right to break the bond, and emancipate all the persons held to service by the rebels, and, as to that matter, also all so held by loyal citizens, only in the latter case a fair compensation might be due. The complete and immediate emancipation of all the slaves or bondmen is thus within the constitutional power of congress, as a war measure, though evidently not as a peace measure.

We have no doubt, as we maintained in our article on *Slavery and the War*, that the president, as commander-in-chief of the army and navy, has the power to emancipate the slaves, when and where in his judgment it is a military necessity, or necessary to the military operations in hand. So, we think, has in his department any general having a departmental command, unless he has received positive instructions from his superior not to do it. The recent order of General Hunter freeing the slaves in the states of South Carolina, Georgia, and Florida, comprised within his military department, was, we have no doubt, a valid order, and the persons previously held to service in those states are now legally free, as are the persons so held freed by General Fremont's proclamation last autumn in the department of the West. The president is bound by the legal acts of his generals, unless he can show, as we presume he cannot, that they have disobeyed orders, or disregarded their instructions. If in these departments the slaves were legally freed by the orders of the generals, the president cannot remand them to slavery by any modification of the orders after they were once formally issued. Either the orders did not free the slaves, or those slaves are now legally free, whatever may have been the subsequent action of the president. If the president disapproved of the policy of those orders, he should have instructed his generals not to issue them. After they are issued it is too late to revoke them. A third party has then an interest.

But the power of the commander-in-chief to emancipate the slaves is confined to strict military necessity, and he can do it only as strictly necessary to his military operations. The commander-in-chief may believe, though it would be highly advantageous to the general prosecution of the war to emancipate the slaves, that it is not in a military point of view absolutely necessary, and, therefore, very properly refuse to proclaim emancipation. The power, therefore, though in certain supposable cases in the president, yet as it is included in the war power of the government, is more properly vested in congress. It is a war power rather than a military power, and emancipation must be regarded as a war measure rather than as a military operation, or military expedient. The military can adopt it only as a measure necessary to its operations, but congress can adopt it as a useful or advantageous war measure, a measure useful in prosecuting the war, in securing its ends, or in bringing it to a more speedy and successful issue.

Judge Trumbull, in his able speech on introducing a bill into the senate, at the opening of the session, for confiscating the property and emancipating the slaves of rebels, has dissipated the notion entertained by not a few, that the war power and the military power are one and the same, and that only the military can exercise the war power. He cleared up no little confusion by showing that the war power is the legitimate power of the government, and vested by the constitution in congress. The executive department, so to speak, of the war power, as of the other powers of the government, is committed to the president, who is made by the constitution commander-in-chief of the army and navy; but the power to declare war, to vote supplies of men and money, and to determine the policy and purposes of the war is expressly vested in congress, and the president acts simply in prosecuting it as the executive department of the government. It is not true to suppose that the war power comes into play only under martial law, and that under the war power the civil gives way to the military. Under our constitution the civil government holds the war power, and it is by the authority of the civil government that the military operates, or has the right to operate. The president, as the chief civil magistrate of the nation, watches over the general welfare, takes care of the republic, and sees that the laws are executed,—and to this end he is made commander-in-chief of the army and navy, or the whole land and naval forces of the Union. His military command is, therefore, subsidiary to his office as chief magistrate. The military is only an arm of the civil government, and can rightly move only by its will, for it is as chief civil magistrate that the president calls out the militia to repel an invasion, or to quell an insurrection; or has the chief command of the land and naval forces.

It is of great importance to keep this always in mind. The civil authority under our system controls the military. The war power is not the prerogative of the military, but of the civil government, and the military operates under and not over it. Were it otherwise, we might become a military despotism, or, in time of war at least, the civil authority would be placed in abeyance, and only the military would rule. Such a case could occur legitimately only when the whole country was placed under martial law. We have not the fears that many of our countrymen have of military despotism, and have no jealousies, common to most civilians, of the army. As a people we have held both army and navy in too low esteem, and are now suffering from it. We have made light of military honors and military glory, and thought we were humane and patriotic in discouraging the cultivation of a military spirit in our young men. In all this we have been wrong. An unmilitary people is sure to become a corrupt and an unpatriotic people. We were personally never a supporter of Andrew Jackson, but we never sympathized in the opposition to him on the ground that he was a "military chieftain," or had proved himself an able and successful general. We said years ago, and we say now, that we should always, other things being equal, prefer a real military man for the chief magistrate of the Union, to a civilian. The military man is usually a better executive officer, and carries into office better formed habits both of obedience and command, more promptness, energy, and activity, and a better *coup d'œil* than a man taken from civil life. If we had a larger sprinkling, not of militia generals and colonels, but of real military men, in congress, we should find our legislation none the worse for it.

But the real danger to our institutions comes from the tendency to devolve more and more of the duties of government on the president. He exercises in times of war extraordinary powers, and prudence requires that no more should be thrown upon him than properly belongs to his office. It is necessary to keep distinct and separate the several departments of government, as was intended by the constitution, and for each department to take care to neglect none of its own functions, and to avoid encroaching upon those of either of the others. The habit of devolving upon the executive duties which properly belong to congress, or calling upon it to do what congress itself can do, is fraught with danger, and may, if not checked, cause or permit the president to grow not into a military chieftain, but into a civil chieftain, which is a great deal worse. For these reasons we prefer that the war measure we insist on should be adopted by congress rather than by the president, for as civil magistrate the president has no power to do more than recommend it to congress, and as the head of the military power he can do it only in a military emergency. In any case it is more in accordance with the spirit of our institutions that it should be done by the civil than that it should be done by the military authority. Besides congress has freer scope under the war power, and may take a larger and a more liberal view of what is called military necessity than the commander-in-chief can. It can decree emancipation as a useful war measure, though not in the strictest sense of the term absolutely necessary, and even though it be not morally impossible to suppress the rebellion without decreeing it. It can do it whenever it regards it in the exercise of its best judgment a wise and prudent measure, and likely to be highly advantageous in prosecuting the war, or in obtaining the desired security for the future.

We assert the constitutional right of congress under the war power to declare universal emancipation as a war measure. But as a war measure it is obvious that congress can adopt it only while the war is pending. When the war is over and peace has returned, congress has no longer any power over it, for we have seen that emancipation in the states does not come within the scope of the peace powers of the federal government. Hence we have not regarded the proposition of the president, embodied in a resolution adopted by congress, to furnish pecuniary aid to those states that may choose to initiate emancipation, as so important as have some of our friends. The proposition is intended to be either a peace measure or a war measure. As a war measure, we doubt its value, for we do not believe any of the states will adopt it, or that it will tend at all to make Delaware, Maryland, Kentucky, and Missouri, one whit more loyal or less disloyal than they now are. Undoubtedly, if it would secure the hearty support of these states to the Union, or tend to detach Virginia, North Carolina, and Tennessee, from the so-called confederacy, it would be justifiable under the war power, and a prudent and advantageous war measure. But we anticipate from it neither of these effects, till the war is virtually over, and both its necessity and its utility as a war measure have passed away. The menace with which the president accompanied his proposition can be carried into effect only while the war continues; and unless the war continues much longer than it is now hoped, it will turn out to be only a *brutum fulmen*, intended rather to divert the pressure of foreign or domestic opponents of slavery, than to have any effect in actually promoting the cause of emancipation.

As a peace measure, the proposition strikes us as unconstitutional. We see nothing unconstitutional in compensating the slaveholders in the District of Columbia for the slaves emancipated by the act of congress, for there slavery existed by the authority of the United States. The United States had, iniquitously if you will, and as we certainly hold, recognized and sanctioned slavery in the district. It ought at once, no doubt, to free the slaves; but as citizens had acquired under its authority a property in the services of the slaves or persons held to service, it could not justly destroy that property without indemnification. You may say it owed a still greater indemnity to the slaves for the loss for so many years of their own services, and we shall not dispute you. But we hold that a state that has authorized slavery cannot justly abolish it without indemnifying the loyal owners of the property it has authorized for the loss they must sustain by its abolition. But we are aware of no clause in the constitution that authorizes the federal government to impose a tax on me for compensating the owners of slave property in the states, where it has never existed by authority of the United States. The government could tax me my proportion for buying up and shipping off to Hayti, San Domingo, Central America, or elsewhere, all the negroes in the country as a war measure, but not one cent for any thing of the sort as a peace measure, nor any other citizen. The tax or the appropriation of money from the treasury for such a purpose would be clearly illegal.

The president, we doubt not, is opposed to slavery, and would be glad to see it abolished; but he is, as he has declared, not in favor of immediate emancipation, and, we presume, favorable to emancipation at all only as it is coupled with colonization, or deportation of the liberated slaves beyond the limits of the territory of the Union. We are ourselves favorable to colonization, or rather to the voluntary emigration of the colored population to a territory where they will not have to struggle against the prejudices of race, as they must if they remain in the Union, and we look forward to such emigration as the final solution of the negro question; but we do not suffer ourselves to couple with the negro question the slavery question, which is a distinct question, and must be disposed of whether the other be or not. The slavery question is now up for solution, and cannot be much longer safely postponed. We have great respect for the chief magistrate of the Union; we have great confidence in his shrewdness and judgment, and should treat with grave consideration any opinions, wishes, or even prejudices of his, however unreasonable they might appear to ourselves; but we must confess that we have great difficulty in not losing our patience when we hear people talk about *gradual* emancipation. What kind of use will gradual emancipation be as a war measure? If you mean to adopt emancipation as a war measure, you must do it at once, and speedily; if you mean to recommend it only as a peace measure, to be carried out after the war is over, we see not what right you have to meddle with it.

The pretence that the negroes, if free, will not work, and cannot take care of themselves is, if you protect them against the oppression of the white men, all moonshine, and is every day refuted by what we see before our eyes. The negroes are far better able to take care of themselves, than are their white masters to take care of themselves, without them. Do you refer us to the free negroes at the North? We grant that as a general thing they do not get along very well. But why? Because prejudice against their race closes to them almost every avenue of success, shuts them out from the public schools, and confines them to a few, and those the least lucrative, branches of industry. They in some places may be farm laborers, they may be barbers, waiters in hotels and on steamboats, and servants in private families, even common sailors; but they cannot get employment in factories or as mechanics, as masons, carpenters, joiners, cabinet-makers, blacksmiths, tailors, tanners, curriers, &c. Yet they do contrive to live, to bring up their families, and some of them acquire handsome properties. At the South, the free negroes, when suffered to live there, do much better. In the District of Columbia they are found to have done well, and we have ourselves seen free negroes in Louisiana that were intelligent and wealthy, who, aside from the question of color, would be accounted accomplished and respectable. Our own barber, a full-blooded negro, is a moral and upright man, and superior in intelligence, wealth, and real respectability, to half of the white men in this city.

We have never heard a respectable argument in favor of gradual emancipation. " Hope deferred makes the heart sick," and the very worst school possible in which to acquire the habits of freemen is slavery. What good purpose do you propose to answer by gradual emancipation that could not be answered equally, if not better, by immediate emancipation? Do you begin to talk of the horrors of San Domingo, and tell us the slaves liberated will turn upon and massacre their late masters, in revenge of past wrongs, or in the mere wantonness of cruelty? The "horrors of San Domingo" were not the consequence of freeing, but of refusing to free the negro slaves. Those slaves rose, not because they were free, but because they were not free,—to assert their freedom, and no doubt they did assert their freedom with fire and blood. But this is a fact that tells the other way. Do you fear the emancipated slaves will come North, and compete with the free white laborers? How will this fear be affected by immediate any more than by gradual emancipation? If they come North, they will leave a demand for labor at the South. Then let our white laborers migrate southward to supply the demand occasioned by the migration of the negroes northward. But this fear is idle; for if the negroes can be free in the South, few, if any, of them will come North. The negro is not a migratory animal, he has strong local attachments, attachments which not unfrequently overcome his love of freedom. His natural tendency is southward, to the torrid zone, for the home of his race is within the tropics. If many come North now, it is to get away from slavery, to a region where they can feel they are freemen. There is, no doubt, need of an apprenticeship to freedom, but not in slavery do men serve that apprenticeship.

The real difficulty and the only difficulty we see in the case, is in the inveterate prejudice of the American people against the negro race. If the slaves were of our race, our own kith and kin, we should hear little of *gradual* emancipation. The non-slaveholding whites in the slaveholding states, who are now fighting with such madness and fury against the Union, detest slavery as much as we of the North do, but they cannot endure free negroes, and they believe that, if the two races are to occupy the same territory, the black race should be the slave of the white race. The president is a native of a slave state, and it may be shares to a certain extent the feelings and prejudices of these non-slave-holding whites, as do a large portion of the population of all the free states. We suppose he wishes gradual emancipation because he couples in his own mind emancipation and colonization, and colonization must in the nature of the case, whether forced or voluntary, go on gradually. In all we have seen of him, he would seem to be more anxious to provide for the removal of free negroes out of the country, than he is to free the slaves. We respect his motives; we respect his loyal intentions; and we readily concede that he may be right in his judgment, and we wrong in ours; but he will permit us to say that, as at present informed, we cannot sympathize with him in his opposition to immediate and his preference for gradual emancipation.

There is another view of the case which so religious a man as the president ought not to neglect. Slavery is an injustice, a sin in the state that authorizes it, and in our case becomes a national sin the moment the government gets the constitutional power to abolish it, and neglects to exercise that power. The war was not and is not waged for the abolition of slavery, but the existence of the war gives to the government the power to abolish it as a war measure. The manifest injustice of slavery and manifest justice of abolishing it should be allowed to have due weight with the government, and predispose it to adopt emancipation as one of its war measures, if it can do so constitutionally. We have shown that it can do so. Then, we say, it is bound to do so, and, if it does not, it makes the sin of slavery a national sin, for which the whole nation is accountable. Now in this case the question of gradual emancipation is like the question of gradually breaking off from sin. The morality we have learned is that sin is to be broken off from immediately, at once, without dallying or delaying a moment. We do not pretend that declaring the slaves free is a complete reparation of the wrongs of slavery, or that it is all that is due in justice to the slaves. But so much must be done and done at once, or the sin does not cease. We must do so much at once, and the rest afterwards as soon as we can, or we continue to sin.

Finally, if we insist on a preparation of negroes for freedom, the best preparation will be to call them out as loyal Unionists, discipline them, put arms into their hands, and let them fight for their own freedom. In no way can men be more readily or more thoroughly trained to freedom than in fighting for it as soldiers with arms in their hands. It makes men of them at once, for it puts them in the way of doing men's work. There is no better school of freedom possible than war for or in defence of freedom. Such a war calls out all the manhood one has in him, and makes him feel the value of freedom by the blood with which he consecrates it, and the costly sacrifices he makes to secure it. This will do infinitely more to elevate the long oppressed negro race, do infinitely more to prepare them to be freemen, than any thing possible while they continue in slavery. Look at it in what light we can, *gradual* emancipation strikes us as nonsensical and absurd. There is no good reason conceivable why gradual emancipation should be preferable to immediate emancipation, while the only power the government has to emancipate at all is to emancipate immediately, not gradually; for gradual emancipation can never be adopted as a war measure, unless we contemplate making the war for the suppression of the rebellion a "Thirty Years War."

Dismissing the question of gradual emancipation, and assuming that congress has under the war power the right to emancipate the slaves, it may still be asked, is it expedient or politic to do it? It can be done constitutionally as a war measure, if congress judges it expedient. Is it expedient? Some say let it alone, why bring constantly the "eternal nigger" upon the tapis? Do leave slavery to take care of itself. But in answer to these we add the government has now power over the question; in a few months it may have none. The life and death of the republic are suspended in the balance, and the solution we give and give now to the slavery question may turn the scale, and save the life or seal the doom of the nation. It is not a question, therefore, to be postponed. The "eternal nigger," as you express it, will not down at the bidding, any more than would Banquo's ghost. We cannot silence the slave question, or stop its agitation. We were to do it with the compromise measures of 1850, and, after that, with a Kansas-Nebraska territorial bill, and we have as the result the present civil war. There is a moral law in the universe stronger than legislative enactments, against which neither the devices of our politicians nor the strategy of our generals can avail—neither armed hosts, nor newly invented artillery. They war in vain who war against OPINION. No despot, even though backed by a million of bayonets and ten thousand guns of the heaviest calibre and the most cunningly devised projectiles, can prevail against the laws of God, or against the moral convictions of mankind. You may as well attempt to silence the ceaseless agitation of the waves, to stop the ebb and flow of the ocean tides, or arrest the course of the viewless winds, as to stop in the American people the agitation of the slavery question, so long as there is a single negro slave left in the land. It is not the wild or silly fanaticism of your abolition men or abolition women, your Garrisons, your Phillipses, your Fosters, your Pilsburys, your Kellys, your Westons, or your Chapmans that convulse the nation, for these are powerless save in the idea they represent; it is God, the moral laws of the universe, the awakening power of justice, the very logic of your own republic, that keeps up the agitation. You might as well point your artillery against the red lightnings of heaven, as against the spirit that moves and agitates the country on the slavery question. Silence, in any way you please the voices of those you call abolition fanatics, and you have done nothing to suppress agitation. Were these to hold their peace, the very stones would cry out. The spirit would pervade your camps, seize upon your soldiers, and turn the heads of your sedatest generals. It can no more be confined or restrained than one of the elemental forces of nature. The time for it in God's providence has come, and you have no alternative but to accept and obey it as freemen, as men who believe in God, who derive from him the courage to do justice, to lighten the load of the oppressed, and to let the bond go free.

It is said emancipation is inexpedient, because it would gravely offend Kentucky, Missouri, Maryland, and even Delaware, and force them out of the Union into open rebellion. This objection has no weight with us. The government has been sufficiently embarrassed already by its concessions to these states, and we shall consider it a cause of abundant thankfulness if its efforts to keep them in the Union do not involve irremediably the dismemberment of the republic and the acknowledgment of the independence of the southern confederacy. If these states are really loyal, the measure, as it affects them only in the market for the surplus produce of slaves, will not drive them out of the

Union; if they are at heart disloyal, and willing to stay in the Union only on condition that it adopt no measure not approved by them, the sooner they openly secede the better. The government is either strong enough to maintain itself against any domestic combination that can be formed against it, or it is not. If it is, they can be subdued along with the other seceding states; if it is not, then let it perish, for it is not worth sustaining. A government that can govern only at the mercy or forbearance of a portion of its subjects, is no government at all. Its stability, its permanence, its consistency, its independence depends on its ability to assert and maintain itself according to its own constitution against any and every combination of domestic enemies that can possibly be armed for its destruction. We wish, also, these border states, that seem to imagine that the nation owes them special gratitude and deference because they did not openly secede with the other slave states, to bear in mind that they stand in the Union on the footing of equality with the other states, and that their insolent pretensions to superiority or to dictate, under threats of making war on the government, its measures and policy, can no longer be tolerated. They have been saved once or twice by the arms of the states they insult, and if need be can be saved again, perhaps at some cost to themselves. The nation owes them no special debt of gratitude for not openly rebelling, which all except Delaware would have done, and perhaps even Delaware herself, had it not been for the presence of the federal forces; and the fact that they hold a portion of their population in bondage entitles their judgment or their wishes to no special consideration. They are an integral part of the one American political people, and as much bound to fight for the Union as Illinois, Massachusetts, New York, or Pennsylvania. Let us have no more of their insolence in or out of congress.

But emancipation will terribly irritate the rebels, and render their future reconciliation impossible. Nonsense. They are already as irritated as they can be. You cannot increase their hatred or malignity. Human nature will bear no more than they already have, even with the assistance of Satan to boot. As for the Union men in the seceding states, save in a few localities, they do not exist. Our armies have not found them, and wherever they go in rebeldom, meet only hatred, sullenness, or insult. Even the wounded rebel prisoners in our hospitals, though unable to deny the care and tenderness with which they are treated, cannot conceal, and do not attempt to conceal their bitter hatred of "Yankees." There need be no fear of irritating the rebels, and the only way possible of conciliating them is to treat them as they treat their own negroes when spiteful or sulky, that is, to flog them, and flog them soundly. They will then begin to respect us, and finally come to love and honor us. The mass of the southern people are not like us here at the North. We are addicted to mammon worship, no doubt, but we do at least recognize a moral power, and confess that we ought to worship God. The southern people as a body worship only force, and to gain their love and respect, you most prove that you are the better man, that you can whip them. Leniency, forbearance, conciliation are thrown away upon them, for they take them as evidence of weakness, of a craven or an overreaching spirit. The government has from the first mistaken their character. It has been too lenient, too conciliatory, and, in endeavoring to conduct the war on humane principles, has been guilty of great inhumanity. Nothing would so much command the respect of the rebels, and so dispose them to live hereafter in peace and friendship with us under one and the same government, as the immediate emancipation of the slaves. They know our principles require us to do it, and they despise us for not having the courage to act up to our principles. The measure would be a bold and manly one ; it would strike them in their tenderest point, and they would think all the better of us for daring to adopt it.

But many of the officers and privates of our army would refuse to fight if the government were to free the slaves. Then let the officers resign and the privates be discharged. Your army will be the better officered and the more efficient for the riddance. The duty of the soldier is to obey his superior, and very few officers in high or subordinate commands would hesitate to fight and do their best, if they must do so or lose their commissions, and still fewer privates when refusal involved dismissal from the service. The government cannot be controlled by subordinates. Let the government prove that it is a government, especially in time of war, and there will be no difficulty. Would not pro-slavery generals show as much submission as the noble Fremont showed when relieved of his command for sympathizing with freedom, or as has probably been shown by the brave Hunter, under the mistimed rebuke of the com-

mander-in-chief ?   If not, the sooner they are relieved from
their commands the better.

Finally, we are told the measure is inexpedient, because
it would have no practical effect.   It would not be recognized by the rebel masters, the knowledge of it would be
kept from the negroes, and they would be so carefully
watched and guarded that they could take no advantage of
it even if informed of its adoption.   The knowledge of
such a measure, if adopted, we apprehend, would in less
than one fortnight find its way to every negro cabin in rebeldom.   As to its efficiency, it would have the effect of securing nearly four millions of people in the very heart of rebeldom as stanch loyalists to the Union. This of itself would
be worth more to us than an army of a hundred thousand
well-appointed and well-disciplined troops.   It would carry
fear, distrust, consternation even to every rebel home, and
render it necessary to keep at home for domestic protection
a large number of troops who now are free to go and swell
the rebel armies in the field.   It would weaken greatly the
forces which can now be placed in the field to operate
against us.   Besides, the negroes knowing the success of the
federal arms would secure their freedom, would find a
thousand ways not easy to point out of injuring the rebel
cause, and serving our own.   Moreover, knowing that by
coming within our lines they would find freedom and protection, they would in spite of the vigilance of their guards
escape in large numbers, and be able to render valuable aid
to the Union cause as laborers in camp and on intrench-
ments, and also as soldiers and sailors.   The able-bodied
among them could be easily organized and disciplined under
white officers, and acclimated as they are, advantageously relieve our unacclimated northern troops of garrison and
guard duty on the southern coast during the sickly season.
They might also be employed as common sailors on our
fleets, and do us good service, as may be gathered from the
brilliant and daring feat of the pilot Robert Small and his
companions in taking the *Planter* out of Charleston under
the guns of the forts, and delivering her over to the Union
naval commander.

The war, let it never be forgotten, is not a war between
the North and the South, between two sections of our common country, but between the United States and an armed
rebellion, seeking the destruction of the government.   All
sections are equally bound to support the United States in

its efforts to suppress the rebellion, and preserve the unity and integrity of the national territory. The government has no right to throw upon any one section the whole burden and expense of prosecuting the war, and is bound to make all sections, as far as in its power, contribute their respective quotas. It is bound to call on the loyal men of the South as well as on the loyal men of the North. It does a manifest injustice to the North, if it refuses to accept the service that four millions of the population of the rebellious states could and would willingly lend it in suppressing the rebellion. We demand, therefore, not as a matter of mere expediency, but as a matter of justice to the free states who are so freely pouring out their blood and treasure to sustain the Union, that the government avail itself of the aid of these four millions of loyal men, not as slaves, but as included in the population of states that are not contributing, and otherwise will not contribute their due share or any share at all to the public cause. These loyal men are an integral portion of the population of those states, and, though under the laws of those states held to service, are known to the United States only as persons. As such the United States has the right to call upon them to support the government, and is bound to grant them in return for their loyalty, freedom and protection; and the loyal people of the other states have the right to insist on its being done.

But there is another reason that proves not only the expediency, or the right of emancipation, but its absolute necessity. It must be done as the only means of saving the integrity of the nation, or of escaping the shame and mortification of acknowledging the independence of the rebels. France and Great Britain, we cannot doubt, will not see their industrial classes suffering the severe distress they are now suffering for the want of the southern staples, much longer without intervening in our domestic affairs, if the war is to be protracted, or if it is to be conducted on the principles on which it has been hitherto conducted. In nearly all protracted struggles in modern times for dismemberment of states, the historical precedents are in favor of the intervention of foreign powers to secure the independence of the rebellious or revolutionary party. It was so in the case of Holland struggling for her independence of the Spanish crown; it was so in the case of the American colonies struggling for independence of the crown of Great Britain, and the United States owe in no small degree their existence as an independent nation to the intervention of foreign powers. The same may be said of the Spanish American colonies, of Greece demanding independence of the Ottoman empire, of Belgium demanding separation from Holland, and of Italy demanding her independence of Austria. The only notable exceptions that we can at this moment recall are Poland and Hungary, but neither of these was able to maintain a prolonged struggle. What reason have we to suppose that the southern rebels will form another exception?

The foreign powers most interested in the conflict have, for over a year, refrained from all intervention, at the expense of great suffering to themselves, and it is no secret that they will not refrain much longer. Nothing can prevent their early effectual intervention in favor of the rebels but immediate, great, and decisive victories by the federal arms, or the emancipation of the negro slaves. We must show that the war is not merely one of subjugation on one side, and of independence on the other, or they will certainly intervene, if the war threatens to be a protracted struggle. We must bring it speedily to a close, or else be compelled to acknowledge the independence of the southern confederacy with such boundaries as the intervening powers shall please to prescribe, for we cannot hope, with the southern rebellion on our hands, to resist successfully the combined power of France and Great Britain, without allies either in the Old World or the New. The only certain way of averting the intervention, and saving the integrity of the republic, is to emancipate the slaves, and enlist the moral sentiments and convictions of the civilized world on the side of the United States.

The government knows the danger, and has sought to avert it, by the resolution adopted by congress proffering pecuniary aid to the states that would initiate emancipation, and relaxing the blockade as to the ports of Beaufort, Port Royal, and New Orleans; but these have failed, for no state has yet accepted the proposition with regard to emancipation, and the rebels have destroyed their cotton and tobacco instead of suffering them to come forward to market. The government now hopes, we presume, to avert it by great and decisive victories at Richmond and Corinth. But at neither of these places shall we obtain a decisive victory, for at either place, the rebels, if they cannot conquer our forces, can retreat, and protract the war indefinitely; and they undoubtedly will do so, for it is their true policy. They feel that we have thus far gained only barren victories, for they are well assured that if they can protract the war a few weeks longer, foreign intervention will come to their aid.   One way, and one way only is open to us; one alternative yet remains, and that is to do what should have been done one year ago,—decree complete and immediate emancipation.   It is the only means left us of escaping a shameful mutilation of the republic.   In the meantime the president hesitates, longs but fears to strike, and congress wrangles, and lets the golden moment glide by.   Terrible will be the responsibility of the government, both executive and legislative, if the rebellion succeeds.   On them, not on the rebels, will fall the blasting curse of outraged humanity.

But events hasten, and in all human probability, the fate of the nation will be decided, before we can issue from the press, and our words will have only an historic value.   The cloud in the East rises, and will perhaps have risen and spread over the whole heavens before our words reach those for whom they are designed.   All we can say is, that since the rebellion broke out we have in our humble sphere endeavored to discharge the duties of a loyal citizen.   We love our country, and as long as we have a country we shall continue to love her, and to hope for her.   If let alone, the United States in a reasonable time can reduce the rebels to submission, and maintain the integrity of the national territory.   If they fail, it will not be republican institutions that have failed.   They will have failed because our northern men consented in the outset to form an unnatural union of freedom with slavery, and because our statesmen and generals have been too anxious to preserve it.   We, however, still hope, before we appear in print, congress will have reconsidered its vote rejecting the emancipation bill, and have passed an act freeing all the slaves of the rebels.

SLAVERY AND THE CHURCH.

[From Brownson's Quarterly Review for October, 1862.]

THERE is no doubt that the majority of our Catholic population are strongly opposed to the abolitionists, and regard
them, very unjustly, however, as the real authors of the formidable rebellion now threatening our national life; but we
should do them great injustice if we supposed them to be
really in favor of negro slavery, or opposed on principle to
emancipation. We think their hostility to the abolitionists,
since the breaking out of the civil war, very unwise, impolitic, uncalled for, and calculated to give aid and comfort to
the enemies of the nation; but we also think it grows more
out of their attachment to the Union, than out of any sympathy with slavery or with the rebels.

Various causes have conspired to render Catholics hostile
to the abolitionists. The majority of Catholics in this country were, not unnaturally, attached to the Democratic party.
They were mostly from the oppressed classes in the mother
country, and have naturally, on coming here, associated with
the party that made the loudest professions of attachment to
liberty and equality, and were, or appeared to be, the most
liberal towards foreigners, and especially towards Catholics
as naturalized citizens. Besides, the great body of the
Catholics migrating to this country, were democrats before
their migration, and, by a very innocent mistake, assumed
that the Democratic party here represented their previously
imbibed democratic views and convictions. The opposing
party, whether called Federal, National Republican, or
Whig, was always less lavish of its promises, both to Catholics and to foreigners, and in its policy, from the time of the
elder Adams to our own day, has been apparently more Protestant and more native American. These facts are sufficient
to explain the general devotion of Catholics, especially Catholics of Irish birth or descent, to the Democratic party. As
that party gradually became a southern party, and strongly
opposed to abolitionism, it was only natural that the Catholics who, though not its leaders, formed a very large proportion of its rank and file, should adopt its views, and follow
its policy.

317

Catholics, especially our Irish Catholics, are strong, not unfrequently intolerant partisans. They have been made so by having been placed for three centuries under the necessity of defending their faith and nationality against Protestant England, seeking constantly to crush and annihilate both. Deprived, to a great extent, of education by the penal laws, and of their natural secular chiefs by apostasy or confiscation, they have had no means of defending themselves and protecting their faith and nationality, but by close party association and intolerance to their enemies, especially such as deserted, or showed symptoms of deserting their ranks. Individual freedom of thought and action were necessarily subordinated to the exigencies of their faith and politics, and they were trained to act as far as possible as a party, according to party tactics, and to carry their points by acting as a great party-machine, sweeping away every thing before it. To desert the party was to desert the church and the national cause, and to prevent desertion they were obliged to treat desertion of party as an abandonment of religion and nationality. The deserter must be hooted, hunted down, rendered unable to live save by taking refuge in the ranks of the enemy. Hence we often find Irish Catholics who regard apostasy from the Democratic party as little less criminal than apostasy from the church.

The leaders of the Democratic party, after the election to the presidency of General Pierce, having adopted the southern policy on the slave question, the Democratic Catholics followed them and their Catholic brethren in the southern states, and became strong and violent anti-abolitionists. They, also, became such by their prejudices against the Puritanism and Sabbath-worship, to which they supposed the abolitionists in general to be addicted, and by the fact that the abolitionists themselves coupled with their abolitionism various other *isms* peculiarly offensive to Catholics,—disunionism, woman's-rightsism, amalgamationism, free-loveism, socialism, and, worse than all, Englishism, at least were charged with doing so. They were led by the Democratic press to regard the abolitionists as miserable fanatics, the enemies alike of religion and civilization, and to believe that the peace and safety of the Union required their suppression. We can, then, easily explain their hostility to the abolitionsts without supposing them to be in the least attached to slavery or desirous of perpetuating a social condition always warred against by the church.

We went as far in our hostility to the abolitionists as any of our Catholic brethren have gone. We regarded them as enemies to the Union of these states, and if not checked we thought them not unlikely to bring about secession or civil war. From 1838 to 1857 we were among their sturdiest opponents, and in our own sphere, we have done as much as any other man in the country to set Catholics against the abolition movement. Yet we know that all the time we were doing it we were an ingrained anti-slavery man, detesting slavery in every form, and desiring liberty for every man, whether white or black, yellow, red, or copper-colored. We have seen nothing to convince us that what we know was true of ourselves is not equally true of the majority of our Catholic brethren. The Union, or as we prefer to say, the *national* question with us always took, and still takes, precedence of the slavery question. We have always believed, and we believe to-day, that liberty and humanity are more interested in maintaining the national integrity and the federal constitution unimpaired, than they are in the abolition of negro slavery. So we have said and repeated any time during the last twenty years. Herein we have differed, differ still, and probably always shall differ from the abolitionists. They place the slavery question before all others, and prefer a division of the Union to a union with slave-holding states. We have differed, still differ, and always shall differ from them on the question of negro equality. They demand the recognition of the negro not only as a man, and as a free man, but as the political and social equal of the white man. They are hardly willing to accept of emancipation unless coupled with negro equality, and we are hardly prepared to accept it if coupled with that equality. We recognize in the negro a man, and assert for him in their plenitude all the *natural* rights of man, but we do not believe him the equal of the white man, and we would not give him in society with white men equality in respect to those rights derived not immediately from his manhood, but mediately from political or civil society, and in this we express, we apprehend, the general sentiment of the Catholic population of this country.

But we have said the national question takes with us precedence of the slavery question. We would not endanger the peace or union of these states in order to abolish slavery; nor would we suffer the national integrity to be destroyed for the sake of preserving slavery. We hold slavery, whether we speak of its abolition or its preservation, subordinate to the Union, or the national existence and welfare. When efforts either to abolish or to save slavery are incompatible with the preservation of the Union, we oppose them with all the zeal and energy we are master of. We opposed abolition, except by the action of the slave-holding states themselves, prior to the breaking out of the rebellion, because we could not effect it without violating the constitution, and endangering the integrity of the nation ; we demand the abolition of slavery, now, because without it we do not believe it possible to suppress the rebellion, vindicate the constitution, reëstablish over the rebellious states the federal supremacy, and secure future peace and harmony between the North and the South. We believe emancipation is now both a military and a political necessity. Differing, as we have always differed, from the abolitionists, in their theoretical views, we are, owing to the change of circumstances, practically with them on the single question of emancipation, and therefore deem it unwise and even dangerous to continue our old hostility to them. They are, at least, some of them, what we are not, conditional Union men. They are willing to accept the Union with emancipation, and we are willing to accept emancipation for the sake of the Union. They are conditional Union men, but unconditional abolitionists. We are unconditional Union men, but conditional abolitionists. We wish they were, like us, ready to accept the Union with or without slavery, but as we do not believe the Union possible with slavery, and as we want all the support for the Union we can get, we have no practical ground of quarrel with them, and can, up to a certain point, coöperate with them.

We do not like a late speech by Mr. Wendell Phillips. The spirit of that speech is : Let the government proclaim emancipation and I will support it ; let it refuse to do so and I will not support it, but perhaps oppose it. We say no such thing. We are as much dissatisfied with the policy of the administration on the slavery question, as strongly opposed to its half-way measures, and to its deference to border-stateism, as he is or can be ; but we must, in order to save the nation, sustain the federal government. Tell it plain truths, if you will, do all in your power to bring it up to your convictions, and to inspire it with wisdom and courage adequate to the wants of the country ; but be loyal to the national cause, which it is its duty to defend and promote.

The conditional loyalism of the extreme abolitionists, consisting of a few hundreds, at most of a few thousands of individuals, may be censurable, but it is far less so than the conditional loyalism of the border.states, for liberty is more respectable than slavery, and a man can be more easily excused for.insisting on conditions in favor of liberty than on conditions in favor of property. The least respectable species of property known to the laws of any state is property in slaves. Your Davises and Wickliffes of Kentucky are excellent Union men so long as the Union protects, your Phillipses and Garrisons so long as it will abolish, slavery; but as it is always more respectable to restore men to their liberty than it is to deprive them or to keep them deprived of it, save as a punishment for crime, we have a respect for the abolitionists who would free the slaves at the expense of the Union, that we have not for the border-state men, who would sooner sacrifice the Union than let their slaves go free. Liberty is a right of all men, forfeitable only by crime, and all our natural instincts are in its favor, and revolt at slavery. Liberty is the principle and end of all our institutions, and the only real fault you can find with any man for asserting and defending liberty for all men, is in respect of the mode or means he adopts to secure it. He is right in principle and right in the end, and can be wrong only as to the means or medium. But slavery is always an abnormal condition, sometimes to be borne with for a season, as is a catarrh, a fever, a boil, rheumatism, or the gout, but never to be admired for its own sake, or regarded as an indication of moral and social health. It is always a moral, political, and social evil, and repelled by all that is free, generous, noble, or respectable in human nature. We confess, therefore, that we have a tolerance for the conditional loyalism of a Phillips which we have not and cannot have for a Wickliffe.

Moreover, the conditional loyalism of the abolitionists is now, in the actual state of things, to say the least, perfectly harmless in practice, while that of the border states joins hands with the rebels, and is a grave obstacle to the suppression of the rebellion, and the preservation of the national life and the integrity of the national territory. On the border-states policy, which has been thus far that of the administration, all clear-headed statesmen see that it is impossible to save the Union. They see that it is necessary to make our election, either the Union and freedom, or slavery and no Union. The preservation of both is no longer a possibility. The abolitionist loves the Union, but he hates slavery more, and in contending to-day for the abolition of slavery, he is not warring against the Union, but contending for a measure absolutely necessary to its preservation. His conditional loyalism, as things stand, is practically unconditional loyalism. Whatever may have been the cause of the rebellion, it is now possible to suppress it, and guard against its recurrence only by appealing to the anti-slavery sentiment of the country, or to the American love of liberty. We need the sympathy and aid of humanity, and humanity will not aid us while we are seeking to perpetuate the grossest outrage upon her rights and dignity. The fault of the administration is, that it has not understood this; it has not felt the pulsations of the large human heart, or been aware that the strength of men is in the strength of man. In the most fearful national crisis it has conceived of nothing higher, nobler, stronger, than the tricks and combinations of second and third rate politicians. It has had no inspirations of genius, no sense of humanity, no understanding of the great moral laws of nations, no consciousness of the presence of God in human affairs. There has been as little genius in our administration as in our generals on the battle-field. In both we have had what democracy gives, common-place, respectable, laborious industry, honest intentions, but no statesman who comprehends the power of an idea, no general at the head of our army who comprehends the value of the dash, the enthusiasm, the *morale* of his troops. The abolition of slavery, as a military and political necessity, should have followed on the heels of the attack on Sumter, and been proclaimed in the president's first call for troops to put down the rebellion. That abolition sooner or later must come, or the United States have ceased to exist, is now no longer a question. It is idle, therefore, to make war to-day on the abolitionists, when, in order to save the Union, we must go practically as far as any of them insist on going.

Catholics have not been quicker than others, we confess, to see the altered circumstances of the country, which have entirely changed the position of the abolition question. Ten years ago to demand of the federal government the abolition of slavery, was to endanger the peace and safety of the Union. To do it to-day, is to demand the means of saving the Union and the national life. Here is the difference. This difference is not fully appreciated by Catholics any more than by a large number of non-Catholics. The archbishop of New York, who we have good reason for believing, is a strong anti-slavery man, in his famous article against us last October, did not see it, nor did he see it in his efforts while abroad to manufacture public opinion in Europe against the immediate emancipation of American slaves, the purpose for which he was sent by his friend the secretary of state, or at least one of the purposes. His article proves him nearly as short-sighted and as weak a statesman as Mr. Seward himself. He, in his article, writes as if the rebellion had made no change in the bearing of the slavery question, as if it was necessary to continue to let off our double batteries on the one side against the abolitionists of the North and on the other against the "fire-eaters" of the South, as the New York *Herald* has constantly done, and continues to do. There was a time when this was wise and just, when it was patriotic and statesmanlike; but it had ceased to be so when the business of the nation was not to ward off but to suppress rebellion. The course taken by the archbishop and his organ, the New York *Herald*, had the effect of preventing Catholics from perceiving and appreciating the new and altered state of the question, and if the Union should be ultimately lost, few men in the country will have incurred a heavier responsibility for it than he. No man has contributed more to keep up old party divisions, and to prevent the union of our people and government on a straightforward and decided policy, such as the crisis demanded. We doubt not his loyal intentions, but had he been decidedly disloyal, he could not have done us more harm. It is owing to the policy he has defended at home and abroad, that we are in our present condition, and that, at the time we are writing (September 3d), the rebels are threatening our capital instead of our possessing theirs. We wish, therefore, that while he insisted upon the people of his charge being loyal, and while he ordered, what he has not done, prayers for the success of our arms, he had judged it compatible with his duty to have refrained from interfering in the party strifes and political intrigues which have brought us to the brink of destruction. He has helped make confusion worse confounded, and done what was in him to place his church and our poor Catholic people, on the question of slavery, in a false position. Yet, could our Catholic population have been left to follow their Catholic instincts unwarped by politicians, and could they have been permitted to see that the abolition question had changed its bearing, and had become a question of saving, not of endangering the Union, they would have proved that they are Americans in their love of liberty, and in their detestation of slavery.

Even the archbishop himself is opposed to slavery in the abstract, and declared himself so to M. Augustin Cochin in Paris, and he was a few years ago regarded by his friends here as a decided anti-slavery man, especially when his particular friends William H. Seward and Thurlow Weed were accounted anti-slavery men. His article against us we presume was inspired by those gentlemen, who persuaded him to adopt their policy of saving the Union by conciliating the party in arms against it, and by convincing them that we are determined to suppress the rebellion without disturbing the existing relation of master and slave—a policy which we should expect from such men as Weed and Seward, but which ought not to have been entertained a moment by the archbishop of New York. It is the policy of narrow-minded and short-sighted politicians, not of a broad-minded and far-sighted statesman. There is nothing in it to command the respect of minds superior to common-place. Still we protest against regarding the archbishop as in any sense a pro-slavery man. He may not be a statesman; he may not be able in political matters to rise above routine; he may not be always careful and exact in his expressions; but he is a Catholic prelate, a Christian, a man, and he must sympathize with freedom. Still more earnestly do we protest against its being concluded from any thing he has said or done, that Catholics, especially Irish Catholics, are in favor of or not opposed to negro slavery. We need but recollect the shout of universal indignation they raised against their favorite and countryman, John Mitchell, when he intimated his desire to own a plantation in Tennessee or Alabama, "well stocked with fat negroes." O'Connell, their representative man, refused to receive contributions to the repeal rent from southern slaveholders, so strongly opposed was he in principle to slaveholding. It is the boast of the Irish that their nation was the first in the world to abolish slavery, and it would be absurd to suppose that a people that has been in a chronic rebellion of seven hundred years' standing in favor of liberty, can be otherwise than opposed to slavery, and friendly to the oppressed everywhere.

The Catholic population of this country have been unfavorable to the agitation of slavery in the free states, because they have not believed the federal government could emancipate the slaves without violating the constitution. It has been their respect for the constitution, not their love of slavery, that has made them anti-abolitionists. They are still opposed to the abolitionists on the same ground. We must concede to them that in this they were right, and that the federal government could not legally emancipate the slaves under the peace powers of the constitution. But that government has constitutionally both peace powers and war powers. Its war powers are as constitutional as its peace powers; and under its war powers, or rights of war, *jura belli*, it has the right or the power to declare the slaves free. It can do it legally and constitutionally as a war measure. In asking the government to do it now as a war measure, we ask no violation of the constitution, and in no respect invade the sacredness of the rights of property it guaranties. Neither congress nor the administration could have done it before the civil war broke out, for the rights of war come into play only when war exists.

The mistake of our Catholic brethren, and of a large proportion of our countrymen generally, arises from their not distinguishing between the rights of peace and the rights of war, and not understanding that in a civil war the government has against the rebels all the rights of a sovereign, and in addition all the rights of a belligerent. The sovereign loses by the rebellion none of his rights as sovereign, and is absolved by it, in relation to the rebels, of all duty of protection, whether of life, liberty, or property. Till they submit, they are out of his protection, and, in case the rebellion assumes the dimensions of a civil war, he has against them all the rights of war as recognized by the law of nations, *jus gentium*, that he would have were they a foreign enemy. When they have thrown down their arms and submitted, the sovereign has no longer the rights of war against them, but simply the rights of peace. Hence the punishment he can inflict on them after their submission, after the war is over, is determined by the peace powers, and not by the war powers of the constitution. War no longer existing, only the peace powers can be lawfully exercised.

These distinctions are important, and if they had been

clearly understood and appreciated in the beginning, we should have been spared the strange anomalies we have seen in both congress and the administration. The administration seems to have had no lawyer in its service, capable of advising it, and has acted as if its war powers were controlled by its peace powers, and while waging war against the rebels it has required its generals to conduct it on peace principles. It need surprise no one that they have everywhere failed, and that after fifteen months of severe and bloody fighting, we are not so far advanced as we were in the commencement. The administration has seemed to proceed on the supposition that while fighting the rebels it owed them the protection it owed them in time of peace, and was as much bound to protect them as it is to protect loyal citizens. Congress, while it did not hesitate to raise armies, arm and equip them to shoot down rebels, hesitated about the right to confiscate their property, and a more complete stultification on the part of both congress and the executive than the confiscation bill actually passed cannot easily be imagined. The president refused to sign a bill confiscating the realty of the rebels for any longer period than the natural life of the person attainted, and yet signed a bill which confiscates absolutely and for ever their personal property. The constitution makes no distinction between the two classes of property. If it is unconstitutional to confiscate real property for a longer period than the traitor's natural life, it is equally unconstitutional to confiscate for a longer period his personal property. If it is not unconstitutional to confiscate for ever the personal property, it cannot be to confiscate the real. The whole difficulty on the part both of congress and the administration grows out of the lack of clear views of the distinction between the rights of peace and the rights of war. If congress in passing a law defining and punishing treason, is acting under the rights of peace, it is restricted in its action by the specific clauses in the constitution ; but in passing a confiscation act as a war measure, it is acting under the rights of war, and is restricted only by the law of nations, and its own judgment of what is expedient or inexpedient.

So of emancipation. Congress has no right to enact and the executive has no right to proclaim emancipation in any of the states held to be still existing as states, as a peace measure, or under the rights of peace, for under the rights of peace neither has any jurisdiction in the case. Neither can touch it, save under the rights of war, as a war measure. But as a war measure neither is restricted by the peace powers of the constitution, or is restricted at all, except by the *jus gentium* or law of nations, regulating civilized warfare. The government is free to adopt the measure or not, as it judges expedient. It can, unquestionably, adopt it as a war measure, without any violation of the constitution ; for the constitution itself confers on it all the rights of war recognized by the law of nations. Hence our Catholic brethren need have no constitutional scruples as to the emancipation of the slaves, as a war measure. While the civil war lasts, the government, either the president, as commander-in-chief of the army and navy, or congress, or both, have the clear constitutional right to adopt the measure, and the slaves so freed would be recognized as free by the law of nations ; for the law of nations recognizes manumission, and treats the manumitted as free ; therefore, as legally emancipated.

Catholics, no doubt, have to some extent, been prejudiced against emancipation as a policy, by the misrepresentation which has obtained respecting the horrors of San Domingo, and the selfish apprehension that the freed negroes would come North and compete with them in the northern labor market. This touches not the right of the government to adopt emancipation, but the expediency of doing so. The horrors of San Domingo, we may remark in passing, were occasioned not by emancipating, but by refusing to emancipate the slaves. If the proclamation of emancipation should excite fears of a servile insurrection, it would not be a thing to alarm us, as it would only compel the rebels to keep at home, to protect their own wives and children, their houses and plantations, those forces which they are now able to employ in the field against the government, and in cutting the throats of loyal citizens. This would be a reason for adopting, not for refusing to adopt the measure. We must not suffer our maudlin sentimentality to ruin our country, and cause the destruction of the nation. We should be much better pleased to see the rebel troops employed in protecting southern homes, and southern property, than in killing the flower of our youth, and carrying sorrow and bereavement into the bosom of every loyal family in the land. Our sympathies are with the loyal, not with the disloyal, and we weep more for the family bereaved of a father, a son, or a brother, by a foul murder, than we do for the murderer about to expiate his crime on the gallows. Our modern sympathy with rogues and criminals ; our misdirected humanity, and our mis-named philanthropy, are giving us over a prey to the spoiler. Let us learn to respect the experience of mankind. The fear that the freed negroes will come North as competitors in the market with white labor, is one Christian men should not indulge, and is also an unfounded fear. They come North now, because they cannot remain free at the South, but let the southern states be free soil, and they will prefer to remain in those states, for the climate is more congenial to them, and they have strong local attachments. Besides, it is probable, when the war is over, if successful for the Union, provision will be made to facilitate the migration of the colored population to a still more southern region, outside of the United States, where there will be no prejudices of color, to keep them for ever an inferior class.

These things, no doubt, have operated to make Catholics unfriendly to the policy of emancipation, but they do not prove that they are in favor of perpetuating negro slavery on this continent. The great body of the Catholics at the North, though by no means partial to the negro race, are anti-slavery in sentiment. For various reasons, given heretofore in these pages, they have more sympathy, or imagine they have more sympathy, with the southern people, aside from their present rebellion, and criminal attitude toward the nation, than with the people of the North, especially of New England; but they are not pro-slavery men, and when they think seriously on the subject, wish that slavery should not be perpetuated. We have, in our intercourse with them, found very few Catholics in the southern states even, who did not profess to us a dislike of slavery, and in Charleston, New Orleans, and St. Louis, we have expressed in public, strong anti-slavery sentiments to Catholic audiences, and been applauded to the echo for them. Catholics in the seceded states have, no doubt, been tainted with the political heresy of state sovereignty, and have therefore supposed that they owe a paramount allegiance to their state, and are bound to obey her when she secedes; but we have not found them, in general, favorable to slavery. They do not like northern interference with what is called the peculiar "institution" of the South, but more because a contravention of state sovereignty, than because hostile to slavery. There is, while we are writing, confined in Fort Warren, living on government rations, a southern Catholic gentleman, one of the most intimate and highly esteemed friends we ever had, and one of the most noble-minded and honorable men we have ever been acquainted with, who never owned a slave, and who has more than once assured us that he could never reconcile it to his feelings or to his conscience to be a slave-holder. He was disloyal to the Union, only because he held the doctrine of state sovereignty, and believed that the Union in using force to coerce a seceding state, outrages and denies that sovereignty. A more loyal man, according to his under-standing of loyalty, never lived, and in opposing, in his ca-pacity as lawyer, and member of the legislature of his state, the action of the federal government in its attempts to coerce a seceding state, he was, in his own mind, opposing simply usurpation, not legitimate authority. The Catholics in the southern army are fighting not to perpetuate slavery, but to sustain state sovereignty. They are wrong, and yet the doctrine of state sovereignty is virtually insisted on by more than one of our northern governors, as strenuously as by them. The federal government has to combat state sov-ereignty in the loyal, hardly less than in the disloyal states. Hence so many of its embarrassments.

The fact is, the political heresy of state sovereignty is not confined to the states in arms against the government, and, save a few arbitrary acts, this war has been conducted by the federal government as the agent of the states, rather than as the supreme government of the land. We have never ac-cepted the true issue. We have accepted, at least acted on, state sovereignty principles, and have not dared to assert na-tional principles. Our state governors have acted and are acting as much on state sovereignty principles as Pickens, Brown, Pettus, or Moore. Our federal government has acted less as a supreme national government, than has the so-called confederate government itself. Neither side is true to itself. We owe our embarrassments, and our reverses, to our failure to oppose national sovereignty to state sover-eignty, and the rebels owe their successes to their disregard of the state sovereignty principle on which they justify their rebellion. Here is the reason why, as yet, neither side has gained a decisive victory. The real question at issue is not slavery or abolition, but are the United States a nation, one political people possessing national sovereignty in its pleni-tude, or are they a mere aggregation of sovereign states? The emancipation of the slaves is, in our judgment, a neces-

eary war measure which the government should adopt without a moment's delay, but the real question is between national sovereignty and state sovereignty, and till that question is met squarely and fairly, there will be nothing settled.
It is because this issue was not made up at first, because,
while the southern states asserted for itself each its own
sovereignty, the federal government failed to make a clear
and distinct assertion of the national sovereignty, that our
confessors found themselves obliged to give absolution to
their penitents, who, by a law of their state, took up arms
against the Union. In the unsettled state of the controversy,
they could do no less. Catholics were generally attached to
the Democratic party, and that party has generally asserted
state sovereignty. Our own writings have done not a little
to accredit that doctrine among Catholics, for when we had
the most influence with them, we held, defended, and
labored to prove, that the sovereignty is not in the nation,
in the states united, but in the states severally. We maintained that heresy for years, and it was only when we saw
some of its practical developments, that we began slowly to
distrust and abandon it. Catholics generally adopted it, and
many of them hold it still. Prior to the outbreak of the
civil war, a Catholic newspaper published in Ohio was in
favor of the South, and defended decidedly secession principles. After the war broke out, it professed to defend the
Union, not indeed on national principles, but on state sovereignty principles. Ohio, it said, having declared for the
Union, it was bound, as loyal to Ohio, to sustain the federal
cause.

No argument, for these reasons, can be deduced from the
conduct of Catholics to prove that the church is not opposed
to slavery. Moreover, it is seldom safe to infer the doctrine
or the spirit of the church from the practice of Catholics.
Nothing is more certain than that the church condemns the
African slave trade, and did condemn it before the discovery
of this continent by Columbus, when first carried on by the
Portuguese. Yet Catholics were the first importers of slaves
into this continent, and Catholics, or nominal Catholics, Portuguese, Spanish, or Hispano-Americans are still the principal slavers, and, save the United States, the only Christian
countries in which slavery now exists are Catholic countries.
All the Protestant states, and France, whose government is
neither Catholic nor Protestant, have abolished slavery in
their colonies, and even schismatic Russia is freeing her

serfs, while Spain, Portugal, and Brazil retain negro slavery. Yet it is in spite of the church they do it, as it is in spite of the church that Catholics continue in all countries practices their religion condemns.

The church, it is true, does not teach with modern abolitionism that slavery is always, everywhere, and under all circumstances, a sin in the individual slaveholder; for she gives absolution to the slaveholder, without demanding as its condition the manumission of his slaves, providing he accuses himself only of simple slaveholding. This proves that she does not regard slaveholding as necessarily a sin, or a sin *per se*, in every individual slaveholder. But it does not follow from this that she approves of slavery, that she does not oppose it, or that she does not regard it as a moral, political, and social wrong, which every individual, according to his lights and means, is bound to do all that he can to mitigate or abolish. Not every individual who participates in a social wrong, and even derives advantages from it, is necessarily a sinner, for often his participation may be a social necessity, and may be innocent on his part, because he sees and intends no wrong in it. Despotism is a great moral, political, and social wrong, but not therefore is every man living under a despotism a sinner, who derives advantages from it, or who does not engage in efforts to overthrow it— efforts which might be fruitless, or which might result in more evil than good. Every man who reduces or aids in reducing a freeman to slavery, is a sinner; but a man who has inherited slaves from his parents or his ancestors, may retain them in bondage without sin, although it is probable that ordinarily he does not. Such is the doctrine of the church as we collect it from her practice and the teaching of her moral theologians.

But the church does not and cannot tolerate what is called chattel slavery—the slavery recognized and sustained by the laws of the southern states, for she regards as a man, and treats as a person, the humblest African slave. She restricts the bondage to reasonable or moderate bodily service, asserting at all times, in all places, and under all circumstances, the moral freedom of the bondman. The bondman is for her a man, a moral being, with a conscience of his own, which the master may not under any pretence whatever invade. She places the bondman and the master under one and the same moral and spiritual law; and makes each alike accountable for his own deeds before the divine tribunal.

She denies with all her divine energy that man has or can have dominion or property in man, and therefore that one man can have any right to exact the bodily service of another, save in consideration of benefits conferred. God, St. Augustine teaches, and in this gives the real doctrine of the church, gave to man dominion over the irrational creation, but not over the rational. Hence the first governors of mankind, he says, were called pastors, not lords, *pastores non domini.* One may owe service to another, as the son owes service to his father, and even the wife to her husband; but this does not imply that one is the lord of another, that is his owner or proprietor. "The relation of master and slave," said Mr. Calhoun to us, in one of his long conversations with us in 1840–'41, "is indefensible. We never call our people our *slaves*, but speak of them as our *people*. The relation between them and us is that of guardian and ward. We are their guardians, and they are our wards, and we defend the relation on the ground that they are virtually minors, and incapable of acting or providing for themselves." We cite his words, because he so far agrees with the church, that he repudiates the doctrine that one man can be the lord, owner, or proprietor of another, and concedes that the master owes to the servant an equivalent for the services he exacts. In calling the slave a ward, he plainly concedes that he is a *person*, and therefore logically entitled to all the rights essential to personality.

The church always insists on Christian marriage for the slave, and in doing so asserts that he is a person, not a thing, a moral agent, not a simple chattel ; for according to her, marriage is a sacrament, and none but persons endowed with free will can be its recipients. Marriage, she teaches, is also a contract, a free voluntary contract, and therefore none but persons capable of contracting can enter into the marriage relation, and the common doctrine of her theologians is, that the *contrahentes* or contracting parties are the ministers of the sacrament of matrimony, and none but persons can be the ministers of a sacrament. Certainly, the church holds bondmen are capable of Christian marriage, and she treats infidelity to the marriage relation in slaves precisely as she does in freemen. In treating the bond as capable of Christian marriage, she asserts them to be persons, therefore capable of family, and hence of a domicile, all of which is incompatible with chattel slavery. Hence we find chattel slavery, after the introduction of Christianity, gradually disappearing from all christianized Europe. The doctrine of the church necessarily, where it was received, if it did not at once free the slave, converted him from a thing to a person, from a chattel slave to a villein or serf; whence in time, he became a free peasant, or freeman.

The church is therefore necessarily opposed to slavery as it exists in our southern states, for, notwithstanding the fine theory of wardship developed by Mr. Calhoun, slavery in them all is chattel slavery. Legally the slaves are things, property, not persons, at least as to all civil relations, though in criminal relations the law, by an inconsistency that operates to his disadvantage, and to the advantage of the master, treats the slave as a person, and holds him to be capable of crime. The law recognizes no Christian marriage between slaves, no family of slaves, or rights of family, and the master seldom respects in them the relation of husband and wife or parent and child. He claims to own both the male and the female, and he regards their offspring as he does the increase of his flocks and herds. The man and woman are regarded as united only temporarily, or so long as it may suit the convenience or pleasure of their owners, and they themselves usually consider their union only as transitory. Hence our missionaries do not treat it as marriage, except when the parties are Catholics, and have been married by a Catholic priest. To a Catholic mind the state in which the slaves are living is far more revolting than the violent rending asunder of family ties; for it is a state incompatible with the practical observance of Christian morality. The almost universal concubinage which takes the place of marriage among the slaves is a thing the church does not and cannot tolerate; and were Christian marriage introduced and legally recognized among them, it would instantly relieve southern slavery of one of its greatest horrors, put an end to its chattel character, and convert it into serfage or villanage, and make the slaves *adscripti glebæ*, fixed to the realty— the first step in the progress from slavery to freedom. Their moral and personal rights, with the rights of family, would soon follow, and the opportunity for improvement and gradual elevation in the social scale, in some measure, be secured. Villanage may coexist with Christian marriage, chattel slavery cannot.

The fathers of the church usually treat slavery as a penalty, as a punishment for crime or sin, not as a penalty for original sin, for original sin is the sin of the race, and all men have alike incurred its penalty, the free as well as the bond. Remotely, slavery may no doubt be traced to original sin, as may all social evils ; but the fathers of the church do not mean that, when they assert the penal and therefore expiatory character of slavery. They have in mind the *jus gentium* or law of nations as asserted by Roman jurisprudence. The law of nations as enforced by the Roman courts, recognized the lawfulness of the slavery of captives taken in a just war, and treated it as a commutation of the punishment of death which they had incurred. "Jure enim naturali omnes homines ab initio liberi nascebantur," say the *Institutes* of Justinian. "Servitus autem est constitutio juris gentium, qua quis dominio alieno contra naturam subjicitur. Servi autem ex eo appellati sunt, quod imperatores captivos vendere, ac per hoc *servare* nec occidere solent." The law of nations, as originally interpreted, allowed the sovereign to put to death the subjects of a foreign prince taken captive in a just war. This rested on the principle that the entire nation against which a prince may lawfully wage war, has forfeited its existence, and the prince may lawfully slay any of its subjects that he can get hold of. We see traces not a few of this in the Old Testament. But, if the conqueror could lawfully destroy the nation, or put the captives taken in war to death, he could, of course, spare their lives and inflict on them the milder punishment of selling them into slavery ; and hence slavery would in some sense be an act of mercy, inasmuch as it *saved* them from the extreme penalty incurred, as the Roman jurists asserted. It was in this way that slavery was introduced, and on this ground it was recognized by the law of nations, though confessedly contrary to nature, the natural law, or the natural freedom with which all men were originally born.

It will be seen from this that slavery, as a constitution of the law of nations, is justified only on the ground that it is a penalty—a punishment for crime. The citizens or subjects of a state or nation were considered as *solidaires* with the state itself, and answerable jointly and severally for its offences. This idea of slavery as a penalty for sin, the sin of the slaves themselves, or their nation, or of their forefathers, is that recognized by the Christian fathers. They, therefore, exhort the slaves to bear their servitude patiently, and to make it, as they may, a means of expiating their sin, and of promoting their own sanctity and final glorification in Christ. Slavery or servitude, as a penalty for crime, the only slavery we ever find countenanced, in principle, by the law of nations, or the fathers, the church has never, to our knowledge, condemned ; and it is not condemned even by our extreme abolitionists. It is condemned by nobody, except certain theorists, who condemn all punishment, and deny that man can be justly compelled to expiate any offence of which he may have been guilty. The fathers and doctors of the church have never, to our knowledge, approved or favored involuntary servitude, except as a penalty or an expiation. But through the influence of Christian principles, developed and applied first by the church and then by Christian society, the law of nations which justified slavery, the slavery of captives, has been greatly modified. That law centuries since has ceased to permit captives taken in war to be either put to death or to be reduced to slavery. Prisoners taken in war might, late in the middle ages, indeed, be held to ransom, but in all Christian nations they are now required to be set at liberty on the return of peace, and the victorious prince seeks indemnification for his wrongs and expenses from the nation through its government, not from subjects or citizens individually. This change in the law of nations, which sweeps away every vestige of the slavery known to that law in Roman jurisprudence, is due to the church, and therefore we have the right to say that she is opposed to slavery.

The children of slaves were held to be slaves on the ground that their parents had lost their personality, were chattels, simply property, and their increase, like the increase of any other kind of property, was the property of the master. This, in ancient times, was less remarked than it would be in modern times, because the ancients indulged less in slave breeding than the moderns, reared comparatively few slaves, and relied chiefly on fresh captives taken in war to keep up the supply of the slave market. But the church, wherever she gained a footing and acquired a predominating influence, exerted herself to put an end to the practice of punishing the innocent offspring for the real or supposed crimes and offences of the parents. She did it by treating the bond as *persons*, not as *things*, and insisting on the right of Christian marriage, which, as we have said, logically implies the right of family and domicile. The prelates of the church, far less the common people, do not always see or suspect at once all the consequences which follow from the principles they assert, when teaching or accepting Christianity, and thus often tolerate or find excuses for continuing practices the church, when her principles are fully developed and carried out, decidedly condemns. Some of them have not much logical capacity to boast of, for not every prelate is a great man, though filling a great office; some of them are indolent, and are quite willing to let things go on as they found them, and spare themselves the labor and trouble of reforming them; some see clearly enough what is needed, but they see also so many difficulties in the way of effecting it, or are so persuaded that society is not ripe for it, that they are appalled by the magnitude of the work to be done, and shrink from undertaking it; some see, undertake, and by their rashness, imprudence, or want of judgment or tact, only make bad worse; so it is that centuries elapse before evils, confessed to be evils, are redressed. It is only when God sends a man of genius, who may or may not pertain to the hierarchy, as he sent prophets under the old dispensation, that much real advance is ever effected in the practical development and application of Catholic principles. Yet from time to time he does send the man of genius, and, though ill-received at first, and looked upon as a restless agitator, as a disturber of the peace, and a seditious fellow, he gradually succeeds in making his voice heard. His words are listened to, and his rich and living thoughts enter into the heart of his age, and become the patrimony of his race. Then the old is changed, the new development is installed, the world advances, and ameliorations long demanded are effected.

We know the principles of the church, and we are not confined to the applications made of them by our predecessors. We, in our age, have understanding and logic as well as they had in theirs. We can, having those principles, judge for ourselves as well as they could for themselves. Any one who knows and understands the principles of the church, knows that she is and must be opposed to slavery and in favor of freedom for all men, whatever their complexion or the condition in which they were born. She asserts the unity of the race, and that by nature all men are free and equal. She treats the negro as a man, and a man with all the rights and properties of an individual of the human race. For her the negro is of the race of Adam, created by the same God, redeemed by the same incarnate Saviour, and destined to the same heaven as the white man. She makes no difference as to their moral and spiritual rights between white men and black men. She has for both the same baptismal, marriage, and burial service, the same doctrine and morality, the same sacraments, the same worship, the same communion, the same promises, the same duties, the same privileges, the same hopes. She takes her Levites and consecrates her priests from both, as she finds them qualified. In this very country of ours, so full of prejudices against the negro, men with large admixture of negro blood, born of slave mothers, are now ministering at her altars, and St. Augustine, the greatest of the Latin fathers, was certainly an African, and some maintain a negro. We have ourselves received holy communion with a negro next on either side of us. She sends out her missionaries to Africa to convert the negroes to her faith, and recently some of her consecrated priests visited the court of Dahomey, and were favorably received by the king, who granted them permission to convert his subjects. Some of the most pious and devoted Catholics we have ever known, were full-blooded negroes. Certain it is, then, that the church holds that negroes, equally with the whites, may share in the regeneration or palingenesia, and then that they share equally in genesis, and are, by origin of the same race, for they could not share in the former without sharing in the latter. Our Lord redeems us, sanctifies and glorifies us, by assuming our nature, and the nature he assumed was taken from the white variety. The blessed Virgin was a white woman, not a black woman. Our Lord, in assuming her nature, could not have assumed the nature of the negro, unless the black and the white have only one and the same identical nature, and, therefore, do and must pertain to one and the same identical race. If the negro were not of the same race, how could he have shared in Adam's sin, since this was the sin of the race, not the sin of the individual? If he does not participate, through identity of race, in the sin of Adam, in original sin, what, in his case, is the use or meaning of baptism?

There is here no need of argument. The moment it is seen that the church holds the negro child over the baptismal font, pours on his head the baptismal waters, and introduces him into the regeneration, it is seen that she holds him to be a man, sprung from the race of Adam, sharing its infirmities, its wants, its privileges, its hopes, its glories. If he were of a different race, to baptize him would be as unmeaning, would be as great a profanation, as to baptize a horse, an ox, or a cannon. It is, then, certain that the church teaches that the negro is a man, and therefore as a man the equal of any other man. To enslave him, then, is just as great an offence in her eyes, as it is to enslave a white man. This narrows the question down to the simple rights of man, eliminates from it all considerations of color, and puts the negro and the white in the same category. Now, does the church teach that one man has the right to enslave another? that the equal has the right to enslave his equal, or that an equal can be the lord and proprietor of his equal? She can do no such thing, for if $A = A$ she cannot say while conceding it, that $A > A$ or $A < A$. The negro may have departed further from the primitive type than has the white man, but that has nothing to do with his rights as a man. In the view of the church, however widely he may have departed, he is a man still. My neighbor may be inferior to me in capacity, in physical strength, in external comeliness, in learning, in intellectual culture and attainments, even in morality, but that does not prevent him from having the same *natural* rights as a man that I have. One man may have certain acquired rights, certain social and political rights, that another has not, and the two may be unequal in property, in social position and influence, in political franchises, power, or trust, but if both are equally men, both have equal natural rights—what we in this country call the rights of man—and among which the American people have solemnly declared are " life, liberty, and the pursuit of happiness."

The church evidently agrees with the law of nations, as interpreted by Roman jurisprudence, that all men are originally born free, that servitude is against nature, and that a man can be deprived of his liberty only in punishment for crime. On this point there is no question, and no need of citing authorities. The church accepts the natural law, and by the natural law man equals man the world over. The proposition that all men are born equal, is as self-evident as the formula $A = A$. The differences between man and man are accidental, not essential. If then, by nature, man equals man, then by nature, or the law of nature, no man has or can have dominion of man, and no man is the property or the subject of another. Slavery or servitude is, then, as the Roman law declares it, *Constitutione juris gentium* CONTRA NATURAM. Hence, under the civil law, as under the common law, the presumption is always in favor of liberty, and no one is obliged to prove himself a free man. The law treats him as free until he is proved to be not free. The claimant must prove the man he claims is a slave before he can take him.

If all men are born free and equal, one man can be the slave of another only by some sin or crime that forfeits his natural freedom. This is what we understand the church to teach; and if she taught any thing else she would stultify herself, which it were blasphemy to suppose. The church teaches more than natural reason can comprehend—truths which transcend reason, and pertain to an order above reason; but she teaches nothing in contravention of reason, and nothing which, so far as it is addressed to our understanding, is not reasonable. There is no discrepancy as there is no separation between faith and reason, and hence Melchior Cano, in his *Loci Theologici*, makes reason one of the topics or sources whence we may ascertain what it is the church teaches. The church undoubtedly does teach that natural liberty may be lost by sin, and that involuntary servitude for crime is defensible. But this is the full extent she goes. She does not teach that it is right to reduce captives taken in war to servitude, for the law of nations which formerly authorized it, has been modified under her influence, and she prohibits the African slave-trade, which she could hardly do if she held it to be lawful to reduce captives to slavery, for most of the slaves brought from Africa are captives taken in war. We have disposed of the question of color, which in her eyes is neither a sin nor a crime; and besides, if to be black were a sufficient reason for reduction to slavery, why should she prohibit the "nefarious traffic," as she calls it, "in blacks"? It is evident from her interdiction under severe pains and penalties of all traffic in blacks, that she does not consider either the complexion, or the peculiarities, moral and physical, of the negro family, such an offence against God or society, as to warrant the reduction of negroes to slavery. Nor does she consider the fact, that men, white men or black men, are infidels, pagans, Obi worshippers, a good reason for making them slaves; for if she did, she would place no interdict on the importation of Africans as slaves into the American states or colonies, since they are nearly all infidels and idolaters. Catholics have sometimes pretended, in order to gratify their revenge or feed their cupidity, that infidel, and especially Moorish and negro captives may be sold into slavery, if they refuse to be baptized. Charlemagne so held, if we may judge from his practice in the case of the conquered Saxons in the ninth century; but his treatment of them has remained a blot on his memory, and the church has never approved of it, or countenanced in others any thing of the sort. She asserts for infidels, pagans, Jews, Mahometans, all the natural rights of man—the same natural rights that she does for Christians or Catholics; for she does not hold that grace abrogates the natural law. Her doctrine is, that grace supposes nature, that the supernatural accepts and completes the natural, but does not supersede it. Hence non-Christian princes retain their natural right to the allegiance of their Christian subjects. Faith, moreover, is voluntary, and must, if accepted at all, be freely accepted, and in no case coerced.

The fact that the parents are slaves, is not with the church a sufficient reason for enslaving the children, for she denies in the outset the principle on which hereditary bondage rests for its only defence, namely: the parents are chattels, not persons; she does not permit the proverb, "The fathers have eaten sour grapes, and the children's teeth are set on edge." She does not allow the children to be punished for the crimes of their fathers. Her doctrine is, that each man must answer for himself, and be rewarded or punished in this world as in the next, according to his own deeds, and not according to the deeds of another. As she always treats the slave as a moral person, and claims for him the right of Christian marriage, therefore of family, she necessarily recognizes the personality of the offspring, and the offspring as owing service to the owner of the parents only so far as they are indebted to him for benefits which he has conferred upon them, such as care, nursing, food, and clothing, in their infancy and childhood, before being able, by their labor, to earn their own living. Beyond, they own their own labor; own, indeed, themselves. Hereditary bondage the church may, in given times and places, find it necessary to tolerate, as Moses tolerated divorce, on account of the intractableness of the people, but she never approves it; never teaches that it is just, and always labors to mitigate it, and ceases not in her efforts till she brings society up to its abolition. No doubt children suffer for the crimes and faults of their parents even to the third and fourth generations, and it is in the order of providence that it should be so; but the enslavement of the offspring for the sin and offences of the parents, is not included in this order, is not a natural and inevitable consequence of the sins of the father. It is clear, that if, as we have seen, slavery is lawful only as a penalty for crime, the children, however much they may accidentally suffer from the slavery of their parents, can no more than could the parents themselves be reduced to slavery, except for their own crimes.

But, furthermore, the church does not confine herself to a merely passive opposition to slavery. She holds and teaches the great principles of Catholic civilization. No doubt, many Catholic writers confine themselves exclusively to the purely ascetic relations of man, and forget that Catholicity, if catholic, that is, universal, embraces both time and eternity, the natural and the supernatural, nature and grace, religion and civilization, the relation of man to his Maker and his relations to his neighbor and to society. To labor for the highest order of civilization is as much man's duty as to labor to save his soul; and his duties to society are no less sacred than his duties to God;—indeed his duties to his God include his duties to society, and those cannot be discharged without discharging these. No man is faithful to God who is faithless to society. No man can love God and hate his brother, for if he loves not his brother whom he hath seen, how shall he love God whom he hath not seen? The Catholic, if true to the letter and the spirit of his church, is never indifferent to any political or social wrong or evil, and is always in earnest to ameliorate the social as well as the individual condition of his fellow-men. The duty insisted on by the church, of alms-deeds, is not fulfilled by throwing a penny to a beggar, or dealing out to him a bowl of soup at the convent gate; but it demands that each one, in his degree and according to his ability, should work earnestly and perseveringly for the amelioration of the condition of all men both individually and socially, for time and eternity. "Do good to all men as you have opportunity." Our Lord condemns, and the church as his spouse condemns the sluggard, the merely negative character, who though he does no positive harm, does no positive good. He condemns the lukewarm, and requires people to be either hot or cold. He declares the servant who wraps the talent he receives in a clean napkin and buries it in the earth, and preserves and restores it entire to his Lord on his coming to reckon with his servants, a wicked and slothful servant, and dooms him to outer darkness, not because he had wasted his talent, but because he had not put it out to the usurers so that he could "receive his own with increase." He demands positive characters, earnest, energetic characters, who have positive virtues, and work to promote a positive good. The admonition to the children of Israel was, " Cease to do evil, learn to do well."

Hence the church is never content with simply disapproving of slavery, with simply letting it alone, or doing nothing to uphold it. She regards it as a wrong, as an outrage upon manhood, a crime against civilization, a sin against God, and therefore requires on the part of all her children an active opposition to it. She knows that where it is wide-spread and deep-rooted in a community it cannot be abolished by simple individual action, and therefore does not impose, under pain of sin, the obligation upon each individual slaveholder to manumit instantly all his slaves, although she applauds him when he does so, honors him for his virtue and his sacrifice ; she knows that the wrong is social rather than individual, and must be redressed by the social or collective action of the slaveholding community ; but she does require each and every individual to do what he can as a member of the community, to bring it up to the point, and to induce it to take the action necessary for redressing it. Every evil she opposes she requires her children individually and socially to oppose, and to do their best to remove. This is a point which Catholics too often overlook. Because the church does not make the immediate emancipation of his slaves by the individual slaveholder a condition *sine qua non* of absolution in every instance, they are apt to conclude that she is not opposed to slavery, and that they are not required by their religion to make any active efforts for its abolition. So they do nothing, and let the evil continue, and grow till it brings on a social convulsion. Know they not that sloth is one of the seven deadly sins, and that the slothful servant who buried his talent in the earth, was cast into outer darkness ? Whatever the church does not approve, she actively opposes, and whatever she actively opposes she requires her children to exert themselves actively, wisely, no doubt, but actively and energetically to remove.

Hence, the church, though tolerating, to a certain extent and under certain conditions, the holding of slaves, is always actively an emancipationist, and requires her children to be the same. Pope Pius IX., gloriously reigning, has just shown the view of the subject taken by the chief pastor of the church, for he has just conferred a knightship on M. Augustin Cochin, expressly for his recent admirable work on the Abolition of Slavery.

The church is certainly anti-slavery and abolitionist, for she has abolished slavery in all the states of Europe, none of which now recognize slavery, save in some of their American colonies. But unquestionably, she does not proceed rashly in her work of abolition, or translate ordinarily by a single bound the individual from a slave to a free man. She looks to the preservation of society, to its well-being, as well as to the liberation and well-being of the slave. This is wise and just, for social changes should as far as possible be effected without social shocks or convulsions. We should, if we were dealing with the question as a peace measure in time of peace, and in a country whose government has by its constitution supreme jurisdiction of it at all times and under all circumstances, be ourselves opposed to instantaneous and complete emancipation. We would proceed gradually, securing to the slave—first his moral rights as a person, his right of Christian marriage, therefore the right of family and domicile. We would convert the slave into a serf, and in due time the serf into a free peasant. But we are not now dealing with abolition as a peace measure, in time of peace, but as a war measure in time of war, which makes all the difference in the world. And as a war measure, to be of any avail, it must be immediate, sudden, and complete. It is not as a moral, economical, or social question we are now to consider it; but as a military question. As a peace question we have always agreed and should now agree with the great majority of the Catholic population of this country, but as a war measure we are obliged to consider it under its military aspects only, and to deal with it according to the exigencies of the war.

The hesitancy in Catholic or in non-Catholic minds about adopting the emancipation policy does not spring, we apprehend, from any love of slavery, or any lack of hostility to its perpetuation on the free soil of America; but from not distinguishing sharply between emancipation as a peace measure adopted for the sake of emancipation, and emancipation as a war measure adopted not for the sake of emancipation, but for the sake of the nation, as a means of weakening the power of the rebels, and enlisting on the side of the nation, struggling to save its integrity and life, the moral aid or the sympathy of all Christian and civilized nations. It is the confusion of the two questions, which obtains in most minds, that disturbs the judgment of nearly the whole American people. This confusion is in great danger of proving, if it has not already proved fatal to us. Some among us want the war a war of abolition ; others, and a much larger number, imagine that if the liberation of the slaves be decreed, it will be a war of abolition, and in an abolition war our armies will not fight, unless on the *other* side. Both of these parties, in our judgment, are wrong. This is and should be no war for abolition. Slavery *per se* enters into it, and should enter, for nothing. The war is to save the life of the nation and the integrity of the national territory, and to vindicate the supremacy of the national government. The abolition of slavery we demand not as an end, but as a means of prosecuting this war to a successful issue. On the slavery question. as a peace question, we presume we agree substantially with Generals Halleck, McClellan, Burnside, and the great majority of the officers of the regular army, as well as with the president, secretary of state, and the postmaster-general. There are insuperable constitutional objections to it as a peace measure, and we yield to no man in our respect for the constitution ; but as a war measure there is no more constitutional objection to it than there is to firing upon the enemy's troops drawn up in line of battle, in capturing or sinking a rebel man-of-war, or in taking possession of a rebel town or village. We demand the measure as a means of prosecuting the war with success, as a means of damaging the enemy, and forcing him into submission. The very purpose of war is to damage the enemy, to inflict on him the greatest possible damage allowed by civilized warfare, in the shortest possible time, and with the least possible damage to ourselves. As a war measure, both abolitionists and anti-abolitionists may demand or sustain it without any compromise of their principles or surrender of their respective convictions. The abolitionist wants emancipation for its own sake, because he regards it as always a sin ; we waive the ethical question, and demand it as a means of saving our national existence. As we both demand emancipation, as a fact, we are both agreed on the practical question, which is enough for both, and there is no occasion for any quarrel between us. They need not quarrel with us, because we do not demand it for the reason they do, nor we with them, because they do not demand it solely for the reason we do. We want the nation saved, not the triumph of our speculative opinions or those of anybody else, and believe it far more important to gain a victory over the rebels, than it is to gain one over the abolitionists, or anti-abolitionists. We do not agree with Messrs. Phillips and Garrison, but as they do not, in this crisis, demand any thing incompatible with the successful prosecution of the war, nay, as what they demand, in so far as it has any practical bearing, is, in our judgment, absolutely necessary to its successful prosecution, we cannot see any propriety or utility in quarrelling with them or denouncing them for their speculative opinions. We might as well quarrel with and refuse to sustain the administration, because the president and secretaries are Protestants.

We say the same of the colonization or migration policy insisted on with so much earnestness by the president. As a peace measure, if the country were at peace, or if the country had leisure to attend to any thing but its own self-preservation, we should give it, if undertaken in a proper spirit, and by capable and trustworthy managers, our hearty support. But the measure is not a war measure, nor to be undertaken while we have a war of the magnitude of the present war on our hands. We regret that either congress or the administration should have raised the question pending the civil war. The civil war itself is alone quite as much as they have the capacity to manage, and they had done better to confine their energies and the resources of the country to the suppression of the rebellion, and securing our national existence, than to raise questions which can receive no practical solution till the return of peace. It is a misfortune, perhaps, fatal to the nation, that we have never been able to make the administration understand and bring home to itself that we are really at war, and a war which leaves the country leisure for nothing else, a war of such formidable dimensions that its successful prosecution demands all our time, all our thoughts, all our energies, and all our resources. Our jaunty secretary of state, a feeble copy of the present English prime minister, appears to have had either no serious intention of saving the integrity of the national territory, or no comprehension of the magnitude of the task of doing it. He seems to have regarded the southern rebellion as a mere bagatelle, that could be suppressed by a diplomatic dispatch, a political juggle, or, that, if let alone, would suppress itself; at any rate a matter that could be taken care of without any interruption of the ordinary pursuits, or the ordinary credit, trade, and industry of the country; while our honest and well-intentioned president, bewildered by a mass of petty difficulties, legal technicalities, and contradictory objections, has hardly known what to do, or been able to take a single firm resolution.   Between them they have suffered the national cause to languish, the national armies to undergo defeat after defeat, disaster after disaster, till the nation stands on the verge of the precipice, waiting only another kick from the rebels to be plunged into the gulf below.   It is high time to attend to saving the nation, and to leave in abeyance all other questions.

If the nation is lost, as there is serious danger that it will be, under the sort of civil and military management we have thus far had, and if present divisions, distractions, confusion of ideas, and party spirit, which render us impotent before the enemy, are to continue much longer, all the questions we now agitate will become alike indifferent.   It matters little who administers the government, if so be it is well administered ; but as yet, it must be confessed, the administration has not refuted the charge of executive incapacity so often brought in past years against our old Whig leaders. For ourselves we are neither Whig nor Democrat; we know, and will know, so long as the nation is in danger, no party but the party of the country, and the whole country; but we demand in the name of the nation and of free institutions, the exhibition of a capacity on the part of the administration, civil and military, which it has not yet shown,—a capacity in some measure equal to the present national crisis, or else that its chief incumbents patriotically retire and give place, before it is too late, to others, who have not only the wish or the honest intention, but the ability to wipe out from the nation its present disgrace, and preserve its unity and life.   Thus far our civil and military administration has proved a miserable failure, and the nation can hardly afford it time to make new experiments.

Our loyalty is known and unquestionable, but our patience is well-nigh exhausted.   Three months ago we wrote, " We are proud of our countrymen ; " we are still proud of our countrymen, but we are pained to see them sacrificed to no purpose, and mortified at the disgrace brought upon our nation by administrative imbecility, and blundering, incompetent generalship. The United States cut at this moment a most sorry figure before the world. We may be sent to Fort Lafayette for saying it, but we tell the administration, and we do so with the most loyal intentions, as well as with sorrow of heart, that it will ere long find itself there or in a southern dungeon, if it does not speedily exhibit a capacity it has not yet given any evidence of possessing, instantly retrieve its past blunders, and prove itself able to use the national resources for the vindication of the national majesty. "The capital is safe;" "The army is safe;" "All is quiet on the Potomac," the stereotyped telegraphic dispatch, with scarcely a variation for so many months, and now resumed again, is a confession of civil and military administrative imbecility, or, what we dare not think, of disloyalty, and cannot any longer be read with patience. The nation must not be lost through tenderness to individuals, civil or military, in high or low places. We have given the administration and its generalship a generous confidence, and a fair trial, and they have failed, miserably failed, and all the world knows it. If they are prepared to do no better—if they are able to do no better, it is time for them to stand aside, and let the really able man, if such we have, take the helm, and rescue the ship from the breakers. Red tape will not save the nation. Confidence in the administration, or in its generals, cannot be preserved, unless they do something to inspire it. The administration has lost the confidence of the nation in its capacity to conduct this war to a successful issue, and it will not regain it by any attempt to suppress the public expression of the fact. Restrictions on the press, the attempt to silence the voice of criticism, will only make matters worse, and increase the growing distrust—will only create the suspicion that it seeks to cover up its imbecility by its tyranny.

But enough, and too much of this; "Out of the abundance of the heart the mouth speaketh." When we touch upon our national disasters, we know not how to restrain ourselves. We have been deceived. We were promised a victory at Corinth, at Yorktown, at Richmond, on the Rappahannock, at Bull Run, before Washington, and we have met only defeat, disastrous and shameful defeat. Our men whenever permitted have fought like heroes, and we have strewn the soil of rebeldom with the dead or wounded bodies of the fairest, noblest, bravest of our sons, and all to no purpose. We demand of the administration and military authorities an account for the dead and wounded, and of our captive heroes; we demand an account for the loss of the brave and indomitable Lyon; for that type of the true soldier, Charles F. Smith; for the noble-hearted, experienced, and accomplished and heroic Kearney; for that true military genius, Isaac Stevens, whose like we shall not soon see again, and whose untimely loss shrouds a nation in mourning, and presages disaster and ruin to the national cause. We lay their loss to the account of the administration, and do not and cannot accept our jaunty secretary of state's assurance that " the war is to be ended in ninety days," as an adequate atonement. Our heart is full of sorrow; our country is on the verge of destruction, and there is no man able to help us. But our chief purpose in this article is not to find fault with the administration, but to vindicate our Catholic brethren from the suspicion of being pro-slavery, to point out the real position of the church on the slavery question, and to convince our Catholic brethren that while the war lasts we have no occasion to quarrel with the abolitionists. The emancipation of the negro slaves, as a war measure, is strictly constitutional, and may be adopted without violating, in any respect whatever, either the letter or the spirit of the constitution, or requiring us to change any conviction we have ever expressed.

Slavery, if respected by the federal government, is, as the events of the war have proved, an element of strength to the rebellious states. The four millions of slaves, with the soil, climate, and simple industry of the South, are equal to twelve millions of our industrial population at the North, with our less genial climate, less productive soil, and more various and more complicated industry, and far larger consumption. It requires in the free states at least twelve millions to provide for our industrial wants, to feed and clothe our population, and to subsist our armies. This leaves us as a military population, from which to draw our troops, able-bodied men for our armies, only about seven millions; and the rebellious states, after deducting four millions required for their industry and subsistence, have a population of just about the same number. Hence they are able to place in the field and subsist as large armies as the federal government can, and the only advantage the government has over them is in its navy, and its command of the sea. The notion that we could starve by a blockade the South into submission could have been entertained only by those who were profoundly ignorant of southern resources. In that kind of wealth which gives military strength, the southern states were and are wealthier than the northern states, for their wealth is agricultural, and ours in great part is commercial and manufacturing wealth, which is necessarily deranged and depreciated by war. The war and blockade have deprived the South of luxuries, but of hardly a single necessary of life, and the stories told of the distress, of the privations of the southern people, especially of the southern soldiers, are only so many silly fictions. As long as southern land remains, and they have four millions of blacks to till it, the southern states can produce in abundance all the necessaries of life within themselves, and subsist their armies and their whole population, and far easier than we can ours. The superiority of military strength, therefore, is not so decidedly on our side as we have pretended, perhaps believed, and we can place it on our side at all, only by detaching from the rebel cause that which sustains it, the southern laboring population. If we could deprive it of the support of its four millions of laboring population, nearly all productive laborers, and consuming in return hardly a tithe of what is consumed by our laboring population, we should almost annihilate their whole military strength, or at least so reduce it as to render it unable to offer any effective resistance. The laboring population of the South can be detached from the rebellion, or rendered a source of weakness rather than of strength to the rebels, for they are mostly slaves desirous of being free, if we will declare their freedom, and enable them to understand that their freedom is bound up with our success, or that our success will make them freemen. Here is wherefore emancipation, as a war measure, is important and even necessary. We do not want the negroes for soldiers to fight in our armies, for we can call out more white men than we can arm; but we want them to sustain the rebellion no longer by their labor. The measure will not be so advantageous to the federal cause now as it would have been had it been earlier adopted, but it would give it a decided preponderance even now, if speedily adopted. It would so diminish the supplies or so augment the fears of the rebels, that they would be obliged to keep some hundreds of thousands of the men now in arms against us at home to protect their families and plantations, and to raise supplies for their armies and their non-producing population.

What we now urge upon our Catholic brethren is the

manifest impolicy of warring against emancipation as a war measure. They are deceived as to the strength and resources both of the loyal and of the disloyal states, as has been and probably is the administration itself, if it has dealt and is dealing honestly with the country. The wealth and resources of the South in time of peace are far inferior to those of the North, and the administration has apparently proceeded on the supposition that they are equally inferior in time of war. But such is not the fact. Organized for peace, for trade, commerce, and manufactures, the North finds war rapidly diminishing its resources and depreciating its wealth. War disturbs its commerce, disturbs its manufacturing industry, depreciates the value of its wares and its rents, cuts off its trade, and renders it really poor, while nominally rich. Why else have we heard the earnest call for a national bankrupt law? On the other hand, the South, chiefly agricultural, and producing within itself all the necessaries of life, is far less disturbed by war in its wealth, and in its industrial and economical relations. Our Catholic as well as our non-Catholic countrymen have not taken this difference between the two sections into the account, and have not seen that a long war, while it would ruin the North if separated from the South, would upon the whole even strengthen the South, separated from the trading community of the North, and secure its triumph. We have supposed that we might give the rebels every advantage, touch them only at arm's length, and still easily crush them. All this is a mistake. We said a year ago, that it would require all our strength and resources to cope successfully with the southern rebellion. We knew the South and its agricultural, mechanical, and military resources, and we knew it would be more than a match for us, unless we should take every advantage allowed by the rights of war. We were not believed by the government, nor by our own Catholic community. Catholics may naturally have presumed the administration understood the matter much better than we, and had intentions at least equally loyal. The government and press adopted a system of boasting, spoke contemptuously of southern resources, southern skill, and southern bravery, and even of southern troops, who were accused of "skedaddling," whenever they made a skilful retreat, or a wise evacuation, or a brilliant strategic movement. The government and the government press have misled us. We now know its calculations were unfounded, and its representations false. The policy or want of policy we have hitherto pursued has left us beaten, the rebels victorious at all points, and from the defensive boldly taking the offensive; and we may soon hear as a piece of gratifying news, "Cincinnati is safe," "Philadelphia can be defended," "New York is in no immediate danger," "Preparations are made to give the rebels a warm reception should they venture to attack Boston."

The republic is really in danger, and, if overthrown, no class of the American population will suffer more than Catholics. Under our free institutions Catholics are gradually taking, in a legitimate way, possession of the country. They already fill the lower strata of American society, constitute, in the free states, our principal laboring class—the real basis of national strength, wealth, and prosperity, and are slowly but surely working their way up to the highest social level. Let the nation fail, or let the Union be reconstructed "on slavery as its corner-stone," and their brilliant prospects are blasted, their glorious national career ended, all hope of making this a Catholic country, or of keeping it a free country must be abandoned. Protestantism has proved its impotence to sustain a free state, and sees itself obliged, in order to escape anarchy, to resort to monarchy, to aristocracy, or to slavery, as its social and political basis. If the South, the truly Protestant section, triumphs, Catholicity will have henceforth little room for expansion on American soil, for the industry of the country will be carried on chiefly by slaves or an inferior caste.

We earnestly beseech our Catholic brethren to review the question, and see if they have not been mistaken in their policy, if real regard for our common country, and our holy religion, dearer to them and to us, than all other interests, do not imperiously demand emancipation as a war measure, as a means of securing victory to the national cause. We are Catholic as well as they, and yield to none of them in the sincerity and earnestness of our faith, or in the heartiness of our devotion to the church. If they are opposed to the abolitionists, let them bear in mind that no man has opposed them longer or more strenuously than we have done, and if we oppose them not now, or write not against them, it is not because we have changed our convictions or our opinion. We stand, on the question of slavery, where we have stood ever since 1838. Not we have changed, but the question itself has changed. Why have you, my brethren, opposed the abolitionists? Because you loved and wished to perpetuate slavery? No. It were a foul slander on you to say it. But because you loved the Union, and believed the agitation of the slavery question likely to endanger its power, and even existence. This was the fact with us, and with you, and with the great body of the Democratic party at the North. Why do we demand emancipation now? For the very reason that before the rebellion we opposed it; because we love the Union more than slavery, as we loved it more than emancipation, and because emancipation is now necessary to save the Union, and prevent the destruction of the nation. When emancipation could not be demanded without endangering the Union, we, and you opposed it; now that it is demanded to save the Union, and is perfectly constitutional as a war measure, we urge it, and why should not you? To do so implies no inconsistency or change of opinion on your part. To be consistent with yourselves, to be faithful to that love of the Union which made you oppose, you must now, in the altered state of the question, demand emancipation.

It is true the greater part of our bishops and clergy, in the beginning believed that emancipation would not need be resorted to, but the archbishop of New York, while apparently opposing us, confesses that, if in the progress of the war emancipation should become a military necessity, it could and should be adopted. Well, it is clearly now a military necessity, and let us not shrink from adopting it. We say, *emancipation*, we say not arming the negroes and placing them in the army on a footing of equality with our white soldiers. That is not a military necessity, and would be unwise and impolitic, as grossly offensive to the deep-rooted prejudices of our countrymen against negro equality. We say nothing in favor of negro political or social equality, to which we have always been personally opposed. It will be time enough to settle the political and social *status* of the negro, when the war is over. All we demand now is the full and complete emancipation from bondage of the whole negro race within our limits, at once and without delay, leaving the question of compensation to loyal slave-holders, if any such there are, to be adjusted after the return of peace. This we demand as legal, constitutional, because a military necessity, and authorized by the rights of war, and the government will, in our judgment, be unfaithful to its trusts, if it hesitates any longer to adopt it.

THE SEWARD POLICY.

[From Brownson's Quarterly Review for October, 1862.]

WHILE from the outbreak of the present civil war we have not hesitated to discuss freely the great questions it involves, and to urge boldly and earnestly the policy on which we have believed it should be conducted, we have taken scrupulous care not to discredit the administration or to impair the confidence of the public in its wisdom and loyal intentions. Mr. Lincoln was not our choice as a candidate for the presidency, but as he was nominated, we gave him our vote, and have aimed to give him a firm and independent support. In the trying times introduced by the defection and rebellion of the slave states, we have felt it the duty of every loyal citizen to stand by the government as the only means of standing by the country. We have suppressed our doubts, our fears, our misgivings, and scrupulously refrained from every public expression likely in the least degree to embarrass the administration either in prosecuting the war, or in dealing with foreign nations, and as far as a man in our humble sphere could, labored to strengthen, invigorate, and encourage the administration. We have so labored, and it is with great regret that we find ourselves compelled in this moment of its greatest embarrassment, to speak to the country plainly and energetically of its faults and short-comings.

We have reached a stage in the conduct of our civil and military affairs, when disguise or suppression of the truth is no longer permissible; when the paramount interests of the nation make it the duty of every loyal citizen to canvass freely, but respectfully, the acts and policy of the administration, and summon it to answer for itself at the bar of enlightened public opinion. Forbearance to criticise the administration were, as we view the matter, now treachery to the country, which is more than any administration. No good citizen can now with a good conscience, as it seems to us, see the administration conducting the country to the verge of destruction, and leaving the national life to be extinguished, and remain silent, or refrain from advertising the nation of its danger. To do so, would be a manifest dereliction of public duty. We know the exigencies of war; we understand the plea of military necessity; and we fully recognize that war does and must impose numerous restrictions on individual liberty, on freedom of speech and discussion, which should never be tolerated in a free country, in time of peace. We would ourselves, if in our power, silence every voice not beyond all question loyal to the national cause. Whether the Union is to be preserved or not, whether the government has the right or not to coerce rebellious states into submission, or whether the government shall or shall not be sustained in its efforts to crush out rebellion, are not open questions, and are not now questions that it is lawful to raise. The nation has authoritatively answered them, and its answer is final in public for the good citizen. Ordinarily, as long as an administration shows the disposition and the capacity to conduct the affairs of the nation, civil or military, with a reasonable measure of success, we should refrain from all unfavorable criticism on even its temporary and minor blunders or failures—for perfection is to be looked for in nothing human. But criticisms, even in time of war, demanded by the public interest, and intended not to hinder, but to forward the work of national salvation, are allowable, and must be tolerated by the public authorities, and will be, if they have any loyal or patriotic intentions. It is useless now to cry out against the danger of impairing confidence in the administration. There is in the country no confidence in the administration to be impaired. The people have confided in it, trusted it, even against their better judgment, and lavished at its call, men and money, blood and treasure, with an unheard of profusion; and now while the nation is on the verge of bankruptcy, and bereavement and mourning have been carried into almost every family in the land, and we find that the administration has nothing to show for it but dilapidated armies, raw recruits, and the victorious armies of the rebellion bringing home war, pillage, rapine, and murder to our own northern homes and firesides, are we to refuse to state the fact and demand an account of it? Tell us not to trust it longer, to give it more time, that it is just agoing to retrieve the past, and speedily suppress the rebellion. We have been told this any time for the last year, and any time for the last year the administration has been just *agoing* to change its policy, just *agoing* to suppress the rebellion, but alas! it moves not at all, or it moves only to defeat and disaster.

We arraign not the army; we will not complain of Halleck, McClellan, or even Pope, till we know what orders have been given them by the administration, or the state policy by which they have been required to govern themselves. We are friends of the army, and we have been ever since we could remember, and we have more than once defended it against civilian censure. We make no invidious distinction between the regular army and the volunteer army. There are in both branches of the army as much bravery and as good fighting qualities as the world ever saw, and as able and as skilful generalship as any nation need desire. Its failures we attribute not to incompetent generalship, but to the policy of the administration. The army is now our only hope, and if the country is to be saved it will save it. Nor do we agree in casting the blame of our military miscarriages, if miscarriages they are to be called, on the secretary of war, whom we know to be a man of large views, loyal intentions, and no mean administrative ability; for he has had no influence in shaping the policy of the administration, and but little in the conduct of the war. He is only one of the president's clerks, and is overruled in his judgment whenever there is a question of any importance to be decided. He opposed with all his might General McClellan's movement upon the peninsula, and was overruled by the president, who, against his own judgment and convictions, consented to it. The policy of the administration, as far as policy it has, or has had, was determined before Mr. Stanton became a member of Mr. Lincoln's cabinet. The secretary of the treasury, we presume, assented to the policy originally agreed upon, but he is understood to have demanded a different policy since. He has, however, confined himself principally to his own department, and has exerted but little influence outside of it on the administration. Mr. Blair is now not counted, and the attorney-general does not count for much. The chief responsibility rests on the secretary of state and the president himself. The president as the executive head of the government and commander-in-chief of the army and navy, is officially the administration, and alone responsible for its policy. But the previous position of the secretary of state, as a Whig leader, and as the recognized chief of the Republican party, his well-known character, and his presumed influence with the president, either personally or through his friends and political managers, have elevated him in the public estimation to a share, and to the chief share in the presidential responsibility. It is the general belief of those best informed on the subject, that the secretary of state has, directly or indirectly, on all questions of importance, a controlling influence, and that he in reality shapes the policy of the administration. This may not be true to the extent alleged, and it is hardly respectful to the president to assume that it is; but a large share of responsibility undoubtedly belongs to the secretary of state—as large a share as in our remarks we shall attribute to him.

Of Mr. Seward, the secretary of state, we speak with great reluctance, and with some reserve, for we may not be as unprejudiced and impartial as we could wish. We have never been personally attached to him, and have nearly always been politically opposed to him ever since he entered public life as a National Republican and an Anti-Mason, under the auspices of Mr. Thurlow Weed, whom we remember as the manufacturer of a "good-enough Morgan till after the election." We never sympathized with him in his National-Republicanism,—although we supported Mr. Adams in opposition to General Jackson,—in his political Anti-Masonry, in his Whiggism, or even in *his* sort of Republicanism. We have never regarded him as a statesman, and have looked upon him merely as a clever and successful politician. Clever he must have been, or he could never have built up so wide a reputation on so narrow a foundation as he received from nature; successful, too, he must have been, for he has been governor of the state of New York, United States senator, and is now secretary of state in Mr. Lincoln's administration. He is a fine rhetorician, a superb phrase-monger, almost equal to Lamartine, though far from being that Frenchman's equal as an elocutionist.

Like all wily politicians who rely on their adroitness and dexterity for carrying their points, the secretary lacks nerve, back-bone, high courage, and firm and generous resolve. His faculties avail him least when the danger he tries to meet is greatest. And, perhaps, no man could have been selected less fitted by constitution and temperament, to meet such a national crisis as has been brought on by southern secession. When the public expected from him, in the winter of 1860–61, in his place in the senate, a speech that should defy or overwhelm the southern disorganizers, and give strength and courage to all loyal hearts, he amused us with an elaborately written essay, worthy of a clever sophomore, on the beauties and grandeur of the Union, and the impossibility of dissolving it, although he knew, or ought to have known, that it was already dissolved, and the question before him was on its restoration. He quailed before the Masons, the Slidells, the Toombses, and the Wigfalls, and evidently showed the white feather. By a sort of common consent of the country, he had been looked upon as the representative man of the Republican party, and we read at the time, in his poltroonery, in his weakness, his trembling before the enemy, the disasters and failures which have since followed the national cause, and gave expression to our despondency at the time. If we have hoped since, it has been because we discovered a spirit and a patriotism in the people, and a generous forgetfulness of party distinctions on the part of many of the old Democratic leaders, especially among those who had the most strenuously opposed abolitionism, and been the most favorable to the South, that we had not looked for. We trusted that the accession of these would give courage to the administration, and strengthen its back-bone. But we have seen all along in Mr. Seward's weakness and moral cowardice, a grave danger to the national cause, which is not yet averted.

Mr. Seward had been a leading anti-slavery man, had given utterance to "the irrepressible conflict" doctrine, and been amongst the most energetic against slavery, of any of our stump orators, in the campaign that resulted in the election of a Republican president. In Illinois, Indiana, Michigan, New York, he showed no lack of courage, was as bold as a lion, and hurled, at a distance, defiance in the very teeth of the southern disunionists; in Washington, confronted with them in the senate of the United States, his courage oozed out at his fingers'-ends, and he was as tame and as meek as a pet lamb. It is no secret that, before the incoming of the present administration, he was the chief, if not the sole originator, aided, as a matter of course, by his familiar spirit, Mr. Weed, of that disastrous policy then adopted by several Republican leaders, of suffering South Carolina, Georgia, and the gulf states to go in peace, and of amending the constitution, so as to secure the loyalty of the border states. He, the irrepressible-conflict man, with his own hand drew up and carried through both houses of congress, by a two-thirds vote, an amendment of the constitution, forbidding the federal government for ever from interfering with slavery in states,—a measure which was quite uncalled for, since that is forbidden by the constitution as it is; could do no good, and served only to demoralize the Republican party, and prove to the country that it was not composed of the right sort of stuff to vindicate the rights of the nation. He has since complained that he is called "a compromising man;" but he was the first and foremost to urge his party to compromise with the slave-power, and that, too, when, if he had the least grain of the sagacity that belongs to the statesman, he must have seen that any offer at compromise, under the circumstances, was to surrender, at least to imperil, the national cause and the existence of the government. The national cause, if maintained at all, could be maintained only by meeting promptly, on the very threshold, every attempt to dismember the national territory, or to set up within it a separate independent state. We have all blamed Mr. Buchanan for not crushing the secession movement in the outset; but Mr. Seward resisted secession not more firmly than did Mr. Buchanan. He yielded at the first summons, quailed before it, begged to compromise the matter, was ready to give up every distinctive principle he had ever contended for, and did what was in him to prove to the world that he and his party had not been contending for principle, and had been only using the anti-slavery sentiment of the country as a stepping-stone to place and power. He carried with him a large portion of the party he represented, and some men from whom better things had been expected.

To Mr. Seward's cowardly surrender to the South of the national cause before the incoming of the present administration, we may attribute the demoralization of parties, and the chief embarrassments loyal men have had to contend with in suppressing the rebellion. He was placed, by an unfortunate concurrence of circumstances, in advance, as the leader of the national cause, and at the first summons ignominiously surrendered it, not from disloyalty, but from his never having comprehended the nature of the struggle, or from having regarded it as only an ordinary struggle of parties and politicians for power. He seems never to have been guided by any principle, or to have understood that there are principles which the statesman, the politician even, is not at liberty to surrender when demanded for party success. It seems necessary even yet to remind him that the nation is more than individuals, more than parties, and that when its honor and dignity, when its very life is at stake, no compromise is admissible. We should never have voted for Mr. Lincoln, if we had really believed his election would be followed by a civil war, for we had never embraced or defended the peculiar doctrines of his party; but having voted for him, and he having been constitutionally elected, we could under no circumstances have compromised with the opponents of his election till they had recognized him as their president, and submitted to his government. The honor and dignity of the nation, the honor and stability of constitutional government forbade it. After the inauguration of President Lincoln, and his appointment as secretary of state, to soothe him for not having been nominated by the Republican party for president, instead of arresting as traitors the commissioners of the seceded states in open rebellion against the federal authority, Mr. Seward received them, unofficially of course, with all courtesy, as high-minded and honorable gentlemen, and conferred at length with them on the matters of difference between them and the federal government, and, it is said, virtually agreed to a separation, and was in a fair way of adjusting the respective boundaries of the two republics, when the attack on Sumter came to interrupt their pleasant interviews, and their interesting negotiations.

Even the motive of that attack appears to have escaped him, and to have been understood neither by Mr. Seward nor by any other member of the administration. It was done to secure the secession of the border states, with which Mr. Seward was coquetting, with a distinct and full understanding with the leading politicians in those states, pledged beforehand to secession. It was as certain in March, 1861, to any one who understood any thing of the plans of the South, that all the slave states would secede, unless prevented by force, as it was in June of the same year when they had all virtually or formally seceded. The resolution to secede was fixed from the beginning, only the border states could not secede without another pretext than that which had served South Carolina and the gulf states. They could secede only in case of an attempt by the federal government to coerce a state into submission. The attack on Sumter and the threatened invasion of Washington were made expressly to compel the government either to resort to coercion or to stand utterly disgraced at home and abroad. Not one of the border states ever intended that its fate should be separated from that of its sister slave states. They never proposed or accepted the offer of compromise in good faith, and

Mr. Seward has from the first been fooled in all his relations with southern statesmen or southern politicians, and has sacrificed his principles and the honor of his party for a shadow. His negotiations even, though unofficial, were a surrender of the national cause, for to allow it to be even unofficially discussed was virtually to surrender it, and were grossly improper, unless the administration contemplated either a separation or abdication in favor of the government of the confederacy, for everybody knew at the time that the differences could not be settled by diplomats or by politicians. There was no middle ground on which the two parties could meet. There was then, as now, no alternative but the unconditional surrender either of the seceders or of the government. Without the one or the other, and neither could be expected, there was no peaceful solution of the controversy possible. But Mr. Seward could not perceive it, and wasted the first six months of the new administration, precious weeks too, in idle attempts to effect by diplomacy and political manipulation what every clear sighted man in the country saw could be effected only by the arbitrament of arms. These precious weeks were not used to put the government in a condition to assert its rights. Nothing was done. The secretary, jaunty, light-hearted, and full of hope, went on with his negotiations, and assured the country that all difficulties would soon be adjusted, peace be made, and "nobody be hurt;" yet we are told Mr. Seward is a sagacious and far-seeing statesman. Did he or did the president honestly believe a peaceful solution practicable? Did either really intend to preserve the integrity of the national territory? Did either expect a resort to arms? The first neither with ordinary sense could seriously believe; if they did not seriously intend to save the integrity of the national territory, they can be excused of treachery only on the ground of their incapacity. If they expected a resort to arms how is their neglect of all preparations to be excused, and if they did not, they deserved to be impeached for their inability. We include the president through courtesy, and because he doubtless acquiesced in the policy, and is officially responsible for it; but the policy was evidently Mr. Seward's, for it was adopted and acted on by him in the senate and by leaders of the Republican party before he became secretary of state. If the president accepted it, we may reasonably presume that he did so, because Mr. Seward had proceeded so far in it before the inauguration, that it was difficult if not impossible for the president, unaided by the leaders of the party that elected him, as he would have been, to adopt and carry out a new and entirely different policy. Mr. Seward had by his arrangement bound the president to his policy, before he was inaugurated. Had the president rejected it on assuming the administration, he would have been isolated from his party, and not known where to look for a friend or supporter.

It is true, if the president had been a different sort of man from what he was and is, if he had fully comprehended the position of affairs, and had had the courage to look beyond party and thrown himself boldly on the country, and continued Dix, Holt, and Stanton, in the departments they filled during the last weeks of Mr. Buchanan's administration, he might possibly have escaped the meshes of the policy Mr. Seward had so adroitly prepared for him; but this would have required the president to have been a man of genius, or a thoroughly trained, and a superior statesman, neither of which can his most partial friends claim for him. Mr. Lincoln is a man naturally of strong common sense, loyal and patriotic intentions, and in ordinary times would have made a decent president, and administered the government without discredit to himself or the country. He is intellectually superior to what he is commonly supposed, and all that is to be said to his prejudice is, that he is not equal to the demands of the country in times which demand at the head of the government a statesman of the first order. What marvel, then, that he felt himself obliged on his inauguration, to acquiesce in the policy Mr. Seward had induced the chiefs of his party to adopt? All the men, unless Mr. Blair be an exception, that the public opinion of his party required him to make members of his cabinet, had already, through Mr. Seward's management, as we maintain, committed themselves to the compromise and peace policy; and, if they did not intend to assent to a temporary dismemberment of the Union, did not contemplate the use of force against the seceded states. He was so placed that he could not make up his cabinet without accepting substantially Mr. Seward's policy. We therefore call the policy of the administration "the Seward policy."

That the Seward policy was one of peace and compromise, if not of at least temporary dismemberment, we know from what came to the public at the time, and authentically from Mr. Seward himself, from an official letter written by him the 10th of April, 1861, to Mr. Adams, our newly-appointed minister at the court of St. James, and published among the documents accompanying the president's message for December of the same year. In that letter, written two days before the attack on Sumter, Mr. Seward professedly lays open by authority for the guidance of the minister himself the policy of the administration. We find the policy to be the same in substance that he had urged in and out of the senate before his accession to office. We recommend the careful persual of this letter to all who look upon Mr. Seward, not as a mere politician, but as a statesman—a "philosophical statesman," as a member of the administration, in apparent seriousness, called him a few weeks since, in our hearing. It will prove that he was wholly at fault in his view of the difficulties of the situation, and the means of removing them and preserving the national life. His political optimism breaks out in every sentence, and he sees nothing in the movements of "our misguided fellow-citizens" of the South that need alarm us for the safety of the Union. The southern confederacy contains in itself the seeds of its own dissolution, and the people after a little time will weary of it, and sigh to return to the Union, as the starving children of Israel in the wilderness sighed to return to "the flesh-pots of Egypt." We extract a few of the more notable passages of this remarkable document:

"One needs to be as conversant with our *federative system* as perhaps only American publicists can be to understand how effectually, in the first instance, such a revolutionary movement must demoralize the general government. *We are not only a nation but we are states also. All public officers, as well as all citizens, owe not only allegiance to the Union, but allegiance also to the states in which they reside.* In the more discontented states the local magistrates and other officers cast off at once their federal allegiance, and conventions were held which assumed to absolve their citizens from the same obligation. Even federal judges, marshals, clerks, and revenue officers resigned their trusts. Intimidation deterred loyal persons from accepting the offices thus rendered vacant. So the most important faculties of the federal government in those states abruptly ceased. The resigning federal agents, if the expression may be used, *attorned* to the revolutionary authorities, and delivered up to them public funds and other property and possessions of large value. The federal government had, through a long series of years, been engaged in building strong fortifications, a navy-yard, arsenals, mints, treasuries, and other public edifices, not in any case for use against those states, but chiefly for their protection and convenience. These had been unsuspectingly left either altogether or imperfectly garrisoned or guarded, and they fell, with little resistance, into the hands of the revolutionary party. A general officer of the army gave up to them a large quantity of military stores and other property, disbanded the troops under his command, and sent them out of the territory of the disaffected states.

"It may be stated, perhaps without giving just offence, that the most popular motive in these discontents was an apprehension of designs, on the part of the incoming federal administration, hostile to the institution of domestic slavery in the states where it is tolerated by the local constitutions and laws. That institution, and the class which especially cherishes it, are not confined to the states which have revolted, but they exist in the eight other so-called slave states; and these, for that reason, sympathize profoundly with the revolutionary movement. Sympathies and apprehensions of this kind have, for an indefinite period, entered into the bases of political parties throughout the whole country, and thus considerable masses of persons, whose ultimate loyalty could not be doubted, were found, even in the free states, either justifying, excusing, or palliating the movement toward disunion in the seceding states. The party which was dominant in the federal government during the period of the last administration embraced, practically, and held in unreserved communion, all disunionists and sympathizers. It held the executive administration. The secretaries of the treasury, war, and the interior were disunionists. The same party held a large majority of the senate, and nearly equally divided the house of representatives. Disaffection lurked, if it did not openly avow itself, in every department and in every bureau, in every regiment and in every ship-of-war; in the post office and in the custom-house, and in every legation and consulate from London to Calcutta. Of four thousand four hundred and seventy officers in the public service, civil and military, two thousand one hundred and fifty-four were representatives of states where the revolutionary movement was openly advocated and urged, even if not actually organized. Our system being so completely federative and representative, no provision had ever been made, perhaps none ever could have been made, to anticipate this strange and unprecedented disturbance. The people were shocked by successive and astounding developments of what the statute book distinctly pronounced to be sedition and treason, but the magistracy was demoralized and the laws were powerless. By degrees, however, a better sentiment revealed itself. The executive administration hesitatingly, in part, reformed itself. The capital was garrisoned; the new president came in unresisted, and soon constituted a new and purely loyal administration. They found the disunionists perseveringly engaged in raising armies and laying sieges around national fortifications situate within the territory of the disaffected states. The federal marine seemed to have been scattered everywhere except where its presence was necessary, and such of the military forces as were not in the remote states and territories were held back from activity by vague and mysterious armistices which had been informally contracted by the late president, or under his authority, with a view to postpone conflict until impracticable concessions to disunion should be made by congress, or at least until the waning term of his administration should reach its appointed end. Commissioners who had been sent by the new confederacy were already at the capital demanding recognition of its sovereignty and a partition of the national property and domain. The treasury, depleted by robbery and peculation, was exhausted, and the public credit was prostrate.

" It would be very unjust to the American people to suppose that this singular and unhappy condition of things indicated any extreme favor or toleration of the purpose of a permanent dissolution of the Union. On the contrary, disunion at the very first took on a specious form, and it afterwards made its way by ingenious and seductive devices. It inculcated that the Union is a purely voluntary connection, founded on the revocable assent of the several states ; that secession, in the case of great popular discontent, would induce consultation and reconciliation, and so that revolution, instead of being war, is peace, and disunion, instead of being dissolution, is union. Though the ordinances of secession in the seceding states were carried through impetuously, without deliberation, and even by questionable majorities, yet it was plausibly urged that the citizens who had remained loyal to the Union might wisely acquiesce, so as ultimately to moderate and control the movement, and in any event that if war should ensue, it would become a war of sections, and not a social war, of all others, and especially in those states, the form of war most seriously to be deprecated. It being assumed that peaceful separation is in harmony with the constitution, it was urged as a consequence that coercion would, therefore, be unlawful and tyrannical ; and this principle was even pushed so far as to make the defensive retaining by the federal government of its position within the limits of the seceding states, or where it might seem to overawe or intimidate them, an act of such forbidden coercion. Thus it happened that for a long time, and in very extensive districts even; fidelity to the Union manifested itself by demanding a surrender of its powers and possessions, and compromises with or immunity toward those who where engaged in overthrowing it by armed force. Disunion under these circumstances rapidly matured. On the other hand, the country was bewildered. For the moment even loyal citizens fell naturally into the error of inquiring how the fearful state of things had come about, and who was responsible for it, thus inviting a continuancy of the controversy out of which it had arisen, rather than rallying to the duty of arresting it. Disunion, sustained only by passion, made haste to attain its end. Union, on the contrary, required time, because it could only appeal to reason, and reason could not be heard until excitement should in some degree subside. *Military spirit is an element always ready for revolution.* It has a fuller development in the disaffected than in the loyal states. Thousands of men have already banded

themselves as soldiers in the cause of disunion, while the defenders of
the Union, before resorting to arms, everywhere wait to make sure that
it cannot be otherwise preserved. Even this cautious and pacific, yet
patriotic disposition has been misunderstood and perverted by faction
to encourage disunion.

* * * * * * * * * *

" The president neither looks for nor apprehends any *actual* and *permanent* dismemberment of the American Union, especially by *a line of
latitude*. The improvement of our many channels of intercourse, and
the perfection of our scheme of internal exchanges, and the incorpora-
tion of both of them into a great system of foreign commerce, concurring with the gradual abatement of the force of the only existing cause
of alienation, have carried us already beyond the danger of disunion in
that form. The so-called confederate states, therefore, in the opinion
of the president, are attempting what will prove a physical impossibility.
Necessarily they build the structure of their new government upon the
same principle by which they seek to destroy the Union, namely, the
right of each individual member of the confederacy to withdraw from
it at pleasure and in peace. A government thus constituted could neither
attain the consolidation necessary for stability, nor guarantee any engagements it might make with creditors or other nations. The movement, therefore, in the opinion of the president, tends directly to anarchy in the seceding states, as similar movements in similar circumstances have already resulted in Spanish America, and especially in Mexico.
He believes, nevertheless, that the citizens of those states, as well as the
citizens of the other states, are too intelligent, considerate, and wise to
follow the leaders to that disastrous end. *For these reasons he would
not be disposed to reject a cardinal dogma of theirs*, namely, that *the federal
government could not reduce the seceding states to obedience by conquest, even
although he were disposed to question that proposition. But, in fact, the
president willingly accepts it as true*. Only an imperial or despotic government could subjugate thoroughly disaffected and insurrectionary
members of the state. This federal republican system of ours is of all
forms of government the very one which is most unfitted for such a
labor. Happily, however, this is only an imaginary defect. *The system
has within itself adequate, peaceful, conservative, and recuperative forces*.
Firmness on the part of the government in maintaining and preserving
the public institutions and property, and in executing the laws where
authority can be exercised *without waging war*, combined with such
measures of justice, moderation, and forbearance as will disarm reasoning opposition, will be sufficient to secure the public safety until returning reflection, concurring with the fearful experience of social evils,
the inevitable fruits of faction, shall bring the recusant members cheerfully back into the family, which, after all, must prove their best and
happiest, as it undeniably is their most natural home. The constitution
of the United States provides for that return by authorizing congress,

on application to be made by a certain majority of the states, to assemble a national convention, in which the organic law can, if it be needful, be revised so as to remove all real obstacles to a reunion, so suitable to the habits of the people, and so eminently conducive to the common safety and welfare.

"Keeping that remedy steadily in view, the president, on the one hand, will not suffer the federal authority to fall into abeyance, nor will he, on the other, aggravate existing evils by *attempts at coercion* which must assume the form of direct war against any of the revolutionary states. If, while he is pursuing this course commended as it is by prudence as well as patriotism, the scourge of civil war for the first time in our history must fall upon our country during the term of his administration, that calamity will then have come through the agency, not of the government, but of those who shall have chosen to be its armed, open, and irreconcilable enemies; and he will not suffer himself to doubt that when the value of the imperilled Union shall be brought in that fearful manner home to the business and the bosoms of the American people, they will, with an unanimity that shall vindicate their wisdom and their virtue, rise up and save it.

* * * * * * * * * *

"Nevertheless, all the world know what are the resources of the United States, and that they are practically unencumbered as well as inexhaustible. It would be easy, if it would not seem invidious, to show that whatever may be the full-development of the disunion movement, those resources will not be seriously diminished, and that the revenues and credit of the Union, unsurpassed in any other country, are adequate to every emergency that can occur in our own. Nor will the political commotions which await us sensibly disturb the confidence of the people in the stability of the government. It has been necessary for us to learn, perhaps the instruction has not come too soon, that vicissitudes are incident to our system and our country, as they are to all others. The panic which that instruction naturally produced is nearly past. What has hitherto been most needful for the reinvigoration of authority is already occurring. The aiders, abettors, and sympathizers with disunion, partly by their own choice and partly through the exercise of the public will, are falling out from the civil departments of the government as well as from the army and the navy. The national legislature will no longer be a distracted council. Our representatives in foreign courts and ports will henceforth speak only the language of loyalty to their country, and of confidence in its institutions and its destiny."

This letter, we must bear in mind, was written for the private instruction of Mr. Adams, who is told that he is not expected to communicate it to the government to which he is accredited, and we may therefore conclude that it is a frank and truthful statement of the real views and policy of the administration, at least up to last December, when the secretary selected it for publication; it may or must be regarded as official and authentic. On the historical sketch of the rise and progress of the rebellion with which it sets out, we have little to say, except the secretary shows in it that he fails to apprehend or appreciate its real cause. The real cause of the rebellion had, no doubt, a close relation to slavery, so close, that if there had been no negro slavery in the land it would never have occurred ; but, at bottom, the cause was not, as the secretary supposes, the rancor of a defeated political party, but the increasing power of centralized democracy at the North, and its alleged tendency to substitute for constitutional government the arbitrary will or caprice of the majority for the time. The southern statesmen, for there were statesmen, as we have learned there are generals, at the South, believed that this sort of democracy was becoming the political order in nearly all the non-slaveholding states, and they saw, or thought they saw, in the growth of the Republican party, hardly less democratic than the so-called Democratic party itself, and in the election of Mr. Lincoln, a sure indication that it might soon be transferred from the states to the nation, placing the whole republic at the mercy of an accidental majority, with no safeguards for the rights and liberties of minorities. Being themselves in a minority the moment parties should be determined by geographical lines, and having a peculiar institution to protect, hateful to northern democracy, and condemned by the public sentiment of Christendom, they were naturally more alive to this, and more ready to resist it, than were the people and politicians of the free states. The southern states were constitutional, not democratic, and the real cause of the rebellion, as it stood in their minds, is to be sought in the determination to sustain constitutionalism against democracy. They having become unable any longer, through ordinary political action, or through the ballot-box, to control the northern democracy, and determined never to be governed by it, thought they had no alternative left but to secede and cut themselves loose from it. This is the simple, truthful explanation of the southern rebellion, and the issue it wished submitted to the arbitrament of arms was not slave labor or free labor, but constitutionalism or democracy.

We have for ourselves, we grant, been always unwilling to meet the rebellion on this issue, or as an issue between constitutionalism and centralized democracy. We are personally, and always have been, opposed to that democracy, and in favor of constitutionalism, and hence the reason why, till we saw the danger to American unity and nationality, we have always in our political sympathies been with the South rather than with the North. We defend, and always have defended, constitutionalism against democracy, and maintained that our system of government is not a pure democracy; but we prefer, first of all, the nation, and demand the preservation of its unity and integrity. These gone, all is gone; but so long as the nation remains, and especially a nation constituted like ours, which provides constitutionally for the amendment of its government, we can correct through legal modes of action the political tendencies that are opposed to the national weal. We have opposed the southern movement not as a movement against centralized democracy, but as a movement against American nationality, represented by the federal government; and we regret that the administration did not meet the controversy as one between national sovereignty and state sovereignty.

The next thing we take up in the secretary's letter is the confession that our government is a "federative government." He calls it "our federative system." "True," he says, "we are a nation, but we are states also." If we are federative states, a federation, or confederation, how can we be politically a nation? There are and can be no federative bonds between different parts of one and the same nation. A federation is a league of different nations or sovereigns, who, bound together only by federative bonds, are not, and cannot be, politically one nation. Here the secretary, on behalf of the administration, concedes in the outset the fundamental principle of the secessionists, and gives up, if he did but know it, the right of the federal government to coerce the seceding states into submission; for he will find in the record of the federation or compact no authority given by the contracting parties to coerce a seceding member. Secession may, indeed, be a breach of faith, but the Union provides no remedy. "All public officers, as well as all citizens, owe," says the secretary, "not only allegiance to the Union, but allegiance also to the states in which they reside." If the sovereignty inheres in the states, as it must if the Union is a federation or league of sovereigns, "a federative system," the allegiance of the federal officer and of the citizen is due primarily to the state, and allegiance to the state must override that to the Union, and then secession is justifiable. But this double allegiance is an absurdity. No man can owe allegiance to two sovereigns at one and the same time, and allegiance is due only to the sovereign. If the state is sovereign, I owe it *allegiance*, and *obedience* to the Union, so long as it commands me to obey it, and no longer. If the Union is sovereign, or rather if the United States, as one political people, is sovereign, then I owe it allegiance, and only obedience, within the limits it allows, to the state in which I reside. If the first alternative is adopted, the southerners in arms against the Union are not rebels, but loyal citizens, for they are evidently acting under the authority of their respective states, whatever may be pretended to the contrary, and you can rightfully wage only a defensive war against them. If the latter alternative be accepted, the federal government, as holding in trust the sovereignty of the nation, has not only the right, but it is bound in duty to treat them as rebels, and to reduce them to their allegiance, if able, whether they act or do not act under state authority, whether they be individuals or states.

The secretary should, as a good logician or as a sound statesman, have taken one ground or the other; but, unhappily, he has tried to take neither and to take both, and alternately asserts and denies both national sovereignty and state sovereignty. Thus he calls the people of the southern states that had already seceded, " our misguided . . . fellow-citizens." And again he says to Mr. Adams, " You will . . . remember that those states are now, as they always heretofore have been, and, notwithstanding their temporary self-delusion, they must continue to be, equal and honored members of this federal Union ; and that their citizens, throughout all political misunderstandings and alienations, still are and always must be our kindred and *countrymen*." If our countrymen and fellow-citizens, notwithstanding secession, the United States is one sovereign nation or political people ; if the states, notwithstanding their secession, are still honored members of this federal Union, the Union is no political sovereignty, and the states, by claiming and exercising sovereignty in seceding from it and arming against it, do nothing incompatible with it! Yet Mr. Seward is a great man, an able diplomatist, and a profound statesman—"a philosophic statesman." If the states are sovereign, the Union is not ; if the Union, or the

United States, is sovereign, the states are not. If the states are sovereign, and their citizens owe them allegiance, then the states that have seceded are no longer members—*honored* or dishonored—of "this federal Union;" nor are their citizens our fellow-citizens or countrymen, whether misguided or not misguided. If they are, then the sovereignty is in the United States, and there is no allegiance, though, while they remain in the Union and perform their constitutional functions, there may be obedience on the part of the citizen to the states. We owe no divided allegiance, for sovereignty is not divisible. Even under feudalism there was no divided allegiance, for allegiance, strictly speaking, was always due only to the national sovereign, the real lord paramount, from whom all grants of fiefs to inferior lords emanated, and to whom they lapsed on forfeiture.

The administration had but one of two grounds to take, either that of state sovereignty or that of national sovereignty. If it took that of state sovereignty, it would have been obliged, at best, to say with Mr. Buchanan, "Secession is wrong, but the government has no right to coerce a state." If it meant to take a ground on which it could pronounce secession rebellion, and assert its right to suppress it by force of arms, it must have clearly and distinctly taken the ground of plenary national sovereignty—that the people of the United States are, always have been, and always intend to be one sovereign political people; and that the states that secede rebel against the sovereign, and cease to exist as states, for they have no longer any legitimate state authority. On no other ground could it justify a resort to arms to bring back the seceding states, and reëstablish the authority of the federal government over the whole Union. On any other ground, the war, if war there should be, though conducted by the federal government, would not be a war between the national government and its rebellious subjects or provinces, but a war between states; in fact, simply a war between the northern states and the southern states—a war which on no legal principles could for a moment be justified. The secretary of state seems to have had some suspicion of this, and, being himself half state sovereignty and half national sovereignty, or, rather, a little more state than national sovereignty, he ventures to propose only a half war; shrinks from open, decided, vigorous war, for the suppression of the rebellion, and trusts for the rest to "the expectant treatment," as we believe the doctors call it. It was neither to be war nor peace. Secession was neither to be accepted nor rejected, but a little of both. Thus he says : " The system " —our federal republican system—" has within itself adequate peaceful, conservative, recuperative forces. Firmness on the part of the government in maintaining and preserving the public institutions and property, and in executing the laws where authority can be exercised *without waging war*, combined with such measures of justice, moderation, and forbearance as will disarm reasoning opposition, will be sufficient to secure the public safety until returning reflection, concurring with the fearful experience of social evils, the inevitable fruits of faction, shall bring the recusants cheerfully back into the family which, after all, must prove their best and happiest, as it undeniably is their most natural home." The rhetoric of this passage is unexceptionable ; but only think of a secretary of state writing such a sentence only two days before the attack on Sumter, and imagine his remarkable credulity, or still more remarkable—reticence. Nearly eighteen months have passed away since this was written, and we can now see, if we could not at the time, how weak and unsubstantial was the "expectant" policy (through Mr. Seward's influence), adopted by the administration, and which up to this time it has apparently retained. It was to wait the effect of the peaceful and conservative forces of the constitution. The government was not to wage war, but to act simply on the defensive. In accordance with this policy, though the government has had, first and last, about thirteen hundred thousand men under arms, and an almost unlimited amount of credit, we may safely assert that, up to this time, it has not waged war, and as safely assert it has never for a moment intended to wage war against the rebellion. The administration never believed itself able, and never intended to suppress the insurrection by force of arms ; and the troops it has called out and armed have been, we may safely assume, only to defend itself and to protect "the public institutions and property."

Do we go too far ? Hear Mr. Seward again : "The president would not be disposed to reject a cardinal dogma of theirs (the secessionists), that the federal government could not reduce the seceding states to obedience by conquest, even although he were disposed to question that proposition. But in fact the president *willingly accepts it as true.* Only an imperial or a despotic government could subjugate thoroughly disaffected and insurrectionary members of a state." This explains all that has been hitherto mysterious in political sympathies, and in the conduct of the war. Every northern press with southern proclivities has been loud in praise of the president, and especially of the accomplished secretary of state, and the men really in earnest to save the integrity of the national territory and to suppress the rebellion, have been cried down as abolitionists, and enemies of the administration. Every commanding officer in the army who has showed that he believed the government wished war to be waged in earnest, has been snubbed or relieved of his command, and one who better understood, or was more willing to conform to the policy of the government, was put in his place. Rear-Admiral Stringham is placed on the retired list, because he was too active—too much in earnest—and did too much to suit the administration. Fremont, whether a great general or not, was relieved not for military blunders or exceptionable financial operations, but because he showed himself disposed to take the war seriously, and not as a make-believe, or simple sham. By earnest national men, General Halleck has been censured for his military *fiasco* at Corinth, but it is evident that he satisfied the administration, for it has promoted him to the chief command of all the land forces of the republic. Great complaints have been made of General McClellan for his failure to take Richmond, but he undoubtedly fulfilled the expectations of the administration, for it has promoted him to the chief command under General Halleck, and made him substantially military dictator. Generals who make war in earnest and win victories, are not the generals the administration honors, because it is not waging war against the rebellion, and is only protecting itself, "the public institutions and property." The matter is plain. The administration never intended and never believed itself able to put the rebellion down by force of arms, and hence it does right to count the campaigns of its generals ending in defeat successful and victorious. Halleck we have no doubt would have captured Beauregard's army, and McClellan Johnston's and Jackson's, and entered Richmond, if the administration had seriously wished it; but to have done so, might have interfered with its policy, irritated our "misguided citizens" in the seceding states, and indicated the intention to "reduce them to obedience by conquest."

We do not misrepresent the administration, if we can believe its own official exposition of its policy, and trust the logic of its own official acts. It began by avowing that it could not, at least did not propose to reduce the seceding states to obedience by conquest, and that it did propose to do it "without waging war" against them, and up to this day it has not waged war against them. When, after the fall of Sumter, it called out the militia to the number of seventy-five thousand, it avowedly did it only to protect the national capital, and if it had proposed any thing more, it would have called out two hundred thousand instead of merely seventy-five thousand men. In the interview with the mayor of Baltimore, the governor of Maryland, and other commissioners, after the attack in Baltimore on the Massachusetts Sixth, both the president and the secretary of state assured them that the troops were called out solely to defend the national capital, not to invade Virginia or to make war on the seceding states. When congress met, and resolved that the rebellion must be put down by force, and voted five hundred thousand men, and five hundred millions of dollars for that purpose, nothing came of it. The administration raised the men, spent the money, and made no attack, if we except that of Ball's Bluff. It is idle to throw on General McClellan the blame of lying before Washington for ten months doing nothing. If the administration had wished him to move during that time he would have moved, or it would have removed him. It was in accordance with the open avowed policy of the administration, that he should not move or fight, unless attacked. The expeditions, partly land and partly naval, to the coast of North Carolina, South Carolina, to New Orleans, up the Tennessee and Cumberland rivers, and down the Mississippi, were political and commercial rather than military expeditions, designed on the one hand to open southern ports to trade, so as to lessen the clamor of foreigners against the blockade, and on the other, to secure an outlet for cotton to feed our own manufactures, and by the presence of Union troops to enable the Union men to rally again under the old flag, and give to Mr. Seward an opportunity to verify the wisdom of his "expectant treatment" of the case. General Sherman, who had the command at Hilton Head, tells us that he was positively forbidden to make a lodgment on the mainland, or to attack either Charleston or Savannah ; and General Burnside was never intrusted with a force sufficient to do more in North Carolina than to capture a few places, open a port, and guard the coast. The same may be said of General

Butler. He may, by the aid of the navy, hold New Orleans a few weeks longer, but he can do little except issue orders and quarrel with the Secesh ladies of the city. The only serious fighting brought on by the Union forces, has been in Missouri, Kentucky, and Tennessee—in Missouri and Kentucky, to expel the rebels from two states, assumed not to have seceded, and in Tennessee and North Alabama, as necessary to protect Kentucky, and therefore within the proper defensive warfare which the administration was carrying on. If there has been any thing more, it has been to amuse and pacify the national party in the loyal states, and nothing has come of it. A little war the administration has been obliged to give us in order to satisfy the war party, but it has taken care that it should do the rebels no serious harm.

We are bound to exonerate the army, and we insist that it must not be made the scape-goat of the sins of the administration. We insist that our commanding generals shall not, till further evidence is furnished than any now before the public, be accused of incompetency, disloyalty, indifference, or neglect. We will not allow that we have not as good generals, as scientific, as accomplished, as brave, and as heroic as any the rebels have. The fault is not in them; it is in the policy of the administration, and which has been obstinately adhered to in spite of warnings, in spite of experience, till the national cause is well-nigh desperate, if not absolutely beyond hope. Those who do not like the manner in which the war has been conducted, and who are dissatisfied with its results thus far, should accuse the administration, chiefly Mr. Seward, the chief author of the policy the administration adopted in the outset, not the army, for the war has been conducted in strict logical accordance with that policy. It would have been incompatible with that policy, and with the theory of the government set forth by Mr. Seward, to have made a vigorous attack on the enemy, or for any general commanding to have followed up any advantage he might happen to gain and secure a real victory. We do not pretend that our generals have always received specific and minute directions from the administration to conduct the war so as to have it fail, but we do say that the best generals in the world could not have conducted it in accordance with the policy of the government without failing. The good general is governed by the policy of the administration, and when that policy is incompatible with military success, succeed he cannot. The wisdom or unwisdom of the policy of the administration is no concern of his as a military man, and his simple business is to conform to it. The policy of the administration controls his military operations, even when he is not conscious of it, and affects his disposition and management of his forces before the battle, if not on the battle-field.

We do not deny that at a later day than the date of the letter we have referred to, the administration accepted civil war, but we do deny that there is any evidence that it has ever contemplated ending the controversy by conquest, or the exertion of military force. The secretary writes to Mr. Adams again, June 8, 1861:

"This government insists, as all the world might have known, that it must and would, under all circumstances, insist on the integrity of the Union, as the chief element of national life. Since, after trials of every form of forbearance and conciliation, it has been rendered certain and apparent that this paramount and vital object can be saved only by our acceptance of civil war as an indispensable condition, that condition, with all its hazards and deplorable evils, has not been declined. The acceptance, however, is attended with a strong desire and fixed purpose that the war shall be as short and accompanied by as little suffering as possible."

Here the administration accepts, no doubt, the civil war, but under two mutually incompatible restrictions, "with a strong desire and a fixed purpose that the war shall be as short and accompanied with as *little suffering* as possible." To be a short war it is necessary that it should be as vigorous and accompanied with as much suffering to the enemy as is possible under the laws of civilized warfare. The very purpose of war is to inflict the greatest damage, and therefore the greatest suffering possible on the enemy in the shortest time possible, to compel him to submit. Wise nations never make war a suit in chancery. War means damage, means suffering, means killing and wounding, mangling by the most destructive engines that can be invented, and the more destructive it is, the greater the horrors and sufferings that accompany it, the sooner must it end. Mr. Seward's policy of conducting a war with the least possible amount of suffering *to the enemy*, which we take it is what he means, is the policy of a sentimental, and therefore of a cruel civilian, not of a soldier. Yet this policy explains the exceeding care taken by our commander in Virginia to do as little harm and afford as much protection to the rebels as

possible, unless when obliged to repel attacks. He has
been blamed for that, but we may be sure that he was only
carrying out the policy of the administration, or as we say
in this city, of "the ring."

Parcere subjectis, et debellare superbos, is a maxim we
understand, and are always prepared to act on. When an
enemy has thrown down his arms and submitted, he is an
enemy no longer; he is our friend and brother, and as such
we clasp him to our bosom. But as long as he resists, as long
as his arm is upraised against us, ours is upraised against
him, to deal him, if possible, a blow that fells him to the
ground. Mr. Seward's humanity has proved to be the most
terrible inhumanity towards our own army, and if a little
of that indignation which he has had the dexterity to turn
against the secretary of war were turned against himself, no
injustice would be done.

But in accepting the civil war forced upon it, nothing
proves that the administration has ever conducted the war
with a view of ending the controversy by military success.
Its theory of the national government is that of a federative
or federal union, a "confederation," and its concession that
allegiance is due to the state as well as to the nation, deprives it of all solid ground on which to defend its right to
attempt it, while it expressly avows that it cannot do it, if
it would, for our federal republican system is "unfitted for
such a task." It is true Mr. Seward tells Mr. Adams that he
will not be expected to promulgate these views, but we have
the right to make use of them, since they are officially published to the world by himself. Besides, all the official acts
of the government, its mode of conducting the war, its studi-
ous avoidance of seizing the strategic points in the enemy's
country, and its careful forbearance to follow up any military advantage it happens to gain, all indicate that it relies
on political manipulations in the last resort to effect a reconciliation. Mr. Seward appears from first to last to have
looked upon the controversy as in its nature an ordinary struggle between two political parties for power or place, and to
be settled as political controversies have usually been settled
in our country, by conciliation, compromise, and the returning patriotism and good sense of both parties. He does not
appear to have as yet given up the conviction that there is
a strong Union party in the seceding states, kept down by
the intimidation and tyranny of a dominant faction, through
which, when that faction is weakened or exhausted by the

war, he can operate to reëstablish the authority of the Union. No hope is or can be more fallacious. There is no Union party worth speaking of in a single seceded state, and it is doubtful, if there could be a free vote to-day in Maryland, Kentucky, and Missouri, whether those states themselves would not secede by triumphant majorities. Certainly their sympathies are strongly with the southern cause, and in not one of them is the loyal part able, unassisted, to hold the disloyal part in subjection. The administration has all along acted on the unfounded assumption that the secessionists are only a faction. They are no faction in their states, but the people. The southern people are substantially a unit against us, and never at any moment, since the secession of South Carolina, was it possible by any political concessions or manipulations to keep them in the Union with the North, so long as the North adhered to its centralized democracy, or remained, so to speak, unsouthernized.

The administration had, on coming into power, but one of two courses to take, either frankly to accept state sovereignty, and let the seceded states go in peace and form an independent nation, or confederation of sovereign states, for themselves and by themselves; or else to take with equal frankness, the ground of full national sovereignty, and to use all the forces at its command to coerce the rebellious states into submission. The former was asked by the South, the latter, with a few dissenters, was demanded by the North. Mr. Seward, by his timidity, his weakness, his lack of backbone, as well as his cowardice, and his failure to comprehend the real nature of the controversy, had so involved the matter that Mr. Lincoln no doubt felt that he could venture safely to take neither alternative; and his administration up to this day has been rendered disgraceful by a miserable attempt to ride astride of both. It has neither accepted state sovereignty nor national sovereignty, nor fully and frankly either peace or war; but a little of each, just enough to irritate both parties without satisfying either. It has not dared accept national sovereignty, with all its logical consequences and duties, for that might have irritated its imaginary Union friends at the South, all state sovereignty men, and interfered with its plans of future reconciliation; and it has not dared to deny it, for that would have brought down upon it, with a few individual exceptions, twenty millions of people in the loyal states. It has therefore neither preserved peace by consenting to an amicable adjustment of the secession question, nor has it preserved the honor and integrity of the Union by war prosecuted on war principles. It has sought to pacify the national party by raising large armies, and the state sovereignty party by conducting the war on peace principles.   The result has been, as might have been expected, the squandering of the national resources, the loss of half a million of as fine troops as the world ever saw, the revival of political and partisan rivalries and animosities, a division of the people, the disaffection of the army, the personal jealousies and rivalries of its superior officers, and the advance of the enemy into the loyal states, with no organized forces to resist them.   This at the time we are writing, 9th of September, is the plain, unvarnished picture of what the Seward policy has brought us to in eighteen months, and yet at this date the president retains him in his cabinet, and refuses to change his ruinous policy.

There is no question of Mr. Seward's loyal intentions, and earnest and laborious efforts to compose our troubles, and to secure the national life and territory ; but the habits of his mind are such as to lead him to believe it hardly possible for any but himself to save us from destruction, to expect salvation from any thing but those political manipulations of which his friend Weed is master, or to desire it, unless the glory of it redounds to himself, and therefore not to be effected by energetic military operations.   Indeed he is no friend of the military.   Doubtless because he feels that he has none of the elements of the soldier in himself. He says, in the letter already quoted from so often. "Military spirit is an element always ready for revolution.   It has fuller development in the disaffected than in the loyal states." That the military spirit has been more cultivated in the southern than in the northern states, is no doubt the fact, but that is because the southern states, on this as on some other points, have observed the conditions of a free and living people better than have the northern.   No people that neglects or despises the military spirit is destined to a long life or a really glorious career.   The military spirit is an essential element of national greatness. It has been the fault of the loyal states, especially of the eastern and middle sections, that they have, ever since the war of 1812, underrated and decried the military spirit, and neglected, to a fearful extent, military education and organization.   The shopkeeper, the lawyer, the pettifogger, has been held in far higher honor than the soldier.   To represent the military

spirit as being "an element always ready for revolution," is
to show a reckless contempt of experience and disregard of
human nature. China has less of the military spirit than
any other nation reckoned as civilized; and in no country
of which we have any knowledge have revolutions been so
common or so disastrous during the last eighteen hundred
years. Revolutions in modern times are preëminently the
work of small lawyers, journalists, politicians, civilians all,
—seldom if ever of the army. The spirit of the army is
always conservative; for the soldier is prepared to command
by being first taught and habituated to obey. The army is
an element of strength and stability, and the habits acquired
by thorough military training are precisely those our people
have most lacked, and are most in need of to preserve and
improve the heritage of freedom and law transmitted to
them by our brave and heroic fathers. If we had had more
of the military spirit among us, our politicians would have
been less craven-hearted before the bold and arrogant men
of the South, and commanded their respect instead of incurring their contempt. Had the military spirit been duly cultivated and honored in the free states, there never would
have been any southern secession or civil war between the
southern states and the United States. We repel with indignation, therefore, the groundless insinuation of the secretary of state against the military spirit.

We know that the army has been blamed, and our military academy has been assailed, because a certain number of
officers of the army, on the breaking out of the rebellion
resigned their commissions and took service with the secessionists. But out of over seven hundred commissioned
officers, only one hundred and seventy-five, if we are rightly
informed, have resigned in order to join the rebels, and
some of the best and most loyal officers now in the national
army were born in states that have seceded. The army
has been the most loyal class of the United States, and the
only class that has not separated by a "line of latitude."
The officers who resigned, did so because their respective
states seceded, and they felt themselves bound to do so by
their state allegiance, asserted by state sovereignty—conceded, not denied at least, to a certain extent, by Mr.
Seward ; for he concedes that allegiance is due to the state,
and nowhere affirms that in case of conflict, the allegiance
due to the state must give way to that due to the Union.
On state sovereignty principles, on which this war has thus

far been conducted on both sides, Generals Lee and Beau-regard are as irreproachable in their loyalty as Generals Halleck and McClellan, equally as high-minded and as honor-able gentlemen, and equally as untarnished in their military character. We hold them to be traitors and forsworn, be-cause we deny state sovereignty, and maintain that alle-giance is due only to the United States. But Mr. Seward cannot do so; and it is observable that he does not so call them, and that he speaks of the states that have seceded as still "equal and honored members of our federal Union," and calls the people in arms against us our "misguided fellow-citizens." He, then, is the last man who should reproach the army, or impeach the morality of the military academy at West Point. No higher-toned morality is taught in any college in our country than in that academy, and not one of them has trained and sent out a larger body of high-minded and accomplished gentlemen. There is no class of educated men, equally numerous, in our community that can surpass, if it can equal, the officers of our army in the highest quali-ties of the gentleman, in their liberal feelings, in their love of order, and in their devotion to sound, conservative polit-ical principles. If the class had been larger, or if there had been more civilians with its spirit, we should not have seen our government plundered by greedy and unscrupulous contractors, coining money out of the blood of our soldiers and the tears of widows and orphans; and if we had duly cultivated the military spirit, instead of stimulating to the highest degree possible, a morbid sentimentality, always cruel, and destitute of honesty, our government would not be now paying monthly for about double the number of volunteers it has in its service. One of the good results we have hoped from the present war is, that it would quicken the military spirit among us, bring the army into repute, and substitute to some extent in the American mind the sense of honor and the love of glory, for habits of political hux-tering, and the sordid love of gain. Our hope for the coun-try is, under God, in the army, and the infusion into the army of the true military spirit; we want the discipline, the habits of obedience, and of *command*, to be acquired by us, with our social and political constitution, only in the army, in order to be a great people, to preserve our institutions and our liberties.

We have spoken in a foregoing article of our blundering generalship; and in a purely military point of view, we have

had little else than blundering, from the famous boa con-
strictor, or anaconda strategy, down to the retreats of Pope
before the rebels advancing on Washington, but we must
remember that the war, from first to last, has been conducted not on military principles, but subordinated to the
political and diplomatic policy of the secretary of state, and
as the administration retains in command the very generals
the public regard as the most unlucky and the least trustworthy, it is only fair to the army to suppose that the whole
responsibility rests on the administration itself, and that
those very generals have acquitted themselves quite to its
satisfaction, or at least to the satisfaction of Mr. Seward,
who, apparently, is afraid that, if the military should be
successful, the glory of saving the national life would not
redound to him, and make him our next president. Military
success might take away his vocation, and put an end to the
reign of pettifoggers and political tricksters, for which the
capital of the secretary's native state is somewhat noted, and
perhaps, also, to the enormous profligacy and corruption
which has for some years been gaining ground in the
national government, as well as in several of the state governments, in which some of Mr. Seward's political friends, as
well as enemies, are supposed to have had their full share.

It is possible that we do Mr. Seward injustice ; but it is
a fact that all the friends of the nation who believe the
nation can be saved only by military success, and the earnest
and vigorous prosecution of the war on war principles, have
found from the first Mr. Seward and his policy in their
way, and him and his policy sustained by all the presses and
men of doubtful loyalty at the North. How is it that all
the enemies of those who are unquestionably in earnest to
save the nation by prompt, vigorous, and decisive measures,
are the friends of the administration, and especially of Mr.
Seward ? The fact is unquestionable and suspicious, if there
is any truth in the old saying, " Birds of a feather flock together." We would not insinuate that Mr. Seward is precisely a man of their sort ; but he evidently is the man in
the administration who comes nearest to representing their
views and wishes. He, we presume, courts them, for he
doubtless holds that at this moment to support him is to
support the administration, and to support the administration is to support the national cause ; but here is precisely
where the doubt or distrust begins. The precise doubt or
distrust is that support of him is support of the administra-

tion, or that the support of an administration controlled or
controllable by him is support of the national cause. A
large portion of the people, especially those the most earnest
in defence of that cause, believe that he, by his timid, conciliatory, expectant policy, has endangered it, and made the
administration play into the hands of the enemy. Here is
the difficulty, and till he clears it up, confidence not only in
him but in the administration itself is shaken, if not lost,
and every move he makes only confirms the suspicions already entertained against him. As matters stand, we see no
way in which he can, even with the best intentions in the
world, serve the national cause, but by a speedy and voluntary retirement to private life in that delightful town of
Auburn, once our own as well as his loved home.

Mr. Seward owes much of the political consideration he
has enjoyed to the position he early assumed on the negro
question, and his enunciation from his place in the senate
of the "higher law" doctrine, and from the hustings of
the "irrepressible conflict" theory, two utterances which
have made him both notorious and famous ; yet he has been
the first to quail before the slave power, and we find him
as late as the 28th of last May, in a letter to Earl Russell,
published in the newspapers, and which we presume to be
substantially authentic, urging the British ministry to withdraw its recognition of the rebels as belligerents, among
other reasons, because it tends to prolong the war, and if the
war be prolonged, it will disturb the institution of slavery,
and perhaps add to the evils of the present war those " of a
servile war." The wonderful aptness of such an argument
addressed to the British government, opposed to slavery the
world over, as is nearly the whole English nation, a diplo-
mat less sagacious than Mr. Seward would have failed to
perceive. But that is not the point. It proves that Mr.
Seward's policy is, and all along has been, to preserve slavery, and to prevent the war from operating its ruin. He
knows, the president knows, that if we had begun the war
by liberating the slaves, as under the rights of war we could
have done, the sympathy of all Europe would have been with
us, and neither England nor France would ever have thought
of mediation, far less of intervention. Yet he prefers to
hazard foreign intervention to touching the institution of
negro slavery. He even sent his friends Thurlow Weed
and the archbishop of New York abroad, to change, if possible, European opinion on the subject of slavery, at least

on the question of immediate emancipation, in this country; and so far as the archbishop is concerned, not without some success. A well known abolitionist in France has written, it is said, a letter to the president, urging him not under any circumstances to suffer himself to be driven into the adoption of immediate emancipation. That letter was virtually dictated by Mr. Seward, through his representative, the archbishop of New York, and we have the proof in a letter from a distinguished French gentleman, a friend of the president's correspondent, urging us not to insist on immediate emancipation, and assuring us that he does so in consequence of an interview with the archbishop of New York. We know what was the sort of public opinion the archbishop of New York labored while in Paris to manufacture, and nobody can doubt that it was the sort of public opinion Mr. Seward, who sent him, desired and approved.

We need not revive here the discussion of the slavery question. We know that the majority of congress and a large portion of the American people believe that this war cannot be prosecuted to a successful issue without detaching, by proffering them freedom, the negro population, whose labor now sustains the rebellion. Yet to any measure of this sort we have found Mr. Seward a wily but steady opponent, and it is not too much to attribute it to his influence that the law of the last session of congress for ever freeing the slaves of the rebels, was not broader and more efficient, and has not yet, even such as it is, been brought to the knowledge of the persons concerned by the proclamation of the president. Congress at its last session passed an emancipation act; it was approved by the president, and is now the law of the land; but it is suffered to stand on the statute book a dead letter. According to that law, all slaves of rebels, or of persons giving aid and comfort to the rebellion, escaping from such persons, and taking refuge within the lines of our army, " all slaves captured from such persons, or deserted by them, and coming under the control of the government, all found on or within any place occupied by the rebel forces, and afterward occupied by forces of the United States, shall be deemed captives of war, and shall be for ever free of their servitude, and not again held as slaves." Is this law executed? Are the preliminary steps taken for its execution? Has the executive issued his proclamation, or a proclamation that sets forth in an intelligible manner, the emancipation features of the act passed by congress, and approved by the president, July 17, 1862? Not at all, and half the people of the country are calling for an emancipation proclamation, in entire ignorance or forgetfulness of the fact that congress has itself passed, and the president has approved an emancipation act, though a feeble one. It is true congress did not fix the time when the president should issue his proclamation, but as we read the law, the emancipation section does not require the proclamation of the president as a condition of its going into effect. It is not conditioned on such proclamation, but is absolutely the law of the land, and the president, by his oath of office, is bound to see it executed. Is it executed in New Orleans, in Nashville, or in any place heretofore held by rebel forces, and now occupied by the forces of the United States? The president is as much bound, we take it, by the will of the nation, when expressed in law, as the meanest citizen, and he may be impeached as well for neglecting his duty in *not* executing the law as in actively doing what the law forbids.

We have made Mr. Seward principally responsible for the policy the administration has thus far pursued, because it is the policy to which he had attached his name before the president was inaugurated, and because, wherever we can trace him since, we find him identified with it. Undoubtedly, the president has accepted it, and is officially responsible for it, but Mr. Seward had artfully, we say not with any sinister intention, prepared it for him, and it has been easy for him, has been precisely in his line, to keep up such a political combination as would make the president regard it as the only practicable policy left him. The president has hardly been a free agent, or had an opportunity of exercising his own unbiased judgment, since his inauguration. Mr. Seward knows how to manage him, without his suspecting it, and when it will not do for him to act in person, he knows enough to call in Mr. Thurlow Weed or some other friend in whom the president has confidence. On the slavery question—a vital question in the present controversy—we regard Mr. Seward as the evil genius of this administration. It was he who obtained the removal of Fremont from the command of the department of the West— a measure, aside from the merits of that general, on which we pronounce no judgment, except to say that we have never been one of his partisans—that has proved disastrous in numerous ways, especially in dividing the national party, not the Republican party merely, but the national party, and in creating partisans for and against other generals. We know Mr. Seward has said that he was the last member of the cabinet that gave his vote for Fremont's removal from his command, which we believe is literally true, in the sense that he was the last member of the cabinet that voted, at the meeting when his removal was finally approved; but we are not aware that he has denied that he urged or dictated the dispatch, two days before, removing him. General Fremont, for good or bad reasons, has a firmer hold on the affections of the loyal people of the country than any other man in it, and his name excites a popular enthusiasm that no other name among us will or can, and, though we interfere not with military appointments, and ask not that he be given an active command, we tell the administration that it cannot afford to alienate and discourage his friends any more than Mr. Seward can afford to dispense with the political support of General McClellan.

We have written plainly, more plainly than the times seem to warrant; but we know we have done so with a loyal heart and a loyal purpose. We want our nation saved, and we care not who saves or has the glory of saving it, if saved it be. If Mr. Seward is that man, all honor to him; but we tell him, we tell the president, we tell the country, if his policy be any longer continued, we shall have no nation to save. On all points he has been outwitted, outgeneralled, and defeated, and the nation stands disgraced at home and abroad. For a moment he may succeed in diverting the indignation of the army, sacrificed to his expectant policy, from himself to the secretary of war, or to the abolitionists; but the truth will ere long be known, and his political juggling or his jaunty airs will fail to save him. For the president personally, we have great respect, and believe that, if he could rid his administration of Mr. Seward, the "irrepressible conflict" man, and put a competent national man in his place, a man of ideas and of practical wisdom, not a mere politician, who understands nothing but rhetoric and the manipulation of party, he might yet succeed in carrying us safely through the national crisis. Perhaps all we ask will be done before what we write issues from the press, perhaps it will not, perhaps it is no longer practicable or possible.

THE PRESIDENT'S POLICY.

[From Brownson's Quarterly Review for January, 1863.]

PRESIDENT LINCOLN's message to congress, at the opening of the present session, is a plain, straight-forward, dignified, and important document, and in tone, spirit, and style, is decidedly superior to any of his previous messages. In it, for the first time since his inauguration, he adopts and defines a policy, or proves that his government has a policy, whether a policy the country will approve, or not. The great complaint has been that he has had no decided policy, and that he has appeared to be carried along by the course of events, without attempting to control them, and shape them to his purpose.

Mr. Lincoln, in our judgment, committed a great mistake in the outset, in supposing that the American people believe practically in the democratic theory, and that he must administer the government on democratic principles, and that he must follow the people instead of leading them, obey the people instead of governing them. All government, in so far as government it is, is imperative, and no people look more to their administration to shape a policy for them than the American. No matter how they talk through the journals, they expect the administration to take the initiative. The present administration erred from the first, in regarding itself as weak and without support in the affections and confidence of the people, and in fearing to adopt the bold and decisive measures the national crisis demanded, lest they should refuse to sustain it. It thought it must temporize, wait for the manifestation of public opinion, and labor to conciliate parties. The consequence has been that by its delays, its indecisions, its half-way measures, now doing a little to gratify this party, and now a little to appease that party, it has lost the confidence of all parties, and found its friends and supporters almost everywhere beaten, and badly beaten, in the late elections. Its supporters,—and its supporters are the supporters of the national cause,—are likely to be in the minority in the next congress, and the national legislation will pass into the hands of the sympathizers with the authors of the rebellion, on whose loyalty we fear we cannot count.

What the administration has regarded as prudence, and what would have been prudence in ordinary times, when there are only the ordinary struggles of political parties for power or patronage to meet, we have regarded from the first as the greatest imprudence, in fact, a blunder. The question the administration had to meet was not a political question, not a question as to what party should govern the country, distribute or share its patronage, but a question far above all party,— a question as to whether we are to have a country for any party to govern,—a question of national existence, in regard to which all loyal men, all men not traitors and rebels, were to be presumed to be of one mind. Whether they were so or not, the administration should have assumed that they were, and boldly adopted and vigorously prosecuted the measures necessary to suppress the rebellion and save the nation. Had it done so, it would have made them all of one mind, or at least have given their differences of opinion no opportunity to embarrass its action. Fear, doubt, hesitation, half-way measures,—now an advance, now a retreat, here a little and there a little,—cannot fail, in times of danger, to be most disheartening and disastrous. The wise administration adopts bold and vigorous measures, measures which confirm its friends and overawe its enemies. The people demand a bold, resolute, and confident leader, who acts as if he regarded himself as invincible, and when they find such a leader, they follow him without much thought as to whither he is likely to lead them. They follow him who proves to them that he is likely to win. Mr. Lincoln had every advantage, if he had comprehended and been equal to his position. With a just cause, with men and money without stint at his command, and a power, derived from the immense patronage he had at his disposal, greater than any king, kaiser, or dictator ever wielded, he might have safely disregarded all party divisions and all differences of opinion, and could easily have carried with him the whole population of the country not in open rebellion to the government. He had no occasion to conciliate conflicting parties and to balance conflicting interests. He should by his boldness, promptness, and vigor have left no time for debate, no time for adverse parties to organize, and taken all minds and hearts by storm, not by the slow and zigzag approaches of a regular siege.

Unhappily, the spirit, or want of spirit, which has characterized the administration, has affected the military operations of the country. Our generals have shown the same lack of enterprise, boldness, and vigor, the same timidity, over-caution, hesitation, and delays, that have marked the civil administration itself. We blame not our generals, for we had no right to ask or expect them to be superior to the administration they serve. If an administration wants its generals to be bold, prompt, and energetic, it must be so itself. The army will always partake of the feebleness and indecision, or of the boldness and vigor of the administration ; and the administration may always have brave, enterprising, and successful generals at the head of its army, if it proves itself worthy of them. Our generals, in their lack of enterprise, in their failure to attack or to follow up their attacks, in uniformly giving the enemy time and opportunity, after a defeat, to recover and more than recover from its effects before renewing the attack, have only followed the example of the administration itself, and Mr. Lincoln, as the administration, is, and will be held, responsible for all our military blunders and failures, for our military inefficiency, and the rapid frittering away of our armies.

But it is of little use to dwell on these things now. If Mr. Lincoln had been a genius or a hero, or if he had listened to the men really in earnest to put down the rebellion and save the nation, and had appealed by his vigorous measures to the living, patriotic, loyal sentiment of the country, and given no heed to the advice or opinions of those whose sympathies were with the rebels, or whose disloyal conduct had involved the country in its troubles, he would have preserved the enthusiasm which broke out all over the loyal states immediately after the attack on Sumter, and restored peace to the country before this. But he let the golden opportunity pass by, and the measures which would have been effectual, if adopted in season, can now do us little good. " It is not true," said Napoleon, *à propos* of the 18th Brumaire, "that the troops fired blank cartridges on the people. It would have been inhuman to have done so." The instant and complete emancipation of all the slaves in the whole United States, as a war measure, immediately after the first battle of Bull Run, with the assurance of reasonable compensation to loyal owners, would have been effectual, and speedily ended the war. The proclamation of the president on the 22d of last September, threatening to emancipate the slaves in such states and parts of states as should be in rebellion on the first day of the following January,

coming when and in the form it did, was fitted only to ex-
asperate the South, and to give strength and expression to
the pro-slavery feeling at the North. The friends of the
administration could not defend it. The president could
not defend the emancipation of the slaves except under the
pressure of military necessity, and what sort of military
necessity is that, it may be asked, which admits of a delay
of a hundred days? If congress, or even the president, had
proclaimed their freedom when General Fremont issued his
modest proclamation, the whole population of the non-slaveholding states would have acquiesced, offered no opposition,
and perhaps have really approved it. Political leaders, unless
in the border states, would have made no capital out of it
against the administration. The hesitation and delay of the
administration, its backing and filling, gave time for discussions, for parties to form, opposition to organize, so that the
proclamation, threatening a partial emancipation, when it
came, created no enthusiasm among the friends of the administration, and gave new strength to its enemies; nobody was
pleased with it but those few who wish the war to be prosecuted primarily for the abolition of slavery, and, if the slaves
are liberated, care for little beyond. These found in it
ground to hope that slavery would finally be abolished, but
scarcely a man saw in it any military advantage sufficient to
justify the extraordinary exercise of executive power. So
it has been with nearly all the measures of the administration. They have either been half-way measures, sufficient
to embolden enemies without winning friends, or they have
been delayed and discussed till the time when they would
amount to something had passed by.

The slavery question, just as it ceases to be the most pressing question, is apparently made the most prominent question by the administration. It is the leading topic of
the president's message. We have no intention of reviving
the discussion of the question in these pages. We have discussed it at full length, under its political, military, social,
moral, and theological aspects, and may for the present leave
it where we left it in our article on *Slavery and the Church.*
Whether the president will issue another proclamation, giving effect to his proclamation of the 22d of last September,
we have no means of knowing at the time we are writing,
but the chances are that he will. But, if he does, we doubt
whether the courts will sustain the freedom of the slaves he
thus declares to be emancipated. We doubt not the power

of the president to emancipate the slaves under the rights of war, as a measure necessary to the military operations of the government; but we do doubt if the courts will recognize this proclamation as having been issued under the rights of war, from the pressure of military necessity. Its being issued as a *threat* only, and allowing a delay of a hundred days before any emancipation can follow, looks to us more like a measure intended to *punish* the rebels, should they not lay down their arms and return to their allegiance before a given time, than as a measure prompted by military necessity, especially as the proclamation was issued on the heels of what was declared to be a decisive victory over the rebel army at Antietam. We are disposed to think the courts will declare it unconstitutional and void. We thought so when it was first issued, and the more we have reflected on it since, the more have we been confirmed in this opinion. We see not how its constitutionality can be sustained.

The president seems himself, if we may judge from his message, to attach no importance to his proclamation, and to regard it as a sort of *brutum fulmen*, issued to appease the anti-slavery party. He lays little or no stress on it, and urges three amendments to the constitution, authorizing the government to give compensation to the states that will free their slaves on or before the first day of January, 1900, as, in his judgment, the great and decisive measure that is to end the war. To giving a reasonable compensation to loyal slaveholders for the loss of the property which the law gives them in slaves, we have no objection; nay, it is only just and right, and we are quite willing that the nation should buy up and set free all the slaves in the country; and if that would end the war and restore the Union, we would hold up both hands to have it done. But we hold that congress can, without any amendments of the constitution, do it as a war measure, if it judges proper; and with emancipation as a peace measure, we desire to have nothing to do till peace is restored. If, in its judgment, the emancipation of the slaves, with compensation to loyal owners, is necessary as a war measure, either for prosecuting or ending the war, congress has ample powers, under the rights of war, to adopt it, and bind the nation to it, and the proposed amendments to the constitution are unnecessary.

The president assures congress that the measure, if adopted, will put an end to the war, and restore union, peace, and harmony to the country. He speaks as if he regarded this as beyond question. Does he merely echo the opinion of border state politicians, or does he speak from some information on the subject not accessible to the public? Has the administration a new policy? or is it merely reviving the policy of securing the border states, and letting the extreme southern states remain out of the Union till they see proper to ask to be readmitted? Is there any connection between the measure proposed by the president, and the offer of mediation by the emperor of the French? Is there an understanding between the two governments, that, if congress will take the necessary steps to alter the constitution, so as to secure gradual emancipation, the emperor will use his good offices with the confederacy, to induce them to lay down their arms? Or is it a measure intended to ward off intervention, and to gain time for fighting out between ourselves alone our own quarrel? We confess that we do not quite understand the confidence of the president in the efficiency of his proposed policy. We suspect he counts by it on securing the border states, and having secured them, he can afford to wait for the gradual acquiescence of the other states; or, perhaps, that they of their own accord will accept the proffered compensation, lay down their arms, and return to their allegiance!

For our part, we place little reliance on the proposed policy, because we do not believe that slavery is the sole matter of difference between the United States and the rebels. We believe the southern states, at least the southern statesmen and politicians have seceded because they want no union with the free states, unless on such conditions that the ruling power shall be in the states which are now slave states. They have not rebelled because they apprehended danger to their slave property from northern abolitionists, but because they would not belong to a country ruled by the northern democracy, northern "mudsills," as they have called them. The protection of slave property, and the prevention of negro citizenship or negro equality, were pretexts used to secure the coöperation of the southern democracy, or non-slaveholding whites, the real people of the South, and in whom lies the real strength of the southern confederacy. We believe, therefore, that the men who have made the rebellion would be as averse to union with us after as before emancipation and compensation. We do not believe the rebellion can be put down and the Union restored by any measures short of the decided military suc-

cess of the national arms. Both parties have appealed to
arms, and it is only by arms the differences between them
can be settled. The rebellion must conquer the government, or the government must conquer the rebellion. We
see no alternative; and we regard the slavery question or
the negro question as of importance now, only in its bearing on our military operations. The parties are on the
ground; each has taken its position; and the duel must be
fought out, till one or the other party falls. We think,
therefore, the administration would do well to confine itself
more exclusively to the work of securing a military triumph
over the rebels, and trouble itself less about the means of
making them friends after it has beaten and dispersed their
armies. "To cook a hare, first catch a hare," says the immortal Mrs. Glass.

But, aside from this, how does the president expect to
secure for his proposed amendments to the constitution the
ratification of the constitutional number of states? For
their adoption it is necessary that they should pass congress
by a two-thirds vote of each house, and be subsequently
ratified by the legislatures or by conventions of three-fourths
of all the states. It may be doubted whether they can secure the requisite congressional vote; but supposing they
do, they must still have the ratification of twenty-five states,
if we accept the theory of the government, that no state has
seceded from the Union, and that the whole thirty-four,
with all their rights as states, are still in the Union. To
secure twenty-five states, seven slave states, at least must be
obtained. The president probably counts on Delaware,
Maryland, Kentucky, Missouri, and Virginia; but even if
he obtains these, and all the free states, then he will lack
two states to make up the constitutional three-fourths.
Now, where are these two additional slave states to be found
that will or can vote on the question? Besides these, all
the slave states are in rebellion, and their legislatures as
much in rebellion as any other portion of the population.
Does the president expect his amendments to be approved
by the rebellious legislature of a single slave state, or by a
convention called by a rebel legislature? If not, how is he
to get for his amendments the ratification of three-fourths
of all the states? Save the five slave states, there is no slave
state not in rebellion, and we are far from conceding that
the Wheeling government is constitutionally the state of
Virginia. The real state government, elected by the peo-

ple known as Virginia, is as much in rebellion as the state government of South Carolina. There is, then, while the rebellion lasts, and till the rebellious state governments return to their allegiance, no way, on the government theory, of getting any amendments to the constitution constitutionally adopted, unless five or six new states can be manufactured out of the territories and admitted into the Union.

We hope the president does not intend to recognize as the state of Tennessee, North Carolina, Florida, or Louisiana, the military government he has himself constituted or proposes constituting in each of the several territories so named. That military government is not the state, is no state at all, and has no power to bind the state, and certainly none to give, directly or indirectly, the assent of the state to amendments of the federal constitution. Whatever authority it has is by virtue of military law, and it can have none when the civil authority resumes its sway, or is reëstablished. The amendments may be ratified by conventions of the people of the several states, instead of the legislatures, if congress so prescribes; but the convention to be legal and binding on the people of the state, must be called by the state authority, and cannot be called by the president, or even by congress. It was never the intention of the convention that framed the constitution, that amendments to that instrument might be adopted by the people, irrespective of state organization or state authority. There is, we hold, one political people of the United States, in whom inheres the national sovereignty; but this one people expresses its will through state organizations, and cannot, as the constitution now stands, express it otherwise. Representatives are representatives of *states*, as the senators, or of certain congressional districts of *states*, as in the case of representatives in congress, and not representatives of a certain population, irrespective of state organization and state authority. Now, the military government established by the president in a state, does not hold from the state, and in no sense represents it; it holds directly from the president, and therefore has no state authority, and can neither itself give the assent of the state, nor call a convention competent to give it, to any amendments of the federal constitution.

We repudiate the doctrine that maintains that the powers of the federal government are derived by delegation from the states, as free, sovereign, independent states; and hold that they are derived by delegation from the one political people called the United States, but at the same time we hold while the sovereignty is in the one political people of the United States, that it delegates the powers it wills the federal government should exercise only through state organizations, and, without altering the constitution this people has ordained, it cannot do otherwise. It is in this way we justify the term *federal*, applied to the general government, and reconcile states' rights with full, indefeasible, national sovereignty. To take the assent of the people of a state, not convened by state authority, as the assent of the state itself, is to supersede the state, and is not only unconstitutional, but revolutionary. To take as the state a government established by the United States, is a direct violation of our federal system, would annihilate the very idea of state rights, and convert our political system into that of complete and undisguised democratic centralism, to be followed at no distant day by a monarchical centralism or monarchical absolutism. We assert most vehemently that the United States, though unhappily lacking a proper name, is, in the strictest sense of the word, a free, sovereign, independent nation ; but we assert, with equal vehemence, the federal character of the government, which does not create, but is created by the United States, and the constitutional rights of the several states. We oppose secession, because it strikes at the unity and indivisibility of the nation, and places the sovereignty in the state, not in the nation. We therefore call secession rebellion, and make war on it as such. But we are not willing, for the sake of putting down the rebellion, to sacrifice the rights of the states or our federal system. The states hold their rights from the sovereign political people of the United States, but not from the federal government,—a real government, indeed, but a limited government, having only the express powers delegated in the constitution. The federal government has received no power to improvise or impose a state government. The most it can do is to institute a territorial government, to govern a certain territory as territory under the Union, not as a state in the Union. The action of the people of the territory of Tennessee, Louisiana, Florida, North Carolina, or Virginia, under a military government established by the federal executive or by congress, may be lawful, but it is not and cannot be the action of the state, or of the people as the state. Any assent given by them to the amendments proposed to the constitution, would be worth no more than the assent given, say, by New Mexico, Nevada, Utah, Colorado, Nebraska, or Dakota.

We dwell the longer on this, for we see, or think we see, in the policy of the government in regard to Virginia, and the orders issued, or said to be issued, by certain military governors, acting by its authority alone, for the election of members of congress, the germs of a most dangerous and deplorable revolution, almost as much so as that of secession itself. A state is one and indivisible. The state is either in rebellion or it is not; if in rebellion, it is the whole state, not a part of it, and the doctrine of the president in his proclamation, that a part of the state may be in rebellion, and a part not, is inadmissible. If the state is not in rebellion, then the president has no right to supersede it, or set at naught its authority, by intruding a government of his own creation, instead of the regularly elected state government. The administration has officially declared that no state has seceded, that no state is out of the Union, that no state, as a state, is in rebellion, but all are in the Union, and entitled to be treated as states, not simply as territories. By what authority, then, does it appoint Andrew Johnson governor of Tennessee, Colonel Hamilton governor of Texas, Mr. Phelps governor of Arkansas, Eli Thayer governor of Florida, Edward Stanley governor of North Carolina, and Colonel Shepley governor of Louisiana? The population and territories designated by these names are either states in the Union, or they are not. If they are, these so-called governors are intruders, without legal or constitutional authority; for it is essential that the state should choose its own officers, and there is no authority in the president or in congress to appoint a single state officer, not even a constable. If they are not states in the Union, then they have neither the right to ratify amendments to the constitution, nor to elect members of congress. If the theory of the government, that no state has seceded or is out of the Union be true, the president, in appointing these governors, is guilty of a flagrant usurpation of power, and a gross revolutionary measure, for which he should be impeached; if not true, then to admit persons elected by the people of those territories to seats in congress, would be illegal and unconstitutional, for only states or the people of states in the Union can be represented in congress.

The administration proceeds, apparently, on the assumption that it has the right to treat the loyal people of a territory in the Union as a state. Its assumption is, undoubtedly, correct, if a state they are. But population and territory do not constitute a state, otherwise all our territorial governments would be states in the Union. Population and territory are necessary conditions of a state, but do not of themselves constitute a state, and by no means a state in the Union. There is no state without a political and civil organization of some sort. Take that away, and you take away the state. All under our system the government can do, when rebellion has carried away the political and civil organization, is to recognize in the loyal population of the territory, the capacity to reorganize or reconstitute the state, and when so reorganized or reconstituted, to admit them as a state into the Union. This is the most it can do, and it may be doubted if it can do as much as this. But while their loyal population remains without state organization, the government cannot treat it as the state, nor can it organize it and make it a state by officers appointed by itself, for officers of its appointment represent no state authority, and can perform no state function; and it is essential to our state system that the people of the given territory should form and adopt their own constitution and elect their own officers.

It is because the state is essentially in its organization, its constitution, by which it is made a political and civil entity, and because the population and territory belong to the United States, and to the state only while it is in the Union, that we have maintained, after Senator Sumner, that state rebellion is state suicide, in opposition to the theory of the administration. The loyal portion of a state, if they retain the state organization, are the state, though the greater part of the population are in insurrection or armed rebellion; but not otherwise. The state follows the organization. The population and territory called Virginia are not population and territory in the Union, for the *state* of Virginia has gone out of the Union, and carried them out of the Union with her. The state of Virginia could go out of the Union, or withdraw from the Union, because it was she herself, not the Union, that made her a state, and the state was *in* not *under* the Union. So far the secessionists are right, and secession is only the assertion of a state's independence. Hence, too, in a certain sense, they are right who deny to the Union the right to coerce a state. You cannot coerce a seceding state back into the Union. That is clear enough. The mistake is in supposing that the state can take the population and territory, not out of the Union, for that it can do, but out of the dominion or jurisdiction of the United States. The *state* of Virginia could take the state out of the Union, but she could not take the population and territory out of the dominion of the United States, because they belonged to her only while she remained a state in the Union. The population and territory are in the Union only after their organization and admission as a state, but before that they belonged as population and territory to the United States, and were under its jurisdiction. They belong to the state only while the state is in the Union, and revert to the United States the moment the state goes out of the Union, for in the United States is the national sovereignty. But as there is no state without population and territory, the moment the state goes out of the Union, she ceases to exist, and therefore her act of secession is simply her suicide as a state. The state having by her own act ceased to exist, cannot be coerced any more than a dead man, and the purpose of coercion is not to force the seceded state back into the Union, but to reduce the rebellious population inhabiting territory belonging to the United States to their allegiance.

The error of the government is in denying that a state can secede, and assuming that the states are all still living in the Union, and that only the population has seceded; the error of the secessionists is not in maintaining that the state can secede, and, in seceding, carry both her population and territory out of the Union, for that it may do; but in asserting that in carrying them *out of the Union*, it carries them *out of the dominion, or beyond the jurisdiction of the United States*. This error arises from the assumption for the state of absolute sovereignty, and therefore that the population and territory belong to the state absolutely, and not simply on condition that it remains a state in the Union. It is the error of a logical, that of the government is the error of an illogical mind. Grant the United States are not a nation, that the people of the United States are not one sovereign political people, and grant further that the sovereignty vests in the state, and that the Union has been formed by the states, each acting in its sovereign capacity, and the doctrine of the secessionists is strictly logical and true, and we are as wrong as they allege us to be in the war we are carrying on against them. But we deny their premises. We maintain that the United States are a nation, and that the sovereignty vests in the one political people, called, for the want of a proper name, THE UNITED STATES; and therefore the state is not a sovereign state, and possesses dominion over population and territory only as one of the united states, and not at all as a seceded, separated, or disunited state. The population and territory are integral in the population and territory of the nation, and inseparable from the national population and domain, save by violence or national consent. The secession of the state places the population and territory out of the Union, indeed, but in precisely the same position, save their rebellion, they would have been in, had they never been organized as a state and existed in the Union. They are foreign to the Union, but not foreign to the nation, or withdrawn from its authority. They remain as population and territory, under, not in, the Union, as do the population and territory of the United States never yet erected into states and admitted into the Union.

We make a distinction between the sovereign people and the government, and between the *Union* and the *Nation*. The one sovereign political people is not created by the federal constitution, but precedes it, and frames, ordains, and establishes it. The government has only delegated powers, it is true, but those powers are delegated by the sovereign people of the United States, not by the states, or the people of the states severally. The sovereign political people and the Union are practically identical. The constitution does not make the Union, but the Union makes the constitution. Yet the Union is not commensurate with the population and territory of the nation, or the United States. The Union is restricted to the population and territory organized into states; the nation embraces the whole population and territory of the United States. The political power of the Union extends over the whole, but is possessed and can be exercised only by the states or people in the Union; and the power is restricted to the population and territory included in the states united, as political power in ancient Rome was restricted to the possessors of the sacred territory marked and bounded by the god Terminus. It is possible, then, to belong to the Union without being in the Union, and to get out of the Union without getting out of the jurisdiction of the United States. Those who get out of the Union cease to have any political power or rights in or out of the Union, for they no longer make a part of the sovereign political people of the United States; but though they lose their rights, the United States or the Union does not lose its right to reduce them to obedience to its authority, by force of arms even, if necessary, as it may do with the population of any organized or unorganized territory within its geographical boundaries.

The government has not distinctly asserted this doctrine, and seems even to deny it. It seems to suppose a *tertium quid* between it and that of the secessionists is possible; or perhaps it persuades itself that no uniform and consistent doctrine on the subject is necessary, and that it may take, now the doctrine of national sovereignty, and now that of state sovereignty, as best suits its immediate purpose, in which it, very likely, conforms to the confused notions of a large number of our politicians, who are not unaccustomed to speak with stammering lips and a double tongue, contradicting in one breath what they assert in the next. But, as far as we can judge, the doctrine we attempt to set forth is the only one on which the administration can justify the war it is waging, or defend its institution of military governments in the territories of the seceded states. If the states were still in the Union as states, these governments, we have said, would be illegal and revolutionary. If they are not, the institution of these governments does not bring them back and reconstitute them states in the Union, or clothe them with any of the rights or powers of states. Consequently they have no power to assent to the proposed amendments to the constitution, and no right to be represented in congress. The persons sent from so-called districts in Virginia, Tennessee, Louisiana, Florida, or North Carolina, may be good men and true, but they can have no legal right to sit and vote in congress.

The fact that each house is made by the constitution the judge of the election and qualifications of its members, does not affect this question; for what the house judges, is, whether the postulant for a seat has the qualifications prescribed by the constitution, and has been elected in accordance with and under the laws of the state and of the United States. The postulant may have received the requisite number of votes, but that does not entitle him to a seat, unless he has received them at an election legally held and legally conducted; and in no seceded state is a legal election now possible. The congressional district must be established and the qualification of voters must be determined by state authority, and cannot be by federal authority; and federal authority is the only authority in the territory. Federal authority cannot, under our constitution, create a state. That must be done by the people themselves of the territory, under an enabling act: and the state is inchoate, and without any authority or political right, till it is admitted by vote of congress into the Union. Till the people become a state, they can elect no representatives; and, till the state is admitted into the Union, and made one of the United States, the members-elect cannot take their seats. What we want understood, is, that the whole political power of the nation is in the United States, and in the state as one of the *United States.* The people outside of the state have no political power,—are under, not a part of, the sovereign people; and, therefore, if the house finds that the applicant has not been elected by the people of a state, under the laws and authority thereof, they cannot admit him to a seat.

We dwell upon this, because we regard it of vital importance to our federal system, and to the legality of the acts of congress. Congress has been greatly to blame in this matter, in not resisting the policy of the administration, when it first developed itself in the case of western Virginia. It should never have recognized, even for an instant, the revolutionary government at Wheeling as the state of Virginia. It is notoriously not Virginia. There has long been manifested by the American people a great indifference to legal methods of doing things. If the thing they want done is but done, they care little whether it is done according to law or in violation of law. It need surprise no one that we have a civil war,—that even the loyal states are overrun with traitors, and even *loyal* men have no scruples in preying on the government to the extent of their ability. The government is not true to itself, and how can it expect the people to be true to it? We acquit the president and congress of all revolutionary intentions, or design of usurping unconstitutional power for the federal government; we believe the acts we complain of grow out of the general misapprehension of popular sovereignty, or the confounding the people as population with the people as the state, and the general disregard of law when it would restrain us from carrying our ends. If we mean to remain a nation, a well-ordered civilized nation, we must clear up our ideas and learn to respect law when it restrains as well as when it authorizes. When the nation is in danger, we cannot, indeed, be over-scrupulous as to the means to be adopted to save it, but in the hour of extremest peril, it is just as easy to save it in a legal and constitutional as in an illegal and unconstitutional way. There has been, since the commencement of our troubles, no occasion for the government to transcend its constitutional powers, or to adopt or sanction any irregular proceedings. It would have saved it infinite trouble if it had adopted in the beginning the true doctrine, and conformed to it in its treatment of the population and territory of the seceded states ; and congress ought to have adopted General Ashley's bill for declaring the seceded states to have lapsed, and erecting the population and territory into territories under governments established by federal authority. But, unhappily, the government flattered itself with the hope that by blockading the ports, raising a large army, and pressing the rebels a little and threatening them much, it could induce the seceded states themselves to resume their attitude as loyal states in the Union, and all would go on again as if nothing had happened. It deceived itself ; its hopes have not been realized.

The government, in both the legislative and executive departments, ought to have looked the question at first directly in the face, and met it fairly and squarely by declaring the lapse of every seceding state government, and establishing for its territory a territorial government, under, not in, the Union ; it would then have proceeded regularly and legally, both in appointing military governors under its own authority, and in reducing the rebellious population to their allegiance to the United States. As it is, all is irregular, unconstitutional and revolutionary ; in direct opposition to our whole system of government. The military governors would then have been governors of territories, and bound only to carry out the laws enacted or recognized by federal authority. Now they are neither governors of territories nor of states, and are in a position legally and politically anomalous. It is, perhaps, not too late for the government to retrace its steps, and do what it should have done in the beginning, that is, recognize and act according to the law and facts of the case ; in other words, simply own and tell the truth and place no longer any reliance on falsehoods or shams. The seceded states exist neither *de jure* nor *de facto* as states in the Union, and it is simply a falsehood to assert that they are. If as states they are

out of the Union, their population and territory are out of
the jurisdiction of the Union, or they are not. If they are,
that ends the question, and you have no right to make war
on them as rebels, and, perhaps, are yourselves the aggres-
sors ; if they are not, and you have the right to use force to
reduce them to submission to your authority, then treat
them as population and territory belonging to the United
States and not erected into states ; provide territorial governments for them, and govern them as you do Nebraska,
Dakota, Colorado, or New Mexico. Be truthful, and deal
with things as they are, and rely on truth to sustain you.
Truth is never made stronger by a modicum of falsehood,
any more than honesty is strengthened by dishonesty.

The president would find this straight-forward and truthful proceeding greatly facilitating the adoption of his emancipation policy. According to our doctrine eleven states
have committed suicide or lapsed, and the whole number of
the United States is now twenty-three, and counting Western
Virginia, admitted by congress while we write, twenty-four,
and the number necessary to ratify a constitutional amendment is eighteen, and it is possible that the president might
obtain that number for his proposed amendments ; but
twenty-five states, the number he supposes to be necessary,
he can never obtain, for there are not that number of
United States now in existence, since, we repeat, the military
governments he has established, or the population acting
under them, are not *states*, and are, if any thing, *territories*,
and, in the present case, territories organized by the executive without the authority of congress. The amendments
ratified by eighteen states would be constitutionally adopted,
for the whole political power of the nation vests in the United
States, or people as states in the Union. They would bind
the people of the seceded states when restored to the Union,
as a new state when admitted into the Union is bound by
the constitution adopted and in force prior to its admission ;
and they would be subject to the amended constitution before such restoration, in like manner as the territories are
subject to the Union.

Of course, it is not as a punishment upon the seceders that
we insist on treating the seceded states as having lapsed, but
for the simple purpose of treating things as they are. The
Union has no power to expel or extinguish a state, and the
lapse is not by virtue of its act but by virtue of the suicidal
act of the state itself. By ceasing to be a state in the Union,

it ceases to be a state at all. We regret, we deplore its lapse; but it, not the Union, is responsible for it. Nor do we contemplate the perpetual existence of the people, who have been so misguided as to declare themselves out of the Union, as territories under the Union, or as the population of a state excluded from the elective franchise. We hope at an early day to see them reëstablished under their old names, and with their old boundaries as states in the Union, on a footing of perfect equality with the states that have remained loyal. Eleven stars have fallen from our political firmament, as the angels fell from heaven; but, unlike Lucifer and his rebel hosts, they may be restored, and we look to see them restored, and to shine anew with all their pristine brightness and glory. They must, however, undergo the purgation of territorial governments first, and it will depend almost entirely on themselves, whether it shall be of longer or shorter duration. We are moved by no hostile feelings toward the people of the lapsed states; we are moved only by our love of the nation, devotion to our country, and respect for the constitution and laws.

But to return to the president's emancipation policy. We repeat, that in itself we are not opposed to it, and even like it; but we do not see how, if adopted, it is to give us military success or put an end to the war. We are as earnest for the emancipation of the slaves as any man is or can be, but we seek it only as subsidiary to the military operations of the country. We say frankly, that with our military success hanging doubtful, the treasury well-nigh bankrupt, the people taxed to the full point of public endurance, and the expenses of the nation running up at the rate of a thousand millions a year, we are not in favor of imposing on the treasury any additional burdens not absolutely necessary. Not believing the president's policy would have the slightest influence in shortening the war, we are not in favor of adopting it. It is simply a policy of the border states, to sell their slaves before they run away, or to get pay for them after they have emancipated themselves. If the rebels will signify to us, say through the British minister, that in case the government will adopt the policy proposed, they will lay down their arms, restore to the United States its forts and arsenals, which they still hold, make restitution for the property they have taken from the Union, pay the legitimate expenses of the war, and return to their allegiance, we will entertain the project, and recommend the government to buy up and liberate, at a fair valuation, in the way and manner proposed by the president, all the slaves, if any such there are, within the geographical limits of the United States. But without such assurance, or at least the assurance that they will accept the proposition and return to their allegiance, it seems to us the project should not be entertained for a moment. The border states men may accept the proposition and honestly believe that the rebels will; but they have, as has been sufficiently proved, no authority to speak for the rebel leaders, and we have already suffered enough from their policy.

If the doctrine we maintain, and on which the government acts, even while denying it, be sound, there are, except in the the non-seceding slave states, no slaves within the geographical limits of the United States to be bought up and emancipated. Except as to the border non-seceding slave states, the president's policy is a pro-slavery rather than an anti-slavery policy. Its adoption would reëstablish and prolong negro slavery where it has already ceased to have any legal existence. The eleven seceded states having lapsed as states, and being no longer states in the Union, but territorial possessions of the Union, slavery, which existed in them solely by virtue of state authority, has necessarily lapsed with them. The lapse of a state carries with it whatever depended on the state for its life and vigor. In these eleven states the slaves are emancipated by the voluntary death of the state; and as the act by which they were emancipated was an act of hostility to the Union, the United States is under no obligation to indemnify their former owners for their loss of property in them.

But it is said that the territorial law, after a lapse of sovereignty, remains in force till altered or repealed by the new sovereign. Thus the territory we acquired from France and Spain was held to be governed by the civil law of those countries till we enacted new laws for its government. The rule is unquestionable, but does not apply in the case of a federal state lapsed by its own act; because, though a change of *status*, it involves no change of sovereignty. The states in our system are, severally, autonomous, but not sovereign. The true territorial law which survives the state is not, and never was, the law of the state, but the law of the United States; and as that law never authorized or sanctioned slavery, save as an institution deriving all its force from the enactments or usages of the state, there can be no territorial law, or law of the land, surviving the lapse of the state, to authorize or to render licit the holding of slaves. But, even conceding that the principle that the territorial law survives the sovereign, and remains in force till the new sovereign ordains to the contrary, applies in the present case, as in that of the lapse of originally sovereign states, these eleven states having lapsed and fallen into the condition of territories of the United States, their slaves are free by virtue of the act of congress at its last session, prohibiting for ever slavery in any of the territories of the United States, thus making liberty, not slavery, the territorial law of the United States, or law of the land. Does the president propose to remand the freedmen to slavery, and then tax the federal treasury to buy them up and emancipate them over again? That these states have fallen into the condition of territories we have proved, and the government, even if it denies it, assumes it to be a fact, by establishing governments for them, for these so-called military governments are simply territorial governments, if they are any thing.

Then, again, what becomes of the president's proclamation of the 22d of last September? Is that to be recalled, and no slave to be freed under it? Or is it proposed to pay for the slaves liberated under it? Or are those liberated under it to be remanded to slavery, and held in bondage till the restored states are willing to emancipate them, on receiving compensation twenty or thirty years in advance from the Union? Out of the slave states remaining in the Union, there is no slavery by virtue of any law now in force, state or national; and the president's policy, if it means any thing beyond the loyal border states, is simply a policy to remand the freed persons to slavery, with a view to having the states emancipate them gradually with compensation from the federal treasury. It may be good policy to offer compensation to loyal men in the seceded states for the loss of slaves by the acts of the rebels, but certainly there is no obligation in justice to do it. The United States are no more bound to compensate the loyal men for their loss of property in slaves, than they are for their loss in horses and mules, hogs and turkeys, by the action of the rebels. Does the government propose to indemnify the loyal men in the rebel states for all the losses of property they have sustained by the action of the rebels and their government?

But passing over this, there is one feature in the president's policy that should not be overlooked. His amendments if adopted, will not authorize the federal government to free a single slave, nor will they render certain emancipation in a single state. They only authorize congress to provide and determine the mode for compensating a state for its slaves in case it chooses to emancipate them. The power to emancipate the slaves will remain, as now, with the state, and it will continue to be, as now, optional with the state, whether it will emancipate them or not. We commend this fact to the consideration of anti-slavery men. The president's policy contemplates issuing bonds, with interest, to the state, before a single slave is actually emancipated. A state may pass a law emancipating all the slaves within its limits, and obtain its compensation bonds for ten, twenty, thirty, a hundred, five hundred, or ten hundred millions of dollars, according to the number and valuation of the slaves, and on the last day of 1899, the state may pass another law making slavery perpetual, and the expenditure of the Union goes for nothing. But in that case the state must return the bonds and pay back the interest received. All very well, to tax the people some three, four, or five millions annually for the benefit of Kentucky or Missouri, and not get the liberation of a single slave. But suppose the state says it can't or it won't pay back the interest received. What will you do then? Compel it? But suppose the state answers, If you attempt compulsion, we will secede; and suppose you have the whole fifteen slave states in the same condition; what would you have but the present rebellion over again? We wish to think well of the president, and we do believe in his integrity and patriotism; but we fear he has been duped, and induced to lend his support, without understanding it, to one of the most stupendous swindles on the government ever contemplated in this or any other country. We honestly believe it nothing but a scheme for depleting our already over-depleted federal treasury, for mortgaging the whole income of the free states to the slave states. We commend this feature of the policy to the tax-paying portion of the community.

We did not intend to enter thus far into the merits of the particular scheme; but we could not forbear calling attention to this feature of it, and showing that the scheme bears on its face the evidence of being a scheme for sacrificing the entire Union to Kentucky, and other slave states. Has the president not yet learned, that however powerful and respectable may be Kentucky, it is not the whole United States? And not for her alone, nor all the slave states included, does the Union exist? The attempt to buy their support, if carried out and persisted in, will prove as fatal in the end as the practice of the old Roman emperors, when the Romans had become too effeminate or too cowardly to defend the empire, of buying the support of the border barbarians. The resources of the Union are large, but not unbounded; and those of the federal treasury are great, but not exhaustless, as Mr. Chase has already ascertained. The administration seems to think the contrary, or that the way to render a nation great and prosperous, is to overload it with debt. We begrudge no expenditure necessary for prosecuting the war and saving the life of the nation, but in all other respects we demand, as one of the people, the most rigid economy.

The expenditure the president's scheme demands is, in no way visible to us, necessary for carrying on the war, and bringing it to a successful issue. If necessary for freeing the slaves in the loyal slave states, it will be time enough to incur it when the war is over and peace restored. In the seceded states, where is the great mass of the slave population, the slaves are now legally free by the lapse of those states, and their conversion by the executive into territories under military governors. It needs only military success to make them practically free. The slave question is now in the way of settling itself, if the government will do nothing to reëstablish slavery, and if it will turn all its energy to gaining complete military success. With the success of the federal arms slavery disappears from all except the loyal border states; if the federal arms fail, and separation or reconstruction follows, slavery is reëstablished, and probably will be more flourishing and vigorous than ever. As one who wishes to see slavery ended, we wish the government to leave the question where it now stands, and exert all its energies to crush by military rather than by political means the rebellion.

We think, however, on further reflection, we catch a glimpse of the real policy of the administration, and of the reason why it so doggedly insists that the seceded states are still in the Union, though its military governments prove that, when it suits its purpose, it can treat them as out of it. It hopes, probably, by means of these governments, to form in each of the seceded states, where it gets a foothold, the nucleus of a Union party, which, though small in the beginning, may gradually, with a little federal nursing, gain to it the majority of the population. So far all is well, and shows statesmanship. But this party can be more effectually and rapidly formed if the military government be treated as the state, and the population adhering to it be allowed the representation of the state in congress. We do not doubt it, and would approve it, if it were constitutional, and not an attempt to put down one revolution by another. If, again, the federal government be allowed to treat the military government as the state, and to issue United States bonds of untold millions to it, ostensibly as compensation for the gradual emancipation of the slaves, which need never take place. the party may grow still more rapidly, and the majority of the population be much more quickly and effectually unionized. That is to say, the president proposes to suppress the rebellion, to end the war, and restore peace, by buying up with United States bonds the rebel population ; and this, the president calculates, would cost less than to do it by means of the military ; so the suppression of the rebellion is to be effected by politicians, on mercantile instead of military principles. Surely this is a mercantile age. But the constitution and laws, what is to become of them ? No matter for them. If the war is ended, rebellion over, and peace restored, the people, in their joy at the end, will overlook the means by which it has been obtained. The merchants and manufacturers will readily condone the violation of the constitution, for trade and business may be resumed ; and the radicals or abolitionists will not complain, if the ultimate extinction of slavery is provided, or apparently provided for. We certainly do not charge our worthy president with originating this policy, or with adopting it with a full knowledge and understanding of its character. It smacks of the astute secretary of state. The policy could be effectual only on the supposition that the mass of the people, North and South, are venal, and have no regard for constitutions and laws; and to adopt and act on it, would serve only to corrupt them still more.

But, setting aside the outrage to public virtue and morality, to the constitution and laws, to fact and truth, the policy implies, we do not believe it would even be successful. We believe, as we have said from the first, that the controversy can be settled only by arms on the battle-field. There is, in our judgment, no road to peace, but through victory, —victory either for the government or for the rebellion. We have as little confidence in, as we have taste for, the corrupt ways and corrupt intrigues of politicians. The federal treasury is not rich enough, the federal credit is not high enough to buy off the southern rebels, and thus end the war. The government is strong in the constitution and the laws, so long as it observes them, and is invincible so long as it relies on the justice of its cause and its army; but if it resorts to other supports it will, in our judgment, fail, and deservedly fail. It will never do to corrupt patriotism in order to intensify it, or to render a people utterly venal in order to render them the better able to appreciate and assert public right and national integrity. The Democratic leaders, who have gained some successes in the recent elections, will find themselves mistaken in their calculations, unless they are prepared to offer either separation, or reconstruction under the confederate government. No; war is our reliance; and our hope is in the God of battles; and if our voice is still for war, it is not that we are Belial, or that we do not love peace. We have no aversion to reconciliation with our southern countrymen, we have no animosities to gratify, no revenges to seek, no vengeances to inflict. We dislike war, as we dislike disagreeable medicines; but it must sometimes be resorted to, as an heroic remedy for diseases which nothing else will cure.

The president seems to us to lack confidence in his military operations, and we doubt if he has ever relied on military success to secure peace and union. In his message, he hardly alludes to the army, and says not a word to encourage it and reward it for its deeds and sacrifices. We regret this, for the army deserves well of the country; and, if it has not yet accomplished all that was expected of it, it is by no means certain that the fault is not the fault of the administration rather than of its generals. For our part, we stand by the army, and have no fears of its failure, if the administration gives it a fair chance, and does not thwart the plans of its generals by panics for the safety of the capital.

We have criticised freely, perhaps severely, what we regard as grave faults in the administration,—faults which we deeply regret; but we have done it not to oppose the administration, or in any way to embarrass its military operations. We have done it solely to urge upon it the necessity of correcting them. What is strictly its war policy, we heartily approve and earnestly support; but its political measures for regaining the people of the seceded states, and reconciling them to the Union, are, in our judgment, to a great extent illegal, unconstitutional, immoral, revolutionary, and unnecessary. The president, as the executive chief of the nation, has, we hold, in time of insurrection or invasion, the right to suspend the writ of *habeas corpus*, and therefore we do not complain of what are called "arbitrary arrests." We do not say that all those who have been arrested deserved to be, but we are confident that very few of those who really deserve to be have been arrested. Justice has not always, and injustice sometimes may have been done; but the constitution has not been violated by the arrests complained of. The violation of the constitution we complain of, is in the manner in which the president is reorganizing state authority in the seceded states. This he is doing by means of a few friends of the government, principled or unprincipled, got together in a seceded state under a military governor appointed by the executive, and authorized to wield the whole representative and electoral power the state was entitled to as a state in the Union. Already the president has *created* two senators for Virginia, and we hear it rumored that Texas is to be divided into four states, and that will be a creation of ten additional senators. The same process may be carried on in all the seceded states, and the president create for himself, or endow creatures of his own with, nearly one-half of the electoral and representative power of the United States. All that is needed is to obtain a military footing in a state, and get together a few dozens of individuals who, under the protection of the federal guns, will consent to meet and resolve themselves the state, and that forthwith the president and congress recognize it as a state in the Union, and admit its senators and representatives to their seats. Against this we protest in the name of the constitution, of legal government, of social order, common honesty, and common sense. But our protest will avail nothing. The house of representatives has just admitted Western Virginia as a state, after listening to the able and conclusive speech of Mr. Conway against it.

Yet the error was not so much in admitting the new state, as in the previous recognition of the Pierrepont government as the state of Virginia. That government was not and is not Virginia, and had and has no power to give the consent required by the constitution for the formation of a new state within the limits of the old state of Virginia. That pretence was well exposed in the debate in the house by Mr. Stevens. But Mr. Stevens himself erred in contending that Western Virginia could be admitted under the war power. The war power is neither unconstitutional nor revolutionary. Under it the government could take possession of Virginia, and govern it by a military governor, but could not create a state, or admit a state into the Union, for a state in the Union is a part of the Union, and is not under the government, either civil or military, of the Union. It is, united with the other states, the national sovereign, and governs instead of being governed. But the *state* of Virginia, having seceded, had ceased to exist, and the territory of Virginia had lapsed to the United States, the national sovereign. It was, after secession, simply territory belonging to the Union and under its jurisdiction, and could be dealt with as any other territory belonging to the United States. It was competent for congress, if it chose, to erect it into two or more territorial governments, and to admit them with a republican constitution, *freely adopted by the people of each,* into the Union as states, with or without an enabling act.

The complaint we make of the administration is, not that it establishes in the several seceded states military governments, but that it treats these governments which it creates, and which depend on the federal government, as states in the Union. This is revolution and usurpation. It allows them the representative and electoral power of states, to which, being at best nothing but territorial governments, they are not entitled. It vitiates the national sovereignty itself. We pray congress, therefore, to refrain from going any further, and when the respectable gentlemen we hear have been elected by the military government of Louisiana, present themselves with Governor Shepley's credentials, it will permit them to withdraw. This it may do, because it is always lawful to correct our own errors; and because Governor Pierrepont, after all, was chosen by popular election, though illegal, while Governor Shepley was simply appointed by the federal executive.

Still, we repeat, the administration, in its war policy, must be sustained, if we would sustain the national cause. It is the legal, constitutional government of the country, and cannot, during its term of office, be separated from the coun-

try. We have full confidence in its patriotic intentions;
we give it credit for a great deal of ability, though not of
the highest sort; and we doubt not that it will, after a manner, carry us through our present difficulties, though not
precisely in what we regard as the best manner. We dislike all finesse, intrigue, and underground working. We
prefer always an open, frank, manly course, and are never
willing to gain even a good end by reprehensible means.
We would rather fail in the right than succeed in the wrong.
We honor only him who seeks noble ends by noble means.
We like and support the end the administration aims at.
We do not like all the means it adopts, for some of them
seem to us unconstitutional, and fitted only to corrupt public virtue. But while we are writing the decisive battle may
be raging, and before we issue from the press, the fate of the
Union may be decided. It is an anxious moment for all
Americans who love their country. Yet our country's destiny, as our own, is in the hands of God, who rears or over-
throws states and empires at his will. In him we put our
trust, confident that whatever he does, he does right. Thy
will be done.

CATHOLICS AND THE ANTI-DRAFT RIOTS.

[From Brownson's Quarterly Review for October, 1863.]

FROM the fact that the immediate actors in the late riots
in New York, got up to resist the draft, and to create a diver-
sion in favor of the southern rebellion, were almost exclusively Irishmen and Catholics, efforts have been made, and
most likely will continue to be made, to excite the hostility
of the non-Catholic American people not only against the
foreign, especially the Irish element in our population, but
against the Catholic religion itself. Non-Catholics judge
the national and political bearings of the church by the
conduct of her members themselves, and, if in a moment
of national crisis, when the nation is struggling for life,
against one of the most formidable rebellions in any age
or country, these are found acting directly or indirectly
against the nation, and giving aid and comfort to the rebels,
they will be very likely to infer that there is something in

Catholicity itself unfavorable to loyalty, or incompatible with national sovereignty and independence.

The standing charge of non-Catholic Americans against our religion is that it is subject to a foreign power, and hostile to free government; that Catholics are not, and as good Catholics cannot be, loyal to our free popular institutions; and that in a struggle of the nation to maintain its existence and independence against either a foreign or a domestic foe, they will be found as a body on the side of the enemy. This charge, false and unjust as it is, many will think, and more will pretend, has been confirmed rather than refuted by the attitude of Catholics during the present civil war, and especially by their participation in the late disgraceful and disloyal riots against the draft, in this city and elsewhere. That these riots were intended to coöperate with the rebel general Lee in his invasion of Maryland and Pennsylvania, and to weaken and overthrow the government by preventing it from obtaining the forces necessary to crush out the rebellion, there is and can be no serious doubt. It is certain, also, that nearly nine-tenths of the active rioters were Irishmen and Catholics. It is, no doubt, true that few, if any, respectable Irishmen, and few, or none, of the better class of Catholics were found actually rioting. The active participators in mobs are usually from the lowest and most degraded social class, even when instigated by men of high social standing. But it is still true, that the mobs were composed principally of Irishmen and Catholics, and of Catholics, too, who were not wholly beyond the reach of the clergy. They were not all of the abandoned, vicious, or vagabond class, who never hear mass, and are at times utterly heedless of their religion. Bad as they were, they were within the pale of the church, and under the charge of the clergy. This was evinced by the influence the clergy had in dispersing them, and by the personal impunity in every instance, except one, with which the clergy went about among them, and snatched from their hands the bludgeons with which they were armed. No, they were not all a hardened and vicious rabble, whom the clergy could not reach or influence, and utterly heedless of the obligations of religion. They were rather a rabble the clergy had neglected, had never labored to instruct, or to bring more directly and completely under religious influences, and for whose conduct, savage as it was, the clergy and their most reverend chief of this city are not wholly irresponsible. Moreover, those rioters only acted out the opinions they had received from men of higher religious and social positions than themselves; and if the general tone of the clergy and respectable Catholics of the city, and especially of the Catholic press, had been decidedly opposed to the rebellion, or heartily in favor of sustaining the administration in its efforts to suppress it by military force, we may be very sure that the riot either never would have occurred, or that the chief actors in it would have been neither Irishmen nor Catholics. Non-Catholics are aware of this, and we Catholics gain nothing by not frankly avowing it.

Yet the riot was not a Catholic riot, and gives, in reality, no confirmation to the standing charge against the Catholic Church. It may prove that all Catholics are not what they should be, and that even our clergy may have been remiss in their duty to instruct and look after the morals of their people, especially the poorer and more exposed classes; but not that the church is disloyal, or incompatible with republican freedom, or national unity and independence. These rioters did not fill our city with horror at their savage deeds in their capacity as Catholics, or as Irishmen. It was not by command of the church or as Catholics that they resisted the draft, attacked the officers of government appointed to carry it into effect, made demonstrations against the Republican presses of the city, burned down the houses of prominent Republican officials, destroyed the Colored Orphan Asylum, murdered negroes, and rifled and demolished their dwellings. These things they did not as Catholics or Irishmen, but as adherents of the DEMOCRATIC PARTY, as partisans of Horatio Seymour, Fernando Wood, James Brooks, Clement L. Vallandigham, and others, who, by their incendiary speeches and by leading articles in the Democratic journals, had for months been exciting them against the government, against the conscription, against the war, and had worked them up to uncontrollable fury. The shouts of the mob tell us what was its *animus*, and under what influence or inspiration it acted, and these were hurrahs for Governor Seymour, Fernando Wood, General McClellan, and Jeff. Davis. A Catholic layman or an Irishman known to be a Republican or a supporter of the administration, was in no less danger from the mob than a Protestant, a native American, or even a negro. Colonel O'Brien, so savagely murdered, was an Irishman and a

Catholic; and one of the best friends of the Irish emigrant in this city, a Catholic and an Irishman himself, escaped the fury of the mob, only by keeping himself concealed. On the other hand, Catholic Irishmen volunteered to aid the authorities in suppressing the riot, and were among the bravest and most efficient in protecting the lives and property of our citizens. No, the mob was literally a Democratic mob, got up at the instigation of the Democratic leaders, and led on by men in sympathy with the enemies of the United States,—a simple pro-slavery Democratic mob. Not a Catholic nor an Irishman, not a German nor an American, who was not a partisan of the Seymours, the Woods, and the Vallandighams, not even a Democrat not hostile to the war, and to negro emancipation, had any part in it, either as instigator or actor.

That the mob assumed developments and entered upon a course of incendiarism, murder, robbery, and pillage, not foreseen or intended by its originators, and was joined by a class of blacklegs, cutthroats, robbers, pickpockets, and thieves, not included in the original programme, is very possible, and that this frightened even its instigators, and disposed them to stop it before it had fully succeeded in its purpose, we can readily believe; but he who wantonly breaks down the dyke that dams out the ocean must expect a deluge, and is responsible for the consequences. The Democratic leaders, the Copperheads are answerable for the mob and its destructive fury; and it will never do to charge it either to Catholics or to the Irish as such, for they are implicated in it only in the respect that they are Democrats or Copperheads. We do not pretend that all who call themselves Democrats, and usually vote with the Democratic party, are disloyal, and opposed to the efforts of the government to suppress by force of arms the southern rebellion. Not every Democrat is a Copperhead; but every Copperhead is a Democrat. The party as a party is disloyal. There are, we know, loyal men, as loyal as any in the country or as ever lived, who are not Republican, but they have no standing in the Democratic party. They are excommunicated by their party as political heretics and schismatics. Who thinks of calling General Dix, General Butler, Daniel S. Dickinson, James T. Brady, and John Van Buren Democratic leaders as they once were? They neither go with their party, nor their party with them. The Democratic party as such support Vallandigham for governor in Ohio, not the old Democrat John Brough; and there is no man in the country they are more bitter against than Mr. Buchanan's Democratic attorney-general, the present patriotic secretary of war. These men are all read out of the party, and placed under its ban. No man enjoys or can enjoy the confidence of the party, who gives the government a loyal and hearty support in its war against the rebellion. These facts prove beyond all cavil that the Democratic party as it now exists, under its present leaders, is disloyal, hostile to the government, and in sympathy with their former political friends and allies, the chiefs of the pro-slavery rebellion.

The rebellion itself was the work of the Democratic party, which, with scarcely an interval, had governed the country for sixty years, and was hatched by Democratic leaders, in Democratic conclaves, under the fostering care and protection of a Democratic administration. The Democratic party originated at the South, was fostered into life, and elevated to power by southern politicians, and has always been a southern party. At first, under Washington, it was called the *Anti-federal* party; under the elder Adams, it called itself the *Republican* party, and continued to do so, till the administration of the younger Adams, when it took the name of *Democratic* Republican, in opposition to *National* Republican. Since the reëlection of Andrew Jackson to the presidency, in 1832, it has assumed and borne the name of the *Democratic* party. Its great strength was always in the political power of the interest created by negro slavery, confined almost exclusively to the southern section. For full sixty years, from the administration of Jefferson, commencing in 1801, to that of Buchanan, ending in 1861, that interest had shaped the policy of the government, dictated its principal measures, and controlled the politics of the republic. Up to 1848 all political parties had courted it, and none had dared openly to oppose it, except in the memorable discussion in congress in 1820, resulting in the so-called Missouri compromise. With all parties the slave interest was held to be sacred, and all parties vied with each other, in their devotion to it, and in their denunciation of the abolitionist agitation. The Whig, Edward Everett, of Massachusetts, went as far as the Democrat, Charles G. Atherton, of New Hampshire, or Mr. Calhoun, of South Carolina, in opposition to the emancipationists. Mr. Everett, as governor of Massachusetts, went even so far as to declare that they ought to be subjected to civil prosecution and punishment. No man who took ground against slavery could aspire to any place of trust or emolument under the federal government. Even Mr. Bancroft's confirmation by the senate, as secretary of the navy under President Polk's administration, was vehemently opposed, on the ground that he had somewhere, in some of his writings, many years before, when a young man, advanced something not favorable to slavery. It was with great difficulty that even the eminent historian of the United States, one of the living glories of his country, could pass the ordeal.

The southern party sustained itself in power by adroitly dividing the free states of the northern and middle sections of the Union. At first, it secured the support of the democracy proper, that is to say, of the lower class of the population, with a few wealthy, intelligent, and aristocratic leaders and managers. The real democracy of a country is always controlled and used by leaders not of their own class. Later the party had maintained itself by gaining the capital, more especially the commercial capital of the free states to its support. But the middle classes of the free states at length grew weary of being virtually excluded from all voice in the federal government, and of being governed by the slave interest. They gradually formed the design of rescuing the government from its subjection to that interest, and of preventing at least any further expansion of the slave power, or increase of slave territory. Hence arose the free-soil party, a party composed of men who had been, some Democrats and some Whigs, and that ran Ex-President Martin Van Buren for president, and Charles Francis Adams for vice-president in 1848, and defeated the pro-slavery Democratic candidates, Cass and Butler, but gained no positive victory, for General Taylor soon dying, was succeeded by the vice-president, Mr. Fillmore, who, though before his election an avowed abolitionist, turned out to be one of the most supple tools of slavery, that ever sat in the presidential chair. In 1852, General Pierce was elected by the Democratic party, and during his administration, and by its influence was concocted and passed the famous Kansas-Nebraska bill, intended, under the pretext of taking the slavery question out of congress, and leaving it to be settled by the people of each territory for itself, thereby asserting the solecism that a territory is a state, to secure for ever the election of the president and the administration of the government to the slave interest. This measure, threatening as it did to render the slave power the permanent governing power of the Union, rallied anew the free-soil party of 1848, for a moment disbanded by the compromise measures of 1850, with a new organization, and under the name of the Republican party. This party came very near choosing its candidate for president in 1856, and succeeded in choosing him in 1860. The multiplication and growth of the free states, the increasing numbers and strength of the party opposed to the political domination of slavery, and its virtual success in 1856, assured the southern wing of the Democratic party, that the policy of the Kansas-Nebraska bill had failed, that the day when the slave interest could govern the country had gone by, and that they must either surrender the power they had hitherto wielded, or secede from the Union, and set up a separate nationality and independence. They chose the latter alternative, and as soon as possible after the election of a Republican president, they seceded with their states, organized a confederate government, and proclaimed their independence. They seceded, not because any of their constitutional rights had been violated, or even threatened, but because they saw that they could no longer, through the interest of their slave capital, retain their old supremacy in the Union. Parties had, through the blunders of the northern Democracy, divided geographically, and left them in a permanent minority.

The secession was expected by both northern and southern Democrats, to be effected peaceably, in consequence of the assumed timidity of the Republicans, and the influence in dividing the population of the free states, that could and would be exerted by the northern Democratic leaders. The northern Democrats had aided, advised, certainly connived at secession, not, however, as a permanent division of the Union, but only as a measure to break up the Republican party, and to last only till they had wrung from the fears and the weakness of the Republicans, such concessions and guaranties to slavery as would satisfy the South, and secure their own return to power. But the firmness of the radical Republicans in refusing the concessions, and the unexpected determination of the administration to put down secession by armed force, disconcerted all their calculations, and placed them in a dilemma from which there was, apparently, no escape. For them openly to side with the rebels was to ruin them for ever in the free states, and to give the administration a full, hearty, and loyal support, was not only to break their pledges to the southern leaders, but to render for ever impracticable the renewal of their old alliance with slavery for the government of the Union.   What should they do? The honest and patriotic among them did what honest men and patriots will always do, placed the country before party, and heartily and loyally rushed to the support of the government in its war to put down the rebellion, and to save the rights and integrity of the republic.   The rest withheld their support, talked Union, intrigued against it, and waited, like Micawber, for "something to turn up," ready to avail themselves of any errors the administration might commit, or any reverses that might befall the federal arms.

For the Democratic party, to enable it to recover its lost ground, two things were indispensable.   1st. If the Union should be dissolved and southern independence gained, the odium, in the public estimation, must rest on the Republican party; and 2d. If the Union should be restored, it must be done without the abolition of slavery, and by a Democratic administration.   Hence their unwearied efforts to cast the blame of secession and the war for the suppression of the rebellion on the Republican party, and to prolong the war beyond the term of office of the present administration.   They must represent the war as a needless war, a war of aggression on the South, provoked and continued by black-republicans and abolition fanatics, for base and selfish purposes, since only in so doing could they justify themselves before even the masses of their own party, for opposing or not actively and energetically supporting it. They must also oppose with all their might all interference, on any ground whatever, with slavery, and cry down the anti-slavery policy of the government, as unconstitutional, wicked, and as rendering the suppression of the rebellion, and all future reconciliation, harmony, and good will between North and South impossible.

Now this is precisely what the Democratic leaders have been laboring, not without some effect, to do.   They for a time made the administration hesitate to avow in an open and straightforward manner all intentions of reducing the seceded states to their obedience by force, and for a still longer time abstain from favoring, and to disavow the intention of favoring any thing like an anti-slavery policy, thereby misleading and disheartening many of its friends and its ablest supporters.   The moment when it became evident that the administration was slowly, timidly, and only partially adopting an emancipation policy as a war measure, they became rabid, denounced it, intrigued against it, threatened to oust it by military force, and attempted, perhaps, as they supposed, perfected arrangements in case any republican opposition should be offered, to have General McClellan unite his command with the rebel general Lee, and suppress it. Proofs of this some day may be forthcoming, and have already been hinted by Lord Lyons in giving Earl Russell an account of the state of things here, and of his interview with the northern Democratic leaders, whose plans were much disconcerted, he says, by the relief of General McClellan from the command of the Army of the Potomac. Lord Lyons's hints are very significant to those who had some previous knowledge of the purposes, plottings, and intrigues of the Democratic leaders during the peninsular campaign, and Pope's campaign in Virginia, and understood why Pope was suffered to fail, and why Lee was induced or suffered to invade Maryland, and the Democrats carried the elections in Pennsylvania, New York, New Jersey, Ohio, Indiana, and Illinois. It was the dark hour of our republic, and we should attribute our escape from destruction to the refusal of General McClellan to carry out the plans of the Democratic leaders, did we not find these leaders laboring to restore him to his command, or to make him general-in-chief of the armies of the Union. But we owe it to his patriotism, to his "unreadiness," or to his fear of not being able to carry his army with him,—or, perhaps, to what they allege, the refusal of the rebels on invading Maryland to consent to the reconstruction of the Union, even on the confederate platform, and under the confederate president and cabinet. That overtures to that effect were made to them by the Democratic leaders, we suppose, nobody doubts; but were entertained by the rebels, we presume, only till they had gained sufficient advantages to render them confident of achieving their independence, and then were scornfully rejected. The rebel chiefs might reasonably hope that with the Democrats in power in the great states named, they could effect their original purpose in seceding.

The Democratic leaders have spared no pains to make the public believe that the Republican party needlessly brought on the war, and are prolonging it for the purpose of securing emancipation, and that if they were in power, they could easily and at once obtain peace without disunion. But certainly they cannot themselves believe what they allege on the first point, and nothing but blind infatuation can enable them to believe on the second. The Republican party did not bring on the war; it was brought on by the secessionists who fired the first gun, and the great error of the administration was that it allowed itself to be attacked, and important strategical points to be seized by the rebels before it offered any armed resistance, and indulged, or affected to indulge, hopes of a peaceable solution of the problem, after its warmest friends felt that no such solution was possible. When it did offer resistance, it had no thought of emancipation, and the emancipation policy, which it has subsequently adopted, was not even publicly urged upon it by the Republicans till it had been insisted on with zeal and energy by some of the best known and strongest anti-abolition men in the country, who saw that without it, the rebellion could not be put down, and future union and peace secured. The war was neither begun nor has it been continued for the sake of abolition; for there never has been a moment when the rebels could not have had peace and amnesty on the simple condition of laying down their arms, returning to their allegiance, and giving the necessary security for their future good behavior; and we may add that had the northern Democrats shown no sympathy with them, no emancipation policy would have been adopted, for the rebellion would have been suppressed before it became necessary. What the Democratic leaders allege on the first point is undeniably false and unjust, and is said not honestly, but for the purpose of deceiving the people, embarrassing the administration, throwing the odium of the war on the loyal portion of the people, and securing their own return to power.

What they allege on the second point is equally unfounded, and deceptive. The southern Democrats have not seceded and carried their states with them for the temporary purpose of getting rid of a Republican administration, or because they did not succeed in the presidential election in 1860; for they had fully made up their minds to secede long before that election took place. They seceded because they had lost and could not again permanently hold the power of governing the Union by remaining in it, and that sooner or later they must either accept freedom as the permanent policy of the government, or separate, and set up an independent republic for themselves. They could have secured the defeat of the Republicans in 1860, if they had wished it; but they did not wish it; because they could more easily carry out secession under a Republican than a Democratic administration. Under a Republican administration they could count on a strong Democratic support from the free states, but on no aid from Republicans under a Democratic administration. Republicans are Union men, and respect the laws. We know, and the Democratic leaders know, that the southern chiefs were determined, as long ago as 1856. that the Republican candidate for 1860 should be elected. They saw in the course taken by politics since the Mexican war, the development of ideas, interests, and tendencies, in the free states,—in the free-soil party of 1848, and the Republican party organized in 1854, immediately after the repeal of the Missouri compromise and the passage of the Kansas-Nebraska bill, that the free states were resolved and were able to restrain and ultimately destroy the usurped political power created and sustained by slavery. They saw that they must soon or late make up their minds either to submit to have the country henceforth governed in the interests of freedom, or to secede, and become a separate and independent power, as we have already said more than once. They saw that by no union among themselves and combination with the northern Democracy, could they render it possible for them, not to retain their slaves, indeed, but to govern permanently the country in the interests of slavery. Therefore they early prepared for secession, and at the first favorable moment which they had, and which they had labored to bring about, they seceded. Now, would the return of the Democratic party to power in the free states offer them any inducement to return to the Union? Can the northern Democrats even in power give them any surer guaranties than they had before secession, that the Union shall be governed in the slave interest?

This is the point our Democratic leaders overlook, or at least do not publicly discuss. The people of the free states have not yet fully made up their minds to abolish slavery, but the great majority of them have made up their minds that this Union shall be restored and maintained, and that its government shall not be controlled by the slave power. Suppose, then, the Democrats should come into power; suppose they should give the most explicit constitutional guaranties that slavery shall have free access to the territories, and never be disturbed in any of the states; what guaranty can they give that the very fact of their doing so will not hurl them from power, or that the people of the free states will stand, or can be made to stand, by those guaranties?   The present Republican party may be suppressed to-day, but what is to prevent a still more formidable and a still more decidedly anti-slavery party from rising to power to-morrow, a party that, constitutionally or unconstitutionally, will sweep away those paper or parchment guaranties, and stop not with warring against slavery as a political power, but even attack it as a social or domestic institution, and utterly extinguish it?   It is against the uprising and onward progress of such a party that the South would ask a guaranty, and a guaranty against such a party the northern Democrats, as the history of the past proves, cannot give.   The South know it; and therefore their leaders will not listen to them, or renew their alliance with them, any further than they can use them in gaining independence. Every step since 1844 taken by either northern or southern Democrats to strengthen and confirm the political power of slavery, has been a step in its downfall.   The annexation of Texas, the Mexican war, the repeal of the Missouri compromise, the passage of the Kansas-Nebraska bill, the exertion of the whole power of Mr. Buchanan's administration to secure Kansas to the slaveholding interest, have all failed, and served only to provoke and consolidate a stronger and more formidable opposition to slavery as an element in American politics; and the South know perfectly well that any attempts of the Democratic party to give new and stronger guaranties to slavery would serve only to prostrate that party, and to hasten the destruction of slavery itself.

The southern politicians never regarded the Republican party as directly or intentionally an abolition party; they did full credit to the constitutional scruples and declarations of its leaders; but they knew that it was a party organized against the political power of slavery, and that it did intend to restrain that power by preventing its expansion into new territory.   This was enough.   To attack the political power of slavery was, in their view, to attack slavery itself, for slavery, they hold, and truly hold, cannot exist if it cannot govern the government, since government is its only basis and protection.   It must be omnipotent, or not be at all. The southern politicians had no fear that the Republicans would violate any of their constitutional rights, or attempt to carry out any thing like an emancipation policy, and yet in the Republican triumph they read the death-warrant of slavery in the Union. In the Republican party there were men, prominent men, in large numbers, who had no real anti-slavery principles, and merely made use of the anti-slavery sentiment as a means of getting into power or place—what the *New York Herald*, calls "Conservative Republicans," ready, if once in power, to make the most liberal concessions to the slave interest, in order to enlist it on their side, and keep their places. But the South understood very well that these "conservatives" were not the real Republicans, the real representatives of their party, that they were not animated by its spirit, and had none of its living earnestness, firm resolve, and indomitable courage. They might for a time clog its movements, and defeat its aims, but they must ultimately be sloughed off, or absorbed by the so-called radicals. Every party that is not simply a faction, has an idea, which is the source of all its vitality and vigor, and ultimately those who are the true exponents of that idea get uppermost, and determine the policy of the party. The idea of the Republican party is not abolition, but that of government administered in the interest of free labor, in opposition to the interest of slave labor. It is an idea, however, not perfectly realizable without the total extinction of slavery itself, and therefore it lay in the nature of the case, that, if obstinately resisted, the Republican party might, in process of time and the course of events, become an emancipation party. The South saw this from the first, and understanding well that the inauguration of a Republican president would be the inauguration of a possible anti-slavery policy, they seceded and set up for themselves; for they foresaw that no moderation of the Republican leaders, no concessions which they might make, or constitutional guaranties that they might offer, could give them more than a momentary and deceptive security for their political ascendency, or for slavery itself, if it undertook to render itself politically significant.

Leading Republicans in the outset thought that separation could be averted by compromise, and some were in favor of making the most liberal concessions to slavery, and giving it the most ample constitutional guaranties; but all to no purpose. The South neither demanded them, nor would accept them. The southern leaders told them plainly, frankly, and sincerely, that secession was irrevocable, that they would accept no compromise, that were they to receive a *carte blanche* and allowed to dictate their own terms, they would not come back into the Union, or be politically connected with the free states. There was and is no reason for doubting their sincerity. They were keener sighted than the Republican leaders, if these expected them to accept of any possible compromise. The matter had gone too far for compromise, and there was in southern eyes, looming up behind the more conservative Republican leaders, a great party who would hold themselves bound by no compromises entered into by their chiefs against their avowed principles and aims. The administration has finally seen, if it did not see in the outset, that the southern politicians understood themselves; and the conservative Republicans have not been able, even with the aid of their Democratic allies, to compel their party to adopt a policy favorable to the slave power. The administration and even the republican members of congress, intended in the beginning to carry on the war for the suppression of the rebellion with the most scrupulous respect for the institution of slavery in the states where it existed, and the secretary of state took the pains to announce officially to foreign powers that the question of slavery would not be involved in the conflict. We all know the extreme reluctance with which the president could be induced to adopt even a partial emancipation policy. Yet ideas are stronger than parties, and events more powerful than individuals. The defeat of the government forces at the first battle of Bull Run, the suppression of the Union party in the South by unheard of tyranny and cruelty, the delay of General McClellan, from October, 1861, to March, 1862, to advance on the rebels, in force far inferior to his own, and the very general discontent with what seemed to be the hesitation, the lack of earnestness, and uncalled-for deference to the timid counsels of the border slave-state Union men, on the part of the government, finally produced an effect on the administration and partially convinced it, perhaps wholly convinced it, that its only chance of success was in adopting an anti-slavery policy, and making emancipation an instrument in the restoration of the Union, on a secure and permanent basis. The so-called radicals have gained the ascendency, and the administration will not attempt to recede from emancipation. All parties now know it, and hence the terrible outcry of the Democratic party against the alleged radical members of the cabinet, and the radical members of congress, for in the anti-slavery policy of the government they read their own annihilation as a party.

The radical members of a party are always sure, in the long run, to gain the ascendency, and, if our Democratic leaders did but understand it, the radical Republicans, under that or some other name, will be, except perhaps for brief intervals, the dominant party in the free states, till the question of slavery is finally disposed of. The South see this, and know that, whatever may be said or honestly meant by the Democratic leaders, they can have no security for the permanent ascendency of the slave power, except in secession and national independence. Hence the southern politicians will not consent to reunion or reconstruction with Democrats in power any sooner than with radical Republicans. Of the two classes they have more respect for and more confidence in the radical Republicans, who know what they mean and say it, than they have in pro-slavery Democrats, who are pro-slavery for the sake of power or place, but, as they have proved on more than one occasion, can be anti-slavery men and form a coalition with free-soilers and abolitionists, to get or retain place or power. It was a coalition of Democrats and free-soilers that broke down the respectable old Whig party in Massachusetts, and elected, for his first term, Charles Sumner, a leading anti-slavery man, to the senate of the United States, and the most prominent of the pro-slavery leaders now in New York, including even Horatio Seymour, were free-soilers in 1848. The southern leaders know that they cannot rely on the northern Democrats, because the northern Democrats can never, as pro-slavery Democrats, be sure of controlling the politics of the free states, or any one of them, and will themselves turn anti-slavery men in their own states, whenever they find it for their political interest to do so. No matter then what party is in power, the seceded states will never come back into the Union or acknowledge the authority of the federal government, till they are compelled to do so by military force, or until they have made up their minds to abolish slavery, and adopt the free-labor system. This may be regarded as indubitable. There is no alternative for the government, but either to subdue them by force or accept disunion, and recognize southern nationality and independence.

That our northern Democratic leaders aided or connived at secession, in the expectation that when it had served a given purpose, it would terminate, and reunion follow, we have no doubt; for we can conceive no motive that they could have had for the permanent dissolution of the Union. They understood, no doubt, that after secession had, if possible, prevented the inauguration of a Republican president, crushed out the Republican party, and restored the Democrats to power, the Union was to be restored on the confederate platform, and under the confederate president. When we discussed this subject in these pages two years ago, we assumed that such was the plan of the southern leaders themselves; but subsequent events and disclosures have proved that it was not, and that they only appeared to entertain it, in order to secure the aid of the northern Democrats in preventing any coercive measures being taken against them by Mr. Buchanan's administration, and, in case of coercion being attempted by the incoming Republican administration, in denouncing it as against the genius of our institutions, in dividing the non-seceding states, in rendering the war unpopular and unsuccessful, and in thus enabling them to consummate disunion, and to establish their independence. They simply played a diplomatic trick upon their northern friends and allies, and used them for a purpose of their own, as they had done any time for sixty years; and when they have no further use for them, they will dismiss them from their service, as an old horse turned out to die. The pretence that the South has a respect for Democrats and will be influenced by their wishes, is preposterous. Men sometimes use the treachery, but always despise the traitor; and traitors to their own section, to their own respective states, and to their own institutions, these pro-slavery Democrats are in the estimation of all southern men, who are firm defenders of state sovereignty. To these Democrats are applied the assurances of the Richmond papers, that "the southern people may consent, after independence, to traffic with them, but only by keeping on the windy side, and holding their noses when in their presence."

Notwithstanding all this, the Democratic leaders and the Democratic journals are continually dinging into the ears of the public, that the continuance of the war is all the fault of the radicals, and that if the Democrats were in power the Union would be restored, and the old flag float again over every square inch of our national territory. It is thus they deceive the poor people, if not themselves, and lead them to the commission of deeds of the blackest criminality, and the most barefaced treason. These poor Irish Catholics

who engaged in the New York riots, are, no doubt, much to
blame, but they are as innocent as angels, in comparison
with the Democratic leaders and journalists. We cannot in
conscience censure them with any great severity. They
were the dupes of men of higher social position and influence than themselves, and not on them alone or chiefly should
fall the merited punishment. They were made to believe
that union and peace could be obtained on honorable terms
without war, but for the wicked black-republicans, or base
and fanatical abolitionists, and they felt that they were only
resisting a piece of gross and superfluous tyranny in resisting
the draft, and securing themselves from being dragged away
from their homes and friends to sicken and die in camp, or
to be mangled, crippled, or slain outright on the battle-field,
for the miserable "nigger," who if freed would be sure to
come North and overstock the labor market, and deprive
them of their means of living. We beseech the public to
have some compassion on them, and reserve their indignation for the men who abused their confidence, who deceived
them by lies and false hopes, and stirred them up to madness. These poor people would have been loyal enough,
and ready enough to fight for the country, but for the influence of their disloyal and traitorous leaders. Hence it is,
we deny, and with justice, that their conduct impeaches in
the least the loyalty of Catholics as such. We deny it, not
on the ground that these poor people are out of the pale of
the church and not to be counted as Catholics, for Catholics
they are, and perhaps have no poorer chance of heaven than
many who occupy well-cushioned seats, in churches up-town,
or than those who disown brotherhood with them and leave
them uncared for, uninstructed, to grovel in ignorance, and
rot in filth, vice, crime, and sin. We own our brotherhood
with them, and deny the inferences drawn from their conduct against the loyalty of Catholics, for that conduct was
instigated not by the church, but by Democratic demagogues and partisans, who had contrived to win their confidence, in order to abuse it, for their own base and disloyal
purposes.

No doubt, among these demagogues and partisans, among
these Democratic leaders, there may be found some who
are Catholics, but none of the first rank and influence, none
who do more than follow the inspiration of men of still
higher standing and more power than themselves. The
Vallandighams, the Seymours, the Woods, the Brookses,

the editors of *The World, The News, The Express*, the *Journal of Commerce*, the *Cincinnati Enquirer*, the *Detroit Free Press*, the *Chicago Times*, are not Catholics, but stanch Protestants, and you cannot charge to Catholicity, that which is inspired and directed by non-Catholics, or done even in common with them. The most you can say is that these subordinate Catholic demagogues and partisans are disloyal in spite of their religion; not that they are so by virtue of it. If there were Catholics in the conspiracy to destroy the Union, or in the intended insurrection in this city designed to coöperate with Lee's invasion of Maryland and Pennsylvania, and to prevent the government from raising the troops necessary to put down the rebellion, nobody can say that either originated with them, or that the eminent Protestants who were in the plot, were their tools or dupes. In both cases the proof is ample that the chief conspirators were non-Catholics. Mallory, the confederate secretary of the navy, may be a Catholic, but Davis, Rhett, Toombs, Yancey, Mason, Slidell, Cobb, Wise, Hunter, Floyd, Thompson, Brown, Buchanan, Toucey, Benjamin, and others, the master spirits of the southern rebellion, the real authors of the conspiracy to take the slaveholding states out of the Union, are or were none of them Catholics; but all either Jews or followers of those renowned secessionists in the sixteenth century, called THE REFORMERS. The master spirits of the northern movement in aid of the southern rebellion are none of them Catholics, and some of them, as James and Erastus Brooks, and Fernando Wood, are or were Know-nothings. We do not excuse the Catholic demagogues and partisans, but they at best merely play second fiddle to others who would scorn to be reckoned as Catholics. The chief responsibility does not rest on them, and therefore does not rest on Catholics in any sense whatever; nor can either the southern rebellion or the northern intended insurrection, be charged with the least show of truth upon the Catholic Church, or be made a reproach to Catholicity.

We do not deny that the sympathies of a large portion of our clergy have been and perhaps still are with the Democratic party, and that the great majority of the Catholic people are, and for some years have been, Democrats; but no bishop or archbishop can be named, North or South, who proposed or defended secession, before it took place; and we are aware of no simple priest that did it, except the editor of the *Catholic Miscellany*, published at Charleston, South Carolina, and Rev. Mr. Perché, of New Orleans. In no case can it be said that our clergy were the prime movers, or among the prime movers, of the rebellion ; and the most that can be said against them before the rebellion broke out, is, perhaps, that they did not exert themselves as wisely and as energetically as they might have done or ought to have done to prevent it. They either remained silent, or followed the lead of the Democratic press, and denounced only the abolitionists and Republicans, as if all the blame was on the side of those who were endeavoring to defeat the southern unconstitutional efforts to extend, strengthen, and consolidate the slave power as the supreme governing power of the Union. Since the rebellion, not more than three or four, North or South, have openly declared in its favor; and we can name a much larger number who have been earnest in their support of the government in its efforts to suppress it by armed force. There are bishops even in the seceded states, who have never wavered in their fidelity to the Union, and we have heard of no bishop or priest, North or South, that has approved of the doings of the New York mob. Several we know, have publicly condemned not only the doings of the mob, but the mob itself ; condemned resistance to the draft, and told their people that it is the law, and that it is their duty to obey the laws, even if they dislike them.

Whatever sympathy the clergy of either order may have had with the Democratic party can be explained without charging them with either secession or pro-slavery tendencies. The clergy, in what does not come within the scope of their divine and ecclesiastical mission, are as much influenced by the laity as the laity are by them, and are acted on by the public opinion of their people as much as they act on it. In matters outside of their mission, and on which they can act only in their human capacity, they are as much under the influence of the Catholic people as Protestant ministers are under that of the Protestant people ; and in political and civil matters they have nothing of that absolute authority over their own people that non-Catholics ascribe to them. They have little control over Catholic demagogues and partisans, and are not seldom controlled and even used by them. It is said that the mob threatened to attack the house of our archbishop, because it was believed that he was in favor of the draft and had advised it. Whether this was

so or not, it is certain that he was frightened; and hence
the explanation of his cruel attack in the *Herald* on Horace
Greeley, when that gentleman was hunted for his life by
the mob, his denial that he had ever done more than suggest a "voluntary draft," his singular card "to the men
called by some of the papers rioters," and his very remarkable address to the crowd he collected together before his
house. His address shows that he felt his impotence to control his people except by diverting their wrath from the
draft to the English, the hated "Anglo-Saxons." In all not
catholic and divine the Catholic clergy respect the public
opinion of their own people, and can hardly be expected, as
a general thing, not to share it.   In this country their people, as to the dominant portion of them, are foreign-born,
and naturalized or simply domiciled amongst us. They
naturally and almost inevitably follow the opinions, the
sentiments, the interests, even the prejudices of this portion
of our population. These are their people, their nation,
their country. With these they do and must identify themselves. Hence, in their view the interests of Catholics and
of foreign-born settlers are in a measure identical, and they
feel that they must look after the interest of the foreign
settlers in order to promote that of Catholics. Consequently, the party the most liberal to foreign settlers, and
the most ready to bring them forward, is naturally the party
which will have their sympathy and support, whether it is
the party best for the country or not.   Their eyes will be
fixed not primarily on this country, but on theirs, the foreign-born, especially the Irish Catholic population, residing
in it. This may be a damage, but it is, for the present, un-
avoidable.

Now, nobody can deny that the Democratic party has,
as a general thing, been more liberal, at least in profession,
to foreign settlers than any of its rivals, and less illiberal to
Catholics. It has favored early naturalization, and it has
had less of that puritanic cant, rigidity, and fanaticism so
peculiarly offensive to Catholics. It has been less positively
Protestant in its political professions and action, and made
a wider separation between the politics and the religion of
its members, and enabled Catholics to act with it without
offence either to their national or religious susceptibilities,
at least in the free states, where are the great mass of the
foreign and Catholic population. Hence we can understand
why it has drawn to itself the great body of Catholics,

especially those of Irish origin, who are with us the ruling Catholic population. Catholics could not support the old Federal party, because it viewed foreigners with suspicion, and for the same reason, few, except natural-born citizens, could support the Whig party. They could not join the anti-slavery movement commenced many years ago, not because they were pro-slavery, but because that movement commenced in a puritanic spirit, and in its progress assumed a character that offended not only Catholic taste, but Catholic conviction and conscience. It was fanatical, and put forth doctrines and projected moral and social reforms which no Catholic could for a moment countenance.

Catholics opposed it, not because it was anti-slavery, but because it sought the abolition of slavery in a fanatical spirit, and in a mode that they did not and could not approve. They have been, like ourselves, at once anti-slavery and anti-abolitionist. The Republican party, again, has not been wholly free from the taint of socialism, fanaticism, and puritanism. Catholics have looked upon it as simply a continuation of the abolition party, only less frank and honest. Its most prominent leaders were *The New York Tribune*, Protestant ministers, and Evangelical laymen, in whose success they could see little hope for the negro, and only disadvantage to themselves. The *Tribune* had become notorious as a journal whose columns were open to Fourierism, socialism, communism, red-republicanism, free-loveism, and all the anti-religious, anti-moral, and anti-social *isms* that had in late years convulsed all Europe, and threatened the very existence of Christian society and Christian civilization. How could Catholics fraternize with a party whose chief organ was such a journal? Nor was the leadership of the New England ministers and the Evangelicals, who can never support a cause without seeking to destroy the good there may be in it, by prostituting it to their own narrow, anti-Catholic, and sectarian views and prejudices—any more attractive to Catholics. Add to this the formal declaration of the *New York Times*, one of the organs of the Evangelical or Know-nothing wing of the Republican party, that "as soon as they had put down the southern rebellion, they must turn round and put down the Catholics," and we can understand very easily the repugnance of Catholics to the Republican party. Moreover, the candidate supported by the Republican party for the presidency in 1856, had first been brought forward and nominated by the American or Know-nothing party, whose nomination he accepted, although, in fact, far enough from being a Know-nothing himself; and, indeed, the Republican party owed its successes to its union with the Know-nothing party. These things have not escaped the observation of our political Catholics, who have been able to carry almost the whole body of the clergy as well as laity against the Republican party.

Nevertheless, we do not urge these things, as a complete justification of the political course taken by our Catholic brethren, otherwise we should not ourselves be found sustaining the Republican administration, exposing ourselves on the one side to the fire of our Catholic brethren, and on the other to that of the Know-nothings. As a matter of fact, *The Tribune* has dropped most of its offensive *isms*, and the Puritan element, strong as it may be, lays aside its sectarianism, and welcomes patriotism wherever it finds it, whether in a Catholic or a Protestant. The statement of the *Times* by no means expresses the policy of the Republican party; and finally, the Know-nothings have drawn off from the Republicans, and are now an integral portion of the Democratic party itself. It was their defection from the Republican ranks that secured the triumph of the Democratic party in so many important state elections last year. The knights of the Golden Circle, a secret society so powerful in the middle and western states, and who are as anti-Catholic as men well can be, are not to be found in the Republican ranks. They are all good Democrats, opposed to the abolition of slavery, and in favor of secession or reconstruction. We have never had an administration so careful as the present to avoid every thing likely to wound the susceptibilities of Catholics or foreign-born citizens, or that has in the army or in civil life been more liberal to Catholics, or made less distinction between them and Protestants. Besides, Catholics who claim to be American citizens, should remember that they are not the country, that the country does not exist solely for their benefit, and that they are as much bound to labor, and, if need be, to make sacrifices for it, as are any other class of citizens. We, as citizens, are bound by our religion to serve our country according to our ability, without stopping to ask what special benefit we are to receive in return; and if, in this hour of the nation's trial, we are found faithful, vying with non-Catholics in self-sacrificing devotion to it, our future here is assured, and no party can ever have the power, even if the disposition, to molest us or deprive us of our equality as freemen and citizens.

Moreover, our Catholic leaders seem not to have reflected that, by associating the church with the Democratic party, and placing Catholics in opposition to the war for national life and integrity, they are adopting the very course best fitted to bring upon them the very fate they are so anxious to avert. Whether the Union be restored or not, the Democratic party can never again permanently control the destinies of the United States. If the Union is divided, and it be proved that Catholics have been, as a body, active on the side opposed to the government, and directly or indirectly aided its enemies, they will, as being mostly a foreign element in the country, and holding a religion opposed by the great majority of the people, be the first to feel the effects of national disappointment and mortification. The whole national and Evangelical, or non-Catholic sentiment of the country will be directed against them, to deprive their religion of its freedom, to take from them their rights as American citizens, and perhaps to expel them from the national territory. Non-Catholic Democrats will have as little disposition as ability to protect them, and, perhaps, as a means of recovering lost popularity, will be foremost in hurrying on the war against them. If the government succeeds in spite of all opposition, and Catholics have aided that opposition, the nation will still take measures against having, on any future occasion, so large and powerful a body in its midst to endanger its existence. The non-Catholic Democrats with whom they have associated will be let off, and they will be made the scapegoat of the nation's sins ; for we must remember that the nation is non-Catholic, and likes not our religion, and is ready at any time to abridge our freedom, if it can get only a fair, or even a plausible pretext for doing so. In fact, we should deserve severe chastisement if we really proved ourselves disloyal; for though the nation has no sympathy with our religion, it has given thus far full freedom and protection to our Catholic conscience. We have had all the rights of American citizenship ; we have lived under the protection of just and equal laws. Annoyances we may, now and then, have had, but persecution none, and our religion has had freer scope here than in even the so-called Catholic countries of Europe. We should prove ourselves the most unprincipled and ungrateful of men if, when we saw the nation in trial, her very life threatened by a most formidable rebellion, we refused to rush to her assistance, remained indifferent, took sides with the rebels and their sympathizers, or thought only of our own special interests as a foreign colony. We should merit the fate Louis XIV. inflicted on his Huguenot subjects, when he deprived them of the rights secured to them by the edict of Nantes, dragooned them into a profession of the Catholic religion, or expelled them from French territory.

Yet we have not thus far merited that fate. We may have been unwise, imprudent, and suffered our tastes and prejudices to carry us much too far; but we have not generally intended to be disloyal, as is evinced by the large numbers of Catholics who, both as officers and men, have entered the army under the different calls of the government for volunteers to put down the rebellion. Several of the early regiments raised were composed exclusively, or very nearly exclusively of Catholics; in many Catholics are the majority; and in few are there not some Catholics to be found. Under the earlier calls, the number of Catholics who responded was more than the Catholic quota. Whatever the motives that have operated with these Catholic volunteers, it cannot be pretended that they were opposed to the Union, or unwilling to fight for its maintenance; and no troops have fought more bravely, endured more hardship, performed more arduous service, or suffered more severely from the casualties of war, and the nation owes them, as well as those not Catholics, a debt of gratitude which, for her honor we hope, she will be slow to forget, and never unwilling to pay. However strongly in this city, where they are nearer being disloyal than anywhere else, except in the border slave states, they have sympathized with the Democratic party, it will always be true that Catholics, both Irish and German, though not born in the country, have in large numbers merited the honor of being ranked as true American patriots, and have put to shame many native-born Americans, who would be indignant were their patriotism or devotion to the cause of the Union in the slightest degree questioned.

It is but simple justice to observe, that even our Democratic Catholics do not regard the present struggle as one of life and death to the nation. They look upon it very much in the light of an ordinary struggle between two political parties, each striving for power and place, and in which a citizen may take either side without any impeachment of his loyalty. They have generally believed that the rebellion cannot be put down and the secessionists reduced to submission by military force, and perhaps they have felt that no great harm would result even from the division of the country into two separate and independent nations. They would prefer the Union should remain undivided, but, if the slaveholding states no longer wish to be united in the same political community with the free states, why not let them go, and go in peace? A forced union is no real union at all, and can be only temporarily maintained. The rebels are ready to let us alone, if we will let them alone. Let us then have peace, and no more useless waste of treasure and uncalled-for effusion of blood. So, we apprehend, the majority of them have looked upon the struggle, and so have most foreigners and foreign governments looked upon it. Not having the feelings and associations of our old American-born population, whose fathers shed their blood to gain us a country and to make us a nation, and reasoning more as foreign residents than as American citizens, they see no vital principle at stake, and think that if we should take a little ghostly advice from the *Catholic Mirror*, the *Metropolitan Record*, and the *Freeman's Journal*, restore the Democrats to power, and allow them to make peace, either by reconstruction on a basis acceptable to the rebels, or by a peaceable division of the Union, all would be well. To them it is much the same whether they live under the stars and bars or under the stars and stripes, since they were born under neither.

It has been with some such view of the case, we suppose, that there has been solicited and obtained a letter from the Holy Father, just published in the papers, though dated last October, to the archbishop of New York, calling upon him and his associate bishops to do all in their power to dispose the American government and people to make peace, and to put an end to the further effusion of blood. This would be very proper, if there were no principle, no right involved, and the belligerents could adjust their difficulties without the absolute surrender of either to the other. But the war in which we are engaged, unhappily, is not one that admits of such adjustment. It is a war between the nation and its rebellious subjects. The rebels demand not a redress of grievances, real or pretended, that might be granted, nor even a change in the form and constitution of the government, which might be conceded, without loss of national unity and continuity; but a division of the country, and the erection of over one third of the population and more than one half of the territory of the Union into a separate and independent nation. Between conceding this and the submission of the rebels there is no middle course practicable or conceivable. Peace, then, either means a continuance of the war till the rebels are forced to submit, or it means disunion, national dismemberment, and the recognition of the confederacy as an independent nation. Such is the very nature of the question; and, therefore, as the government cannot, without surrendering its inherent rights, and sacrificing the unity, dignity, and sovereignty of the nation, concede division, and the erection out of its population and territory of a separate and independent state, it has refused, very justly, all offers of foreign mediation. There is nothing to mediate, for there is no medium between recognizing the separate nationality and independence of the so-called Confederate States and denying it, and doing our best to reduce the rebels to submission to their legitimate national sovereign.

We revere the paternal care of his Holiness for our country; but we must be permitted to say that he cannot require the nation to surrender its rights and dignity, and voluntarily, even for the sake of peace, consent to dismemberment. We have not learned that he has himself as yet consented to the secession of his Æmilian provinces, made peace with Victor Emanuel, and recognized the kingdom of Italy. His Holiness must be well aware that we are doing only what his own government attempted, when it raised the Irish legion and collected all the military forces it could, and placed them under the command of the brave and accomplished General Lamoricière. His government would have recovered his seceded states and brought them back under his temporal authority, if it had been able, and we presume would do it to-morrow if it had the requisite military force. The popes have, in times past, waged more than one war against their rebellious subjects or vassals, for the recovery or maintenance of the integrity of the Roman state. When the Holy Father was asked, for the peace of Italy and the interests of religion, to resign his temporal rights, with ample indemnification for their loss, he answered, *Non possumus.* He said he could not do it without violating his oath and betraying the trust he had received from God, through the church; he surely then cannot complain of our government if, when asked to consent to national dismemberment, it answers, *"Non possumus;* we cannot do it without violating our oath, and betraying the trust we have received from God, through the nation." The bishops from all parts of the world, assembled at Rome last year, in an address to the pope, warmly applauded his conduct; and how can our American bishops disapprove a parallel conduct in the case of our government, since, in both cases, the question concerns the temporal sovereignty alone?

Our filial reverence for the chief of our religion, and our high-toned views of the papal power, which we have never hesitated to assert and defend, and which are well known to our readers, do not permit us to regard with indifference such a letter as this, which is ascribed to his Holiness, if assured of its authenticity. We cannot treat as of no importance the pope's recommendation to peace, for the mission of peace is peculiarly his as the vicar of Jesus Christ on earth. But we are certain that the letter published as his in the newspapers either has been forged in his name, or has been solicited and obtained on a gross misrepresentation of the actual state of American affairs. It is no Catholic doctrine that the magistrate bears not the sword, or that a sovereign nation has not the right to defend itself, to maintain its unity and the integrity of its territory, so far as able, against any and every foe, foreign or domestic. The only ground on which his Holiness could urge our government to put an end to the war before gaining its legitimate ends, is, that those ends are not attainable, that it cannot suppress the rebellion and restore the Union, and, therefore, that the further prosecution of the war is unlawful, a criminal effusion of blood, and consequently a war which God and humanity forbid—one of those wars which justify the armed intervention of civilized nations to bring them to a close, if they cannot otherwise put an end to them. But this involves a question of fact as well as a question of law, and one of those questions of fact in regard to which all the world admit the pope may be misinformed as well as anybody else, since it is not a divinely revealed fact, or even what is called a "dogmatic fact." Nothing warrants the assumption of the letter that our civil war is a war carried on by our government from mere pride, obstinacy, or revenge, without any reasonable hope of success; nothing warranted it last October, the date of the letter, to any one who knew the real facts in the case; and far less was there any thing to warrant it when the letter was first published, after the splendid and important, if not decisive, victories recently won by the federal arms. The federal army, considering the difficulties it has had to contend with, has accomplished more in two years and a half than was ever accomplished, in the same space of time, by any of the armies of modern Europe, or the world; and we never, for ourselves, expected the war to be a short war; we never expected it to end short of seven years, and, if necessary, the United States can carry it on, with a fair prospect of success, for a much longer period. We cannot concede, then, that our war is hopeless, and one of those wars which may not be prosecuted by our government without crime against humanity, or sin against God.

The war, it is true, is, on the part of the rebels, even supposing what cannot for a moment be conceded, that their cause is just, instead of being as it is void of all right and wholly indefensible, a hopeless war, and therefore a crime against humanity and a sin against God; and it is not the federal government and loyal people of the United States that the pope and American bishops should exert themselves to dispose to peace, but the confederate government and the rebellious population of the seceded states. They are the party carrying on a hopeless war; a war that nothing, without foreign intervention in their favor, which were a gross indignity and wrong to us, or traitorous sympathy and aid from northern Democrats, can possibly render successful. It is singular that in this war all the appeals at home and abroad for peace should be addressed to the federal government and loyal people of the Union, and that nobody should appear to be aware that the rebels can have peace any day they wish, by simply laying down their arms, dissolving their illegal confederate government, returning to their allegiance, and giving reasonable security for their future good behavior, that is, by doing what is only their simple duty! That there ever was war was their crime, and that the war continues is solely their fault. The government and loyal people do not want war; they never wanted war, and will not continue it one moment after the rebels have thrown down their arms and disbanded their armies. There never was any need of his Holiness or the American bishops to labor to dispose the government and loyal people to peace, for they are and have been so disposed from the first; and the quickest and surest way of getting peace is for our bishops and priests, backed by the earnest wishes of the Holy Father, to use all their influence to prevent divisions at the North, and to persuade their own people to give their united and hearty support to the government. It is not the government nor the loyal people that prolong the war, but the opposition they meet with from the Democratic party, with which the great body of our Catholic people are associated. Detach from the Democratic *peace* party its Catholic supporters, and it would be too weak seriously to embarrass the government, for there is not a state that has not seceded, in which, without the Catholic vote, it would not be in a hopeless minority. Strengthen the loyal party by the cordial and united support of the Catholic population, and the government could speedily bring the rebels to terms, and put a just and honorable end to this frightful civil war.

But the letter ascribed to his Holiness is calculated, as far as it has any effect, though of course, if authentic, not so intended by the Holy Father, to encourage the copperhead peace party, and to array Catholics against the war; that is, practically against the nation. It is true, the letter says another of similar import has been written to the archbishop of New Orleans; but that amounts to nothing, for the Catholic population is nearly all in the loyal states, and there are not Catholics enough in the seceded states to have any appreciable influence for peace or war on either the rebel government or the rebel people. There are not over a hundred thousand Catholics all told in the seceded states, and a considerable portion of them are Gallicans of the lowest type, and would pay very little respect to a papal letter admonishing them to make peace, or to submit to the national authority. The letter can have any appreciable influence only in the loyal states, where there are probably two and a half millions or three millions of Catholics, and its only influence on them must be to withdraw them from the support of the government, and place them in opposition to the Union. The well-meant mediation of his Holiness, like all meditation in the case, as far as practically efficacious, is all on one side, against legitimate authority and in favor of rebellion and revolution, and, if successful, would secure the dismemberment of the Union and southern independence; for peace, without the submission of the rebels, means that, nothing more, nothing less. His Holiness, then, either could not have authorized the letter, or else he has been imposed upon, and wholly deceived as to the real state of our affairs, and as to the practical effect of his intervention. It could at best only tend to unite the Catholics in the loyal states with the copperheads against the government to which they owe allegiance.

But we are told that " the North can never conquer the South." We concede it ; but that the government cannot conquer the rebels, and reëstablish the national authority over the whole territory of the Union, we do not concede. The war is not a war between the North and the South, and should never be spoken of as such ; but a war of the nation, under its legitimate authority, to reduce its rebellious subjects in arms against it to their obedience, and this it can and will do in spite of foreign mediation or foreign intervention—in spite of rebel sympathizers, aiders, and abettors in the states that have not revolted, and in spite of good, well-meaning, but weak and timid men, who are always afraid of a battle, and cry out for peace. The republic is not yet dead, nor yet in its agony. But its life will not be saved, and it restored to health and soundness, without the patriotic devotion of the people, and their readiness to make any and every sacrifice for their country. The war which the nation is waging is not a war of ambition, of conquest, or of national aggrandizement. It has no aggressive character, no oppressive feature. It is purely a war of self-defence, for the defence and maintenance of the nation itself in its inherent rights and legitimate authority. It is not a war the benefit of which is to inure to this generation only, but to all coming generations. It is not a war for party, but for country, and we, as American citizens, have no right to desist from it, to oppose it, or refuse to aid its prosecution, because it imposes upon us great and painful sacrifices. Men who will not, at the call of their country, give up all personal interest, and even life itself, are no true patriots, and are unworthy to be counted citizens. Men who will do no more for the country than they can personally secure from it in return, fail to comprehend and appreciate their civil duties. No meaner wretch breathes than he, who, when his country is in danger, asks : " What am I to gain by defending her ? " Never is there any thing great or good won without sacrifice, and he who lacks the power of sacrifice is no true man. Patriotism is love of country, and all love is sacrifice. The true lover sacrifices all he has, and gives even himself to the beloved. A generation that asks only what it is to gain for itself by defending its country, is a mean and contemptible generation, and not fit to be counted among the generations of men. It denies the continuity and solidarity of the human race, and practically denies both God and man. The present generation had predecessors and will have successors. It has inherited a rich and noble patrimony, won by the toils, and labors, and sufferings, and blood of our fathers, and held IN TRUST, to be transmitted unimpaired and even augmented to its successor. Woe to us if we waste it in riotous living, on our own pleasures and selfish indulgence, and leave nothing to our children but our debts and the shame of our prodigality! Country is lost when the people expect the nation to live and thrive without love, sacrifice, heroism. We must think not simply of what we are to gain by defending our country, but of what we owe it and are able to do for it. We must not isolate ourselves from the future, as if the race were to end with us, but identify ourselves with all the generations to come, feel that we survive in them, are one with them, and serve ourselves in serving them. We live in the life of our country, and no sacrifices are too precious or too costly to make for her preservation, her honor, or her glory. Hitherto we have only been recipients of the benefits of the government; it has done all for us, we nothing for it. Now is the time to repay the benefits we have received, and to prove that we know how to appreciate them. Now is the time to be grateful, generous, disinterested, self-sacrificing, heroic and thus save the patrimony received from our fathers, and transmit it unimpaired and augmented to our children.

The secessionists, their Democratic and pro-slavery sympathizers, and our kind-hearted northern peace men, we should bear in mind, are only playing the game of the European cæsarists, aristocrats, and conservatives, intended to deprive the republic of its rank as a great power, and to destroy its republican prestige and influence. This republic is offensive to them, because it lends a formidable moral support, to the European liberals, and may one day lend a material support which will render every European throne insecure, and every despotic government impracticable. It is necessary then, to check its growth, break up the Union, throw American society into chaos, render republicanism odious, and compel the American people either to come under the protection of the European powers, as has been the case with the Ottoman empire, or to seek the reëstablishment of order through the institution of monarchy or a military despotism. To this end the European cæsarists and conservatives find the preservation of slavery necessary—necessary as being in itself a great drawback upon the influence of the great republic in favor of popular freedom, and as furnishing an instrument for dividing and breaking up the republic itself. The existence of a strong anti-slavery party at the North, and of a strong pro-slavery party at the South they desire, as favorable to disunion; but the abolition of slavery, with all the states united, is the thing of all others to be warred against. Secession was concocted chiefly with France and England, who pledged it their moral support, and all the material aid they could give it without coming to an open rupture with the United States. Faithfully, so far, have both France and England redeemed their pledge. England has given it all her moral influence, supplied it with arms and munitions of war, built, armed, and manned a navy for it, with which to prey on our commerce, and secure it success. France has aided it by all her moral power, by proffers of mediation, which, if accepted, could operate only to secure its success, making indirect war upon us by invading Mexico, and setting up a monarchy on the ruins of its republican institutions. Secession chiefs, whether they know it or not, are only the tools of France and England, used by them to discredit or destroy republicanism, to deprive the New World of all power to influence through European liberals the politics of the Old.

Now we beg our Catholic readers to note that the Catholics of nearly all Europe give their sympathies to the two western European powers in their real if not avowed war on our republic and the popular freedom it represents. They favor the confederacy, wish it success, and set up a yell of exultation at every disaster that befalls the federal arms. The only notable exception is the small band of liberal Catholics whose organ is *Le Correspondant*, and whose leaders are the bishop of Orleans, the Count de Montalembert, the Count de Falloux, Augustin Cochin, and a few others, who remain faithful to the *parti-catholique*, that from 1830 to 1850 rendered such important services to liberty and religion throughout the civilized world. In Ireland we may have a few Catholic friends, in England we have none; in the rest of Europe none, except the supporters of the new kingdom of Italy. Nowhere has our republic more bitter enemies, and nowhere is there a stronger desire to see its power and influence destroyed, than among European Catholics, who seem to have resolved, since the terrible fright they got in 1848 from the Mazzinians in Italy, and the red-republicans in France, on linking the Catholic cause throughout the world with that of cæsarism. It is easy to explain this inveterate hostility to our republic and to republicanism, or that form of republicanism known as *democracy*, without charging our religion with hostility to freedom ; but it is not easy for us American Catholics, the majority and dominant portion of whom are of European birth or education, from being influenced and carried away by our European brethren, or from being drawn, unconsciously and unintentionally, into the conspiracy against American union, freedom, and greatness, which they unquestionably support.   Here is the danger against which we warn our brethren, and have not ceased to warn them at any time since 1852, when the reaction against revolutionism had reestablished, with the approbation and joy of the French bishops, the Napoleonic empire in France, and when the European conspiracy against our republic was formed.   Unconsciously and involuntarily no small portion of our American Catholic population have been drawn into the support of its plans, and even the Holy Father himself, if the letter ascribed to him is authentic, has been induced to lend the conspiracy his powerful aid.   The letter in itself, taken without reference to the use intended to be made of it by those who solicited it, is precisely what we should expect from the goodness of heart and paternal affection of Pius IX., and is only a proper manifestation of his solicitude as the father of Christendom, and the spiritual guardian of the rights and duties of both sovereigns and subjects.   He had and could have no thought of doing or saying any thing prejudicial to this great republic, where the church has enjoyed perfect freedom and protection, and where he himself has been more truly pope than in any other country on earth.   There has been the most perfect freedom of communication between the head and the members, and no civil proclamation, *placet*, or permission has been demanded or thought of. The civil government has in no manner interfered with ecclesiastical affairs, and has left them entirely to the management of the ecclesiastical authorities.   It has never interfered in the selection, recommendation, nomination, or appointment of pastors, and has neither had nor claimed any right to be consulted. The pope could have no hostility as pope to our republic. But the enemies of the republic may have had a purpose in soliciting and publishing his letter, which he did not suspect. They abused his kindness of heart, and obtained a document perfectly fair and just, and generous and noble, in his intention and on its face, which they could use to aid them in their purpose of breaking up the Union, perpetuating slavery, and checking the spread of popular freedom.

Our Catholic readers will now see why we attach so much importance to a letter which seems only a priestly exhortation to peace, and why we take so much pains to warn them against allowing themselves to become associated with the peace Democrats. These peace Democrats are the dupes of the secessionists, as the secessionists themselves are the dupes of England and France, and used by wily European statesmen to destroy the greatness, the power, the influence, and the glory, if not the independence of their own country, for the purpose of giving security to European aristocrats and absolutists. American Catholics, whether foreigners or natives by birth, either as Catholics or as citizens, cannot prudently or safely go with them. We are free here in the general freedom of the citizen ; and when we lose our freedom as citizens, we lose our freedom as Catholics, for the nation is not Catholic, but anti-Catholic. Throughout the world the interests of Catholicity are inseparably united to those of popular freedom, and popular freedom is now represented by the government and loyal people of the United States, and is warred against alike by southern secessionist, and European despot. Our government may have committed blunders, and the loyal people may have, as we believe they have, pushed their republicanism too far, and given it a too democratic development, but with all their faults, they are the representative, and the only acknowledged representative, of the liberal and popular tendencies of the age. The ruin of the American republic would be the most serious calamity that could befall the Catholic Church, not only here, but throughout the world, for henceforth her freedom must be secured not by assertions of her supremacy as a corporation, nor by concordats or treaties between her and secular governments, but in the freedom of the citizen ; and the loss of civil freedom by the citizen involves her enslavement to the civil power. Catholics, therefore, in warring against our republic, and laboring to extinguish republican liberty, are really warring against the interests alike of their church and of humanity. One is practically a traitor to the church in taking sides with the rebellion, no less than to his country.

We need not repeat what we have already said of the dangers to which we, as Catholics, expose ourselves here in this country by joining with the formidable conspiracy against liberty and the rights of humanity, or by refusing to give our hearty and energetic support to the government in its efforts to defeat it. If we do so, we shall be deprived of our citizenship, and our church will suffer gravely from our disloyalty, or lack of loyalty. We are already suspected of being governed more by the opinions, character and example of our brethren abroad than by our sense of duty to our own country ; and we may easily imagine the indignation and wrath with which we should be visited, if the proofs that we really are so were furnished and shown to be conclusive against us. The war we are waging reaches far, and involves far greater consequences than the generality of the people imagine. The slavery question is not confined to the simple question whether the four millions of persons and their posterity, now claimed as slaves in this country, are to be free or to remain bondmen, but involves the whole question of liberty or despotism for the world. The question whether civilization is to advance, or is to be arrested for an indefinite number of ages, turns now for its decision on the question, whether these persons are to be set free or to be held in bondage. The cause of humanity and of the church is to-day on the side of these poor, despised, degraded, and unhappy four millions of negro slaves ; and we decide against both, if we decide against emancipation. Oh, stupid and blind, how is it that we discern not the signs of the times ? Sneer not at the "nigger," for to-day it is in him we must find our Lord, and in serving him that we are to serve the church of God. "Inasmuch as ye did it unto the least of these my brethren, ye did it unto me."

The kings, kaisers, aristocrats and oppressors conspire together against the righteous cause ; but he that sitteth in the heavens shall laugh at them, and shatter them in pieces as a potter's vessel. The conspiracy will not succeed. This nation will not be destroyed, nor its mission in modern civilization be revoked. No matter how weak, short-sighted, or incapable may be the persons to whom are committed the reins of power, they are working with a strength greater than their own, are doing more than they know, and going further than they see. With them God will confound the wise, bring down the mighty, and take the wicked in their own craftiness. The nation had sinned and deserved to be chastised; it had become foul, and needed to be purified; but it will not fail. Not the strength, skill, or bravery of the rebels, aided by foreign mediation or intervention, or by divisions in the loyal states, peace parties and New York mobs or insurrections, traitorous governors, traitorous members of congress, and common councils, will prevent it from winning the victory, and continuing its majestic march in harmony with the noble and irrepressible instincts of humanity, in securing freedom and equal rights for all of the human race. God has given it this mission, however unworthy it may be of it, and will not suffer it to fail. As a people, we shall prove equal to the sacrifices demanded of us.

Yet let us not suppose the battle is fought and the victory won. There are, no doubt, reverses still in store for us, and our fortitude may be tried as it has not yet been tried, and the hearts of many may grow faint and fail them. It is altogether too soon to talk of peace, and to discuss its conditions. Our brave and true hearted soldiers have yet many a weary march before them, and more blood to shed to enrich and consecrate American soil, before each state becomes hallowed ground; but the reverses will be borne up against, the marches will be made, the blood will be willingly poured out, and victory crown in peace her heroes with fresh and fadeless laurels. France may mediate, and England, while pretending to be neutral, may exert all her power to give success to the arms of the traitors and oppressors; but in vain. We dare defend our cause with all the world in arms against us, for we defend rightful authority, the rights, dignity, and independence of nations, the freedom and interests of religion, the deliverance of the oppressed, and the rights and honor of our common manhood, and fail we cannot. It were impious to think it.

RETURN OF THE REBELLIOUS STATES.

[From Brownson's Quarterly Review for October, 1863.]

ALTHOUGH the military suppression of the rebellion is as yet far from being effected, the politicians of all parties are already busy discussing the mode and conditions of the return of the seceded states to the Union. The question raised, though premature, is one of great importance, and much of the future strength and glory of the republic depends on the solution the government shall finally adopt. It is a question that will severely tax American statesmanship,—far more severely than the military suppression of the rebellion has taxed American generalship ; since it is always easier to win victories than it is to secure their fruits. It is, also, a question in regard to which there is much confusion of thought in the public mind, and broad differences of opinion even among men equally loyal and equally determined to maintain at all hazards the life of the nation and the integrity of its territory ; and every one who has thought at all on the subject, is called upon, since the question has been raised, and is widely discussed, to contribute his share to the formation of a wise and just public opinion in regard to it.

There are publicists among us, affecting to sustain the government, but really in sympathy with the rebels, and more intent on preserving slavery than on saving the nation—who call upon the government to be generous and magnanimous, and tell it that since its recent important victories it is strong, and can afford to offer the rebels the most liberal terms of peace. Satan, when he would deceive honest and noble-minded men, always takes care to assume the guise of an angel of light, and to appeal to their generous and magnanimous sentiments. We have gained important victories, it is true, but the military power of the rebels, though weakened in a greater ratio than our own, is not yet destroyed, and we are not yet secure against serious, though, we trust, only temporary military reverses. The military suppression of the rebellion is yet a work of far more difficulty than these publicists pretend, and till that is completed the civil suppression can hardly be attempted. The

448

government cannot as yet afford to offer the rebels any advantage, or to relax in the least its military operations. The talk of peace is premature; and, besides, there are, strictly speaking, no terms of *peace*, liberal or otherwise, to be offered in the case. The war is between sovereign and subject, and there is no party to whom the government can offer peace, or with whom it can negotiate peace. Peace is made only between independent states, or between powers that have each the right of peace and war. The so-called confederacy, or any one of the seceded states, is no such power. Neither is competent to receive or to accept peace. For the government to offer either peace on any terms, would be to recognize it as an independent power, and to compromise the national dignity and the national sovereignty. The government makes peace with its rebellious subjects only after it has acknowledged their independence. There is no peace with rebels; the government may grant them, on condition of their laying down their arms and returning to their obedience, an *amnesty*, if it judges proper; but nothing more. To proffer terms of peace to them, is to abandon its claim of authority over them, and to condemn the war it wages against them. The proffer of any terms of peace to the rebels, would be a virtual recognition of all they have been contending for; and any union of them with us, or of us with them, that might follow, would be simply a league, or an alliance between independent states or nations.

No government that respects itself and is conscious of the power to sustain its own dignity and authority, can treat of peace with its own subjects, or offer terms to rebels with arms in their hands. They have no will or voice in the matter, and must submit to the disposition, if subdued, that it sees proper to make of them. No terms can be offered them till they have laid down their arms and sued for mercy. When they have ceased to be rebels, and have submitted to the government, the war is ended, and liberal terms of pardon may or may not be offered them, as the government sees proper, but not before. The government, if wise and just, will even then consult, not their feelings, their honor, or their interests, but the honor and interests of the nation. It owes them nothing; they have no right to plead against it, and whatever it grants them it grants as a favor, and they must take it as a grace. It has no right to be generous to them at the expense either of the nation or of the loyal population that have poured out their blood and treasure to subdue them. They gave up their rights, their faith, their honor, when they became rebels; betrayed their country, and took up arms to subvert its government, and they have no right to complain if compelled to drink, and to drink even to the dregs, the bitter cup of humiliation. It is a mawkish and mischievous sentimentality which no nation can tolerate and live that consults only the feelings and interests of traitors, rebels, and revolutionists, and would place them at the earliest practicable moment on a footing of equality with the loyal citizens who have stood by the country and saved it from destruction. The government may find it expedient, or even necessary, as a means of extinguishing the rebellion, to adopt a liberal policy towards the seceded states, and to permit them on very easy and liberal terms, to resume their former *status* in the Union; but, if so, it will be for its own sake, not for theirs. The question of policy in this case is distinct from the question of right; so let us have no appeals to the magnanimity or generosity of the government. Such appeals have cost us already two thousand millions of dollars, and half a million of lives, and clothed almost every family in the land with mourning. We have made sacrifices enough to gain the good will of the slaveholding states.

There are, unhappily, even among the earnest friends of the government, grave differences of opinion as to the proper mode of dealing with the rebellious states, when they shall have thrown down their arms, and submitted to the national authority. Some among us gravely maintain that the rebellious states are still states in the Union, standing on a footing of perfect equality with the other states that have remained loyal. Having never gone out of the Union, they must retain all their political rights under the constitution, and consequently whenever they choose to cease their hostility to the government, they have the right to elect representatives and senators in congress, who on taking the oath to support the constitution, are entitled to seats in like manner as others. As the confederate government is simply no government at all, and no state is bound to it or by it, any state may resume its *status* in the Union whenever it chooses by simply sending its representatives to the federal instead of the confederate congress. This doctrine has been officially promulgated by the secretary of state as that of the administration, and it is sustained by all the journals supposed to be in the especial confidence of the secretary, and to speak his sentiments. This doctrine treats the state as still a state in the Union, and the Union people to be found in it as the political people of the state, although only a pitiful minority, and without any state organization. Thus Virginia, the main stay at this moment of the rebellion, is represented in both houses of congress as a state in the Union. A handful of Union men, in no way competent to speak in behalf of their state, are allowed equal political power in the Union with Massachusetts or Illinois, while the whole force of their state is directed against it, and armed for its destruction.

Others, and without whom Mr. Lincoln's administration had never existed, or had long since ceased to exist, very emphatically deny this doctrine, and maintain that the rebellious states *are* rebellious states, that they have actually seceded from the Union, and fallen, in regard to the government, into the condition of population and territory belonging to the Union indeed, but not yet erected into states and admitted into the Union, and, therefore, population and territory without political rights or powers. Even supposing them to have ceased to war against the government, to have thrown down their arms, and submitted to the federal authority, they have as yet regained no political rights or powers, are no part of the political or sovereign people of the United States, and have no right of representation in either house of congress. The secession ordinance was suicidal, and by adopting it the state lapsed, ceased to exist as a state, and must be reorganized and admitted into the Union by an act of congress, before it can be entitled to any federal, or even any state representation. This is the view taken by Mr. Solicitor Whiting in his letter in the *New York Tribune;* it is the view which has uniformly been taken in the pages of this *Review,* and is the only honest and statesmanlike view that can be taken by any one who understands the constitution of the American state.

The administration may have been excusable in April, 1861, if not justifiable, in taking the ground that no state had seceded ; for the facts in the case were then but imperfectly known, and it might honestly believe that the secession ordinance was in no state the act of the state itself, but of a faction that had usurped its power, and professed, without authority, to act in its name. It might, also, have believed that the best way to put down the rebellion was to encourage the Union party in the seceding states, and wait for them to get the upper hand in the state elections, to repeal the secession ordinances, and resume their functions as states in the Union.   But it is now known that the policy of consulting the Union men in the seceded states, and seeking through their political success in their respective states to suppress the rebellion and restore the order it had interrupted, was a blunder, and all but fatal to the nation. There is and can be no doubt now that in every instance the secession ordinances were, in each state, the act of the state itself, as much so as any act ever is or can be, and, therefore, that all the states that passed secession ordinances have really seceded, and, though subject as population and territory to the Union, are no longer states in the Union. There is such a state as West Virginia, but Virginia, North Carolina, South Carolina, Georgia, Florida, Alabama, Mississippi, Louisiana, Texas Arkansas, and Tennessee, are not states in the Union, nor out of it, but simply geographical expressions.

To argue that the act of secession is illegal, therefore null and void, no act at all, is as ridiculous as to argue that since murder is illegal, nobody ever is or can be murdered.   Besides, it is not so certain as some suppose that simple secession *is* illegal, or that a state is not as competent to secede from the Union, if it chooses, as is a king or emperor to resign his crown, and abdicate his sovereign authority.   Secession, in itself, is neither rebellion nor revolution ; it is simply the abdication by the state of all its political rights and powers, the renunciation of all participation in the sovereign power of the Union, and the subjection of itself to the Union.   We know nothing in the written or unwritten constitution that forbids it to do this ; and we know no law whatever, except the law of good sense, that it violates.   A single glance at the constitution of the American state will make this evident.   Our republic is a federal republic, and the sovereign power is vested, neither in the states severally, nor in the federal government itself, but in the one political people of the United States.   This political or sovereign people, which is called the United States, exists, not as a consolidated mass, but in organized bodies, at first called colonies, and afterwards called states, united into one body politic called the Union.   To belong to this political people, it is necessary to be a citizen of a particular state, and of a particular state in the Union, or, that is one of the *United*

States. The people not in such a state, but in territories not yet erected into states and admitted into the Union, do not belong to the political or sovereign people, have no political rights, faculties, or franchises whatever, and are citizens of the United States only in that general sense in which all subjects of a national government, even women and children who do not vote, are, or are sometimes called, citizens. It is not compulsory on the people of a territory, say Dakota, Colorado, or New Mexico, to organize themselves into a state, and apply for admission into the Union. If they choose to remain outside of the Union, and be governed by it, instead of coming into it and governing in it, we know no power in the Union to prevent them. The ratification of the federal constitution by each of the original states, the condition on which the state participated in the sovereign power of the Union after the adoption of that constitution, was a free, voluntary act of the state itself. What a state is competent by its own voluntary act to do, it is competent to undo, in the absence of all express law to the contrary. Since, then, a state comes into the Union by its own free act, it must, if it chooses, be able by its own free act to go out of the Union. We have never seen this reasoning of the secessionists answered, nor do we believe it can be answered ; and if the slaveholding states had simply seceded from the Union, and there stopped, we should have had no occasion and no right to have used force against them, with a view of coercing them back into the Union. But they did not stop with secession simply, but they declared themselves not only out of the Union, but independent of it, set up a new government for themselves, and made war on the Union, that is, they added to secession, rebellion and revolution, and it is not as secessionists, but as rebels and revolutionists that we are fighting them. Moreover, we are fighting them not to force them back into the Union, but to compel them to submit to the authority of the Union.

The mistake of the secessionists was in supposing that in seceding from the Union the states became independent states. Precisely the reverse is the legal effect of secession. While in the Union, the people of the state are an integral portion of the political or sovereign people of the United States, and participate in the government of the country. By secession they cease to belong to that people, cease to participate in the government of the country, cease to have any political power or rights anywhere, and become completely dependent on the Union, and subject to be governed by it, as are the so-called territories. Secession is undoubtedly a great folly, and no state would be guilty of it, if it did not mean it as a stepping-stone to rebellion and revolution. The people of the seceding states by seceding abdicated their sovereignty, ceased to be a political people at all, and fell into precisely the condition we have described, and in that condition they remain when the rebellion and revolution are suppressed. They do not then, as a matter of course, resume their former *status* or their former political rights and powers in the Union, and they have not, and cannot have, any right of representation in congress, till reorganized as states and readmitted, on application, by act of congress, in the same way that new states are formed and admitted.

This doctrine is sustained by the act of congress passed July 13th, 1861, commonly called the "non-intercourse act;" by the act authorizing the blockade, which has been recognized by foreign powers; by the president, in appointing governors without military command, in the seceded states; by the erection of Western Virginia into a state, with a representation in congress; and especially by the decision of the supreme court in the Hiawatha case, that the war between us and the rebels is a "civil, territorial war;" and it directly negatives the absurd doctrine that none of the states, as states, have seceded, and that all the states pretending to have seceded, are states still in the Union, and standing on a footing of perfect equality with the other members, and having the right, whenever they choose, to their former representation in congress. The war, by the highest judicial authority, is declared a "civil, territorial war," as it must be, or the blockade of the southern ports and the prohibition of all intercourse with the states proclaimed by the president to be in rebellion, or insurrection, are indefensible; and "civil, territorial war" it cannot be if none of the states have rebelled and the rebellion is confined simply to insurgent individuals. To make the war territorial, the states must not only have seceded, but have joined the revolution, united in the declaration of independence, and in the war intended to establish it by the subversion of the government, as everybody knows is precisely what the rebellious states have done, or are engaged in doing.

That in all the rebellious states there were and still are persons who are loyal to the Union, persons of high character and distinguished patriotism, persons whom we may be proud to own and honor as our countrymen and fellow-citizens is very true; but they are not the state, nor do they inherit its rights and powers in the Union. They follow the territory and their state organization so far as their political *status, rights,* and *powers* are involved. The civil war is not simply a war against insurgent individuals, but a civil, *territorial* war, as the supreme court has formally and unanimously decided; and as Mr. Solicitor Whiting, himself no mean authority, justly remarks, "when the civil war becomes a territorial war, every citizen residing in the belligerent districts becomes a public enemy irrespective of his private sentiments, whether loyal or disloyal, friendly or hostile, unionist or secessionist, guilty or innocent," as is by international law every citizen or subject of a foreign country with which our government is at war. No doubt the loyal men in the belligerent districts have a claim upon our sympathy, and many of them, as individuals, deserve our highest esteem, but they have no political power, no political rights, no political existence whatever, save as they escape from the belligerent territory and become citizens of a loyal state. If the Union citizens of the rebellious states constituted and continued the state, the war would not and could not be a civil, territorial war, and could not be carried on as such. The blockade of the ports of the seceded states could not be legally sustained, and neither foreigners nor our own citizens would be obliged to respect it, for they would be friendly, not belligerent ports, and the captured blockade runners would not be lawful prizes. The administration, doubtless, was aware of this fact, when it decided to proclaim the blockade, instead of taking the alternative authorized by congress, of closing the southern ports as ports of entry. The non-intercourse act of July 13, 1861, instituting an internal blockade, and prohibiting all trade and communication with the districts declared by the proclamation of the president to be in a state of rebellion, would be equally indefensible, and for the same reason neither the congress that passed the act, nor the president who issued the proclamation, could have regarded those districts as still states in the Union. It would be an insult to their understanding to pretend it.

They who maintain that the belligerent states are still in

the Union, and that persons in each state holding loyal sentiments are the state, and possess in themselves all its rights and powers in the Union, overlook the fact that the Amercan states, though autonomous, are not complete, independent, sovereign states, and that the people of a state as population and territory, have no inherent political rights or faculties. In an independent, sovereign state, the sovereignty survives the loss of the political organization, and inheres when the organization is subverted or usurped by rebellion, revolution, or by unconstitutional means, in that portion of the population that have loyally adhered to the constitution, and done what they could to sustain it. They are *de jure* the political people of the state, and have the right to claim and exercise all its authority, if able to do so, either by themselves alone or by foreign assistance, against any number of persons or any organization claiming to act as the state; for every such organization is illegal, and all such persons are rebels and revolutionists, and without political right or authority. But this is not the case with a state that is not an independent sovereign state, and is a state at all only as organized under and admitted into the Union. Under our system the political power does not inhere in the people simply as population and territory, and a state that has lost by secession, rebellion, or revolution, its organization as a state in the Union, has lost its political existence, all its political rights and powers, even its autonomy, and its population have in themselves alone no right or power to reconstitute themselves a state, even though loyal. With us the sovereignty inheres in the political people called the United States or the Union, and it is this sovereign people that gives both to the federal and state governments all their respective rights and powers. Both derive from the same source, and both are delegated governments, with only such powers as the Union has delegated to them respectively. The American nation is one nation, with one national sovereignty; but neither government alone represents that sovereignty. The national sovereignty is not divided between the federal government and the several state governments. It is one and indivisible, and inheres in the political people of the *United* States. But though governing always as one national sovereign, it governs partly through a federal government and partly through state governments; and when either lapses the power delegated to it reverts necessarily to the Union, and it is only by the power of the Union that either can be restored or reconstructed. The Union or national sovereign governs in the state governments just as much as in the federal government, and the states govern in the federal government just as much as in the state governments. In both the one sovereign authority that governs is the same, and they are only distinct organs through which it exercises its several powers, or expresses and carries out its will. The population and territory do not, under our system, constitute a state, as democracy teaches, nor is the state an independent sovereign as the seceders pretend. Population and territory are a state only when organized by authority of the Union, under a state constitution, and admitted into it by act of congress. The loyal people in the seceded state not being so organized, have no state rights or state authority. The others being in rebellion, and without any political rights of any sort, the state has lapsed to the Union, and there is not so much as the veriest abstraction that remains.

The doctrine we maintain applies equally to the original states and to the new states. Not one of the original states had a purely democratic origin, or was self-created. The original states were at first colonies, created such by the British crown, in which was vested the sovereignty. By the revolution they ceased to be colonies, and became what we call *states;* but not sovereign states, for the sovereignty which was originally in the British crown, and which created them colonies, and gave them their autonomy, and their rights and powers as colonies, did not by the revolution and the acknowledgment of American independence revert to them severally, but to the *United* States. As it was by virtue of the sovereignty vested in the British crown that they held their rights and powers as colonies, so it is by virtue of the same sovereignty, vested now in the *United* States, that they hold their rights and powers as states. Our politicians fall into error on this subject by attempting to apply to the American system of government the theory that derives the state from simple population and territory, and which asserts what with us has been called, "squatter sovereignty;" or to give to our political institutions a purely democratic interpretation. This attempt, so little creditable to American statesmanship, has done much harm, and all but ruined the republic. The American government, state or federal, has had a historic origin, and rests on a legal basis. The United States, unhappily without a proper name, is a nation constitutionally organized—a state, not a confederation of states—and is democratic only in the respect that the sovereignty vests in the political people, who have the power, according to prescribed forms, to alter or amend the constitution as they see fit; and the affairs of the government are carried on through the agency of popular elections, in which, however, none have the right to vote unless they belong to the political people; and none but citizens of states *in* the Union belong to that people. The government is constitutional, republican in form, as it should be, not strictly speaking, democratic, in the present political sense of the word.

But to return. The supreme court of the United States has decided that the present war is a "civil, territorial war," and, therefore, that the states engaged in it are public enemies, and, consequently, like all public enemies, they have no rights or standing in the Union. Having ceased to be states in the Union, or to make a portion of the sovereign political people, they necessarily, since not independent of the Union, fall, even supposing their rebellion and attempted revolution suppressed, into the condition of population and territory, subject to the Union, but not yet erected into states and admitted into the Union. They have no political *status* or existence. All in them that lived only by state authority has died, and can be revived only by a new act of the national sovereign, according to the forms of the constitution. The government is bound neither by their old constitutions nor by the laws passed under them, and is free to deal with them precisely as it may deal with any population and territory acquired by purchase or by conquest. By ceasing to be states, they become completely subject to the Union, and are to be governed according to its pleasure.

We can now approach, with a tolerably clear understanding of the legal and constitutional aspects of the case, the grave question as to the mode and conditions of the return of the rebellious states to their former *status* in the Union. They have now no standing in the Union. The suppression of the rebellion by military force, and subjection of the rebellious population and territory to federal authority, will relieve them of their character of public enemies, but will not reinstate them in the Union, or make them again a part of the political or sovereign people of the United States, any more than are the people of Idaho, Colorado, Nevada, Utah, or New Mexico; nor indeed so much, unless congress erects them into territories under territorial governments, created by and subject to the federal government.   There is only one regular way by which the seceded states can be reinstated in the Union, and that is precisely the way in which new states are erected and admitted out of territory belonging to the United States.   Congress must first erect them into territories with a territorial government.   It must then pass for the territorial people what is called an " enabling act."   After this the territorial people must organize, under authority of this act, draw up and adopt a state constitution—republican in form, and containing nothing repugnant to the constitution of the United States, elect their state officers and representatives, also their federal representatives and senators, and apply to congress for admission. They are not yet a state, but only prepared to be a state. To make them a state, congress by a formal act must entertain their application, recognize them as a state, and admit their representatives and their senators to seats in the federal legislature.   The initiatory act is on the part of congress; so also is the final or complementary act.   The whole action is partly the act of congress, and partly the act of the territorial people, and without the concurrent act of both parties can no territory be regularly and legally transmuted into a state, and be aggregated to the political or sovereign people of the United States.   Each of the seceded states must go substantially through the process here described, before it is or can be legally and constitutionally restored to the Union.

It is important, however, to bear in mind that the part of the action that belongs to the federal government belongs to congress, and not the executive.   Neither the initiation of the movement for the restoration of the seceded states, nor its consummation belongs to the executive.   Nor does it belong to the executive to determine the time or the conditions of the return.   The whole matter belongs to congress, and the executive has nothing to do with it but to execute faithfully the laws of congress.   The president has, indeed, a veto on all acts of congress, but as included in the legislature, not as the executive.   Every act of congress constitutionally passed is mandatory on him, and he must execute it, if in his power, whether he likes or dislikes it.   Congress is not bound by the views or policy of the administration, and it fails in its duty to the public when it attempts to devolve on the executive any responsibility which properly rests on itself. When it does so, it is unjust both to itself and to the executive. The views and wishes of the executive are no law for congress, and deserve its respect only so far as they commend themselves to its own judgment. Congress of late years has been too chary of assuming the responsibility that belongs to it under the constitution, and has shown itself quite too ready to be governed by the policy of the administration. The executive has an enormous patronage; and members of congress have shown themselves for years quite too willing to yield up their independence to the executive in exchange for an effective voice in the distribution of executive patronage, on which, perhaps, depend their chances for reëlection. In measures necessary or expedient for the executive in either civil or military administration, congress should, undoubtedly, consult the president and chiefs of departments, and, as far as practicable, conform to their views and wishes; but in other measures, it should follow its own judgment irrespective of the policy of the executive. The administration, as the executive branch of the government, has nothing to say as to when, how, or on what conditions the seceded states, or any one of them, may return and be admitted into the Union. They are all three questions within the province of congress, and it is for congress to settle them in accordance with its own sense of right and of public duty under the constitution.

The fact, if fact it be, that the administration has committed itself to the doctrine that the rebellious states engaged in a civil, territorial war against the Union, are still states in the Union, imposes no restraint on congress, and it is free to treat them simply as population and territory subject to the United States; nor does the fact that the last congress, in a moment of confusion, when the question had not been fully discussed, and was only imperfectly understood, admitted to seats in either house, very respectable gentlemen from Virginia, Tennessee, and Louisiana, establish a precedent that its successor is bound to follow. Western Virginia, on the doctrine we maintain, is a state in the Union, standing on a footing of equality with any other state, but only on that doctrine; for it is ridiculous to pretend that Mr. Pierrepont's establishment, formerly at Wheeling and now at Alexandria, is the state of Virginia, and competent to give the assent required by the constitution to the erection of a new state within its limits. Such a pretence is a burlesque on constitutional law. Western

Virginia is a state, because Virginia in which it was formerly included had ceased to be a state under the constitution, and fallen into the condition of unorganized population and territory. The act admitting the state is defensible, but the reason that was assigned is bad. Virginia, Tennessee, and Louisiana have no more right to representation in congress than Timbuctoo, Dahomey, or Senegambia. Representatives from old congressional districts of a seceded state, which are subjected to federal authority and placed under charge of military governors, are inadmissible, till those districts are erected into a separate state, and admitted into the Union by act of congress. If the administration has blundered—if the last congress blundered—it is not necessary that the next congress should also blunder, and give the *coup de grâce* to the contempt already cast on constitutional government in general, and our own in particular. Let us lose no time in repairing past blunders. It is better to lose the majority in the next congress or even to offend Old Kentucky, than sanction the solecism of treating as in the Union a state that has declared herself out of it, and by the law of the land is a public enemy.

It is not necessary to interpret even the official statements of the secretary of state literally, or to regard his declaration to the French minister that the seats of the representatives of the seceded states are vacant, and that whenever they choose they can fill them, and discuss the terms of settlement on the floor of congress itself, as any thing more than a little diplomatic badinage, for which the secretary is somewhat noted. The thing is preposterous both as law and as policy; and the secretary asserted it, we presume, only as a good joke, as a fair offset to the French joke of offering to mediate between our government and its rebellious subjects. It was a jocular and not uncivil way of telling his imperial majesty to mind his own business, and that we hold ourselves competent to manage ours, and to settle our internal disputes without foreign intervention or foreign advice. We trust congress and even the country will not commit the blunder of taking the secretary's jokes in earnest, however exquisite or witty they may be. There are no vacant seats in congress belonging to seceded states. This is the fact; and no jocularity or sophistry can make it otherwise. Those states and all their inhabitants are declared to be public enemies by the supreme court; and public enemies have no political or civil rights, and no rights at all, except those conceded them by the laws of war. The policy that would permit these states a full representation in congress—an equal voice in legislating for the whole country, while they are in arms or avowed hostility to the government—is a policy no government could adopt till resolved on self-destruction. The population and territory of these *ci-devant* states belong to the Union; but since they have seceded—since they have become public enemies, engaged in carrying on a civil, territorial war against the Union, they are no part of the political or sovereign people of the United States. They may again, by action of their inhabitants and that of congress, become states, but to treat them as such now, is a gross violation of our whole constitutional system.

The *mode* of the return of the seceded or rebellious states must, as we have said, be precisely that in which new states are formed and admitted into the Union. We have given that mode in its regular form, but some departures from it have been admitted. Territories have been organized as states without an enabling act, applied for admission, and been admitted. Such proceeding is irregular, but as the irregularity affects only the rights of congress, congress is competent to condone it, if it chooses, and to pass an act recognizing the organization and admitting it as a state. The essential points are, that the state organization be the act of the territorial people, and the admission be the act of congress, which can, if it chooses, dispense with the other formalities. The admission in every case must be by a formal act of congress. There is no smuggling of a state into the Union by executive treaty without the act of congress, nor under the constitutional clause, making each house the judge of the election and qualifications of its members. Texas, it is true, was admitted by treaty, but it was, in the first place, the admission of an independent state, not subject to the United States; and in the second place, the executive was authorized by an act of congress to make the treaty. The constitution, indeed, makes each house the judge of the election and qualification of its members, but it presupposes the community sending them is a state in the Union, previously recognized as such by congress, in which both houses have concurred.

Here we must note an error of fact into which a writer in *The New York Times* has inadvertently fallen. He asserts that Kentucky and Missouri both seceded, and he proposes the mode in which they have been reinstated in the

Union, as an example of the way in which the other seceded states may be reinstated; but these two states, if we have been rightly informed, never seceded. The position Kentucky assumed, at first, was that of neutrality, an untenable position indeed, but recognized and respected, under instructions, we presume, by General McClellan, the commandant of the military department to which the state was then attached. Missouri was disposed to assume the same position, and arrangements to that effect were entered into between General Harney, the federal general, and General Sterling Price, the state general, but were set aside through the influence of the Blairs. Both states, though containing each a large disloyal population, soon wheeled into line as Union states—Missouri, by the action of her state convention, which had been previously legally convened, and Kentucky, by her regular election resulting in the success of the Union candidates. We are far from approving the attitude assumed by the authorities of these states in the beginning, but we cannot admit that they ever seceded. Perhaps it would have embarrassed the Union less, if they had, but they did not, and we concede willingly their present loyalty and legal *status* in the Union. Their example cannot be adduced in the way assumed, for though the authorities favored secession, there was no ordinance of secession adopted by the people legally assembled in convention, without which no state can take itself out of the Union.

This writer and some others, especially the authors of the resolutions adopted by the Union convention, or more properly, caucus of this state at Syracuse, last September, to nominate candidates to be voted for in the ensuing state election, seem to us to look more at what they deem expediency than at what is strict constitutional law. They seem anxious to find out some way by which the seceded states can resume their place and their political rights and faculties in the Union without any formal surrender to the federal arms, and, by diplomatic or executive action, without the intervention of congress. They appear to be afflicted still with the old lack of "backbone," and a little of our old northern flunkyism, without which there had been no civil war. They are afraid of exasperating the public enemies of the country, and wish to prove to them that we of the loyal states are liberal, generous, magnanimous, good-hearted fellows, and have no disposition to resent the wrongs done by them to our country; and that we will take it **very** kindly in them if they will only overlook the past, let bygones be bygones, and come back into the Union, and continue, as of old, to be our masters. We must forbear to mortify or humiliate them, or to wound their feelings. But we have no patience with such flunkyism. We wish to mortify them, to humiliate them, and to subject them, unconditionally, to federal authority. This is what we are fighting for, if we are fighting for any thing. We care not, save for their sakes, whether they are reinstated as states in the Union or not. To be so reinstated is a favor for them, not to us; and to permit them to be so reinstated is to permit them to become again an integral portion of the political or governing people of the United States, and to be clothed anew with political rights and powers of which they have wantonly and wickedly divested themselves. There will be no little magnanimity on the part of the loyal states in consenting to their reëstablishment in the Union on a footing of perfect equality with themselves, after having done their best to subvert the government, and to ruin the nation. It is a great privilege to be a state in the American Union, and we own that we wish the rebels to be made to feel it such, for till they feel it such, and we also feel it such, the nation will never be safe; there will be no real union between North and South, and the South, as of old, will gamble on the northern devotion to the Union, and on every occasion of discontent threaten to dissolve it. Till we compel them to feel that the Union is as essential for the South as for the North, there will be no affection between the two sections. We have given the rebels a taste of our military superiority; let us prove now our civil superiority, and the reconciliation will be complete. Love is never yielded to humble entreaty or to unmanly solicitation.

The *conditions* of the return of the rebellious states to the Union, when the military suppression of the rebellion is completed, and the rebels have submitted and sued for mercy, it will be for congress in its wisdom to determine. First, however, it is necessary to dispose of the military question. "To cook a hare, first catch a hare," and never count your chickens before they are hatched. There is serious military work yet to be done, and we can receive no state back into the Union till it has ceased to be in rebellion, has unconditionally surrendered, and asked to be restored. Till then we can offer no terms, and entertain no conditions. The rebels must, first, throw down their arms and submit unconditionally to the federal authority.   Till then the war must continue, and if the rebels choose, it must be continued to the bitter end.   When the work of military suppression is completed, and there is no longer any armed resistance offered to the government, then we may freely discuss and determine the future *status* of the seceded states, what disposition shall be made of them, and on what conditions they may be safely restored to the Union.   The time for conciliatory measures had passed when the resort to arms became necessary.   Our business now is to fight, not to conciliate, and to fight till the rebels are subdued.   When they are subdued we are far more likely to err by dealing too leniently than by dealing too severely with them ; for, as a people, we are much more ready *parcere subjectis* than we are *debellare superbos*.   The Yankee may know anger, but he knows no revenge ; and when he has caught the criminal, he is much more easily induced to pardon than to punish him.   The appetite for blood will have been satiated when the rebellion is put down, and Jeff. Davis's life will be in as little danger as our own.   There will be no executions for treason, and no one need be surprised to see Mason and Slidell, Toombs and Hunter, Benjamin and Mallory, occupying their old seats in the senate, as arrogant and as impudent as ever ; or even to see Lee and Beauregard, Hill and Longstreet, Bragg and Johnston, reinstated in the federal army.   Our people will be anxious to push them forward, in order to show that they have no grudge against them, and those only will have reason to complain who have stood by the Union and saved the nation.   It is much more pleasant to our Anglo-Saxon race to be generous than it is to be just.   The worst terms that any man amongst us dreams of imposing upon the seceded states, if subdued by our arms, is, after a brief probation, to place them, if they can make up their minds to accept the boon, in the Union on a footing of perfect equality with ourselves.   All we insist on is, that care be taken not to violate the constitution in order to reward these *ci-devant* states for their treachery and rebellion, and that we do not absolutely sacrifice the real interests of the nation in order to atone to them for their failure to destroy it.   We insist that an effort at least shall be made to take advantage of the opportunity that will be presented by the suppression of the rebellion, in case it is suppressed, to obtain not indemnity for the past, but security for the future.   The present rebellion the nation may survive ; but such a rebellion is no joke, or bit of pleasantry, that will bear repetition, and the wise statesman will take all reasonable precautions that it be not repeated. A recognition of the seceded states as still states in the Union, or permission for them to resume the exercise of their old political rights and faculties in the Union whenever they choose, settles nothing, and leaves all the causes that have produced the present secession, rebellion, and revolution in full operation, to reproduce our present dangers. Our only safety is in removing the causes themselves—in expelling the disease from the system. If we lack the power to do this, we must do the best we can. But we are writing on the supposition that we shall be masters of the situation, and, as strange as it may sound in northern ears, able to dictate to the enemy our own terms, instead of being obliged to accept his. If we cannot save the integrity of the national territory on our own terms, we must, undoubtedly, do it on the best terms we can get, and leave it to our children to meet the difficulties that may hereafter arise, as best they may. The integrity of the national territory is to be saved at all hazards, and no foreign power, under any conditions, is to be suffered to be erected anywhere within its limits. This must be insisted on at any and every cost. Yet it is our duty not only to save the integrity of the national territory, but to save it, as far as we are able, free from all causes of future discord and rebellion, and we shall stand condemned as dishonest, cowardly, or incapable statesmen, if we leave any root of bitterness to spring up hereafter that it is in our power to eradicate.

The causes of the war are in and inseparably connected with slavery, and without the abolition of slavery it is idle to dream of any security for the future. The federal government, under the present constitution, has no authority to prosecute the war for the abolition of slavery as its direct purpose and end, we concede, any more than it has for the purpose of killing, wounding, or disabling the enemy's soldiers. But as it may disable, wound, or kill the enemy's soldiers, destroy or take possession of his property, in prosecuting a war for a lawful end, so it may in a war for a lawful end, abolish slavery, if necessary to gaining and securing that end. War, according to the authorities, may be lawfully waged either to redress a wrong committed, or to prevent a wrong about to be committed ; that is, as usually expressed, indemnity for the past and security for the future.

The war we are waging is unquestionably a lawful war, and as it is a civil, territorial war, we have against the rebels all the rights both of belligerents and of a sovereign. We have in this war the right to reduce the rebels to submission; that is our right even as sovereign. And we have the belligerent right to demand indemnification at least for the expenses of the war, and reasonable security for the future. Under the head of indemnity for expenses, we can lawfully confiscate any amount of rebel property judged necessary; and under the head of security for the future, we can, if necessary, abolish slavery, throughout all the seceded states, and in all the other states that authorize it, only in the case of loyal states, we must give a reasonable indemnification to the loyal slave-owners. Slavery may be abolished for either of the ends named, under the rights of war, which we have shown, over and over again, are as constitutional as the rights of peace, since the constitution clothes the government with them. If congress believes that the abolition or prohibition of slavery is necessary to our future security, it can lawfully and constitutionally abolish or prohibit it everywhere and for ever within the United States and its territories. It certainly can, then, lawfully refuse to admit into the Union any state with a constitution that does not prohibit slavery, except for crime, within its limits. This much it could do under even its peace powers; at least such is the doctrine of the Republican party, as laid down in the Chicago platform.

We do not pretend that no other considerations than that of preserving slavery have moved the secessionists; but we say only what all the world knows, when we say that slavery is the primal cause, and without it there would have been no secession, no rebellion, no attempted revolution. But for the existence of slavery, there never would have been that difference of character and interest between the North and the South which has, no doubt, counted for much in bringing about our present troubles. Nay, that very centralized democracy, which several northern, middle, and western states have pushed to a dangerous extreme, and which some of the chiefs of the rebellion profess to be warring against, is of southern origin, has been fostered amongst us by southern politicians, and if they now war against it, it is only because being in the minority they see in its progress a power not unlikely to sweep away their cherished domestic slavery. If they insist on constitutionalism, and strict construction, it is not because they are constitutionalists in principle, but because they cannot otherwise save their peculiar "institution." Even the doctrine of state sovereignty, which is only the wildest democracy applied to the states, has been defended both North and South mainly for its bearing on the slave question. Pro-slavery men have asserted it as a barrier to all interference with slavery by the Union, and anti-slavery men in the free states have resorted to it as an answer to the charge against them of belonging to a slaveholding republic, and of sustaining slavery. This last was our chief motive for insisting on it in our long war against the abolitionists. It is idle to attempt to deny that slavery is at the bottom of all the differences that have culminated in the present rebellion. Hence, so long as slavery exists in any portion of the United States, the cause of our present troubles remains, and we are in constant danger of another outbreak, as soon as the wounds of the present are partially scarred over.

It is again only through slavery that foreign powers do or can carry on their machinations against our republic, and work with any prospect of success for its division and destruction. As long as slavery exists in America, there will be a geographical party seeking its abolition, and a geographical party seeking to sustain it. This lies in the nature of things, and no wisdom, prudence, or forbearance can prevent it. You cannot prevent freemen, who honestly believe that slavery is a moral, social, and political evil, a crime against humanity, and a sin against God, from speaking, writing, and, if they have or can make the opportunity, of voting against it. Thirty years of experience with abolitionists, has proved it. Nor any more can you prevent men who own slaves, who believe slave property as inviolable as any other species of property, and hold it to be a primary duty of government to protect property, from combining and using all their political, as well as moral and social influence for the maintenance of slavery. You have, then, two geographical parties pitted against each other. The thing is inevitable. Here opens the chance for foreign machinations. Great Britain, or France, or both, may, in a thousand subtle and unsuspected ways, urge on the anti-slavery party of the North, inflame its zeal and encourage its efforts, till worked up to the fighting point, and at the same time encourage the pro-slavery party at the South to resist, offer them their sympathy, promise them their moral and diplomatic influence, and such indirect material aid as can be rendered without provoking open war with the United States. So encouraged the South secedes, and makes war on the Union. This is precisely what has been done under our very eyes, and what will be repeated if slavery is retained, till the moral influence of the republic is lost, till its material strength is wasted in internal dissensions, and republicanism stands disgraced before the world by the utter ruin of its great American representative.

Foreign powers, especially the two great western powers of Europe, France and Britain, wish, and are plotting the destruction of this republic as a great power, because its existence as a great power is in the way of the policy they are pursuing, and because, by its republicanism, it exerts a moral influence on their own subjects, by no means to their liking. These two powers have entered into a league or alliance for regulating and settling, as they deem best, the political and international affairs of both hemispheres. This was openly declared, some years since, by Lord Clarendon, in the British parliament, and is no secret. Our republic must, as the great power on this continent, be broken up, and either thrown into hopeless anarchy, or divided into a number of petty states and confederacies, each too feeble to stand alone, as preliminary to their settlement of the affairs of the western hemisphere, *if not indeed to their undisputed control of the affairs of the eastern.* Our present civil war is, in great part, their work. They have brought it about by operating with the internal dispute between the free states and the slave states on the subject of slavery. Secession was resolved on in concert with them, and the revolution would never have been attempted without their approbation, and promises, at least, of moral and diplomatic assistance. They hoped that, if once we got to fighting amongst ourselves, that we should devour each other, like the far-famed Kilkenny cats. The mass of the French people and of the English are, no doubt, honestly opposed to slavery ; but neither the French government nor the English wants it abolished in the United States, and we are not certain but either would, if necessary, make open war on us sooner than suffer it to be abolished ; for if once abolished, there would exist no element of serious division amongst us, with which they could operate to involve us in civil dissensions or civil war ; and united as one homogeneous people, with a single national sentiment and national will, as we should be if slavery were abolished, we should be the great power of the modern world, and make it somewhat hazardous for both France and England combined to attempt any interference with the affairs of this continent not meeting our approbation. We could defy alike their diplomacy and their arms. Slavery is the pivot on which turns the whole policy of France and England, and indeed of the cæsarists and conservatives of Europe, with regard to this western hemisphere, and its abolition is as sure defeat to them as to the southern revolution.

The true policy for our statesmen, in view of the Anglo-French alliance, is, at home, the abolition of slavery, which is a source of internal division, and a great drawback upon our moral influence with the European liberals, and abroad, a closer alliance with Russia, Austria, and Italy. Russia is emancipating her serfs, and preparing, as rapidly as possible, to give to the empire a liberal constitutional government; Austria has adopted, and has in full operation, a constitutional *régime*, as liberal as is desirable, and which is resisted only by the wrong-headed and sulky Magyars, and Italy is preparing to take her place as a free constitutional state. Our natural bond of political sympathy is with these states, which must soon reckon Prussia and the smaller German states on the same side. These European powers are now on the side, or preparing to be on the side, of freedom, liberal, constitutional governments. They are reforming and liberalizing powers, and are opposed as such by both the French and British governments. Between them and us there can now be foreseen, notwithstanding the French policy in Mexico, no cause of quarrel, and in them our diplomacy should find a counterpoise in the Old World to the two western powers, who have forever forfeited our friendship by their intrigues with the secessionists for the destruction of our great republic. Both of these powers threaten us, and with one or both of them we are not unlikely, before our difficulties are settled, to be at open war; but whether so or not, as long as the Napoleonic policy reigns in the French court, and the Palmerstonian policy in the English, there can be no cordial friendship between them and us. If there had been no slavery in the Union we could smile at their hostility, and even with our domestic affairs unsettled, we shall not allow ourselves to fear it, though we would bear much in order to avert it.

Now, if we adopt the policy which seems to be insisted

on by the so-called "conservative Republicans," as well as by the copperhead Democrats, of treating the seceders as still states in the Union, and with their old state constitutions still in full life and vigor, and hold ourselves bound to admit their representatives to seats in congress whenever they choose to send them, we have guarded against no danger, and taken no precaution against the recurrence of the very evils we are now struggling with. In this wise? Is this statesmanlike? We will not say that we may not lawfully stretch the constitution, if absolutely necessary, to save the nation; but we positively deny the right to do it for the detriment of the nation, to prevent the removal of dangers, or to expose it without protection to both its internal and external foes. There is no constitutional obligation on the part of congress to recognize the seceded states as in existence, or their old constitutions as in force; nay, it has, as we have shown, over and over again, no constitutional right to do it, save as a military necessity, and such necessity is hardly conceivable. It would settle nothing. These states, though they might have fewer slaves, would all be slaveholding states as much as they were before the outbreak of the civil war, and would be even more tenacious of remaining such. Slavery would enter as much as before into our politics, be as fruitful a source of internal discord, and offer as fair an opportunity for foreign powers to foment sectional divisions amongst us, and to weaken, if not ruin, our civil and military power. The nation remains exposed to all its present dangers, both internal and external, and nothing will have been gained by the two thousand millions of debt we have incurred, and the loss of half a million of lives from the very flower of our population. The statesman, having the power to do better, who should adopt such a policy, would deserve, we will not say to be hung, but to be held in universal and everlasting execration.

Let us not be deceived by the vain talk that slavery is dead, that the system is so shaken that it cannot survive, and that we need trouble ourselves no more about it. When we in our last *Review* intimated as much, it was on the supposition that public opinion had already set in so strongly against it, and that the government had so decidedly resolved on an anti-slavery policy, that it could not survive the military suppression of the rebellion. Moreover, we wished to fix public attention on the military question, then the only important question, as perhaps it is still.

We believe now that slavery will die, but not at present, unless the proper measures to prevent its living are taken. It will not die, but revive in more than its former ferocity, if the policy apparently recommended by the secretary of state in his official correspondence is sanctioned by congress. We say *apparently* recommended, for the secretary of state is not a man, as we have already intimated, to be always taken *au sérieux*, or *au pied de lettre*. He usually masks his purpose from his adversary, and sometimes in his efforts to mislead him he misleads his partner, as one who over-finesses at whist. We once undertook to expose the *Seward Policy*; we confess that we were rash, and we shall not be surprised to find that his real policy all along has been the same as our own, and that his organs are constantly talking one thing and meaning another. He labors to conceal his real purpose from the enemy, which is all well, only we hope that he will not in his laudable desire to overreach him, end by overreaching himself and his friends. We say then the policy *apparently* recommended by the secretary of state and his special organs. That policy suppresses the rebellion indeed, but leaves slavery unabolished, and the slave interest as powerful as ever, and even more virulent. On that policy slavery is not dead nor likely to die. It is alive and kicking, as the next congress will find, when it assembles, to its no trifling embarrassment, and as may be seen in the inaugural, or what purports to be the inaugural of the newly elected governor of Kentucky.

No. Slavery is not yet dead, and there is a powerful party even in the loyal states determined that it shall not die. The president's proclamation, allowing it all the force claimed for it, only emancipates the slaves in a part of Virginia and Louisiana, and in North Carolina, South Carolina, Georgia, Florida, Alabama, Mississippi, Texas, and Arkansas, and leaves them unemancipated in Tennessee, Kentucky, Missouri, Maryland, Delaware, and a part of Virginia and Louisiana. It moreover abolishes slavery nowhere, and could not do it. There is a wide difference between emancipating the slaves actually held in bondage and abolishing slavery. Suppose North Carolina should abandon the confederacy, and be permitted to return to the Union under her old, as we maintain, defunct state constitution, she comes into the Union as a slaveholding state, and what is to prevent her from remanding to slavery all the negroes and colored people heretofore held as slaves by her state laws or her state usage remaining within her boundaries? Neither congress, nor the president, nor the courts can interfere. A state may declare any portion of its population slaves that it chooses, so long as slavery is held to be not repugnant to the constitution of the United States, or inconsistent with a republican form of government. Nay, more, suppose that in order to be readmitted to the Union, the state should, before admission, alter her constitution so as to prohibit slavery, or so as to make it mandatory on the state legislature to adopt some scheme of gradual emancipation, what is to prevent her, the day after admission, from calling a convention and altering the constitution so as to authorize slavery? If we treat the seceded states as territories subject to the Union, slavery is abolished in them while they remain territories, both by the lapse of the state authority, on which slavery depended, and by the act of congress, prohibiting for ever slavery in any district or territory subject to the United States; but neither prohibits the reëstablishment of slavery in any territory when it becomes a state in the Union.

There are but two conceivable ways in which full security against the reëstablishment of slavery can be obtained. The one is, to refuse to admit any state into the Union whose constitution does not contain a clause, unalterable by any future convention, prohibiting for ever all involuntary servitude, except for crime, within its limits; the other, an amendment to the federal constitution, prohibiting for ever slavery in any and every state in the Union or territory subject to it. Either would be a sufficient guaranty. But the first is unconstitutional, for the constitution places the new state, when once admitted, on a footing of equality with the original states, and all the states now in the Union may authorize slavery to-morrow, if they choose. The second would be constitutional, for the loyal states now in the Union are the United States, and the political and whole political power of the Union vests in them. They are the national sovereign, and perfectly competent to amend, in a constitutional way, the constitution, and to insert such a prohibitory clause, if they see proper. We, however, are reluctant to urge such a measure; and we prefer to leave the constitution as it was left by our fathers, and if it must be altered, we prefer it should be by the concurrence of the people of the seceded states, when reinstated—as we trust they soon will be—in the Union. We therefore fall back on the principle laid down by the Republicans in the Chicago platform, and insist, simply, that no state be admitted into the Union whose constitution does not exclude slavery, except for crime. This is not, indeed, absolute security, we grant, but it will probably prove practically sufficient. At any rate, it is all that we deem it prudent to ask, and certainly it is all that can be obtained even from the loyal states in their present temper.

In answer to the question as to the *mode* of the return of the seceded states, we contend that it should be substantially that in which new states are organized and admitted into the Union; and in answer to the question as to the *conditions*, we insist that they shall not be permitted to return, save as organized under constitutions that prohibit slavery. We do not want the war prolonged a moment to secure even that condition. The war, strictly speaking, is not waged either against secession or to force the seceded states back into the Union with or without slavery, but against rebellion and attempted revolution, and its object is gained when the revolution is defeated and the rebellion is suppressed. The task of the military is accomplished when the rebels have thrown down their arms, and submitted to the government. The war is then ended, and can no longer continue. The task of reorganizing the seceded population and territory, and readmitting them to the Union, is the work of peace, and to be performed by the civil authorities. So we propose no prolongation of the war, for the purpose of securing the abolition of slavery. We do not say the war must continue till slavery is abolished, or till its abolition is secured; we ask nothing of the sort; we simply ask that it be continued and prosecuted with the utmost vigor against the armies of the revolution, till there is no longer any armed resistance offered to the government, and the rebels have unconditionally submitted to its authority. When no armed resistance is any longer offered, the war is over, because there is no longer anybody to fight, nothing to war against. We here accept fully, in its plain literal sense, the resolution of congress in the beginning of the war, proposed, if we recollect aright, by the late Mr. Crittenden, of Kentucky, as to the purpose and end of the war. It has had and should have no other object than the suppression of the rebellion, and the reëstablishment of the constitutional authority of the United States over the whole population and territory of the Union. We ask nothing more and nothing less from the war. Nor do we pretend that no one of the seceded states may be restored to the Union till the rebellion has been put down in them all. Any seceded state may be restored whenever it has withdrawn from the confederacy, abandoned the revolution, returned to loyalty, and is ready to return to the Union on the conditions required; but not so long as the great body, or even a very considerable portion of its population are disloyal, and require a federal army within its borders to enable loyal men to vote peaceably and freely according to their wishes. If Kentucky had seceded, we should insist on her remaining a territory under a military government, till a much smaller portion of her population were disloyal than is now the case. When the rebels are driven out of Tennessee, and her population can peaceably and freely vote, assemble in convention by their delegates freely chosen, and that convention reorganizes the state under a constitution that abolishes and prohibits slavery, she must be admitted into the Union upon formal application, but not till then, if the constitution or wise policy be consulted. So of any other seceded state. The confederacy is nothing. The government may deal with each *ci-devant* state separately, and may even divide its territory into two or more states, as it has done in the case of Virginia, if it chooses; but we hope, for the sake of geography and old associations, that it will not. We want the old boundaries, and the old names religiously retained, for we hope that some day the memory of the present sad attempt at revolution will be obliterated. But let it be understood, that the work of restoration, whether the seceded states be restored singly or all at once, is to be performed by the civil and not by the military authority, by congress, and not by the executive.

We have urged the abolition of slavery, and, as far as practicable, its perpetual exclusion from the United States, for reasons of state, and chiefly as necessary to the future internal and external security of the republic. We have in no instance taken the ground of the abolitionists, and we have refrained from doing so partly because we do not wholly agree with them, and partly in deference to the passions and prejudices of our countrymen. But it is by no means improper for a statesman to reflect that slavery is a sin on the part of the nation that, having the power to remove it, authorizes, or tolerates, or connives at its existence; and that as nations have no future life, national sins are and must be punished in this world. Our indifference to the wrong done by slavery, both to the slave and to his master, has already been visited upon our nation with one of the most formidable civil wars that history records; and it will not render the Great Arbiter of nations less disposed to smile on our patriotic efforts, and to give success to our arms, if he sees us resolved to put away the evil of our doings, to remember his poor, to raise up the bowed down, to help the helpless, and to set the captive free. The government has now the right under the constitution to wipe out from our national escutcheon the foul stain of slavery; and if it refuses, or if the factious spirit, the bitter prejudice, or the cold-hearted selfishness of the people prevents it from doing so, what right have we either to expect or to ask God to give us success in the field, or to endow us with wisdom in council to defeat the machinations of our enemies? He fights in vain who fights against an offended God, or without the Lord on his side. His very victories are defeats, and his triumphs are failures and death. He is thrice armed who hath his quarrel just; and ours can hardly be called just, if we are resolved not to use the victory we may win, to remove from our midst that grossest outrage man can commit against humanity, negro-slavery. We own that even on moral and religious grounds, we should fear that we had taken no security for the future, if we suffered slavery to be reëstablished anywhere within the American Union. We are not in the secrets of the government; but we are confident that it has no intention of restoring any seceded state to the Union as a slaveholding state, or without having given a constitutional pledge to abolish it.

The government has given a pledge of freedom to the negro race, by organizing negro troops, and using them to fight the battles of freedom. We have never urged it to do that; nay, we have opposed it,—for we hold none but freemen can be justly called upon to bear arms in defence of the country, since slaves have no country,—unless there is a determination on the part of the supreme authority to recognize and treat them henceforth as freemen and citizens. As we read it, the government, in raising negro troops, and employing them side by side with white troops, has given a solemn pledge of negro freedom and negro equality; and though we did what we could to dissuade it from giving that pledge, now it is given, we insist that it shall not be broken. It is too late now to talk of gradual emancipation, of colonization, or to oppose negro troops. Their blood has been mingled on more than one battle field with that of white men ; and it is idle to wrangle about the brotherhood of race, when we have established the brotherhood of arms. Henceforth, whatever have been or still are our prejudices, we are bound in honor to treat the negro as our countryman, and as a free citizen, having as much right to call this his country as we have to call it ours.   No man has a better right to call a country his than he whose blood has consecrated its soil ; and never let the man or the man's race be enslaved in a country that he has poured out his blood or given his manhood to defend.   The government has gone further than we wished, further than we believed wise or prudent, but we accept what it has done as *un fait accompli*, and hold it to the logical consequences of its action, as far as in its power to follow them.

Yet we are far from believing our troubles are over.   The land is full of cowards, imbeciles, half-way men, selfish men, well-meaning but timid men, conceited men, incapable of becoming wise, even from experience, and who are always at war with earnest, clear-sighted, and strong-hearted men, and who are constantly catching hold of wise and brave men's skirts, and trying to hold them back.   These are always a terrible clog on every great and noble enterprise ; and in every age and nation they are numerous enough to prevent it from being more than half successful.   Hence it is that human progress is so slow, and terrible evils remain so long unredressed.   Hence it is, too, that so many noble reforms, nobly begun, bring with them not seldom as much of evil as good.   These men of the past, who should be in their graves, compel their advocates to leave them incomplete and unfinished.   But this is one of the miseries of our human condition in this life, and we must bear up against it as well as we can, and "bate not a jot of heart or hope."

THE FEDERAL CONSTITUTION.

[From Brownson's Quarterly Review for January, 1864.]

THERE is apparently, as we have shown, a serious difference of opinion among loyal politicians as to the actual condition in regard to the Union of the several states that have
seceded, declared their independence, and entered into a
confederacy among themselves. Are they states still in the
Union, or have they lost, by their act of secession, their
state character, and become simply population and territory
subject to the Union, in like manner as any other population and territory belonging to the United States, but not
yet erected into states and admitted into the Union? A
great cry is raised against those of us who maintain that state
secession is state suicide, and we are asked if we propose to
blot out their stars from our political firmament, and to reduce
them to territories? The affected horror is quite misplaced,
and the question quite impertinent. Nobody proposes to
inflict any injury on the seceded states, or to deprive them
of any constitutional rights to which they are entitled. All
we and those who think with us demand is, that the seceded
states be treated for what they really are, or by their own
act have made themselves. There is no question of reducing
them to the condition of territories subject to the Union;
but the question is, Have they or have they not, by their
own act, so reduced themselves? If they have, we must unless we choose to go against both law and fact, treat them,
not as states in the Union, but as unorganized population
and territory under the Union, or subject to the Union, and
in rebellion against it.

The question is one of grave importance, and we cannot
agree with a leading Republican journal, that we should
leave it to be settled by the administration, because we do
not believe that its determination belongs to the executive
branch of the government, and because much of the future
peace and harmony of the Union, and the stability of the
government itself, depends on its being settled by the
proper authority, in strict accordance with the constitution.
If we had from the first understood ourselves, North and
South, as to the real character and provisions of the consti-

tution, and strictly adhered to it, and had not endeavored to evade difficulties by affecting not to recognize them, or by creating false issues to divert attention from the real issues, we should have had no secession, no rebellion, no civil war, and no such questions as we have now to meet and dispose of. We are required now, as it were, to take a new start, and we should be careful to avoid former errors, and to set only such precedents as may hereafter be safely followed. It is always better to prevent the evil from coming, than it is to rely on our ability to remedy it after it has come. There is wisdom in the homely proverb, "An ounce of prevention is worth a pound of cure." We ought now to fix the understanding of our constitution, at least as to its essential principles, and place the government, in its policy and administration, on a strictly constitutional ground. We should guard against all irregularities, and admit as few theoretic or practical anomalies as possible with the imperfections and infirmities of human nature. The easiest way of getting over a present difficulty may not prove in the long run the best, and as a rule the right will be found the truest measure of the expedient. In common with all loyal Americans, we want the rebellion suppressed, and all the states that have seceded reinstated in the Union on a footing of perfect equality with the states that have remained faithful, and by their fidelity, their bravery, and their sacrifices, saved the nation. But we want this done by the constitutional authority, and in a legal and constitutional manner, so as to take away all pretext for any future disturbance, and all precedent justifying future irregularity.

What is the legal or constitutional *status* to which the seceded states, by their own act, have reduced themselves, can be determined only by a correct and profound understanding of the American constitution, or the real constitution, written and unwritten, of the American state, or republic, called, for the lack of a proper name, the UNITED STATES. If our republic in the outset had had a proper name, much difficulty would have been avoided, many questions which have agitated us would never have been raised, and doubts as to our national unity would never have been entertained. The illustrious Count de Maistre, in the beginning of the present century, predicted the failure and dissolution of our republic, precisely on the ground that it had no proper name, and therefore no national unity. The name adopted, that of United States, is expressive of union, indeed, but may be understood to designate a confederacy of states rather than a nation, and it tends to fix attention on the elements of which the republic is composed, rather than on the unity or oneness of the nation itself. Nevertheless, though the lack of a proper name is an inconvenience in more ways than one, the thing does not depend on the name; and the republic may, notwithstanding, be one polity or state, as much so as if it had a name less cumbersome and more expressive of its unity. What, then, is the constitution of the United States? Who made it? Whence does it derive its authority? And what is the rule of its interpretation?

We reject in the outset the theory that the constitution of a state is or can be made. Constitutions are generated, not made, and antecedent to all written instruments, or constitution of the government. The constitution of the United States is not the instrument drawn up by the convention of 1787, and which we call the constitution; for that constitution was the sovereign act of the United States, and therefore the United States preceded it, and must have been anterior to that convention. The convention represented the United States, but it could not represent what did not exist. Either it was no convention at all, but an assembly of very able and respectable private gentlemen, or there was already a United States, possessed of supreme political power. Now the real constitution of the republic of the United States, what we call the unwritten constitution, was that preëxisting constitution of the people themselves, by which they were constituted one political people of the United States. The people were already constituted as states and as *United* States prior to the convention, and as such they assembled by their delegates in that convention, drew up and *ordained* the written constitution, or constitution of the government.

The fundamental and essential constitution is the constitution of the people themselves, as United States, or as distinct states united. The sovereignty that governs with us is the sovereignty of the people, but of the people organized and existing in bodies called states. They exist as the sovereign people, or the American state, only in these states or organizations, and in these only as united as one political people; or the one political people, the political sovereign from whom all laws emanate, exists only as organized into states *united*. There is, then, by the essential constitution of the American people, no political sovereign without states, and none with states without the Union. Such is the constitution as we understand it. To this view, no doubt, many objections, more or less plausible, may be urged, and we do not pretend that many historical facts may not be cited which appear to contradict it, or that no opinions of great weight have been entertained not in harmony with it. But we are satisfied that this view is the only one that really meets the thought and intention of the men who won our independence, and gave us a national status among the nations of the earth.

We are told, and many people honestly believe, that the American state has had a democratic and revolutionary origin, and that our government is to be interpreted on democratic and revolutionary principles. But we must bear in mind that though a state may owe its origin to a successful revolution, yet no state is ever founded, or can stand, on revolutionary principles; for the very idea of a state is repugnant to that of a revolution. Revolution is the subversion of the state, and the moment the new state is organized and established, it is obliged in its own defence to repudiate revolutionary principles, and to punish those who conspire to subvert it, as criminals, traitors, and rebels. Our fathers understood this, and sought to guard against all future revolutions by providing, in the institutions they founded, for their legal, orderly, and peaceful amendment. The fact that we acquired our national independence by a successful revolution, has nothing to do with the principles of the American state, or the constitution of the American government. Our fathers were revolutionists, if you will, in asserting national independence, but not in organizing and founding the government, whether state or federal; and we must take the government they established, and interpret it precisely as if it had been preceded by no revolution, but had always been the legitimate and established government of the country.

The American state had a democratic origin, and is a democratic state in the sense that it was founded by, and on the principle of, popular sovereignty. With us sovereignty vests in the people, but in the political people, or the people organized as the state, and acting through and under constitutional forms, not the people regarded simply as inhabitants or population of the national territory. That it is the right of the people in this latter sense, where there is no civil constitution, where there is no state, no government, to come together in convention, or by a *plebiscitum*, as Napoleon III. calls it, and organize themselves into a state, and institute such government as they judge best, we freely concede. Indeed, this right rests on the natural equality of all men, and grows out of the necessity of the case. But we must beware of confounding the right of the people to institute civil society where none exists, with their right where it already exists, and there is a civil constitution in force and operation. Where civil society exists the constitution defines the rights of the people, and prescribes the conditions on which their power is to be exercised, as well as who among them are to exercise it. The government is to be interpreted, when established, by governmental principles, as government, precisely the same as any other government.

This is one of the points on which we are the most liable to mistake the character of our government, and many of us, in fact, do so interpret American democracy as to nullify the government itself, or to make it the government of mere arbitrary popular will, popular passion, or popular caprice, and so as virtually to deny the right of the authorities to enforce any law not in accordance with popular opinion. But this is not American democracy—it is European democracy, invented by the old Jacobins, and brought here principally from France and Ireland. It is only popular autocracy substituted for imperial autocracy, or what we call cæsarism. The sovereignty with us vests in the political people, indeed, but who are the political people is determined by the constitution, and their will only as constitutionally expressed is law. They, in a constitutional way, may enlarge or contract their number, decree universal suffrage, or restrict it to property-holders, as they see proper; but outside of the constitution and constitutional forms they are simply population, and without a particle of political power. It is important that we bear this in mind, lest we confound the caucus with the convention.

The democratic question is, in fact, no question for the American statesman, and the term *democrat*, as applied here to a political party, has, if the party is not a revolutionary party, no meaning. The democratic question is properly raised, and is important only when there is no government, no civil society, and the question is that of founding civil society, and organizing government; or where there is a question as to the right of revolution, or of overthrowing by violence an existing government, and introducing a new one. In neither sense is it a legitimate question in the United States, for we have a government, and the people have a constitutional way of amending our institutions, and therefore can introduce such ameliorations as they judge desirable without any resort to revolution.

The simple fact is, that the men who resisted what they regarded as the tyranny of Great Britain, asserted American independence, and made us a nation, were not democrats, and rarely, if ever, appealed for their justification to democratic principles. They argued their case on the principles of the British constitution, and their grievance against the mother country was not that she was monarchical, aristocratic, or oligarchical, but that she, by her acts, in which she persisted, violated their rights as British subjects, as set forth in magna charta and the bill of rights. There is in the whole controversy scarcely an appeal to the democratic theory, of which so much has since been said, and in whose name so much blood has been shed and so many crimes committed. In reorganizing government, and providing for the administration of justice, our fathers took care to observe as far as possible the law of continuity, and to admit no break. no innovation, even, that could be avoided. Whether they were justified or not in throwing off the authority of the British crown was a momentous question for them, but is none for us, for the acknowledgment of American independence by the British sovereign legitimated their act and condoned any offence against loyalty or legality which they might have committed. The American state properly dates from that acknowledgment, and since then, whatever it was before, it has been an independent sovereign nation, with the acknowledged and unquestionable right of self-government. The government which then existed may have been incomplete, imperfectly organized, but it was the legitimate government of the country, and the people, collectively and distributively, were bound by it. We, in interpreting the constitution, must begin with it, take it as we find it, without going into any inquiry as to the justifiableness of the revolutionary acts preceding it, or whether it be or be not necessary to assert, in order to justify them, the modern democratic theory of popular sovereignty.

Certain it is that the American system is not democratic in the present popular sense of the word, for democracy in that sense, as we showed in 1844, in our controversy with the

Democratic Review, is tantamount to no government at all.* The American system is what we may term, with strict propriety, a constitutional system, and is a system of real government. It is not a constitutional monarchy, not a constitutional aristocracy, but, perhaps, may be defined, with sufficient accuracy, a constitutional democracy, although the terms are to us a little incongruous. We would, if the thing were possible, exclude the word democracy altogether, as unnecessary, and apt to mislead. " We committed a great mistake," said John C. Calhoun to us in 1840, " when we dropped the name *republican,* and suffered ourselves to be called democrats ; names are things, and by adopting the name *democrat* we are led to substitute democracy for the constitutionalism founded by our fathers." The Jeffersonian party, in Jefferson's days, never went by the name of the Democratic party, and to call, in our younger days, a member of that party a Democrat, was regarded as an insult. The party called itself officially *Republican,* and never assumed generally the name *Democratic* till the reëlection of Andrew Jackson in 1832, when an effort was made to assimilate the American Republican party to the Democratic party of Europe. It is too late to get rid of the name, but not too late to understand and conform to the real constitution of the American state, and to employ the name in the American sense, and not in the European.

Dismissing all questions relating to the revolutionary and democratic origin of American independence, we return to the real constitution of the United States. What was the American constitution at the moment George III., our former sovereign, acknowledged the American people to be a free and independent nation ? Two facts are certain : the people existed as distinct states, and as states united. They had been constituted colonies, independent in relation to each other, by their former sovereign, and were united as one by being dependent on one and the same supreme national authority. As colonies they were distinct and mutually independent, but under the relation of nationality they were one people, so far as people they were. They, therefore, remained one after the separation from Great Britain, unless in the act of separation, or immediately or subsequently, something was done to destroy their national

---

* *Origin and Constitution of Government,* Brownson's Works, Vol. XV., pp. 405 *et seq.*

unity. The essential constitution then was a federal constitution ; that is, the people acknowledged to be one people or sovereign nation constituted a federal republic, with the political sovereignty vested in them as a federal body, distributed, so to speak, between a general government representing the states united and state governments representing the states in their severalty. Such was the fact. How they became so united and so divided is of no consequence in determining what was or is the real constitution of the American people. It is enough to know that they were so constituted, and that their constitution was legitimate.

The states succeeded to the colonies. Now the colonies were not independent sovereign states, under the British crown, as the electorate of Hanover after the accession of George I., or as was Hungary under the crown of Austria prior to 1848. They were colonies, and were and claimed to be British subjects, with the rights and duties of British subjects. Their independence of the British crown did not necessarily convert them into separate and independent sovereign states, or states in the full and proper sense of the word. They retained the political, civil and corporate rights which they held as colonies, but did not necessarily, or by the act of separation, receive any accession of rights, or become separate and independent nationalities. We find, also, bating a few irregularities not to be counted, that, in point of fact, they never acted as such nationalities. Whatever may have been the theory of the time, or the doctrines contended for by individuals, they never acted as sovereign states, or performed the functions of sovereign states. They declared their independence in common, carried on in common, under the authority of the United States, the war for independence, were acknowledged as the United States, and as the United States they took their rank as a nation. No foreign power has ever recognized any national character in any one of the states, or held any national relations with any one of them in its separate state capacity, or save as one of the *United* States, through the general government. Complete state sovereignty has therefore never existed either in law or in fact,—certainly never in fact.

That from the first there has been more or less widely entertained the theory that under our system sovereignty inheres in the states severally, or that the sovereignty which in colonial times was in Great Britain inured on independence to the states severally, that the articles of confederation were drawn up on that hypothesis, and that the weight of judicial opinion, especially in later times, favors it, we do not deny; but that amounts to nothing, unless we find some political act of the political sovereign recognizing it, and asserting it in the legal constitution. The judicial opinions favoring it in recent times have little weight with us, because they have been more or less influenced by the conflicts and controversies of parties growing out of the slavery question. The prevalence of the theory at the time that the articles of confederation were drawn up and adopted, is by no means conclusive in its favor, because it was a time of revolution, when almost every thing was unsettled, and men's minds were chiefly intent on gaining national independence. Our fathers had no historical precedent to guide them, and even our ablest statesmen only imperfectly comprehended the providential constitution of Anglo-American society. Besides, the question at the moment did not seem to them one of any great importance. They generally held the now exploded doctrine of the origin of the state in the *contrat social*, or the foundation of civil society in compact or agreement between sovereigns, or equal and independent parties. In their view, government formed *de novo* by compact or agreement between independent sovereign states was a real civil society or state, for all civil society, they held, originates in convention, in an express or tacit pact between sovereign individuals. Thus the preamble of the constitution of the commonwealth of Massachusetts, drawn up in 1780 by the elder Adams, the profoundest and most thoroughly accomplished statesman, and perhaps the greatest man our country has ever produced, defined a state or commonwealth to be a voluntary association or agreement of individuals,—a definition that would answer as well for a debating club or a temperance society. It accorded perfectly with the political theories of the time to regard the Union as formed by an agreement or compact between sovereign states. But if the articles of confederation assumed the sovereignty of the states severally, they also assume the contrary, in the rights they assert for the United States as represented by the congress and in the rights they deny to the states respectively. The articles, however imperfect they may have been, were intended to bind the several states together in an inseparable union, and to distribute the exercise of sovereignty between a general government and several state governments. They accorded, indeed, to the states severally, much the larger portion of power; yet they recognized the essential national and political constitution of the American people as a federal people.

The articles of confederation, it is well known, proved a failure, did not meet the wants of the country, and precisely because they left the central government too weak. Their failure proves that they were not in harmony with, or did not fully express the national constitution, the unwritten but real constitution of the American people. The constitution could not endure so weak a centre, or find its expression in simple state sovereignty. Why? Simply because the people had a national instinct, and did and could regard the several states only as parts of one whole, and as unable to stand alone. The articles of confederation did not satisfy this instinct or national sentiment for the whole Anglo-American people. State sovereignty broke the nation into pieces, and destroyed not only the life of the whole, but the life of each of the parts. The very failure of the articles of confederation, proves that the American people were, and felt themselves, one people; a nation, not a confederation of nations. Hence the necessity and explanation of the convention of 1787, called to amend the articles of confederation; and to provide for a more perfect Union; that is, a more complete national government.

The idea that constitutions are made, not generated, no doubt predominated in the minds of the men of 1787, and they supposed that a nation is formed by the constitution agreed upon and adopted by the people. Whether the Anglo-American people were really one nation or not prior to the adoption of the constitution, was to them a matter of no consequence, because they regarded as the constitution only the written instrument, and the written instrument as constituting the nation, or civil society. If that asserted or implied nationality, it was enough. Hence Mr. Webster, in his controversy with Hayne and Calhoun, of South Carolina, concedes that the states severally were originally sovereign, and the first union formed under the articles of confederation was simply a congress of sovereign states; but that the new federal constitution, when adopted, made the states one state, or rather constituted the people of the several states one people. Mr. Calhoun, taking a more philosophical view of political constitutions, maintained that, if the states were sovereign prior to the

adoption of the federal constitution, they remained so
after its adoption, and that the federal government could
only be a compact between independent sovereigns, and
however great or numerous the powers conceded to it, they
are simply delegated powers, and powers delegated by sovereign states.   Hence, the United States are not a civil society, and the federal government is not a government proper, but is and can be only an agency created by the states.
The states are principals, and the Union must be interpreted
by the law that governs the relation of principal and agent.
Mr. Webster, still adhering to the doctrine that civil
society is founded in compact, the doctrine of the *contrat
social*, continued to assert that since the adoption of the
constitution we are one people, but could not succeed in re-
futing Mr. Calhoun's reasoning.   This concession, which
could be safely made on his theory of the foundation of the
state in compact, was fatal to his argument on Mr. Calhoun's
theory, which denies that a state is created by agreement or
convention, and maintains that it exists prior to the adoption
of the written constitution.   Mr. Calhoun always maintained
that the real constitution is in the constitution of the people, and is anterior to the written constitution ; for only a
constituted people, a political people, a people already existing as a state or organized nation, can draw up and ordain a written constitution.   In this he was, in our judgment right, and therefore, if the people of the United States
did not exist as one political people prior to the convention
of 1787, they did not afterwards, and do not so exist now ;
for the convention could not create what did not exist ; and
could only regulate or determine the mode or manner in
which a preëxisting power, which it represented or was,
might or should be exercised.

The written constitution is the fundamental law of the
government, but it always presupposes a state or political
sovereign that draws it up and ordains it.   It is a sovereign
act, and the act or creature of the political sovereign ; and
where there is no sovereign people, there can be no such
constitution established, because there is no power competent to establish it, and impress upon it the character of law.
The people cannot establish a constitution unless they are,
or exist.   They must exist as a people before they can meet
in convention and agree on a constitution.   But who are
the people that can meet in convention ?   Are they a people previously defined, the people of a certain defined terri-

tory? Or are they any number of persons inhabiting such territory or not, coming together fortuitously, and irrespective of any preëxisting authority or law? Can any number of persons who choose, without reference to territorial boundaries or preëxisting law, come together, and constitute themselves into a sovereign state? If so, we have no right to complain of the secessionists, or to brand them as rebels, or traitors. Here is the insuperable objection to the theory that founds civil society in compact, and maintains that the state is created by the written constitution, or that written constitutions are law when they are framed by no political power competent to ordain and enforce them.

The real starting-point for the American statesman is the convention of 1787. The constitution drawn up by the convention, and subsequently ratified by the states respectively, or by conventions of the people thereof, purports to emanate not from the states, but from "the people of the United States." Thus in the preamble we read " We, *the people of the United States*, in order to form a more perfect Union, establish justice, insure domestic tranquillity, provide for the common defence, promote the general welfare, and secure the blessings of liberty to ourselves and our posterity, do ordain and establish this constitution for the United States of America." Can any thing be more clear, explicit, and to the purpose? Who ordain and establish this constitution? The states severally? No. " We, the people of the United States." For whom do the people of the United States ordain and establish it? For "the United States of America." The constitution does not emanate from the states severally, but from the people of the United States. Then there must have been such a people already existing, for, if there had been no people of the United States, they could not have ordained and established, or assume to ordain and establish, a constitution. This people could not have been created by the constitution, for it ordains and establishes, or creates the constitution, and it is absurd to suppose that the creature creates its creator. There not only was, then, a people of the United States, but a sovereign political people, for none but a sovereign political people can ordain and establish a constitution. Hence, with the constitution before our eyes, we assert, and are obliged to assert, that the political sovereignty with us resides not in the states, nor in the people of the states severally, but in the political people of the United States, or of

the states united. Therefore, we have maintained that the
sovereignty which before separation and independence, was
vested in the British crown, or the mother country, lapsed
to the states united, not to the states severally, and therefore
the Anglo-American people have always been one people,
and since the acknowledgment of independence by Great
Britain, one sovereign people, with all the inherent unity
and rights of self-government of any other free, sovereign,
and independent nation.

That the political sovereignty is in the people of the United States is still further evident from Article X. of the
amendments. "The powers not delegated to the United
States by this constitution, nor prohibited by it to the states,
are reserved to the states respectively, or to the people."
The article would have been more consistent with itself,
and more consonant with the general spirit of the constitution, if it had said "delegated to the general government,"
instead of the United States; but, though drawn up and
adopted to satisfy the scruples or the fears of the Anti-
federal or state-rights party of the time, it recognizes the
political people of the United States. The reserved powers
are "reserved to the states respectively, or—to the people."
What people? The people of the states respectively? No,
otherwise it would have read, "are reserved to the states
respectively, or to the people thereof." The "thereof" is
omitted, and therefore we must understand, by the people,
"the people of the United States. This interpretation is
confirmed by Article V., which provides for amending the
constitution without the unanimous consent of all the states,
or the people thereof. Amendments proposed by two-
thirds of the members of both houses of congress, or by
conventions called by congress, on application of the legislatures of two-thirds of the states, when ratified by the legislatures of three-fourths of the states, or by conventions
in three-fourths thereof, are valid, to all intents and purposes, as parts of the constitution. These amendments, so
proposed and ratified, are as binding on the states opposing
them as on the states ratifying them. This supposes a political sovereign distinct from state sovereignty, competent
to alter the constitution, and to enlarge or contract the
powers of either the general government or the state governments.

But we have asserted the political people of the United
States, and asserted them as vested with full and complete

sovereignty. But this sovereign people is the people of the United *States*. There is with us no political people out of either the states or the Union. The sovereign people are the people organized as states, but as states united. This is the essential constitution of the American state; and is the creature of no pact or convention. We owe it to the fact that the Anglo-American people existed while under Great Britain as distinct and mutually independent colonies under one sovereign authority. The people who asserted their independence were one people, but they existed as thirteen colonies, and they could act only as they existed, and as they had been accustomed to act; that is, through such organizations as they had. Each colony was an autonomous body. It had been so under British rule, and continued so under independence, making as little alteration or change in its internal organization or structure as possible, simply supplying by election or appointment such officers, political, legislative, executive, or judicial, as the change from colonial subjection to independence rendered necessary, and supplying, by union with the sister colonies, the loss of national sovereignty occasioned by the lapse of that of Great Britain. The internal social structure remained unchanged. The same people voted that had voted in colonial times, the laws were continued, and the courts were retained merely with patriotic judges, instead of royal judges. The people accustomed to vote chose their legislators and their delegates to the congress of the United States in the way previously established, or according to customary forms. We say not that every thing was done by a strictly legal authority, for we do not understand how any revolution can be effected by legal authority; but we do say that all was done constitutionally, or that what the people did they did in their constituted or organic character.

So in the convention of 1787 That convention was the convention of the political people of the United States, a national convention, as much so as that of France in 1793, or the later one in 1848; and even more so than the latter, because it was called by a recognized legitimate public authority. But this people was represented in it by delegates chosen by states, or the people existing and acting through state organizations. They could be present in no other way, because in no other way did they exist as civil society. The constitution agreed on by the convention was submitted to the people as organized into states for ratification.

This was a measure of prudence, not of necessity, for the people in convention were the people, and in their plenary sovereignty. But it was wise to get, as it were, their reiterated assent, their assent given in convention, repeated out of the convention, or, as in our days it is called, a *plebiscitum*, though this added nothing, except as they chose to submit to it, to the legality of their act in convention. But choosing to demand the popular ratification of their act, the people could give it only as states, either through the state legislatures, or through conventions of the people of the states legally convoked.

If this is borne in mind, taking the convention of 1787 as our point of departure, the American people will be found to have in some sense a two-fold capacity, state and federal, or to exercise their sovereignty partly through a general government and partly through state governments. They are in each one and the same people, and the two governments combined constitute only one full and complete government. There are not two sovereigns, one of the Union and the other of a particular state, but the one sovereign people governs alike in both the state and the Union. The Union does not derive from the states, nor the states from the Union, but both coexist as the one political sovereign, acting as one sovereign through a two-fold organization. Historically considered, the same sovereignty represented in the United States is the creator of the states, regarded simply as colonies of Great Britain, transformed by independence into what, under our system, we call states. The colonies were created, organized, or constituted bodies politic and corporate by the sovereignty of Great Britain, whose subjects the colonists were. That sovereignty on independence inuring to the United States, the states depend on the United States, and can be bodies politic only as states united, as they were British colonies only under British sovereignty.

The existence of the people of the United States as one people prior to the adoption of the federal constitution, we think, is sufficiently proved by what we have now said, and by what has been said on several previous occasions. But whether so or not we are obliged to assume it, because that constitution asserts such existence, and, as the sovereign people, ordains and establishes it. We cannot go behind its assertion and question its truth. On that point the declaration of the convention is conclusive, for the convention was itself that people assembled by its delegates. We are not disposed to deny that prior to the adoption of the federal constitution the people in their federal capacity were but imperfectly organized and represented, and therefore that the constitution was incomplete. The practical organization and measures for expressing and governing according to the internal constitution of the people were in an inchoate state, and the people never really came into the full practical possession of their sovereignty till the convention was called. Its organs were not fully formed and were defective, and the nation was struggling to get full possession of its faculties, and to exert them according to its will. In fact, we may regard the nation, politically considered, from 1776 to 1787, as in an embryonic state. The convention is the real date of its birth, and in interpreting its constitution we must take it precisely as the convention presents it to us. Whatever facts or opinions may be encountered at a prior period adverse to indivisible nationality, or to the unity of the national sovereign, must count for nothing, for the assertion of the convention in the preamble of the constitution overrides them, or is the law of their interpretation.

The written constitution is not the creator of the political sovereign, for only the political sovereign can write it. It is never a constitution of the state, That is the constitution of the state by which the people are constituted in themselves, and by virtue of which they are not only a political people, but a political people of such or such a character. It is the essential and differential principle of a given people, and is generated and born with it. Hence we say constitutions are generated, not made. The written constitution is really only a solemn act of the political sovereign, already existing and constituted, or declaration of the rules by which the sovereign state is to be governed in the exercise of its power. With us it is the solemn declaration of the political people, and the manner in which they will govern, for with us sovereignty vests in the political people. It is in the nature of an ordinance or supreme law enacted by the sovereign people, binding alike upon them as governors and as governed. It is an act of the sovereign will, and is a constitution, not of that sovereign will, but of the several branches of the government it chooses to create. Governments have three distinct functions, with us separated into three separate as well as distinct departments—the legislative, the judicial, and the executive. But back of and over all these is the political or sovereign power of the state, which organizes according to its will these several departments of government, delegates to them their powers, which they hold and exercise according to the constitution publicly ordained and established in free states, by the arbitrary orders of the monarch in despotic states.

The political sovereignty always exists and is inherent in the nation, and inseparable from it. Hence most writers on government hold, that even in monarchies the sovereignty vests in the people or nation, and that kings hold their power only as a trust from the people, and forfeit it when they grossly and persistently abuse it. Hence the doctrine that kings and emperors are justiciable, and that even armed resistance when the monarch becomes a tyrant is lawful, and sometimes a civic duty. The early fathers of the church and the mediæval doctors were, we believe, unanimous in maintaining this doctrine ; and the doctrine of the divine right of kings and passive obedience, the irresponsibility of rulers, and the inamissibility of power, seems to have been unknown or without defenders prior to the Stuarts in England, and Bossuet in France. All power is indeed from God, but it comes to kings, kaisers, rulers, and magistrates from God through the people or nation. The political power or sovereign with us, whence all legislative, judicial, and executive powers are derived, and to whom they are responsible, is what we call the political people of the United States, whose supreme organ is the convention. The convention is supreme, and can modify, in the prescribed way, the powers now possessed by either the general government or by the several state governments, or by any branch of either. We see the unity and political sovereignty of the United States in the convention, not in the several state governments, nor yet in the general government, all of which are subordinate to the convention, and possess only the delegated and limited powers it concedes them. That the convention is supreme, and the people assumed to be present in it is sovereign, we know, from the fact that it can enlarge or contract the powers held by either the general government or the several states at its will. Were it not so, the provision adopted for amending the constitution would be nugatory, and there would be no way of getting amendments but by revolution. If the preamble asserts the existence of a sovereign people of the United States, the fifth article of the constitution asserts equally the supremacy of the convention. It is true, three-fourths of the states must give their assent to any proposed amendment before it can become a part of the constitution ; but that provision itself, which we regard as a wise concession to the minority, and also very necessary to render constitutional changes difficult, and to preserve the stability of the government, is alterable by the convention, and a simple majority of the states may be made competent to adopt new amendments.

If now you ask, What is the constitution of the United States ? we answer, It is the original and inherent constitution of the American people as a federal republic, or people existing in several state organizations, united in one general organization, as one people in many, and many in one. Is it asked, Who made this *constitution ?* we answer, It was not made, it grew ; grew up with the people, with the circumstances in which they were placed, and came into play with national independence. It was the work, not of human foresight, forethought, or deliberation, but of Providence, using men and their circumstances as his agents. Is it asked, What is the constitution of the government ? we answer, It is the written instrument before us. Are we asked ? Who made it ? or who ordained and established it ? we answer, the convention, or people of the United States acting through their several state organizations, because there is no political people of the United States existing outside or independent of state organizations. The sovereignty that ordains and establishes it is the people of the United States in convention, exercising their sovereignty, not as a consolidated mass, but as divided and organized into states. In answer to the question, What is the rule of interpretation or construction of the written constitution ? we answer, The antecedent unwritten constitution, or providential constitution of the people of the United States ; that is, on the one hand so as to save national unity, and on the other, so as to save the rights and autonomy of the states.

It will be perceived that we distinguish between civil society or sovereign state and the government. The sovereign governs in the government, whether state or general; but in either case, the government has only delegated powers. We distinguish also between the United States and the general government. The states united, or the states in their unity, are represented in the general government ; but the United States are anterior to that government, and create it instead of being created by it. This distinction is not always observed, and has been overlooked through the influence of the theory that confounds civil society with the government, and founds government in compact, or the *contrat social*.* Civil society is anterior to the government, and institutes the government, instead of being instituted by it. The government is never the sovereign ; the sovereignty is civil authority itself providentially constituted ; the government, whatever its form, is created and constituted by civil society, or the convention. The people of the United States are sovereign, but the United States government is not sovereign, and has only delegated and limited powers. This distinction is important, although the framers of the constitution seem not to have always kept it in view, as when they speak of the powers " conceded to the United States." They, however, evidently mean, not the United States as represented in convention, but as exercising sovereignty in the government they were creating or organizing. The government is subordinate to the convention, and therefore is not supreme. The several state governments do not derive their powers from the general government, and therefore are not subordinate to it; but they derive their powers from the convention, and, like it, are subordinate to the convention, or to the political people called the United States.

This view of the constitution, whether of the United States or of the general government, guards equally against consolidation and dissolution. The United States are states,

---

* The constitution of civil society, or the sovereign state, is providential, and, as the illustrious Maistre maintains, generated, not made ; but the constitution of the government originates in convention, and is founded in compact expressed or implied. The constitution of the government may be said to be made, but not the constitution of civil society itself. The error arises from confounding the government with the state, or civil society, as Louis XIV. did, when he said, *L'état, c'est moi.* The government, as in absolute governments, may be constituted with unlimited powers, or they may be, as in free states, only with limited powers. That is, the convention may delegate all the powers of sovereignty to the government, as in the present imperial government of France, or it may delegate only certain portions of the powers of civil society, and reserve the others to itself, as is the case in our government, general or state. But the constitution of the government should correspond as nearly as practicable to the inherent, unwritten, providential constitution of the state ; and if it does not so correspond, it will not work well, and the government can maintain itself only by armed force, as in the greater part of the European governments.

and act, whether in the convention or in the general government, only as states, or as a people existing in distinct and mutually independent state organizations. The states, or the people of the states, elect delegates to the convention, representatives and senators in congress, their votes for president and vice-president are given and counted by states, and no enlargement or contraction of their powers can be effected without their consent as states, or people organized as states. This sufficiently secures and asserts state rights. But they have none of these powers or rights save as *united* states, or in national unity. The individual citizen has political power only as a citizen of a state, and of a state only as it is a member of the Union. This guards sufficiently national unity, for the state loses its state rights, all political rights whatever, the moment it ceases to be one of the United States, and its people cease to be an integral portion of the political people of the United States. The Union cannot subsist without the states, nor the states without the Union, since the sovereignty is in the convention, and the convention is the convention of the states, or people of the states united. Dissolve the states, you dissolve the Union; dissolve the Union, and you dissolve the states. The one is as essential to our system as the other, which eschews alike the disintegrating doctrine of state sovereignty, and the centralism which denies state rights, and asserts the federal government as the supreme national government of the land. As we understand it, all are but parts of one people or nation, and both governments are alike essential to one complete national government. The same sovereign governs in both, and the state governments are no less national than the general government. The states govern in the general government as truly as they do in their own, and the nation governs in them as truly as in the general government. The two governments are simply two distinct modes through which the political sovereign, which is one, sees proper to exercise its power; or in other words, the exercise of the indivisible sovereignty is distributed in two distinct organizations, instead of being concentrated, as in all centralized states, in one alone. But this distribution in nothing impairs its unity, for one and the same sovereignty governs in them both.

This, if we may so call it, federal unity, which it requires some little thought and philosophical culture to understand, is the peculiarity of the American state, and the chief merit of its constitution.   We have found in our reading no state or national constitution like it.   The union of separate independent states under one crown is not rare, and formerly existed between England and Hanover, and has long existed between Austria and Hungary; but in these and similar cases, each state is complete in itself, and the union of both under one crown is a personal and not a political union. The emperor of Austria in Hungarian affairs, before the new constitution, not yet accepted by the Hungarians, acted not as emperor of Austria, but as king of Hungary.   There have been numerous examples of the confederacies of states, ancient and modern, as that of the Greek cities, that of the Swiss cantons, and that of the united states of Holland, and that of the present German states.   But none of these were or are a federal state.   The states confederated are each a state complete in itself, and its constitution is as complete without as with the confederation.   But with us the constitution is federal, the state is strictly a federal state.   The central government has no bottom, nothing to rest on without the states, and has its complement in the state governments; and the state governments are complete in themselves, and find their complement as governments proper, only in the central or general government.   Either without the other is like man without men, or men without man. The two subsist synthetically, and constitute together not a syncretic, but a real synthetic state and government, and their separation would be the destruction of both.   Hence we assert a real American state, instead of a confederacy or congeries of states, and call its constitution a federative instead of a unitary constitution, or a government that contains essentially the idea of unity in plurality, and of plurality in unity.   Herein is the originality and the peculiarity of the American constitution expressed in the name UNITED STATES.

The merit of the system is in this originality or peculiarity.   Suppose each state complete in itself, and you have in each a simple unitary state, which within its own limits, like all unitary or centralized states, is a despotism, whether monarchically, aristocratically, or democratically organized. The central government, in such case, would, and could, be no protection for liberty within the particular state.   The power of the states severally might be a check on the power of the central government, as under the feudal *régime* the feudal barons were a check or restraint on the power of the monarchy, but no protection to the people in their respective fiefs against their own tyranny and oppression. The feudal baron limited the power of the monarch, but was not in turn limited by him in his own power over his own vassals and serfs. Within his barony or fief he was absolute, and could govern as he pleased. So it would be in a confederacy of states as distinguished from a federal state. Remove the principle of unity, and the state is dissolved ; take away the principle of plurality, and the Union would be a simple centralized despotism. The true American statesman, who loves and resolves to maintain American freedom, either for the nation or the citizen, will guard with equal vigilance against consolidation and against disintegration—against encroachments on the rights of the states by the central government, and against encroachment on the powers of the central government by the states, or state governments.

It will be seen from what we have said that the constitution of the United States, or, as we prefer to say, the American state, is profoundly philosophical, and accords perfectly with that synthetic philosophy which we have for years defended. We even doubt, if we had not found in that philosophy a key to it, we should ever have been able fully to understand it. It is a complex state, and is founded neither on the simple idea of unity, nor on that of confederation, but on the two ideas dialectically united. This creates the difficulty in understanding it. All, or nearly all, foreigners either interpret it on the unitary principle, suppose the states to be not constituent elements of the nation, but the creatures of the Union, and therefore that the constitution is unitarian, and the government in principle a consolidated or unitarian government ; or else they interpret it by the simple idea of confederation. They can understand that the Union is sovereign, or that the states are severally sovereign, but not that sovereignty is conjointly in both. The majority of our own citizens come very near falling into the one or the other error. The rebels and their sympathizers adopt the theory of state sovereignty, that each of the states is in itself a complete state, and that the Union is merely a confederation, a league, or an alliance, and that when a state in its sovereign capacity secedes, it becomes, *ipso facto,* an independent sovereign state, as much so as France or Great Britain. According to them allegiance is due to the state, and only obedience to the United States by virtue of state enactment. This view is simple, and is easily taken in, and we confess we held and defended it down almost to the breaking out of the rebellion. We were led to it not only by its simplicity, but by supposing that there could be no alternative between it and the opposite view,—the denial of state rights, and the assertion of the Union as a consolidated, or centralized state, which, with our love of liberty, we could not accept. The fact is, that those among us who reject the doctrine that the states are severally sovereign, are apt to favor the doctrine that ours is a consolidated or unitary state. Since the rebellion broke out we have found even our most loyal statesmen defending now the one extreme, and now the other. Obliged to reëxamine the question for ourselves, we have found that our system of government accepts neither as excluding the other, but both dialectically united and harmonized. We may reject both as extremes, and yet accept each as containing an element of truth. There is in each a truth that must be accepted, and in each an error to be rejected. The error is avoided, and the truth asserted in a single judgment, as we have now shown. The constitution of the American state is the synthesis of the rights of the whole and of each of its constituent elements,—what we mean by a federal or federative constitution. What our people need is not to study theories that have been adopted for interpreting the constitution, but to study the constitution itself, as it really is in the written constitution of the government, and the unwritten and providential constitution of the American people, from whom the written constitution has emanated. In this deeper sense the constitution has been little studied amongst us. If it had been, the people of the southern states had never rebelled or seceded, for they, with very few exceptions, never intended to be rebels or traitors to the government to which they owed allegiance. The mass of them have only done what they sincerely believed they had a perfect moral and civil right to do. Hence, while we feel it the duty of the Union to suppress their rebellion by force of arms, we entertain for them personally no ill-will, and indeed entertain sentiments of respect for their sincerity, as well as for their bravery, and we deeply commiserate them in their delusion, and the fearful sufferings which it has occasioned them, and which they have borne so manfully.

But no man can really understand the American constitution without long, deep, and earnest study. It is easy to master the routine, the external forms, the practical methods of conducting a canvass, elections, or of enacting laws, and the like, but the deeper, the inner sense of the constitution, the mass of our citizens neither understand nor suspect. They can talk fluently, sometimes flippantly, if they read the journals, about democracy, aristocracy, monarchy, liberty, despotism, but are at fault whenever required to speak of the constitution of the state. Indeed, not a few of them have no conception of what a state is, and still less of what is the American state. A state, a real state, is a mysterious existence. It is not a voluntary association, a collection, or an aggregation of individuals, with no existence, no life, no activity, except what it derives from them. It is a real existence, not a mere abstraction; an organism, not a mere organization. It has its own unity, its own central life, of which individuals participate, and which enables them to live at once a national and an individual life. It does not subsist without individuals, nor does it subsist in individuals as formed by them. They must obey at once the law of national life, and of individual life, and have in them a national, no less than an individual element, so that every individual pertains partly to the state, and partly to himself. The mystery of the state is, in some sense, the mystery of the race itself, distinguishable, never separable, from the individual, any more than the individual is separable from the race, or men from man. It is analogous to the mystery of the church, what is called the mystic body of Christ, and, perhaps, is only a lower phase of that same mystery. Of all conceivable states, the American state is the most complex, the most mysterious, and demands the most intelligence, the most study, and the most thorough mental discipline for its scientific understanding. No people ever had greater need than we of the profoundest political philosophy, and hardly a people can be found with less, or that has not a better understanding of the constitution of its country. Liberty, in the American sense, is a boon that can be received, retained, and enjoyed only by a people that stands in the front line of modern civilization, and even further advanced than any other nation that has hitherto existed. Let us hope that the present life-and-death struggle of the nation will force the American mind to the study of political science, and to master the profound and philosophical constitution of the American state.

Returning to the question regarding the rebellious states with which we set out, we can now easily dispose of it.

The simple question to be settled is, are these states a part, an integral part, of the *political* people of the United States, in whom vests the national and state sovereignty? The sovereignty is one and indivisible, and vests in the political people of the United States. But the whole population and territory belonging to the Union, and within its jurisdiction, are not included in the *political* people of the United States, and none not so included have any political rights or existence under the constitution as it is. None are so included except those who are organized into states, and states existing in the Union; that is, none but citizens of a federal state. The people of the territories, not yet organized into states and admitted into the Union, are no part of the political people of the United States. They have no political rights, no political existence, and are simply subjects. The powers of the territorial government derive solely from congress, not from the territorial people. The non-political people have duties, and may have equal *civil* rights, but no *political* rights or powers.*

The fact, then, that the rebellious population and territory belong as population and territory to the United States, does not make them states in the Union, or give them any political rights or existence; otherwise the territories would be states in the Union, and the territorial people would have political rights, and there would be no distinction conceivable between a state and a territory, which, indeed, seems to have been the doctrine of the Kansas-Nebraska bill, but which the supreme court, in the *Dred Scott* case, very decidedly rejects. The rights of suffrage and eligibility belong only to citizens of an organized state which is in the Union as a state, not merely as population and territory.

---

* We call *civil* rights, the rights of persons and property, some of them natural, some of them acquired, which the law recognizes and protects for all persons, without distinction of age or sex; we call *political* rights, the rights of sovereignty, or the right of the citizen to participate in the government of the country. In a monarchy proper, these rights are the rights of the monarch alone; in an aristocracy, they are the rights of the nobles; in a democracy, they are the rights of every freeman; with us, they are, in most of the states, the rights of all free white male persons, and in some, of all free male citizens, without regard to color, over twenty one years of age, of sound mind, and not having been convicted of any infamous or disqualifying offence, and who are at once citizens of the United States, and of a particular state. They may all be included in the right to vote, and the right to be voted for, or suffrage and eligibility. The American citizens who have the rights of suffrage and eligibility, are what we call the political people, and may include a larger or smaller number, according to the will of the convention.

Now we do not pretend to deny that the people and territory in rebellion belong to the United States, and are, though rebellious, a part of the population and territory of the Union. It is only on the ground that they are that we can make war against them as rebels. The simple question is, are they a part of the *political* people and territory of the United States? To be so, they must be states legitimately organized and in the Union; that is, they must be *federal* states. Are they federal states? They certainly are not. They were such states, but have ceased to be, and have so ceased by their own free, voluntary act. They have seceded from the political people of the Union, and, by doing so, have lost for their population and territory all their political rights in the Union. As they could be states and possess political rights only in the Union, they have, by their act of secession, ceased to be states, or to have any political rights at all. Their legal *status*, even were they not rebels, would be simply that of population and territory of the Union, not yet organized into states and admitted into the Union, which as we have seen, have no political rights or existence whatever.

But it is said that the states have not seceded. They have not seceded, because they could not. We might retort, they could secede, because they have seceded, and *valet argumentum ab esse ad posse*, as all logicians maintain. The states have not seceded from the population and territory of the Union, and could not, except by a successful revolution, we grant; but we see no reason why they could not secede from the political people of the Union, and thus deprive themselves of all political *status*, or political rights under our system in the Union. To be a state in the Union, is a privilege conferred by the convention or supreme political power; but the convention compels no one to accept or to retain the privilege. There is no authority in the state or nation to compel me to avail myself of my political rights —to compel me to vote at any election, although I have the right, or to accept of an office, although I am eligible. The territory needs the permission of congress to organize itself as a state and to come into the Union, but the organization and the application are voluntary acts, and there is no power under our system to compel them. What an actor may freely do, he may as freely undo. The state in the Union, as a federal state, has certain very important and much coveted rights, but if it chooses to forego or to abdicate them, what is to hinder it?

Moreover, a state under the federal system, though it has not full and complete sovereignty, for it is sovereign only in union with others, has, nevertheless, autonomy, and is capable of standing on its own feet, and acting from its own centre. It is a constituent element of the Union, but a living, self-acting element. In performing its revolutions with its sister planets around the common centre, it revolves in an orbit of its own, and on its own axis. This is what is said when we say it is autonomous, or self-acting. Now by virtue of this autonomy, not derived from the Union, but possessed only in the Union, it is competent to withdraw itself from the political people, or to abdicate all the political rights it holds as being an integral part of that people. The seceded states claim to have done so. Grant that in doing so they have annihilated their own political existence, killed themselves, committed political suicide; even that does not exceed the limits of their free agency, and is only the extreme exertion of their autonomy. Cannot a man, if he is wicked enough, or foolish enough, commit suicide? To deny this would be to deny the autonomy, the substantive existence of the states—would be to deny the federal constitution of the American state, and to make the states simple provinces, prefectures, dependencies, and the republic a simply unitary state—the doctrine which seems to have been that of the president himself, for in some of his early speeches after his election, he compared the relation which a state bears to the Union to that of the county to a state, forgetting that the county is a simple creature of the state, and that the state is a constituent element of the Union, not created by it, any more than the hand is created by the head.

In the exercise of its autonomy, or its free agency, the state secedes, declares itself out of the Union; that is, no longer a state in the Union. Eleven states have so seceded. What, then, remains of these *states* as states in the Union? Not the political people of the state, for that people exists only in the political organization, and that organization is gone, since it exists only as a federal organization, or as an organization in the Union, and loyal to it. What remains, then, as the state? Nothing. No. The state, we are told again, has not seceded; only the rebellious part of the population has seceded. The state remains in the loyal Union men. But the act of secession, if an act at all, was the act of the state. The authority of the state is personal and territorial, and binds both population and territory; alike secessionists and non-secessionists, the loyal to the Union no less than the disloyal. Otherwise it would not be a state. Was the act of secession an act of the state? It has pleased our administration to assume the contrary, and to maintain that secession was the work of a faction in the state, and not the work of the people of the state at all. This we now know was not the fact. In every case the secession ordinance received the votes of a majority of the political people of the state, and was as literally and as truly the act of the state as any act is or can be. No doubt, if the great body of the people had been let alone, or if an active and energetic few had not stirred them up, they would not have voted as they did; but that, we apprehend, is the case in all elections, even in the loyal states. The few always lead and govern the many, and the real contest in every election is a contest between two opposing minorities. Even if there had been irregularities in the state action, it would have been only a question between the citizens of the state themselves, and none between them and the general government, which can, constitutionally, interfere in the internal affairs of a state, only to suppress insurrection or to guaranty a republican form of government. Neither case existed. There was no insurrection against the state authorities, and no attempt to set up in the state other than a republican form of government.

The secession evidently was not the work of a faction in the state itself, but undeniably was, as we have maintained from the first, the act of the state, or the political people of the state, acting as a political organized community, in their highest political capacity, through the forms of law and the constitution of the state government. Therefore the state has seceded, and in seceding has ceased to be a state. Certainly there were in all the seceded states differences of opinion among the citizens, and in them all many citizens who in their sentiments and convictions were loyal to the federal Union; but these, if they still remain, be they more or be they fewer, are not the state, for they have no political organization, and no unorganized people are a state. The Union men in the rebel territory may, under an enabling act of congress, be organized politically, and become states, but it is idle to pretend that they are states in the Union now.

Having settled this, we can understand the political condition of the rebel population and territory. They are, seclude the fact of rebellion, simply population and territory belonging to the Union, and in precisely the condition of any other population and territory belonging to the United States, but not yet erected into states and admitted into the Union. The process by which they may be restored as states is precisely that by which new states under our system are formed and admitted into the Union.

We are not in the secrets of the administration, but from all we have been able to learn, its plan is to treat the seceded states as still states in the Union, and the Union men as the state. These are to be allowed or encouraged to organize under the old state constitution, now really defunct, to elect their officers, state and federal, and to resume all the functions, rights, and immunities of a state in the Union. But if the states are held to have never seceded, and to be still states in the Union, there is already a state organization existing, and the state is in that organization, and can act only through it. The new organization formed without and against its authority, would be illegal and revolutionary, in direct violation of every principle of constitutional government. This plan would do more credit to a ranting Jacobin than to a constitutional lawyer, and can be favored by none who really understands that the American state is a constitutional state, and that it is only the organized political people, acting through constitutional forms, and according to law, that is sovereign.

But what is to prevent the disloyal and rebellious population, the unquestionable majority in all the rebellious states, from outvoting the Union men? "None but Union men," Mr. Henry Winter Davis tells us, "are to be permitted to vote." By what authority are others to be prevented? In passing an enabling act, as it is called, congress can prescribe the qualifications of electors, and say who may or may not vote in the organization of the state. In the question of organizing a new state, congress may declare disqualified, both in relation to suffrage and eligibility, all disloyal persons, and all persons whose loyalty is suspected ; but when the state is once constituted, the qualifications of voters, even for electors of the president and vice-president of the United States, and for members of congress, are determined by the state. Hence, we have never fully understood by what right the government interfered in the recent elections in Maryland and Delaware. Where does it find its authority for proposing a test oath, and to prevent by its military police any citizen from voting who refuses to take it? The government may come, as in Kentucky and Missouri, in aid of the state authorities to enable them to enforce the law of the state, but to interfere in its own name, without any pretence of state law, is, it seems to us, an unauthorized interference, at war with constitutional government, incompatible with the freedom and purity of elections, and going far towards rendering them null and void. We concede that persons ought not to be permitted to vote for officers of a government they are striving to overthrow, or to which they are really disloyal; but it is the business of the state authorities to exclude them. If the state authorities cannot exclude them, send them sufficient federal force to enable them to do it; if they can, but will not, then treat the state as disloyal, place it under martial law, in a state of siege, and thus for the time being suspend the elections. The convention, in framing the constitution of the government, made ample provisions for such cases, by clothing the government with the war power; and a state constitution, when perverted to shield traitors and rebels, can be suspended under that power, or by martial law, without being violated, or the principle of constitutional government being attacked.

Yet the end contemplated in this plan can be as speedily and as effectually attained in a constitutional way as in an unconstitutional way, and even more so. The rebels in each of the states in question had the state organization, and by their rebellion have destroyed it. All loyal men are agreed that the rebels have ceased to belong to the political people of the United States, that is, have ceased to have any political rights whatever, and the purpose, both of those who oppose us, and of those who agree with us, is to prevent them while remaining rebels, or disloyal, from exercising any political rights in the state or in the Union. Both alike wish to reconstitute the lapsed states in the hands of the loyal Union men inhabiting their territory. Constitutionally, this cannot be done, if we hold these states to be still *states* in the Union. But concede what is the obvious fact, that these states by their act of secession have ceased to exist as states, and every difficulty vanishes. Let congress declare the surcease of the states, organize the rebel population and territory into territorial governments, and then, when the territory is ready to become a state, pass an enabling act authorizing the territorial people to organize as a state, elect state and federal officers, and claim admission into the Union. In this enabling act, who may or may not vote in the organization of the state, may be prescribed by congress, without exceeding its constitutional powers, and therefore all who will not take the oath of allegiance may be excluded, and the state organization secured to Union men. All that is necessary to make the plan we have criticised legal and constitutional is, that the Union men should organize *de novo*, not as the continuation of the seceded state, and under a new constitution, not the old. The new may be a duplicate of the old, if the convention pleases, or it may be different from it. The convention may revive and confirm as many or as few of the rights acquired under the old as it sees fit. The matter is plain enough, and less difficult than the unconstitutional way which we oppose, and which seems to be favored by the administration.

It is greatly to be regretted that Gen. Ashley's bill did not become a law. Early in the regular session of 1861–2, this distinguished member of congress from Ohio introduced, as far as we can judge, a carefully drawn bill for the organization of the rebel population and territory into territories under governments established by congress. The bill took a legal, constitutional, and statesmanlike view of the subject, and if it had become a law, much confusion would have been avoided, several very questionable things would not have been done, and the loyal men of the country would not have been divided as they now are, on a question on which there should be no disagreement. We hope Gen. Ashley will revive his bill early in the present congress, and meet with better success than he did when he originally introduced it. The subject is eminently one for congressional action, for under our system of government, congress alone has the constitutional power to deal with it. The executive has no authority to act on it, save under the war power, and he has the war power only in its executive branch. The president, in his letter to a meeting of friends of the Union at Springfield, Ill., last August or September, quietly remarks, " I suppose I have the war power." We have been in the habit of supposing the contrary : that the constitution vests that power in congress, and that the president carries on war as commander-in-chief of the army and navy only in the execution of the law or laws of congress. We have supposed, also, that congress does nothing under the war power that it can do under its peace power. If we are not on our guard, with a war of such formidable dimensions on our hands, and all minds and hearts intent on military success, we shall overload the war power, or forget, till too late, that there is such a thing as the civil power. We must remember that our own brave and noble army, to which we owe more than we are always aware of, is enduring all its fatigues, all its hardships, sickness in camp, wounds and death on the battle-field to reëstablish the supremacy of the civil power, not to install the war power as the government of the country.

We know our most excellent president shrinks from no responsibility, except severity to criminals, especially traitors, and is willing to take his own and that of congress too; but we do not think it becoming in congress to suffer a free horse to be ridden to death. It has no right to throw on the executive, who must have his hands full with the business of his own department, the responsibility devolved by the constitution of the government on itself. We have every possible confidence in the patriotic intentions and business capacity of the executive, but we do not feel ourselves at liberty to regard him as alone and in himself the whole government, and we want each branch of the government to assert its independence, and to do its own work. At present, the whole question in regard to the treatment of the rebel population and territory is left to the discretion of the executive. There may be serious danger in this—a danger so much the greater because we cannot fully expose it without assuming an attitude which, in these times, might be mistaken for that of hostility to the administration. We have no wish to restrict, in the smallest respect possible, the constitutional sphere of the executive, nor have we any disposition to enlarge it. We are neither monarchists nor democrats; we are constitutionalists, and we raise as our battle-cry, and demand, "The Union as it was, and the constitution as it is;" but in our sense, as explained in this article, not in the sense of those who seek only to embarrass the government, and to preserve intact the fondly cherished institution of negro slavery.

We say, then, in conclusion, that we believe it of vital importance to the safety of our constitutional system that congress should take possession of the whole subject, and dispose of it in its wisdom. If congress do not do it, we fear the consequences will be such as every loyal American will deplore as long as he lives, and his children after him. Let congress look to it.

THE PRESIDENT'S MESSAGE AND PROCLAMATION.*

[From Brownson's Quarterly Review for January, 1864.]

ALL will agree that this message, including the proclamation appended to it, is one of great importance, perhaps the most important that has ever been sent to congress by a president of the United States. It tells us plainly the executive plan for reorganizing the rebellious states as states in the Union, and the terms on which the rebels may be restored to their rights of property and citizenship. The plan of reorganization in its outlines, however, has been well understood to be that of the administration since the first advance of our army into Tennessee, and was criticised in this *Review*† in April, 1862, and has been uniformly opposed by us ever since. It will be found discussed at length in the article on *The Federal Constitution*, written and in type before the message was delivered. We find nothing in the president's reasoning in his message, or in the details of the plan as set forth in his proclamation, to induce us to change our opinion of the plan. We honestly believe the plan unconstitutional, and fraught with hardly less danger to our republican institutions than the southern rebellion itself, and all the more dangerous because it is not unlikely to enlist in its support a large portion of the most fearless and most devoted friends of the Union.

The executive plan is ingenious; it is astute, but it seems to us the plan of the politician, rather than of the statesman, and to look more to the next presidential election than to the real welfare of the nation. If accepted by congress it secures Mr. Lincoln's renomination, and reëlection to the presidency; no serious objection in itself, indeed, for it matters not who administers the government if it is well administered; and our rule is to retain the present incumbent so long as he faithfully and efficiently discharges the duties of his office. It is better to put up with evils that we know

---

* *Third Annual Message of President Lincoln to both Houses of Congress,* December 9, 1863.
† *Emancipation and Colonization, ante,* p. 253.

than fly to others that we know not of.   There are many reasons why we should prefer the reëlection of Mr. Lincoln to the election of a new man.   He has acquired experience, and knows the ropes.   He is far better qualified to administer the government for a second term than he was for the first.   We do not, therefore, object to the executive plan on account of its probable bearing on the next presidential election.   We object to putting forth so important a plan with such a view, and for such a reason.

We object primarily to the plan of reorganization proclaimed, because it is an executive plan, and as an executive plan without the sanction or acquiescence of congress cannot be carried into effect.   If the president had simply recommended the measure to congress, with his reasons for wishing it to be adopted, he would have done his duty, and whether congress approved the plan or not, he would have been free from all blame.   What we object to is the attempt by executive action to forestall the action of congress, or to place the whole question in such a position as to render it next to impossible for congress to refuse its sanction.

The president proceeds on the supposition that he is clothed with the whole war power of the nation, and as the war power is unlimited, while the war lasts he may do any thing he judges proper.   Judge Trumbull, of Illinois, in his speech in the senate early in the session of 1861–62, corrects this error into which the president and many others appear to have fallen, and proves, what we all ought to have understood, that the war power is vested by the constitution in congress, and in congress alone.   It was that able speech that set us right on the question, and showed us that we had written our essay on *Slavery and the War*, with a wrong impression as to the constitutional powers of the president. The president is the chief executive of the nation, and has the executive branch of the war power, but only that branch. As commander-in-chief of the army and navy, he has authority to make such disposition of the land and naval forces placed by congress at his command, as he judges most proper to gain the military ends congress has designated.   He can issue such orders and do such things as are allowed by the laws of war to commanders-in-chief, and are of strict military necessity.   He can take enemy's property and enemy's slaves, or declare them emancipated, appoint military governors for conquered territory, where no civil government is acknowledged, and govern it by military law.   But he cnnot organize such territory under a civil government, or say on what terms its inhabitants may or may not regain a civil organization, for that, under our system, is the prerogative of congress alone.

The civil organization of government cannot be done even by congress under the war power, and if done at all, must be done under its peace powers, as specified in the constitution. The seceded states are still states, that is, civil and political organizations in the Union, or they are not. If they are, the executive; neither under the war power, nor any other power, has any authority to establish military or any other governments within their limits. If they are not, their reorganization is the work of congress under its peace powers. The executive has then, in either case, nothing to do with their civil reorganization till congress has acted, and then only to carry out the law of congress. Congress is competent to reorganize them under the peace powers of the government, or it is not; for under the war power only military governments can be instituted. The institution or reorganization of civil government is always the act of the supreme political power, of the sovereign authority of the state or nation, and is the work of peace, not of war. The president, then, when he tells congress it must hold on to the war power, as the power under which the rebellious states are to be reorganized, forgets that neither he nor congress can reorganize them under that power. The moment we come to the civil reorganization of conquered territory, the belligerent rights have ceased, and only the rights of peace are in operation.

The president, in his proclamation, tells the rebels on what conditions or terms they may escape the penalties of their treason and resume the exercise of their political and civil rights. He has, unquestionably, the right to except from the confiscation and emancipation laws of congress, to the extent that those laws give him power to do so, but it may be questioned if he has not, in the amnesty and general pardon he has proclaimed, exceeded his powers. He claims, by virtue of his power to pardon, a general dispensing power, for daring to exercise which, James II. of England lost the crown of three kingdoms. We are the last man in the world who would deprive the president of the power to pardon, of mercy, but we do not wish to see it *very* grossly abused. The terms of the amnesty should have been settled by congress, and the proclamation would have been more in order, and had more weight, if it had been issued in obedience to an act of congress. An amnesty, general pardon, and restoration to civil rights are not proclaimed under the war powers, but under the peace powers of the government, and when proclaimed on certain conditions they are null, if the conditions are not complied with. And also when the authority proclaiming them is not competent to fix the conditions, which the executive is not. Congress may to-morrow, if it chooses, overrule the proclamation, or pass a law prescribing entirely different conditions. Nothing the president has done beyond what the acts of congress authorize, binds congress in the slightest degree. It would, then have been much better to have submitted the whole matter to congress, with such suggestions and recommendations as the executive judged proper. It would have been far more in consonance with the constitution which distributes the functions of government in three departments, instead of concentrating them in one alone, and that the executive.

We have, we admit, no grave objections to the terms on which the executive proposes amnesty and pardon to the rebels. We have no vindictive feelings to gratify, and we ask not for vengeance. The terms the president proposes are as severe as we have ever contemplated, perhaps severer. But we would offer no terms at all to rebels till they have submitted. Submission first, is our rule. When rebels have submitted and thrown themselves on the mercy of the government, we will then offer terms, and treat them humanely, liberally. The submission of rebels at discretion, is the homage they owe to the authority they have unlawfully and wickedly resisted, and it is needed to vindicate the honor of authority, the majesty of the state. The rebels had, in the beginning, liberal terms enough offered them, and this proclamation looks like an act of weakness on the part of the government, and will be taken as such by the rebels themselves. It is an exhibition of northern doughfacedness, and want of manliness. The rebels are still in arms against the government, and it is folly to pretend that their military strength is not still formidable. They have large armies still confronting us, and our army of the Potomac hesitates to attack their army of northern Virginia, on equal terms. We have but just barely escaped the greatest disaster of the war in northern Georgia and eastern Tennessee. The rebels have suffered, and suffer much, but their spirit is not broken

nor their resources exhausted. Is this a time to proclaim
an amnesty, and attempt to coax them back to their allegiance? We feel that the proclamation belittles the nation,
and throws away the opportunity the government might
soon have to gain some credit for real magnanimity.

We are surprised that after his experience, the president
should still continue to place reliance on the oath of allegiance. All he asks of the rebels, of any rebel, while the
war is still raging, while rebel corsairs are driving our mer-
chant ships from the ocean, and rebel gangs go aboard our
steamers in our own harbors, and overpower and murder
their peaceful crews—all he asks of any rebel, as the condition of a full pardon and a full restoration to his political
and civil rights, is that he take the oath of allegiance. All
the prisoners of war we now hold, under the rank of colonel,
have the right, under the president's proclamation, to demand the oath, and to be treated as free and loyal citizens
as soon as they have taken it. They would then be free to
go where they please, to return to their homes, if they can
get through our lines,—no difficult matter,—and to reënter
the rebel army; that is, just as free as they were before
taking the oath. All citizens are bound by an express or
tacit oath of allegiance, and every rebel breaks it, and does
so either because he does not believe in the sanctity of
oaths, or because he does not believe in the right of the
government to impose an oath that conflicts with his allegiance to his particular state. In either case the oath of
allegiance to the Union has no binding force on the rebel
conscience. Political oaths have never offered any real security for political fidelity. In all ages and countries they
have been found worthless, as weak as cords made of burnt
flax. The only men they would bind, who would not be
bound without them, are precisely the men who refuse to
take them. They are, as a rule, worse than worthless, and
yet the president places his whole reliance upon them,—and
he has been a practising lawyer! If the rebels could be
bound by oaths of allegiance to the Union, they would never
have been rebels. The oath is only a profanation, and the
rebels who have taken it, or may hereafter take it, will keep
it no longer than they are forced to do so, or than it suits
their convenience. In the summer of 1861, as the story
goes, a company of New York troops, sent out as a scouting
party, captured a rattlesnake, which they brought with them
into camp, where they kept his snakeship a day or two, as a

plaything. But growing tired of him, they held a council of war to determine what they should do with him. Some proposed to cut his head off, others said hang him, but one, who had made a little too free with commissary whiskey, exclaimed, "Swear him, and let him go." The president is fond of a good story, and we tell this for his benefit; "Swear him, and let him go," is the executive way of disposing of traitors and rebels, on whom an oath has about as much influence as on a rattlesnake.

But does the president really hold that to determine the conditions on which the seceded states may return as states to the Union is within the province of the executive? We confess we read with some surprise the following extract from his proclamation:

"And I do further proclaim, declare, and make known, that whenever, in any of the states of Arkansas, Texas, Louisiana, Mississippi, Tennessee, Alabama, Georgia, Florida, South Carolina, and North Carolina, a number of persons, not less than one-tenth in number of the votes cast in such states, at the presidential election of the year of our Lord 1860, each having taken the oath aforesaid, and not having since violated it, and being a qualified voter by the election law of the state existing immediately before the so-called act of secession, and excluding all others, shall reëstablish a state government, which shall be republican, and in nowise contravening said oath, such shall be recognized as the true government of the state, and the state shall receive thereunder the benefit of the constitutional provision which declares that

"'The United States shall guarantee to every state in this Union a republican form of government, and shall protect each of them against invasion, on application of the legislature, or of the executive, when the legislature cannot be convened, against domestic violence.'

"And I do further proclaim, declare, and make known, that any provision which may be adopted by such state government in relation to the freed people of such state, which shall recognize and declare their perfect freedom, provide for their education, and which may yet be consistent, as a temporary arrangement, with their present condition as a laboring, landless, and houseless class, will not be objected to by the national executive.

"And it is engaged as not improper that, in constructing a loyal state government in any state, the name of the state, the boundary, the subdivisions, the constitution and the general code of laws as before the rebellion, be maintained, subject only to the modifications made necessary by the conditions herein before stated, and such others, if any, not contravening said conditions, and which may be deemed expedient by those framing the new state government.

"To avoid misunderstanding, it may be proper to say that this proclamation, so far as it relates to state governments, has no reference to states wherein loyal state governments have all the while been maintained. And for the same reason it may be proper to further say, that whether members sent to congress from any state shall be admitted to seats constitutionally, rests exclusively with the respective houses, and not to any extent with the executive.

"And still further, that this proclamation is intended to present the people of the states wherein the national authority has been suspended, and loyal state governments have been subverted, a mode in and by which the national authority and loyal state governments may be reëstablished within said states, or in any of them.

"And, while the mode presented is the best the executive can suggest with his present impressions, it must not be understood that no other possible mode would be acceptable."

Here, it strikes us, is an extraordinary assumption of power. Where in the constitution does the president find it? Does he claim it under the war power? But we have already shown that under the war power congress can establish military governments for conquered territory, that neither he nor congress can under that power organize civil government, or determine the conditions on which it may be organized or recognized. If the rebellious states are still states in the Union, the president violates their constitutions, and wars against the essential principle of every state organization in the Union; if they are not states in the Union, but, as we maintain, population and territory belonging to the Union, then he transcends his province as the executive branch of the government, and undertakes to do on executive authority alone what only congress can do. By what right, then, does the president issue his proclamation prescribing on what conditions the rebellious population and territory may reorganize themselves and be recognized as states in the Union?

We said we objected primarily to the executive plan, because it is an executive plan. Every feature of it is marked by what seems to us an extraordinary assumption of power on the part of the executive. The president prescribes the oath, prescribes on what conditions the states in rebellion may reorganize state governments, and be recognized and represented in congress as loyal states in the Union. Any one of them, with not less than one-tenth of the number of persons who voted in the presidential election of 1860, may reorganize itself as the state, and have the full federal representation in congress to which the state under the census of 1860 was entitled! Why, the president could easily, by the distribution of federal offices and patronage in any seceded state, unless there are fewer Union men than is pretended, induce at least one in ten, if assured of federal protection, to swallow without scruple the prescribed oath, or any number of oaths he might prescribe, and elect state and federal officers, whom he may choose to prescribe. With the federal representation of eleven states, who would be his nominees and creatures, and the number from the other states he could always command by the distribution of the patronage of the government, the executive could easily grasp for himself the whole power of the Union, reign as an absolute prince, perpetuate by reëlections his reign during life, and reduce the functions of congress to that of simply registering his edicts; or, if it should now and then show a disposition to demur, he could, after the manner of Louis XIV., hold a *lit de justice.*

We are far from pretending or from believing that the president has concocted his scheme with a view of practically concentrating the whole power of the government in the hands of the executive. His motives are no doubt unselfish and patriotic, and he seeks power only as the means of doing good, and settling in the easiest and readiest way possible the terrible difficulties of the nation. But his scheme is only the more dangerous on that account. All dangerous usurpations of power are made from good motives, for desirable ends, by men in whom the public confide. The scheme is cunningly devised, and admirably fitted to make the executive practically the government, even the state, and to open the door to wholesale political corruption, and to force the people to cheat themselves out of their honesty and their liberty. Nobody imagines for a moment that the president has adopted his scheme for the sake of the evil sure to flow from it. He adopts it for the good he hopes to effect by it. We hope we shall be pardoned if we say the president seems to have inherited something of the doctrine of his old English Whig ancestry, that government can be carried on only by trickery and corruption; also that he seems to have confused the peace powers and the war powers of the government, to have supposed that in time of war the peace functions of the government are in abeyance, or absorbed in its war functions. So, holding that he has the war power, he sees no impropriety in assuming that he can settle by his own authority any questions growing out of the rebellion, and settle them in any way that seems to him advisable, without seeking any legislative authority, or legislative sanction. In no other way can we explain or account for that part of his proclamation under review. Our friends of the *Times*, in this city, the organ of the secretary of state, claim the message and proclamation as decisively discarding the doctrine of state suicide; but will they tell us on what principle the president authorizes one-tenth of the legal voters under the constitution to organize and assume to be the state, if the old state is still a state in the Union? If the state is still in the Union, it is in it with its old constitution, its old organization and laws, and neither the president nor congress can authorize a reorganization, or treat one-tenth of its voters as the state. To do so would be in the last degree revolutionary. The assumption of power on the part of the president to prescribe the conditions of reorganization and the qualifications of voters, can be defended only on the ground that the old state is dead, and that the population and territory have ceased to be a state. If the presidential scheme for the return of the rebellious states has any sense, any principle, it must assume that the states by their secession have ceased to be states; and what is this but the assumption that state secession is state suicide? They who can approve the president's message and proclamation, and still reject Mr. Sumner's doctrine, and which we after him have defended, that the territory and population in rebellion are not states in the Union, but simply population and territory belonging to the Union, have minds very differently constituted from ours, and are capable of maintaining, in spite of the logicians, that of contradictories both may be true; and they who suppose that they can palm off such an absurdity upon the public must count largely upon popular ignorance, popular stupidity, or popular credulity. The general government cannot interfere in the internal affairs of a state recognized to be a state in the Union, and is as much bound to respect the state constitution and laws not repugnant to the constitution and laws of the United States, as the state is bound to respect the constitution and laws of the general government. If the president denies the seceded states have ceased to exist, he has no right to institute either military governments or civil governments, for them, or to prescribe the conditions on which they may become states again, and be restored to their rights as states in the

Union, for they are, on the supposition, already states in the Union. So much must be clear to the veriest tyro, and ought to be clear even to our radical-conservative friends of the *Times*. But if the seceded states have ceased to be states, and become simply population and territory belonging to the Union, then, again, the president has no authority either to reorganize them, or to prescribe by proclamation or otherwise the conditions on which they may reorganize and be recognized as states. In either case the executive action is revolutionary and indefensible, as much so as the act of secession itself. There is no principle known to our constitution, written or unwritten, on which the action of the executive can be justified or even palliated.

The president, no doubt, calculates that his extraordinary assumption of power will be overlooked by those who might otherwise oppose it, because in the test oath which he prescribes, he requires adhesion to his proclamation emancipating the slaves in certain states and parts of states. But it should be remarked that he requires an oath to adhere to it only in case it is not set aside, or till it is set aside by congress or the supreme court. If congress can set aside the emancipation proclamation, as the president clearly concedes that it may, he cannot suppose that his proclamation really frees the slaves he declared to be free, for nobody can pretend that congress has the right to reduce freemen to slavery, unless it be for crime. That the supreme court will sustain the freedom of slaves under the proclamation, unless they have become free in fact before the conclusion of the war, we suppose nobody expects. For ourselves, we do not believe a single person can sustain his freedom in the courts under that proclamation ; and more than this, we have, and all along have had doubts whether it was ever intended that any one should. Moreover, this new proclamation asserts, in terms somewhat obscure indeed, but still intelligible enough, that, should the revived states see proper to hold the persons declared free by the emancipation proclamation as slaves for an indefinite period, no objection will be offered by the "national executive." If the president believes that his proclamation really freed the slaves, how can he proclaim that he will not object should they for any reason whatever even for one moment be detained in servitude? We have always regarded the emancipation proclamation as intended not so much to free the slaves as to silence the clamor of the anti-slavery men at home, and to amuse the philanthropists abroad, and by so doing guard against foreign intervention.

Mr. Lincoln, as everybody knows, however much in general thesis he may be opposed to slavery, is invincibly opposed to any and every scheme of immediate emancipation, and in no sense will he willingly or cordially favor it. In this we might ourselves agree with him, if we were considering emancipation as a peace, and not as a war measure; but certain it is that he is no immediate emancipationist, and we have no doubt that he has sought to prescribe himself the mode of reorganizing the rebellious states instead of leaving it to congress, lest congress should insist on immediate emancipation. His whole course with regard to Missouri, if not also to Maryland, proves that he is determined to use all his power and influence to prevent immediate, and in favor of what is called gradual emancipation. Here is the trouble. The emancipation of the slaves as a military necessity is and must be immediate. Having issued a proclamation emancipating the slaves immediately and for ever, the problem came up, how to prevent it from taking immediate effect? The only valid reason for proclaiming emancipation was military necessity, to deprive the rebels of the labor of their slaves, which enabled them to draft nearly the whole able-bodied free white population into their army; and yet it will be remembered that the president, in the very proclamation in which he declares them free, exhorts them to remain peaceably where they were, and to *continue laboring for their masters as before!* Now he issues a proclamation telling the rebels how they can reorganize their states and recover their lost rights in the Union, and adds, that if they choose to retain their slaves, that is, the men he had professed to free, in bondage for a time, he shall make no objection! The key to this singular inconsistency is in the fact that the president is opposed to immediate emancipation, and is determined to do what he can to prevent it. Mr. Lincoln is an able man, a shrewd man, and no man is less likely to commit a blunder, or to act without deliberation. He has a logical mind, and never does any thing without knowing what he is doing, and intending it. He knew perfectly well why he emancipated the slaves by proclamation instead of by a military order to his generals commanding military departments, and is lawyer enough to know that the latter would hold good in the courts, and that the former would not, unless in the case of those who became actually free during the war.

We do not doubt in the least that the president is opposed to slavery, and intends that this rebellion shall be made use of for its ultimate abolition. He did not so intend in the beginning; he *hoped*, as he himself says, that the rebellion might be suppressed without emancipation, but finding the public opinion of the only party he could rely on to sustain his administration too strong to be resisted, he, after long deliberation and with evident reluctance, yielded in appearance, not because he believed the emancipation would in itself aid his military operations, but because without it he saw he could not carry on the war. We presume he is now in earnest to secure the ultimate abolition of slavery, but only gradually, and by what may seem to be the action of the slave states themselves. Such, we suppose, to be the actual facts in the case, and such the true explanation of the extraordinary acts and apparent inconsistencies of the course of the executive on this momentous subject. We find no fault with him, for, given the man and the circumstances, we see not how he could have done better or differently. Yet we personally have a great dislike to a tortuous course, and we like a man, whether in public or private, to act openly, in a straightforward manner. We want him to tell us plainly and without ambiguity what he means. We will not ascribe what displeases us in Mr. Lincoln's policy to the subtle advice of Mr. Seward, for we believe the president the abler man and the shrewder politician. Besides, Mr. Lincoln is the principal, and we hold the principal, not the agent, responsible. The convention organized the government with a single responsible executive head. The president has no cabinet ministers, he has only clerks, or heads of departments, responsible to him and removable at his will. The journals speak of his *constitutional* advisers; but he has no constitutional advisers. The heads of departments or secretaries are no more the president's constitutional advisers than we are, and no more responsible for the advice they give him, than we are for the advice we give him, and he is no more constitutionally bound to follow their advice than he is ours. In Great Britain the ministry are responsible, and may be impeached for the advice they give the sovereign, but it is not so here. We ought to bear this in mind, and place the responsibility where the constitution places it. The president is responsible for all the acts of his secretaries.

The executive plan does not appear to us to give any adequate security even for the ultimate abolition of slavery. It will, if the states are restored, and still hold their slaves even temporarily, be easy for them to alter their constitutions, prescribed by the executive, and make slavery perpetual. When once recognized as states they are competent to do it. The states will then be perfectly competent to take off the restriction from suffrage and eligibility, in state matters at least, restore the disloyal population excluded by the president's test oath, and in ten or a dozen years slavery, in all the states, may be reëstablished as firmly as ever, perhaps more firmly than ever. Slavery is now more flourishing in Kentucky than it was before the rebellion. That state has become the grand slave mart of the Union, whence the slave masters from localities where slave property is insecure send their slaves to be sold, at a low price. Kentucky alone, after peace, will be able in a very few years to restock a large portion of the South. The president, by the exceptions he inserted in his proclamation, secured plenty of nest-eggs for slavery.

But, the president's plan of reviving the seceded states would, in many respects, be objectionable, even if proposed and adopted by congress. We do not think a tenth of the votable population of a seceded state, while the other nine-tenths are in rebellion, or at least opposed to the Union, ought to have the whole federal representation of the state. It is neither just nor fair to the loyal states who have borne the whole burden of suppressing the rebellion. A state with nine-tenths of its population disloyal and excluded from the ranks of its political people, evidently could not sustain itself and discharge its proper functions as a state in the Union. It would have to be held up and nursed by the government, and thus would be opened the door to political intrigue and corruption, exceeding any thing we have yet known, even in this city. Its representatives in congress would be virtual nominees of the administration, and the congressional districts would be only so many "rotten boroughs" owned by the government. No election would or could be free. Besides, with here and there an individual exception, the men who would take the oath and be allowed to vote, would be the weakest and least energetic portion of the population. The portion of the southern people who have the most character, and are the best fitted to govern and look after the interests of the state or the Union, are precisely those who would be excluded by the test oath. The majority of the voters would be composed of government employés, adventurers from other states, with very little honesty or principle of any sort, and without any permanent interest in the state, or connection with it. Here is a grave consideration.

We know there has been some talk about changing the population of the rebellious states, of getting rid of the present population, and supplying their place with Yankees or emigrants from Europe. We contemplate, we wish nothing of the sort. We wish to save and keep the present southern population, with most of its characteristics. It has elements that the North has not, and with which the nation cannot dispense without great loss; and we look forward to the time when the seceded states will be restored, and their politics will be in the hands of the very population now in arms against us. We are neither for exterminating nor changing the southern people. After they have been well whipped they will abandon their disloyalty, and become the most loyal people of the Union, and the most politically honest and trustworthy. We are a New Englander, and like New England, but we have no wish to see the South new-englandized. We want it free; we want slavery abolished, but we do not want to see disappear the simplicity of manners, the warmth of feeling, and the hospitality we were accustomed to find in southern homes. We should be sorry to see even plantation life disappear, or the large plantations cut up into small farms, cultivated either by black or white owners. A nation is nothing without families, and families soon disappear without estates, without homesteads, transmitted from father to son, through generation after generation. We demand political equality, in the sense secured by our institutions; but we regard equality of property and of social position as neither practicable nor desirable. It is long since we had faith in *la république démocratique et sociale*. We do not believe the whole past has been simply a blunder, and that nothing that has been approved of by those who went before us deserves to stand. We have not to begin the world anew; we have only to develop and perfect what we have received from our fathers. We want the conservatism of the South to balance the radicalism of the North, as we want the radicalism of the North to balance the conservatism of the South. We want both sections to make a complete nation, a full and rounded national character.

The executive plan would transform the South for the worse. We think ours, though less favorable to speculators, political jobbers, and Jewish Yankees, or Yankee Jews, is far more favorable to the southern people, and likely much sooner to reinstate them in their rights as an integral portion of the political people of the United States. Our plan is given in the article on *The Federal Constitution*, in the present number of our *Review*. It is simply for congress to establish in each of the seceded states a territorial government, and then as soon as any one of them gives satisfactory evidence of its ability to maintain itself as a loyal state in the Union, with simple protection by the general government from exterior invasion and disturbance, for congress to enable it to form a state government and enter the Union with a federal representation and electoral vote, determined by its actual population. That this plan supposes that the seceded states have lapsed, we grant; but so does the executive plan. The president and all loyal men hold that all legal government in the rebellious states has been subverted, and therefore there is, unless the doctrine of complete original state sovereignty be conceded (and if it is, the secessionists are not rebels), no state remaining. They who oppose Mr. Sumner's doctrine that state secession is state suicide, and contend that the seceded states are still states in the Union, are at best contending for the veriest abstraction, for an airy nothing, to which not even the poet, of imagination all compact, and his eye in a fine frenzy rolling, can give a local habitation and a name. The president himself concedes that to all practical purposes the seceded states are dead, and he proposes, as we have seen, to deal with them as such. We have heard no one ever pretend that the governments now in rebellion against the Union are legitimate state governments, or that they are to be reinstated in the Union. Mr. Winter Davis, in his speech elsewhere alluded to, while denouncing rather flippantly Mr. Sumner's doctrine about state suicide, scouted the idea that these disloyal concerns were legitimate governments. or that they would ever be recognized as such. Well, what then are he and his friends fighting for, or quarrelling about? The states have lapsed as actually living states in the Union by their own concession, and can be living states in the Union only by being reorganized as such; and the president, in his proclamation, points out the mode in which they may be reorganized. Practically, then, all we contend for is conceded, and asserted by all loyal men, if, as we suppose they do, they understand themselves.

The difficulty which some honestly feel on the point grows out of the fact that they well understand that a real sovereign state may be disorganized or lose its entire government, and yet retain its existence and all its rights as a state. It is a sovereign state still, and has in itself the power to reorganize its government. The government is gone, but the convention remains. All this is true, and is assumed in the distinction we have made in the article on *The Federal Constitution* between the state or civil society and the government, between the constitution of the government and the constitution of civil society or the state. Every half-fledged politician knows, or ought to know this much; for if we did not concede it we should recognize in a nation no recuperative power, no power when its government has once been subverted to reorganize and reëstablish legitimate government. But this applies to a state proper, to a complete, sovereign state, but not to a state in the Union, unless we hold the states in the Union are severally complete states, states proper, possessing all the attributes and faculties of free, independent, sovereign states. In an independent sovereign state, the sovereignty, in the absence of government, or any constitution of government, vests in the national territory and population. But to assume that it vests in the territory and population of one of the American states, when its organization and government are gone, have been subverted, destroyed, is plainly and undeniably to assume that these states are each a sovereign state, a full and complete state in itself. But assume this, and you have no right to make war on the seceders as insurgents or rebels. Here is the dilemma in which these good people place themselves. They can contend that the seceded states are still states in the Union, only on the assumption of full and independent state sovereignty; and they cannot make that assumption without denying the right of the general government to prosecute the war against the seceders. They must either condemn the war as a war of invasion and conquest, or they must reject state sovereignty as we do. Then they must concede that the state under our system is not population and territory, but is population and territory organized as a state and admitted into the Union. Then they must concede that the lapse of the state organization is the lapse of the state; and as they admit that the state organization has been subverted or destroyed by secession, and therefore lapsed, they must, whatever wry faces they may make, concede that they have lapsed as states, and accept the doctrine that "state secession is state suicide." Mr. Sumner's phrase will live.

By the concession of the president and the so-called conservative republicans themselves, the state organization is gone, and nothing but population and territory, as a practical fact remains. What we ask of congress is, that it deal with the practical fact as it is, and establish for this population and territory regular territorial governments, in like manner that it is accustomed to do for any other unorganized population and territory belonging to the Union. This it can do under the exercise of its ordinary or peace powers. It requires no assumption of extraordinary powers, and no resort to the war power. It is simply the sovereign exercising his civil power, in establishing a civil government, not exercising his belligerent rights.

But we are told that this is to reduce the seceded states to provinces, and to place them under provincial governments. That is something terrible, we suppose. But how much better off are they now, placed as they are under military governors appointed by the commander-in-chief of the army and navy, and governed by military law, so far as by any law at all? They would, under our plan, be placed at least under a civil government, a civil administration, and the protection of civil law, which we regard as an advantage of no slight moment. Then, again, under our system, the territorial organization is provisional, and is never intended to be final or permanent. It is merely preparatory to a state organization, and looks to the transformation of the territory into a state at the earliest practicable moment. Nobody dreams that the population and territory of the seceded states are to be held for any considerable length of time under territorial governments, and the territorial people will always have it in their power, by returning loyalty, to abridge the period of their probation, and hasten the day of their reinstatement in the Union. In some cases it may be only a few months before the transformation may be safely effected, and in no case will the territorial government need to be continued beyond the period of the complete military suppression of the rebellion. When the southern people once find that they are really whipped, that they have not the slightest chance of securing separation and independence, they will cease resistance, and, if permitted, return to their allegiance. They may then be safely intrusted with the powers of self-government. There is, no doubt, humiliation for a people once a state in being placed under a territorial government, but less, in our judgment, in being placed under a civil than under a military government, and the transformation from the civil territorial government is easier, more regular, and more speedy than from a military government. We cannot sympathize, then, with the men who affect such a holy horror at treating the rebel population and territory as territories, and yet are quite willing to see them treated as military departments, under military governors, and subjected to military law.

No objections can be made to this simple and constitutional way of restoring the rebellious states that do not bear with far greater force against the executive scheme, and, unless there are, as is not unlikely, some political interests, party or personal, at stake, we can understand no reason why that scheme should be preferred. Its adoption would, indeed, enable a few thousands of voters in each of the eleven states to cast in the next presidential election the entire electoral vote of those eleven states, representing a population of some twelve millions, nine-tenths of whom are in hearty sympathy with the rebellion. This, supposing Mr. Lincoln to be a candidate for reëlection, would render his election well-nigh certain, even should a Republican as well as a Democratic competitor run against him. But we cannot suppose a thought of that sort could influence in the least our honest and high-minded chief magistrate, or the high-souled and patriotic admirers of the secretary of state. Such a scheme, adopted for such a purpose, would be an outrage, and a death-blow to honest constitutional government. And yet, for the life of us, we cannot understand why else the especial friends of the secretary of state should persist so strenuously against law, fact, and common sense, in maintaining that the seceded states are states still in the Union. They know, as well as we do, that there is no truth or reason in maintaining that those states are states still in the Union. Mr. Lincoln knows they are not, for his very scheme, while it assumes that they are, denies it.

We are utterly opposed to allowing one-tenth of the population of a seceded state, while the other nine-tenths are in rebellion, to cast the whole electoral vote to which the state would be entitled if loyal and in the Union, under the United States census of 1860. We are not opposed because we fear it would secure the defeat of our candidate for the next presidency, for it would be very sure to elect him; but because we do not believe that so small a number as one-tenth of the assumed voters in a state have the right to a federal representation and an electoral vote, based on a census that gives ten times their number. If the Union men are to be treated as the state, be it so; but let, at least, their electoral vote and federal representation be no more than their actual number under the census entitles them to. We cannot understand why one Union man in South Carolina, Tennessee, or Louisiana, should count for ten in Massachusetts, New York, or Pennsylvania. We know no reason why they should have any vote at all, while the great, the overwhelming majority of the population are in rebellion. "But that majority are politically dead." Then do not count them as a basis of representation. Abstract them from the whole population given by the census of 1860, and take only the remainder as the representative population. You cannot do that legally? The state is the state, and you must count its whole population or none? Then do you not see the gross inequality and absurdity of pretending that they are states in the Union, with all their federal rights unimpaired? Moreover, the Union men in the eleven seceded states are not citizens of the United States. They are enemies, and are declared to be so by the supreme court in the Hiawatha case, and have been since the 13th of July, 1861, and their territory is enemy's territory, otherwise the president could never have placed it under military governors, or blockaded the southern ports. The supreme court have decided that the war we are carrying on is not a simple war against insurgent individuals, but a territorial civil war, which makes every man, woman, and child in the rebellious territory an enemy. The interdict must be removed from that territory before these Union men cease to be enemies; and that cannot be removed so long as the law of congress of the 13th of July, 1861, remains unrepealed, and the great majority are still hostile, without a gross abuse of executive power. We do not know that even these Union men in the seceded states are any better than the Union men in the organized territories under the government of the United States. And why should they, any more than these, have a federal representation and an electoral vote?

But happily the executive scheme is naught unless sanctioned or acquiesced in by congress. Congress has the supervision of the whole matter, and nothing is concluded but by its will, unless it be the exceptions from the confiscation and other penal laws, which the president was authorized by congress to make. Congress has clothed the executive with too large a discretion in the case, and we hope it will be more cautious for the future. But it has not yet given up to the executive its authority to say on what conditions the rebels may return and resume their political rights as states in the Union; at least we hope not. There are good men and true in congress, and we count on their vigilance and fidelity to the constitution. The last congress, in the novelty of the questions and the confusion of the times, set one or two very bad precedents, but the present congress need not follow them. If congress will but assert its independence, and do its own work, no harm can come from the executive scheme. Even the scheme itself, though still objectionable, would be shorn of some of its dangerous features, if adopted by congress along with the establishment of civil territorial governments for the lapsed states, till such times as they are able to organize state governments in accordance with the conditions prescribed by the president in his proclamation. But what we insist on is, that the reorganization of the seceded states, whether under state governments or territorial governments, is a thing that neither the president nor congress can do under the war power, and must be done by the simple exercise of the ordinary peace powers of the government. It is not a thing which needs or admits a resort to the war power, in whose hands soever that power may be vested; for it is not necessary to military operations, and is determined not by international law, but by the national law, the constitution and laws of the national government. The rights of war, however extensive they may be, are yet restricted to the legitimate object and purposes of the war, and never exceed what is necessary to gain and secure that object and those purposes. This understood, it is certain that the subject is one for congressional action, not for the executive action.

We insist, perhaps to wearisomeness, on the importance of proceeding constitutionally, and of each branch of the government confining itself to its own department and to its strictly constitutional functions. We are and always have been a constitutionalist of the strict constructionist school, and we believe the constitutional way the best and safest. Yet we have never urged the constitution in any way to impede the government in doing any thing necessary to suppress the rebellion or to save the life and integrity of the nation. We have no sympathy with those who can see in the constitution only a restriction on power, and appeal to it only when they want to prevent some very useful and necessary thing from being done. The constitution grants powers, as well as imposes restriction on power, and we believe it confers on the government all the powers that in any emergency it needs or can find useful. We have never complained of what are called "arbitrary arrests," for we see them provided for in the constitution, when the public safety requires them. We have been much more disposed to complain of arbitrary discharges from arrest and imprisonment. We have never complained of the suspension of the writ of *habeas corpus*, because we find the constitution allows it to be suspended in certain contingencies which obviously now exist; and as the object of that writ in our jurisprudence is not to restrain the executive from making necessary arrests, but to compel the courts to bring the person arrested to a speedy trial, or to grant him his discharge, we believe the power to suspend it in times of war, invasion, or insurrection, is vested in the president. It may often be necessary to suspend it when congress is not in session and cannot be assembled in season. We have given great extension to the war power, not as an extra-constitutional power, for the constitution confers it on congress. Under it congress and even the president can do legally and constitutionally many things in times of war, foreign or domestic, which neither can do under the peace powers of the government, or in times of peace, when the higher law of public safety does not come in. Congress has the ordinary peace right to prescribe the terms of the reorganization and restoration of fallen states to their *status* of states in the Union, but the president has not, because the convention did not see proper to confer it on him; and he cannot do it under the war power, for it is not one of the ends of the war, is not necessary to the success of our arms, or to his military operations as commander-in-chief. He has in regard to it in time of war all the power that he has in time of peace, and no more. The constitution gives to no branch of the government under the rights of peace the right to abolish slavery within the limits of any state in the Union, but it gives to congress, perhaps even to the president, the right, under the war power, to abolish it everywhere in the Union and in the territories of the Union, if judged necessary as a military measure, or to obtain indemnity for the past or security for the future.   A military order of the commander-in-chief, or an act of congress abolishing slavery for such reasons, if correct in form, would be valid, and repealable only by the convention, for congress has no more right to establish slavery than it has to abolish it.   We were among the first, except the abolitionists, to urge the abolition of slavery as a war measure, and we are proud of it.   It is a legacy we leave to our children.   Our complaint of the president has been, not that he issued his proclamation, but that he did not in his proclamation adopt, in our judgment, the proper legal form.   We think it should have been by military order to his generals commanding military departments.   We have always preferred, however, emancipation by act of congress, because congress has more freedom in the case, and there could be no doubt of the validity of its act.   It is true, the proclamation cites an act of congress emancipating certain classes of slaves, and professes to be based upon it, but it is not merely executory of it, but goes beyond it, and it may be a question in the courts whether in the respect that it transcends that act, or goes beyond what is necessary to its execution according to its true intent and meaning, it has any legal force.   We hope congress in its present session will remove all doubts on the subject by passing for the purposes we have named, an act emancipating the slaves for ever, not only in the states and parts of states included in the proclamation, but in those states and parts of states not so included.   We have not a doubt of its constitutional right to do it as a military measure, or as a measure necessary to guaranty the nation against a new outbreak of the rebellion.

It is idle to expect peace and union, henceforth, between free states and slave states; and as we cannot be forced to become all slave states, we must look to it that all become free states, and let the value of the slaves, as property, be set off as an indemnity to the United States, for the expenses they have been obliged to incur in the suppression of the slaveholders' rebellion, and for which the Union has the right to indemnify itself, by levying on any property belonging to rebels it can find.   They ought to feel that they are let off easily, if they are let off with simply the loss of their slaves.   The few really loyal slaveholders in the non-seceding states may receive a reasonable compensation; the others deserve and should receive none. The seceded states may adjust the matter with their own citizens as they see proper. The proclamation relieves them, with very few exceptions, if they choose to return to their allegiance, of all other penalty for their treason and murders. The people of these states rebelled as states, and they deserve to lose their slaves; for, if they had remained loyal, they might have enjoyed their property in slaves, and "wallopped their own nigger," with nobody to disturb them. Let the dispossessed slaveholders seek redress from their own states, when those states are restored.

The president, we have said, is evidently opposed to immediate emancipation, and so are we; he favors gradual emancipation, and so should we, so that the transition from slavery to freedom should disturb society as little as possible, though we do not understand the same thing by gradual emancipation that the president does. If the government had had under its peace powers the constitutional right to deal with the question of slavery, we should not have favored immediate emancipation. But such was not the case. It could deal with it only under the war power, and under that power emancipation must be immediate or not at all. We cannot understand, then, why in Maryland and Missouri, where slavery can be abolished without any serious social shock, the president should set his face against immediate emancipation. As the slaves in all the rebel states, with the exception of Tennessee, and parts of two other states, have had their immediate emancipation declared, the federal executive might, we should think, prudently suffer the people of the loyal slaveholding states to adopt immediate emancipation, if they saw proper.

We see Mr. Wilson, of Iowa, has given notice, in congress, of his intention to move an amendment to the constitution of the United States, abolishing and prohibiting for ever involuntary servitude, in the Union and the territories thereof, except for crime, and empowering congress to carry it into effect by the requisite legislation. Seeing the turn things are taking, we withdraw our former objections to such an amendment. It would be the shortest, and most effectual way of disposing of the slavery question at once and for ever. The supreme political power is in the convention; the convention is composed of the political people of the United States, and is as complete and as sovereign with the states now in the Union, as it would be were all the seceded states restored. An amendment passed by the requisite majority of both houses of congress, and ratified by three-fourths of all the states actually in the Union, would be, to all intents and purposes, a part of the constitution. It would always remain such, for there would always be at least over one-fourth of the states that would never consent to its being changed. If such an amendment could be carried, it would be a grand thing; whether it can be or not, can never be known till the experiment is made. We hope Mr. Wilson may succeed, for our mind is made up on this slavery question. We demand the utter extinction of negro-slavery. The nation has recognized the negro as a man. It has done more: it has put arms in his hands; incorporated him into its armies; bid him fight manfully as an American, for the life and integrity of the nation. In doing so, it has naturalized and nationalized him. Never will we consent to see a man who has shed his blood for our country, for the maintenance of national right, liberty, and law, held in slavery, and counted, not as a person, but as a chattel; and never will we consent to enslave a race that has produced such a man. The government, by arming the negroes, has made them our countrymen; and never shall our countrymen, whatever their complexion, be held as slaves, without our doing every thing in our power to prevent it. To so much we solemnly pledge what remains to us of life. That flag, under which the freedman and the freeman have mounted the parapet side by side, side by side met death from rebel fire, and side by side been laid in the same soldier's grave, must henceforth wave only over the free, and never again be profaned to protect the slave-owner, or the trafficker in human flesh.

"Liberty," said Mr. Calhoun, in a letter to us in 1838, "we consider a boon which they only are entitled to, who are able to take it." It is a harsh, pagan doctrine, and overlooks the obligation of the strong to help the weak, and the powerful to defend the defenceless. But the negro is fast proving that he is entitled to the boon, even on Mr. Calhoun's hard conditions. Nothing sooner calls out one's manhood, than to make him a soldier, and to let him feel that he is counted worthy to bear arms and do a man's work. Yet, we are far from feeling that the battle for abolition is over. The rebellion is not yet suppressed, and the war is not yet ended; nor, in our judgment, so near being ended as many of our friends flatter themselves. The president's proclamation, we do not believe, will have much effect on the rebel population, one way or another. They do not look upon their cause as we look upon it, and they fight for it with all the determination, ardor, and desperate bravery of patriots. Not easily or speedily will such a people succumb, and give over the struggle. They will hope against hope, and yield only when they find that all possible chances are against them. Nearly one-half of the people of the loyal states are bent on preserving slavery, as essential to their political combinations and influence ; even in the ranks of the professedly loyal, there are large numbers who have little or no manliness or pluck, and are ready for almost any compromise that will secure peace, and not deprive them of their political importance. So we do not yet feel sure that a reconciliation will not be effected, without obtaining sufficient guaranties that slavery shall cease, and cease for ever. Even the president's proclamation weakens, instead of strengthening our assurance. We have so few politicians that place right as the measure of expediency, justice above interest, or their country's good before their own, that we always are in doubt till the thing is done, and so done that it cannot be undone.

We have taken up so much space in commenting on the executive plan for restoring the fallen states, that we have left ourselves no room for commenting on the other important matters in the message,—the ablest and best written message Mr. Lincoln has ever sent to congress. It has more dignity, and more the character of an official document, than its predecessors. We have criticised freely, but honestly and conscientiously, the executive scheme for reorganizing the rebellious states, or transforming them into loyal states ; but, we hope, with becoming respect for our chief magistrate, and without any gratuitous offence. We may have misconceived its intent and what is likely to be its practical bearing, and we are led to distrust, in some measure, our own judgment, by finding the message and proclamation cordially endorsed by some of our most earnest and judicious political friends. We are never above acknowledging and correcting our errors when we detect them, or when they are pointed out. Better that we should suffer in public estimation than that the truth should.

We have, in the course of our remarks, twice alluded to the next presidency. We are no president makers or president breakers. We voted for Mr. Lincoln in 1860, and we shall vote for him in 1864, if he is the candidate of the loyal Union party, and with less reluctance, for though not, as we need not say, precisely a man after our own heart, he is an abler man, and has made a better president than we had looked for. We have expected him to be a candidate for reëlection as a matter of course. In 1860, Mr. Chase, secretary of the treasury, was our first choice, and if he is the candidate we shall cheerfully support him. We have heard the names of two eminent loyal military men mentioned in connection with the next presidency, either of whom would meet our wishes. We recorded years ago our conviction that a *real* military man, other things being equal, should be preferred for president. A military training is better than a mere civilian training to fit a man for the executive duties of the presidential office. He who has led the life of a soldier, acquired the discipline of the army, and learned to command men in the battle-field, is likely to have a more manly character, a better judgment of men, and more promptness and energy in emergencies. Wellington was England's greatest soldier, but he lives almost entirely in the memory and affections of his countrymen, as her noblest, greatest, and most disinterested statesman. No man as president would be more likely to keep the nation out of war, or to help it in case it was unhappily involved in a war, than a real soldier. Personally our preferences are for the soldier, and our only hesitancy is the fear that the soldier we should prefer will be required for active service in the field; for we by no means expect the war to end this year, or even the next. But, be this as it may, we shall support the candidate of the loyal Union party, be he soldier or civilian; and the present incumbent will have the advantage of four years of valuable experience.

Since writing the foregoing, we have seen the bill reported to the house by General Ashley for organizing the rebellious states under military governors, and providing for their reorganization as states, on the basis of the scheme set forth in the president's proclamation. Should congress pass the bill, it would relieve the scheme of our objections to it on the ground of unconstitutionality, and of its being purely an executive measure. We, however, still object to the " one-tenth " provision, and should demand a decided majority, for reasons we have already given. The president's proposition is unfair, and it is unjust to the other states to give to so small a number the whole representative and electoral vote of the former state. The military governments may

be instituted under the war power, but the *civil* reorganization of seceded states can be effected only under the peace
powers of the government, and therefore the scheme, whether
congressional or executive, is unconstitutional and revolutionary, if the seceded states are held to be still states in the
Union. It is only on the supposition that they are not,
that Mr. Ashley's bill is defensible ; and if they are not,
there is no defence of the one-tenth provision, which allows
a federal representation and electoral vote due only to ten
times their number. It is all very well to get over difficulties by way of compromise when one can, but here is a question of law, and an unconstitutional mode of proceeding
even by congress may vitiate the whole. It is folly to assume in one part of the act the nullity of the seceded states,
and in the other their legal existence and vitality. We suppose then that the bill, as it evidently does, assumes the legal
nullity of the seceded states. We ask congress to provide
for a larger percentage. Regarded as a new state organization, it has no right, and congress can give it no right to
count as a portion of its population, the disloyal population
of the old state ; and if it does not regard it as a new organization or the creation of a new state, it has no right to
effect or authorize it. The whole difficulty we see in the
way of Mr. Ashley's new bill is precisely here, in the matter
of federal representation and the electoral vote. If the bill,
before it passes, can be so modified as to obviate this difficulty, we shall heartily approve it. We are willing and
even anxious that congress should make the executive plan
the basis of its own legislation, for we want no quarrel between congress and the executive that can be avoided ; but
we presume the president himself will consent to such modifications as are necessary to save its consistency and constitutionality.

We see also, with great pleasure, that Mr. Lovejoy has introduced a bill giving effect to the president's emancipation
proclamation. If it becomes a law it will settle all disputes
as to the legality or illegality of the proclamation, and fix
the status as freemen of the persons professed to be liberated
by it. Let congress do its duty on these great questions, and
it will soon be able to rally all Union men around it and the
executive, and secure with the hearty good-will of the nation
the reëlection of Mr. Lincoln, which is on many accounts
desirable, for there will questions come up in the next four
years which can be much better settled under a second presidential term than under the first.

ABOLITION AND NEGRO EQUALITY.*

[From Brownson's Quarterly Review for April, 1864.]

THAT Mr. Phillips is one of the ablest and most eloquent men in the United States cannot well be doubted; and that he is perfectly honest and sincere in his devotion to the abolition of slavery, and the elevation of the negro race in the country, is just as little to be doubted. No one can read one of his speeches and not say to himself, Here is an honest man speaking his honest thought; here is an able man, an educated man, a cultivated man, of large and liberal views, a man of genius, of heart, of soul, devoting all his mind, all his intelligence, and all his energy, to the cause of the poor and oppressed. Such a man, however we may differ from him on this or that point, we are forced to respect and love. He had, and could have, no selfish or sinister motive for espousing the cause of the slave, and giving up his life to the negro. He started life from a social position, with talents, learning, genius, and accomplishments which could not fail, with ordinary industry, to open to him the doors to the highest professional honors, or to the highest political distinctions his country had to offer. The beaten track was for him, if he chose to follow it, the sure path of ambition, both smooth and easy of ascent. He chose to forego his advantages, to brave public opinion, to bind himself to an unpopular cause, to suffer reproach for it, and to be branded as an incendiary, to be hissed by the mob, and to incur the wrath and hatred of all the sleek respectabilities in both church and state. Such a man does not so expose himself from vulgar ambition, or without being governed by lofty principles, and animated by noble and generous sentiments. He has in him the stuff of a true man.

It has never been my lot to be a coöperator with Mr. Phillips in his special work; indeed, he has found me always one of his most steady, persevering, and determined opponents. Yet have I always loved his noble and genial

---

*Speech of Wendell Phillips, Esq., at the Annual Meeting of the Anti-Slavery Society, Tremont Temple, Boston, January 28, 1864.

spirit, respected his humanity, and honored his disinterestedness. I have always regarded him as a genuine man, a
living man—one who thinks and has the courage to act out
his thought. I have always sympathized with him as to the
end he proposed, but rarely as to the means by which he
sought to gain it. Mr. Phillips was, and is, a philanthropist
—a sincere and earnest believer in the democratic principle,
and I am not, and never have been. Philanthropy is a
great word ; but nature has not made me a philanthropist.
I am a Christian, and aim to discharge my Christian duties,
both to God and to my fellow-men. But philanthropy is a
sentiment, not a principle, and I never suffer myself to
build any system, religious, philosophical, ethical, or political, on any sentiment, however generous or noble it may be,
for all sentiments are subjective, individual, and variable.
Even the religious sentiment, the highest and noblest sentiment in man, cannot be trusted, unless enlightened and directed by truth, principle, independent of both the human
mind and the human heart. Without truth, objective truth
—what we call idea or dogma, it becomes a grovelling superstition, or a wild and destructive fanaticism. Love is one
wing of the soul, no doubt ; but with one wing alone, the
soul does not, cannot soar. It must have two wings, and
the other wing is intelligence, which grasps a reality which
is not soul, but above soul—God ; and hence the apostle re-
proves those who have a zeal for God which is not according to knowledge.

In democracy, as expounded by Locke and Rousseau, and
advocated by Jefferson and his school, we do not believe.
We have studied philosophy too long for that. Democracy
is the political expression of the materialistic and sensistic
philosophy of the last century, which nobody of any brains
pretends now to defend. · Liberty we love ; the equality of
all men as to their natural rights we recognize—hold as a
part of our Christian faith. We believe in republican government, in the election by public suffrage of all rulers and
magistrates, and dislike all hereditary monarchy and all hereditary political aristocracies. We are not Jews, but Christians. Judaism rested on natural generation, and, therefore,
on the hereditary principle ; Christianity is palingenesiac,
and under it all goes by election, the election of grace.
Every man's philosophy, religion, and politics should unite
in a common principle, and every man's does, if he thinks
and is master of his thought. We believe in popular suffrage,

and so far accept democracy; but we hold that suffrage is a trust, not an inherent and indefeasible right, and so far we reject democracy. The right to vote, and to be voted for is a trust from civil society, not a natural right inherent in every man by virtue of the fact that he is a man. On this point we disagree with Mr. Phillips and all the disciples of Rousseau; and, disagreeing on this point, we naturally disagree, supposing us equally logical, on all the points growing out of it and dependent on it.

Mr. Phillips is an abolitionist; his one primary object is the abolition of negro-slavery. Slavery is an injustice, and no injustice should be tolerated. The right of the man to his freedom is higher than that of any civil constitution or human enactment to obedience. The right of the slave to his freedom rests on the patent of the Almighty; is incorporated into the very charter of his existence by his Creator. Any human enactments or civil constitutions that deprive him of that freedom, or prevent me from rushing to emancipate him, are repugnant to the law of God, and may be lawfully resisted or disregarded. Hence, Mr. Phillips subordinates the constitution of the United States to emancipation, and places the question of emancipation above that of preserving the Union. If the Union abolishes slavery, he sustains the Union; if it refuses to do any thing of the sort, then he is for disunion, so as to be able to wash his hands of the sin of slavery. Now, on this last point, not being a philanthropist, and holding the support of the constitution as it is, till constitutionally altered, to be a public duty, binding by the law of God on every citizen, I have always held that I must sustain the Union whether it did or not abolish slavery, and seek the abolition of slavery under it, not against it. My duty to the constitution, to the Union, to the country, I have always held to be, if the two came in conflict, paramount to my duty to free the slave. Here was and is the fundamental difference between me and the abolitionists. If we must choose between the dissolution of the Union, the loss of our national life, and the continuance of slavery, I choose the latter. But Mr. Phillips must bear us witness that the first moment that we were able to demand the abolition of slavery without danger to the Union or lesion to the constitution, we did it, and the echo of our essay on *Slavery and the War*, written in August, 1861, has not yet died away.

We grant slavery is an evil, an injustice, and that it is a

sin to continue it a moment after it is possible to abolish it; that is, possible to abolish it without a greater evil, or a greater injustice. Of two evils choose the less; and unhappily in this world, such is the complication of human affairs that often it is not possible to repair one wrong without committing another, and, perhaps, a far greater wrong. We believed slavery, till it rose in rebellion against the Union, a less evil than the dissolution of the Union; and on the principle that we may not do evil that good may come, we separated from the abolitionists. We did so because we acted from principle, not sentiment, or from sentiment guided by principle; not from impulse, but judgment. Whether we erred in judgment or not is another question, which others may answer or not answer, as they think best. But this much we say, and say cheerfully, that the country owes a deeper debt of gratitude to the abolitionists than it is prepared to acknowledge, or will be during this generation. Much in their manner as well as in their principles was offensive; and their overlooking the claims of patriotism, or seeing their country only in the negro, and counting every man their countryman and fellow-citizen who went for abolition, cannot be commended. Nothing did more to excite prejudice against them than their affiliation with English abolitionists, and importing George Thompson to help them abuse their own country and countrymen; and we regret to see the same gentleman amongst us again, as we regretted Mr. Ward Beecher's mission to England. We are not cosmopolitans; we believe in nationalities, that God for wise purposes has divided mankind into distinct, separate, and independent nations; and we are so old fashioned as to believe that each nation should manage its own internal affairs for itself. We have not yet accepted the modern doctrine of "the solidarity of peoples;" nor can we even go with our friends of the *Tribune* for national dismemberment in Schleswig, which is not and never was any part of the German empire, and against it in our own southern states. The cause of Denmark in relation to Schleswig, not in relation to Holstein, is the same as our own in relation to the seceded states. We have no acquaintance with George Thompson; he is no doubt an able, a worthy, and eloquent gentleman, but we are sorry to see him here as an abolition lecturer. We are not believers in English philanthropy, and disclaim all solidarity with it; yet we honor those earnest men and women amongst us who have so long and so perseveringly battled for the slave, amid obloquy and reproach, borne calmly being laughed at, sneered at, persecuted, mobbed, stoned by the Pharisees of the day, and we devoutly hope that the freedom they have so bravely, if not always wisely, battled for, will be obtained and secured.

These remarks define well enough our relation with the abolitionists. It is not a relation of hostility, nor a relation of perfect sympathy and agreement. Yet we have read the speech by Mr. Phillips, which we have cited, with deep and thrilling interest, and wish our worthy president would himself read and ponder it. It is a great speech, and while it indulges the hope that slavery is to end, it eloquently expresses well grounded apprehensions that the republic is in danger, through the readiness of the government, in its haste, to sacrifice the interests and honor of the nation to a sham peace. While we are writing there comes the news of the election of a civil governor in Louisiana; and we may before long hear similar news from Arkansas, and from Tennessee, unless the federal forces are driven out of the latter state before the election can come off. These elections, hailed as triumphs for the Union cause by the journals, we hear of with much misgiving and sadness. They are triumphs only for the vulpecular policy of our accomplished secretary of state, by which he seeks to transfer the struggle from the control of generals to that of politicians and demagogues. We are told General Banks favored the election of Michael Hahn, the successful candidate for governor of Louisiana, and that is proof enough that his election is to be regretted by every friend of the Union; for who knows not that Butler was superseded, because he was in earnest to carry out a straight-forward, honest anti-slavery policy, and that Banks was appointed because he was an ally or tool of Seward, and would do what man could do to defeat such policy and to save slavery from utter annihilation, at least for a time? So it will be everywhere else. Mr. Phillips is right. There are grounds for serious apprehensions, for matters have gone so far that it is impossible ever to establish the Union in peace and harmony without the immediate and total abolition of slavery throughout the whole United States and the territories thereof, and that will not be done if it is in the power of the Sewards, the Blairs, the Bateses, the Bankses, aided by the weakness, vanity, and timidity, and crotchets of the president, to prevent it.

We believe the president, if emancipated from the influence of the selfish politicians represented by the Sewards, Blairs, & Co., would take and consistently pursue an anti-slavery policy, and would not broach the question of reconstruction till he had made sure of abolition; but of such emancipation there is no longer any hope. Perhaps after all, what we wish we shall have to look for from another and an unexpected quarter. Who has not observed of late that a change has come over the Democratic party in congress and elsewhere? Do they not say slavery is dead? and is it not possible that they are shrewd enough to throw the odium with their own friends, of killing it, on the Republican party, and to secure for themselves the honor of burying it, and saving the nation? Democrats love slavery no more than do the Republicans, and are just as willing to get rid of it as Republicans are, if they can do so without loss of prestige, or if by doing so they can again govern the republic. Suppose then, that having discovered that it is political ruin to wed themselves for better or worse to the cause of slavery, they have resolved or are resolving to avail themselves of the opportunity the indecisive and double-faced and no-faced policy of the administration affords them, to take the ground that the abolition of slavery is *un fait accompli*, plant themselves on the principle of universal freedom, elect the next president, and the next congress, and gain to themselves, for their own party, the glory of burying slavery, putting an end to the war, and saving the nation? Why not? They can do it in spite of Seward, Thurlow Weed, and the Blairs, if they choose, and who knows that they will not so choose? It is their wisest and best policy, and if they adopt it, they can carry nearly every state and every loyal man in the Union with them. We are not in their secrets, but are very much disposed to believe that their leaders are already meditating something of the sort.

"But they cannot carry the anti-slavery sentiment of the North with them." Be not so sure of that. They could not, if the Republican administration had not trifled with that sentiment, played fast and loose with it, or if it had fairly accepted it, and proved itself capable of conducting the war with spirit, energy, wisdom, and success. Thus far, as a war administration, as a civil administration, as an anti-slavery administration it has been, in public estimation, comparatively at least, a failure. Suppose then, the Democratic party should take the ground that slavery is dead, that it is no longer in question; also take high national ground, such as has been taken by General Dix in his letter to certain gentlemen in Wisconsin, and put in nomination a strong man, a man of character, capacity, untainted with Copper-headism, possessing eminent ability, and high moral and civil courage; who doubts they would carry the next election with a rush, redeem their own political character, and gain a lease of power for another half century?

Taking the ground we have supposed, and putting up such a man as we have described, not General McClellan, Fernando Wood, or Governor Seymour, from the ranks of their own party, they would have no difficulty in securing the anti-slavery sentiment of the country, for it would have more to hope from them, than from Messrs. Seward & Co., or even Mr. Lincoln himself. We recommend no such policy, for we are not of their party; but were we in the Democratic ranks as we once were, we should recommend it, nay, we would carry it, and believe that we were serving our party and our country in so doing; and even now we care not what party does the right thing, if so be that the right thing is done.

The nation has now the opportunity, without any violation of the constitution, without any danger to the Union, nay, as the necessary means of restoring and consolidating the Union, of emancipating the slaves and putting an end to slavery; and it makes itself responsible henceforth for the sin of slavery, if it does not. If it did not insist on the absurd theory that the seceded states are still states in the Union, it might obtain a constitutional amendment for ever prohibiting slavery in the United States and everywhere within their jurisdiction; but that is not to be hoped for. We hear on every hand that slavery has received its mortal wound, nay, that slavery is dead; but we do not believe it. The Republican party, though opposed to the extension of slavery into new territory, is not and never professed to be opposed to the existence of slavery in the states. There was, no doubt, a strong anti-slavery element in the party, but it was not, and is not the predominant or controlling element. Mr. Seward had been looked upon as an anti-slavery man, and had even been put forward, or had put himself forward as the representative man of the Republican party, but he was opposed to slavery only as a political power, and saw no reason for being opposed to it at all, when he found his party in place without being himself president; and his whole study since the election of 1860 has apparently been to strengthen his party, or himself, by an alliance with the slave interest. Mr. Lincoln was perhaps an anti-slavery man, but opposed to immediate emancipation, and to emancipation at all without colonization, and we are not aware that he has changed his views in the least since he became president. He has from external pressure opposed some anti-slavery measures, but no one with a good grace, as though his heart was in it, and no one that goes far towards immediately or ultimately extinguishing slavery. He has defeated immediate emancipation in Missouri, most likely in Maryland, carefully protected the slave interest in Kentucky, forborne to touch it in Tennessee, and secured to the anti-free-state party the electoral victory in Louisiana. His emancipation proclamation we count for nothing. It was ostensibly issued on the ground of military necessity, and yet, he waited for military success before issuing it; and though one great purpose of issuing it was to deprive the rebels of the labor of their slaves, he in the very proclamation itself, advises them to remain and labor for their masters as usual. This looks very little like military necessity. In his amnesty proclamation, he consents that the returning states should still hold their slaves for a time, as slaves, although he had proclaimed them free, which time he leaves indefinite. In the oath he requires to be taken, the person taking it only swears to sustain his emancipation proclamation *till set aside by the courts or by* CONGRESS, implying that it can be set aside by either. All he pledges himself to is that he himself will not rescind it. We do not ourselves regard, and we presume he does not himself regard it in law, as worth more than so much waste paper. It was one of his jokes. Anti-slavery men thought they had got something and lauded him to the skies; but they will find that they got only fairy gold, except not being obliged to return as fugitives, slaves escaping from states and parts of states included in the proclamation. But is a slave escaping from Mississippi, Alabama, Georgia, or North Carolina into Tennessee or Kentucky, not liable to be imprisoned as a runaway slave, and after a certain time to be sold into slavery to pay the sheriff's fees and jail expenses? It is well to look at things as well as at words. Our president has the reputation of being a confirmed joker.

We cannot with these facts before us concede that Mr.

Lincoln has killed or has any disposition to kill slavery; while his plan of reconstruction is, to our apprehension, expressly devised, if not to perpetuate, at least to prolong its existence. Let half a dozen southern states return to the Union, under the president's plan, and slavery will command a working majority in congress, and may speedily recover from the wounds it has received. The only really anti-slavery measure of much magnitude that has been adopted has been that of arming the negroes. That is a great measure, and may have consequences. All the others are shams, or of little moment. Suppose the patched up state governments in rebel states even abolish slavery, what then? It will, when the proper time comes, be the easiest thing in the world to show that those governments and the state organizations under them are illegal, without the slightest constitutional vitality, and that all their acts are null and void from the beginning; for, be it remembered that the government not only concedes, but maintains, that the seceded states are still states in the Union, and therefore any government set up in opposition to them is revolutionary, and to be treated as *non avenu*. These governments extemporized under military commanders and in presence of federal bayonets are not states, or state governments, and no court that respects itself will ever pronounce them such. It is idle to praise or blame the administration for pursuing an anti-slavery policy. It has no policy but that which Thurlow Weed had in anti-masonic times, in making the body of Timothy Monroe look that of Morgan. " But it is not the body of Morgan." "No matter, it is a good enough Morgan till after election."

But this is not the point we intended to discuss when we commenced. Mr. Phillips, and he is a better judge on that question than we are, thinks, after all, that slavery is as good as dead, and that the measures of the administration will result in its abolition. Perhaps he is right in assuming that slavery is virtually dead, though not in supposing that the measures of the administration have killed it, but that public opinion, coming round so rapidly and so fully to the conviction that the Union cannot be restored, and peace obtained without getting rid of slavery, it cannot be permitted to survive. Slavery has made us trouble enough, and now our hands are in, let us make an end of it. Such we believe is or is every day becoming the general conviction. This is pretty sure to compel the administration to adopt measures that will kill it, or if not, compel it to give way for another administration that will. But this is not enough for Mr. Phillips, and he has given us fair warning that he will not be satisfied, unless the negro is not only emancipated, but clothed with the elective franchise, placed on a footing of perfect political and social equality with the white man. The negro is a man ; he has the rights natural and common to all men, and what right have you to make any political or civil distinction between him and the white man ? It is little you do for the negro in declaring him free. You must go further, and give him the right to vote, so that he may be able to protect his freedom. IT IS HIS RIGHT. Nay, you must go further still, and cut up the large estates at the South, and give him a farm, so that he may have a home and wherewith to support himself and little ones. So under abolition lie concealed agrarianism and negro equality. Let philanthropy once get astride of her hobby, and she is sure never to stop till she has ridden it into the ground.

We think the abolitionists might be satisfied with the abolition of slavery, and the recognition of the equal rights of the negro as a man. That is further than any portion of the human race ever yet advanced at a single stride. It is, at least, sufficient for one instalment ; for, after all, the negro is not the only man in existence. The white man is a man, and has the rights of a man, and in our worship of the negro we cannot prudently leave him out of the account. He is not very patient nor very fond of Cuffey, and if you undertake to do more than he thinks is about right, he will be very likely to break Cuffey's head, hard as it is, and exterminate the whole negro population of the country. You may induce him to consent to let the negro be free, but if you undertake to incorporate him to political society, and make him an equal member of the civil community with himself, he will revolt and insist on remanding Cuffey to slavery, sending him out of the country, or cutting his throat. There are rough customers both North and South, both East and West, who have no special love for the negro, and who will never willingly meet him anywhere on terms of equality. You may philosophize, philanthropize, senti- mentalize, moralize, and sermonize as much as you will, but you will never make the mass of the white people look upon the blacks as their equals. Attempt to force them to do it, and you will raise an Anglo-Saxon devil that you will not be able to exorcise.

We may talk as we will, spin any fine theories we like, praise the negro as we please, and sneer at the boasting Caucasian to our heart's content, but we cannot alter the fact of negro inferiority, or make it not a fact that the negro is the most degenerate branch of our race. This is no reason why we should enslave him, oppress him, throw obstacles in his way, but it is a reason why we should not seek to form one community with him, or seek to mould blacks and whites into one people. The basis, under God, of society, is family, and the basis of family is marriage, and where there are classes between whom intermarriage is inadmissible or improper, they do not and cannot form one common society. Society proper did not exist in the middle ages between the nobility and the serfs, for they did not intermarry. It exists now in France, Italy, and Great Britain, to some extent, because intermarriage between the nobles and commons has ceased to be infrequent. Between blacks and whites marriage is anomalous and never desirable. Both races suffer by it, because the distance between them is too great to be leaped by a single bound. The mulatto is intellectually inferior to the white man, and as an animal, inferior to the black man. All observation proves that the mixed breed is shorter lived and less prolific than either parent stock. Mixed breeds even in animals, without frequent new crossings, soon run out. One or the other race gets the upper hand, and eliminates the other, as English agriculturists and stock farmers know very well. Whites with abnormal tastes may now and then marry a black, but as a rule, both blacks and whites prefer to marry each with their own color. Even if they inhabit the same country, the blacks and the whites are, and will be too diverse to constitute really one people, one society. We are not, therefore, in favor of placing them on a footing of even political equality. In the northern states, where there is but a small negro population, the right of suffrage can be extended to them without any serious disadvantage to them, or exciting much hostility or prejudice against them; but in the southern states, where " the negro vote " would be large and able to decide the election, the case would be quite different, and the whites would not and could not be made to submit to negro suffrage, far less to negro eligibility. The experiment we fear would result in no benefit, but in grave injury to the negro population. We remember when a negro was elected a member of the house of representatives of Massachusetts and the indignation that was felt even in that anti-slavery and negro-loving state at his taking his seat.   He did not occupy it long.

"But do you not wish to elevate the negro?" My dear madam, I am getting to be an old man, and don't believe much in elevating negroes or any other class of men.   We are for knocking off the fetters of the slave, recognizing the negro as a man, but not for elevating the negro to the level of the white man, any more than we are for lowering the white man to the level of the negro.   We would leave the negro free to raise himself to equality with the white man, and above him, if able, but we have never discovered that we did any man, black or white, any good by elevating him above his natural level.   Our romance, my dear madam, has fled with our once dark, thick, glossy locks, and remains not with our dimmed eye and white hair.   We talk no more of elevating the laboring classes, and we believe it would be a great deal better for our country, if we had a much larger class inured to toil, contented to remain an honest laboring class through life, and to earn and eat their bread in the sweat of their faces. All cannot stand at the top of society, for if all were at the top there would be no bottom, and society would be the bottomless pit.   The merit of the negro is that as a rule he is not remarkably anxious to accumulate, or over ambitious of rank or place for which he is not fitted.   Give him the right of suffrage or eligibility, and make him feel that he may indulge political ambition, and you destroy the simplicity and charm of his character, wake up in him all the base passions of the white man, and make him as restless, as discontented, and as great a nuisance as a Yankee pedlar or speculator.   We do not believe that the poorer class even of white men have gained any thing by being entrusted with suffrage and eligibility.   They vote as honestly and as intelligently as the easier classes, but their votes avail them little.   All is not gold that glisters.   There is much philanthropy, madam, that overshoots itself, and aggravates the evils it would cure.

"But it is the negro's right."   I am not sure of that, sir. The negro has the right to himself, his wife and children, to the free use of his limbs, to his savings, his earnings, to the property he honestly acquires or inherits, the same as you or I.   He has the same right to be protected by civil society in his natural rights, his rights of person and property, for he is a man, a free man, and so far the law should

recognize no distinction based on color; but when it comes
to political rights the case changes. All men are equal before the law, but not therefore does it follow that all men
have an equal right to a voice in making or in saying who
shall make the laws. I told you, sir, that I am no disciple
of Jean Jacques Rousseau. The right of suffrage is not one
of our natural, inherent, and inalienable rights, like the right
to "life, liberty, and the pursuit of happiness." Suffrage
confers political power, makes him who possesses it, in a
certain sense, a governor, and we cannot concede that any
man has a natural right to govern; no, not the king of Prussia, or even the Turkish sultan. We do not believe in governors, who govern by a natural, inherent, and indefeasible
right. All power is a trust, and is amissible. Civil society does not simply regulate, it confers the right of suffrage,—trusts whom with it she judges it proper, or most
expedient. We told you that we believed in election. If
the voters elect the rulers and magistrates, society in her
own way elects the voters. There is on this point no higher
law than that of society, in the exercise of its highest prerogative. So do not talk to me about the right of the negro
to be a voter. When and where civil society has invested
him with that right he has it, and you and I are bound to
respect it; but only then and there.

"But he needs it to protect himself against the overbearing insolence and oppression of white men in general, and
his former master in particular. With a vote in his hand,
he can bid the oppressor defiance." I beg your pardon. I
do not believe quite so much in votes as you do, my democratic friend. In my youth I listened to all these fine theories and said myself some fine things, about the power of
the ballot-box. Don't insist upon my believing them now.
Many of the things you say, I seem to have heard centuries
ago, and it is hard to persuade myself that they are uttered
by a living voice to-day in my ears. Is it that our friends
have for these many years been asleep, or that I have for
the last twenty years been living in quite another world from
that in which they have been living and moving? I did
not expect to hear a live man of to-day pretending that the
vote of a poor man, and that man a poor black man, could
afford him any protection, save on election days. His vote
may be worth something to you if you are a candidate for
office, but precious little to himself. We talk of independent voters. What independence! I had to vote in 1860

for Abraham Lincoln, for fusion, or throw my vote away. This was all the independence and freedom of choice I had. We manage our elections better than by encouraging or permitting independent voting. Ordinarily, the managers have got the question narrowed to a simple question between your party and mine. I must vote for my party, and you for yours, or else each of us be branded a renegade; and to vote for one's party means to vote for its candidates, very likely about as scaly a set or at least as incompetent a set of scapegraces as can be selected. They are selected on the principle of availability, and the more worthless the candidate, usually the more available he is. This city has judges of a high court, and representatives in congress, that I would on no account shake hands with, or invite to a seat in my parlor, poor as it is. We cannot understand, then, what protection his vote will give the freedman, for we may be sure that he will not be one of the wire pullers or party managers, and of the candidates presented, it does not matter him a groat which is elected or which defeated. Do not suppose for a moment, sir, that I would, if I could, abolish or restrict suffrage. "It is often," says the sage Dr. Johnson, "misery to lose what it is no happiness to possess." I do not believe that suffrage is an adequate protection, or much of a protection at all, to a poor man, black or white, but I would not take it away from any one who has it, any more than I would a toy from my child. We need through every period of life our playthings, whether as individuals or as nations. Suffrage to those who, aside from their social position, intelligence, profession, wealth, or personal character, have no means of asserting their independence, can afford little or no protection; but it may serve to amuse them, and when they are not all on one side, led on by a few adroit, able, but unscrupulous demagogues, it can do no great harm. So, sir, let suffrage and eligibility remain as they are, and for what they are worth. The objection is not that the poorer and less educated classes make a bad use of suffrage, but that the wealthier and better educated classes make a bad use of them. They are not the poor who bribe the poor; it is quite another class who do it—they who have plans for robbing the treasury, or compelling the government to countenance their swindles, or to aid them in their speculations.

Now, my dear friend, let me not shock you, but I do not believe your poor, ignorant, and inexperienced negroes, whose religion is for the most part mere sensibility or animal excitement, and whose moral habits are those of lying, stealing, and cheating on a small scale, are better than white men of a corresponding class, or any less likely to be used by wily and unprincipled demagogues. The gentleness, docility, and even affectionateness, you admire so much in them, are due in the main to the dependent condition in which they have lived, to their habits of deferring to superiors, and consulting only the will of their master or mistress. Free them, give them votes, and put them on the footing of political equality with their former masters, and these amiable qualities, these virtues, if you please, will disappear, and your beloved negroes will become vain, proud, insolent, overbearing, and exhibit the usual vices and manners of freedmen. They are nothing without leaders, and at present their leaders are their preachers; and the demagogues have only to gain their preachers to gain them. These preachers, for the most part themselves very ignorant and vain, can be bought, wheedled, or deceived, and gained over to the support of measures any thing but advantageous to their own people. Hence, your "negro vote" will only go to swell the ever-rising tide of political corruption. Do not, my dear sir, flatter yourself that, because negroes have been oppressed, they are all saints, or that because they have been more wronged and degraded, they are more conscientious, more self-reliant, or personally firm and independent, more proof against temptation, or less corruptible than white men of the lower class. You, my dear madam, having made the negro for a long time your pet, and defended him against wrong, abuse, and contempt, have, woman like, come to regard him as faultless. I will not undertake to reason you out of your persuasion, for you would be very sorry to lose it; but he will set you right at the first opportunity.

Seriously, then, we honestly believe that you are doing the negro great harm by your proposal to elevate him above his sphere, and to do for him what no man or society can successfully do for any one. Already have you done him harm by placing him on a footing of equality in the army with white soldiers, and insisting that no distinction shall be made between him and them as to pay and bounties. Some time since, I received a memorial to congress, for me to sign, praying congress to make the pay and bounties of negro soldiers the same with those of white soldiers. I threw it into the waste basket. With all deference to the negro-lovers, we do not believe black soldiers are worth as much as white soldiers, and ten dollars a month and emancipation pay them even better than white soldiers are paid. The negro and everybody else would have been satisfied, if nobody had had a pet theory to be crammed down our throats against the stomach of our sense—that of negro equality. Philanthropy shrieked at the cruel injustice of giving a white man a few cents a day more than was paid to a black man, as if it were an unheard of thing in armies, to make a distinction in the pay of different classes of troops. There is no tyranny so relentless or so universal as that of passion or sentiment, and the better the sentiment or the nobler the passion the more galling and universal the tyranny. A theory based on sentiment instead of reason is the grave of all freedom, and hence it often, nay, usually happens, that those who vociferate loudest in the name of liberty are the greatest despots in power. Does not the world agree to call the reign of LIBERTY, EQUALITY, BROTHERHOOD, in France, the REIGN OF TERROR? The Lord save us from men whose sentiments frame their theories, and whose reason is used only to enable their passions to grasp their victims? Half truths are worse than whole falsehoods, and the best sentiments of our nature, when perverted, are more destructive than the worst. Men will commit infinitely greater iniquity in the name of liberty than they dare commit in the name of tyranny; in the name of justice than in the name of injustice. The great crime of the world is ignorance, and hence all the great theologians make ignorance the origin of sin. Under this pet theory of negro equality, a perversion, as understood and applied, of the Christian dogma of the unity of the race, no discrimination is allowed, but every thing is brought to its Procrustean bed. The government has no freedom of administration, individuals no freedom of action, justice itself no free course, and common sense is cast to the dogs. Pardon me, my dear madam, you know I have the misfortune not to be a philanthropist, and while I say *chacun à son goût*, I add in plain English, to each one according to his works, and of those works the supreme authority of the state is in relation to suffrage the supreme judge.

But while we protest against many of the positions taken by Mr. Phillips, we do not oppose, absolutely, the recognition of negro equality before the law. The government has gone so far that to be consistent it must go further. The general government having enrolled the negroes, and placed them in its army on a footing of equality with white soldiers, and allowed them to mingle mutually their blood on the battle-field in defence of the country, has naturalized and nationalized the negro. We opposed, till opposition was useless, making negroes soldiers. We took the ground that this is the white man's country, and the white man should defend it. But the government has overruled us, wisely or unwisely it is needless to inquire or to say. It is enough that it has done so. The negro, having shed his blood in defence of the country, has the right to regard it as his country. And hence deportation or forced colonization is henceforth out of the question. The negro here is as much in his own country as we are in ours, and the government is bound to protect him as much as it is us in the right of domicile, and in the inalienable right to "life, liberty, and the pursuit of happiness." Having placed the two classes in the army on a footing of equality it is but a step to do so in the state, at least so far as depends on the general government. If the special friends of the negro demand it, we certainly will not oppose them, though what they demand we think will in the end turn out an injury rather than a benefit to their *protégés*.

We are the more ready to yield this point, because we foreseee very clearly and distinctly, if we get abolition without equality, we have not got rid of the everlasting negro question. The abolitionists have been agitating the whole country for over thirty years, for abolition, and Mr. Phillips's speech assures us that the same party are prepared to agitate thirty years longer, if need be, for negro suffrage, or negro political equality; and with the democratic notions generally adopted by our countrymen, they will be able to agitate with effect. We are growing old and irritable; we dislike agitation, indeed never liked it; and we think, since we have gone so far, in order to avoid greater evil and have done with the negro, it may be the wisest and safest plan for the general government to abolish within its jurisdiction all distinctions founded on color, and, so far as it is concerned, to give the negro a chance to compete successfully with the white man, if he can. We say, therefore, let the general government, within its jurisdiction, recognize all persons as equal before the law. If this should make negroes and white men equal before civil society, it would not necessarily make them equal in their domestic and social relations, with which the government has and ought to have no right to interfere. The negro may accompany me to the polls and vote, but I will not be obliged to ask him to visit me, to open my drawing-room to him, or to give his son my daughter in marriage. The chief evil of this will be in the fact that the negro or colored population will constitute a distinct or separate class in the community, that will vote collectively rather than individually, even more so than do the Irish or the Germans. This will be an evil, a permanent evil of no small magnitude, not a mere temporary evil, as in the case of naturalized citizens of our own race, who, after a generation or two, become absorbed in the general population. But, I suppose, we can put up with it and contrive, in some way, to survive it.

But we confine negro equality within the jurisdiction of the general government, which extends only to the federal courts and territories not yet admitted into the Union, because the states, each in its own limits, have the exclusive right of settling the question for themselves. The state, not congress, under our system, says who may or may not be entrusted with the elective franchise. The general government, in an enabling act, may indeed define the qualification of voters in the first election under it, but the state in framing its constitution is not governed by the definitions or prescriptions of congress, and fixes itself the qualification of voters as it sees fit. It may exclude or include negroes as it judges best, and the general government has no right to intervene one way or another, even as to the election of president and vice-president of the United States or members of congress. The state fixes the qualification of voters for members of the general government as well as of its own, subject only to the constitutional provision that voters in presidential and congressional elections shall be the persons qualified to vote for members of the most numerous branch of the state legislature. If the government had declared the seceded states no longer states in the Union, congress could have authorized negroes to vote for delegates to a convention for organizing the state or framing a state constitution, and on the question of accepting or rejecting the constitution proposed by the convention, but there its jurisdiction ends. Having, however, fallen into the absurdity of treating these states as still states in the Union, the question of negro suffrage lies beyond its jurisdiction, and is solely a state question. We have never been willing to change the constitution for the sake of the negro, and we are not now. The preservation of the states in all the constitutional rights they now have is as necessary to the preservation and free working of our political system as the preservation of the general government in all its constitutional rights and, powers. Beyond the line we have designated, the question of negro suffrage or negro equality is one for the states themselves, for it comes under the rights of peace, not under the rights of war. The rights of war authorize the government to do whatever is necessary to put down the rebellion, and secure peace; but they do not authorize it to subvert or change the constitution, general or state. It may, as a military necessity, declare martial law and suspend for a time the local civil authorities; but the necessity passed, they revive, *ipso facto*, and resume their functions, as if there had been no suspension or no martial law declared. All that the general government can do in the subject is, then, very little, and not worth quarrelling about.

The states can do as they please about negro suffrage. We should be glad to stop all agitation on the subject, but we are not willing to see the general government attempt to force, without a law, negro suffrage upon states opposed to it. That would be a greater evil than abolition agitation itself; nor is it desirable to change the constitution, even if it were possible, as it is not, so as to prohibit the states from ever making any distinction between its inhabitants based on color. There are some things government can do, and some things the strongest and most absolute government cannot do. We cannot urge upon the states the adoption of negro suffrage, because it is, out of own state, none of our business. We honor the Old Bay State, and we like many, very many, of the traits of the New England people, but not Massachusetts, nor yet all New England, is the whole Union, and we do not know that if we could, we would yankeeize the whole nation. We are not fighting in this war for Massachusetts ideas any more than we are for New York ideas, Pennsylvania ideas, or western ideas. It is as much to us what Illinois or Indiana thinks, as it is what Massachusetts thinks. We live in New Jersey, and are a Jerseyman. If the several states are willing to adopt negro suffrage, we shall not object, and if any of them refuse, we shall not abuse them, or agitate to make them change their mind. We are willing, in view of the circumstances, that the general government should, within its jurisdiction, abol-

ish all distinction founded on color. We wish the several
states, as a means of forestalling agitation, would do the
same, providing they do it voluntarily, of their own accord,
without any attempt to compel them to do it by external
pressure. If forced to do it, especially the southern and
southwestern states, they would make short work with the
negro. Some states have adopted negro suffrage, others
will, if let alone, perhaps all will in time. So much we
say, lest we should be understood as conceding more than
we mean.

As to cutting up the large estates of the planters, and dividing them among the negroes, the agrarian feature of the
plan, rather whispered than strongly urged, and yet to some
extent favored by the government operations in South Carolina, we remark that, "to cook a hare, first catch a hare."
We have not got the great planting states in our possession
yet, and shall not get them without much more hard fighting, even if then. Every military movement this spring,
thus far, has proved a failure, and appearances now are that
we are to have a most unsuccessful spring campaign. We
hope it will turn out otherwise, but we have serious misgivings. The best generals and the best army in the world
cannot carry on a successful campaign with an inefficient or
uncertain civil administration. But, however this may be,
we are not in favor of cutting up the large estates either
North or South, Governor Aikin's no more than General
Wadsworth's, and are not at all disposed to give negroes
farms or homesteads. If the negroes can earn farms or
homesteads, or the means to buy them in the market, we
are quite willing that they should have the opportunity, and
the same protection for their property, when they have
acquired it, that white men have. We have no liking for
what is called the homestead law, and never advocated it,
for we never like any law which is enacted for another purpose than that which appears on its face. We like no un-
derhand measures. The homestead law was intended to operate as an anti-slavery measure, by parcelling out the public
lands among small white farmers, who would cultivate them
with their own hands—a democratic policy, if you will, but
illusory. For our part, we frankly own, that we are in favor
of large estates, of heavy landholders, as an offset to manufacturers and merchants, or what we call business capital
and urban wealth. You will need them yet, when you find
yourselves in a death struggle with the huge corporations

and mammoth monopolies with which you have covered over the whole land. Yet, if the negroes emigrate and settle on the public lands, give them the same rights and advantages you give white men, but no more; and if, as you pretend, they are equal or superior to white men, they need no more. We protest, however, against creating a privileged class, even though that privileged class should be negroes.

Under existing circumstances, and for reasons that we have assigned, and with the reservations we have made, we believe it wisest and best for the country and the government, general or state, to prohibit slavery, to recognize the equality of all men before the law, and make no legal distinction founded simply on color. Let the negro have a fair chance, and compete successfully with the white man, if he can. We see no other prudent course now possible. We do not believe him able to compete successfully with the white man, and if we were the special friends of the negro, and anxious to preserve the negro race in our country, we should be very unwilling to expose him to what we regard as so unequal a competition; but as we seek even abolition in the interest of the whites rather than in that of the blacks, and as we believe the gradual extinction of barbarous and inferior races, when they cannot be or ought not to be absorbed by the superior race, is no loss to humanity or civilization, but a gain, we are willing that he should be exposed to it, if those who claim to be his especial friends and to have charge of his interests insist upon it. We do not believe the colored races can, starting with equal chances, maintain equality on the same soil with the white race. Slavery abolished, they will soon be crowded out of the southern states as laborers, by the heavy emigration from the northern states and from Europe pouring in. They will live in little huts, cultivate a small patch of ground, and eke out a scanty and precarious subsistence, for a time, by fishing, hunting, trapping, and pilfering. Some will enter the ranks of the army, some the navy; others will drift away to Central America, to Hayti, to the British West India Islands, or to the South American continent. Hemmed in or crowded out by an ever advancing tide of white population, more vigorous, more energetic, and more enterprising, their numbers will diminish day by day, and gradually the great mass of them will have disappeared, nobody can tell when, where, or how. It will take several generations, perhaps centuries, to complete the process of elimination, but the process is sure to go on till consummated.

Could we have had our way, and had we wished to preserve the negro race in the United States, we would never have emancipated the slaves; we would have changed the form and condition of their servitude, and converted them from chattels into *adscripti glebæ*, or serfs. We would not have made them freemen, but we would have made them in law persons, have recognized for them the sanctity of marriage, family, and domicile, have secured them their moral and religious freedom, but not have released them from their obligation of bodily labor. But we could not have our way, we could not try the efficacy of our "Morrison pill," for the South would not have consented to it, and we could not reach the slaves at all except under the rights of war, and these rights know nothing of any emancipation, but immediate emancipation. Moreover, we had, and have no wish to preserve, here or elsewhere, the negro race. Do not be shocked, my dear madam, you know I am no philanthropist, and you must expect me to speak as a reasonable man, who respects things, not fine phrases. I would not wrong a negro any quicker than a white man. I would deal out to him and his far off cousin, the American Indian, the same even handed justice, and discharge towards either, promptly and cheerfully, all the claims of humanity and Christian charity; yet I own that I should joy rather than weep to see both races disappear from our continent, if they should disappear without any wrong or injustice on the part of our own race. Let the disappearance be by the operation of a law of Providence, not by human wrong and oppression, and we shall have no tears to shed over it. We respect the amiable feeling which sympathizes with the inferior races, and dreams of their elevation, but, although I have a mellow spot in my heart, as well as you, my dear madam, in yours, I do not yield to it, for I never allow myself knowingly to attempt the impossible, or to war against the inevitable. I cannot make "a silk purse out of a sow's ear." The inferior races had the same origin that you and I had, but they are inferior, because they have, with or without their fault, degenerated further from the normal type of the human race than we have. Pray, do not doubt, whatever you think of me, that you, with your tall queenly figure, your graceful walk, your Grecian face, your sparkling eyes, bright golden hair, and bewitching smile, approach nearer to our common mother Eve, than that black, greasy, thick-lipped, flat-nosed, woolly-headed, tub-figured, and splay-footed Dinah. Treat Dinah kindly, speak gently to her, don't despise her, don't turn away disdainfully from her, for she, too, is a daughter of Eve, a creature of God, and has both a heart and soul; but don't ask me to regard her as the type of womankind, and yourself as the one who has departed from it.

The inferior races, the yellow, the red, or the black, nearly all savage, barbarous, or semi-barbarous, are not, my dear sir, types of the primitive man, or so many stages in man's progressive march from the tadpole, chimpanzee, or gorilla, up to Bacon, Newton, Napoleon Bonaparte, George B. McClellan, and you and me. They mark rather so many stages or degrees in human degeneracy. The African negro is not the primitive man, the man not yet developed, the incipient Caucasian, but the degenerate man, who, through causes which neither you nor I can explain, has fallen below the normal human type, and stands now at the lowest round in the descending scale of human degeneracy, and for him, save by the transfusion of the blood of a less degenerated variety, there is no more development. He has ceased to be progressive, and when a race has ceased to be progressive, nothing remains for it but to die. Get a deeper philosophy, my friend, and read history anew. Why is it that you can rarely get a negro to embrace any thing of Christianity but its animality, if I may so speak, or its exterior forms, and that after generations of Christian worship and instruction, he falls back to the worship of Obi? Why is it that you can scarcely get a single Christian thought into the negro's head, and that with him religion is almost sure to lapse into a grovelling superstition? Why, because he is a degenerate man, and superstition is degenerate religion, and the religion of the degenerate.

Well, my dear friends, I have said my word. An honest, conscientious, outspoken word it is, too, and wiser than you believe; but you will not like it, nobody will like it, because it is not sophistical, flatters no one's prejudices, favors no one's crotchets, helps on no one's party. My word will return to me without an echo. Well, be it so. If a true word it will not die. If fitted to the times, and the times will not hear it, so much the worse for the times, and for those whose duty it is to manage them and shape things to bring about better times. I like, my dear abolitionist, your earnestness, your intensity, your resoluteness, your invincible energy, and wish I could find as much elsewhere in loyal ranks; but not being able to do so, I tell you, either the federal arms will fail to crush the rebellion, or you will succeed alike with your good and your bad. Life is stronger than death, and you represent the only living body just now in the loyal states, and Wendell Phillips is bound to carry it over William H. Seward. So much we see; and forced to a choice between the two, we prefer Phillips, for "a living dog is better than a dead lion."

ARE THE UNITED STATES A NATION?*

[From Brownson's Quarterly Review for October, 1864.]

No series of essays could possibly have been written, better adapted to the questions with regard to the new constitution agitated by the public at the time of their publication, than these masterly and profound essays, by Hamilton, Jay, and Madison, so well known, so widely studied, and so universally esteemed, under the collective title of *The Federalist.* There was, at the time, nobody who was not in favor of the several states remaining united under a federal congress or general government, and hardly any one who doubted that the adoption of the new constitution would constitute the American people one political people or nation; but there were those who believed the new constitution would strike a fatal blow at the independent rights of the states respectively, and who for that reason strenuously opposed its adoption. The writers of the essays do not deny that the states under the new constitution would not be severally sovereign, but confine themselves to questions, then uppermost in the public mind, of the necessity and utility of union, the fitness of the proposed constitution to secure it, and to the nature, extent, and limitation of the powers of the government to be created by it, if adopted. On these

---

* *The Fœderalist: A Collection of Essays written in favor of the new Constitution, as agreed upon by the Fœderal Convention, September 17, 1787.* Reprinted from the Original Text. With an Historical Introduction and Notes. By HENRY B. DAWSON. New York: 1864.

questions they have left nothing to be said. On the necessity and utility of union, on the constitution and powers of the general government, their essays are, and must be, high authority as long as that government lasts.

But the question which the American statesman has now to consider in regard to the depositary of American sovereignty prior to the adoption of the constitution, the writers in the *Federalist* do not expressly discuss, or furnish us the means of answering. All agreed then, as now, in the doctrine of popular sovereignty, or that the people are sovereign; but left undecided the question, What people? the people of the states severally, or the people of the *United* States? This question, indeed, was hardly raised at the time, or, if raised at all, was considered of no practical importance. In the eighteenth century, all who rejected the doctrine of "the divine right of kings and passive obedience," as asserted by the Stuarts and their adherents, held that government, however constituted, originates in convention, and is founded in compact, expressed in the constitution of the state, or the written instrument that can be folded up and put in one's pocket, or filed away in a pigeon-hole, to use the language of Thomas Paine. Whether the people of the United States were sovereign as united, or as separate and independent states, was a matter of little importance when once the constitution was adopted, or the contract duly ratified; for by that, for certain purposes at least, they would undeniably be created one political people. That was enough for all practical purposes; for the federal government rested then in compact, and no political authority more ultimate than the compact itself was recognized. The age, we should remember, whatever its practical belief, embraced a purely atheistic philosophy, and held, theoretically at least, that nothing is simpler than effects without causes, or for things to make or create themselves.

There can be little doubt that the strongest nationalists in 1787, if they had been asked where was our political sovereignty prior to the adoption of the federal constitution, would have answered, In the states, or the people of the states, severally; and would have maintained, if pressed, that the national sovereignty they asserted was created by the surrender of a certain portion of the rights of the states to the general government. The possibility of such surrender nobody questioned, and nobody saw any thing absurd in the assertion at once of the sovereignty of the Union and of the

states severally.   John Locke was generally followed in politics as well as in metaphysics.   All through the works of
John Adams, the profoundest statesman of the epoch, runs
the theory of the origin of government in compact, or the
voluntary agreement of the individuals composing the community, like that entered into by the Pilgrims on board the
Mayflower.   Even in the preamble to the declaration of independence, by the congress of 1776, we find the assertion
that "government derives its just powers from the consent
of the governed."   Holding this doctrine, the statesmen of
1787 could concede without difficulty that the states, or the
people of the states, severally, were sovereign prior to the
adoption of the federal constitution, and yet deny them to
be sovereign afterwards, as did Mr. Webster, in his celebrat-
ed controversy on state rights with General Hayne and Mr.
Calhoun, of South Carolina.

    Yet the doctrine of the origin of government in compact,
in the sense asserted in the eighteenth century, is now,
though frequently asserted by small politicians, maintained
by no statesman worthy of the name.   There is no political philosopher now who does not see that Rousseau's doctrine, in his *Contrat Social*, has no foundation in fact, is
a mere theory, and one that establishes, under the specious
garb of liberty, the most odious of all tyrannies,—that of
an ever-varying and irresponsible majority. Rousseau maintains that all individuals are equal, and that each is sovereign
in his own right.   But as government is necessary, these
sovereign individuals meet, or are imagined to meet, in convention, and agree that the majority shall govern, and govern absolutely; whatever the majority wills is to be law,
and whatever it commands must be done, because each individual surrenders his individual sovereignty to the majority,—a doctrine that our little politicians still assert, and
which is still the theory of the whole body of European
democrats, who, as a rule, are at least a century behind
the times.   God save us from the theories of European
democrats, radicals, and revolutionists!   This doctrine is
not only repugnant to all individual liberty, but to all legitimate authority.   Its very general prevalence among us has
been most fatal to the development of personal freedom, individual independence, manliness, and frankness of character, on the one hand, and to the maintenance of legitimate
authority, and the impartial administration of justice, on the
other.   Under it, minorities have no protection, and indi-

vidual freedom no guaranty. The will of the majority governs, and he who dissents from the opinion of the majority, is for that reason alone virtually outlawed. Popular opinion becomes the criterion of truth and the standard of morality. Everywhere in Europe, in proportion as it has obtained, it has deluged the land in blood, and led to a reign of terror, to the introduction of anarchy, and to the most intolerable despotism; and in our own country, so far as acted on practically, it has swept away all the guaranties originally retained of the rights of minorities and of individuals, and subjected them to the interest, the caprice, or the fanaticism of the majority for the time.

But the doctrine has no foundation in reason. The rights of the state are not made up of the rights surrendered by individuals. If individuals are individually sovereign, they may delegate certain powers to the commonwealth, but cannot surrender their sovereignty. They necessarily retain the right to revoke the powers delegated whenever they choose. So of the states in the Union. Concede that they were severally sovereign and independent states before the adoption of the federal constitution, and you must concede that they are so still. The powers of the general government are in that case not made up of rights surrendered, but simply of powers delegated, to it by the several states, and the sovereignty vests in the states severally, or the people thereof, as before. The federal government, in such case, is not, strictly speaking, a government, but an agency, as the southern leaders contended, created by the states, which retain to it precisely the relation of the principal to the agent. Each state is then free, whenever it judges proper, to revoke the powers it has delegated, and withdraw from the Union, as the seceded states now making war on the Union profess to have done. To concede the original sovereignty of the states severally, and then to deny the right of secession, is simply to outrage common sense. Yet most American citizens, in theory at least, concede that the states, severally, were originally sovereign, and that prior to the adoption of the federal constitution there really was no such national existence as the United States. Even the weight of judicial authority, from first to last, inclines to the side of state sovereignty. It is this fact, which the loyal American instinct combats, that gives so much strength to the so-called confederacy, and secures it the sympathy of nearly all foreign states and statesmen. We say our cause against it is just, and so it unquestionably is; but not on the ground assumed by the administration and the majority of its adherents.

Up to the breaking out of the rebellion by the secession of South Carolina, in December, 1860, we had held and maintained the theory of state sovereignty, and contended that, under our political system, the original and ultimate sovereignty still vests in the states, or the people of the states, severally; that allegiance is due only to the state; and that the citizen owes obedience to the United States only because his state has by her ratification of the constitution enacted it, and made it, and the legislation by congress under it, a part of her own state law. The state that enacts the Union and its legislation is as competent to reject it as she is to repeal any other of her legislative acts; and, when she does so, her citizens cease to owe even obedience to the federal government, and may, at her command, lawfully resist it, and even fight against it, as against any other foreign power. The sovereign, saving his faith, is always competent to resume the powers he may have delegated, and to unmake any agency he may have created. The sovereign states that have severally made the Union, may, then, each of them, or any one of them, for itself, unmake it, whenever they judge it advisable. Hence, on the doctrine of original and persistent state sovereignty, the secessionists may have acted in good faith, from loyal and patriotic motives, in the simple exercise of their unquestionable rights, and the federal government has no right to denounce them or to make war on them as rebels. Rebels they certainly are not, if that doctrine be true. All this we saw as clearly as did the leaders of the secession movement themselves, and we felt that we must either give up the state-sovereignty theory, or consent to secession.

But give up that theory for its opposite, the theory of consolidation, we could not. Nothing is more certain than that the states do not hold from the Union, for their existence is implied in the conception of Union itself, and we are not one consolidated people under one supreme, omnipotent central government. Nothing is or can be more false than the doctrine put forth by the president before his inauguration, that a state under our political system and a county in a state stand on the same footing, and hold one and the same relation to the government. The right of secession certainly was never contemplated by the framers of the constitution, or by the several states when they ratified it; but it is equally certain that they did intend to retain the federal character of the government, to maintain certain state rights or powers not derived or dependent upon the federal constitution, or the government created by it; so much is certain. What, then, shall we hold? Is there a middle term, equally removed from these two extremes? Is it not possible to maintain state rights without state sovereignty, and the unity of the political people of the United States without asserting consolidation, or making the states mere dependencies on the general government? In the article on *The Federal Constitution*, we attempted to answer these questions, and proved, as we think, that the sovereignty with us vests neither in the states or the people of the states severally, nor in the Union created by the constitution of 1787, but in the political people of the *United* States, who have ordained and established both the several state governments and the general government; and that this political people is one people, yet capable of existing and acting only as organized into mutually independent political societies called states, and into states united. Hence, their union and their division into states are equally essential to our political system.

Two facts must be borne in mind: 1, the political people of the United States have never existed as a consolidated mass, without organization or distribution into separate and mutually independent states, corporations, or political societies; and, 2, these political societies, corporations, or states, have never existed and acted as free, independent, sovereign states, or nations. These are facts, and facts never contradict facts. No interpretation of our system of government that does not recognize these two facts, harmonize them, and show them consistent the one with the other, is an adequate interpretation. The American people existed primarily as colonies of Great Britain. These colonies were, politically, or as political bodies, mutually independent, and they remained so when, by the revolution and the acknowledgment of Great Britain, they became states; of this there is and can be no doubt. But the colonies, though possessed of certain political rights pertaining to political sovereignty, and though politically independent in face of each other, were not free, independent, sovereign nations. They had, politically considered, all one and the same nationality, yet the supreme and sovereign national authority vested not in them alone, but in the British crown, or the British crown and parliament. Here was political unity with political diversity, and political diversity with political unity. The two facts we have asserted certainly existed and were facts during the colonial period. They existed equally after independence. The political rights of the states hold from or continue the political rights of the colonies, while the Union inherits and continues the political rights or sovereignty held by the British crown, prior to independence.

The question turns, it will be seen, on the assumption that the national sovereignty, originally vested in Great Britain, inured, on the acknowledgment of American independence, to the political people of the United States, not to the states or people of the states severally. Is this assumption warranted? It rests on the historical fact that the assertion of independence was made by the colonies united—by one joint act—and not by the colonies severally; that the war for independence was carried on by the *United States*, or states united; that treaties negotiated with foreign powers were treaties with the United States; and that the new national sovereign acknowledged by Great Britain in the preliminary treaty of 1782, as well as in the definitive treaty of 1783, was the United States. No one of the states of the Union has ever been known or recognized by any foreign power as an independent sovereign nation, or has ever exercised the supreme political rights of a sovereign nation. It has done so no more, in fact, than it did when a colony of Great Britain. As a simple historical fact, that portion of political sovereignty which in colonial times vested at first in England, and after the Scottish union, in Great Britain, and could in no sense be exercised by the colonies, unless through the British crown, or as an integral portion of the British people, has never been exercised by any one of the United States, separately considered, and has been exercised since independence by, and only by, the political people of the United States—under the old confederation through congress, and under the federal constitution, through the general government. This is the plain, undeniable historical fact, and it clearly and fully supports the assumption, that on the acquisition of independence the national sovereignty inured not the states severally, but to the United States; which would also seem to be corroborated by the fact recorded by the elder Adams in his *Diary*, while a member of the old congress, of the several states, or at least some of them, asking and obtaining permission of congress to form for themselves state constitutions, as well as by the process of receiving new states into the Union.

The decision of the question rests on historical, not on legal grounds. The nation exists historically prior to law in its strict sense, as the will of the sovereign, as has been amply proved by Mr. Hurd, in his able and learned work on *The Law of Freedom and Bondage in the United States,* for law, in its juristical sense, as distinguished from its ethical or political sense, presupposes a national sovereign competent to ordain and promulgate it. We cannot, then, appeal to the written constitution, for that is of the nature of positive law, and supposes the preëxistence, historically, of the national sovereign, or political people, competent to ordain and establish it. Who, what, or where this sovereign or political people are, can be determined only historically ; for they exist as an historical fact, prior to all positive law. The sovereignty may be transferred, and the mode or manner of its expression or exercise may be changed, but it never expires. Wherever there are men, there is for them a political sovereign, to whom they owe allegiance. Every people, no matter how few or how many, that owe allegiance to no other power, are themselves sovereign, and may constitute or organize a government according to their own judgment of what is right or best for them. But even in such a case, the people precede the state, and their existence, as independent of all foreign powers, must be settled as an historical fact; so, if we prove that in becoming independent of Great Britain, the only power that had any claims of sovereignty over us, the British sovereignty, as a simple historical fact, passed to the states united, and not to the states severally, we have proved all that the case demands. The courts cannot go behind the historical fact, and are and must be bound by it, whether it comports with their political or ethical theories or not. The fact stands independently of all theory or speculation, and determines the law. What we mean, whether we clearly express it or not, is, that the historical fact controls the law, not the law the fact ; for the law follows the fact and depends on it. We may say, the constitution or the law ought to be different, might have been different; but different it cannot be, as long as the fact remains unchanged.

There is no reason, *a priori*, that we know of, why the original British sovereignty could not have inured to the states severally. There was no positive law in force, or legal principle, prohibiting it. If the colonies had each, by its separate individual action, thrown off the authority of the mother country, won its independence by its separate action, and obtained its recognition as an independent sovereign power or nation, an independent sovereign power or nation it would certainly have been. In such case, the sovereignty would have passed to the states severally, and not to the states united ; but solely because the historical facts would have been different. The historical fact determines who is the sovereign, who are the sovereign people, where, in a sovereign nation, the sovereignty is lodged, and through what channels it is exercised ; because the existence and constitution of the national sovereignty is an historical fact, anterior to all written constitutions and to all positive legislative enactments. What might have been, what it is desirable should have been, are political and ethical questions,— very interesting, very important, no doubt, but of no moment in determining what is.

Relying on the historical fact, we assert that the sovereignty, which, prior to independence, was vested in the British crown and the British parliament, or the British people over the colonial people, after independence inured to the United States ; and hence, the United States are a free, independent, sovereign nation, as truly one single nation as any other nation that can be named. This settles the question of state sovereignty as distinguished from national sovereignty, and accepts the truth asserted by the consolidationists, though it denies consolidation. But the sovereignty inures to the United States as states *united*. The Canadas, the West Indian Islands, the northeastern provinces, and other colonies of Great Britain, even had they asserted and gained their independence, at the same time the " Old Thirteen " asserted and gained theirs, would not have had any participation in the sovereignty of the United States, unless they were historically a part of that political people which was acknowledged as an independent nation, under the style and title of the United States. It was necessary, in order to share in its national rights and powers, to be states, and states united. But the union in the British nation, and under the British sovereign, did not and could not, of itself, constitute them one united sovereign nation after independence. They must have been united in declaring and winning their independence. Yet the Union, before as well as since the acknowledgment of independence, was not the union of the people as simple individuals, but as political communities or states. This fact is historically as certain and as essential as the fact of union. The diversity is as certain and as important as the unity ; and the rights of the states are no more to be denied than the rights of the Union ; —both are alike sacred and inviolable.

We place the sovereignty in the political people of the several states united and forming one complex sovereign nation,—we say *political* people, that is, the electoral people. We do so, because neither historically nor constitutionally is the whole population included in the political people, either of the states severally or of the United States. The people are sovereign,—certainly ; but only the electoral people, or the people who have the elective franchise, which in no state includes more than one-fourth of the actual population. The talk about universal suffrage is nonsense. Universal suffrage never has existed, never can exist as a fact ; for in no civilized country, however democratic, are women permitted to vote, and children, at a tender age, do not and cannot vote. Yet these are integral parts of the population, and without them there would soon be no population at all. They who assert the electoral franchise as a natural right, as an incident of human nature, speak very loosely, and are never to be understood *au pied de la lettre*. Suffrage is a civil not a natural right ; and monarchy or aristocracy, however we may dislike them, are not necessarily repugnant to natural right, or to what is called the law of nature, and are as legitimate, where they are the historical or existing forms of government, as democracy. The right of the government rests on an historical basis, not, as actual government, on a speculative or theoretical basis. Democracy may or may not be the best form of government ; but it is not the only legitimate form of government, as our stupid journalists and pothouse politicians pretend. The political people, in the beginning, was determined by the colonial law ; or, in other words, after the colonies resolved on resistance, and till they had become states, and formed constitutions for themselves, the various political acts done, whether regular or irregular, legal or revolutionary, were done or held to be done, by those who, under the colonial laws or usages, were electors, or by representatives or delegates chosen by them. Hence the political people all along acted as formed into colonies or states. The colony, or state, in its separate action, determined who were to be included in the electoral, or sovereign people; and outside of its determination there were and could be no political, electoral, or sovereign people. The electoral people of the several states in union constitute, and from the first have constituted, the sovereign people of the United States.

We are not theorizing here; we are simply stating facts. There are amongst us, no doubt, politicians who regard these facts as of no importance; who hold that the people are inherently sovereign, and tell us that they are always and everywhere sovereign. They sneer at what is called historical right, and, like Napoleon III., settle every question of right by a *plebiscitum;* but these politicians forget to tell us who are the sovereign people, or by what authority it is determined who are the people who are to vote the plebiscitum. Is it said the majority? But the majority of whom? Of all the male citizens of the nation over twenty-one years of age? But you suppose in this a nation, and the existence of a nation is a fact to be determined only historically. Exclude the historical fact, you have no nation, and no citizens; for where there is no nation there is no state, and where there is no state there are no citizens. We told you this twenty years ago, in the *Democratic Review.* Without the recognition of historical right, you cannot talk a moment intelligibly about the sovereignty of the people, popular rights, popular will, or plebiscitums. Grant that the will of the majority is the sovereign will, and all you need for the constitution or the laws; you have still to settle who are the people to be counted in ascertaining the will of the majority. Nobody is absurd enough to pretend that the will of any two men, who are the absolute majority of three, is sovereign, and that any three men, wherever found, are the sovereign people. Myself and any two others might otherwise unite, and declare ourselves a sovereign state, and secede from the city, the state, and the Union, and scornfully refuse to recognize your magistrates, your laws, your police, your conscription, and your tax-bills. This would be democracy run mad, and too absurd to be asserted even by the *Evening Post* or the *N. Y. Tribune.* We might call it democracy gone to seed. No, your sovereign people must exist, and their number and territory be defined, before it can ordain a constitution, enact laws, or perform any political function; and who are the political or sovereign people in any given case is a question of history, of fact; not of ethics, not of metaphysics, nor even of law, in the sense of the will or ordination of the sovereign. The sovereign people can, no doubt, alter or amend their written constitution, as they can make or unmake laws; but we must always ascertain who the sovereign people are in point of fact, before we can determine who can make or amend the constitution, establish or abrogate laws. The historical fact, what we call the unwritten constitution, is providential, like all historical facts; but the written constitution is *lex scripta*, is positive law, and constitutes not the sovereign, but the government under the sovereign. The convention of 1787 did not create or constitute the sovereign people of the United States, for it was that people, present in its delegates in convention, that drew up, ordained, and established the constitution under which our present general government is organized and exists. That constitution is the act of the sovereign people, and not their creator,—is the law they have in their sovereign capacity enacted, ordained, and promulgated; to remain unaltered and in force, for all branches of the government, state or national, and for all individuals within their jurisdiction, during their pleasure. They derive none of their rights or powers from the constitution, for they are antecedent to it, and it is the creature of their sovereign will; as much so, as any law enacted by the supreme legislative power of the state is the creature of the will of that legislative power. Written constitutions emanate from the sovereign; they never create or constitute the sovereign; they proceed from the supreme political power, but confer no political power; and hence it is, that neither the general government, nor the state governments, have any political powers whatever. All constitutional governments, whether their chief magistrate be called governor, president, stadtholder, king, or kaiser, are republican governments; and in all republican governments, the sovereign and the government are distinct, and their peculiarity, as their glory, consists in distinguishing the political power from the administration. This is a fact the people, and even politicians, do not sufficiently consider. Words are perverted from their original meaning, or come to have for them no distinct meaning at all. Our parties are named as if the great questions to be decided by our elections were political, that is, questions relating to the constitution of the sovereign power, as the *Democratic* party, the *Republican* party, &c. The political power is the sovereign power, and with us is identically the sovereign, or, as we say, the political or electoral people, and they speak and act politically only in the convention, for only in the convention can they decide or act on questions of polity. The notion that has prevailed to a fearful extent, especially since the reëlection of General Jackson, in 1832, that the people outside of the convention, as simple population, are sovereign, is unwarranted, anarchical, tends to the despotism of the mob, and has had the chief agency in bringing about the present formidable rebellion, which we have for nearly four years struggled in vain to suppress. Webster, Clay, Calhoun, were right in their opposition to that reëlection, though generally wrong in the reasons they assigned for it; and hence their opposition was unavailing. The people with us are unquestionably sovereign; yet not as population, or a mass of individuals; but as the political or electoral people, really or virtually, in convention duly assembled, and in which vests the supreme political power of the nation.

Now, who are this political people? Who they are to-day, we can settle by referring to the constitution and laws of the Union and of the several states; but who were they when we became a nation independent of the mother country? Who chose the delegates to the congress that declared independence? Who chose the representatives in the several state legislative assemblies that superseded the colonial assemblies? Who chose the delegates that in convention drew up the several state constitutions, and voted on their adoption? To these questions there is but one answer, namely : they who were the electoral people of the colonies, by virtue of the colonial charters or colonial legislation. Hence, the new institutions, though they modified, continued the old ; and though there were irregularities and acts strictly revolutionary in their character, the transformation from colonies to states, and from British to American national sovereignty, was effected without a total disruption of political or legal continuity, as the history of the times and the decision of the courts amply prove. Whatever powers the colonies had, they derived legitimately from Great Britain ; and it was by the exercise of these powers, not by an out-and-out assumption of the original and abstract rights of man, about which Tom Paine and others babbled so much nonsense, that our independence was declared and won, that we were transformed into an independent nation, and our present institutions were founded. Grant there were un-constitutional assumptions, a stretch of powers, and great irregularities,—these were condoned by the sovereign against whom they were committed, if condonement they needed, when Great Britain acknowledged us a free, independent, sovereign nation. The historical, and therefore the real basis of our government, state or federal, rests on these colonial rights, or the will of the colonial electoral people. Here is the simple fact, whatever democratic or anti-demo-cratic theories and speculations may be entertained on the subject.

The states, then, hold from the colonies, and therefore not from the federal Union. They stand on as firm and as ultimate a footing as the nation itself. In fact, they are, in their origin of the colonies, older than the political peo-ple of the Union; for the colonies were mutually separate and independent political corporations, or, if you prefer, political communities, before the Union existed, and, unless in the British people, did in no sense constitute one politi-cal community. We do not pretend, and do not recollect, that we ever have pretended, that, distinguished from their unity under the British crown and parliament, they were *always* one political people, as seems to have been the doc-trine of Mr. Quincy Adams. They were originally sepa-rate and mutually independent political communities; and if they had, as a fact, formed no political union before being transformed from colonies into states, and their acknowledg-ment as such, they would have been, as the defenders of state sovereignty maintain, on becoming independent, sov-ereign states, each with all the political attributes of a free, independent, sovereign nation. They became one nation by their mutual action while yet colonies, by declaring their in-dependence by one joint act, by assuming the style and title of a nation, exercising never separately, but always in unity, the proper national functions, and by being acknowl-edged and received into the family of nations as one nation, not as several nations. This union was effected before in-dependence, and it was as the *united* colonies that they met in congress, and as *united* states, not as *confederate* states, that they declared independence, and prepared to carry on the war in its defence, as we have already shown over and over again. By this union, to which inured the sovereignty previously vested in the British crown and parliament, or British nation, including the people of the colonies as well

as those of the British Isles, as some of our fathers contended against the British ministry of the time, the people
of the colonies were transformed into one political people,
or a sovereign American nation. But, and this is the point
we are laboring to establish, the integral elements, or, so to
speak, the units of this political people or sovereign nation,
are not individuals, but the electoral people of the states
severally, as the continuators or legitimate heirs of the
colonies. This being so, the political sovereign, or political
people of the nation, exists essentially as the political people
of the states, and has no existence independent of the several state organizations in the Union.

Here is the foundation of what we call state rights, as
distinguished from state sovereignty. The states are not
severally sovereign, for the colonies under the British
crown, though they had certain rights, were not sovereign,
and the complement of sovereignty which they lacked is
now in the *United* States. Yet without states there can be
no united states ; without the political people of the several
states there can be no political people of the United States.
The destruction of the states as elementary political bodies
would be the destruction of the United States. The United
States, or political people thereof, in convention, may enlarge
or contract the powers either of the several states or of the
general government ; but they cannot abolish the states, as
distinct and autonomous political communities, without committing an act of suicide, and overthrowing all legitimate
government in the country. Viewed as an existing fact,—
the way in which we must view it,—the states and the
United States are correlative and each connotes the other,
and the destruction of either is the destruction of both. It
is this fact that makes our republic a federal republic. The
nation itself is federally constituted. The states are federal
states, just as much as the Washington government is a federal government. The one political sovereign reigns in all
our political institutions, but that sovereign is itself a federal sovereign,—not the government created by the convention but the political people of the several states federally united into one political people that met in the convention, and that may meet again whenever they choose.

Now the fact that theories have been entertained, that
popular opinion, or even juridical assumptions, have opposed
this view of our national sovereignty, does not move us.
The courts exist by and under the constitution, and cannot

go behind it. They have no political functions, and can adjudicate upon no political question. They hold from the sovereign power, and have nothing to say of its constitution. They presuppose it, and simply seek to ascertain and apply what, under the constitution, is the law. What they say beyond is *obiter dictum*, and, though entitled to more or less respect, as the opinion of eminent men, binds nobody. Popular opinion is never a safe rule of judgment. It is seldom any thing but a compound of ignorance, prejudice, passion, caprice, and interest, constantly varying, condemning a Socrates one day to drink hemlock, and the next erecting a temple to his memory. Never were there greater crimes committed in the government of the world than since, under the direction of journalism, the effort has been made to govern by popular or public opinion. With us, public opinion is the opinion created by a few unprincipled journals, demagogues, and what Sir Richard Steele calls "coffee-house politicians." As for theories, they must conform to facts, or they are valueless, and are mischievous whenever they attempt to make facts conform to themselves. Facts exist independent of theory, and seldom is a theory constructed, whether in philosophy, politics, or the so-called exact sciences, that rightly explains facts. Men may have a good understanding of facts, and yet fail utterly, and become grossly absurd, when they attempt to construct theories for their explanation. The question for us is, not what theories our fathers held with regard to the seat of the sovereign power, but where it was actually lodged as a matter of fact, for the fact overrides all theories on the subject; and we have proved, we think, that, as a fact, the sovereign power of the new nation that sprang into existence, and was recognized in 1783 as an independent sovereign nation, was vested in the political people of the United States, represented by the convention, and actually governing, partly through a general government, and partly through state governments. Such being the fact existing prior to law in the sense of the ordination of the sovereign, and prior to all written constitutions, whether of the general government or of the state governments, no theories can be for a moment entertained that impugn it, either by denying it outright, or by explaining it away.

Indeed, all political theorists must fail in their attempts to explain our political system, for it is constructed in accordance with no theory. It is *sui generis*, logical, but complex, and falls under the head of none of the recognized systems of government. It is not monarchical, aristocratic, or democratic; it is neither a confederacy nor a centralized state, and the attempt to reduce it to any one of these recognized systems is to destroy it. It is like and unlike them all. It is as far removed from European democracy as from European aristocracy or imperialism, and analogies borrowed from any one of these are sure to mislead, if relied on as the principle of its interpretation. Neither the general government nor the state governments are sovereign. These governments are all created by written constitutions, therefore by positive law, and suppose a sovereign anterior to them, who has ordained them, and governs in them. Nor are the people as population, either of the states severally or of the United States, sovereign, but only the political or electoral people, always determined by the states severally, and never in any state more than a small portion of the whole people. Nor is sovereignty in the political people of the several states as represented in the state governments, nor in the political people of the several states united, as represented by the general government. It is in this political people of the several states united and assembled in convention. The political people in convention is the sovereign, and the only political power, properly so-called, under, or known to, our system.

Our political system, so original, peculiar, and complex, has been from the first exposed to dangerous misconstructions. Some, observing the priority to the Union of the states as political communities, and their absolute necessity to the system, conclude that the sovereignty vests in the states severally, and therefore that we have no national sovereignty. According to them, the Union holds from the states, and the general government holds its powers as delegated not by the political people of the United States, but by the states or the people of the states severally. Others, observing that the constitution in its preamble professes to be ordained and established by the people of the United States, that it was actually formed by a convention of the United States, and that the supreme national functions have always been exercised by the United States, and never exercised, or allowed to be exercised, by the states severally, regard the general government as the supreme national government, and overlook the rights of the states as states to share in the national sovereignty. They conclude that the states hold from the nation, instead of being its constituent elements. These make the nation a consolidated instead of a federal nation. To this view the old federalists inclined, and it has been generally taken by those who have combated either nullification or secession. The present administration alternates between it and the state-sovereignty theory, sometimes acting on the one, sometimes on the other, and apparently without being aware of any radical difference between them. Moreover, our politicians, as distinguished from statesmen, observing that we have no king, no nobility, no political aristocracy, and that nearly all elections are by popular suffrage shared in by the great body of the freemen, and ordinarily decided by a majority of voices, have favored the consolidation doctrine, by concluding that our republic is a pure democracy in theory, and always to be interpreted and administered on democratic principles. We do not mean here the principles of the so-called Democratic party, which, as a party, is less democratic than the Republican party, as formed and led by the *New York Tribune;* but we mean democracy in the political sense, or as one of the three simple forms of government which writers on the constitution of government recognize, and which they distinguish from what they call mixed governments. Democracy, in the political, not the party sense, asserts theoretically, that each man is sovereign in his own right, by virtue of his manhood, and in this sense it resides in the people as population, but practically in the majority, who, save such ethical restraints as they may recognize and submit to, are free to do as they please. It asserts the right of the majority, or what demagogues and political tricksters make pass for the majority, of the people of a state, to rule in the state, and of the people of the United States to rule in the United States. People who believe themselves democrats, who boast of being democrats, may entertain and insist on very just views of government, and hold that constitutions are not merely to secure the right of the majority to govern, but to protect the rights of minorities and individuals; in other words, not to confer power, but to guaranty liberty; but these are not really democrats. The genuine democrat, he who fully understands the democratic principles, holds no historical right, no constitution or vested rights, sacred or inviolable, any further than they suit the ideas, the interests, the passion, or the caprice of the majority; and the constant and invincible tendency of democracy, when it is

practically asserted as the political order, is to sweep away
every thing that interposes an obstacle or an impediment to
the direct, immediate, and absolute rule of the majority.
Such, under the democratic interpretation of our political
system, has been our American experience. All the amendments to our old state constitutions, as well as all the new
constitutions that have been adopted for new states, have
been formed on the democratic theory, and reject at least
some of the guaranties of liberty that our fathers had the
wisdom to institute or retain. This is a fact that cannot be
denied, and which very few would wish to deny. It is cited
and boasted as an evidence of our political progress, as it
certainly is of our progress in democracy.

Our institutions do not admit of a democratic interpretation, and the very general attempt made to explain and administer them on democratic principles is a fatal mistake, if
it is wished to preserve them, or our republic as a federal
republic. The tendency to democracy in the states is necessarily followed by a tendency to democracy in the United
States; for the same people, with the same ideas, convictions, and sentiments, act in both; and its realization in the
United States is, evidently, the destruction of our federal
system, and the subjection of all minorities and individuals
to the will of one irresponsible, unrestrained, and generally
factitious majority. This result is inevitable, though neither
intended nor attempted with "malice aforethought." It
comes naturally, like all things of the sort, from the silent,
unsuspected efforts of the people to realize their ideal.
Democracy, like monarchy, like aristocracy, seeks always to
realize its ideal, and to mould all things after itself. Whatever judgment may be formed of it, democracy is not the
American system of government, nor the idea on which
our political and governmental institutions are based. Our
government, whether state or national, though original and
peculiar in its combinations, belongs to the general order of
what are termed mixed governments, and is destroyed whenever reduced to any one of the simple forms of government.
Our political institutions are designed to protect the rights
of minorities and individuals, or, as we have said, to guaranty liberty; but none of the simple forms of government
do, or pretend to do, this. A pure monarchy knows no
liberty but the liberty of the monarch to govern as seems
to him good; a pure aristocracy knows no liberty but the
liberty of the nobility to rule as they see fit; and a pure

democracy knows no liberty but the liberty of the majority to govern as it pleases. The moment you talk of constitutions, or political contrivances to limit the power of the majority, or to restrain its will, and demand political guaranties, you are out of the purely democratic order, as much as you are out of pure absolute monarchy when you seek to impose constitutional restrictions on the power of the monarch. All simple governments are unlimited absolute governments, and therefore despotisms, democracy no less than the others. We, for ourselves, love freedom too well to be in favor of any of them. We know no natural and indefeasible right of one man, of a few men, or of the majority, to govern. If all men before the law of nature are equal, as the Justinian Institutes assert, and as we firmly hold, one man has no natural right to govern another, and the larger number none to govern the smaller number; that is, a right anterior to the institution of civil society, or positive law. The sovereign is given in the providential constitution of civil society itself, or in the historical existence of the nation; and written constitutions in free states are not adopted so much to guaranty the right of the majority to govern, as to restrain them from oppressing minorities and individuals, or depriving them of the exercise of their natural rights.

But the larger portion of the people of the United States, having adopted democracy as their ideal, and having arrived at the conclusion that majorities can do no wrong, that they may always be safely trusted, and that they ought to have free scope to govern as they please, have well-nigh converted our constitutional government into what we call a centralized democracy, under which the states and the nation hold their rights at the good pleasure of an ever-varying and irresponsible majority, although obtained by lying, cheating, trickery, bribery, stuffing ballot-boxes, miscounting votes, or downright violence. Providence, as manifested in historical events, counts for nothing; historical rights, vested rights, and political guaranties, are swept away before the ruling majority. The people are always equal to themselves, and are as sovereign to-day as they were yesterday, and nothing they did yesterday can bind them to-day, or that they do to-day can bind them to-morrow. We pretend not that the American people have as yet reached this extreme length; but this is only the practical realization of the idea they are developing and applying, and which they will not permit to be called in question. As yet, constitutional habits, acquired when no man, as in our own boyhood, would allow himself to be called a democrat, have to some extent practically restrained us. But we have been hastening to it, hurried on by the influence of European democrats and European democratic literature, and not a little by northern humanitarianism or philanthropy, manifesting itself in various ways; but chiefly in the abolition movement, which, threatening the rights of property, led Mr. Calhoun, one of the most sagacious of our statesmen, to protest against absolute majorities, to insist on state sovereignty, and to contend for government by *concurrent* majorities as our only protection.

The southern leaders have not, as many suppose, it is well to remark, asserted the right of secession, and carried their states out of the Union, and caused the present formidable civil war, for the purpose solely or chiefly of preserving negro slavery; and their opposition to the abolitionists is not, and never has been, solely on account of their anti-slavery sentiments and convictions. We know many of them well, and have shared their friendship and their confidence, and we have found them never impugning, but always respecting, genuine anti-slavery sentiments. Indeed, the South were always as anti-slavery and as wedded to liberty as the North, as every one knows who knows thoroughly both sections. The South were always less sentimental and less speculative than the North, but they were always more serious, and more in earnest. What they opposed, and what has induced them to secede, and involved them in rebellion, was the centralizing democracy rapidly gaining the ascendency in the northern, middle, and western states, and of which abolitionism was one of the most striking characteristics. The abolitionists were not, and are not to-day, simply anti-slavery men, who recognize themselves as citizens of the United States, and bound in their modes of action by the constitution; but democrats of the most ultra stamp, who hold that the constitution and laws have and can have no sacredness any further than they conform to their convictions, or to what they choose to call the "higher law." Slavery, in the United States, is a local institution, existing by local or state law, so far as legal existence it has; and its preservation or abolition is within the jurisdiction of the several states that authorize or tolerate it, and the general government has no constitutional right to meddle with it.

Hence, it is only on the ground that our republic is a centralized or a consolidated republic, that citizens of non-slaveholding states have any responsibility for it, or any right to meddle with it, otherwise than by the simple expression of their approval or their abhorrence of it. The abolitionists, not by their anti-slavery sentiments or expressions, but by their movement, and the principles on which they based and justified it, overlooked the federal character of our government, and violated not simply state sovereignty, but state rights; and their movement could not go on without revolutionizing our whole system of government. The slaves, by the *lex loci*, were property, and the abolitionists struck at the inviolability of that right. If you can, through the majority, deprive a man, in a state of which you are not citizens, of his property in slaves, you may just as well deprive him of his property in his plantation, his farm, his cattle and horses. Property itself, which is one of the bases of society, is held then at the mercy of the majority. The southern statesmen saw this, as we ourselves saw it, and hence their secession movement—a movement not for the defence of slavery, as we have said, so much as of the right of property, and was in principle directed not so much against the abolition of slavery, as against its abolition by unconstitutional means, and by persons who have no political right to demand its abolition.

Undoubtedly, we ourselves have demanded the emancipation of the slaves, and even the abolition of slavery, everywhere within the jurisdiction of the United States; but we have never done it on abolition principles, as every abolitionist feels and knows. There is not an abolition journal in the country that regards us, or treats us, or ever has treated us, as an abolitionist. We have never urged emancipation on the ground of the natural equality of all men—never on the ground that slavery is a moral wrong, a crime against society, and a sin against God. On this question of slavery we formed and published our views in April, 1838,* and we have never changed or modified them since. We are, and always have been, an anti-slavery man; we do, and always did, regard slavery as a great moral and social wrong, though not the only nor the greatest in the country; but we have demanded emancipation only under the war power as a military necessity, or means of putting down the

---

Slavery—Abolitionism, Brownson's Works, Vol. XV., p. 45.

rebellion, just as we demand the taking of any other species of property as a means of strengthening the government, and of weakening the enemy, and compelling him the sooner to submit.   On this ground, not as an abolitionist, but as a loyal citizen, determined to save the life and integrity of the country by all means permitted by the laws of civilized warfare, we have demanded emancipation,—on the very principle on which the government takes the enemy's cotton, rice, tobacco, wheat, corn, cattle, sheep, hogs, and horses.   In our whole argument, the slaves are assumed to be property—not justly, but legally, property ; and their emancipation is defended on the ground that it weakens the enemy's means of resistance.   This no more violates the right of property, than the shooting down in battle an enemy violates the precept of the Decalogue, "Thou shalt not kill." It comes within the acknowledged belligerent rights of the government.

It is true, in attempting to reconcile the public to the measure, and to persuade the military authority to adopt it, and issue the necessary orders for carrying it into effect, we have urged the natural equality of all men, the detestable character of slavery itself, and all the considerations of humanity bearing on the subject,—not as giving the right to emancipate, but as a reason why the government should not hesitate to exercise its belligerent right to emancipate. Neither Wendell Phillips nor William Lloyd Garrison will recognize in this their doctrine, though they may see in it a disposition to get rid of slavery by legal means.   The policy of emancipation we have urged is lawful under the belligerent rights of the government, and would have been, we doubt not, most efficient, if it had been promptly adopted at the time we first urged it, and in the way and for the reasons we urged it.   If the president, as commander-in-chief of the army and navy, had sustained General Fremont's proclamation and General Hunter's order, neither of which could he, in our judgment, lawfully rescind, and given orders to his other commanders of military departments to issue similar orders in their respective commands, if they found them necessary, we believe the measure would have been wise and just, and would have aided in suppressing the rebellion.   But it is the misfortune of Mr. Lincoln always to adopt wrong measures, or right measures at a wrong time or in a wrong way.   The measure, at the time and in the way he has adopted it, has been unwise, and even disastrous.

He has so bemuddled the matter, as he does every thing he takes in hand, that we see now no way of getting rid of slavery, but by a fresh grant of power from the sovereign, that is, by an amendment to the constitution in the way pointed out by the constitution itself. We cannot do it now under the war power, for the president has so abused that power that we cannot appeal to it; and the attempt to prolong the war one moment after the restoration of the Union has become practicable, for the sake of forcing the seceded states themselves to abolish slavery, would be highly criminal, as well as of no practical use.

We have never ceased, for more than twenty years, to warn our countrymen of the danger of encouraging this centralizing tendency, and of its hostility to the federal constitution of the nation; but they have considered it a sufficient reason for not reading or not heeding us, that we are said to be eccentric and paradoxical,—a man who never knows his own mind, and changes his opinions with the moon,—as if truth depended on the personal character of him who utters it, or as if the people have no judgment of their own, and no capacity in themselves to recognize truth when presented to them. Doubtless we have changed our opinions on many subjects, for we do not happen to be of the number whom experience cannot profit or events enlighten; but on the question of abolitionism and slavery, or the danger of attempting to interpret our institutions by the democratic or Jacobinical theory, we have never changed our views. For nearly twenty years, indeed, we held the doctrine of state sovereignty, and defended it with earnestness and such poor ability as we had, because we saw not how otherwise we could consistently assert state rights, and resist the tendency to consolidation; but never did we do it with a view to the denial of the federal character of our political constitution, which, however we may have erred in explaining, we have always held; nor with a view of obtaining a ground for dissolving the Union, which we have always loved, and which we have always been prepared to do battle for with our tongue, our pen, our property, and our life. We have, since secession took place, rejected state sovereignty, but not state rights, and we have done it for the reasons we have given, and for which we are chiefly indebted to Mr. Hurd, in his masterly work on *The Law of Freedom and Bondage in the United States*. We know not whether Mr. Hurd intended to teach the doctrine

as to the federal constitution that we have defended, but we
do know that we have been led to it by reading his work,
more especially his Chapter XI., to which our readers are
respectfully referred. We have changed our method of explaining state rights and American nationality; but we have
not changed our views as to the fact of such rights and of
such nationality. When we first formed our opinions on the
subject, then a very young man, we supposed that we had
no alternative but either state sovereignty or consolidation,
and we adopted the former instead of the latter, as we
should do now, if we must take one or the other. Mr. Hurd,
however, has shown us, intentionally or not, that we are not
obliged to adopt either, and enabled us to perceive that the
historical facts in the case authorize us to assert, as mutually
compatible, national sovereignty on the one hand, and the
rights and mutual independence and autonomy of the several states on the other. Whether the reasons we have given
are sufficient to establish our conclusions, they who conde-
scend to read them must judge for themselves. The explanation of our federal constitution we have given is not original with us, and does not rest on our personal authority. If
accepted, it must be accepted on the authority of historical
facts, which nobody can deny, and which must control the
decision.

In our judgment, the southern states would never have
seceded if they had not embraced the theory of state sovereignty; or even with that theory, had it not been for the
fact that they found themselves in the minority, and their
special interests threatened by the rapidly increasing tendency in the northern, middle, and western states to democratic or Jacobinical centralism, threatening to change our
federal republic into a huge democracy, restrained by no
constitution, and under the absolute sway of the majority
for the time. They saw that the practical working of the
democratic idea, so widely adopted in modern society, was
silently undermining our American constitutionalism, and
depriving them of all guaranties for their rights of property.
Hence they seceded. In this, all the wrong has not been on
their side. We of the North have our share in the blame.
No doubt they wished to keep their slaves, at least to prevent their emancipation by northern interference; no doubt
they wished to rule in the councils of the nation, for all men
love power; but we know not that the slave states had any
stronger wish to rule than had the free states. If the South

wished their policy to prevail, the free states equally wished theirs to prevail, and held that, being in the majority, they had a *right* to have it prevail. Here was an error of the free states.

Yet we do not and cannot exonerate, or even excuse, the slave states. The ablest champions of democracy as the American idea were southerners and slaveholders—Thomas Jefferson and Andrew Jackson, the idols of American democrats. Jefferson was, no doubt, an ardent patriot, and rendered important services to the cause of American independence; but he was no philosopher, and, in the higher sense of the word, no statesman. He, as he himself avows, deliberately violated the constitution in the purchase of Louisiana, and justified himself on the ground that the measure was highly expedient, and was sure to be popular—thus placing expediency and popularity as rules of action above the constitution. Indeed, he was a revolutionist on principle, denied the inviolability of vested rights, recognized no historical rights whatever, maintained that one generation cannot bind its successor, and contended that there should be in every country a revolution once in every generation—that is, as he counted, about once in every nineteen years. Andrew Jackson was a man of indomitable energy of character—what we call a magnetic man; but he was no statesman. He placed the caucus on a par with the convention, maintained that the will of the people collected from demagogues, newspapers, and informal assemblies, is as authoritative as the will of the people expressed through legal and constitutional forms; and he claimed to be bound even by the constitution, only as he interpreted it for himself: thus asserting in principle both *mobocracy* and cæsarism. The South, in point of fact, was foremost in giving a Jacobinical interpretation to the American system; and the measures, such as the war of 1812, the protective tariff, internal improvements by the federal government, the stealing and annexation of Texas, the Mexican war measures, which have given such an impulse to the centralizing tendency, have all been southern measures. The Kansas-Nebraska bill was introduced and carried in the interest of the slave states; and the demand of the South of positive legislation by the general government to make slavery national, and to protect it in territories where it was not authorized by local law, which gave rise to the Republican organization and to the geographical division of parties, was one of the most thoroughly centralizing and unconstitutional demands ever made on the general government. Indeed, the South have had even more to do with fostering the dangerous tendency, which they make their excuse for secession, than the North; and it has only been when they felt the necessity of constitutional guaranties for their own special interests that they have asserted constitutionalism in contradistinction from democracy, and insisted on concurrent instead of absolute majorities.

The southern leaders did wrong in seceding; because, if they were more constitutional and freer from the influence of Jacobinism than the North, the Union needed them to aid in correcting the dangerous centralizing tendency, and in bringing back the people of all sections to the principles of American constitutionalism. The southern states, had they chosen to remain in the Union, could, aided by the true conservatives of the northern states, have controlled the policy of the general government, and, in time, as Mr. Calhoun, who was no secessionist, always maintained, brought back the people of all the states to sound constitutional doctrine, and rendered effective the constitutional guaranties of the rights of minorities and individuals. They may allege that they made the attempt, and found it vain; but if they found it vain, it was their own fault. They dictated their terms, as if they had but to speak to be obeyed; and they dictated them under threats that, if they were not accepted and conformed to, they would dissolve the Union. These threats were impolitic and offensive. The North loved the Union, but they did not like to be coerced into adopting measures, even if they did not disapprove them in themselves, by threats of its dissolution. The threats provoked defiance. The editor of this *Review*, who had always sympathized with the South, gave, at a public meeting in 1860, as his reason for supporting Mr. Lincoln, a man he did not like, and in whom he had no confidence even then, the fact that for thirty years he had voted under threats that, if he did not vote in a certain manner, the South would dissolve the Union; and he was tired of voting under threats. He said he wished to have the question, whether the Union was to be dissolved or not, brought to the issue, and settled once for all, so that he might know whether he was a free man or a slave. Thousands and thousands of those who, in 1860, voted for Mr. Lincoln, no doubt did so for the same or a similar reason. People do not like being threatened, especially by their equals. The South failed through their arrogance and dictatorial spirit. Their leaders assumed for years such an attitude, and so shaped the issues, that we of the North could not support even their just rights without acknowledging them to be our masters, with the right to dictate to us as they were in the habit of dictating to their slaves. They supposed us to lack the spirit of freemen, and addressed us as if we had no manhood—as if we were a herd of miserable fanatics, a pack of cowards, or, at best, of low mechanics and mean-spirited shopkeepers, unworthy to come between the wind and their nobility. They thus rendered it impossible for us to act with them without sacrificing our own rights and dignity as men, and as free and equal citizens of the United States. Had they not assumed our immense inferiority to themselves; had they withheld their insolent and disloyal threats; had they met us as equals, whose lot was, in their own feelings as well as ours, indissolubly bound up with that of the nation, there could have been harmony and concert of action, and they and the real conservatives of the eastern, middle, and western states could have saved the Union and reaffirmed American constitutionalism. Their conduct was more than a crime—it was a blunder.

The people of the seceded states were not and had never been a complete political people in themselves: they were an integral portion of the one political people of the United States, and their secession was at once treason to the sovereign, and a disruption of the American nation. The people of a nation may, when oppressed beyond all reasonable endurance, and they have no other means of redress, depose their tyrannical rulers, and even change their form or constitution of government; but a part of the national population has never the right to separate, and set up to be an independent nation by itself. If they will separate from the national authority, and seek to place themselves out of its jurisdiction, they must emigrate, for the national jurisdiction always extends to the whole national territory, and to all persons resident within it. The wildest French revolutionists held sacred the French nation, and the integrity of the French territory. They attempted, illegally and criminally if you will, to gain possession of the national authority, and to govern without right in the name of the nation; but to divide the nation, or to create for themselves a separate nation out of a portion of the French population and territory, was a thing they never dreamed of. In the midst of all revolutions, the nation is assumed to persist, and its authority to remain inviolate and supreme. Secession, with us, either means the abdication by the state of all its political rights, and its lapse into the condition of population and territory under the United States, or it means national disruption, expatriation without emigration,—a thing never admissible under any circumstances whatever, and hitherto unheard of ; for the part separated from remains in possession, with unrestricted jurisdiction. To contend otherwise, would be to maintain that the nation is purely personal, and not territorial as well as personal. This would be democracy with a vengeance.

The slave states, even waiving these considerations, had no right to resort to the extreme measure of secession till they had exhausted all legal and constitutional means of redress of their grievances, if grievances they had. This they had not done. They might have appealed from the government to the sovereign, that is, to the political people of the United States assembled in convention. If the convention had been called, their grievances would have been redressed ; or, if not, and no means of reconciliation were found practicable, a peaceable and friendly separation would have been authorized, and its conditions settled. The North wished the Union, but it had no disposition to insist on a Union that could be maintained only by force, or to compel states to remain in it against their will. The North, in point of fact, felt that it had as much to complain of in the South, as the South had to complain of in the North, and would never have withheld its assent to separation, had it been asked in a proper spirit, and in a constitutional way. It would not assent, and ought not to have assented, to secession, when claimed as a right; for under our system as it is, it is not a right. At any rate, the southern leaders should have tried, or made a serious and honorable effort to try, the experiment of the convention, before appealing to the questionable right of revolution. As they acted, they have no excuse.

The government, which is always to be distinguished from the convention, had its constitutional duty to perform. Its action had caused none of the grievances complained of, and the South had and have made out no charge against it, or the United States. For the government to have made, under threats of dissolving the Union, the concessions which would have contented the disaffected states, or even those which leading Republicans in the spring of 1861 were prepared to make, would have been to violate its constitutional powers, virtually to abdicate its own authority, and to betray the nation itself. It would have sacrificed its dignity, and furnished a precedent for yielding to the demands that might thereafter be made by any factious combination of states, whether northern or southern, eastern or western. The government had no option in the case; it could not rightfully, or safely, make concessions to those who denied its authority, and asserted, and continued to assert, the right of secession. It must assert, and if able, cost what it might, maintain its constitutional authority, and compel the secessionists to recognize and obey it. They, therefore, who blame the government for not having made peace at the price of concessions which it had no right to make, and could not have made without sacrificing its own dignity and the authority of the nation itself, are hardly less criminal than the secessionists themselves, and a great deal more despicable. They are as despicable as the Scotch Whigs, who sold their king, Charles I., to the commissioners of parliament, to be beheaded. If they are not traitors, they are miserable cowards or simpletons, incapable of appreciating the rights or the duties of government. Hence we said, and we say now, let there be no compromise till the authority of the United States, represented by the government, is recognized and submitted to. Till then, let there be war, terrible war, carried on in dead earnest; and let the government hang, emancipate, confiscate, do any thing and every thing it judges necessary, that is permitted by the laws and usages of civilized warfare. But then, when the authority of the United States is recognized, when there is no longer armed resistance, we have always felt that the uncertainty in the public mind as to the seat of sovereignty, and the provocation given the South by the growth of the unconstitutional centralizing democracy in the free states, threatening to lay the whole Union at the mercy of an irresponsible and irresistible majority, should be taken into the account, and allowed to have due weight in adjusting the terms of final settlement. When the war is over, there need be, under the circumstances, no vengeance sought, and a general act of oblivion would be good policy, even if not demanded in strict justice. Each state, when it chooses to reorganize itself as a loyal state, and return to its former place in the Union, we would receive on a footing of equality with the states that have not seceded, and forget the past.

But the terrible civil war now raging, we think, will practically explode the doctrine of state sovereignty, and practically establish national unity, at least for all the states that remain united, or are recovered to the Union. What we now most fear is, that in the reaction in favor of national unity, we shall lose the rights and independence of the states as the units of our political system. We fear that the federal element will be virtually eliminated, and our republic transformed into a consolidated republic, and the state governments be converted into simple prefectures, holding, not immediately from the political people of the United States federally constituted, but from one supreme, omnipotent central government, as in the French empire, or the new kingdom of Italy. The tendency was that way before the war, and the war has strengthened it. The public mind has never yet been prepared to reject state sovereignty, otherwise than in favor of consolidation, or to distinguish sharply between state rights and state sovereignty ; and as it recedes from state sovereignty it verges towards consolidation or centralism. This is wherefore we have taken so much pains, while asserting the unity of the political people of the United States, before the adoption of the written constitution, or even the old articles of confederation, to show that our political people exist only as federally constituted. This we have maintained to be the historical, the providential fact, prior to all positive law, and from which all positive laws, with us, whether written constitutions or ordinary legislation, emanate, and derive, under God, their legal force. Yet this original federal constitution of the political sovereign, though instinctively held by the American people, has never been fairly understood and avowed by the public mind. Hence, the public mind in its reflective and deliberate action tends to assert either state sovereignty, or centralism and state nullity. It now rejects state sovereignty, and yet does not understand how state rights can be still asserted, save as grants from the state, or what distinction there is or can be between state autonomy and state sovereignty. When any one to-day insists on state rights in the face of the general government, struggling to suppress the rebellion, he is at once charged with sympathizing with secession, and his loyalty is suspected, if not out and out denied. All war has a centralizing tendency, because it demands a concentration of powers in the hands of the government; and any thing that looks like a decentralization of power is regarded as hostile to the government and the national sovereign. In a civil war like the present, it looks like attempting to with-hold from the government the power necessary to sustain the national life and integrity, and to embarrass its free and necessary action. Hence our fears.

The danger is aggravated by the obvious centralizing ten-dency of the administration, of the last and the present con-gress, and indeed of the Republican party itself. The Re-publican party holds from the old Whig party, as the old Whig party held from the old Federal party. The old Federal party labored to give to our institutions, by interpretation, a non-federal character. The Democratic party, so called, though it has inclined too far, at times, to the state sover-eignty theory, and has never well understood our complex national sovereignty, has, upon the whole, been less unfaith-ful to the federal character of our institutions, and more opposed to centralization, than any other party we have had. The party in power, whether in congress or the administra-tion, have favored and strengthened the centralizing tenden-cy, already so strong as to be exceedingly dangerous to liberty. The restoration of the Union on consolidation principles would in our judgment, be of little value. We want the Union with the federal constitution as it is. The Union without that constitution is hardly worth fighting for, for its restoration under one supreme, omnipotent central government would be only its transmutation into a consolidated republic, and effectively the introduction of a pure and unmitigated des-potism; and in our estimation despotism is not a less evil than disunion. Our federal constitution—we mean not the written, but the unwritten constitution, which is antece-dent to the written constitution—is a providential fact, and if once lost, it can never be recovered. We would rather have confederation than consolidation, for it is easier to reconstruct federalism from confederation than from con-solidation; and we would rather be joined to the southern confederacy, as much as we abhor it, than to have central-ism, which is sure to pass, in a democratic country, without much delay, into imperialism, with which the kind of de-mocracy we as a people have encouraged, has a natural affin-ity. No man is more anxious to have slavery abolished than we are, but we prefer the preservation of our constitutional-ism, even to the abolition of slavery; and should the presi-dent succeed in abolishing it in the way he is now attempting it, in his plan of reconstruction, which he assuredly will not and cannot do, we should think liberty would have lost more than it had gained. His plan of reconstruction contravenes at once the rights of congress and the rights of the states. No state can be organized or reorganized by military authority, or under the war power. We are anxious, no man more so, to have the Union restored, and the integrity of the national territory maintained, but we wish it done in a way that leaves us, unimpaired, all our old guaranties of liberty. We do not want to be ruled by majorities any more than by minorities, unless their will is restrained by the constitution. We approve heartily the American system of constitutional government, but we do not love or respect the European democracy we are substituting for it. We believe not in the democracy of Mazzini or Garibaldi, any more than we do in the czarism of Russia, or the imperialism of France, the filibusters that stole Texas from Mexico, or those who attempted to steal Cuba from Spain. We sympathize with filibusters and revolutionists neither at home nor abroad. We believe in liberty, we love it, and will die sooner than surrender it; but we do not believe liberty practicable in a democracy not limited by constitutions, any more than it is practicable in a pure autocracy. We will stand by our country, whatever the form of government it may adopt, even should it become a pure despotism; but while liberty of action and liberty of speech are allowed us, we will speak honestly our mind, and resist with all our feeble power every tendency that we regard as a tendency to despotism, whether of the one, the few, or the many.

In writing this article, as well as the series which it concludes, we have aimed to set forth the American political system as it is—not as it ought to be, not as it might be, not as political theorists have explained it, but simply as it is, according to the simple historical facts which it embodies, and on which it rests. We have never seen a theory of our institutions that we could accept, for the constitution of the sovereign power in any particular nation is a fact, not a theorem, and a fact that precedes both the institution and the constitution of the government. The constitution of the government is the work of the national sovereign, and is of the nature of positive law, or law in its strict sense, and its interpretation and application belong to the courts instituted under it. The difficulty in the case of the American polity has always been in regard to the constitution of the sovereign power, which most writers in the eighteenth century, and the early part of the nineteenth, confound with the constitution of government. The sovereignty is unquestionably in the nation, but the nation may be constituted in different ways, and the business of the political philosopher is not to determine how it ought to be constituted, how it might be constituted, but how it is constituted. He seeks not the law, but the fact that precedes and makes the law. The fact, we have contended, and we think have shown, is, that the sovereign power with us is not simply but federally constituted. The states are not sovereign without the Union, nor the Union without the states, for without states there is and can be no union of states. The sovereign power is complex in its constitution, embracing unity with diversity, and diversity with unity. It is the work of Providence in his ordering of events, and, like all his works, is dialectic. The states as primitive elements are as essential as unity, and unity as essential to the national constitution as the diversity of states. This complex sovereign governs through a complex organ, composed of a general government and of state governments, according to their respective organizations. The two governments are really, in relation to the sovereign power, but one government; only they operate in distinct spheres, and are in their respective spheres equally supreme and independent. The error of state sovereignty is, that it denies the fact of national unity; and that of consolidation or centralism is, that it absorbs in the national unity the rights of the states. The government, whether that of the Union or that of the states severally, is bound to guard alike against each of these errors, and to preserve national unity with state diversity, and state diversity with national unity.

The secessionists lose the nation; and the Republican administration is in danger of losing the states; and the one evil is hardly greater than the other. The administration has evidently never had any clear understanding of what we call the constitution of the sovereign power, which in every nation is one, and can be only one; or what, perhaps, might better be called the constitution of American civil society, or the American state. At one time it apparently concedes state sovereignty, and at another it fails to recognize state rights or state autonomy in any sense. In no instance does it appear to understand that our civil society is federally constituted,—the only ground on which it can call the secessionists rebels, or justly carry on war against them. The president has never yet, in any of his messages or speeches on the subject, met the arguments of the secessionists, and given a good reason why their secession ordinances are null, and do not absolve them from their obedience to the United States. We have endeavored to do what he ought to have done in the beginning, but has not done. He has proceeded blindly from the first, and kept "pegging away" at the rebellion, though with indifferent success, leaving himself and the nation to follow the course of events without seeking to control them. The journals on either side have nowhere met the real difficulties of the case, but have merely echoed the crude and unphilosophic views of their respective parties, as is their wont. Congress, while manifesting excellent intentions, has followed in the wake of the administration, apparently as much at a loss as the journals themselves. Of the president not much was ever expected, for nobody ever dreamed that he was or could be a statesman, and his cabinet, if they had statesmanship, could never display it under so incompetent a chief. The consequence is, that we have been for nearly four years carrying on a disastrous war, without any tolerable understanding of the grounds of its justification. The popular mind has remained confused on the subject, and honest and even loyal men take opposite grounds with regard to it.

We have aimed to grapple with the difficulties of the case; to show on what grounds the war was not only inevitable on the part of the government, but strictly just, if conducted in a proper way. We have shown that the secessionists are really rebels, and wherefore they are rebels; and that it is the right and the duty of government to use all its force, if necessary, to reduce rebels to submission, no man who believes in government or civil society at all can question.

END OF VOLUME XVII.